The Documentary History of
the Supreme Court of
the United States, 1789-1800

Volume Three
The Justices on Circuit
1795-1800

The Documentary History of the Supreme Court of the United States, 1789-1800

Volume Three
The Justices on Circuit
1795-1800

Maeva Marcus, *Editor*

Associate Editors
Mark G. Hirsch
Christine R. Jordan
Stephen L. Tull
Natalie Wexler
Marc Pachter, *Illustrations Editor*

James R. Perry, *Co-editor, 1980-85*
James M. Buchanan, *Associate Editor, 1980-88*
Emily Van Tassel, *Associate Editor, 1985-87*

COLUMBIA UNIVERSITY PRESS
NEW YORK

The Press gratefully acknowledges the assistance of De Witt Wallace and of The William Nelson Cromwell Foundation in the publishing of this volume.

KF
8742
.A45
D66
1985
v. 3

Library of Congress Cataloging in Publication Data
(Revised for vol. 3)

The Documentary history of the Supreme Court of the
United States, 1789-1800.

Includes bibliographical references and index.
Contents: v. 1. pt. 1. Appointments and proceedings—
v. 2. The justices on circuit, 1790-1794—v. 3. The
justices on circuit, 1795-1800.
1. United States, Supreme Court—History—Sources.
I. Marcus, Maeva, 1941–   . II. Perry, James R.,
1950-   . III. United States. Supreme Court.
KF8742.A45D66 1985   347.73'2609   85-3794
347.3073509
ISBN 0-231-08867-1 (lib. bdg. : v. 1, pt. 1 : alk. paper)
0-231-08870-3 (v. 3)

Columbia University Press
New York   Oxford
1990

Printed in the United States of America

Casebound editions of Columbia University Press Books are Smyth-
sewn and printed on permanent and durable acid-free paper

10 9 8 7 6 5 4 3 2 1

To the Memory of Richard B. Morris, 1904-1989

Contents

1795-1800

List of Illustrations

Maps

Maps showing the Eastern, Middle, and Southern Circuits follow page six.

Acknowledgments

The institutions, organizations, individuals, repositories, projects, and libraries whose assistance has contributed to the preparation of this volume are included in the acknowledgments printed in volume 2. We would like, however, to thank especially James C. Brandow, our National Historical Publications and Records Commission Mellon Fellow, who worked with us for the academic year 1989-1990. Although his primary focus was on learning the craft of documentary editing, he has made many contributions to this volume. We greatly appreciate his efforts.

Guide to Editorial Method

In producing volume 3 of *The Documentary History of the Supreme Court of the United States, 1789-1800,* the editors have followed the "Guide to Editorial Method" used in volume 1. The editors have, however, made a few adjustments in that method, described below under the same headings used in the first volume. An additional heading has been provided to describe the particular organization of volume 3.

Organization of Volume 3

The documents published in volume 3 consist of private and official correspondence, grand jury charges and replies, and newspaper reports. Each document is presented in chronological order. The editors provide a short introduction at the beginning of each calendar year. The documents are also interspersed with opening notices for the meetings of the circuit courts; each opening notice is placed according to the date when each court was required by law to convene. These notices give the opening and closing dates of the court, the Supreme Court justices and United States district court judges present, whether a charge was delivered, and whether a copy of the charge exists (for a table of the dates of holding court and which judges attended, see Appendix C). As the focus of this volume is on the justices of the Supreme Court and not on the operation of the circuit courts, we do not note grand and petit jury rolls and attorney admissions. We include a short biography of each United States district judge, because of his role in the circuit court system, in the notice marking his first appearance at a circuit court. A collection of six undated charges by William Paterson can be found in Appendix A of volume 3. In Appendix B there is a separate section on legislation relating to the details of holding the circuit courts.

Selecting Documents for Publication

Except for grand jury charges, subsequent reprintings of newspaper articles and/or variations in printings are not noted. Grand jury presentments were selected from circuit court minutes and newspapers. We did not search the criminal case files of the circuit courts for presentments.

Dating Manuscript Grand Jury Charges

Manuscript charges present a particular dating problem. Because the charges were written in advance of their delivery and, unlike correspondence, have no dateline, we have chosen to date them on the day the justices first delivered them to a grand jury. Specific information for the dating of each charge can be found in its source note.

Annotating Documents

The circuit court system of the 1790s resulted in the justices going to places they had never been to before, meeting new friends, and renewing old acquaintances. As these people and places form the narrative of their letters to wives, friends, and relatives, we try to provide date of birth, date of death, occupation, and, where appropriate, any other important information identifying persons mentioned in the documents. Persons identified in volume 2 of this series are not identified again in volume 3 unless a change in their position warrants it. The index to volume 3 contains references to first mentions and identifications in volume 2.

Cases before the circuit courts mentioned in unofficial and official correspondence and which do not eventually come before the Supreme Court are identified to the extent that the editors have been able to obtain records from repositories.

When the justices quote laws of the United States we do not note minor differences between their quotation and the text of the act printed in the *Statutes at Large.*

Transcribing from Printed Sources

In volume 3, documents obtained from newspapers have been silently corrected where type was inverted, where type did not imprint, or where there were obvious typographical errors.

Guide to Editorial Apparatus

Descriptive Symbols for Documents

The following table includes the symbols used to describe the documents available for publication and citation. When more than one version of a document exists, preference for publication is given in descending order according to this table. Thus, we publish a recipient's copy of a document in preference to a draft. In the source note, all versions are listed, the first being the one we are publishing.

R Recipient's copy of a letter or other document. We determine whether a letter or document is a recipient's copy by any indication of endorsements, the presence of an address cover, or the collection in which it was found. If the letter or document is identifiably a duplicate, triplicate, presscopy, or polygraph copy made and sent to offset possible loss of the original, then we mention that fact in the source note; but the letter or document is still considered a recipient's copy.

D Document. When used to describe commissions and other official documents, this symbol indicates that we cannot identify whether the document is a recipient's copy or a retained copy. When applied to diaries, notes, and journal entries, this symbol means that we are describing an original. If the document is identifiably a duplicate, triplicate, presscopy, or polygraph copy, that fact is explained in the source note; but the document is still marked as "D."

L Letter. We use this symbol when we cannot determine whether a letter is a recipient's copy or a retained copy. If the letter is identifiably a duplicate, triplicate, presscopy, or polygraph copy, then that fact is mentioned in the source note; but the document is still considered an "L."

C   Retained copy of a letter or other document. It is assumed that such copies are kept for personal or official files unless otherwise stated. This designation also is used (with appropriate editorial explanation) for copies of letters sent to individuals other than the addressee. If the letter or document is identifiably a duplicate, triplicate, or polygraph copy, that fact is mentioned in the source note; but the document is still marked with a "C."

Pc   Presscopy. Used only for a retained copy of a letter or document. A presscopy was made by impressing thin dampened paper onto the original document, thereby transferring some ink to the thin paper. The result is frequently blurred and difficult to read.

Lb   Letterbook copy. A letterbook copy of a letter or document is a retained version copied into a bound volume.

Df   Draft of a letter or document.

Pr   Printed version of a letter or document. Usually published substantially later than a contemporary version.

Tr   Transcript of a letter or document made substantially later than a contemporary version. If a transcript is typewritten, that fact is mentioned in the source note. When the origin of a transcript can be identified, an explanation is provided in the source note.

The symbols above are used in combination with the following descriptive symbols.

A   Autograph text (text in the handwriting of the author).

[A?]   Probably autograph text.

S   Signed by the author.

[S?]   Signature cropped, clipped, or obliterated.

Seals are represented by the following symbols.

SEAL   An official seal.

Seal   A handwritten drawing of a seal.

LS, etc. The abbreviations "LS," "L.S.," "LS.," "L.S" as well as the words "Seal" and "SEAL" appear as in the original document.

Three special situations must be noted. First, if we transcribe from a photocopy made from another photocopy or facsimile, we mention that fact in the source note. If we are relying on a text which is itself an extract or abstract, we note that also. Finally, if we translate the text from another language, we explain that in the source note.

Repository Symbols

The following list includes all repository symbols used in this volume.

A-Ar	Alabama Department of Archives and History, Montgomery, Alabama
CtHi	Connecticut Historical Society, Hartford, Connecticut
CtY	Yale University, New Haven, Connecticut
DLC	United States Library of Congress, Washington, D.C.
DNA	United States National Archives and Records Service, Washington, D.C.

      RG 21   Records of District Courts of the United States

      RG 46   Records of the United States Senate

      RG 59   General Records of the Department of State

      RG 217   Records of the United States General Accounting Office

      RG 267   Records of the Supreme Court of the United States

GEpFAR	United States Federal Archives and Records Center, East Point, Georgia

      RG 21   Records of District Courts of the United States

MB	Boston Public Library, Boston, Massachusetts
MH-H	Harvard University, Houghton Library, Cambridge, Massachusetts
MHi	Massachusetts Historical Society, Boston, Massachusetts
MWalFAR	United States Federal Archives and Records Center, Waltham, Massachusetts

      RG 21   Records of District Courts of the United States

MiU-C	University of Michigan, William L. Clements Library, Ann Arbor, Michigan
NHi	New-York Historical Society, New York, New York
Nc-Ar	North Carolina State Department of Archives and History, Raleigh, North Carolina
NcD	Duke University, Durham, North Carolina
NcU	University of North Carolina, Chapel Hill, North Carolina
Nh	New Hampshire State Library, Concord, New Hampshire
NjBaFAR	United States Federal Archives and Records Center, Bayonne, New Jersey

      RG 21   Records of District Courts of the United States

NjR	Rutgers—The State University, New Brunswick, New Jersey
PCarlD	Dickinson College, Carlisle, Pennsylvania
PHarH	Pennsylvania Historical and Museum Commission, Harrisburg, Pennsylvania
PHi	Historical Society of Pennsylvania, Philadelphia, Pennsylvania
PP	Free Library of Philadelphia, Philadelphia, Pennsylvania
PPFAR	United States Federal Archives and Records Center, Philadelphia, Pennsylvania
	RG 21 Records of District Courts of the United States
PPIn	Independence National Historical Park, Philadelphia, Pennsylvania
PPiHi	Historical Society of Western Pennsylvania, Pittsburgh, Pennsylvania
PRO	Public Record Office, Kew Gardens, Surrey, England
	FO 5 Foreign Office, Class 5: General Correspondence, America, United States-Series II, 1793-1905.
	FO 115 Foreign Office, Class 115: Embassy and Consular Archives: America, United States, Correspondence, 1791-1929.
PSC-Hi	Friends Historical Library of Swarthmore College, Swarthmore, Pennsylvania
Vi	Virginia State Library, Richmond, Virginia
ViMtV	Mount Vernon Ladies' Association of the Union, Mount Vernon, Virginia
ViU	University of Virginia, Charlottesville, Virginia
ViW	College of William and Mary, Williamsburg, Virginia

Short Titles and Abbreviations

Ames	Seth Ames, ed., *Works of Fisher Ames,* 2 vols. (Boston: Little, Brown, 1854).
Annals	*Annals of the Congress of the United States,* 42 vols. (Washington, D.C.: Gales and Seaton, 1834-1856).
ASP	*American State Papers: Documents, Legislative and Executive, of the Congress of the United States,* 38 vols. (Washington, D.C.: Gales and Seaton, 1832-1861). This series is divided into ten classes: *Foreign Relations, Indian Affairs, Finance, Commerce and Navigation, Military Affairs, Naval Affairs, Post-Office Department, Public Lands, Claims,* and *Miscellaneous.*

BDAC	U.S., Congress, House, *Biographical Directory of the American Congress, 1774-1961,* 85th Cong., 2d sess., H. Doc. 442, Serial 12108.
Black's Law Dictionary	Henry Campbell Black, *Black's Law Dictionary,* 4th ed. (St. Paul, Minn.: West Publishing, 1951).
Bl. *Comm.*	William Blackstone, *Commentaries on the Laws of England,* 4 vols. (Philadelphia: Rees Welsh, 1897).
CCD	Circuit Court for the district of: e.g., CCD Massachusetts means Circuit Court for the district of Massachusetts.
2 Coke *Inst.*	Edward Coke, *The Second Part of the Institutes of the Laws of England, Containing the Exposition of Many Ancient and Other Statutes,* 2 vols. (London: printed for E. and R. Brooke, 1797).
3 Coke *Inst.*	Edward Coke, *The Third Part of the Institutes of the Laws of England: Concerning High Treason, and Other Pleas of the Crown, and Criminal Causes* (London: printed for E. and R. Brooke, 1797).
DAB	*Dictionary of American Biography.*
Dallas, 1	Alexander James Dallas, *Reports of Cases Ruled and Adjudged in the Courts of Pennsylvania* (Philadelphia: T. Bradford, 1790).
Dallas, 2-4	Alexander James Dallas, *Reports of Cases Ruled and Adjudged in the Several Courts of the United States, and of Pennsylvania,* vol. 2 (Philadelphia: Aurora, 1798); vol. 3 (Philadelphia: J. Ormrod, 1799); vol. 4 (Philadelphia: printed for P. Byrne, by Fry and Kammerer, 1807).
DC	District Court for the district of: e.g., DC Virginia means District Court for the district of Virginia.
DHSC	*The Documentary History of the Supreme Court of the United States, 1789-1800,* 2 vols. to date: vol. 1, ed. Maeva Marcus and James R. Perry; vol. 2, ed. Maeva Marcus (New York: Columbia University Press, 1985-1988).
DNB	*Dictionary of National Biography.*
FFC	*Documentary History of the First Federal Congress of the United States of America,* 6 vols. to date: vols. 1-3, ed. Linda Grant De Pauw; vols. 4-6, ed. Charlene Bangs Bickford and Helen E. Veit (Baltimore: Johns Hopkins University Press, 1972-1986).

FFC, Maclay
Diary

Documentary History of the First Federal Congress of the United States of America, vol. 9, The Diary of William Maclay and other notes on Senate Debates, ed. Kenneth R. Bowling and Helen E. Veit (Baltimore: Johns Hopkins University Press, 1988).

FFE

The Documentary History of the First Federal Elections, 1788-1790, 3 vols. to date: vol. 1, ed. Merrill Jensen and Robert A. Becker; vols. 2-3, ed. Gordon DenBoer (Madison: University of Wisconsin Press, 1976-1986).

HRJ

Journal of the House of Representatives of the United States, vols. 1-9 (Washington, D.C.: Gales and Seaton, 1826).

JCC

Journals of the Continental Congress, 1774-1789, vols. 1-15, ed. Worthington C. Ford; vols. 16-27, ed. Gaillard Hunt; vols. 28-34, ed. John C. Fitzpatrick (Washington, D.C.: Government Printing Office, 1904-1937).

LPAH

The Law Practice of Alexander Hamilton, vols. 1-2, ed. Julius Goebel, Jr.; vols. 3-5, ed. Julius Goebel, Jr., and Joseph H. Smith (New York: Columbia University Press, 1964-1981).

MBBP

John Hill Martin, Martin's Bench and Bar of Philadelphia (Philadelphia: Rees Welsh, 1883).

Miller, Treaties

Hunter Miller, ed., Treaties and Other International Acts of the United States of America, 8 vols. (Washington, D.C.: Government Printing Office, 1931-1948).

MJI

Griffith John McRee, Life and Correspondence of James Iredell, 2 vols. (1857; reprint ed. in 1 vol., New York: Peter Smith, 1949).

OED

Oxford English Dictionary (1933).

PAH

Harold C. Syrett, ed., The Papers of Alexander Hamilton, 26 vols. (New York: Columbia University Press, 1961-1979).

PGM

Robert A. Rutland, ed., The Papers of George Mason, 1725-1792, 3 vols. (Chapel Hill: University of North Carolina Press, 1970).

PGW, Diary

The Diaries of George Washington, vols. 1-3, ed. Donald Jackson; vols. 4-6, ed. Donald Jackson and Dorothy Twohig (Charlottesville: University Press of Virginia, 1976-1979).

PGW, Journal   *The Journal of the Proceedings of the President, 1793-1797,* ed. Dorothy Twohig (Charlottesville: University Press of Virginia, 1981).

PJA   Robert J. Taylor, ed., *Papers of John Adams,* 6 vols. to date (Cambridge: Belknap Press of Harvard University Press, 1977-1983).

PJA, Diary   Lyman H. Butterfield, ed., *Diary and Autobiography of John Adams,* 4 vols. (Cambridge: Belknap Press of Harvard University Press, 1961).

PJA, Legal   L. Kinvin Wroth and Hiller B. Zobel, eds., *Legal Papers of John Adams,* 3 vols. (Cambridge: Belknap Press of Harvard University Press, 1965).

PJI   Don Higginbotham, ed., *The Papers of James Iredell,* 2 vols. to date (Raleigh: Department of Cultural Resources of the Division of Archives and History, 1976).

PJJ   Richard B. Morris, ed., *John Jay,* 2 vols. to date: vol. 1, *The Making of a Revolutionary,* and vol. 2, *The Winning of the Peace* (New York: Harper & Row, 1975-1980).

PJM   *The Papers of John Marshall,* 5 vols. to date: vol. 1, ed. Herbert A. Johnson; vol. 2, ed. Charles T. Cullen and Herbert A. Johnson; vol. 3, ed. William C. Stinchcombe and Charles T. Cullen; vol. 4, ed. Charles T. Cullen; vol. 5, ed. Charles F. Hobson (Chapel Hill: University of North Carolina Press, 1974-1987).

PMad   *The Papers of James Madison,* 15 vols. to date: vols. 1-7, ed. William T. Hutchinson and William M. E. Rachal (Chicago: University of Chicago Press, 1962-1971); vol. 8, ed. Robert A. Rutland and William M. E. Rachal (Chicago: University of Chicago Press, 1975); vols. 9-10, ed. Robert A. Rutland (Chicago: University of Chicago Press, 1977); vols. 11-13, ed. Robert A. Rutland and Charles F. Hobson (Charlottesville: University Press of Virginia, 1977-1981); vol. 14, ed. Robert A. Rutland and Thomas A. Mason (Charlottesville: University Press of Virginia, 1983); vol. 15, ed. Thomas A. Mason, Robert A. Rutland, and Jeanne K. Sisson (Charlottesville: University Press of Virginia, 1985).

PTJ   *The Papers of Thomas Jefferson,* 22 vols. to date: vols. 1-20, ed. Julian P. Boyd; vols. 21-22, ed. Charles T. Cullen (Princeton: Princeton University Press, 1950-1986).

RFC   Max Farrand, ed., *The Records of the Federal Convention of 1787,* 4 vols. (1937; reprint ed., New Haven: Yale University Press, 1966).

ROC   *The Documentary History of the Ratification of the Constitution,* 8 vols. to date: vols. 1-3, ed. Merrill Jensen; vols. 8 and 13-16, ed. John P. Kaminski and Gaspare J. Saladino (Madison: State Historical Society of Wisconsin, 1976-1988).

SEJ   *Journal of the Executive Proceedings of the Senate of the United States of America,* vols. 1-3 (Washington, D.C.: Duff Green, 1828).

SLJ   *Journal of the Senate of the United States of America,* vols. 1-5 (Washington, D.C.: Gales and Seaton, 1820-1821).

Stat.   *The Public Statutes at Large of the United States,* vols. 1-17 (Boston: Little, Brown, 1845-1873); vols. 18-94 (Washington, D.C.: Government Printing Office, 1875-1981).

Statutes (in chronological order of passage)

Collection Act of 1789—"An Act to regulate the Collection of the Duties imposed by law on the tonnage of ships or vessels, and on goods, wares and merchandises imported into the United States," July 31, 1789. *Stat.,* 1:29.

Compensation Act of 1789—"An Act for allowing certain Compensation to the Judges of the Supreme and other Courts, and to the Attorney General of the United States," September 23, 1789. *Stat.,* 1:72.

Judiciary Act of 1789—"An Act to establish the Judicial Courts of the United States," September 24, 1789. *Stat.,* 1:73.

Process Act of 1789—"An Act to regulate Processes in the Courts of the United States," September 29, 1789. *Stat.,* 1:93.

Crimes Act of 1790—"An Act for the Punishment of certain Crimes against the United States," April 30, 1790. *Stat.,* 1:112.

Collection Act of 1790—"An Act to provide more effectually for the collection of the duties imposed by law on goods, wares and merchandise imported into the United States, and on the tonnage of ships or vessels," August 4, 1790. *Stat.,* 1:145.

Circuit and District Court Act of 1790—"An Act to alter the Times for holding the Circuit Courts of the United States in the Districts of South Carolina and Georgia, and providing that the District Court of Pennsylvania shall in future be held at the city of Philadelphia only," August 11, 1790. *Stat.,* 1:184.

Excise Act of 1791—"An Act repealing, after the last day of June next, the duties heretofore laid upon Distilled Spirits imported from abroad, and laying others in their stead; and also upon Spirits distilled within the United States, and for appropriating the same," March 3, 1791. *Stat.,* 1:199.

Compensation and Circuit Court Act of 1791—"An Act providing compensations for the officers of the Judicial Courts of the United States, and for Jurors and Witnesses, and for other purposes," March 3, 1791. *Stat.,* 1:216.

Invalid Pensions Act of 1792—"An Act to provide for the settlement of the Claims of Widows and Orphans barred by the limitations heretofore established, and to regulate the Claims to Invalid Pensions," March 23, 1792. *Stat.,* 1:243.

Circuit Court Act of 1792—"An Act for altering the times of holding the Circuit Courts, in certain districts of the United States, and for other purposes," April 13, 1792. *Stat.,* 1:252.

Excise Act of 1792—"An Act concerning the Duties on Spirits distilled within the United States," May 8, 1792. *Stat.,* 1:267.

Process and Compensation Act of 1792—"An Act for regulating Processes in the Courts of the United States, and providing Compensations for the Officers of the said Courts, and for Jurors and Witnesses," May 8, 1792. *Stat.,* 1:275.

Invalid Pensions Act of 1793—"An Act to regulate the Claims to Invalid Pensions," February 28, 1793. *Stat.,* 1:324.

Judiciary Act of 1793—"An Act in addition to the Act, entitled 'An Act to establish the Judicial Courts of the United States,' " March 2, 1793. *Stat.,* 1:333.

Circuit Court Act of 1793—"An Act to alter the times and places of holding the Circuit Courts, in the Eastern District, and in North Carolina, and for other purposes," March 2, 1793. *Stat.,* 1:335.

Adjournment Act of 1794—"An Act further to authorize the Adjournment of Circuit Courts," May 19, 1794. *Stat.,* 1:369.

Excise Act of 1794—"An Act making further provision for securing and collecting the Duties on foreign and domestic distilled Spirits, Stills, Wines and Teas," June 5, 1794. *Stat.,* 1:378.

Neutrality Act of 1794—"An Act in addition to the act for the punishment of certain crimes against the United States," June 5, 1794. *Stat.,* 1:381.

Invalid Pensions Act of 1794—"An Act concerning Invalids," June 7, 1794. *Stat.,* 1:392.

District and Circuit Court Act of 1794—"An Act making certain alterations in the act for establishing the Judicial Courts, and altering the time and place of holding certain courts," June 9, 1794. *Stat.,* 1:395.

Invalid Pensions Act of 1795—"An Act supplementary to the act concerning Invalids," February 21, 1795. *Stat.,* 1:418.

Circuit Court Act of 1797—"An Act concerning the Circuit Courts of the United States," March 3, 1797. *Stat.,* 1:517.

Alien Act of 1798—"An Act concerning Aliens," June 25, 1798. *Stat.,* 1:570.

Alien Enemies Act of 1798—"An Act respecting Alien Enemies," July 6, 1798. *Stat.,* 1:577.

Sedition Act of 1798—"An Act in addition to the act, entitled 'An act for the punishment of certain crimes against the United States,' " July 14, 1798. *Stat.,* 1:596.

Crimes Act of 1799—"An Act for the punishment of certain Crimes therein specified," January 30, 1799. *Stat.,* 1:613.

Judiciary Act of 1801—"An Act to provide for the more convenient organization of the Courts of the United States," February 13, 1801. *Stat.,* 2:89.

Repeal Act of 1802—"An Act to repeal certain acts respecting the organization of the Courts of the United States; and for other purposes," March 8, 1802. *Stat.,* 2:132.

Judiciary Act of 1802—"An Act to amend the Judicial System of the United States," April 29, 1802. *Stat.,* 2:156.

Newspaper Coverage, 1787-1801

As extensive as our newspaper search has been (see the "Introduction" to volume 1), we have not been able to locate complete runs for every newspaper we wanted to read. We have given priority to reading all hard copy and microcopy available at the Library of Congress. Next, we have sought to borrow microform copy on interlibrary loan from a number of libraries and historical societies. Despite our best efforts, we often have been unable to secure all copies of every newspaper.

The list that follows presents the newspapers that were read and the extent of the coverage for each. Our short titles correspond to those used by Clarence S. Brigham in his two-volume *History and Bibliography of American Newspapers, 1690-1820* (Worcester, Massachusetts: American Antiquarian Society, 1947) and in his "Additions and Corrections to *History and Bibliography of American Newspapers, 1690-1820,*" included in the *Proceedings of the American Antiquarian Society* 71 (1961): 15-62. Brigham's bibliography and supplement provide full newspaper titles, changes in those titles, dates of publication, as well as printers and publishers. Following the name of the newspaper, we place in parentheses the years that the newspaper was published between 1787 and 1801—the years included in our search. Finally, we indicate how many issues of the newspaper we were able to find and read. We note the coverage by these terms:

> "full" means all issues (sometimes with a few exceptions) were available
> "very good" means three-quarters or more was available
> "good" means one-half to three-quarters was available
> "poor" means less than one-half was available
> "scattered" means only a few issues were available.

CONNECTICUT

Hartford
American Mercury (1787-1801): 1787-1791 missing, 1792-1797 very good, 1798 missing, and 1799-1801 full.
Connecticut Courant (1787-1801): full.
Hartford Gazette (1794-1795): good.

New Haven
Connecticut Journal (1787-1801): full.

DELAWARE

Wilmington
Delaware and Eastern-Shore Advertiser (1794-1799): scattered.
Delaware Gazette (1787-1799): good.
Mirror of the Times (1799-1801): very good.

GEORGIA

Augusta
Augusta Chronicle (1789-1801): 1789-1794 very good, 1795 good, 1796-1801 missing.

Augusta Herald (1799-1801): scattered.
Georgia State Gazette (1787-1789): full.
Southern Centinel (1793-1799): scattered.

Savannah
Columbian Museum (1796-1801): 1796-1797 good, 1798-1801 poor.
Gazette of the State of Georgia (1787-1788): full.
Georgia Gazette (1788-1801): very good.

MARYLAND

Annapolis
Maryland Gazette (1787-1801): 1787-1789 scattered, 1790 very good, 1791-1794 missing, 1795-1798 very good, 1799-1801 missing.

Baltimore
American (1799-1801): very good.
Baltimore Daily Intelligencer (1793-1794): full.
Baltimore Daily Repository (1791-1793): full.
Baltimore Evening Post (1792-1793): scattered.
Baltimore Telegraphe (1795-1801): scattered.
Edwards's Baltimore Daily Advertiser (1793-1794): scattered.
Federal Gazette (1796-1801): full.
Federal Intelligencer (1794-1795): full.
Maryland Gazette (1787-1792): 1787-1790 poor, 1791-1792 missing.
Maryland Journal (1787-1797): 1787-1792 full, 1793-1794 good, 1795-1797 missing.

Easton
Maryland Herald (1790-1801): scattered.
Republican Star (1799-1801): scattered.

MASSACHUSETTS

Boston
American Apollo (1792-1794): very good.
American Herald (1787-1788): very good.
Argus (1791-1793): 1791 poor, 1792-1793 full.
Boston Gazette (1787-1798): full.
Boston Gazette (1800-1801): full.
Boston Price-Current (1795-1798): scattered.
Columbian Centinel (1790-1801): full.
Courier (1795-1796): poor.
Federal Gazette (1798): poor.
Federal Orrery (1794-1796): good.
Herald of Freedom (1788-1791): 1788-1790 good, 1791 scattered.

Independent Chronicle (1787-1801): full.
Massachusetts Centinel (1787-1790): full.
Massachusetts Gazette (1787-1788): full.
Massachusetts Mercury (1793-1801): 1793-1796 poor, 1797-1801 full.
Russell's Gazette (1798-1800): full.
Times (1794): scattered.

New Hampshire

Exeter
Herald of Liberty (1793-1796): scattered.
Lamson's Weekly Visitor (1795): good.
New Hampshire Gazetteer (1789-1793): scattered.
Political Banquet (1799-1800): scattered.
Ranlet's Federal Miscellany (1798-1799): scattered.

Portsmouth
Federal Observer (1798-1800): scattered.
New-Hampshire Gazette (1787-1801): 1787-1789 missing, 1790-1792 very good, 1793-1794 missing, 1795-1801 very good.
New-Hampshire Spy (1787-1793): 1787-1788 very good, 1789-1793 missing.
Oracle of the Day (1793-1799): 1793-1796 missing, 1797-1798 full, 1799 missing.
Republican Ledger (1799-1801): scattered.
United States Oracle (1800-1801): full.

New Jersey

Trenton
Federalist (1798-1801): full.
Federal Post (1788-1789): poor.
New-Jersey State Gazette (1792-1796): 1792-1794 missing, 1795-1796 very good.
New-Jersey State Gazette (1799-1800): good.
State Gazette (1796-1799): scattered.

New York

Albany
Albany Register (1788-1801): scattered.

New York
American Citizen (1800-1801): poor.
American Minerva (1793-1796): 1793-1794 poor, 1795-1796 missing.
Argus (1795-1800): very good.

Commercial Advertiser (1797-1801): full.
Daily Advertiser (1787-1801): 1787-1793 full, 1794-1795 poor, 1796-1797 missing, 1798-1801 very good.
Diary (1792-1798): 1792-1793 poor, 1794 full, 1795 scattered, 1796-1798 good.
Forlorn Hope (1800): full.
Gazette of the United States (1789-1790): full.
Greenleaf's New York Journal (1794-1800): scattered.
Impartial Gazetteer (1788): good.
Mercantile Advertiser (1798-1801): scattered.
Minerva (1796-1797): full.
New-York Daily Gazette (1788-1795): 1788-1789 full, 1790-1795 missing.
New-York Gazette (1795-1801): scattered.
New-York Journal (1787-1793): very good.
New-York Morning Post (1787-1792): scattered.
New York Packet (1787-1792): scattered.
New-York Weekly Museum (1788-1801): 1788-1791 scattered, 1792-1794 very good, 1795-1796 missing, 1797-1801 very good.
Time Piece (1797-1798): full.

NORTH CAROLINA

Edenton
State Gazette of North-Carolina (1788-1799): very good.

Fayetteville
North-Carolina Minerva (1796-1799): good.

New Bern
Newbern Gazette (1798-1801): scattered.
North-Carolina Gazette (1787-1798): scattered.
State Gazette of North-Carolina (1787-1788): scattered.

Raleigh
North-Carolina Minerva (1799-1801): good.
Raleigh Register (1799-1801): full.

Salisbury
North-Carolina Mercury (1798-1801): scattered.

Wilmington
Wilmington Centinel (1788): full.

PENNSYLVANIA

Norristown
Norristown Gazette (1799-1800): scattered.

Philadelphia
   Aurora (1794-1801): full.
   Claypoole's American Daily Advertiser (1796-1800): full.
   Complete Counting House Companion (1787-1790): scattered.
   Country Porcupine (1798-1799): scattered.
   Daily Advertiser (1797): good.
   Dunlap's American Daily Advertiser (1791-1795): full.
   Evening Chronicle (1787): scattered.
   Federal Gazette (1788-1793): full.
   Freeman's Journal (1787-1792): full.
   Gales's Independent Gazetteer (1796-1797): full.
   Gazette of the United States (1790-1801): 1790-1793 full, 1794-1798 good,
      1799 missing, 1800-1801 very good.
   General Advertiser (1790-1794): full.
   Independent Gazetteer (1787-1796): full.
   National Gazette (1791-1793): full.
   New World (1796-1797): very good.
   Pennsylvania Evening Herald (1787-1788): full.
   Pennsylvania Gazette (1787-1801): 1787-1796 full, 1797-1801 missing.
   Pennsylvania Journal (1787-1793): full.
   Pennsylvania Mercury (1787-1792): full.
   Pennsylvania Packet (1787-1790): full.
   Philadelphia Gazette (1794-1801): full.
   Philadelphia Minerva (1795-1798): full.
   Porcupine's Gazette (1797-1799): full.
   Poulson's American Daily Advertiser (1800-1801): full.
   True American (1798-1801): scattered.
   Universal Gazette (1797-1800): full.

York
   Pennsylvania Herald (1789-1800): 1789-1793 full, 1794-1795 missing,
      1796-1798 full, 1799-1800 missing.
   York Recorder (1800-1801): full.

RHODE ISLAND

Newport
   Companion (1798-1799): scattered.
   Guardian of Liberty (1800-1801): scattered.
   Newport Mercury (1787-1801): 1787-1791 very good, 1792-1801 full.

Providence
   Providence Gazette (1787-1801): very good.
   Providence Journal (1799-1801): full.
   State Gazette (1796): poor.

United States Chronicle (1787-1801): 1787-1799 very good, 1800-1801 missing.

SOUTH CAROLINA

Charleston
City Gazette (1787-1801): 1787-1788 missing, 1789 full, 1790-1795 missing, 1796 full, 1797 missing, 1798-1801 very good.
Columbian Herald (1787-1796): 1787-1792 missing, 1793-1794 poor, 1795 missing, 1796 poor.
Federal Carolina Gazette (1800): scattered.
South-Carolina State-Gazette (1794-1801): 1794-1796 poor, 1797 missing, 1798-1799 poor, 1800-1801 missing.
State Gazette of South-Carolina (1787-1793): 1787-1790 good, 1791-1792 missing, 1793 very good.
Times (1800-1801): full.

VERMONT

Bennington
Vermont Gazette (1787-1796): 1787-1792 full, 1793 poor, 1794-1796 missing.

Rutland
Farmers' Library (1793-1794): full.
Herald of Vermont (1792): full.
Rutland Herald (1794-1801): 1794-1800 full, 1801 missing.

VIRGINIA

Norfolk
Norfolk Weekly Journal (1797-1798): full.
Virginia Chronicle (1792-1795): good.

Richmond
Examiner (1798-1801): scattered.
Friend of the People (1800): scattered.
Observatory (1797-1798): scattered.
Press (1800): scattered.
Richmond and Manchester Advertiser (1795-1796): poor.
Richmond Chronicle (1795-1796): scattered.
Virginia Argus (1796-1801): 1796-1798 missing, 1799-1801 good.
Virginia Federalist (1799-1800): scattered.
Virginia Gazette, and General Advertiser (1790-1801): 1790-1796 very good, 1797-1798 scattered, 1799 very good, 1800-1801 scattered.
Virginia Gazette and Independent Chronicle (1787-1789): scattered.

Virginia Gazette, and Richmond and Manchester Advertiser (1793-1795): very good.

Virginia Gazette & Richmond Chronicle (1793-1795): scattered.

Virginia Gazette, and Weekly Advertiser (1787-1797): 1787-1789 full, 1790-1797 missing.

Virginia Independent Chronicle (1787-1790): full.

The Documentary History of
the Supreme Court of
the United States, 1789-1800

Volume Three
The Justices on Circuit
1795-1800

—

Spring and Fall Circuits 1795

The Supreme Court opened its sixth year with its chief justice, John Jay, still over-seas. After completing the negotiations for a commercial treaty with Great Britain, Jay—never a good sailor and now in ill health—had elected to remain in England tem-porarily rather than risk the dangers of a winter crossing of the North Atlantic.[1] "Much of the dignity of the Court is lost by the absence of the Chief Justice," remarked an observer of the Court's opening session in February. According to this same com-mentator, Jay "was the ornament of the Bench."[2]

With the chief justice in England the leadership of the Court fell to the senior as-sociate justice, sixty-three-year-old William Cushing. Suffering from a cancer on the lip, Cushing guided the Court through a lengthy February term, attending either when he was well or if needed to make a quorum.[3] For eight days the justices heard argu-ments in the highly political *Penhallow v. Doane's Administrators,* a revolutionary war prize case that had been the subject of several remonstrances by the New Hampshire legislature. On February 24 the Court handed down its decision against the plaintiffs, citizens of New Hamsphire who repeatedly had been victorious in that state's courts.[4]

Because of the importance attached to the pending trials at Philadelphia of those who participated in the Whiskey Rebellion, a spring circuit arrangement was contem-plated that would allow two justices to preside. James Iredell would begin riding the Eastern Circuit and Paterson the Middle Circuit. Once the Philadelphia court opened, Iredell would return to assist Paterson. William Cushing would then take the remain-der of Iredell's Eastern Circuit, James Wilson the rest of Paterson's courts on the Middle Circuit, and John Blair the Southern. Cushing's medical condition, however, may have forced a change in the assignments, for Iredell ended up riding the entire Eastern Circuit, and Paterson presided over the trial of the whiskey rebels by himself. Those trials ended on June 3, just three days before the scheduled opening of the Delaware circuit court, and Paterson made a hurried departure from Philadelphia in order to open court in New Castle. Wilson held the courts in Maryland and Virginia.

Riding the Eastern Circuit did spare Iredell the task of sitting with Paterson at the Whiskey Rebellion trials in Philadelphia, something Paterson found "a disagreeable necessity."[5] The government sent thirty-six bills for treason to the grand jury, which returned twelve *ignoramus*. Of the remaining twenty-four accused, only ten were brought to trial, and of these, two—Philip Vigol and John Mitchell—were found guilty and

---

1. Frank Monaghan, *John Jay* (New York: Bobbs-Merrill, 1935), pp. 228, 370-71; *PJJ,* 1:680; *PAH,* 17:390.

2. *DHSC,* 1:752, 753.

3. Ibid., 1:752.

4. Ibid., 1:233, 235-38, 241; Julius Goebel, Jr., *Antecedents and Beginnings to 1801,* vol. 1 of *The Oliver Wendell Holmes Devise History of the Supreme Court of the United States* (New York: Macmillan, 1971), pp. 765-70. A more complete treatment of this case will appear in a subsequent volume of the *DHSC.*

5. William Paterson to Euphemia Paterson, February 20, [1795] (q.v.).

sentenced to be hanged.[6] Paterson's charge to the petit jury at the Vigol trial seemed to preclude any possibility of acquittal: "With respect to the evidence, the current runs one way," he told them. "With respect to the intention, likewise, there is not, unhappily, the slightest possibility of doubt."[7]

Before the executions of Vigol and Mitchell could be carried out, they were pardoned by the president.[8] But the events of the Whiskey Rebellion provided rich material for the justices as they made the rounds of the spring circuit courts. Paterson's grand jury charges warned that "civil liberty and order consist in and depend upon submission to the laws." Those "turbulent and refractory" individuals violently opposed to the government were guilty of the "highest crime of a civil nature": treason.[9] Delivering a charge in Georgia, John Blair characterized the rebellion as the work of "licentious abusers, of liberty" who, if left unchecked, would plunge all men into a state of nature where evil roamed freely. Like Paterson, Blair saw education as the best antidote for rebellion. "[L]et us all inculcate upon the minds of our more ignorant brethren," he concluded, "the high advantages of our social compact, and the eminent interest which we all have in its inviolable preservation; and let us prove to them the sincerity of our professions, by a dutiful obedience even to such laws (if such there be) as do not in themselves meet our approbation."[10]

Three weeks after the conclusion of the trials, John Jay, recently returned from Europe, resigned from the Court to become governor of New York.[11] For the first time the office of chief justice fell vacant. Moreover, one of the remaining five justices had health problems that affected his attendance on the bench and circuit. John Blair suffered from "a rattling, distracting noise" in his head that forced him to adjourn prematurely the spring South Carolina circuit court and to cancel entirely the North Carolina court.[12] When the Senate adjourned and no replacement for Jay had been named, James Iredell was "extremely mortified." "I have too much reason to fear that owing to that circumstance it will be unavoidable for me to have some Circuit duty to perform this fall."[13]

Unbeknownst to Iredell, on July 1 the post of chief justice had been offered to his former associate on the bench, John Rutledge of South Carolina. Rutledge, aware that Jay would probably resign after his election to the governorship, had written to President Washington expressing interest in the position. Coincidentally, Rutledge's application arrived on Washington's desk the same day as Jay's resignation. For Wash-

6. Albert Gallatin to Thomas Clare, May 30, 1795, Albert Gallatin Papers, NHi; Engrossed Minutes, May 1795 term, CCD Pennsylvania, RG 21, PPFAR; Thomas P. Slaughter, *The Whiskey Rebellion* (New York: Oxford University Press, 1986), pp. 219-20. We wish to thank Mary K. Bonsteel Tachau for her help in ascertaining the number of rebels accused and tried.

7. Francis Wharton, *State Trials of the United States During the Administrations of Washington and Adams* (Philadelphia: Carey and Hart, 1849), p. 175.

8. Ibid., pp. 176n, 183n.

9. William Paterson's Charge to the Grand Jury of the Circuit Court for the District of New Jersey, [April 2, 1795], and William Paterson's Charge to the Grand Jury of the Circuit Court for the District of Pennsylvania, [May 4, 1795] (qq.v.).

10. John Blair's Charge to the Grand Jury of the Circuit Court for the District of Georgia, April 27, 1795 (q.v.).

11. *DHSC*, 1:7, 13.

12. See John Blair to William Cushing, June 12, 1795.

13. James Iredell to Hannah Iredell, July 2, 1795 (q.v.).

ington the choice was easy, and the following day he dispatched a reply offering Rutledge an interim appointment, subject to confirmation by the Senate on its return.[14]

As Jay prepared to leave the bench, the treaty that bore his name was becoming an object of heated controversy. His mission had been to negotiate a commercial treaty with Great Britain while securing concessions that would prevent war between the two countries.[15] In the sense that war was averted (or postponed until 1812) the negotiations were successful, but the terms of the treaty and the negotiator came under harsh criticism. Even what appeared to be a unilateral concession by the British—a promise that by June 1796 they would surrender their military posts along the United States' northwestern frontier—was scorned, as the withdrawal had been a condition of the Definitive Treaty of Peace (1783). The treaty made no provision for compensating the owners of slaves confiscated by the British during the Revolution; there was no mention of ending the impressment of American seamen by the British navy; and the commercial arrangements were viewed as too favorable to English interests. Other outstanding issues between the two countries, such as compensation for the capture of American merchant ships and the repayment of British debts, were left for future determination by arbitration boards.[16]

The treaty arrived in Philadelphia in early March, after the Senate had adjourned. It reconvened for a special executive session on June 8. Sixteen days later, the Senate consented to the treaty's ratification by a vote of twenty to ten, but only on condition that Article 12 be eliminated.[17] Parts of the treaty were unacceptable even to its backers; the whole, unacceptable to many others. Hamilton, an avid supporter of the treaty, criticized the provisions of two of its articles; Washington also expressed reservations.[18] Republicans denounced the treaty as harmful to the interests of the country and to those of a faithful ally, France. Jefferson referred to it as an "execrable thing . . . which is really nothing more than a treaty of alliance between England & the Anglomen of this country against the legislature & people of the United States."[19]

The Senate's deliberations on the Jay Treaty had been conducted under an injunction of secrecy, but after the conditional vote on June 24, opponents of the treaty leaked copies to the press, and its publication sparked a wildfire of public protest. The terms of the treaty were denounced at public meetings in Portsmouth, Boston, New York, and Norfolk.[20] In Philadelphia, a crowd celebrated Independence Day by parading through the streets with a caricature of Jay selling his country for British gold; afterwards, it burned Jay in effigy.[21] At a public meeting in Charleston on July

14. *DHSC*, 1:94-97.

15. Ibid., 2:436.

16. For a discussion of the terms of the treaty, see Jerald A. Combs, *The Jay Treaty: Political Battleground of the Founding Fathers* (Berkeley: University of California Press, 1970), pp. 151-58.

17. *SEJ*, 1:177, 186. Article 12 of the Jay Treaty allowed small American ships to trade in the West Indies for the first time, but in exchange for this privilege the American exportation of molasses, sugar, coffee, cocoa, and cotton, including goods brought from the West Indies, was prohibited. Combs, *Jay Treaty*, pp. 152-53.

18. *PAH*, 18:432, 443, 461-64.

19. Thomas Jefferson to Edward Rutledge, November 30, 1795, Paul Leicester Ford, ed., *The Works of Thomas Jefferson*, Federal Edition, 12 vols. (New York: G. P. Putnam's Sons, 1904), 8:200.

20. George Hammond to Lord Grenville, July 27, 1795, vol. 4, FO115, PRO; John A. Carroll and Mary W. Ashworth, *George Washington*, vol. 7, *First in Peace*, completing the biography by Douglas Southall Freeman (New York: Charles Scribner's Sons, 1957), pp. 268-69.

21. *Independent Gazetteer* (Philadelphia), July 8, 1795.

16, a group of citizens met to "consider whether the impending treaty . . . is not degrading to the national honour, dangerous to the political existence, and destructive of the agricultural, manufacturing, commercial and shipping interests of the people of the United States."[22] Among the speakers was the Supreme Court's next chief justice, John Rutledge. Rising from his seat, he characterized the treaty as a "surrender of our rights and privileges." Jay should have demanded, Rutledge argued, an unconditional return of the frontier posts. The one article that had "the appearance of reciprocity"— the twelfth, allowing small American ships access to British West Indies ports—was on further examination revealed to be "a deception, a trick that add[ed] insult to injury." In addition, the plan permitting commissioners to arbitrate claims by British creditors was "ridiculous and inadmissible," denying the state courts and the Supreme Court their rightful authority. Dearly as he loved the president, Rutledge concluded, he would rather see him die than have him sign that treaty.[23]

Rutledge's remarks would doom his chances for confirmation as chief justice. His lack of circumspection outraged the Federalist-controlled Senate, which had yet to approve his appointment, and greatly embarrassed key members of the Washington administration. After all, asked Secretary of the Treasury Oliver Wolcott of Alexander Hamilton, "what must the British Government think of the United States, when they find . . . the Country rising into a flame, their Ministers house insulted by a Mob— their flag dragged through the Streets as in Charleston & burnt before the doors of their Consul—[and] A driveller & fool appointed Chief Justice."[24]

On August 12 Washington took the first step to end the controversy over the Jay Treaty by announcing to his cabinet his intention to ratify it;[25] that same day, the newly appointed chief justice took the oath of office in Philadelphia.[26] On August 13 Rutledge presided over a Court that already had been sitting for one week and would not adjourn until August 24.[27] The length of the term was caused in part by one case, *Talbot v. Jansen,* which had the distinction of being the first to appear before the Court that involved a violation of the Neutrality Act of 1794.[28]

Although there is no extant record of the circuit assignments for the fall of 1795, it is clear that neither Iredell nor Blair thought that he should have to ride circuit, and that Cushing believed it was his turn to take the Middle Circuit. But something happened during the August meeting that threw the circuit assignments into disarray. Iredell was apparently assigned to the Middle Circuit but balked and tried to get Blair to substitute for him. Blair, for his part, wondered why either of them was asked to

22. *DHSC,* 1:765.

23. A newspaper account of the meeting in Charleston and John Rutledge's speech is printed in *DHSC,* 1:765-67.

24. Oliver Wolcott, Jr., to Alexander Hamilton, July 30, 1795, *PAH,* 18:531n.

25. Two days later Washington signed the treaty. Combs, *Jay Treaty,* p. 167. Upon hearing the news, a thankful British minister reported to Whitehall that this and other actions "will, I trust, completely supress that Spirit of Faction and Turbulence, which has, of late, been excited without Cause, for mere Party Purposes." Phineas Bond to Lord Grenville, August 16, 1795, vol. 4, FO115, PRO. On October 28, 1795, instruments of ratification, including an additional article suspending Article 12, were exchanged in London, and the treaty was proclaimed by George Washington on February 29, 1796. Miller, *Treaties,* 2:245.

26. *DHSC,* 1:97, 248.

27. Ibid., pp. 244-53. It was the Supreme Court's longest August term of the decade.

28. *DHSC,* 1:246-52; Goebel, *Antecedents and Beginnings to 1801,* pp. 770-75. A more complete treatment of this case will appear in a subsequent volume of the *DHSC.*

Engraving by an unknown artist, ca. 1795. Courtesy Historical Society of Pennsylvania, Philadelphia. Journalist William Cobbett, otherwise known as "Porcupine," is shown being paid by the devil to write in support of Great Britain. He is encouraged by the British lion upon whose back rides John Jay, represented as a bird holding a copy of the Jay Treaty in his beak.

ride a circuit so soon after his last one. Unable to continue his judicial duties because of an "overbearing noise in my head" which rendered him "utterly unfit" and "incapable of business," Blair informed Iredell in September that he could not ride circuit and would probably soon resign from the Court.[29] Somehow an arrangement was reached whereby the Middle Circuit was divided between Paterson (who took New Jersey and Pennsylvania), Wilson (Maryland and Delaware), and Iredell (Virginia). Cushing escaped the Middle Circuit and rode the Eastern, while Rutledge took the Southern Circuit.

On October 25, 1795, with no prospect of recovery from his longstanding illness, John Blair tendered his resignation from the Supreme Court.[30] This reduced the number of justices to five, and it would not be long before another vacancy arose. When the Senate reconvened in December, one of the first things it took up was the con-

---

29. John Blair to James Iredell, October 10, 1795, *DHSC,* 1:802-3; John Blair to James Iredell, September 14, 1795 (q.v.).
30. *DHSC,* 1:59.

firmation of John Rutledge's recess appointment. On December 15, 1795, by a vote of fourteen to ten, the Senate rejected the nomination.[31]

The controversy over his remarks in Charleston had taken its toll on Rutledge. For months Rutledge had endured rumors regarding his sanity, finances, and sobriety that had circulated freely in the Federalist press and in the inner circles of the administration. With his health and spirits battered, Rutledge even made an unsuccessful attempt to drown himself in Charleston; two days later, pleading ill health and probably unaware of the Senate's rejection of his nomination, he resigned his commission.[32]

31. Ibid., pp. 98-99; *SEJ*, 1:186.
32. *DHSC*, 1:100. For commentary on Rutledge's appointment, his speech, and allegations of insanity, see *DHSC*, 1:772-831.

James Iredell to Hannah Iredell

February 13, 1795   Philadelphia, Pennsylvania

...The Circuits are not yet assigned, but it is understood I am to go the Eastern Circuit, though it is in contemplation at present that I shall only go part of it, and Judge Cushing the remainder, that I may return here to assist Judge Paterson [in?] trying the Insurgents.[1] If this be so, Judge Wilson will attend the remainder of the Middle Circuit, and Judge Blair the Southern.
. . .

ARS (Nc-Ar, Charles E. Johnson Collection). Addressed "Edenton, North Carolina." Postmarked "[13?] FE."
1. Participants in the Whiskey Rebellion.

William Paterson to Euphemia Paterson

February 20, [1795]   Philadelphia, Pennsylvania

...M? Blair, will go the southern circuit _ It is probable that I shall be under the disagreeable necessity of trying the insurgents at this place. If so, I shall be here all the months of April and May, and perhaps part of June. ...

ALS (NjR, William Paterson Papers). William Paterson dated this letter February 20, 1794. The reference to the insurgents, however, indicates that it was written in 1795.

James Iredell to Hannah Iredell

February 26, 1795   Philadelphia, Pennsylvania

...It is expected that the insurgents will have their trial at the Circuit Court here; and therefore that Judge Patterson will not be able to attend any other

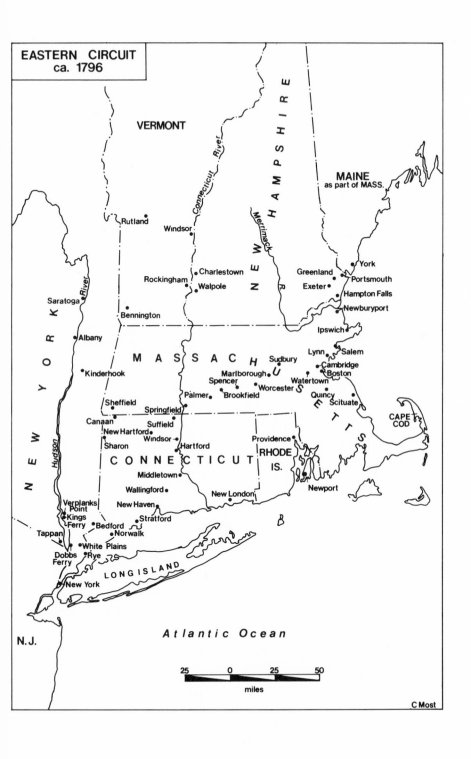

**EASTERN CIRCUIT
ca. 1796**

VERMONT

Connecticut River

NEW HAMPSHIRE

MAINE
as part of MASS.

Rutland

Windsor

Merrimack R.

Charlestown
Rockingham
Walpole

Greenland
Exeter

York
Portsmouth
Hampton Falls
Newburyport

Saratoga

River

Bennington

Ipswich

Albany

MASSACHU

Kinderhook

Sudbury
Marlborough
Spencer
Brookfield
Palmer
Worcester

Lynn
Cambridge
Boston
Watertown

Salem

SETTS

Quincy
Scituate

Sheffield
Springfield
Canaan
New Hartford
Suffield
Sharon
Windsor
Hartford

CAPE
COD

Providence

CONNECTICUT
RHODE
IS.

Hudson

Middletown
Wallingford

New London

Newport

N
E
W

Y
O
R
K

Verplanks
Point
Kings
Ferry
Tappan
Bedford
Norwalk
White Plains
Dobbs
Ferry
Rye

New Haven
Stratford

B

LONG ISLAND

New York

N.J.

Atlantic Ocean

25   0   25   50
miles

C Most

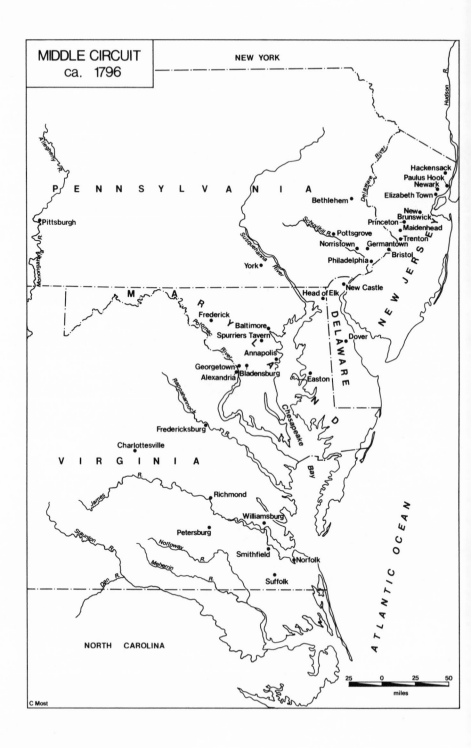

MIDDLE CIRCUIT
ca. 1796

NEW YORK

PENNSYLVANIA

Allegheny R.

Pittsburgh

Monongahela R.

Bethlehem

Schuylkill R.

Pottsgrove

Norristown

Germantown

Philadelphia

York

Susquehanna River

Hackensack
Paulus Hook
Newark
Elizabeth Town
New
Brunswick
Princeton
Maidenhead
Trenton
Bristol

NEW JERSEY

Delaware River

Hudson R.

Head of Elk

New Castle

MARYLAND

Frederick

Potomac River

Baltimore

Spurriers Tavern

Annapolis

Georgetown
Alexandria
Bladensburg

Easton

DELAWARE

Dover

Chesapeake Bay

Fredericksburg

Rappahannock R.

Charlottesville

VIRGINIA

James R.

Staunton R.

Richmond

Williamsburg

Petersburg

Nottoway R.

Meherrin R.

Dan R.

Smithfield

Suffolk

Norfolk

ATLANTIC OCEAN

NORTH CAROLINA

25   0   25   50
miles

C Most

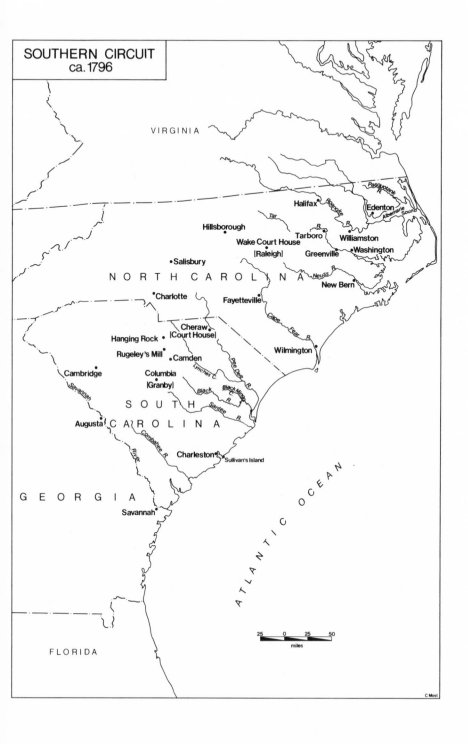

SOUTHERN CIRCUIT
ca. 1796

VIRGINIA

Halifax

Edenton

Hillsborough

Tar

Wake Court House
[Raleigh]

Tarboro

Williamston

Greenville

Washington

Albemarle Sound

Pasquotank

Roanoke

Salisbury

NORTH CAROLINA

Neuss

Charlotte

Fayetteville

New Bern

Cheraw
[Court House]

Hanging Rock

Cape Fear

Rugeley's Mill

Camden

Wilmington

Cambridge

Columbia
[Granby]

Lynches C.

Pee Dee

SOUTH

Black River

Black Mingo C.

CAROLINA

Santee R.

Savannah

Augusta

Combahee R.

Charleston

Sullivan's Island

GEORGIA

River

ATLANTIC OCEAN

Savannah

FLORIDA

25   0   25   50
miles

C Most

Court in the Middle Circuit, in which case (if the C. Justice does not come in time) Mr. Wilson has promised to attend the other Courts.[1] There was no offer to exchange with me, or I should have liked it very much. Agreeable as the Eastern Circuit would be to me in all other respects, it distresses me beyond measure to think of the painful situation in which it places me with regard to you, and my dear children. The last Court will be held in Rhode Island the 19th of June, and probably continue until the latter end of the month, if not till sometime in July, for there is always a good deal of business there, so that I have no expectation that I can get home until after the Supreme Court in August...

Pr (Printed in *MJI*, 2:440-41).
    1. Chief Justice John Jay did not return from England until late May, 1795. Monaghan, *John Jay*, p. 387.

Circuit Court for the District of New Jersey ——————————————
April 2, 1795   Trenton, New Jersey

    The circuit court for New Jersey opened on April 2, with Associate Justice William Paterson and Judge Robert Morris in attendance. Paterson delivered a charge to the grand jury. The court met twice again before adjourning on April 4 until the next term.[1]

    1. Minutes, CCD New Jersey, RG 21, NjBaFAR; William Paterson's Charge to the Grand Jury of the Circuit Court for the District of New Jersey, [April 2, 1795] (q.v.).

William Paterson's Charge to the Grand Jury of the Circuit Court for the District of New Jersey ——————————————
[April 2, 1795]   [Trenton, New Jersey]

Gentlemen of the grand jury.
    The office, into which you have been sworn, is of the utmost importance to the good order, peace, and prosperity of the government under which we live. ~~Your~~ Offences of an indictable nature create distrust, excite terror, and disturb the public tranquility ~~and mind~~; their example too is contagious and alarming, especially if ~~they~~ be suffered to pass without legal and speedy animadversion_ For the security, then, and uninterupted enjoyment of our civil liberties and rights, it became necessary that crimes should be inquired into, and their perpetrators denounced by some competent authority. ~~And~~
                                                    invent
The wisdom of ages has not been able to ~~discover~~ and establish any institution so adequate for the purpose as that of grand juries. The justice of the nation is, in criminal matters, committed to their care; for they must present before courts can punish; they are the medium through which offences receive

judicial discussion and reproof. To the execution of this high office you are gentlemen at present called upon by the laws of your country. These laws prescribe your duty, and direct to the investigation and presentment of almost every offence, which may have been perpetrated, in this district, against the United States. No offender, whatever may be his condition, can hope to elude the vigilance or avert the justice of a tribunal, whose duty and interest happily coincide , and lead to in the detection and punishment of crimes, and whose authority descends to the lowest and reaches to the highest character in social life. The proper exercise of your function protects the innocent and brings forward the guilty for conviction, allays the fears of the good, and chastens the outrageous spirit of the bad, checks vice, promotes virtue, preserves order, and vindicates the violated supremacy of the laws. I shall not, gentlemen, enter into a particular enumeration of the offences, which are indictable by the laws of the United States. Their penal code is plain and concise, and reduced, in the most important points, to written exactitude and precision.[1] But another reason, which supersedes the necessity of a detail, arises from the improbability of any crimes having been committed in this district against the United States. The citizens of this state are distinguish[ed] for their love of social order, and submission to the laws. Of this they exhibited an illustrious proof on a late interesting occasion. The suppression of that dangerous insurrection, which, in the course of the last year, agitated a sister state, may, in a great measure, be ascribed to the promptitude and ardour, the prowess and exertion of the militia of New Jersey. Their names stand high on the role of patriotism, and may they be emulous to sustain that honorable rank, which they have so justly acquired.[2]

Deeming a description of presentable offences to be at present an unnecessary, as it is always an unpleasing task, let me call your attention to preventive justice, which, though connected with penal jurisprudence, is more congenial with the feelings of humanity, and the principles of policy, than punishing justice. The best and most effectual method of preventing the commission of crimes is to render the system of education as general and perfect as possible. For supporting good government, cherishing republican principles, and promoting the interests of virtue, and the cause of freedom, schools and seminaries of learning are of primary importance. The mind, without literature or science, is in a rude and dark state, and incapable of high or useful exertions; even genius, uncultivated, loses half his force; he soars, but with unequal wings. Ages have passed away, generations have rolled on in rapid succession, ere civil liberty and the rights of man were ascertained or understood. Seek we the reason? Man was ignorant. Ignorance may be called the mother of slavery as well as of superstition. When The mind, when is destitute of morals and of knowledge, it is in a fit state for the reception of every species of falshood and oppression. While overshadowed by ignorance, our mental faculties are unable to discern the subtilties, and to

resist the artful impositions of designing and factious men; but the moment that knowledge begins to break in upon our minds, we think, and judge, and act for ourselves; the film is removed from our eyes, we see things, and discern political operations and characters as they really are and not through the false and imposing medium of error and deception. Before the torch of science or education, all illusive appearances vanish, like darkness before the dawning of the day. To act well our parts in society, we must know the true interest of the community in which we live; to perform in a proper manner the various duties incumbent upon us as men and as citizens, we must know what those duties are, what we owe to others, and what is due to ourselves. Knowledge lies at the foundation of social order and happiness. What then can be expected from uninformed and ignorant minds? They know no country and have no patriotism. Enough, if they know the spot, on which they were born and rocked; ~~enough,~~ that is their country: enough if they know and consult the little interests, and narrow politics of the neighbourhood, in which they live and move; that is their patriotism. But of country, which comprehends towns, counties, and states, and their numerous inhabitants; which comprehends thousands and millions of men, as well as the earth on which they live, and of patriotism, which views those thousands and millions with equal eye, and clasps them all in the same generous embrace; of such a country, and of such patriotism what do they know. Persons ignorant and uninformed are easily imposed upon and led astray; they are unable to detect
                                        projects
error, or to discern and frustrate hostile but colourable schemes and views; they have no resources within themselves, and generally repose implicit confidence in others; they are the fit, and, indeed, usual instruments in the hands of designing men to serve the purposes of party, or to work out the ruin of a state. Zeal they may have in great abundance; but it is a zeal without knowledge, which is dangerous equally in political and religious life. Without mental and moral improvement, neither order, nor republicanism, nor civil liberty can be long preserved. Ignorance is freedom's worst foe _ Permit me, therefore, gentlemen, to impress upon your minds the importance of diffusing knowledge through the state by the means of proper and well-conducted schools. Believe it, no money is so well bestowed as upon the education of children. They are the hopes of our infant republic. Give them education, give them morals, and thus make them useful men and valuable citizens. Remember that without morals, there can be no order, and without knowledge no genuine liberty _

To a proper system of education, let me subjoin as the further means of preventing the commission of crimes, an uniform attachment to, and an habitual love and veneration for the constitution and laws. This indeed ought to be interwoven in the system of a good education. To reverence the laws is, perhaps, the first political maxim in a republican government. Observance of the laws and obedience to legal authority are the great bulwark of public liberty, and which free states find it difficult to maintain; because their restraint sits uneasy upon turbulent spirits, and is mistaken ~~for~~ for slavery by the thoughtless and ill-informed part of the community, who delight in irregularity and licentiousness, as sure ~~indication~~ symptoms of freedom, and certain indications of a manly spirit. The truth is, that civil liberty and order consist in and depend upon submission to the laws. The constitution and laws contain the articles of our political faith; they point out the path we are to go, and the rule by which we are to walk. They are the work of the people, declarative of their will, and as such ought to be reverenced and obeyed. To fashion our temper, character, and conduct, as citizens, by the principles and spirit of the constitution and laws is both our interest and duty; and while we do so, we shall insure internal order and repose, preserve our civil rights and liberties pure and entire, and be united at home and respected abroad. But why enlarge? The citizens of New Jersey love the constitution, venerate the general government, and obey the laws; nay more, they are prompt and active in compelling the turbulent and refractory to submit to legal authority. The supremacy of the law they acknowledge; it is the only sovereign they know. These are the brightest virtues, that can adorn the republican character. Long may they live, and highly may they be cherished in the bosom of every American!

AD (NjR, William Paterson Papers) Date and place determined from evidence in the charge and the circuit court minutes. Passages in this charge parallel some of the passages in a newspaper essay Paterson wrote under the signature of "Aurelius" during the early months of 1793. Those essays are published in Richard P. McCormick, "Political Essays of William Paterson," *Rutgers University Library Journal* 18 (June 1955): 38-49.

1. Crimes Act of 1790. *Stat.*, 1:112.
2. A reference to the Whiskey Rebellion in Pennsylvania during the previous year. New Jersey was one of four states called upon to contribute militia to help quell the insurrection. Carroll and Ashworth, *George Washington*, pp. 188-93.

Circuit Court for the District of New York ———————————
April 6, 1795   New York, New York

Associate Justice James Iredell and Judge John Laurance convened the circuit court, after which Iredell delivered a "learned and ingenious" charge to the grand jury. The court met again on the following day before adjourning to the next term.[1]

1. Minutes, CCD New York, RG 21, NjBaFAR; *Daily Advertiser* (New York), April 7, 1795. See James Iredell's Charge to the Grand Jury of the Circuit Court for the District of New York, April 6, 1795.

James Iredell's Charge to the Grand Jury of the Circuit Court for the
District of New York ————————————————————————
Gazette of the United States
  April 6, 1795   New York, New York

Gentlemen of the Grand Jury,

IT is a custom, I believe, founded in great utility, that before you enter
on the performance of your duty after being sworn to the faithful discharge
of it, you should meditate for a few moments at least on its high importance.
In a country which is happily governed by law, and by that alone, and in
which no distinction as to rights is made between one individual and another,
no trust can be of more consequence to the community than that which
holds in an impartial balance the scale of justice between the public on the
one hand, and individuals on the other. The security of each individual
consists in a due obedience, being voluntarily paid or properly enforced to
the laws framed, by common consent for the common welfare of the whole,
and in those laws being administered in such a manner as to be a terror
only to the guilty, and a protection to the innocent. This impartiality, which
ought in all countries to prevail in the administration of public justice, ought
to be attended to with the utmost possible strictness in a Republic, the very
basis of whose government it is that no one is superior to an other, but the
law is superior to all. She is the depositary of the common happiness and
security of all the citizens. Without her voice none ought to be condemned.
From her awful censure none ought to be exempted.

The peculiarity of our political situation which requires essential duties to
be performed, not only as citizens of a single state, but as citizens of the
United States, should be frequently revolved in our minds, in order that we
may comprehend its true nature and importance. It has arisen from a necessity
we have all felt, and from an anxiety in which I trust we all participate, the
necessity of maintaining a strong and cordial union with each other, and an
anxiety to promote the real and effective purposes of that union by the best
means calculated to secure it. Whatever difference of opinion may have been
entertained as to the means, the end has certainly been long the object of
the most anxious solicitude in every part of the United States. It has been,
I believe, as generally as justly thought, that the mischiefs of disunion,
however lightly contemplated at a distance, would upon an unhappy
experience be felt in a manner we should have eternal reason to regret. To
prevent so great a calamity, rendered too probable by former examples, and
of which we had in some degree felt the symptoms among ourselves, the
present constitution of the United States was formed.

The objects of this constitution being solely the preservation and security

(Philadelphia) April 16 and 17, 1795. Date and place are those given in a headline to the charge,
which also indicates that it was published at the request of the grand jury.

of the union, it in no instance interferes with the internal regulations of any state in cases which concern the interests of such state only.

There are therefore two governments to which we owe obedience: The state government to which we particularly belong, in all instances which concern the interests of the state alone; the government of the United States in all instances which concern the interests of the union at large. Each of these governments deserves our equal confidence and respect. Each is calculated to promote, tho' in different ways, the security[1] of those blessings we have now the happiness to enjoy. Both are restricted within those bounds which the people have thought proper to prescribe, and neither can violate, without violating a most sacred duty, the peculiar province of the other.

The formation of the criminal law of the United States, as distinguished from that of each state in particular, would naturally have devolved, (as it must do in every government where power is unrestricted) upon the Legislature alone, if the constitution had not imposed restrictions on this authority, calculated to prevent its possible abuse. It may be interesting to enquire into the nature of these restrictions and to see upon what footing the Legislative authority of the United States in this respect is placed.

The following are the restrictions which the constitution (including amendments to it which have received the requisite consent) has provided:

1. "The privilege of the writ of *Habeas Corpus* shall not be suspended, unless when in cases of rebellion or invasion the public safety may require it."[2]

2. The nature of a *Habeas Corpus*, so far as concerns our present subject, is well known. It is a writ which upon an application of a prisoner he is entitled to, in order that he may be brought before some legal authority, and the cause of his commitment examined, in consequence of which if entitled to a discharge or to bail, he is to be discharged or bailed as the case requires, otherwise to be remanded that he may be proceeded against further as the law directs. The many thousand instances which have taken place at one time or other in every country of Europe of arbitrary and unjust imprisonment, by which innocence has been basely sacrificed, sometimes to motives of unprincipled policy, and not unfrequently to the gratification of mere private malice, or for the purpose even of family or personal convenience, might well excite the vigilant precaution of a free and enlightened people, altho they had been remarkably distinguished in their own country by a happy exemption from such tyranny and oppression. A practice of this kind indeed would be at this time so abhorrent to the feelings

---

The charge was also printed in the *Philadelphia Gazette,* April 17, 1795, and the *State Gazette of North-Carolina* (Edenton), May 14, 1795.

1. In the *Gazette of the United States* (Philadelphia), April 16, 1795, this reads: "haurity." In the *Philadelphia Gazette,* April 17, 1795, and the *State Gazette of North-Carolina* (Edenton), May 14, 1795, it appears as "security."

2. Article I, section 9.

of the most callous mind, that it certainly could not be indulged without meeting universal resentment and indignation. But what precaution can be too great where personal liberty is concerned, the natural and just claim of every honest man unoffending against the laws of his country? There may, however, be occasions where the public danger is so imminent, that a power of discretionary imprisonment may for a time be necessary to save the public from destruction. Such critical emergencies have been in all countries. We well recollect periods of the late war when this authority was indispensable. The occasions named in the exception must be admitted to be such where a discretionary power may be necessary to be lodged. It can, however, I apprehend, even then be alone authorised by an express act of the legislative body, who for their own sakes as well as the safety of their constituents will take good care that the authority never shall be allowed but where the danger shall be imminent, and the necessity real indeed, and a severe responsibility will be annexed to the abuse proportionate to the detestation in which an abuse of so formidable a power must be held, by every virtuous mind.

2. "No Bill of attainder or *ex post facto* Act shall be passed."[3]

An act of attainder may be defined to be an act of a legislative body deciding in a single case, upon mere arbitrary discretion, on the life and fortune of an individual—The very definition of the power shews of what an outrageous nature it is. No trial by jury, no certainty of defence, no security in innocence. All those guards against injustice which have been wisely established in all other cases are taken away in this, the most dangerous of any, in which a bare majority of a legislative body, governing themselves by no rule, and under the influence of violent party prejudices, too apt to sway even virtuous minds, may rashly take away the life of the most innocent man. Justly has so despotic a power been rejected by our constitution, which takes care not only of whole classes of men, but also of each individual, whose rights are deemed too sacred to be left to the mercy of any party upon pretexts easily assumed, and naturally susceptible of abuse, and which have in fact been productive of the grossest abuses in countries where such a power was possessed.

An act of attainder is in some degree and that indeed very essentially an *ex post facto* law, since it subjects a man accused of a crime not to an ordinary trial and a fixed punishment, but to a legislative condemnation, which may be without a trial at all, and to a punishment altogether discretionary. But as it usually, if not always proceeds, upon the presumption of the commission of a capital crime which the ordinary proceedings at law, for some cause or other, are not competent to reach; it may naturally enough stand as a case upon its own footing, and, as some respectable law book tells us,[4] may rather

---

3. Ibid.
4. In the *State Gazette of North-Carolina* (Edenton), May 14, 1795, this phrase reads: "as some respectable law books tell us."

be regarded as a sentence than a law. An *ex post facto* law, so far as it respects crimes (its only meaning we have now occasion to consider) means, as I understand it, a law that in any manner alters the consequences of an act from what they were at the time when the act was done, whether the action at the time was wholly innocent, and afterwards made criminal, or was at the time criminal in a less degree than it was made by the legislative act afterwards passed.—The same principles of regard to private rights which occasioned the rejection of acts of attainder naturally dictated a rejection of every species of *expost facto* acts as grounded on no better foundation, and equally violative of that security of individuals which it was an invariable object of the constitution to protect.[5]

3. "The trial of all crimes, except in cases of impeachment, shall be by Jury; and such trial shall be held in the State where the said crimes shall have been committed, but where not committed within any State the trial shall be at such place or places as the Congress may by law have directed."[6]

This was the original provision in the constitution; but as a great many respectable persons, and even some of the Conventions that ratified the constitution, did not think it particular enough, the amendments contained in the following articles were proposed by Congress at their first Session—and have since been ratified, and now form a part of the constitution.

"No person shall be held to answer for a capital or otherwise infamous crime; unless on a presentment or indictment of a Grand Jury, except in cases arising in the land or naval forces, or in the militia when in actual service in time of war, or public danger: nor shall any person be subject for the same offence to be twice put in jeopardy of life or limb; nor shall be compelled in any criminal case to be a[7] witness against himself; nor deprived of life, liberty, or property, without due process of law; nor shall private property be taken for public use without just compensation."[8]

"In all criminal prosecutions the accused shall enjoy the right to a speedy and public trial, by an impartial Jury of the State and District wherein the crime shall have been committed, which District shall have been previously ascertained by law, and to be informed of the nature and cause of the accusation; to be confronted with the witnesses against him; to have compulsory process for obtaining witnesses in his favor—and to have the assistance of Counsel for his defence."[9]

The most innocent man, I apprehend, cannot wish for greater securities than these. But how happy is that country where protections like these are no novelties, but have long been so familiar that our sense of the value of them, perhaps is not sufficiently strong! If we desire, however, to be truly

5. In the *Philadelphia Gazette,* April 17, 1795, "prevent."
6. Article III, section 2.
7. The article "a" is not part of the text of the Constitution.
8. Fifth Amendment.
9. Sixth Amendment.

sensible of their value, let us turn over a few pages of any ancient, or almost of any modern history, and we shall be devoutly thankful for the uncommon share of personal, as well as political liberty, these States are blessed with.

4. "Treason against the United States shall consist only in levying war against them, or in adhering to their enemies, giving them aid and comfort. No person shall be convicted of treason unless on the testimony of two witnesses to the same overt act, or on confession in open court."

"The Congress shall have power to declare the punishment of treason, but no attainder of treason shall work corruption of blood, or forfeiture, except during the life of the person attainted."[10]

The crime of treason in all countries where arbitrary power has prevailed, or personal freedom has been too little regarded, has either been so indefinite in its nature, or such latitude has been taken in its construction, that perhaps it has occasioned more victims than any other instrument of tyranny. Resentment, full as often as justice, has whetted the sword of State, and caused many an innocent man to fall, and many a worthy family to perish. The mischiefs indeed that under a colour, and sometimes barely a color of justice, have been wantonly occasioned to mankind by prosecutions for this offence, cannot be contemplated without horror and indignation. Justly therefore have precautions been taken against such abuses here. The crime itself, it is true, when real, is of deep malignity. An attempt to throw a free government and a happy people into disorder and confusion; to dissolve all social ties, and to risk the security and happiness of every private family, is certainly the highest offence which can be committed against society. Such a crime must be of peculiar aggravation when committed against a government deliberately established by the people themselves, and susceptible in itself of regular and peaceable alterations. But in proportion to the interest, which every man feels in the preservation of a government, will be the warmth of his passions in its defence, and consequently it is of extreme moment that he should be upon his guard to prevent their misleading him, which all violent passions are apt to do, and none so much as those which have the public, as well as private interest for their object. The law therefore, in all such cases ought to be peculiarly circumspect, in order to secure by every possible means a fair and impartial trial; and this appears to have been anxiously aimed at, not only by the provisions in the constitution which I have read to you, but by very material legislative provisions which concern this important subject. The declaration as to corruption of blood and forfeiture, (formerly no slight objects of rapacity to abandoned men) is an additional and pleasing proof of the liberal and manly spirit with which the whole of these excellent constitutional provisions were framed.

Besides the provisions in the constitution I have already noticed, there are other provisions in it calculated to secure still farther the invaluable

10. Article III, section 3.

possession of personal liberty, so that it may not be unjustly sacrificed to any arbitrary measures. They are as follow:

"The right of the people to be secure in their persons, houses, papers, and effects, against unreasonable searches and seizures, shall not be violated: and no warrants shall issue but upon probable cause, supported by oath or affirmation, and particularly describing the place to be searched, and the persons or things to be seized."[11]

"Excessive bail shall not be required, nor excessive fines imposed, nor cruel and unusual punishments inflicted."[12]

The above contain all the restrictions in the constitution I proposed to enumerate. Subject to these, the following authority in regard to the criminal law is vested in the legislature of the United States.

1. They have express authority given in the constitution to define and punish piracies, and felonies committed on the high seas, and offences against the law of nations.[13]

Crimes that are committed on the high seas, are not the objects of any law merely territorial; that is, a law resting entirely on the discretion of the legislature of the country, but being crimes equally against all the nations in the world, are equally punishable in any, and therefore must have some common principle. For this reason, laws concerning crimes of this nature ought to be materially the same in every country. But in every country there must be some authority which has a right to expound and enforce this law, so that every violation of it may be properly punished. In our country this authority naturally devolved on the Government of the United States, as having alone the care of the public interest with foreign nations, and it is peculiarly proper that the right of defining and prescribing the punishment of such crimes, should be vested in the legislature,[14] with whom the important power of declaring war, or authorizing any inferior species of hostility, is entrusted, otherwise they might be accountable for breaches of the law of nations committed without their sanction.

Other offences of individuals against the law of nations consist chiefly of such as are a violation of the duties owing from an individual of one nation to an individual of another, in respect of the public relation which subsists between the two nations.

The offences of this kind, which I think most material to enumerate and observe upon, are these:

1. A violation of the privileges of an Ambassador, or other public Minister.[15]

---

11. Fourth Amendment.
12. Eighth Amendment.
13. Article I, section 8.
14. Crimes Act of 1790, sections 8-13, 16. *Stat.,* 1:113-16.
15. Ibid., sections 25-27. *Stat.,* 1:117-18.

Such persons, by all the civilized nations in the world, have been esteemed entitled to an exemption from either insult or injury. Considering the little acquaintance the different nations of the world have with each other, the apparent opposition of their interests (which is much more common than a real one) their mutual jealousies and suspicions, and the difficulty of judging at a distance, and without local knowledge of the true causes of measures which are found to be injurious, it was a happy expedient to propose an interchange of public Ministers, in order to promote a better understanding between different nations, and thereby to preserve both nations in amity with each other; or if unfortunately that should be found impracticable, to convince the world that every honorable method had been pursued to avoid their coming to extremities. Such men, when employed in so noble an object, ought not only to be secure, but deserve all possible respect, when they do not glaringly violate the pacific and conciliatory purposes for which we ought to presume they were sent. It shews, therefore, a wanton disregard of the peace of mankind when such characters are ill-treated; and as such ill-treatment tends to defeat altogether the just purposes of their mission, and may aggravate, in a most dangerous degree, any subsisting differences (if there be such) between the two nations, if not occasion a fatal hostility between them, whatever were the dispositions before, no real offence of that nature can, either with safety, or consistently with its duty, be passed over by that government in whose country such an offence is committed. If it be, it may then be considered as a national act of hostility, and resented accordingly.

2. A violation of any safe conduct or passport issued under the authority of the United States.[16]

This is an offence nearly similar to the former, with this difference chiefly, that this offence is more peculiarly adapted to a state of war, and the former to a state of peace. But in this case, as the restoration of peace may be one of the objects for which the safe conduct or passport was granted, or if not as it may have been granted to discharge some duty incident even to a state of war, or perform some act of humanity from which no state ought to be exempted, it is highly incumbent on all individuals to respect and obey the authority from which it flows.

3. A violation of the duties of neutrality incident to a neutral nation, which this is in regard to the powers engaged in the present war.[17]

When a war unfortunately takes place among other nations, if there be one so happily situated, that neither its duty nor its safety requires it to take a part in the war—it becomes immediately placed in a peculiar and critical situation, deserving of its utmost attention. It owes to the hostile powers a fair and disinterested impartiality in its conduct—neither assisting one or the

16. Ibid., section 28. *Stat.*, 1:118.
17. Neutrality Act of 1794. *Stat.*, 1:381.

other to promote the hostile purposes of either—at the same time observing inviolable faith with both correspondent to the general law of nations; where there are no treaties, or in a perfect conformity to them where there are. By the most impartial and disinterested conduct, a neutral nation is too apt to give offence to one party or the other, who seldom, in the midst of the violent passions, which a state of hostility occasions, will regard with sufficient candour and good faith the independent rights of a nation which does not share in their hostility. But men are not answerable for the consequences of their conduct; they are answerable only for the integrity of it, and therefore when they exercise with good faith, all the duties which they owe to the rest of mankind, they can with true dignity, and composed fortitude, meet all consequences to which such integrity may expose them. If it were possible for any rational man to doubt whether peace be a great blessing, or whether the true interest of the United States does not require that an exact neutrality shall be maintained in the present war—it is sufficient to observe, that this is a policy which the government of our country hath thought proper to pursue, and it is remarkable, that in the midst of all the controversies which other subjects have occasioned not one member of that most respectable body, with whom the people of the United States have entrusted the great authority of declaring war, hath proposed our taking any share in the unhappy one now subsisting. Such being the policy—such the conduct of those with whom the whole authority of the people of the United States in this respect is entrusted; it is surely the duty of every citizen to conform his own personal conduct, to those principles which the situation of his country requires him to observe. The conduct of the government is of little consequence—if every individual is at liberty to act according to the dictates of his own will, or the impulse of his own passions, because one purpose for which government was instituted, was to make the will of each individual, in all cases of public concern, conform to the general will of the community; to prevent the selfish or wicked views of a few from injuring the rest; and so far as foreign nations are concerned, government is answerable even at the hazard of a war, for the proper conduct of every individual belonging to it. Each individual, therefore, is answerable in this respect, as in all others, to the community of which he is a member, or in which he resides; if he commits a breach of the laws of neutrality, while his country continues a neutral nation, he commits a public offence, for which he may be prosecuted and punished.

II. The Congress have also express authority given in the Constitution "To provide for the punishment of counterfeiting the securities and current coin of the United States."[18]

Upon the propriety of this, there can be no room for any doubt.

III. They have also express authority to exercise exclusive legislation in all cases whatsoever, not only over such district as may, under the constitution,

18. Article I, section 8.

become the seat of the government of the United States (a district which, as is well known, is already fixed upon, tho' not to be the actual seat of residence till a future day,) but also over all places purchased by the consent of the legislature of the State, in which the same shall be, for the erection of forts, magazines, arsenals, dock-yards, and other needful buildings.[19]

This general authority of course includes a right of providing for the punishment of all crimes committed within such places.

IV. As incidental to the power of legislation over the great objects of the general government, the legislature has authority to enforce its laws by proper sanctions, without which laws would be useless.

Thus, for instance; if a Record or process of any Court of the United States, should be stolen or falsified, this is an offence against the United States, and therefore a proper subject of trial in some of its Courts.[20]

In like manner, if perjury should be committed in any of the Courts of the United States, this must be admitted as a proper instance of the jurisdiction of the United States.[21]

So also, if any process issuing out of a Court of the United States, should be resisted, it follows that this is a case within the jurisdiction of the Courts of the United States, or some of them.[22]

Authority for these purposes, and others of a similar kind, is plainly given in the following words, which are contained at the end of the special enumerated powers of Congress, viz.

"To make all laws which shall be necessary and proper for carrying into execution the foregoing powers, and all other powers vested by this constitution in the government of the United States, or in any department or officer thereof."[23]

Tho' these words do not convey more real authority than would perhaps have been understood to be conveyed by fair implication arising from the special powers of legislation before expressed; yet in an instrument of this high importance it was certainly wise and safe to leave as little room as possible for any doubt in its construction.

These, gentlemen, are the grounds upon which the legislative authority of the United States as to this interesting subject is placed. We find no power conveyed that does not appear to be necessary, nor I believe are any restrictions wanting that the general safety would admit. Legislative provisions, equally wise and judicious, have been made in the execution of this authority, but the particulars of which I do not think it now material to detail; neither do I think it necessary to point out the peculiar criminal jurisdiction of this

19. Ibid.
20. Crimes Act of 1790, section 15. *Stat.*, 1:115.
21. Ibid., sections 18-20. *Stat.*, 1:116.
22. Ibid., section 22. *Stat.*, 1:117.
23. Article I, section 8.

Court, it being a very general one, tho' I am sensible some doubts may arise concerning its extent, the solution of which it might be improper for me now to anticipate. No human system can be so perfect as to be entirely clear of difficulties; but I trust the general tenor of the legislative provisions on this subject will be found, on examination, to be congenial with the same high spirit of freedom and liberality which dictated the constitution itself. In many other countries the criminal law is the dread and terror of the people, and they are afraid to look at it. Ours, thank God, courts the light, instead of shunning it; and never can suffer but by being defectively seen. If ever any people indeed had reason to repose confidence in their governments, the people of the United States surely have. The people in each state, solemnly and deliberately, by Representatives fully authorised, have chosen their forms of government for themselves. They have chosen their own State constitutions. They have agreed to and ratified the constitution of the United States. A higher degree of freedom, consistent with any government at all, is not exerciseable by human nature. So high a degree was never exercised until America tried the noble experiment. May she prove, by the support of her own work, that she has not been in search of an unattainable good! and that after passionately following that LIBERTY which she has constantly adored, she has at length succeeded in fixing her by bringing to her her best beloved and only safe companions ORDER and JUSTICE.

James Iredell to Hannah Iredell ———————————————————————
    April 7 and [8], 1795   New York, New York

... I left Philadelphia on Friday morning, but the roads were so bad that we did not get further than Newark on Saturday night, and here on Sunday forenoon _ I have very good lodgings in Wall Street, have my health perfectly well, and pass my time agreeably. The consideration only of the distance between us, the length of time I must still expect to be absent from you, and the dangers of the approaching Summer, affects me very sensibly.[1] I have engaged a new Servant, who was very well recommended to me in Philadelphia. He is a young Mulatto Boy that had been set free under his
                                                                    State
Master's Will in Maryland, has since lived in the Delaware‸, and was working day by day when I heard of him in Philadelphia. His name is David,[2] he seems very good tempered, and has hitherto behaved remarkably well _ I aim to find[3] him in every thing, and pay him 4 dollars a month _ he asked more, but agreed to take this, and tho' it appears to be high wages it is comparatively low according to the rate of wages in Philadelphia. I must leave entirely to your own judgment your coming or not to the Northward _ but if you could not accomplish this, would it not be better to try if possible some situation in our Western Country for 3 or 4 months? I confess I dread

inexpressibly your being a whole summer in Edenton again. But, whatever you decide on, I commend you all, with inexpressible tenderness and anxiety, to the good providence of God.

[8]ᵗʰ Our Court ended yesterday, having sat but two days. I dined with Judge Laurance. His Wife[4] is really a very agreeable Woman. To day I am to dine with Mͬ MͨCormick,[5] and have 3 invitations more ahead, so that I am likely to experience a good deal of the New York hospitality. Gen. Schuyler[6] came and sat with me two or three hours last night. I never saw him look better, & he was in high spirits. Mͬ and Mͬˢ Hamilton[7] are in Albany, having now no house here, but are expected in May. It is said he has already received more than a year's Salary in retaining fees. At the dinner given to him here all Parties attended, and shared in the hilarity of the day. A number of Mechanicks here have declared they will build a house for him at his own expence. Mͬ Jay is expected soon. It is thought he will certainly be elected Governor if he returns soon _ some think he will at all events, C. J. Yates[8] is the other Candidate. ...

ARS (Nc-Ar, Charles E. Johnson Collection). Addressed "Edenton, North Carolina." Date in brackets is inked out and is determined from reference to the closing of the New York court "yesterday," April 7, 1795.

    1. Iredell was concerned about the health of his family in the climate of coastal North Carolina; see James Iredell to Hannah Iredell, June 5, 1795, and July 2, 1795.

    2. David replaced Andrew as Iredell's servant.

    3. "To supply, provide, furnish." *OED.*

    4. Elizabeth (Lawrence) (Allen) Laurance (d. 1800), widow of James Allen of Philadelphia. American Antiquarian Society, "Index of Deaths in *Massachusetts Centinel* and *Columbian Centinel,* 1784-1840," typescript, 12 vols. (Worcester, Mass.: American Antiquarian Society, 1952); *DAB* under John Laurance.

    5. Daniel McCormick, a director of the Bank of New York, resided in New York City. Frank Monaghan and Marvin Lowenthal, *This Was New York* (Garden City, N.Y.: Doubleday, Doran & Co., 1943), pp. 33-34; *PAH,* 7:444; information courtesy of Alice Wolfe, The Bank of New York.

    6. Philip John Schuyler (1733-1804) was a major-general of the Continental Army during the Revolution. He also served as a member of the Continental Congress, the New York Senate, and the United States Senate. *DAB; BDAC.*

    7. Elizabeth (Schuyler) Hamilton (1757-1854), wife of Alexander Hamilton and daughter of Philip John Schuyler. *PJJ,* 2:545n.

    8. Robert Yates (1738-1801), chief justice of the New York Supreme Court, lost to John Jay in the gubernatorial election of 1795. *DAB.*

Circuit Court for the District of Pennsylvania

April 11, 1795   Philadelphia, Pennsylvania

On April 11 the circuit court convened with Associate Justice William Paterson and Judge Richard Peters in attendance. The grand jury was then called and dismissed

until May 4, when Paterson delivered a charge. On June 5 the court adjourned to
the following term.[1]

1. Engrossed Minutes, CCD Pennsylvania, RG 21, PPFAR; William Paterson's Charge to the Grand Jury
of the Circuit Court for the District of Pennsylvania, [May 4, 1795] (q.v.). The grand jury was dismissed
until May 4 to allow the court to clear most of its civil docket before proceeding with the indictment and
trial of the Whiskey rebels.

James Iredell to Hannah Iredell

April 15, 1795   New York, New York

... Our Court ended the second day, and as the Court at New Haven does
not begin till the 25th I expect to be here a week longer. I receive very
great civilities indeed, but nevertheless my time drags on heavily, as none
of my intimate Friends are near me, and whatever you may think of it I
prefer them to the most agreeable Strangers. I am almost opposite to M[r]
Bayard's Family[1] with whom M[rs] Edwards lives, and have dined with them
and been there three or four times besides. M[rs] Jay, I think, looks younger
than ever. She is in high spirits, in expectation of M[r] Jay's arrival, tho' she
has had no letter from him of a later date than the 11 December. He had
gone down to Bath, and there has been no arrival this spring from England
except a Vessel from Liverpool. You remember Warrand said—M[rs] Jay had
her night.[2] She has still so far, that she is always at home every Thursday
evening. She enquired very kindly after you and M[rs] Johnston, and I have
drank tea with her on a special invitation. I called to see M[rs] _____(I
forget her name _ the Doctor's Wife whose house M[rs] Dawson[3] was at in
the Country). She seemed much obliged to me for calling, and desired to
be very kindly remembered to you and M[rs] Dawson and M[rs] Lowther.[4] I
have not seen Miss Marshall[5] that was tho' she is in town. Neither have I
seen D[r] Romaine.[6] He lives somewhere now about Cuyler's hook. I called
at his house, but found it full of Frenchmen who had lately rented it. M[rs]
King[7] has lately brought her Husband another Son _ I dined with him soon
after I came, but she was not then visible. This City is increasing and
beautifying very fast _ The Walk at the Battery I am persuaded is one of
the finest in the World. They have planted some young Trees, which when
grown up must add greatly to it. The Governor's house appears to great
advantage. There are many more elegant houses in Broadway than formerly,
and several more building. There are also some very elegant ones towards
the lower end of Broad Street. Property is even dearer here than in
Philadelphia. ... The Servant I have hired continues to behave extremely
well, and is as useful to me as Peter ever was in his best days. He has been
much used to horses, so that I hope he may be useful in many ways at home.
Be pleased to direct your next letter to me at Portsmouth in New Hampshire,

New York by Alexander Robertson (1772-1841) and Archibald Robertson (1765-1835). Etching, 1793. Courtesy New York Public Library, Astor, Lenox and Tilden Foundations, New York. Eno Collection, Miriam & Ira D. Wallach Division of Art, Prints & Photographs Division. Visible in the background to the right of the flagpole are the Battery and the houses of State Street.

to be kept 'till called for. I expect to be there about the 25ᵗʰ of May. After
that be pleased to direct to me in Boston. I expect to be there on the 7ᵗʰ of
June, perhaps sooner _ and at Newport in Rhode Island on the 19ᵗʰ _ ...

ARS (NcD, James Iredell Sr. and Jr. Papers). Addressed "Edenton, North Carolina."
Postmarked "N York APR 15."

1. The family of William Bayard (ca. 1761-1826), a prominent New York City merchant,
included his wife of fifteen years, Elizabeth Cornell, daughter of Samuel Cornell, a New Bern,
North Carolina loyalist merchant. Iredell represented Mrs. Bayard's interests in *Bayard v.
Singleton*. Sarah R. Van Rensselaer, *Ancestral Sketches and Records of Olden Times* (New York:
Anson D. F. Randolph, 1882), pp. 143-44, 179; 1 *Martin's Reports* 48, in *North Carolina Reports*,
ed. William H. Brattle (Raleigh: Turner and Hughes, 1843), p. 48.

2. During the period that John Jay served as secretary for foreign affairs (1784-1789), whenever
his family resided in New York, his wife, Sarah Jay, customarily entertained company on
Thursday nights. The identity of "Warrand" is unknown. Rufus Wilmot Griswold, *The Republican
Court; or, American Society in the Days of Washington* (New York: D. Appleton, 1864), pp. 96-
98.

3. Penelope (Johnston) Dawson (1744-1797), colonial North Carolina Governor Gabriel
Johnston's daughter and the widow of lawyer John Dawson (d. 1770), lived at Eden House,
across the Chowan River from Edenton, North Carolina. *PJI*, 1:88.

4. Penelope (Dawson) Lowther was the widow of Tristram Lowther, who had died a few
months earlier. She was the daughter of John and Penelope (Johnston) Dawson. Armistead C.
Gordon, "The Stith Family," *William and Mary Quarterly*, 1st ser. 22 (July 1913): 48, 50; *PJI*,
1:88n; *MJI*, 2:439.

5. "Miss Marshall that was" may be the woman Iredell mentioned in a letter to Helen Blair,
July 9, 1779, and who was to be "married to some unknown somebody tonight." *PJI*, 2:100.

6. Nicholas Romayne.

7. Mary (Alsop) King (1769-1819), wife of Rufus King and daughter of New York City
merchant, John Alsop (1724-1794). Douglas Leffingwell, "Alsop Genealogy," typescript, Library
of Congress (1928), pp. 5-6; *DAB* under Rufus King.

James Iredell to Hannah Iredell

April 21, 1795   New York, New York

... I continue perfectly well, and am to set off to morrow for New-Haven,
the Court beginning on Saturday. My time has passed in an agreeable manner
in the midst of very great civilities. The Cornell Family and all their
Connexions have been particularly kind.¹ I am sorry you did not mention
the locks and a bell sooner, as my expences are unavoidably so great that I
am afraid the money I have left will scarcely be sufficient. My Board here
for 2½ weeks only, amounts to 35 Dollars. ... Mʳ Lenox has been particularly
obliging, and I did not fail to present him with your and my own thanks for
his civility in mentioning me. He pressed me to accept of a room at his
house, but I declined it. He wishes very much that George Blair was here
that he might give him a Ship in the Liverpool trade. It would not be too
late perhaps if he could come soon. ...

ARS (Nc-Ar, Charles E. Johnson Collection). Addressed "Edenton,   North Carolina."

1. Iredell is referring to the family of North Carolina merchant Samuel Cornell, who had four daughters living in New York. Mary Cornell married Isaac Edwards and later lived on Wall Street with her sister Elizabeth, wife of William Bayard; Hannah Cornell wed Herman Le Roy; and Sarah Cornell married Matthew Clarkson. Van Rensselaer, *Ancestral Sketches*, pp. 143-45; *William and Mary Quarterly*, 1st ser. 15 (1906-1907): 196; William Duncan, *The New-York Directory and Register, for the Year 1795* (New York: Thomas and James Swords, 1795); James Iredell to Hannah Iredell, April 15, 1795 (q.v.).

Circuit Court for the District of Connecticut ————————————
April 25, 1795   New Haven, Connecticut

Associate Justice James Iredell and Judge Richard Law opened the circuit court for Connecticut, and Iredell delivered a charge to the grand jury. On May 5 the court adjourned until the following term.[1]

1. Docket Book, CCD Connecticut, RG 21, MWalFAR; James Iredell's Charge to the Grand Jury of the Circuit Court for the District of Connecticut, April 25, 1795 (q.v.).

James Iredell's Charge to the Grand Jury of the Circuit Court for the District of Connecticut ————————————————————————————
Gazette of the United States
April 25, 1795   New Haven, Connecticut

Gentlemen of the Grand Jury,

YOU being now assembled to discharge one of the most awful and important trusts which can be executed in any Country, particularly in one which enjoys the highest share of rational liberty of which perhaps human nature is capable, I doubt not you are sufficiently impressed with a sense of the great interest which your Country has in a due performance of it. In vain are laws made if an obedience to them is not enforced. In vain have the people chosen their own constitutions of government (as well general as particular) if the governments established under them are not submitted to. In vain does government act one way, if the individuals by whose authority collectively that government was instituted, or a considerable portion of them act another. Common sense, as well as common justice and the lowest notions of republican government, revolt against the absurd idea that when once a majority constitutionally authorised has passed a law, which all are bound to obey, any may disobey with impunity. Courts of Justice, therefore, are established to punish a disobedience to all such laws as are obligatory on all the citizens, in order that the common will of the whole community, when collected in a constitutional manner, may be truly and not nominally carried into execution, whatever opposition it may meet with from weak or wicked members of the community who may disregard the will of the whole when it comes into competition with their partial or indistinct views, their interests, their passions, or mischievous designs of any sort, if such should be entertained by any.

But, gentlemen though it be thus obviously necessary that an obedience to the laws of our country be enforced, yet the manner in which it is to be done is a consideration of extreme moment to the happiness, the security, the peace of mind of every citizen. The suspicions which are often unjustly cast upon the best men the jealousy with which a great part of mankind view the conduct of each other, the envy of some the malice of others, the two great readiness in all to indulge their passions, when not checked by a powerful sense of duty operating strongly on their consciences,—all these circumstances, the reality of which is well known to every man,—indispensably require, in a land of liberty, that prosecutions should not be too rashly undertaken, that they should be undertaken with deliberation and solemnity, that they should be undertaken impartially, being "no respecter of persons,"[1] and that their sole object should be the security and interest of the community at large, disdaining every consideration of private favour or ill will, as alike incompatible with the eternal principles of justice, and the sublimity of those principles of freedom which regard with an equal eye the richest and the poorest, the most powerful and the most weak, the best befriended members of the community, and those whose sole protection, under God, is the justice and humanity of the community itself. To attain an impartiality so just and so desirable no institution can be better calculated than that of a Grand Jury, composed, as it usually is (and always ought to be) of a select number of respectable and disinterested members of the community, selected for a single time only, and who may justly be presumed to have no views but to promote the interest and happiness of their common country. From such men innocence has every thing to hope, and guilt every thing to fear, and their country at large every blessing to expect that can flow from a steady, upright, and discerning administration of criminal justice.

This duty, gentlemen I am persuaded you will perform with the greater cheerfulness from a recollection of the prosperity your country has attained in consequence of the sacred regard which it has paid to the principles of justice both public and private, and which hath afforded an illustrious proof of the value of genuine liberty, which is founded on the basis of law and order and cannot exist without them. It's true mean is undoubtedly fixed between anarchy and tyranny, the two extremes which all rational governments have to guard[2] against, and which I trust, are sufficiently guarded against by ours, if the people (as I doubt not they will) cordially support the governments of their own formation. A glorious evidence of this has indeed lately been given which will astonish most other nations in the present age, and perhaps be felt in its effects, as well as admired in it's example by generations yet to come.

Having no reason to believe that any important business is likely to come before you upon which it may be material for me to make any particular observations, I shall therefore only observe generally, that your duty is to present offences committed against the United States, not any that are committed against this State solely. The offences against the United States consist in violations of the law of nations, or violations of some duty to the United States in particular. Of the former the courts of the United States have cognizance because the United States have the sole management of the interests of all as they concern foreign nations: They therefore are to take care that all offences of that sort when known meet with a proper prosecution, it being a duty necessarily incident to their sovereign superintendency over all cases of that nature, and also because in case of any palpable injury to a foreign nation, or any individual belonging to it, the United States as a nation are accountable for proper redress being given. The courts of the United States also have naturally authority to enforce the laws of the United States, as it of course devolves on every government to enforce obedience to its own regulations. But in order that such obedience be properly enforced, without hardship or oppression, the constitution hath provided important checks even upon the Legislative power itself (a thing without example until happily introduced in the American governments,) and the Legislature hath made many excellent provisions of its own calculated for the fair and impartial trial of every person under prosecution. They are well worthy of your study and attention as individuals, whether you have occasion at present to consult any of them in your capacity as Grand Jurors or not. If there should be any prosecutions, you may, I am confident, safely rely on the abilities and integrity of the gentlemen whose official duty it is to conduct the prosecutions on behalf of the United States in this district. You may be assured, upon application of receiving every proper assistance from the court. I doubt not, if you should have occasion to consider of any prosecutions whatever you will exercise the same diligence, impartiality, and regard to justice which hitherto, so far as I have observed or heard, have done so much honour to American Grand Juries, and which, I trust, will be evinced in all future instances of the like kind in all times to come.

(Philadelphia) July 14, 1795. Date and place are those given in a paragraph preceding the charge. That paragraph reads: "*A CHARGE delivered to the Grand Jury for the District of Connecticut, in the Circuit Court of the United States, held at New-Haven, April 25, 1795; and also delivered to the Grand Jury for the District of Vermont, in the Circuit Court of the United States held at Windsor, May 12, 1795.*"

The charge was also printed in the *Connecticut Journal* (New Haven), July 29, 1795, and in the *State Gazette of North-Carolina* (Edenton), August 6, 1795.

1. Iredell may be equating the power of prosecution with the biblical saying that "God is no respecter of persons." Acts, 10:34.

2. In the *Connecticut Journal* (New Haven), July 29, 1795, "reguard."

Circuit Court for the District of Georgia

April 25, 1795   Savannah, Georgia

On April 25 court convened with Associate Justice John Blair and Judge Nathaniel Pendleton in attendance. A grand jury was not formed until Monday, April 27, when Justice Blair delivered his charge. The court adjourned on May 5.[1]

1. Minutes, CCD Georgia, RG 21, GEpFAR; John Blair's Charge to the Grand Jury of the Circuit Court for the District of Georgia, April 27, 1795 (q.v.).

John Blair's Charge to the Grand Jury of the Circuit Court for the District of Georgia

Georgia Gazette

April 27, 1795   Savannah, Georgia

Gentlemen of the Grand Jury,

THE office of a Grand Jury is of a very important nature, whether we consider its efficacy for the detection of guilt, the protection of innocence, or the support of freedom. It may be considered as one intermediate station between the public avenger and the supposed object of his vengeance; he bears, indeed, the drawn sword, but suspends its fatal stroke, till the peers of the accused, under the guidance of the laws of the land and evidence of facts, consecrate it as the sword of justice. And so greatly is innocence favored, so carefully guarded under our happy government against the oppressions which uncontrolled power would be too apt to produce, that after a presentment by a Grand Jury (which cannot be made but by a majority of them, nor by a less number than twelve) a prisoner has a right to a fair trial by other twelve impartial men, and cannot on his arraignment have a verdict pass against him, without their unanimous consent; so that no free man can be convicted of any crime, of which the punishment would affect life or member, without the concurrence of, at least, twenty-four legally qualified men.

Miserable, on the one hand, is the slavery, where obedience is exacted to men, and not to the laws, but miserable too, on the other, is the anarchy, where the laws lose their tone, are violated and despised. Neither of these conditions can be the lot of Americans, while the office which you, Gentlemen, now fill, is exercised with firmness, circumspection, and impartiality.

As the good of the community, Gentlemen, requires all your activity and zeal in bringing forward to justice real guilt, so it would be a subject for mutual congratulations, if the true state of our country were such as to defy

(Savannah) May 7, 1795. Date and place are derived from the minutes of the circuit court. The charge was also printed in the *Gazette of the United States* (Philadelphia), June 23, 1795.

the keenest researches of your inquisitorial office, if just information on the subject of public happiness, added to the general prevalence of virtuous habits, were universally displaying a better security for order and good government than can be expected merely from a fear of the laws; and this I flatter myself is now not far removed from the truth. However this may be, it will be salutary to keep in perpetual memory, that a scene of convulsive disorder, exhibited in some of the western counties in the state of Pennsylvania, threatening a calamity no less dreadful than the eversion of our happy government, stood forth lately a melancholy exception to such a pleasing state of things.[1] To those who wish the general prosperity of our nation, it will afford a useful lesson, how dangerous it is to indulge too freely discontent with respect to the measures of government, to oppose with pertinacious petulence private to public opinion, and to urge the removal of grievances, imaginary or real, without the line of constitutional redress. And to those who though they have not undergone so diabolical a perversion as to feast on distress, and delight in disturbing the orderly course of things, though they love not evil for its own sake, can yet consent to introduce it for the sake of advancing their own ill understood, their own distorted good, it will afford the only instruction their principles permit them to receive, how unavailing for the attainment of its object is all their sinister policy, how strong its tendency to produce nothing but what is the most opposite to its aim. In such men we expect not to see the influence of more generous motives; but it will be happy for the public if by fear they may be restrained from annoying the general peace.

Whatever other objects there may be reason to think these disturbers of the public tranquility had in view, that which they avowed was, to prevent forcibly the collection of the excise duties;[2] a species of tax, which, however unfortunate in its name, by which it stands undistinguished from a tax which in other countries has with reason been held odious, is perhaps in cool argument capable of being defended, under the modifications which the Legislature have imposed upon it. Whether this be so or not, is not, however, for me to say; it will, I suppose, one day become a subject of discussion before the Honorable Body to whom the law imposing that tax owes its existence, who alone can correct or annihilate it, as on the one hand they will feel too much for the dignity of Government to give up, through the impulse of faction, any measure which may appear to them essential to the public good, so on the other will, no doubt, be well disposed to remove every real grievance, every occasion of just complaint. But what chiefly concerns us, what principally affects all the good people of the United States, takes place on the contrary supposition. Admit that the principle of the law is untenable, that the law ought to be repealed, or never to have been enacted, yet this,

1. The Whiskey Rebellion.
2. Excise Act of 1792. *Stat.*, 1:267.

surely, will not justify a forcible resistance. Such a conduct is going back to a state of nature; it is to renounce all the advantages of civil society, and abandon all to the evils which men by civil associations seek to avoid. For it would be too absurd to expect a participation of all the benefits of the social compact, without sharing its burdens; such a privilege would be a political monster. Men, therefore, who refuse to be governed by the general will, declare (as far as they have a right to do so) that they are not members of the community; and if not brought back to a sense of duty they are effectually expatriated, the honor of Government is tarnished, its authority set at nought.

Unanimity in the counsels of republican states is seldom to be expected, and in every society the public will is sought for in the sense of the majority. Government, which unites and concentres the strength of every individual, in any case of refractory behavior uses the greater force, or of the many, for the subduction of the lesser, or of the few; as naturally, in the case of different wills, is that of the few merged in the will of the many. But if a minority can persuade themselves that they have a right to oppose a law enacted by the majority, with equal reason might they deny the existence of the law; with equal reason might they insist, that the will of the few is that which is to prescribe a rule to the society; but this is repugnant to the common sense of mankind, to the principle of every consociation.

If this opposition had been made to any self constituted authority, it would have been only a resistance of tyranny, and the exertions of those engaged in it would have merited the highest praises which their contemporaries could bestow, or the faithful historian record: If resistance should, in another form, be made to an unconstitutional act of Congress itself, it would have some degree of merit, and be entitled to the protection of the law. But what can be said for a violent opposition to the constitution itself, that constitution which, whatever may be its faults, is the deliberate act of the people, and provides, in a similar course of deliberation, for its own amendment? For, surely, the constitution is attacked whenever resistance is made to a law enacted under its authority. If such a fabric, erected by the public will, should ever fall a sacrifice to the rage of a few, what fairer edifice is likely to rise on its ruins? If liberty be the object, how is it likely, or rather, how is possible to be built up with more stability? If tyranny be dreaded, where is its hideous form more likely to shew itself than in the rear of wild and licentious anarchy? Against such a constitution as, through the indulgence of Heaven, we have the singular felicity to have established for ourselves, can there be ever an apology for violence? All the evils which can intrude from whatever quarter (for no work of man is exempt from imperfection) may here meet with ready correctives. Have bad laws, the mere effect of inexperience, been enacted? Wisdom will be acquired from their operation. Are the Legislative Body, or any of its Members, suspected of indulging a private interest inconsistent with the general good? the Constituent Body may either try the milder means of admonition, in the form of instructions, or if the occasion seem to demand a more energetic remedy, it may withdraw its confidence, and repose it where it may be less likely to be abused; and in addition, all men have a right in a decent manner to lay open their grievances before the whole Legislature, and explain the ground of their complaint. All these modes of redress, if none beside, may be also used, where the evil complained of is an unconstitutional exercise of legislative authority, or an extension of the legislative powers beyond their prescribed limits; and if the evil lie in the constitution itself, even there also, (as has been already said) not indeed with equal facility and as little ceremony, (for that would seem liable to great objection) it is capable, by the mere volition of the people, by that general will which first spoke it into being, in this mild form it is capable of purgation, and even of annihilation. What just occasion can there ever be, then, to withhold obedience and make a desperate appeal to arms? the event of which, whatever it may be, cannot possibly put us in a better situation, but after all the cruelty and distraction inseperable from civil war may possibly end in destroying fundamentally one of the fairest fabrics the world has yet seen, and in putting to a hopeless end one of the best political establishments the wisdom of man has yet formed for public felicity.

Led, as we are, to deplore the late melancholy occasion, it may not be amiss, Gentlemen, to trace the evil (if we may) to its root; we may then more happily apply the cure. Whatever other causes may have concurred to produce it, (for I pretend not to accurate information on this subject) may we not suppose one to be a spirit, which in various parts of the Union has been too much encouraged, and even by some who probably[3] never meant to extend its baneful influence to such unhappy consequences; a spirit incompatible with order and the temperate provisions of regular government? Happy will it be if the dangerous crisis to which we were once reduced shall engage some men to reflect, how much easier it is to fret the minds of the ignorant with sour discontent, than to confine their rage at a certain point. Happy too will it be, if the final event which has taken place shall induce the deluded multitude to open their eyes and be guarded against future deception, if not from a love of their country, at least from a fear of its laws. When we consider how much we are indebted, for the advantageous political ground on which we happily stand, to the military aid of a nation,[4] who are now engaged in the defence of their own rights, as men, against the invasions of a powerful combination, it is no wonder that in generous minds a grateful sympathy should arise, with fervent wishes for their success: That the outrages which our commerce, in contempt of our unquestionable rights, as a neutral nation, has suffered in the progress of the present war, should call in to the aid of fraternal affection, on the one hand, the keen force of resentment on the other, is perfect nature; the sentiments themselves deserve no reproof. But there may be, and

3. In the *Gazette of the United States* (Philadelphia), June 23, 1795, "probably" is omitted.
4. I.e., France.

there certainly are, other motives, to which even these ought to yield. War is undoubtedly one of the greatest evils a nation can fall into, next to those to which it may be exposed from an opinion of its importance or pusillanimity; and that nation which hastily engages in it, even in resentment of real injuries, without trying the success of those pacific negotiations which sometimes spare the effusion of human blood, can scarce be acquitted of the charge of neglecting its indispensable duty. Is there not, then, reason to be pleased with the moderation of our political rulers, who have so happily known how to reconcile a firm resolution to maintain our national rights with a prudent caution to pursue all healing measures for the redress of our wrongs to prevent the necessity of making the last awful appeal? and that these measures have been probably crowned with success beyond our highest hope affords an occasion at once of mutual joy and national gratitude.[5] Was it not then to be lamented, that the wise and salutary exertions of our Government were exposed to the danger of disappointment from the unruly temper and over hasty zeal of a part of our citizens? It is a truth we cannot too earnestly inculcate, that no partial collections of the people have a right to decide for the whole, or to hazard their dearest interests; that the impossibility of exercising dominion by the immediate agency of the people indispensably requires that they have their Representatives to be clothed with their authority and strengthened by their confidence; that in such representation alone is displayed the majesty of the people; and that every exercise of power, derogatory to the authority so delegated, whatever pretences it may make to popular dignity, is in truth a presumptuous invasion of the rights of the people, a bold usurpation of their sovereignty; and the acts of such collective bodies are to be classed with those disorders, to repress which is one of the great ends of all government.

I have been induced, Gentlemen, to make those strictures, from an opinion I have conceived, that the spirit of those proceedings, though operating upon a different subject, was the governing principle of the late commotions; an overstrained conception of liberty, deriving to certain combinations of men, and almost to individual characters, all the sacred rights of the people, and dignifying with *their* name and authority their own pernicious systems. But if it be the just end of government to restrain the licentious conduct of unauthorized agents, what title can such men have to think themselves the defenders of our rights? They are not the supporters, but the licentious abusers, of liberty.

Government is a thing so interesting to every member of the society, that it could have no pretensions to the character of free, if it should aim at a

---

5. A reference to the Jay Treaty, negotiated by Chief Justice John Jay, which was aimed at lessening tensions between the United States and Great Britain. Although the existence of the treaty was publicly known, the Senate did not begin consideration of it until June 8, 1795. Miller, *Treaties,* 2:267-70; *SEJ,* 1:178.

coercion of the minds as well as of the actions of the citizens; while men pay an external obedience to the laws, they have a right to think of them as they please, and even to *express* their opinion decently, yet strongly, as a mean of obtaining an alteration; but one step farther is culpable; actual disobedience, or prompting others to disobey, can never be justified; for the evil of such behavior must ever outweigh infinitely the evil (whatever it may be) of the law itself.

But why have we had occasion to complain that this disorderly, this headlong temper of some of our citizens was able to progress to so dangerous a crisis? Can it be true, that some stronger power, than that which is derived from the people themselves, is necessary to keep men within just bounds? Can chains be necessary to preserve order? If the sacred and unalienable rights of man must bend at the shrine of power, and be sacrificed to protection, what will remain worth protecting? Must we be constrained to confess, that good and evil are so inseperably allied, that the general interest, joined to proper information as to its true centre, will never be able, in a republican shape, to do as much for promoting political harmony, as the strong hands of a tyrant? For the honor of human nature let us exemplify the falsity of such a creed. We have already exhibited the grateful proof in the suppression, by our militia alone, of that insurrection of which I have spoken; and most cordially, Gentlemen, do I congratulate you on the event, and still more that it has been accomplished without bloodshed: All government, except the divine, being the work of man, must of necessity partake of human imperfection; each system may have its peculiar advantage and disadvantage; and if it were undeniably true, that our own is less powerful for the prompt restraint of popular ferment; if some few excrescences (the natural price of freedom) cannot be so easily lopped, let us be consoled by the reflection, that the good order of government is substantially effected, and, as far as is practicable, without bearing its reins so tight as to frustrate the most valuable object of the social compact. Slight irregularities give us no reason to undervalue our government, and the grosser I trust it will always have energy enough to restrain. Powerful auxiliaries may also be applied: A general diffusion of knowledge, and a system of virtuous and religious education, are the great desiderata. Our Constitution, to be valued, needs only fair play, and to be seen as it is. A state of ignorance may be well adopted[6] to those governments which have much to conceal, and are afraid of investigation; but a government founded on the only legitimate basis, if, though it stand on a rock, it should, through the madness of the people, or the languor of general corruption, fall at last to ruins, must probably owe its fall to the neglect of making proper provision for the general circulation of knowledge and purity of manners. Something towards this general instruction, as far as concerns our political happiness, may be done by every one of us; let us all inculcate upon

6. In the *Gazette of the United States* (Philadelphia), June 23, 1795, "adapted."

the minds of our more ignorant brethren the high advantages of our social compact, and the eminent interest which we all have in its inviolable preservation; and let us prove to them the sincerity of our professions, by a dutiful obedience even to such laws (if such there be) as do not in themselves meet our approbation.

I have been so absorbed, Gentlemen, by a subject of this magnitude, as to have little room for notice of others, which yet are of importance too great to be neglected. I would say of them in general, that none of them are to be slighted. All the laws of the Union, more or less momentous in themselves, stand upon one level considered in their character of being laws. You will therefore, Gentlemen, pay a proper attention to the whole system of Congressional legislation. If, in the course of your inquiries, you should happen to doubt respecting the presentability of any fact, or its prohibition by any of the acts of Congress, you may expect from the Court every assistance in their power to give you.

I will no longer detain you, Gentlemen; you will be pleased to retire to your chamber, and enter upon those consultations which the present service may require.

Roger Griswold to Fanny Griswold
April 28, 1795   New Haven, Connecticut

... A Judge of the Supreme Court whom I have never before seen, attend this Session_ Judge Iredell is a Man of the most amiable manners conceiveable_ without a spark of that haughty superiority of manners, which too often characterizes the man in office, he never appears without a decent a dignity with which is decent & respectable_ his conversation is not only instructive, but extriemly amusiing_ always possessing a flow of Spirits, which animates not meerly himself but other[s.] He discovers an openness a candour in opinions & benevolence of heart which commands the attachment of all those with whom he converses_ such is the Judge who now sits in this Court & who may be considered not only great but good_

I have met the usual Company in this Town Lawyers from every part of Connecticut_ & of all descriptions_ Suitors of all colours & Witnesses of all characters_ and I aught to add people of all religions_ We have in this House a Company of Quakers, of the ^most valuable Characters I have ever met in that denomination ^of Christians_ they are men of Sense modesty & benevolence, & in short have so far gain'd upon my estimations that I am half persuaded to change my Religion & become a member of the Society of friends_

The business of the Court proceeds very slowly, & when the Session will close is very uncertain_ certainly not before the next week, if then ...

View of the New Haven Green in 1800 by William Giles Munson (1801-1878). Oil on canvas, ca. 1830. Courtesy New Haven Colony Historical Society, New Haven.

AR[S?] (ViU, Nevins, Perkins, Griswold Papers). Addressed "Norwich." Sent via "Mr. Perkins." The letter is torn where the signature should appear.

A Connecticut lawyer and an outspoken federalist, Roger Griswold (1762-1812) represented Connecticut in Congress from 1795 to 1805. *DAB.*

Fanny (Rogers) Griswold (1767-1863), wife of Roger Griswold. Glenn E. Griswold, comp., *The Griswold Family: England-America,* 3 vols. (Rutland, Vt.: Tuttle Publishing, 1935), 2:156-57.

Presentment of the Grand Jury of the Circuit Court for the District of Georgia

April 29, 1795   Savannah, Georgia

We the Grand Jury for the District of Georgia on our Oaths present as a grievance that the Courts of Admiralty in the United states have a power too unlimitted _ We therefore recommend to the next Congress seriously to consider on the propriety of restoring to the people of the United States a priviledge the most sacred _ that of tryal by Jury in those Courts[1]

We are happy in the pleasing opportunity afforded us of Congratulating his Honor the Judge and our fellow Citizens in General on the restoration of peace & tranquility in the Western Counties of Pensylvania and feel a confidence in the readiness displayed on that alarming occasion (to quell so daring an attack on the liberties of a free people) that no other Attempt of a like nature will be made to disturb our happy Government _ the sentiments expressed in the excellent Charge delivered us by his honor the Judge and the moral and patriotic lesson it contains, wou'd if properly disseminated add much to the order and good Government of our Country, to promote so desirable an end, we recommend that the same together with our presentment be published in the Gazettes of this state

We perfectly agree with His Honor the Judge that every Attempt towards a redress of real or Imaginary Grievances if not applied for in a Constitutional manner is highly Injurious to the Community and frought with the most dangerous Consequences and as it is our duty so it shall be our endeavour to prevent every Infringment of our happy Constitution   Savannah the 29th April 1795

Tho⁵ Stevens foreman	Barth Waldberger (LS)
F T Smithson (LS)	Joseph Miller (LS)
Timothy Staley (LS)	Jonathan Rahn (LS)
Edwᵈ Harden (LS)	Soloman Grover (LS)
Wᵐ Hunter (LS)	Benj. Butler (LS)
Richᵈ Leake (LS)	Ebenezer Jackson (LS)
Luke Mann (LS)	Joel Walker (LS)
James Kirk (LS)	

D (GEpFAR, RG 21, CCD Georgia, Minutes).
1. During the two decades prior to the Revolution, admiralty cases were heard primarily by colonial vice-admiralty courts presided over by crown-appointed judges and conducted without juries. A reaction against this system, especially the use of vice-admiralty courts to enforce navigation and revenue acts, led most states to take the unprecedented step of providing jury trials when they established their own admiralty courts during the Revolution. By 1789 such a system was deemed a failure. The First Congress attempted to remedy the situation in section 9 of the Judiciary Act of 1789 by providing that judges in the newly created federal district courts would try admiralty and maritime cases without a jury. Henry J. Bourguignon, *The First Federal Court: The Federal Appellate Prize Court of the American Revolution, 1775-1787* (Philadelphia: American Philosophical Society, 1977), pp. 25, 32-33, 192, 339, 342; Goebel, *Antecedents and Beginnings to 1801,* pp. 159, 473-74; *Stat.,* 1:76.

William Paterson's Charge to the Grand Jury of the Circuit Court for the District of Pennsylvania ————————————————————————
[May 4, 1795]   [Philadelphia, Pennsylvania]

All free governments are instituted to protect and secure the property, liberties, and lives of the people, and, in a word, to promote their prosperity and happiness. The more effectually to attain these important ends, the legislative, executive, and judicial authorities have been established by the constitution of the United States, and have, as far as possible, distinct and independent existence. In the construction of the judiciary department, juries compose a capital and distinguished figure; they stand next to the legislature in point of utility and importance. The more we contemplate their formation and nature, their powers and duties, the higher they rise in celebrity and esteem. They are indeed the best preservative of civil liberty and order, and essentially necessary for the support of good government. It is, therefore, a radical and vital principle in the government of the United States, that no person can be affected in his property or life, for the commission of any offence, except by the judgment of twenty four good and lawful men; that is, one jury to find the preparatory bill of indictment, and another to pass a verdict upon it. The first of these is denominated the grand inquest or jury, principally, perhaps, on account of ~~their~~ the plenitude of their power. They are judges both of law and fact; judges upon whose presentment, frequently awaits life or death. The due execution of the system of penal jurisprudence depends almost entirely upon the diligence and rectitude, the ability and firmness of grand juries. They must present before courts can punish. The proper exercise of their function protects the innocent, and brings forward the guilty for conviction and punishment, allays the fears of the good, and chastens the outrageous spirit of the bad, checks vice, promotes virtue, preserves order, and vindicates the violated supremacy of the laws. It may, therefore, truly be said, that the justice of the nation is, in criminal matters, committed to their discretion and care. These observations apply with peculiar force to the scheme of government, which has been formed for, and adopted

by the citizens of the United States. It is a government of laws, and not of men; a government, which has freedom for its basis, and the happiness of the people for its object. Crimes perpetrated against such a government ought
to be considered as pointed as pointed against the peace, the well-being, the political existence, and, if I may so prase it, the majesty of the people themselves. The duties, gentlemen, designated and enjoined upon you by law, extend to the investigation and presentment of all offences, which have been perpetrated against the United States, within this district, or on the high seas by persons in it. To detail these offences would be an unnecessary expence of time. It is sufficient to observe in general, that the penal code of the U. States is plain and concise, and reduced, in its most important points, to written exactitude and precision. But as some offences will, perhaps, claim your particular notice, it may not be improper for the court to specify and observe upon them. Of these one is the forgery of bank bills,[1] which, beside its moral turpitude and fraud, has a direct and powerful tendency to impair the credit, and impede the currency of this species of circulating medium. An other offence, consists in the violation of neutral principles.[2] The power of declaring war is, by the constitution, vested exclusively in Congress, and until they exercise that power and announce hostilities, it becomes us to remain in the line of neutrality and peace.[3] The last offence, worthy of notice, is treason. Alas! gentlemen, that any circumstances should have arisen to render it necessary for courts to take cognizance of this crime.[4] But while we regret and deplore the occasion, we must be mindful of our duty, and be faithful to our country and its laws, to our oaths, our consciences, and our God. Treason, gentlemen, is the highest crime of a civil nature, and consists in levying war against the United States, or in adhering to their enemies.[5] It is the first part only of the description, which at present merits attention. All persons, who rise in
rebellion, and take up arms against the government, or who by numbers and open force in a violent and forcible manner resist and prevent the regular administration of justice, and due execution of the laws, come within the description of levying war. The guilt of this species of treason may also be contracted by persons, who make insurrections under the pretence of redressing national or public grievances, whether they be real or imaginary, or who attempt, by intimidation and violence, to force the repeal of a law, or an alteration in governmental measures.*

*If persons assemble to act with force in opposition to a law, and hope thereby to affect get it repealed; or if they endeavour in great numbers and force to work or bring about a reformation, without pursuing the methods prescribed by the constitution and laws [it w]ill be a levying of war and of course treason.

Such acts amount to an usurpation of legislative powers, and, if tolerated, would prove destructive to civil liberty and legal authority. To aid and assist in a rebellion against the government is a levying of war; and so also is an insurrection with an avowed design to pull down all inclosures, to open all prisons, and the like. In such cases the universality of the intention marks the line of discrimination between acts of treason and acts of riot. The truth is, that such ~~practices~~ outrages are highly criminal; they are contrary to the constitution, contrary to the law, and endanger our political existence. While it is the duty of every good citizen to be active in quelling all insurrections, it is peculiarly your duty, gentlemen, to present their authors and abettors for judicial discussion and reproof. May the like occasion never more occur! But if the spirit of rebellion or insurrection should again break forth, and bid defiance to government, may the militia of the United States exhibit the same promptitude and ardour, prowess and exertions to suppress it, as was displayed on the late trying emergency. Ever obedient to the voice of their country, may they be ready to repel all attacks upon her peace and prosperity, her government and laws. Illustrious example! Ye disorganizing spirits from henceforth obey. To reverence and obey the laws is the first political maxim and duty in a republican government. Observance of the laws and obedience to legal authority are the great bulwark of public liberty, which, however, free states find it difficult to maintain, because their salutary restraint sits uneasy upon turbulent spirits, and is mistaken for slavish subjection by the ~~ignorant~~ thoughtless and ill-informed part of the community, who delight in irregularity and licentiousness, as sure symptoms of freedom, and certain indications of republican virtue. Ah licentiousness! thou bane of republics, more to be dreaded than hosts of external foes. The truth is, that civil liberty and order consist in and depend upon submission to the laws. The constitution and laws contain the articles of our political faith; they point the path we are to go, and the rule by which we are to walk. They are the work of the people, declarative of their will, and as such ought to be reverenced and obeyed. To fashion our political temper, character, and conduct by the principles and spirit of the constitution and laws is both our interest and duty, and while we do so, we shall insure internal order and repose, preserve our civil rights and liberties pure and entire, and be united at home, and respected abroad. But why enlarge? The citizens of the U. States love the constitution, venerate the government, and obey the laws; nay more, they are prompt and active in compelling the turbulent and refractory to submit to legal authority. The supremacy of the law they acknowledge; it is the only sovereign they know. These are the brightest virtues, that can adorn the republican character. Long may they live, and highly may they be cherished in the bosom of every American _

AD (NjR, William Paterson Papers). Date and place derived from evidence in the charge. Readings supplied in brackets where document is torn.

1. Crimes Act of 1790, section 14. *Stat.*, 1:115.
2. Neutrality Act of 1794. *Stat.*, 1:381.

3. Article I, section 8.

4. A reference to the Whiskey Rebellion.

5. Punishment for treason is provided for in Article III, section 3 of the Constitution and in the Crimes Act of 1790, sections 1 and 2. *Stat.*, 1:112.

James Iredell to Hannah Iredell
May 7, 1795   Springfield, Massachusetts

... I left New Haven yesterday morning, and arrived here ~~yesterday~~ this morning (which is about 70 miles distance), after travelling through a delightful Country, passing several very pretty Towns, and enjoying (almost for the first time this spring) most charming weather. I preserve my health perfectly well, and am to set off in the stage for Windsor in Vermont tomorrow. I am told the road is a very fine one, which is more than I expected till lately. I am afraid my letters from you will now reach me with great uncertainty, tho' I leave directions for them to follow me _ Remember I am to be at Portsmouth in New Hampshire on the 25 of May, at Boston on the 7th of June, and at Newport in Rhode Island on the 19th of June. ...

ARS (Nc-Ar, Charles E. Johnson Collection). Addressed "to the care of Samuel Johnston Esq Williamston,   North Carolina." Postmarked by hand "May 7 _ Spring^d."

Circuit Court for the District of Maryland
May 7, 1795   Annapolis, Maryland

Judge William Paca appeared in court, but Associate Justice James Wilson's absence caused Paca to adjourn the court until the following day. On May 8 the court commenced its session with Wilson and Paca in attendance, after which Wilson delivered a charge to the grand jury. On May 9 the court adjourned to the next term.[1]

1. Minutes, CCD Maryland, RG 21, PPFAR. Charge not found.

Circuit Court for the District of South Carolina
May 12, 1795   Columbia, South Carolina

Court opened on May 12 with Associate Justice John Blair and Judge Thomas Bee in attendance. On May 14 the court was adjourned to the following term because John Blair was "so much indisposed" that he was "incapable of proceeding to Business."[1]

1. Minutes, CCD South Carolina, RG 21, GEpFAR. For an account of Blair's illness, see John Blair to William Cushing, June 12, 1795 (q.v.).

Sharon, Connecticut attributed to Ralph Earl (1751-1801). Oil on canvas, ca. 1796. Courtesy Litchfield Historical Society, Litchfield, Connecticut.

Circuit Court for the District of Vermont
May 12, 1795   Windsor, Vermont

On May 12 the circuit court commenced its session with Associate Justice James Iredell and Judge Samuel Hitchcock in attendance. Iredell then delivered a charge to the grand jury. The court adjourned on May 16.[1]

1. Circuit Docket, CCD Vermont, RG 21, MWalFAR; James Iredell's Charge to the Grand Jury of the Circuit Court for the District of Vermont, May 12, 1795 (q.v.).

James Iredell's Charge to the Grand Jury of the Circuit Court for the District of Vermont
May 12, 1795   Windsor, Vermont

[*For the charge to the grand jury, see James Iredell's Charge to the Grand Jury of the Circuit Court for the District of Connecticut, published above under date of April 25, 1795.*]

James Iredell to Hannah Iredell
May 18, 1795   Windsor, Vermont

...I have been here about a week, and am to set off to-morrow for Portsmouth. My health, thank God, is perfectly good; and I have passed my time very agreeably in this place, where there is a small but genteel society, who have shown me many pleasing civilities. They gave a ball one night in a very elegant room, and where there was so agreeable a company that I danced with pleasure till after two in the morning.[1] The country in general is very rough and mountainous, not only in this neighborhood but almost all the way up the Connecticut River from Springfield, in Massachusetts (about 115 miles below), but it is relieved in many places with fine fertile valleys, and some of the mountains are cultivated almost to the summit. In many places on the road the prospects are more extensive, variegated and romantic than any I have seen in any inland part of America. You see not only a great many distant waving mountains, but very large plains below dotted with houses, detached from each other, and here and there pretty little towns ornamented with handsome steeples. These are chiefly on the New Hampshire side of the river, for about 60 miles below this the Massachusetts line ends, and New Hampshire and Vermont are divided by the river. I am now sitting in a room with the river close by me in front, and on the other side a lofty mountain. This town is indeed surrounded with mountains. In Charlestown, New Hampshire, about eighteen miles hence, a very pretty place, there are two more elegant houses than any I saw in Connecticut. Having occasion to stay one day on the road, at a little town called Walpole,

View from Stacey Hill, Stoddard, New Hampshire by Thomas Doughty (1793-1856). Oil on canvas, 1830. Courtesy Museum of Fine Arts, Boston. Gift of Mrs. Maxim Karolik for the Karolik Collection of American Paintings, 1815-1865.

in New Hampshire (27 miles from this place), I heard Dr. Cutler[2] lived at Rockingham in this State (about 6 miles distant). I accordingly went and spent the day with him. I met him within a little distance of his house, as he was coming in search of me, having heard a day or two before of my being expected up. His wife[3] and daughter are at Hartford in Connecticut. He has only that daughter and two sons, who are both fine boys. I was very much affected to find that he had called his youngest (about three years old) after me—James Iredell.[4] ...

Pr (Printed in *MJI*, 2:444).

1. James Iredell wrote Helen (Blair) Tredwell that he left the dance "with regret. I was introduced to a Stranger to dance with, but I liked her so well that I changed Partners with great reluctance, and barely in deference to the custom, as seldom as possible." James Iredell to Helen Tredwell, May 27, 1795, Charles E. Johnson Collection, Nc-Ar.

2. Samuel Cutler (1744-1821), a medical doctor and an old friend of the Iredells, resided in Rockingham, Vermont. Lyman Simpson Hayes, *History of the Town of Rockingham, Vermont* (Bellows Falls, Vt.: published by the town, 1907), pp. 635-36.

3. Jennette (Caldwell) Cutler (ca. 1765-1851) of Hartford, Connecticut. Hayes, *History of the Town of Rockingham, Vermont*, p. 636.

4. James Iredell Cutler (1792-ca. 1878). Hayes, *History of the Town of Rockingham, Vermont*, p. 637.

James Iredell to Hannah Iredell
May 20, 1795   Greenfield, Massachusetts

... I am now about seventy miles below Windsor, on my way to Boston, by which I am obliged to go to get to Portsmouth, though a great way round, there being no stage across the mountains above, nor scarcely a practicability of travelling on horseback[1] ...

Pr (Printed in *MJI*, 2:445).

1. James Iredell also wrote to his niece Helen (Blair) Tredwell from Portsmouth, New Hampshire on May 27, 1795, that "the mountains are so formidable between that side of New Hampshire and this, that no Stages attempt to cross, and I was obliged to come back to Springfield, & come by way of Boston to this Town_" (Charles E. Johnson Collection, Nc-Ar).

James Iredell to George Simpson
May 22, 1795   Springfield, Massachusetts

Springfield, Massachusetts,   May 22[d] 1795.
Sir,

I hope you will excuse the liberty I take in requesting you to enquire if the President and Directors will be pleased to advance me two hundred Dollars on discount, to be deducted by them out of my next quarter's salary, in which case I hereby authorise such deduction to be made, and you will

much oblige me in inclosing a draft for the amount on the Branch Bank in
Boston, inclosed in a letter to me directed to be left_{kept} at the Post office in
Boston till called for— But if such advance be inconvenient or not agreeable
to them I beg the favour of you to inclose me directed as above Post Notes
to the above amount, or a draft on the Branch Bank payable on the day
that I shall be entitled to credit on your books.

I am,   Sir,   with great respect and esteem,   Your obliged and   obedient
Servant

Ja. Iredell.

ARS (PHi, Etting Papers). Addressed "George Simpson Esqʳ Cashier of the Bank of the United
States Philadelphia."
  George Simpson (1759-1822), cashier of the Bank of the United States from 1795 to 1811.
Henry Simpson, *The Lives of Eminent Philadelphians, Now Deceased* (Philadelphia: William
Brotherhead, 1859), pp. 890-93; *PAH*, 17:329n.

Circuit Court for the District of Virginia ——————————————

May 22, 1795   Richmond, Virginia

Associate Justice James Wilson and Judge Cyrus Griffin opened court, and a charge
was delivered to the grand jury. After completing its business, the court adjourned
on June 8 to the next term.[1]

1. Order Book, CCD Virginia, Vi. Charge not found.

James Iredell to Hannah Iredell ——————————————

May 27, 1795   Portsmouth, New Hampshire

... I arrived here the day before yesterday, and never was in better health
in my life than I am at this moment, tho' I had to travel almost the whole
way in the rain from Windsor in Vermont to Boston, we having had the
latest, wettest, and most disagreeable spring that I am told can be remembered
in this Country. Yesterday and to day the weather has assumed something
like a summer appearance— I was received with the greatest cordiality and
kindness by all my old Friends in Boston whom I had an opportunity of
seeing. I found Mʳˢ Hancock just going to comfort herself for a slavish
confinement for many years to a goutified ill tempered Husband by marrying
a Capt. Scott,[1] an old Captain in Gov. Hancock's employ who sails in the
London trade, and who arrived much to her satisfaction on Sunday last. ...
Mʳ Gerry has been in very ill health, and is travelling with his Wife & 5
Children to recruit it. He went from the house in which I am the morning
of the day I arrived, & obligingly left his compliments for me. Her eyesight,
I am told, is better, but her health otherwise not good— They have the

A View of Portsmouth, in New Hampshire, taken from the East Shore by an unknown artist. Engraving, 1778, from *The Atlantic Neptune*, 1778. Courtesy New Hampshire Historical Society, Concord.

misfortune of having nothing to do but to enjoy life, and accordingly it is said feel the <u>ennui</u> of the French, tho' I believe it is what they know only by name. I wish however we had the trial of such a disadvantage. This Town is on a pretty situation very near the Sea, and with an admirable harbour, but it is laid off in a very irregular disagreeable manner, with narrow streets, but there are here and there interspersed very handsome houses. The road from Boston to it (about 65 miles) is a remarkably fine one, but the Country does not look at all like Connecticut, nor have the little Towns the same neat appearance as even in Vermont_ I met Dr Cutler at a place on the road the evening I left Windsor, but could not stay with him more than 5 minutes, which we both greatly regretted. He desired to be very respectfully remembered to you and M.^r and Mrs Johnston, and his other old Friends in Carolina. The improvements in almost every part of America are wonderful. The Bridge between Boston and Cambridge far exceeded my expectations.[2] The causeway leading to it from Cambridge, which is now as good a road as the road by Roberts's, and railed in like the bridge, is a mile and a quarter long, and the bridge itself 3 quarters of a mile, the whole as ~~straight~~ strait as an arrow, the carriage way very wide, with passages on each side for foot passengers, beautifully painted, and with an astonishing number of fine lamps all along on each side—The River is deep and very rapid—notwithstanding which the whole of this bridge was completed, so as to be passable at least, in about 6 months. We passed an excellent and beautiful bridge over the Merrimack River near Newbury Port, which was building when I was there before, and they have a very fine one, I am told, over the Piscatiqua River which runs by this Town a few miles above.

... I think you had better direct your next letter to me in New York "to be kept at the Post office till called for". ...

ARS (Nc-Ar, Charles E. Johnson Collection).

1. Dorothy (Quincy) Hancock married James Scott (ca. 1746-1809) on July 28, 1796. H. Hobart Holly, *Descendants of Edmund Quincy, 1602-1637* (Quincy, Mass.: Quincy Historical Society, 1977), pp. 5-6; American Antiquarian Society, *Index of Deaths in Massachusetts*.

2. The West Boston Bridge, also known as the Cambridge Bridge, opened for traffic on November 23, 1793. Nathaniel B. Shurtleff, *A Topographical and Historical Description of Boston* (Boston: Alfred Mudge & Son, 1871), pp. 419-20.

Circuit Court for the District of New Hampshire —————

May 27, 1795   Portsmouth, New Hampshire

Court convened with Associate Justice James Iredell and Judge John Pickering in attendance. The court was adjourned May 29 to the following term.[1]

Following graduation from Harvard in 1761, Judge John Pickering (ca. 1738-1805) returned to his native New Hampshire and entered law practice. He settled in Portsmouth (1771), married Abigail Sheafe, and embarked on building up a large but not particularly profitable law business. During the Confederation period Pickering

A chain bridge across the Merrimac at Deer Island, near Newbury by Pavel Petrovich Svinin (1787-1839). Watercolor on paper, ca. 1811-1813. Courtesy Metropolitan Museum of Art, New York. Rogers Fund, 1942.

John Pickering by an unknown artist. Watercolor on ivory, ca. 1795. Courtesy New Hampshire Historical Society, Concord.

held a number of positions in the New Hampshire government and was influential in the state's ratifying convention. In August 1790 he was made chief justice of the New Hampshire Superior Court of Judicature, a position he held until his confirmation on February 11, 1795, as United States judge for the district of New Hampshire. In 1803 the House of Representatives voted to impeach Pickering. One of the impeachment articles charged that on two occasions in 1802, Pickering, "being a man of loose morals and intemperate habits," appeared on the bench "in a state of total intoxication ... and did then and there frequently, in a most prophane and indecent manner, invoke the name of the Supreme Being, to the evil example of all the good citizens of the United States." The Senate found him guilty and removed him from office on March 12, 1804.[2]

1. Records, CCD New Hampshire, RG 21, MWalFAR.
2. *DAB; SEJ,* 1:172; *HRJ,* 4:383-84; *SLJ;* 3:493, 497, 506-7.

Albert Gallatin to Hannah Gallatin ————————————————
June 1, 1795   Philadelphia, Pennsylvania

[*Gallatin, attending the trials of those arrested in the Whiskey Rebellion, notes that the*] trials go still very slowly _ only two since I wrote to you; the men called Curtis and Barnet both indicted for the attack upon & burning Nevil's house and both acquitted; the first without much hesitation, as there was at least a strong presumption, that he went there either to prevent mischief or

at most only as a spectator _ the second was as guilty as Mitchell[1] who has been condemned; but there were not sufficient legal proofs against either _ The difference in the verdict arises from the difference of Counsel employed in their respective defences and chiefly from a different choice of jury _ Mitchell was very poorly defended by Thomas (the member of Senate) who is young unexperienced, impudent and self conceited _ [2] He challenged (that is to say rejected, for you know the accused person has a right to reject 35 of the jury without assigning any reason) every inhabitant of Allegheny and left the case to 12 Quakers, (many of them probably old tories) on the supposition that Quakers would condemn no person to death; but he was utterly mistaken _ Lewis[3] defended Barnet made a very good defence, and got a jury of a different complexion _ the consequence of which was that although the evidence, pleadings and charge took up from 11 in the forenoon till 3 °Clock the next morning, the jury were but 15 minutes out before they brought in a verdict of not guilty _ Brackenridge[4] says that he would always chose a jury of Quakers or at least Episcopalians in all common cases such as murder, rape & so forth _ but in every possible case of insurrection, rebellion & treason, give him Presbyterians as the jury, by all means _ I believe there is At least as much truth as witt in the saying _ The why and wherefore I will explain at the next politico-religious lecture I will give you _ I have been quite lonely since I have been in town _ not a single time have I called on Miss Armstrong, and what is worse I have not been once at Mrs Pettit's _ [5] Bad as I am I would have called at the last place had it not been
                                                  lives
that Judge Patterson ~~was~~ there and, from prejudice I guess, merely on account of his connection with Gen. White,[6] I did not wish much to meet him. By the bye, he [is an?] excellent Judge, a sound lawyer and as impartial as cou[ld be?] expected _. His colleague on the present occasion Judge Peters has not thought fit to improve by his example, but has behaved during the whole course of the trials not as a Judge but as a Prosecutor _ I have drawn, at the request of the jury who convicted Philip Vigol, a petition to the President recommending him as a proper object of mercy; they have all signed, but what effect it will have I do not know, and indeed no body can form any conjecture whether the persons convicted will be pardoned or not _ It rests solely with the President _ ...

ARS (NHi, Albert Gallatin Papers). Addressed "William Street   New York." Postmarked "1 IV." Readings in brackets supplied where letter is torn.

   Abraham Alfonse Albert Gallatin (1761-1849) was a witness on behalf of John Corbley and Thomas Geddes, two men indicted for offenses resulting from their participation in the Whiskey Rebellion. In 1795 Gallatin was a member of the House of Representatives from Pennsylvania. *DAB;* Albert Gallatin to Hannah Gallatin, May 12, 1795, Albert Gallatin Papers, NHi; Engrossed Minutes, May 11, 1795, CCD Pennsylvania, RG 21, PPFAR.

   Hannah Nicholson (1766-1849) and Albert Gallatin were married in 1793. William Plumb

Bacon, ed., *Ancestry of Albert Gallatin ... and of Hannah Nicholson* (New York: Press of T. A. Wright, 1916), title page and p. 27.

1. John Mitchell.

2. Probably Joseph Thomas (b. 1765), a Pennsylvania state senator in 1795. *Journal of the Senate of the Commonwealth of Pennsylvania,* vol. 5 (Philadelphia: Zachariah Poulson, Jr., 1794), p. 3; University of Pennsylvania, *Biographical Catalogue of the Matriculates of the College, 1749-1893* (Philadelphia, 1894), p. 24.

3. William Lewis (1751-1819), the former United States judge for the district of Pennsylvania. *DAB.*

4. Probably Hugh Henry Brackenridge (1748-1816), a resident of Pittsburgh, who attempted to mediate the dispute between the rebels and the government. *DAB.*

5. Possibly Elizabeth (McKean) Pettit (1767-1811), wife of Philadelphia merchant Andrew Pettit and daughter of Pennsylvania's chief justice, Thomas McKean. Wilfred Jordan, ed., *Colonial and Revolutionary Families of Pennsylvania,* vol. 5 (New York: Lewis Publishing, [1934-1936]), pp. 473, 479.

6. Anthony Walton White, Paterson's brother-in-law, was a general in the army that rounded up the Whiskey Rebellion participants. Mary D. Ogden, *Memorial Cyclopedia of New Jersey,* 3 vols. (Newark: Memorial History Co., 1915-1917), 1:55; Elizabeth Morris Lefferts, comp., *Descendants of Lewis Morris of Morrisania* (New York: Tobias A. Wright, 1907), Chart L.

Circuit Court for the District of North Carolina

June 1, 1795   Wake Court House, Wake County, North Carolina

No court was held in North Carolina this term. Associate Justice John Blair was scheduled to attend the court, but the same illness that caused him to adjourn the South Carolina court prevented him from holding the court in North Carolina. Blair claimed to have done everything he could "to prevent the fruitless attendance of others."[1]

1. For Blair's account of his illness, see John Blair to William Cushing, June 12, 1795 (q.v.). We cannot determine if Judge John Sitgreaves attended court this term. The minutes of the court do not note his attendance. According to a 1796 statute, "a sufficient quorum of judges did not attend" the spring 1795 session of the North Carolina circuit court. This may indicate that Sitgreaves did appear at that session inasmuch as the same act specifically notes that "no judge attended" the fall 1795 session. Minutes, June 1, 1795, CCD North Carolina, RG 21, GEpFAR; "An Act making certain provisions in regard to the Circuit Court, for the district of North Carolina," March 31, 1796. *Stat.,* 1:450-51.

James Iredell to Hannah Iredell

June 3, 1795   Boston, Massachusetts

Boston June 3[d] 1795.

My dear Hannah,

I arrived here very well on Monday last, and have since received a letter from your Brother[1] dated the 9 of May. I am much obliged to him for writing, but extremely concerned that you were too much indisposed to write yourself. I have been afraid for some time your health was not good. I hope you will not neglect to do every thing you can to restore it, tho' I have too often had reason to lament you are so much less careful of your own health than that of your Friends. I write this by a Vessel to Pasquotank _ but intend to write by the post too. Give my tenderest love, and many warm kisses, to our lovely Children. Rememember me most kindly to your Brother and his Family and all my other Friends. I am obliged to write now very hastily. I have preserved my health remarkably well _ God grant I may soon hear you are perfectly recovered _

I am ever,   my dear Hannah,   Your most affectionate

Ja. Iredell

ARS (Nc-Ar, Charles E. Johnson Collection).
  1. Samuel Johnston.

James Iredell to Hannah Iredell

June 5, 1795   Boston, Massachusetts

Boston,   June 5th 1795.

My dear Hannah,

I wrote to you a day or two ago by a Vessel bound to Pasquotank. I shall feel great anxiety till I receive an account of the recovery of your health. I hope you will not always rely on the fortnight post alone, but try other opportunities of writing to me. I have preserved my health remarkably well, in the midst of the most disagreeable rainy weather ever known at the same season, notwithstanding which I have had no other indisposition but a slight cold, unaccompanied with any fever, which I have entirely subdued by a little medicine and abstinence for one day. I now scarcely feel the effects of it. Tho' there have been two plays performed here since I came I have been at neither, but as the weather is very fine at present I believe I shall go tonight. I continue to receive the kindest civilities, and can't help wishing you were here to partake of them. I met M[rs] Cabot[1] in town one day. She looked very well, and enquired kindly after you. M[r] Cabot was just then setting off for Philadelphia. He sent me a very obliging message, not being able to come himself. M[rs] Cabot invited me to go and see her, which I intend to do _ She lives only about four or five miles from town, just beyond Judge Lowell's, with whom I shall spend next Sunday. I have received several kind invitations into the Country, which my time will not admit of my accepting. I called on M[rs] Howard, but did not find her at home.

I hope to be in New York early in July, and probably shall stay there but a short time before I go on to Philadelphia. As to the approaching summer, I know not what to advise for you and our dear Children. I must depend on your determination, and rely on the good providence of God. But I confess I dread another experiment at Edenton.

Mrs Langdon desired her compliments to you. I received great civilities
from Mr Langdon & her, who gave me a very kind invitation to their house$_\wedge$. which I declined
I staid two days with Mr Parsons on my way here, & was obliged to force
myself away at last, so importunate was he with me that I should stay longer.
Mrs Parsons, tho' unknown, desired to be mentioned to you. She is an amiable
Woman, and they have 5 lovely Children _ 4 Daughters & a Son. They have
lost 3 Sons, tho' Newbury Port is generally reckoned a very healthy place.
Last year they had a fatal Dysentery among them. Mr Parsons's Family then
escaped. The loss of his Children was before.

I earnestly hope I shall soon hear from you. Kiss with great earnestness
our lovely Children for me, and beg them not to forget me. Remember me
to Annie & her Husband _ [2]

I am ever,   my dear Hannah,   Your most affectionate

Ja. Iredell.

ARS (Nc-Ar, Charles E. Johnson Collection).

1. In 1774, Elizabeth (Higginson) Cabot (1756-1826) married her cousin, George Cabot (1752-1823), who became a senator from Massachusetts (1791-1796). L. Vernon Briggs, *History and Genealogy of the Cabot Family, 1475-1927,* 2 vols. (Boston: Charles E. Goodspeed, 1927), 1:185-93; *BDAC.*

2. Iredell could have been referring to Annie (Johnston) Hunter who was the niece of Hannah Iredell. *MJI,* 1:37.

William Paterson to Edmund Randolph ———————————————————
June 6, 1795   Philadelphia, Pennsylvania

Dear Sir,

At the request of the President through Mr Attorney-General, I have given
a short narrative of the cases made out in the trials of Mitchell and Vigol.[1]
Time would not permit me to go more into detail, as I shall be obliged to
set off for Delaware early to-morrow, and have many things to do before
my departure _

Y^r obed. hb. serv.

Wm Paterson.
6th June, 1795

The Honble
Mr Randolph _

ARS (DLC, George Washington Papers). Place determined by evidence in the letter.

1. Paterson's case narratives probably were written in response to a petition for a presidential pardon. President Washington granted a respite of execution to Philip Vigol on June 16 and to John Mitchell on June 17. Both men received a full pardon on November 2. Petitions for Pardon, 1789-1869, RG 59, DNA; Pardons and Remissions, 1793-1893, RG 59, DNA.

Circuit Court for the District of Delaware
June 8, 1795   New Castle, Delaware

On June 8[1] the circuit court convened with Associate Justice William Paterson and Judge Gunning Bedford, Jr., in attendance. Paterson delivered a charge to the grand jury. The docket of the circuit court does not record the court's closing, but the "teste" day was on June 9.[2]

1. Section 2 of the District and Circuit Court Act of 1794 changed the date of the spring circuit court from April 27 to the second Monday of June. *Stat.,* 1:396.
2. Appearance Docket, CCD Delaware, RG 21, PPFAR; William Paterson's Charge to the Grand Jury of the Circuit Court for the District of Delaware, [June 8, 1795] (q.v.); Reply of the Grand Jury of the Circuit Court for the District of Delaware, June 9, 1795 (q.v.).

William Paterson's Charge to the Grand Jury of the Circuit Court for the District of Delaware
[June 8, 1795]   [New Castle, Delaware]

The situation of the United States is the most happy in the world. In consequence of the moderation, firmness, and wisdom displayed by the administrators of our government, and of the pacific principles, which they early adopted, and have invariably pursued, we have not been involved in the present war, which rages with such destructive fury in Europe. War is a dreadful calamity; nothing but a case of extreme necessity should prevail on any people to engage in it. The evils attendant upon a state of war are many and great; to a young and rising republic, like ours, it might be productive of fatal effects; clear it is, that it could produce no good. Peace promotes industry, agriculture, manufactures, arts, commerce, and good morals; it cherishes all the benevolent and domestic virtues, and diffuses an air of calmness and benignity over the face of the country. War, on the other hand, delights in bloodshed, rapine, and devastation, injures agriculture, destroys commerce, retards population, and ruins the morals of a people; it exhausts the resources of a nation, and entails a debt of millions on posterity; thousands of men fall beneath its stroke, while pestilence and famine often stalk in its rear and close the disastrous scene. Happy America! the land of peace and plenty, the asylum for the oppressed of every clime. May no factions nor disorganizing spirits arise within thy ~~peacef~~ peaceful vales to generate and foment internal discord and strife; may insurrection never more rear her crest; may neither foes at home nor foes abroad disturb this our rare and high felicity. But may we all, as becomes good citizens, lead quiet lives under the guidance and government of the laws. From our political situation arise certain duties with respect to the powers at war, which ought to be observed with fidelity, and performed with punctuality and honor. The United states are neutral in the present war; they take no part in it; they remain common friends to all the belligerent powers, not favouring the arms of one to the detriment of the others. An exact neutrality must mark their conduct towards the parties at war; if they favor one to the injury of the other, it will be a departure from pacific principles and indicative of a hostile disposition. It would be a fraudulent neutrality. To this rule there is no exception but that which arises from the obligation of ~~tre~~ antecedant treaties, which ought to be religiously observed. All contracts should be held inviolably sacred. This principle, so just in itself, ^will^ apply with particular force to treaties, which are conventions or contracts between ~~nat~~ states, and have for their object national measures, adjustments, and regulations. In forming treaties, as in forming contracts between individuals, the will and advantage of one party alone, in exclusion of the other, cannot, in reason and the nature of the thing, be the governing motive or rule. The will and benefit of both ~~mu~~ ^are to^ ~~st~~ be consulted, and must conspire before the compact can be completed. The misery, however, is, that we are apt to look at one side only of the question, and this unavoidably leads to incompleteness and of course to inaccuracy of view. Hence the difficulty of making treaties, so as to give general satisfaction. Besides, they require talents and information, integrity, and skill in conducting them to a proper termination. Much coolness and reflection, political discernment and knowledge are also requisite in forming a just estimate of their merit, and in discriminating between their good and bad properties. In order to form a fair decision many particulars must conspire; we must have a sound knowledge of the law of nations, and a correct view of existing treaties; we must take a just survey of our own country, its agriculture and manufacturers, its population and resources, its navigation and commerce, its strong and weak points, and whether a state of war, if it can be honourably avoided, is to be preferred to our present state of prosperity and peace. In short, we must consider and combine that immense variety of interests, which arise from fifteen states almost infinitely diversified; and whose safety and welfare depend upon their co-operation and confederacy. Nor is this all, we must likewise have extensive and accurate information respecting the state and resources of the nation, with which the treaty is made, and of the relative situation of the other powers abroad. Taking all these circumstances under consideration, it will admit of some doubt, whether it requires more talents and temper, political sagacity and information to form a just treaty than to decide upon its merits when formed. Upon full investigation a dispassionate inquirer will terminate his research with observing, that the constitution has placed the power of making treaties in the most sagacious and vigilant, the safest, best-informed, and most trust-worthy persons; that he will in this respect, as in every other, confide in the constituted authorities of his country; and therefore will, with full assurance, rely upon the wisdom, rectitude, and patriotism of the President and senate of the United States. These are the men, to whom the people, by [the?] constitution, have delegated the power of making treaties; it is their interest and duty to consult and advance the prosperity and happiness of the Union at large; and from thence it may be fairly inferred, that they would not conclude and ratify a treaty with any nation, which, under all circumstances, and in a collective point of view, they considered to be radically wrong, or eventually prejudicial. Sentiments of this kind will naturally arise in the mind of every person, who reflects upon the present state of things; they will, indeed, extend themselves, and embrace all the branches of our political establishment. The interest and honor, the prosperity and safety of the United States are committed to Congress; they are men of our own choice, and, doubtless, will direct and pursue the most effectual measures for the advancement of our national welfare and happiness. In them is exclusively vested the power of declaring war, and until they exercise that power and announce hostilities, it becomes us to remain in the line of neutrality and peace. The station of neutrality, which the United States have assumed, point to a certain course of conduct, which it is incumbent upon us invariably to observe. Neutrality implies two things. 1. That we are not to afford any succours to any of the belligerent powers, when there is no obligation to do so, nor voluntarily to furnish troops, arms, ammunition, or other articles of direct use in war. 2. In things, which do not respect war, a neutral nation must not refuse to one of the parties, on account of its present quarrel, what it grants to the other. These rules import exact impartiality, and must be strictly observed by neutral nations. A deviation from them denotes an active preference, a favoring of one to the detriment of the other, whereas a neutral must steer an even course between hostile nations, without leaning as̲ to̲ conduct to the one side more than to the other. Every active or improper preference is founded upon a predilection for one of the belligerent powers, or hatred to the other. If the United States for instance should furnish troops or ammunition to Great Britain or France in their present state of hostility to each other, no person would hesitate in pronouncing it to be incompatible with the principles of neutrality. Such supplies would make us confederates and parties in the war. If the United States should knowingly suffer any of the powers at war to equip and fit out privateers within their jurisdiction or territorial limits, it would be considered as an infraction or abandonement of neutral principles. Hence it follows, that if any of our citizens should fit out or aid in fitting out privateers in any of the ports of the United States to cruize against friendly powers, it would be deemed an offence highly criminal, and justly punishable by the law of nations. The same may be said of a citizen of the United States accepting therein a commission from any foreign nation to act against the enemies of that nation, but who are at the same time our friends. Such acts are dangerous to the peace and happiness of our country, as they have a direct tendency to involve us in disagreeable disputes, and, perhaps, in long and expensive wars. For friendly powers will assuredly resent such hostile

conduct, and call upon our government at once to disavow the offence and punish the offender. And yet so ignorant or regardless of duty, so perverse or prejudiced, selfish and fond of gain have some of our citizens been found, that they have, in direct violation of the principles of neutrality, committed offences of the foregoing description, and set both law and government at defiance. Transgressions of this kind became frequent in some parts of the union, and at length attracted the notice of Congress, who, in June 1794, passed an act declaratory of the law of nations, and enforcing its observance by vindicatory sanctions. The parts of the act material on the present occasion
are contained
and worthy of your attention lie in the first five sections.[1] They run in the following words—Here read them_

If therefore, gentlemen, any offenders of the foregoing description should come to your knowledge, it will be your duty to present them. The principles of neutrality, the law of nations, and the laws of the United States, require, that such transgressors should be proceeded against and punished according to their respective demerits. The prosperity and peace of our country depend in a great measure upon grand juries; they must present before courts can punish. The execution of criminal law, or, in other words, the justice of the nation, so far as it relates to indictable offences, is committed to their care. I shall close this address with recommending an observance of the principles of neutrality, a regard for the constituted authorities, and an habitual obedience to, and veneration for, the laws of our country. While we pursue this line of conduct we shall live in peace at home and be respected abroad, we shall cherish a spirit of candor and unanimity, promote good order, justice, and social happiness, maintain the independence and dignity of the United States, and be at once the envy and dread of the world. May the God of Heaven be our protector and guide, and enable us all to discharge our official, relative, and social duties with diligence and fidelity_

AD (NjR, William Paterson Papers). An examination of the text of this undated charge narrows its probable date to a period between the passage of the Neutrality Act on June 5, 1794 and Senate approval of the Jay Treaty on June 24, 1795. Paterson sat at four circuit courts during that period: New York, New Jersey, Pennsylvania, and Delaware. The grand jury charges delivered at two of those courts, New Jersey and Pennsylvania, are already identified (qq.v., under dates of April 2 and May 4 respectively). Uncertainty about the state of Jay's negotiations (news of even a preliminary draft was not known until November 11, 1794), would seem to exclude the September 1794 New York court, leaving the Delaware court as the only remaining possibility. Coincidently, on the day the Delaware circuit court opened, June 8, 1795, the Senate began consideration of the Jay Treaty.

1. Neutrality Act of 1794. *Stat.*, 1:381.

Circuit Court for the District of Massachusetts

June 8, 1795   Boston, Massachusetts

Court was opened on Monday, June 8, by Associate Justice James Iredell and Judge John Lowell. On June 16 after completing its business, the court adjourned until the following term.[1]

1. Final Records, CCD Massachusetts, RG 21, MWalFAR.

Reply of the Grand Jury of Circuit Court for the District of Delaware

June 9, 1795   New Castle, Delaware

New Castle   June 9th 1795.

Sir/.

The Grand Inquest for the district of Delaware, impressed with the importance of your address deliv[ere]d to them yesterday;[1] presume the publication thereof, will tend to diseminate and inculcate Ideas, that may be usefull to our fellow Citizens: We therefore, the undersigned, in behalf of the Grand Inquest, take the liberty of Soliciting your Honor for a Coppy or Transcript thereof.

With Sentiments of esteem & respect we are Sir, your obt Humb St

Jno Stockton
Saml Hollingsworth
Jos Barker

RS (NjR, William Paterson Papers). Reading supplied in brackets where document is torn.
1. William Paterson's Charge to the Grand Jury of the Circuit Court for the District of Delaware, [June 8, 1795] (q.v.).

John Blair to William Cushing

June 12, 1795   Williamsburg, Virginia

... Your letter on my last leaving Philadelphia,[1] inclosing me a hundred dollars on account of my taking the Southern circuit,[2] expressed a wish that you might be excused from attending the Supreme Court in August next, as in that hot season little is to be done, & as the middle circuit would probably be assigned to you, at that siting, which would make it necessary for you to leave home in Septr after _ As far as this was to depend upon me, I was determined to do every thing in my power, for gratifying your desire, & had fully ~~determined~~ resolved to attend the August-Term my self _ ~~and~~ This is still my design, if a calamity which has befallen me do not prevent it _ I think,

however, I ought to inform you, that a malady which I have had for some years, in a smaller degree, has since I had the pleasure of seeing you increased so greatly as to disqualify me totally for business _ It is a rattling, distracting noise in my head _ I had much of it at Savannah, besides almost continual
there,
cholic. I would fain have declined the decision of several Admiralty cases‸if I had not been told that delay would be greatly injurious, on account of the prize-goods being stored at a very great daily expense _ This circumstance prompted me to go thro that business, altho in a condition not fit for any; & I have some reason to fear that in doing so I have effected nothing but
to
work for the Supreme court, b̶y̶ undo̶i̶n̶g̶ what I have done.[3] It is, however, a consolation to me, that there is yet a court where my errors may be corrected _ When I came to Columbia, I found much business of the same sort; but as in those cases bond & security had been given, & the goods not stored, altho I heard an argument on two of them, I thought it adviseable (my disorder still increasing) to decline making any decree & adjourn the court _ The same cause induced me to decline holding the court at
but make the best of my way home,
Raleigh,‸having   first done every thing I could to prevent the fruitless attendance of others . . .

ARS (MHi, Cushing Family Papers, 1650-1840). Addressed "Massachusetts." Postmarked "W͟m͟.burg June 12 1795."
    1. Letter not found.
    2. Blair is referring to an agreement among the justices that each of them give one hundred dollars to the justice assigned the Southern Circuit. For further information, see James Iredell to James Wilson, November 24, 1794, and note, *DHSC*, 2:497-98.
    3. Three admiralty cases decided at the April 1795 term of the Circuit Court for the district of Georgia were appealed to the Supreme Court. *John Wallace v. Brig Everton and John Cotton,* also known as *Cotton v. Wallace,* and *Wallace v. Brig Caesar,* were affirmed by the Court at its February 1796 term. Minutes, May 5, 1795, CCD Georgia, RG 21, GEpFAR; *DHSC*, 1:265-66. *Walter Ross v. Ship Elizabeth and Hills, May & Woodbridge* was reversed under the name *Hills v. Ross* at the August 1796 term of the Supreme Court. Minutes, May 1-5, 1795, CCD Georgia, RG 21, GEpFAR; *DHSC*, 1:282.

James Iredell to Hannah Iredell ─────────────────────
June 12, 1795   Boston, Massachusetts

. . . General Knox[1] and his family came to town a few days ago, all very well. A subscription is going about for a public dinner to the General, which undoubtedly will be given him. Here where he is known so well he is universally beloved and respected. I believe the Court will end to-morrow, and that I shall go to Rhode Island on Monday. We yesterday tried a man for manslaughter on the high seas, and he was convicted on the most satisfactory though affecting evidence.[2] The circumstances were so aggravated, that the Court deliberated whether they should not direct an acquittal on that indictment on purpose that he might be found guilty of murder. But, finding that it had been under consideration of the grand jury, we did not think ourselves at liberty to do so. I went on Saturday evening to Judge Lowell's (three miles from town), and staid at his house, which is delightfully situated, till Monday morning. He has a very agreeable family, and I always pass my time very agreeably with them. His third daughter, who is a charming girl, is shortly to be married, with the approbation of the whole family, to a young gentleman, who lodges in the same house with me, of the name of Gardiner,[3] with whom I am much pleased, and who is a merchant of a very respectable and amiable character. On Sunday evening we went and drank tea with Mrs. Cabot, at a beautiful place Mr. Cabot has lately bought. She looks much better than I ever saw her. She and Mrs. Lowell expressed a great desire to see you in this country...

Pr (Printed in *MJI*, 2:446-47).

1. Henry Knox, formerly secretary of war, had retired to private life in December 1794. *DAB*.

2. Joseph Hood, master of the schooner *Nancy*, was convicted of killing a young sailor aboard the ship while on a voyage from the West Indies to Boston. *United States v. Joseph Hood*, General Case Files, CCD Massachusetts, RG 21, MWalFAR.

3. Rebecca Russell Lowell (1779-1853), daughter of John and Rebecca (Russell) (Tyng) Lowell, married Boston merchant Samuel Pickering Gardner (1767-1843) on September 19, 1797. Delmar R. Lowell, comp., *The Historic Genealogy of the Lowells of America* (Rutland, Vt.: Tuttle Company, 1899), pp. 34, 58-61.

Rebecca (Russell) (Tyng) Lowell by Edward Savage (1761-1817). Oil on canvas, date unknown. Courtesy Mead Art Museum, Amherst College, Amherst, Massachusetts. Bequest of Herbert L. Pratt, '95.

Circuit Court for the District of Rhode Island ——————————
June 19, 1795   Newport, Rhode Island

Court opened with Associate Justice James Iredell and Judge Henry Marchant in attendance. The *Newport Mercury* reported that Iredell delivered a "concise and judicious Charge" to the grand jury on June 19. On June 27 the court adjourned until the following term.[1]

1. Minutes, CCD Rhode Island, RG 21, MWalFAR; *Newport Mercury* (Newport), June 23, 1795. Charge not found.

James Iredell to Hannah Iredell ————————————————————
June 20, 1795   Newport, Rhode Island

...I left Boston, and not without considerable pain in parting with the many respectable people who had shown me the greatest kindness, on Wednesday last. I had dined the day before at a very superb public dinner given to General Knox, and received marks of the personal regard of the company to myself which were extremely affecting. I arrived here the evening before last...

Pr (Printed in *MJI*, 2:447).

James Iredell to Hannah Iredell ————————————————————
June 22, 1795   Newport, Rhode Island

...I continue to enjoy my health very well. I expect to be detained here but a few days, and then to go in one of the Packets to New York. From there I shall have more leisure to write, and hope to write to several of my Friends. I find an infinite difference between this place and Boston, tho' we have very agreeable Company in the house where I lodge, and I dined yesterday with a very genteel South Carolina Family with whom I was well acquainted, and for whom I had a great regard. I have not yet called to see Mrs Lopez,[1] but intend it. I wrote to your Brother[2] by way of New York the day before yesterday. ...

ARS (Nc-Ar, Charles E. Johnson Collection). Addressed "Edenton."
   1. Sarah (Rivera) Lopez was the widow of Aaron Lopez (1731-1782). Iredell probably became acquainted with Aaron Lopez after 1772, when Lopez shifted some of his whaling business to Edenton, where Iredell was port collector. Morris A. Gutstein, *Aaron Lopez and Judah Touro: A Refugee and a Son of a Refugee* (New York: Behrman's Jewish Book House, 1939), pp. 15, 17-18; Virginia Bever Platt, "Tar, Staves, and New England Rum: The Trade of Aaron Lopez of Newport, Rhode Island, with Colonial North Carolina," *North Carolina Historical Review* 48 (1971): 1-22; *MJI*, 2:28.
   2. Samuel Johnston.

S.W. View of the Seat of [Honorable?] Henry Marchant Esq. [in?] South Kingston, State of Rhode Island by an unknown artist. Pen and ink on paper, ca. 1785-1790. Courtesy Rhode Island Historical Society, Providence.

James Iredell to Hannah Iredell ————————————————————
    July 2, 1795   New York, New York

...I arrived here the day before yesterday, after a very agreeable passage
from Newport of about 51 hours. The latest letter I received from you was
of the 7ᵗʰ of June, but Mʳ Lenox told me he forwarded one to Newport,
which I expect will be returned here. I am perfectly well, but extremely
mortified to find that the Senate have broke up without a Chief Justice being
appointed,[1] as I have too much reason to fear that owing to that circumstance
it will be unavoidable for me to have some Circuit duty to perform this
fall _ Four Judges out of five were upon duty the last time, and there is
some business, which will make it indispensably necessary that two Judges
shall be on the Eastern Circuit. Judge Blair (owing to the Chief Justice's
absence) went upon the Southern Circuit this last spring when he was entitled
to stay at home if possible, and Judge Wilson had also several Courts to
attend tho' it was his turn to stay, and they had additional duty on the same
account 12 months before _ At least four Judges must be on the Circuit
this fall, and I hear with great concern that Judge Blair was so sick in South
Carolina that he was not able to do any business there. If I have to attend
any I presume it will be the middle Circuit, which begins at Trenton on the
2ᵈ October.[2] Should I be so unfortunate as to find this unavoidable, I will at
all events go home from the Supreme Court if I can stay but a fortnight _
but how distressing is this situation? It almost distracts me. Were you & our
dear Children any where in this part of the Country I should not regard it
in the least _ But as it is, it affects me beyond all expression. The state of
our business is now such, that I am persuaded it will be very seldom that
any Judge can stay at home a whole Circuit, so that I must either resign or
we must have in view some residence near Philadelphia, I don't care how
retired, or how cheap it is. The account of your long continued ill health
has given me great pain, and I am very apprehensive you will suffer relapses
during the Summer. My anxiety about you and the Children embitters every
enjoyment of life. Tho' I receive the greatest possible distinction and kindness
every where, and experience marks of approbation of my public conduct
highly flattering, yet I constantly tremble at the danger you and our dear
Children may be in without my knowing it in a climate I have so much
reason to dread. May God Almighty, in his goodness, preserve you all! At
this distance, & not capable of judging, I must depend altogether on your
discretion to do what is for the best, whether to remain in Edenton during
the summer or not _ Draw upon me for what ~~you~~ money you want...

ARS (Nc-Ar, Charles E. Johnson Collection). Addressed "Edenton, North Carolina."
Postmarked "N York July 2."
    1. Chief Justice John Jay had resigned on June 29, 1795. *DHSC*, 1:13.
    2. On June 18, 1795, William Cushing had written to John Jay that "The middle circuit will
of course fall to me next." As it turned out, James Iredell, James Wilson, and William Paterson

divided the Middle Circuit among them. William Cushing to John Jay, June 18, 1795, *DHSC*, 1:759.

James Iredell to Simeon Baldwin ————————————————
July 15, 1795   Philadelphia, Pennsylvania

Philadelphia   July 15th 1795.

Dear Sir,

I take the liberty to inclose you a Copy of the Charge, which the Grand Jury at New Haven did me the honour to wish to have published.[1] I could not with propriety have it published sooner, as I had to deliver the same substantially at other Courts. You will be so good as to dispose of it as you think proper.

I returned here a few days ago, having gone by water from Newport to New York. My Circuit upon the whole was a very agreeable one. It would give me great pleasure to hear that you and M[rs] Baldwin[2] and the Children continue quite well. I expect to be in this City until after the Supreme Court is over.

You will oblige me in presenting my best respects to M[rs] Baldwin. I shall always gratefully remember your kind attention to me, and am,

Dear Sir,   with great respect and esteem,   Your faithful and   obedient Servant

Ja. Iredell

ARS (CtY, Baldwin Family Papers). Addressed to Baldwin as "Clerk of the Circuit Court of the United States, New-Haven, Connecticut." Postmarked "17 IY."

1. See James Iredell's Charge to the Circuit Court for the District of Connecticut, April 25, 1795.

2. Rebecca (Sherman) Baldwin (ca. 1763-1795), daughter of Roger and Rebecca (Prescott) Sherman of New Haven, Connecticut. Franklin Bowditch Dexter, *Biographical Sketches of the Graduates of Yale College,* 6 vols. (New York: Henry Holt, 1885-1912), 4:179.

Simeon Baldwin to James Iredell ————————————————
July 28, 1795   New Haven, Connecticut

... I ~~also~~ have also the pleasure to acknowledge the rec[t] of yours of the 15th ins[t] inclosing a Copy of your charge to the grand Jury _ I have handed it to the printer who will gratify the Jury & the public by the publication of it in his paper of this week _ [1]

~~I am h It give me pleasure~~ I am happy to hear that your circuit has been agreeable to you...

ADf (CtY, Baldwin Family Papers).

1. The charge was printed in the *Connecticut Journal* (New Haven) on July 29, 1795 (q.v. under date of April 25, 1795).

Circuit Court for the District of New York
September 5, 1795   New York, New York

Associate Justice William Cushing and Judge John Laurance opened court. A charge was delivered to the grand jury, after which the court adjourned to the next term.[1]

1. Minutes, CCD New York, RG 21, NjBaFAR. Charge not found.

John Blair to James Iredell
September 14, 1795   Richmond, Virginia

Mr. Blair,[1] of this place, informed me that he received from you, in your way to Edenton, a letter for me, which he had forwarded to Col. Bell, of Charlottesville,[2] where he expected I should get it earlier than if he had kept it till my return. Unfortunately, however, I have never yet seen the letter.[3] Yet I must endeavor to answer it from the information of Mr. B. with regard to the probable subject. ... the design of it was to propose to me, if not too inconvenient, to ride the Middle Circuit, otherwise that you would do it yourself. This makes it proper that I should inform you that my trip up the country has not brought me any relief from the strange disorder, which for a considerable time past has afflicted my head, and renders me incapable of business, which I have been obliged to neglect, in a degree very painful to me. Sensible of the advantages of my official character, I have not been in haste to resign. I have been willing to take every chance for a removal of the complaint, consistent with a resolution I have taken, in case an unexpected recovery should not prevent it, to resign so long before the court in February next, as to give the President sufficient time to supply the vacancy against that court. The time I had limited for that purpose will shortly expire, and then I shall not think of any further experiment.[4] As the performing the duty of the Middle Circuit, would in other respects be less inconvenient to me than to yourself, as it would not take me quite so far from home, I would most freely assume it, if I had not ample proofs that I am utterly unfit for it. But I am utterly at a loss to conceive why that course of duty should have been assigned to either of us, when both of us had taken a tour in the spring, you in the Eastern Circuit, myself in the Southern, besides having had the Middle Circuit in the fall.[5] When I last had the pleasure of seeing Mr. Cushing, he expected to have the Middle Circuit at this time. ... My infirmity will, I fear, deprive me of the pleasure of ever seeing you again. ...

Pr (Printed in *MJI*, 2:454-55).
   1. Identity unknown.
   2. Thomas Bell (d. 1800), resident of Albemarle County, Virginia. *PTJ*, 17:325.
   3. Letter not found.

4. John Blair sent George Washington a letter of resignation from the Supreme Court on October 25, 1795. *DHSC*, 1:59.

5. While attending the August 1795 term of the Supreme Court, at which time the circuit assignments were made, James Iredell wrote that he had "great hopes of resting entirely this fall" (James Iredell to Hannah Iredell, August 13, 1795, Charles E. Johnson Collection, Nc-Ar). It was, however, Iredell who attended the November term of the Circuit Court for the district of Virginia.

Circuit Court for the District of Connecticut
September 25, 1795   Hartford, Connecticut

On September 25 the circuit court was convened by Associate Justice William Cushing and Judge Richard Law. After the court opened, a charge was delivered to the grand jury. The court adjourned on September 30.[1]

1. Docket Book, CCD Connecticut, RG 21, MWalFAR. Charge not found.

William Paterson to Euphemia Paterson
October 1, 1795   Princeton, New Jersey

... I shall be obliged to set out to-morrow morning for Trenton for the purpose of holding the court. I shall write from that place before I set off for York Town. ...

ARS (NjR, William Paterson Papers). Addressed "Brunswick."

Circuit Court for the District of New Jersey
October 2, 1795   Trenton, New Jersey

The circuit court commenced its session with Associate Justice William Paterson and Judge Robert Morris in attendance. Justice Paterson delivered a charge to the grand jury on October 2. The court adjourned the same day to the next term.[1]

1. Minutes, CCD New Jersey, RG 21, NjBaFAR. We have been unable to identify the specific charge given. For undated Paterson grand jury charges, see Appendix A.

William Paterson to Euphemia Paterson
October 6, 1795   Philadelphia, Pennsylvania

... I arrived at this place last evening, and shall set off for York Town some time to-day. The roads were extremely dusty about the city, but the rain of last night will have a happy effect, and render the travelling more agreeable. There is nothing new in this place; except the great number of vessels arrived from England with Winter goods, which, however, bring no recent intelligence as they had long passages. ...

ARS (NjR, William Paterson Papers). Addressed "New Brunswick."

Circuit Court for the District of Massachusetts
October 12, 1795   Boston, Massachusetts

On October 12 the circuit court convened with Associate Justice William Cushing and Judge John Lowell in attendance. Boston newspapers described Cushing's charge to the grand jury as "elegant and patriotic" and "judicious and elegant." The court adjourned on October 19.[1]

1. Final Records, CCD Massachusetts, RG 21, MWalFAR; *Columbian Centinel* (Boston), October 14, 1795; *Federal Orrery* (Boston), October 15, 1795. Charge not found.

Circuit Court for the District of Pennsylvania
October 12, 1795   York, Pennsylvania

Associate Justice William Paterson and Judge Richard Peters opened court on Monday, October 12, and adjourned it on October 23.[1]

1. Engrossed Minutes, CCD Pennsylvania, RG 21, PPFAR.

Circuit Court for the District of New Hampshire
October 24, 1795   Exeter, New Hampshire

On October 24 the circuit court convened with Associate Justice William Cushing and Judge John Pickering in attendance. Cushing delivered a charge, after which the court adjourned to the following term.[1]

1. Records, CCD New Hampshire, RG 21, MWalFAR; Reply of the Grand Jury of the Circuit Court for the District of New Hampshire, October 24, 1795 (q.v.). Charge not found.

Reply of the Grand Jury of the Circuit Court for the District of New Hampshire
Massachusetts Mercury
October 24, 1795   Exeter, New Hampshire

SIR,

You will permit us unanimously to express the great satisfaction we have felt from the charge you delivered us at the opening of the Circuit Court. Persuaded that society is necessary for man—that Government is necessary for the due regulation of Society—and that the Government of the United States, which the people have established, is more calculated to produce their happiness, than that of any other country. Persuaded too, that the Government has been administered with wisdom and virtue and that its citizens enjoy an unexampled degree of prosperity under it—we will in our situation as Grand Jurors, and private citizens, exert ourselves to maintain it against every attack. If any foes to our peace, and the endeavours of our Government to preserve it, exist within this district, we shall be gratified to unite in detecting and bringing them to punishment. If any are so rooted in their discontent as to attempt to subvert a Government, because any important late acts, founded in the highest wisdom and regard for the happiness and welfare of our country, are opposed to their views or designs, no exertions of ours shall be wanting to defeat them. We most heartily disapprove of all *mobs* or riotous proceedings, as directly tending to endanger our peace and our constitution, to introduce confusion and anarchy—and are happy that this opportunity exists to express these our decided sentiments.

JEREMIAH FOGG, *Foreman.*

(Boston) November 6, 1795. Date and place are taken from an introductory paragraph to the reply.

Circuit Court for the District of South Carolina
October 26, 1795   Charleston, South Carolina

The South Carolina circuit court opened on Monday, October 26, with Chief Justice John Rutledge and Judge Thomas Bee in attendance. The court adjourned on November 5 to the following term.[1]

1. Minutes, CCD South Carolina, RG 21, GEpFAR. A temporary commission appointing John Rutledge chief justice was issued on July 1, 1795. *DHSC,* 1:96.

Circuit Court for the District of Delaware
October 27, 1795   Dover, Delaware

Court convened with Associate Justice James Wilson and Judge Gunning Bedford, Jr., present. The docket of the circuit court does not record the court's closing. The "teste" day was October 29.[1]

1. Appearance Docket, CCD Delaware, RG 21, PPFAR.

Circuit Court for the District of Maryland
November 7, 1795   Easton, Maryland

On Saturday, November 7, court was opened by Associate Justice James Wilson, who delivered a charge to the grand jury. The court met again on November 9 before adjourning to the next term.[1]

1. Minutes, CCD Maryland, RG 21, PPFAR. Charge not found.

Circuit Court for the District of Rhode Island —————————
November 7, 1795   Providence, Rhode Island

Associate Justice William Cushing and Judge Henry Marchant were present to open court. On November 12 the court adjourned to the following term.[1]

1. Minutes, CCD Rhode Island, RG 21, MWalFAR.

Circuit Court for the District of Georgia —————————
November 8, 1795   Augusta, Georgia

The Georgia circuit court did not meet this term.[1]

1. For accounts of why no court was held, see the *Augusta Chronicle* under date of November 12, 1795, and John Rutledge to George Washington, December 28, 1795.

Augusta Chronicle ————————————————————
November 12, 1795   Augusta, Georgia

☞   THE Chief Justice of the United States arrived here the last evening; but the Records being all in Savannah, and the Clerk who had the custody of them lately dead,[1] and no person appointed to succeed him, so that no business could be proceeded upon, and the Judges not attending: I therefore adjourned the Court to the next Term being at Savannah.

THOMAS GLASCOCK,
Federal Marshal.[2]

Augusta, Nov. 12, 1795.

(Augusta) November 21, 1795. Date and place are those of the notice.

1. James Whitefield, clerk of the federal district and circuit courts and register of probates for Chatham County, died on November 7, 1795. *Georgia Gazette* (Savannah), November 12, 1795.

2. The marshal was empowered to adjourn the court by the Adjournment Act of 1794. *Stat.,* 1:369.

James Iredell to Hannah Iredell ————————————
November 19, 1795   Smithfield, Virginia

... I arrived in very good time at Mitchell's on Tuesday evening, and yesterday at Suffolk, and got here to day about one o'clock, intending to go 19 miles further, but I heard they were horse racing at the house where I intended to stop, and I had suffered too much before from such a set to encounter a similar one again. There being no other public house between this and that

View down James river from Mr *Nicolson's house above Rocketts* by Benjamin Henry Latrobe (1764-1820). Pencil, pen and ink, and watercolor on paper, 1796. Courtesy Maryland Historical Society, Baltimore. Benjamin Henry Latrobe Papers.

I am obliged to stay here, which much mortifies me, tho' I must have very bad luck if I don't get to Richmond on Sunday.

. . .

I shall not be able to send you a letter later than this to reach you by the next Post. My health is extremely good. . . .

ARS (Nc-Ar, Charles E. Johnson Collection). Addressed "Edenton, North Carolina."

Circuit Court for the District of Virginia
November 23, 1795   Richmond, Virginia

On Monday, November 23, the circuit court commenced its session with Associate Justice James Iredell and Judge Cyrus Griffin in attendance. After court opened, Justice Iredell delivered a charge to the grand jury. Court adjourned on December 12.[1]

1. Order Book, CCD Virginia, Vi; James Iredell's Charge to the Grand Jury of the Circuit Court for the District of Virginia, November 23, 1795 (q.v.).

James Iredell's Charge to the Grand Jury of the Circuit Court for the District of Virginia
November 23, 1795   Richmond, Virginia

Gentlemen of the Grand Jury,

The business for which you are now assembled is of no small consequence to the peace and happiness of the Community. The People of the United States having thought proper to establish a Government for the management of all its general concerns, in which not one State only but all the States are equally interested, it is necessary to take care that their intentions may not be defeated by the misconduct of any Individuals. All who love their Country may be expected to obey its laws; those who have right notions of a and possess a proper degree of zeal and virtue to support it,
Republican Government, ^ will chearfully submit to the only terms upon which it can be enjoyed, a deference of private sentiment to that of the Public constitutionally expressed; Men of morality will in all instances abstain from any criminal conduct which may injure any Individual, or Community, or Mankind at large. Were all Men of these happy dispositions, criminal Laws would be useless, and we should in fact see something like that <u>millenium</u> which has been too sanguinely the theme not only of heated Divines, but of some enthusiastic Politicians. Experience too forcibly teaches us, that in all Countries, even in those most happily situated, even in our own enjoying every political blessing to which the mind of Man can aspire, there are bad

AD (Nc-Ar, Charles E. Johnson Collection). Readings in brackets supplied where text is obscured.

Men incapable of being restrained by any moral or political tie, from devising the most nefarious schemes, and perpetrating the most wicked actions. The instances, I trust, are rare, but we are well convinced of the reality of [some].

The general objects of the Criminal Law of the United States, are the following.

1. Offences against the United States, considered in their national Character, for the internal purposes of Union, and wherein their own Government is alone concerned.

2. Offences against the United States, considered in their national character, as one among the Nations of the Earth holding a common cognizance of Offences against the Universal Law of Society, committed out of the limits of any particular Territory.

3. Offences against the United States, considered in their national Character, as connected with other Nations either by the common tie of the Laws of Nature, or by any particular Treaty or Compact.

× Under the first head may be comprised the following Offences.

I. Treason. As it is not only natural, but the duty of every Government to Happily for the United States, such scenes have been known to them only by the history of other Nations. The mildness of their own Governments Government itself, and of course of all the order, peace, security, and happiness connected with it, thus involving (whe[re] the Government is a good one) the greatest accumulation of public and private misery which any crime can possibly occasion. But where so much is at stake, an extraordinary degree of Jealousy is usually proportioned to it, which Jealousy will be entertained by a bad Government as well as a good one, and always in a greater degree from a consciousness of deserving ill. Accordingly it has in fact happened, that in most Countries, at almost all periods, and under all forms of Government _ the abuses which have been committed in prosecutions for this offence have been among the most atrocious ever perpetrated to

suffered the punishment

the injury of Mankind. Innocence, as often as Guilt, has [*passage inked out*].
of the latter, and thousands of helpless Families have perished with it.

Happily for the United States, such scenes have been known to them only by the history of other Nations. The mildness of their own Governments has long been one of the most distinguished, as well as one of the most honorable Characteristics of their Country. But the Framers of the present Constitution of the United States were too wise to depend for permanent security on occasional temper, or even the strong and tried basis of a national Character. Knowing well the mischiefs which prosecutions for this offence had occasioned, glowing with proper indignation at the tyrannies of other Countries, and thinking no precaution too great to exclude them from their own, they took especial care to guard against the danger of such by provisions in the Constitution which appear judiciously adapted to that end. Every Person conversant in such subjects knows, that the great engines of this species of

Judicial Tyranny, have been these. 1. So loose a definition of the Crime that it was easy, by means of plausible subterfuges, to charge that as an act of Treason which was never intended to be deemed such. 2. The admission of such slender proof that an unprincipled Government, in tempestuous times, taking advantage of favourable conjunctures, could often find means to obtain the conviction of an obnoxious tho' innocent Man. 3. (And which is scarcely credible, if the proofs of it were not too numerous and too plain to be questioned) A spirit of Rapacity, which dictated accusations of Treason upon very insufficient grounds, in order to obtain the benefit of the forfeiture of property annexed to the Crime. Thus infamously taking away a Man's life to rob himself and his Family of his Estate! Such have been the methods by which Man has preyed on his Fellow Man, and inhuman Tyrants, without one spark of feeling, have sported with the happiness, the peace, the security of the human race! The provisions in our Constitution meet each of these causes of so many Evils, and I trust will for ever prove a sufficient barrier against them, should it be the fate of this Country, at any future unhappy period, to have to dread a tyrannical disposition they have never yet experienced. The provisions in the Constitution are as follows:

"Treason against the United States, shall consist only in levying war against them, or in adhering to their Enemies, giving them aid and comfort. No Person shall be convicted of Treason, unless on the testimony of two Witnesses to the same Overt Act, or on confession in open Court.

"The Congress shall have the power to declare the punishment of Treason, but no Attainder of Treason shall work corruption of blood, or forfeiture, except during the life of the Person attainted."[1]

By the Constitution too, it is provided, in respect to Crimes generally (including this) "That the trial of all Crimes, except in cases of Impeachment, shall be by Jury; and such trial shall be held in the State where the said Crimes shall have been committed; but when not committed within any State, the trial shall be at such place or places as the Congress may by law have directed."[2]

Besides these Constitutional Provisions, the Legislature hath enacted the following, part of which hath reference to other capital crimes as well as this, which Congress hath made such.

It is Enacted, "That any Person who shall be accused and indicted of Treason, shall have a Copy of the Indictment, and a list of the Jury and Witnesses to be produced on the Trial for proving the said Indictment, mentioning the names and places of abode of such Witnesses and Jurors, delivered unto him at least three entire days before he shall be tried for the same, and in other capital offences, shall have such Copy of the Indictment

---

1. Article III, section 3.
2. Article III, section 2.

and list of the Jury two entire days at least before the trial: And that every Person so accused and indicted for any of the Crimes aforesaid, shall also be allowed and admitted to make his full defence by Counsel learned in the law, and the Court before whom such Person shall be tried, or some Judge thereof, shall, and they are hereby authorised and required immediately upon his request to assign to such Person such Counsel, not exceeding two, as such Person shall desire, to whom such Counsel shall have free access at all seasonable hours; and every such Person or Persons accused or indicted of the Crimes aforesaid, shall be allowed and admitted in his said defence to make any proof that he or they can produce, by lawful Witness or Witnesses, and shall have the like process of the Court where he or they shall be tried, to compel his or their Witnesses to appear at his or their trial, as is usually granted to compel Witnesses to appear on the prosecution against them."[3]

The Legislature hath also enacted, "That no Person or Persons shall be prosecuted, tried, or punished for Treason or other capital Offence, wilful Murder or Forgery excepted, unless the Indictment for the same shall be found by a Grand Jury within three years next after the Treason or capital Offence aforesaid, shall be done or committed." _ The Prosecution of other Offences is limited to two years. But in all cases there is an exception of those fleeing from Justice.[4]

It is also further provided by Law, That in cases punishable with death (of which Treason, as I before observed, is one) the Trial shall be had in the County where the offence was committed, or where that cannot be done without great inconvenience, twelve Petit Jurors at least shall be summoned from thence.[5]

These are the wise and equitable Provisions calculated to secure the Citizens of the United States against unjust convictions in prosecutions for this offence. Before I dismiss this subject I cannot avoid recalling to your recollection with emotion and gratitude the memorable events of the last year, a year which will form as bright a page as any in the American Annals. A large and very considerable part of one of the first States in the Union appeared in open insurrection against the Government, after having been gradually seduced to it by the basest artifices and the grossest misrepresentations of a few designing Men, whose views in all probability were much deeper and more malignant than they were avowed to be.[6] The Executive Branch of the Government, in duty bound to suppress this insurrection by every constitutional means in its power, but willing before the exertion of force to try the effect of lenient measures, altho' justly irritated by some very

3. Crimes Act of 1790, section 29. *Stat.*, 1:118-19.
4. Ibid., section 32. *Stat.*, 1:119.
5. Judiciary Act of 1789, section 29. *Stat.*, 1:88.
6. The Whiskey Rebellion in western Pennsylvania.

exasperating instances of private injury in defiance of public authority, sent, in concurrence with the Executive of the State, a very respectable delegation of Men standing high in the public estimation, to state to the Insurgents the criminality and danger of their conduct, and to try every pacific means of rendering a recourse to arms unnecessary, even offering a general pardon on condition of general submission. But this humane effort failed of its effect: tho' it conciliated many, the conduct of others too plainly shewed that nothing but arms could restore the law to its wonted energy. This means was then employed, _{but} ^in a manner worthy of the Government of a free People, by a Militia of different States chearfully obeying the orders they received, among whom were found many who, sacrificing all private considerations, engaged voluntarily in the service with a disinterestedness, alacrity, and zeal which, I _{believe I may safely say} sup~pose~, have seldom been equalled, and never exceeded on any similar occasion. Nor was this merit confined to those who were personally partial to the Government, and supported it with warmth from affection and sympathy. Several who had strong prejudices against some of its most important measures, even the [*word inked out*] one which afforded the pretext if not the ground of the insurrection, readily engaged with them in support of the common cause of their Country, of Republicanism whose principles were so daringly attacked, of order in danger of being immediately subverted, of Justice which was set at defiance, of those social ties without which Liberty is a name, and Existence of no value. Success beyond the most sanguine expectations followed measures so honorably begun, and so nobly conducted. In 3 months the Insurrection was suppresse[d.] The principal Fomentors of it, for the most part, either fled from the danger as it approached or by disgraceful means sheltered themselves from the punishment of their Crimes. Many, who had been more deluded than criminal (so far as their intentionswere concerned) were probably seriously convinced of their errors, and disposed to repair them[.] Not a drop of blood was hostilely shed in the field. Vast numbers partook of an Amnesty freely offered; _{[to those] brought to trial} ^a ~few only, com-~ ~was shewn~ which humanity as well as justice could declare; _{experienced every indulgence} _{two alone ~have been~} ~paratively were reserved for trial, two alone (as I have yet heard)~ have been _{were capitally convicted to whom has since been extended} convicted, ~whose fate has hitherto been suspended by~ the sceptre of Mercy.[7] The whole scene has exhibited a lesson to Governments and People which never before was displayed on the theatre of the world. God grant it may not be without its effect on other times and other Countries, nor ever be obliterated from the memory of our own.

7. See William Paterson to Edmund Randolph, June 6, 1795.

Pardon, Gentlemen, this digression, if it be one. We will now proceed to the consideration of other Crimes under the present head, which I shall think it sufficient to state to you, without any comment, in the very words of the law.

(Here read the following sections of an Act, entitled "An Act for the punishment of certain Crimes against the United States", passed at the second Session of the first Congress.[8]

Volume 1. _	p.	145	sect.	2.
		148		14.
				15
		149		18.
		150		21.
		151		22.
		151		23.[9]

It having been thought proper by the Legislature, in order to excite greater horror against the crime of Murder, to authorise the Court, at their discretion, to add to the usual Judgment of death, that the body of the offender, after execution done, shall be delivered to such Surgeon as the Court shall direct, for dissection, it is enacted

(as, p. 145   sect. 5).[10]

Besides the above, there are some other Offences which might be ennu-
merated under the present head, but as they are of the same species with others which belong to the next (differing only in the place of their commitment), and it will save time to consider them altogether, I shall reserve them for that place.

II. The next Class of Offences to be considered is of such as are committed against the United States, considered in their national character, as one among the Nations of the Earth holding a common cognizance of Offences against the Universal Law of Society, committed out of the limits of any particular Territory.

The following are Crimes of this description, of which the Legislature hath taken cognizance, blended with others which (as I before observed) in strictness belong to the foregoing head, but were purposely reserved for this place for a reason I have already alledged.

(Here read the following Sections from the Act mentioned before.

	p. 145	sect.	3
	146		6
			7
			8

8. Crimes Act of 1790. *Stat.*, 1:112.

9. Iredell's citation is to *Laws of the United States of America* (Philadelphia: Andrew Brown, 1791).

10. Ibid.

147	9
	10
	11
	12
148	13
149	16
	17[11]

III. The next and last Class of Offences to be considered is of such as are committed against the United States, considered in their national Character, as connected with other Nations either by the common tie of the Laws of Nature, or by any particular Treaty or Compact.

#The Legislative Provi[s]ion as to this class of Offences in particular, are the following.

(Here read as follows:

Vol. 1.	p. 151	s. 25
		s. 26.
	152	27.[12]

Vol. 2.   Acts of third Congress, first Session.

p. 97. Chap. 50. "An Act in addition to the act for punishment of certain Crimes against the United States."[13]

of this Act the following Sections.

p. 97	sect. 1.
	2.
98	3.
99	4.
100	5.
101	9.[14]

The duration of this Act is limited to the term of two years, and from thence to the end of the next Session of Congress. _ The Session at which this Act was passed began Dec. 2ᵈ 1793: The Act was signed by the President June 5ᵗʰ 1794.

Besides these Provisions by the Legislature, there are the following in sundry Treaties between the United States and other Nations.

1. In the Treaty of Amity and Commerce between the United States and France. The 21ˢᵗ Article is in these words. (See 1 Vol. p. 286).[15]

I need not observe, that tho' this Treaty was made when the French Gov-

---

11. Ibid.

12. Ibid.

13. Neutrality Act of 1794. *Stat.*, 1:381.

14. Iredell's citation is to *Acts passed at the Third Congress of the United States of America* (Philadelphia: Francis Childs, 1795).

15. Iredell's citation is to *Laws of the United States of America* (Philadelphia: Andrew Brown, 1791). For article 21 of the Treaty of Amity and Commerce (1778), see Miller, *Treaties*, 2:17.

ernment was a Monarchy, and of course the stipulations on the part of France were in the name of their King, yet it being a national compact, the Treaty is equally binding between the United States and the present French Republic, as if it had been expressly formed with the latter.

2. In the Treaty of Amity and Commerce between the United States and the States General of the United Netherlands

The 19th Article is as follows.

(See 1 Vol. p. 308)[16]

3. In the Treaty of Amity and Commerce between the United States and the King of Sweden.

The 23[d] Article is thus expressed.

(See 1 Vol. p. 340).[17]

4. In the Treaty of Amity and Commerce between the United States and the King of Prussia.

The following is the 20th Article.

(See p. 368)[18]

5. In the Treaty of Peace and Friendship between the United States and the Emperor of Morocco.

The 2[d] article is as follows.

(See p. 391.)[19]

I omit Indian Treaties, and Legislative Provisions in regard to Indians, because they are of a local nature, and not likely in any manner to come under your consideration.

The above Treaties, from which I have read Extracts, were formed and ratified previous to the establishment of the present Constitution of the United States.

In that Constitution there is a Provision in regard to these and other Treaties which I will now read to you. The whole of the Clause, in which it is comprehended, is as follows:

"This Constitution, and the Laws of the United States which shall be made in pursuance thereof; and all Treaties made, or which shall be made, under the authority of the United States, shall be the supreme Law of the Land; and the Judges in every State shall be bound thereby, any thing in the Constitution or Laws of any State to the contrary notwithstanding."[20]

16. Iredell's citation is to *Laws of the United States of America* (Philadelphia: Andrew Brown, 1791). For article 19 of the Treaty of Amity and Commerce (1782), see Miller, *Treaties,* 2:76.

17. Iredell's citation is to *Laws of the United States of America* (Philadelphia: Andrew Brown, 1791). For article 23 of the Treaty of Amity and Commerce (1783), see Miller, *Treaties,* 2:142.

18. Iredell used *Laws of the United States of America* (Philadelphia: Andrew Brown, 1791), but the citation should be to page 363. For article 20 of the Treaty of Amity and Commerce (1785), see Miller, *Treaties,* 2:175-76.

19. Iredell's citation is to *Laws of the United States of America* (Philadelphia: printed by Andrew Brown, 1791). For article 2 of the Treaty of Peace and Friendship (1786), see Miller, *Treaties,* 2:213.

20. Article VI.

× These subjects, being of infinite importance, suggest a great many interesting considerations, but they would exceed the proper limits of a discourse of this nature, and probably they are not necessary for your immediate attention. I shall therefore, Gentlemen, not detain you further, but merely to assure you that if in the course of your enquiries, or any prosecutions that may be depending, you should want any assistance which it is proper for the Court to give, it will be most readily and chearfully afforded.

James Iredell to Hannah Iredell —————————————————————
November 27, 1795   Richmond, Virginia

... I arrived here on Sunday evening. ... There is so much business here, that I don't think we shall finish till the latter end of next week. I receive great civilities and distinction here. I dined the other day with Mr. Hylton,[1] and in the evening went with his wife[2] and daughter[3] to the play ("As you like it"), which was very indifferently performed, except by a Mrs. West, formerly Mrs. Bignall,[4] who is really a pleasing actress. In the farce (Le Foret Noir[5]) a little boy of five or six performed admirably. They have a neat little theatre. ... Mr. and Mrs. Randolph[6] have arrived. He was so obliging as to call on me yesterday, and had begun to enter into a very interesting conversation concerning the circumstances of his resignation,[7] when we were interrupted. The town was so full that for three or four nights I was obliged to lodge in a room where there were three other beds, but my landlady was so obliging as to engage another room immediately opposite her house, where I lodge very comfortably, and am entirely alone. ...

Pr (Printed in *MJI*, 2:456).

1. William Hylton (ca. 1749-1837), a Jamaican planter residing in Richmond. *History of the Cauld Lad of Hilton*, (1875; reprint ed., Newcastle upon Tyne, England: Frank Graham, 1968), p. 28; *MJI*, 2:456; James Iredell to Thomas Iredell, November 29, 1795, James Iredell Association, Edenton, North Carolina.

2. Mary (Johnson) Hylton. Robert Surtees, *The History and Antiquities of the County Palatine of Durham*, [*England*], 3 vols. (Sunderland, England: Hills and Co., 1908-1910), 1:105.

3. This could have been either of William and Mary Hylton's two daughters: Mehitable (b. 1773) or Lucy (b. 1777). Surtees, *History and Antiquities of the County Palatine of Durham*, [*England*], 1:105.

4. Anne West (d. 1805), an actress in Richmond's Virginia Company. Brent Holcomb, comp., *Marriage and Death Notices from The (Charleston) Times, 1800-1821* (Baltimore: Genealogical Publishing, 1979), p. 103; *PJM*, 3:4.

5. "Le Forêt Noire," described as "one of the most popular Ballets of the day," was performed in theaters in England, France, and America. Eola Willis, *The Charleston Stage in the XVIII Century* (1924; reprint ed., New York: Benjamin Blom, 1968), p. 323.

6. Elizabeth (Nicholas) Randolph (d. 1810), wife of Edmund Randolph. *DAB* entry under Edmund Randolph.

7. Edmund Randolph resigned as secretary of state on August 19, 1795. His position in President Washington's cabinet had been compromised by the British capture of French dispatches which seemingly incriminated Randolph in a plot to influence United States policy toward France

in return for money. One particular document—labeled Dispatch No. 10, dated October 31, 1794, and written by Jean Antoine Joseph Fauchet, French minister to the United States—was shown by George Hammond, British minister to the United States, to Secretary of the Treasury Oliver Wolcott on July 28, 1795. Wolcott shared it with other members of the cabinet the next day. President Washington returned to Philadelphia from Virginia; and on August 19, Washington, with Wolcott and Secretary of War Timothy Pickering present, confronted Randolph with the document and asked for an explanation. Believing that the interview was unfair and humiliating, Randolph resigned. *PAH,* 18:527ff.

Circuit Court for the District of North Carolina ———————————————
November 30, 1795   Wake Court House, Wake County, North Carolina

The circuit court for the district of North Carolina did not meet this term. Chief Justice John Rutledge did not attend because he had fallen ill while traveling to the North Carolina court and was resting at a tavern northeast of Camden, South Carolina. Judge John Sitgreaves did not attend the court either; it is not known why.[1]

1. *Stat.,* 1:450. For accounts of Rutledge's illness, see the *Aurora* under date of December 1, 1795, and John Rutledge to George Washington, December 28, 1795.

Arthur Iredell to James Iredell ——————————————————————————
December 1, 1795   "near Lewes," Sussex County, England

... Your high Office is certainly an onerous one; but you had the Reasonable Expectation of some Relief; and I trust your Legislature, or the Executive Power, if it rests with that, _ will afford it. ...

ARS (Nc-Ar, Charles E. Johnson Collection). Addressed "Philadelphia   N America." Sent "By the New   York Packet."

Aurora ——
December 1, 1795   Charleston, South Carolina

By a gentleman who left Camden on Wednesday last, we are informed that the Chief Justice of the United States left that place on the Saturday preceding, on his way to hold the Circuit Court in North Carolina; that on the evening of that day he reached Evan's tavern, on Linch's Creek, which he left the next morning, a few hours after, he was taken so unwell that he was obliged to return to Mr. Evans's. When the account came away, he was so much indisposed as to make it doubtful whether he would be able to proceed in time to hold the court in North-Carolina.

(Philadelphia) December 23, 1795. Date and place are those of the article.

James Iredell to Hannah Iredell ——————————————————
December 2, 1795   Richmond, Virginia

...I am extremely mortified to find, that owing to very stupid regulations
at the Post office, the nature of which I totally misunderstood, a letter which
I put into the Post office last Friday will not reach you till Tuesday next.[1]
We are very busily engaged here, being in Court generally 6 or 7 hours
every day, but notwithstanding I have too much reason to fear that the Court
will not break up this week __ I am resolved however, let me suffer what I
may, no charge of neglect or delay shall be imputable to me. I had a
troublesome cold lately, as many have had, for two or three days, but it did
not confine me, and by abstinence and going early to bed I am almost entirely
recovered from it. ...

ARS (Nc-Ar, Charles E. Johnson Collection). Addressed "Edenton, North Carolina."
Postmarked "RICHM'D. Dec. 3, [1795?]"
   1. Iredell is referring to his letter to Hannah, dated November 27, 1795 (q.v.). Postal
regulations enacted in 1794 allowed some post offices to delay until the next mail letters posted
one-half hour to an hour prior to the mail's departure. *Stat.,* 1:358.

James Iredell to Hannah Iredell ——————————————————
December 7, 1795   Richmond, Virginia

Richmond   Dec. 7. 1795
My dear Hannah,
   I am this moment come out of Court, after being there about 8 hours. I
do every thing possible to dispatch business, but fear I may still be detained
all this week. I write that you may not be surprised at my stay, hoping M^r
Stith may find an opportunity to forward the letter. My disappointment is
very vexatious.
   My tenderest love to our dear Children, and pray remember me to all my
Friends.
   I am, my dear Hannah,   Your most affectionate

                                                              Ja. Iredell

ARS (Nc-Ar, Charles E. Johnson Collection). Addressed "Edenton   North Carolina."

John Rutledge to George Washington ——————————————————
December 28, 1795   Charleston, South Carolina

[*After informing the President that he is resigning his commission as chief justice,
Rutledge adds that*] on my return to this State, I found a Variety of Causes,
ready for Trial, before the Circuit Court, on all of which I gave Decrees in

View of Richmond from Washington's Island by Benjamin Henry Latrobe (1764-1820). Pencil, pen and ink, and watercolor on paper, ca. 1796. Courtesy Maryland Historical Society, Baltimore. Benjamin Henry Latrobe Papers. Latrobe painted this scene from an island in the James River, which belonged to future Supreme Court Justice Bushrod Washington. The neoclassical building that dominates the landscape is the state capitol, in which were held both the state and federal courts.

the Course of a Fortnight _ [1] That after having rested from the Fatigues of the Court for a day or two, I set out, tho' in ill Health, to attend my duty at Augusta, but, the death of the Clerk of the Court, at Savannah, the Want of the Records, & the Absence of M[r] Justice Pendleton, in whom the right of appointing another Clerk was vested, prevented my proceeding to Business, at Augusta:[2] I then set out for Raleigh, in N[o]Carolina, but was so indisposed on the Road, as to be incapable of reaching it & was ultimately obliged to return to this Place, convinced by Experience, that it requires a Constitution less broken than mine, to discharge with Punctuality & Satisfaction, the Duties of so important an Office _ [3] ...

ARS (DNA, RG 59, Miscellaneous Letters).

1. Rutledge is referring to the admiralty cases *Moodie v. Ship Mermaid; Moodie v. Ship Phyn; Moodie v. Brig Eliza and John Gaillard; Moodie v. Brig Tivoly; Moodie v. Brig Favorite; Moodie v. Ship Alfred; Moodie v. Ship Phoebe Ann; Moodie v. Ship Britannia; Moodie v. Snow Potowmack; Moodie v. Brig Eliza and Paul Beltrimeaux; Morphy v. Ship Sacra Familia; Delcol v. Arnold* (also known as *Lavergne v. Arnold*); and *Geyer v. Michel (Mitchell)*, all of which were appealed to the Supreme Court. These cases will receive fuller treatment in subsequent volumes of the *DHSC*. Rutledge also decided two other admiralty cases, *Moodie v. Ship Brothers* and *Vidal v. Moodie*, which were not appealed to the Supreme Court. Minutes, November 5, 1795, CCD South Carolina, RG 21, GEpFAR; *DHSC*, 1:504-7.

2. See *Augusta Chronicle* (Augusta), November 12, 1795.

3. For documents relating to John Rutledge's resignation as chief justice, see *DHSC*, 1:94-100.

Spring and Fall Circuits 1796

As war continued to rage in Europe, foreign affairs dominated both politics and the courts in 1796. Maintaining peace with Great Britain was the major concern in the first half of the year. While the Supreme Court prepared to decide "the great British debt question," which had aggravated Anglo-American relations since the end of the Revolution, the House of Representatives debated whether to provide funding for implementation of the Jay Treaty. By the latter part of the year, emphasis had shifted to salvaging deteriorating relations with France. New restrictions mandated by the Jay Treaty on the rights of French privateers in American ports, combined with French attempts to influence the American presidential election, made for many instances of misunderstanding and friction.[1]

The Supreme Court opened its February term with only four justices present to hear the most crowded and important docket to date. In addition to the British debt case, *Ware v. Hylton,* the Court would hear the question of the constitutionality of the carriage tax and several important prize cases in which the British alleged French violations of the Neutrality Act of 1794.[2] Samuel Chase, appointed to fill the vacancy left by the resignation of John Blair, arrived at Court several days late. Because William Cushing declined Washington's attempt to elevate him to the chief justiceship after the Senate rejection of John Rutledge, the Court was without a chief justice for most of this term. The president appointed Oliver Ellsworth in early March, and he took his oaths in Court on March 8. Ellsworth, however, attended Court only once during the remaining days of the session.[3]

In the course of its lengthy six-week term, the Court heard and decided two landmark constitutional cases. After a full week of argument and three weeks of deliberation on *Ware v. Hylton,* the Court, on March 7, finally handed down a judgment in favor of the British plaintiffs' right to recover bona fide debts contracted by Americans before the Revolution. In so doing, the Court invoked the supremacy clause of the Constitution and declared that Article 4 of the Definitive Treaty of Peace (1783), barring lawful impediments to the recovery of debts, superseded state sequestration laws.[4]

The following day the Court passed on the constitutionality of a federal statute. Daniel Hylton, also the defendant in the British debt case, had agreed to be sued by the United States for non-payment of the carriage tax. At issue was whether this was a direct tax which, under the Constitution, had to be apportioned according to a cen-

---

1. John C. Miller, *The Federalist Era, 1789-1801* (New York: Harper & Row, New American Nation Series, 1960), pp. 171-80, 193-208; Goebel, *Antecedents and Beginnings to 1801,* pp. 748-49.

2. The British consul in Charleston, Benjamin Moodie, had filed libels in eleven prize cases that eventually came before the Supreme Court. Four of these were decided at the February term and the remaining ones at the August term of the Court. Goebel, *Antecedents and Beginnings to 1801,* pp. 776-77; *Stat.,* 1:381; *DHSC,* 1:265-78. These cases will be treated more fully in subsequent volumes of the *DHSC.*

3. *DHSC,* 1:113-14, 59, 103, 98-99, 120-22, 269, 272.

4. Ibid., pp. 257-59, 268-69; *Dallas,* 3:199; Miller, *Treaties,* 2:154. See also *DHSC,* 2:123, 339. This case will be treated more fully in a subsequent volume of the *DHSC.*

sus of each state. Having been ill during oral argument on the case, William Cushing did not participate. James Wilson, who had sided with the government in a split decision in the court below, concurred in the judgment but issued no opinion. The three remaining justices wrote opinions unanimously upholding Wilson's view that the carriage tax was not a direct tax and therefore was constitutional under the government's general power to lay and collect taxes.[5]

While the Supreme Court was deciding these cases, Chief Justice Ellsworth was helping the Federalists deal with a constitutional crisis in the House of Representatives over the Jay Treaty. As a member of the Federalist-dominated Senate, Ellsworth had voted for ratification of the treaty the previous summer. At the moment of Ellsworth's appointment to the Court, Republican forces in the House, led by Edward Livingston and James Madison, opened fire on the treaty by demanding to see executive documents relating to the negotiations before voting the funds necessary to implement the treaty.[6] Ellsworth privately advised Senator Jonathan Trumbull that the Constitution gave the treaty-making power to the president and the Senate and that once made, treaties became the supreme law of the land without the passage of any statutes. "The claim of the House of Representatives to participate in or control the Treaty making power is as unwarrented as it is dangerous," he concluded.[7] Having received similar advice from Alexander Hamilton and most of his cabinet, President Washington informed the House on March 30 that he would not release any documents.[8]

The president's action unleashed a storm of controversy both in and out of Congress.[9] While the House heatedly debated whether to fund the treaty in light of Washington's refusal to submit documents, the grand juries of the circuit courts in both New Jersey and Pennsylvania included in their responses to James Iredell's grand jury charges explicit statements of support for the treaty.[10] In Philadelphia this sparked heated correspondence in the city's leading Republican newspaper denouncing the grand jury for having overstepped its bounds.[11] The treaty controversy finally reached a political and rhetorical climax on April 28, when Fisher Ames of Massachusetts, weak-

5. The constitutionality of the carriage tax had been a subject of heated debate in the House of Representatives during passage of the statute, and the government decided to bring a test case when the tax and penalties became due in September 1794. Article I, sections 8 and 9; *DHSC*, 1:269; Goebel, *Antecedents and Beginnings to 1801*, pp. 680, 778-82; *Dallas*, 3:171. This case will be treated more fully in a subsequent volume of the *DHSC*.

6. *SEJ*, 1:184-86; Combs, *Jay Treaty*, pp. 174-87.

7. Oliver Ellsworth to Jonathan Trumbull, March 13, 1796, George Washington Papers, DLC. Jonathan Trumbull of Connecticut, a former colleague of Ellsworth's in the Senate, was a leading Federalist supporter of the treaty. It is not known how or when Ellsworth's letter to Trumbull became part of the Washington Papers or whether it was shown directly to Washington. In a letter of March 4, Jonathan Trumbull indicated to John Trumbull, his brother and an artist living in London, that he had had a private conversation with the president about the treaty. As Washington was in close communication with Trumbull and was actively seeking advice about the treaty from a number of people, he may have seen Ellsworth's letter at the time it was written. Jonathan Trumbull to John Trumbull, March 4, 1796, H. W. Hubbard Collection, Ct; Carroll and Ashworth, *George Washington*, pp. 349, 353-54.

8. Carroll and Ashworth, *George Washington*, pp. 354-55.

9. Ibid., pp. 355-70.

10. See Reply of the Grand Jury of the Circuit Court for the District of New Jersey, under date of April 2, 1796, and Reply of the Grand Jury of the Circuit Court for the District of Pennsylvania, under date of April 12, 1796.

11. See "A Friend to Order," April 23, 1796, and Letter from an Anonymous Correspondent, April 25, 1796.

ened by serious illness, rose and addressed the House for more than an hour, eloquently calling upon its members to fund the treaty as a matter of the country's honor. Iredell, who had been attending the debates as regularly as his judicial duties allowed, exclaimed on hearing Ames's plea, "My God! How great he is!"[12] Two days later, by a margin of three votes, the House approved funding of over eighty thousand dollars.[13]

Even before this crucial vote, the justices of the Supreme Court appeared prepared to enforce the Jay Treaty. On April 22 Tench Coxe predicted that the Court would side with the president when presented with the question.[14] Coxe's prediction was borne out in May, when Chief Justice Ellsworth, riding the Southern Circuit and probably unaware of the House vote, decided a prize case in Charleston that raised the issue. The federal courts in the south had for several years been swamped with large numbers of French prize cases, and there had been instances of French privateers refusing to obey legal process issuing from American courts. In Savannah, Ellsworth's first stop on the circuit, a French prize ship had even defied arrest.[15] Passing through Charleston on his way to Columbia, Ellsworth entertained a petition of the British vice-consul to stay the sale of the prize ship *Amity*, which had been captured and brought into port by the French cruiser *Leo*. Although the circuit court was due to meet in Columbia on May 12, Ellsworth took the unusual step of hearing the case "at his chambers" on May 9. Ellsworth not only issued the injunction, but he also declared that Article 24 of the Jay Treaty barred the sale of French prizes in American ports.[16]

12. James Iredell to Hannah Iredell, March 18, 1796 (q.v.); Carroll and Ashworth, *George Washington*, pp. 370-75.

13. Carroll and Ashworth, *George Washington*, p. 375.

14. Tench Coxe to Thomas Jefferson, April 22, 1796, Thomas Jefferson Papers, DLC.

15. On March 5, 1795, District Judge Nathaniel Pendleton had notified Secretary of State Edmund Randolph of an incident in Savannah where "A French prize ... manned her guns; lay two day before the Town, in defiance of the Officer, who had a Warrant to arrest her; and then went to Sea." Pendleton also reported that in another case in Georgia the marshal had been resisted by open force from retaking a ship unlawfully removed from his custody and from arresting the offenders. Furthermore, Pendleton enclosed evidence that the French vice-consul in Charleston was responsible for the incident. Miscellaneous Claims, ca. 1798-1804, France: Convention of 1803 (Spoliation), RG 76, DNA.

16. On April 23, 1796, the United States district judge in Charleston, Thomas Bee, issued an opinion in the admiralty case *Moodie v. Ship Amity,* in which he denied the jurisdiction of the court. Judge Bee held that jurisdiction was precluded by Article 17 of the Treaty of Amity and Commerce between France and the United States (1778), which permitted duly commissioned French privateers to carry their prizes into American ports without any examination being made "concerning the Lawfulness of such Prizes." Minutes, April 23, 1796, DC South Carolina, RG 21, GEpFAR; Thomas Bee, *Reports of Cases Adjudged in the District Court of South Carolina* (Philadelphia: William P. Farrand, 1810), p. 89; Miller, *Treaties,* 2:16-17.

The British vice-consul, Benjamin Moodie, who was frustrated by the recent loss of six prize ship cases on appeal to the Supreme Court, turned to Chief Justice Ellsworth for an injunction to stay the sale of the ship *Amity* as being "in contravention to stipulations contained in the 24th article" of the Jay Treaty. The injunction was granted pending a hearing at the Circuit Court for the district of South Carolina scheduled to meet at Columbia on May 12. Benjamin Moodie to Phineas Bond, April 23, 1796, and John Shoolbred to George Hammond, June 14, 1796, vol. 15, FO5, PRO; *Gazette of the United States* (Philadelphia), May 19, 1796; Miller, *Treaties,* 2:262.

At this point the history of the case of the ship *Amity* becomes unclear, because the case files for the United States Circuit Court for the district of South Carolina no longer exist. Although Benjamin Moodie wrote to his superiors on May 14 that he expected to hear at any moment that the circuit court in Columbia had "confirmed" Ellsworth's opinion, the court minutes record only the name but not the disposition of the case. In early June the French Minister in the United States, Pierre Adet, reported his disappointment with Ellsworth's decision and assessed the chances of obtaining a reversal on appeal. In what appears to be a justification for

Continuing on to North Carolina for the opening of the circuit court at Wake Court House, Ellsworth encountered another case involving the supremacy of treaties. In keeping with the Court's recent decision in *Ware v. Hylton*, he issued a major opinion on the Definitive Treaty of Peace (1783) and the confiscation of British debts. In *Hamiltons v. Eaton* he invoked the supremacy clause of the Constitution to invalidate the North Carolina confiscation act, declaring, "Surely then, the treaty is now law in this State, and the confiscation act, so far as the treaty interferes with it, is annulled."[17]

Ellsworth returned to the north to find that word of his opinion on the Jay Treaty had preceded him. Secretary of State Timothy Pickering wrote to him on June 30 with regard to an incident in Boston involving two British ships, the Brig *George* and the Ship *Tartar*, recently captured and brought into that port by a French privateer. Pickering asked Ellsworth to inform the district judge in Boston immediately of the particulars of Ellsworth's decision at Charleston and to advise the district judge whether a similar injunction could be issued in Boston.[18] Without waiting for Ellsworth's advice, Pickering directed government officers in Boston to prevent the sale of the ships and their cargoes and through Secretary of the Treasury Oliver Wolcott, Jr., issued a circular letter to all customs collectors forbidding the sale of prize ships brought in by French privateers. Despite the speed with which Pickering acted, he was too late to prevent the sale of the prize ships' cargoes and could only ordain that in the future, agents of the captors would be held accountable for such illegal sales.[19]

The circular letter further strained Franco-American relations. Pierre Adet, the French

---

not pursuing the case in the circuit court at Columbia, Adet argued that Ellsworth would issue the same decision again, and that his decision would be controlling whether or not the district judge agreed. He continued with the gloomy prediction that the Supreme Court would also rule against the French position, as Ellsworth and two other justices were pro-British and only Samuel Chase could be counted on to rule in favor of the French. Benjamin Moodie to George Miller, May 14, 1796, vol. 15, FO5, PRO; Minutes, May 12-13, 1796, CCD South Carolina, RG 21, GEpFAR; Pierre Auguste Adet to Charles Maurice Talleyrand-Perigord, June 3, 1796, France: Ministry to the United States (1795-97), NN. We are grateful to Amy Simowitz for translating Adet's letter.

Two months later the injunction granted by Ellsworth was apparently no longer in force, because Benjamin Moodie was lamenting the "sham condemnation" and sale of the *Amity* and was left with only the promise from the collector of customs not to allow the ship to sail without explicit instructions from the Secretary of the Treasury. In what may have been a final footnote on the fate of the *Amity*, a ship by the same name belonging to Claude Delcol, a known French privateer owner, was ordered sold by Judge Bee in July 1797 in order to satisfy a debt owed to the ship chandlery firm of North and Vesey. Benjamin Moodie to Phineas Bond, August 19, 1796, vol. 15, FO5, PRO; *Delcol v. Arnold, Dallas,* 3:333; Minutes, July 12, 1797, DC South Carolina, RG 21, GEpFAR; *North and Vesey v. Ship Amity and Claude Delcol,* Admiralty Final Record Book, vol. 2, 1795-1800, DC South Carolina, RG 21, GEpFAR.

17. 2 *Martin's Reports* 1, in *North Carolina Reports,* ed. William H. Bartle (Raleigh. Turner and Hughes, 1843), p. 131.

18. Timothy Pickering to Oliver Ellsworth, June 30, 1796, Miscellaneous Letters, RG 59, DNA; Russell & Soley to Harrison Gray Otis, July 7, 1796, Harrison Gray Otis Papers, MHi.

19. Timothy Pickering to John Lowell, June 30, 1796, Timothy Pickering Papers, MHi; Timothy Pickering to Harrison Gray Otis, June 30, 1796, Harrison Gray Otis Papers, MHi; Timothy Pickering to Benjamin Lincoln, June 30, 1796, Timothy Pickering Papers, MHi. As early as July 3 the British Minister to the United States, Robert Liston, was familiar with Ellsworth's decision in the ship *Amity* case and was offering his advice to Pickering as to the measures necessary to prevent the sale of the two ships at Boston. On July 12 Pickering further advised Otis, the acting United States attorney for the district of Massachusetts, that under the Judiciary Act of 1793 Justice Cushing could issue an injunction, and that he expected Ellsworth would communicate the same information to Judge Lowell. Three days later, Pickering wrote to President Washington that although he had not yet received a reply from Ellsworth, the government had issued a circular letter to all customs collectors. Robert Liston to Lord Grenville, July 3, 1796, vol. 14, FO5, PRO; Timothy Pickering to Harrison Gray Otis, July 12, 1796, Harrison Gray Otis Papers, MHi; Timothy Pickering to George Washing-

minister to the United States, wrote the first of many letters of complaint about treatment accorded French ships in American waters.[20] As far as the French and their American supporters were concerned, their worst fears of the Jay Treaty had been confirmed. They viewed the treaty as an alliance between Britain and the United States, one that worked to Britain's advantage in the ongoing war in Europe, and one that violated treaties formed with France when it was America's wartime ally. Not even Ellsworth's opinion in support of the French privateer *La Vengeance* at the August term of the Supreme Court could mollify them.[21]

In the fall of 1796, as President Washington delivered his Farewell Address warning of the dangers of entangling alliances and counseling neutrality, relations with France continued to deteriorate. French Minister Adet attempted to influence the course of the presidential election in favor of Thomas Jefferson by publishing in American newspapers his dealings with the Washington administration. When John Adams narrowly won the presidency in late 1796, France increased its attacks on American shipping.[22] In the course of a few months, controversy over the Jay Treaty had led from the threat of war with Great Britain to the threat of war with France.

With the winds of the European war sweeping over the country and occupying the attention of Congress, the justices' faint hopes of circuit riding reform were quickly dashed. Setting out to ride the Middle Circuit in the spring of 1796, James Iredell contemplated moving his family back to Philadelphia from Edenton and commented to his wife that as the Senate committee on the judiciary had made no report, "We are still doomed, I fear, to be wretched Drudges."[23] A shorter circuit ride, made possible by arranging for James Wilson to take the Delaware circuit court in June, did little to lessen Iredell's longing for his family or his concern over their susceptibility to the dreaded malaria during the hot months in Edenton.[24]

The Eastern Circuit continued to be the easiest, despite the passage of a statute requiring the Vermont circuit court to alternate between Windsor and Rutland.[25] By

---

ton, July 15, 1796, Timothy Pickering Papers, MHi; Russell & Soley to Harrison Gray Otis, July 7, 1796, Harrison Gray Otis Papers, MHi. No letter from Oliver Ellsworth to John Lowell or Timothy Pickering has been found.

20. *ASP, Foreign Relations,* 1:653-55, 579-88.

21. The United States had seized the French privateer *La Vengeance* for violation of the Neutrality Act of 1794, which barred the outfitting of foreign privateers in American ports. The district judge had ruled in favor of the United States, but on circuit Samuel Chase reversed the judgment after determining that the armaments on board had been transferred from another French ship. Attorney General Charles Lee appealed the case to the Supreme Court on the grounds that the proceeding was a criminal matter and that the judgment of the district court should have been final under the Judiciary Act of 1789. The Supreme Court decided that the case came within the admiralty jurisdiction, and that it had been properly decided on circuit. *United States v. La Vengeance, Dallas,* 3:297; Goebel, *Antecedents and Beginnings to 1801,* pp. 776-77.

22. Ballots for presidential electors were cast at different times in different states between November 4, the date of the first state election, and December 7, the date set by statute for voting by the electoral college. Although the official tabulation by Congress did not occur until February 9, 1797, the results were widely known by early January. Carroll and Ashworth, *George Washington,* pp. 419-25; "An Act relative to the Election of a President and Vice President of the United States, and declaring the Officer who shall act as President in case of Vacancies in the office of President and Vice President," *Stat.,* 1:239; Richard B. Morris, ed., *Encyclopedia of American History* (New York: Harper & Brothers, 1961), p. 128; Miller, *Federalist Era,,* pp. 196-202, 205.

23. See James Iredell to Hannah Iredell, March 31, 1796.

24. See letters from James Iredell to Hannah Iredell, dated March 11 and April 8, 1796.

25. "An Act altering the Sessions of the Circuit Courts in the Districts of Vermont and Rhode Island; and for other purposes" (May 27, 1796). *Stat.,* 1:475.

booking passage on ships sailing from Philadelphia to Charleston, Oliver Ellsworth and William Paterson were able to manage the spring and fall circuits respectively in the south. Ellsworth soon joined the other justices in his distaste for the arduous Southern Circuit. "It will not fall to my lot again to go into that Country in less than three years & probably never," he told his wife Abigail. "Nor is it likely that I shall hereafter have occasion to be from home more than about two months at any one time, which indeed is quite long enough."[26] Ellsworth's prediction regarding the length of his absence from home proved wrong, but not because of the demands of circuit riding. Like John Jay, the new chief justice would eventually be called into the service of his country in foreign affairs, and the circuit riding duties of his fellow justices would consequently increase.

26. See Oliver Ellsworth to Abigail Ellsworth, March 20, 1796.

Samuel Johnston to James Iredell ————————————————————
February 27, 1796   Williamston, North Carolina

... I am glad to understand that the Senate have again taken up the Judiciary System and hope they will at last see the necessity of having a seperate set of Circuit Judges leaving the Judges of the Supreme Court to hold that Court only, reducing the number to one half as the present Judges resign or die, the expence can be the only objection to the plan, which in so important a business should not be an object.[1] ...

ARS (Nc-Ar, Charles E. Johnson Collection). Addressed "Philadelphia." Endorsed "Ans^d."
   Samuel Johnston, former senator from North Carolina (1789-1793), was living at "Hermitage," his plantation in Williamston, Martin County, North Carolina. *MJI,* 1:40; 2:385.
   1. No such revision was attempted at this session. Although the Senate appointed a committee on January 13, 1796, to consider alterations to the judiciary system, the committee made no report. *SLJ,* 2:206.

William Paterson to Euphemia Paterson ————————————————
[March] 8, 1796   Philadelphia, Pennsylvania

... The court will continue through this week; so that I shall not reach home till sometime in the next. We have this moment settled the Spring circuit. The Chief Justice, Mr Ellsworth, goes the southern, Mr Iredell the middle, and Mr Chase the eastern circuit. You see that I escape the Spring circuit, which is a great point gained, so far as respects the southern states. ...

ARS (NjR, William Paterson Papers). Addressed "New Brunswicke, New Jersey." William Paterson dated this letter "8 May, 1796;" however, as he was attending the February term of the Supreme Court when he wrote the letter, March 8, 1796, is more likely.

Samuel Chase by Charles Willson Peale (1741-1827). Oil on canvas, date unknown.
Courtesy Independence National Historical Park, Philadelphia.

Samuel Chase to William Cushing ————————————————
March 10, 1796 Philadelphia, Pennsylvania

Philadelphia 10 March 1796
Thursday
Dear Sir

If on your Return Home You could make it convenient to hold, for Me, the Circuit Court at New York on the 5ᵗʰ of next Month, You would greatly oblige Me. this favour would enable Me to stay with my Family twenty Days longer. I came from Home with only three Days Notice, and I wish some time to arrange some private Business. If You can render Me this Service be pleased to write Me, at Baltimore Town.¹

I request my respectful Compliments to Mʳˢ Cushing, and am,

With great Respect & [Esteem],   Your Most Obedᵗ Servant

Samuel Chase

ARS (MHi, Cushing Family Papers, 1650-1840).
   1. Apparently, Cushing could not comply with Chase's request. Justice Chase did attend the Circuit Court for the district of New York, although he arrived there April 6, a day late. Minutes, CCD New York, RG 21, NjBaFAR.

James Iredell to Hannah Iredell ————————————————
March 11, 1796 Philadelphia, Pennsylvania

... Our new Chief Justice (Ellsworth) goes to the Southward _ Mʳ Chase to the Eastward _ and I am to attend the middle Circuit, all but Delaware, which is after Virginia, and Judge Wilson or Paterson has promised to take that in my room.¹ Though this Circuit be by far the easiest and most convenient for me yet I don't expect I can be at home till the middle of June, and I must leave it the middle of July to return here again. It is impossible I can lead this life much longer, and I see no prospect of any material change. To lead a life of perpetual travelling, and almost a continual absence from home, is a very severe lot, to be doomed to in the decline of life after incessant attention to business all the preceding part of it. I mentioned before Judge Wilson the other day, that I probably might be under the necessity of bringing my Family to reside some where in the neighbourhood of the City, and he recommended Potts-grove to me. I wish you would endeavour to reconcile yourself to the thought of residing some where in the neighbourhood of Philadelphia, and it would encourage me to make particular enquiries about a proper place. I know how painful the thoughts of another removal will be to you, and therefore only request you to reflect on all the circumstances of our situation, & consider what upon the whole you think most adviseable. The advantages in respect to our Children's

Fairmount and Schuylkill River by William Groombridge (1748-1811). Oil on canvas, ca. 1800. Courtesy Historical Society of Pennsylvania, Philadelphia.

education I know you have as much at heart as I have, and I am very sensible of the necessity of attending to œconomical regulations. ...

ARS (Nc-Ar, Charles E. Johnson Collection). Addressed "Edenton, North Carolina." Postmarked "11 MR."
    1. James Wilson attended the Circuit Court for the district of Delaware. Appearance Docket, CCD Delaware, RG 21, PPFAR.

James Iredell to Hannah Iredell ───────────────────────────
    March 18, 1796   Philadelphia, Pennsylvania

... I have been very much concerned in receiving no letter from you this week, and should have been more so if I had not been told no Edenton Post had arrived. I hope therefore it may have been delayed by some accident on the way, and that that has been the only cause of one not arriving. It is the first week I have not received a letter and I shall not recover my tranquillity of mind till I hear from you. Our Court broke up on Monday last, but unavoidably left so much business unfinished that I suppose we must at least sit 3 or 4 weeks in August. There are several plans in contemplation for our relief, but none that will prevent my being absent from you at least 6 months in the year while we reside in Carolina.[1] For Gentlemen who live near this one or two plans thought of would prove a great relief. The House of Representatives are still debating upon the call for Papers concerning the British Treaty. I have attended the debates regularly since our Court broke up, and heard many able speeches on both sides. The Papers in some mode or other will be undoubtedly called for, and I believe on the final question a Majority will be for carrying the Treaty into effect. The uncommonly warm and animated terms in which some of the Gentlemen unfavourable to the Treaty have spoken in favour of the President personally have done them honour, and must have warmed the heart of every Person present, whose feelings were not totally dead to all sensibility. There are no late accounts from Europe, but some accounts have just arrived from the West Indies of very villainous treatment by some Captains of Men of War to American Seamen. M[r] Ellsworth is to sail in a few days for Charleston upon the Southern Circuit. ...

    ... I send a line to each of our dear Children. God Almighty bless and preserve you all! And may I soon be happily relieved from the anxiety I now feel. ...

    Kiss all the children for me _ [2]

A[R]S (Nc-Ar, Charles E. Johnson Collection).
    1. In two earlier letters to his wife, James Iredell had mentioned the possibility of Congress reforming the judiciary system. James Iredell to Hannah Iredell, February 10 and 19, 1796,

Charles E. Johnson Collection, Nc-Ar. For one possible plan, see James Iredell's "Alterations Proposed in the Judicial System," ca. March 18, 1796.
   2. This sentence appears as a postscript after Iredell's signature.

James Iredell's "Alterations Proposed in the Judicial System" ————
[ca. March 18, 1796]   [Philadelphia, Pennsylvania]

One Session of the Supreme Court to begin 1st Wednesday in January, Seat of Government.[1]
14 States to be divided into 6 Districts, viz

   1.   { Georgia
        { South Carolina

   2   { North Carolina,
        { Virginia

   3   { Maryland
        { Pennsylvania[2]

   4   { Delaware,[3]
        { New Jersey,
        { New York

   5   { Connecticut
        { Vermont

   6   { Massachusetts
        { New Hampshire,
        { Rhode Island

Circuit Courts to be held once a year in the Spring, by ~~the~~ a Judge of the Supreme Court and the Judge of the District Court:[4] And by the District Judge alone in the Fall _ [5]

Circuit Court to commence, in the Spring, viz.
        Georgia, at Savannah _ 20 April

                            Charleston
        South Carolina, at ~~George Town~~ _ 1 May.

        North Carolina, at Raleigh _ 10 May.[6]
        Virginia, at Richmond _ 26 May.

        Maryland, at Baltimore Town _ [word illegible] 20 April
        Pennsylvania, at Philadelphia _ ~~10 March~~ 25 March

Delaware, at Wilmington _ March 25th
New Jersey, at Trenton _ April 10
New York, at New York _ April 20

Connecticut, at Hartford _ April 10th
Vermont, at Windsor _ May 1st

Massachusetts, at Boston _ April 20th
New Hampshire, at Portsmouth _ April 25th
Massachusetts, at Boston _ May 10.
Rhode Island, at Providence _ May 26th

Circuit Courts in the Fall, at the times now established, and at the places above mentioned.

District Courts, at the times now established, and in the places above mentioned, with the following alterations, viz.

In North Carolina, at New Bern.
In Virginia, at Richmond   Williamsburg alternately.
In New Hampshire
Maine _
In Vermont _

The following Provisions.

When the Circuit Court is held by the District Judge alone, & there shall be a Demurrer, Case agreed, Special Verdict, or Bill of Exceptions / Evidence,
                    if desired by either Party
the same   shall be continued for argument to the ensuing Circuit Court to be argued before both the Judges _   If divided, [*phrase inked out*] a Writ of Error may be immediately brought to the S. C. by Agreement in cases where a Writ of Error will now lie after a Judgment there.

Power to the District Judge to hold the Court alone, & to decide all cases
                       or interested
in which he is not a Party [*phrase inked out*] or has not given a decision.

In the District or Circuit Courts, Upon a Writ [of Error] issued subject to the opinion of the Court, upon both Parties consenting by the same there may be Judgments [& Decrees?] subject to the opinion of the S. C. [*phrase inked out*] Circuit Court or Supreme Court (as Parties may agree) upon a
                 transmitted by   agreed by
case stated & counsel and ₍the Court   C. C. Judgment or Decree, in like manner.

Case alone to be transmitted, & no part of the Record _
   S. C. to return the Case, with an opinion, & Procedendo[7]
   No Discontinuance for non attendance of the Judges. Qu[8]__.
   Mem[9] _ Juries to be provided for

AD (Nc-Ar, Charles E. Johnson Collection); ADf (Nc-Ar, Charles E. Johnson Collection). The draft version is on one sheet and contains only a portion of the full text. Because the draft describes the "present" circuit court arrangement as consisting of one Supreme Court justice and one district judge, we are certain that the plan was created after March 2, 1793, when the Judiciary Act of 1793 reduced the number of justices required to attend a circuit court from two to one. *Stat.,* 1:333. There was a new flurry of activity over circuit riding in Spring 1796; we have tentatively dated these proposals ca. March 18, 1796, because they more closely resemble a plan mentioned by James Iredell in his letter of the same date than any other plan discussed during the 1790s. A reordering of the spring circuit riding into six circuits, one for each justice, and the elimination of fall circuit riding fits with Iredell's description of a plan which would still cause him to be absent from North Carolina "at least 6 months in the year," but which would provide great relief for justices living closer to Philadelphia. By 1798, when judicial reform efforts resurfaced, the main proposal, in the form of a Senate bill, eliminated circuit riding altogether. James Iredell to Hannah Iredell, March 18, 1796; Oliver Ellsworth to Abigail Ellsworth, March 20, 1796; and Oliver Ellsworth to William Cushing, April 15, 1798 (qq.v.).

1. Iredell also proposed changing the meeting of the Supreme Court from February to January in a letter to John Jay of January 24, 1794. *DHSC,* 2:441.

2. In the draft Pennsylvania and Delaware are reversed.

3. In the draft Delaware and Pennsylvania are reversed.

4. In the draft this sentence reads "Each of these Circuits to be attended, once a year, by one of the Judges of the Supreme Court, and the District Judge, as at present."

5. In the draft the following paragraph appears here:
"If they disagree, in opinion, upon a Demurrer, [*word inked out*] or a case stated for the opinion of the Court, and either Party ~~desired~~ desire it each of the Judges shall state his opinion and reasons in writing, ~~and lay them~~ which shall be laid before the Judges of the S.C. during the next Session of the Supreme Court, where both Parties may be heard by Counsel if they please, but unless both shall chuse to employ C. the Judges ~~may~~ shall decide upon it, in Court, without hearing Counsel."

6. The circuit court for North Carolina did not meet in Raleigh until 1797, but the Judicary Act of 1793 had provided for this relocation as soon as a courthouse was built. *Stat.,* 1:333.

7. A writ by which a superior court returns a cause to a lower court for that court to issue judgment. *Black's Law Dictionary.*

8. Quaere. "Question."

9. Memento. "Remember!" Adriano Cappelli, *Dizionario di abbreviature latine ed italiane,* 6th ed., reprint (Milano: Hoepli, 1973). We are grateful to Charles Donohue for this information.

Oliver Ellsworth to Abigail Ellsworth ——————————————
March 20, 1796   Philadelphia, Pennsylvania

... It will give you some pain to read this letter as it does me to write it. I expected that as soon as the Supreme Court here should be ended I should return home and attend the Spring Courts in the Eastern States, but a different arrangement has taken place and I go this time to the Southward. I expect to sail for Georgia this week.[1] And after holding a Court there & also one in each of the Carolinas I shall return home by land. My last Court in North Carolina will terminate about the Middle of June, & it will probably take me about three weeks afterwards to get home. I take with me a trusty servant, & shall pay all the attention I can to my health & comfort as well

Oliver Ellsworth and Abigail Wolcott Ellsworth by Ralph Earl (1751-1801). Oil on canvas, 1792. Courtesy Wadsworth Atheneum, Hartford. Gift of Ellsworth Heirs. The house visible through the open window is Elmwood, the Ellsworth family home in Windsor, Connecticut.

as to the discharge of my publick duties. My health is now good, & as I shall not be in the Southern Country in the sickly season I hope it will continue good. It will not fall to my lot again to go into that Country in less than three years & probably never. Nor is it likely that I shall hereafter have occasion to be from home more than about two months at any one time, which indeed is quite long enough and a great deal [too?] long. ... I shall write to you when I can but that will not be often & you probably will not receive any letter from me after this sooner than the middle of May. But wherever I am you may rest assured it will be my daily prayer that you & my dear children may be safe & happy. _ ...

    ...

Daddy sends his best love to Martin[2] and all the rest of the his little Children. ... Daddy is going about a thousand miles further off, where the oranges grow _ And then he will begin to come home & come as fast as he can, and will bring some oranges.[3]

ARS (CtHi, Oliver Ellsworth Papers). Addressed "Windsor." Reading in brackets supplied where letter is torn.

    Abigail (Wolcott) Ellsworth (1755-1818), daughter of William Wolcott, was born in East Windsor, Connecticut. She married Oliver Ellsworth in 1772; they had six sons and three daughters. Henry R. Stiles, *A Supplement to the History and Genealogies of Ancient Windsor, Connecticut* (Albany: J. Munsell, 1863), p. 58; William Garrott Brown, *The Life of Oliver Ellsworth* (New York: Macmillan, 1905), pp. 23-24; Henry A. Rowland, "A Sermon, Occasioned by the Death, and Delivered at the Funeral of The Honorable Oliver Ellsworth" (Hartford: n.p., 1808), p. 10.

    1. On March 25, 1796, James Iredell noted that Ellsworth had set sail for Charleston from Philadelphia the day before. He arrived there March 30, 1796. James Iredell to Samuel Tredwell, March 25, 1796 (Charles E. Johnson Collection, Nc-Ar); *City Gazette* (Charleston), March 31, 1796.

    2. Martin Ellsworth (b. 1783). Stiles, *Supplement to the History and Genealogies of Ancient Windsor, Connecticut,* p. 58.

    3. This paragraph appears after Ellsworth's signature.

James Iredell to Hannah Iredell

March 31, 1796   Philadelphia, Pennsylvania

... I am perfectly well, and going to Trenton tomorrow. The Court here will be held on the 11th I rejoice that day after day brings me nearer to you, though so many are yet to intervene. It made me very happy to hear by your last letter that you and our lovely Children were well _ ...

    ...

... The Judicial Committee, after a great re-port [parade?] have made no report, and I expect no alterations of moment, after the fairest prospects. We are still doomed, I fear, to be wretched Drudges. ...

ARS (Nc-Ar, Charles E. Johnson Collection). Addressed "Edenton, North Carolina." Postmarked "31 MR."

Circuit Court for the District of New Jersey ─────────────
    April 2, 1796   Trenton, New Jersey

Associate Justice James Iredell and Judge Robert Morris opened court, and Iredell delivered "a very pertinent Charge" to the grand jury. The court adjourned on April 5 to the following term.[1]

1. Minutes, CCD New Jersey, RG 21, NjBaFAR; *New-Jersey State Gazette* (Trenton), April 12, 1796. Charge not found.

Reply of the Grand Jury of the Circuit Court for the District of
New Jersey ──────────────────────────────
New-Jersey State Gazette
    April 2, 1796   Trenton, New Jersey

May it please the Court,
    THE Grand Jury of the District of New-Jersey have, with great pleasure, heard the Charge which has been delivered to them from the honorable Bench.
    While contemplating on the important ideas which have been communicated, they have thought it a duty in this manner to express an entire conviction of the truth of such sentiments, and of the utility of holding them up to public view.
    We are sensible that the opinions, passions and interests of individuals, or of any particular part of the community, should be subordinate to the *general will*, and that a deviation from this principle, in the recent instance which you have mentioned, produced that most daring and dangerous insurrection[1] which you have described, and which eminently threatened us with all the evils consequent from discord, disorder, anarchy and civil war. We trust, however, that the rise, progress and suppression of this enormous outrage upon law, order and true republicanism, will form so instructive a page in our history, that it will long indeed, we hope forever, remain a solitary instance in the annals of our country.
    When we look on the world around us, and view almost every country in Europe torn by the ravages of war, and behold thousands, nay millions of its late peaceful inhabitants, deluged in their own blood—When we see the calamities of war extending themselves to Africa and the Indies—When we see whole nations in array, contesting that liberty which we enjoy, when danger and fatigue conducts the van, while famine, with all her horrid train of evils, is bringing up the rear—We say, when we look around us and see these things, how do we felicitate ourselves that we are Americans;—with what complacency, with what superlative delight, do we turn our eyes on our own happy, thrice happy, country—blessed with peace—blessed with freedom—blessed with plenty, where no rude hand dares approach the

peaceful dwelling; where even the meanest cottager enjoys his pittance and his sentiment; where every man without hyperbole, sits under his own vine and under his own fig-tree, and enjoys the fruits thereof, while there is none to make him afraid—Surely no nation on earth has greater reason for thankfulness and content: The measure of our enjoyment is full, and scarce a reasonable wish remains unsatisfied. With all these blessings in store, with our cup full and overflowing, are there yet those among us who are dissatisfied? Sorry are we to say, there are—there are who complain—there are who find fault—with our constitution, with our government, with public men and public measures—surely, if we are to judge of these by their effect, and if the maxim be just, that by the fruit ye shall know if the tree be good, we must all with united voice exclaim, that we live under the happiest constitution, and under the best government that ever blessed a nation.

But let us examine if there be real cause of complaint. The late treaty with Britain[2] seems to be the present foundation on which those complaints are built; this instrument we have seriously considered, both in its causes and consequences. After a seven years contest with that nation, in which every thing dear to freemen was at stake on our part, we at length succeeded; a treaty was formed, in which our independence was fully acknowledged, and we took place among the nations of the earth.[3]

But, alas! we soon discovered that our confederation, formed amidst the din of arms and the confusion of war, was of too weak a texture to combine so many discordant interests, and that nothing but the sense of common danger had united us so long—A solemn pause ensued—The good sense of the union at length formed a Constitution of Government for the whole, and the people willed it should be permanent—A constitution of checks and balances—A constitution which secures to every class of citizens their equal rights, and to every order of government its regulated powers—A constitution which has been the admiration of the world, and which we hope will be co-existent with it.

To the head of the government, organized under this constitution, the unanimous voice of the exulting people called that great man, whose wisdom, whose prudence, and whose fortitude, had led them through all the various fortunes of the war, and whose patriotism and invincible fidelity had shone conspicuous thro' the whole course of it.

Was it not natural to suppose that between two nations, just separated by the violent effects of a civil war, and irritated by the events of it, disputes would arise respecting the fulfilment of the articles of that treaty by which they were separated?—Such disputes have arisen—It has *not* been fulfilled on *their* part, say we—it has *not* been fulfilled on *our* part, say they—The peace contemplated by that treaty was affected, hostile appearances were seen, mens minds were agitated, a rupture was likely to become the consequence, war with all its concomitant horrors rose in our view.—The Executive at this important moment stepped forward and mildly said, before we plunge into a gulph so profound, into a situation so distressful to *any* country, so destructive to a *young* country, and so *uncertain* in its consequences, let us make one more peaceful effort, let us try negociation!—A negociation is set on foot, a new treaty is formed, not with all the favourable features we could have wished, *could we have dictated*, but in our opinion much more favourable to us than the dire alternative: Suppose it does not embrace all the objects we conceive it ought, yet it opens to us a considerable share in the commerce of the European as well as of the Eastern and Western world.—It gives us an opportunity of possessing ourselves of by much the most considerable part of the fur trade, by securing to us the possession of those keys to the Indian country—the western posts.—It secures to us a general peace with the Indian tribes, by enabling us to extend our own influence and prevent that of other nations amongst them, an object of more consequence to America than all the others contended for—and, it puts in a state of settlement the disputed boundaries of our territory—shall we then spurn at such a treaty? we answer no, and are free to say, that, in our opinion, both they who advised and he who ratified this treaty, have *deserved well of their country.*—Confirmed and ratified as it has been, we hope no obstacles which may be thrown in its way, will prevent its being carried into effect; and have no doubt but those parts which now appear least favourable, may hereafter, by peaceful negociation, be accommodated to mutual interest and satisfaction.

Finally—We cannot but indulge the hope, enthusiastic as it may seem, that a steady and inviolable adherence to the true principles of our excellent constitution, may establish peace, law and order, upon such a firm basis as to render a political millenium not altogether a visionary and ideal thing.

Signed by direction of the Jury,

JAMES EWING, Foreman.

(Trenton) April 12, 1796. Date and place are from an introductory paragraph to the reply.

The reply was published earlier in the *Gazette of the United States* (Philadelphia), April 9, 1796.

1. The Whiskey Rebellion.

2. The Jay Treaty was signed in London on November 19, 1794, ratified by the United States on August 14, 1795, by Great Britain on October 28, 1795, and proclaimed February 29, 1796. Miller, *Treaties,* 2:245.

3. The Definitive Treaty of Peace (1783).

Circuit Court for the District of New York

April 5, 1796   New York, New York

Because no Supreme Court justice was present on April 5, court did not open until April 6. Associate Justice Samuel Chase and Judge John Laurance were in attendance, and a charge was delivered to the grand jury. Court adjourned on April 20.[1]

1. Minutes, CCD New York, RG 21, NjBaFAR. Charge not found.

James Iredell to Hannah Iredell
April 8, 1796   Philadelphia, Pennsylvania

... I returned from Trenton on Tuesday night, ... I am very sorry what I wrote about our residence gave you pain.[1] I know a change ought not rashly to be resolved on, but really my situation at present is extremely distressing, and I am convinced no material change in the Court System will take place. Painful as my situation is in all other respects, I could bear it with more composure if we had not so much reason to dread the effects of every Summer at Edenton. My apprehensions on that account continually present themselves to prevent my having any durable satisfaction from any other. However, I will avoid as much as possible dwelling on ideas which make me miserable whenever they occur to me. I had a letter yesterday from your Brother,[2] and am truly distressed to hear so melancholy an account of M[rs] Johnston's[3] situation. He flatters me with the hope of my meeting him in the course of this month or the next. I fear I shall not meet with him if it be not in the course of this month, because early in May I am to go to Annapolis, which will be out of the post road. ... The Court here is to begin on Monday next, and I suppose will employ me from morning till night till the beginning of May when I am to go to Annapolis, there being a great deal of very important business depending. ...

A[R]S (Nc-Ar, Charles E. Johnson Collection).
  1. See James Iredell to Hannah Iredell, March 11, 1796, in which Iredell proposed moving his family near Philadelphia.
  2. Samuel Johnston.
  3. Frances (Cathcart) Johnston.

Circuit Court for the District of Pennsylvania
April 11, 1796   Philadelphia, Pennsylvania

Court opened with Associate Justice James Iredell and Judge Richard Peters in attendance. On April 12 Justice Iredell delivered a charge to the grand jury. The court adjourned on May 2.[1]

1. Engrossed Minutes, CCD Pennsylvania, RG 21, PPFAR; James Iredell's Charge to the Grand Jury of the Circuit Court for the District of Pennsylvania, April 12, 1796 (q.v.).

James Iredell's Charge to the Grand Jury of the Circuit Court for the
District of Pennsylvania ————————————————————————————
Claypoole's American Daily Advertiser
    April 12, 1796   Philadelphia, Pennsylvania

Gentlemen of the Grand Jury,
    THE business for which you are now assembled is of no small consequence
to the peace and happiness of the community. The people of the United
States having thought proper to establish a government for the management
of all its general concerns, in which not one state only, but all the states are
equally interested, it is necessary to take care that their intentions may not
be defeated by the misconduct of any individuals. All who love their country
may be expected to obey its laws; those who have right notions of a
Republican government, and possess a proper degree of zeal and virtue to
support it, will chearfully submit to the only terms upon which it can be
enjoyed, a deference of private sentiment to that of the public constitutionally
expressed; men of morality will in all instances abstain from any criminal
conduct which may injure any individual, or community, or mankind at large.
Were all men of those happy dispositions, criminal laws would be useless,
and we should in fact see something like that *millenium* which has been so
sanguinely the theme not only of heated divines, but of some enthusiastic
politicians. Experience too forcibly teaches us, that in all countries, even in
those most happily situated, even in our own, enjoying every political blessing
to which the mind of man can aspire, there are bad men incapable of being
restrained by any moral or political tie, from devising the most nefarious
schemes and perpetrating the most wicked actions. The instances, I trust,
are rare, but we are well convinced of the reality of some.
    The general objects of the criminal law of the United States, are the
following:
    1. Offences against the United States, considered in their national character,
for the internal purposes of union, and wherein their own government is
alone concerned
    2. Offences against the United States, considered in their national character
as one among the nations of the earth, holding a common cognizance of
offences against the universal law of society, committed out of the limits of
any particular territory.
    3. Offences against the United States, considered in their national character

(Philadelphia) April 18, 1796. Date and place are those of the headline. The newspaper notes
that Iredell's charge was published "at the request of the Grand Jury."
    The charge was reprinted by *Gazette of the United States* (Philadelphia), April 19, 1796; *Phil-
adelphia Gazette,* April 19, 1796 (supplement); *Pennsylvania Gazette* (Philadelphia), April 20, 1796;
Federal Gazette (Baltimore), April 21 and 22, 1796; and the *Independent Gazetteer* (Philadelphia),
April 23, 1796.

as connected with other nations either by the common tie of the laws of nature, or by any particular treaty or compact.

A full discussion of each of these branches of jurisdiction would take up your time in a manner equally tedious and unuseful. I shall therefore only observe upon such detached parts of the subject as may appear most interesting in a discourse of a general nature on the present occasion.

Under the first head I shall mention only one offence, but that of the greatest importance, and which cannot be too frequently the object of consideration. The offence I speak of is that of *Treason*.

As it is not only natural, but the duty of every government to take care of its own preservation, this crime in all countries is considered of the highest rank; the object of it being the total destruction of the government itself, and of course of all the order, peace, security, and happiness connected with it, thus involving (where the government is a good one) the greatest accumulation of public and private misery which any crime can possibly occasion. But where so much is at stake an extraordinary degree of jealousy is usually proportioned to it, which jealousy will be entertained by a bad government as well as a good one, and always in a greater degree from a consciousness of deserving ill. Accordingly it has in fact happened, that in most countries, in all ages, and under all forms of government, the abuses which have been committed in prosecutions for this offence have been among the most atrocious ever perpetrated to the injury of mankind. Suspicion has supplied the place of evidence, the most distant approaches of danger have armed the hand of power against the greatest of men, and not unfrequently the highest instances of public virtue have been doomed to the punishment of the highest public offences. Happily for the United States, such scenes have been known to them only by the history of other nations. The mildness of their own governments has long been one of the most distinguished, as well as one of the most honorable characteristics of their country. But the framers of the present constitution of the United States were too wise to depend for permanent security on occasional temper, or even the strong and tried basis of a national character. Knowing well the mischiefs which prosecutions for this offence had occasioned, glowing with proper indignation at the tyrannies of other countries, and thinking no precaution too great to exclude them from their own, they took especial care to guard against the danger of such, by provisions in the constitution anxiously adapted to that end.[1] Every person conversant in such subjects knows, that the great engines of this species of judicial tyranny have been these. 1. So loose a definition of the crime that it was easy by means of plausible subterfuges, to charge that as an act of treason which was never intended to be deemed such. 2. The admission of such slender proof that an unprincipled government in tempestuous times, taking advantage of favourable conjunctures, could often find means to obtain the

1. Article III, section 3.

conviction of an obnoxious though innocent man. 3. (And which is scarcely credible, if the proofs of it were not too numerous and too plain to be questioned,) A spirit of rapacity, which dictated accusations of treason upon insufficient grounds, in order to obtain the benefit of the forfeiture of property, annexed to the crime. Thus infamously taking away a mans life to rob himself and his family of his estate! Such have been the methods by which man has preyed on his fellow man, and inhuman tyrants, without one spark of feeling, have sported with the happiness, the peace, the security of the human race! The provisions in our constitution meet each of these causes of so many evils, and I trust will for ever prove a sufficient barrier against them, should it be the fate of this country, at any future unhappy period, to have to dread a tyrannical disposition it has never yet experienced.

Before I dismiss this subject I cannot avoid recalling to your recollection with emotion and gratitude the memorable events of a very recent period, a period which will form as bright a page as any in the American annals. A large and considerable part of this important state appeared in open insurrection against the government, after having been gradually seduced to it by the basest artificers, and the grosest misrepresentations of a few designing men whose views in all probability were much deeper and more malignant than they were avowed to be.[2] The executive branch of the government, in duty bound to suppress this insurrection by every constitutional means in its power, but willing before the exertion of force to try the effect of lenient measures, although justly irritated by some very exasperating instances of private injury in defiance of public authority, sent in concurrence with the executive of the state, a respectable delegation of men standing high in the public estimation, to state to the insurgents the criminality and danger of their conduct, and to try every pacific means of rendering a recourse to arms unnecessary, even offering a general pardon on condition of general submission. But this humane effort failed of its effect: though it conciliated many, the conduct of others too plainly shewed that nothing but arms could restore the law to its wanted energy. This means was then employed, with decision though with reluctance, but in a manner worthy of the government of a free people, by a militia of different states chearfully obeying the orders they received, among whom were found many who, sacrificing all private considerations, engaged voluntarily in the service with a disinterestedness, alacrity and zeal which I believe have seldom been equalled, and never exceeded on any similar occasion. Nor was this merit altogether confined to these who were personally partial to the government, and supported it with warmth from affection and sympathy. Several who had strong prejudices against some of its most important measures, even those which afforded the pretext if not the ground of the insurrection, readily engaged with them in support of the common cause of their country, of republicanism where principles were so daringly at-

2. The Whiskey Rebellion in western Pennsylvania.

tacked, of order in danger of being immediately subverted, of justice which was set at defiance, of those social ties without which liberty is a name, and existence of no value. Success beyond the most sanguine expectation followed measures so honourably begun, and so nobly conducted. In three months the insurrection was suppressed. The principal fomentors of it either fled from the danger as it approached, or by disgraceful means sheltered themselves from the punishment of their crimes. Many who had been more deluded than criminal were probably seriously convinced of their errors, and disposed to repair them. Not a drop of blood was hostilely shed in the field. Vast numbers partook of an amnesty freely offered; a few only, comparatively, were reserved for trial; two alone have been convicted, to whom has since been extended the sceptre of mercy.[3] The whole scene has exhibited a lesson for governments and people, which never before was displayed on the theatre of the world. God grant it may not be without its effect on other times and other countries, nor ever be obliterated from the memory of our own.

2. The second class of offences I proposed to speak of was, such as are committed against the United States, considered in their national character as one among the nations of the earth holding a common cognisance of offences against the universal law of society, committed out of the limits of any particular territory.

Crimes of this description, among others, are piracy and murder committed on the high seas. These being committed out of the particular territory of any state must either go without any punishment at all, or be equally punishable by any nation into whose country the criminals may afterwards arrive. They being unquestionably a violation of that law of nature by which man is bound to abstain from injuring a fellow creature wherever he meet with him, and more especially from robbing or murdering him; all civilized nations concur in the punishment of such offences, each nation proceeding to enforce the law of nature in such instances, in the manner which it conceives most conducive to justice. The laws of the United States have made special provisions on this important subject.[4]

3. The remaining class of offences I stated is, such as are committed against the United States considered in their national character as connected with other nations, either by the common tie of the law of nature or by some particular treaty or compact.

The principles which regard the former class of offences are principles, in general much better understood than the principles of this class. But yet this in itself is of great importance, and ever since the present unfortunate war has prevailed in Europe it has been of the greatest. I hope therefore you will not think your time mispent, while we employ a little consideration upon it.

---

3. See William Paterson to Edmund Randolph, June 6, 1795.
4. Crimes Act of 1790, sections 8-12. *Stat.,* 1:113-15.

Though particular incidental duties may be incumbent upon individuals, when their own nation is engaged either wholly or partially in a war, yet as in such a case it is most probable they will receive express injunctions from the legislature, and there is no present appearance of such an event, I shall confine any attention under this head, to those which result from a state of general peace, as to the world in general or a state of Neutrality in respect to other nations at war when our own is at peace.

The first, though it gives occasion to the exercise of many humane and benevolent virtues, seldom can occasion offences of a kind peculiar to itself. It will therefore be sufficient, to observe generally, that no nation, when in a state of peace with another nation can justify doing it any injury whatever; that if any injury is committed by authority of the government itself, the government is immediately answerable for it, and if due satisfaction be not given, it is a justifiable cause of war, or of any lesser species of hostility which may be deemed adequate to the object; that if an injury is committed, though without the authority of government, by a citizen of one nation against another nation, or any individual of it, when no redress can be otherwise obtained, it is a cause of complaint which may be presented by the one nation against the other, in consequence of which it becomes the immediate duty of the government of the aggressor to enquire into the complaint, and upon satisfactory proof to afford all the redress it is susceptible of; and if this be not done, it may be considered as an indication of a hostile disposition in the government, and the nation injured may proceed to such vindicatory measures as upon a fair construction of all the circumstances of the case it shall deem most adviseable. Since therefore a whole nation may be answerable, even at the hazard of a war, for any violation of the law of nations which its citizens may commit, and since each citizen is entitled to the full protection of his own government upon the principles I have stated, it follows that each citizen must be answerable to his own government for a disregard of his duty in this particular, he being indispensably bound to serve his country by every means in his power, and not to injure, much less disgrace it by any. This being a result of national[5] reason and propriety, it forms a part of what is called *the common law*, though statutes, to give it greater force and efficacy, frequently make express provisions on the subject, as has been done by the Congress of the United States.[6] But as it is altogether a subject of national concern, as those entrusted with the national authority in this particular must be responsible for the rules of action observed in relation to it within their own boundary, as various unforseen diviations from general principles, not capable in their nature of reaching every possible case, may be rendered justifiable by extraordinary exigencies of which alone each nation must judge for itself, each nation has the power of prescribing rules for the observation of its own citi-

5. In *Gazette of the United States* (Philadelphia), April 19, 1796, "natural."
6. Neutrality Act of 1794. *Stat.*, 1:381.

zens in this particular, and in our nation this power is expressly delegated to the Congress of the United States. If therefore they should prescribe different rules on this subject for the observation of their own citizens, than those which theoretical writers on the law of nations teach, I apprehend the citizens of the United States must obey that rule prescribed by the competent authority of their own government, which in the exercise of this, as well as every other species of constitutional authority, binds the whole because it is appointed a trustee for the whole to whose wisdom and discretion the subject is submitted. Consequently, when an individual is guilty of a violation of what is usualy termed the law of nations in our own territory, he is not chargeable with this in our courts merely as violation of the law of nations, but as a violation of the law of his own country of which the law of nations is a part, and of which Congress is the sole expositor as to us when it takes that duty upon it. When no act of Congress interferes it is an offence at common law, in the same manner and upon the same principle as any other offence commited against the common law, and in respect to which no particular statute had passed. Where there is any special act on the subject, it is an offence against that act in the same manner and upon the same principle as an offence against any other act would be. In short, my idea is, that in all such instances each citizen is answerable to his own nation, and the nation itself answerable to other nations, for the proper conduct of its own citizens, over whose actions the nation necessarily must have controul, so far as they affect the interests of other nations, otherwise upon no principle of justice, could each nation be fully responsible for the conduct of its own citizens in such instances, which all the writers on the law of nations agree they are. The same observations as to citizens will almost in every case equally apply to others residing in the country and ameanable to its laws, as to citizens themselves.

2. Those general duties incumbent upon the government and its citizens as to mankind at large, when in a state of universal peace, cannot be changed merely by the event of two other nations being at war, with which the United States have no connection. In regard to them, however, certain new duties arise superadded to the former, which being relative to the peculiar nature of the case, may be called duties of neutrality, it being inconsistent with the pacific conduct due to both to favour the hostile purposes of either. What may be construed to do so would open a large field of enquiry, with which I shall not now trouble you, but of which, within these few years you have heard a great deal. If one of the hostile powers should even be an ally, which the United States are bound by an antecedent treaty, either generally or partially to assist, I apprehend no individual citizen could be justified in actually affording assistance, unless the Congress of the United States, with whom the power of declaring war or authorising any actual hostilities is invested, should direct or authorise such assistance to be given, they being to judge in relation to those objects, in all cases of that description, of the nature of the

obligation, as it originally existed, whether any change of circumstances has since intervened to do away or weaken its force; or if assistance is to be afforded, at what time and in what manner, and also to what extent it shall be afforded; since in all these respects the nation, whom Congress represent on this occasion, is accountable on the one hand to the other contracting power for a proper observance of the public faith pledged by such treaty; and on the other hand the Congress are responsible to their own country, that any reciprocal rights of the United States are duly protected and secured, and their real interest and safety not disregarded. Until therefore some active measure of this kind be taken, each individual is undoubtedly bound to act according to the existing situation of his country, which is a state of peace until a state of war, or any inferior state of actual hostility is created by the authority constituted for that purpose. In this situation the United States were at the commencement of the present European war, and have uniformly remained since. Upon these principles was grounded that proclamation of the President, the propriety and utility of which have become more apparent under every discussion.[7] The Congress, though so often in session since the war began, never have decided that any obligation of duty required, or any motive of policy induced the United States to take a part in the war either wholly or partially. Much less have they by any act authorised any hostilities whatever. On the contrary, they have passed laws more strictly to enforce those duties of neutrality, which, upon general principles, it is conceived were incumbent upon all before, tho' certainly it was a desirable thing on so important an occasion to obviate all possible doubts by express provisions of the legislature itself, which none could mistake, and accompanied with sanctions less indefinite than those which existed before.[8]

Independently of what I have already said, the subject under discussion, if fully investigated, would naturally lead me to a consideration, under many aspects, of the nature and effect of treaties, those solemn national compacts in which the peace and happiness of mankind are so deeply interested, and which acquire a peculiar sanctity from the good faith they indispensably demand. But though no topic can be more interesting to us as individuals, especially at the present momentous crisis, yet as I know no case likely to arise upon which a judicial consideration of it will be requisite, for any official business before you, I forbear any particular observations upon it.[9]

I shall now, gentlemen, only add, that the government we enjoy can alone

---

7. George Washington issued the Neutrality Proclamation on April 22, 1793. *ASP, Foreign Relations,* 1:140.

8. See, for example, "An Act prohibiting for a limited time the Exportation of Arms and Ammunition, and encouraging the Importation of the same," May 22, 1794 (*Stat.,* 1:369); "An Act to authorize the President of the United States to lay, regulate and revoke Embargoes," June 4, 1794 (*Stat.,* 1:372); Neutrality Act of 1794 (*Stat.,* 1:381); Resolutions I-IV (*Stat.,* 1:400-401).

9. Iredell is referring to the Jay Treaty and the debate in the House of Representatives about appropriations to execute it.

be supported by a due mixture of vigilance and moderation; by inviolably adhering to the principles of the constitution, but at the same time making reasonable allowances for real differences of opinion, whenever they occur, and the various difficulties to which the affairs of a great country will always be subjected; by paying proper obedience to the constituted authorities of our country, relying upon those guards against abuse which the constitution has not only carefully, but I am persuaded efficaciously provided; and by constantly bearing in mind, that that law which protects others protects ourselves, and therefore that we shall arrogate what no true friend to liberty can consistently claim, if we fail in that measure of obedience to the government of our country in cases that are not perfectly agreeable to us, which we expect from all others in those that are.

Reply of the Grand Jury of the Circuit Court for the District of Pennsylvania

Claypoole's American Daily Advertiser
   April 12, 1796   Philadelphia, Pennsylvania

To the CIRCUIT COURT *of the* UNITED STATES *for the Pennsylvania District of the middle Circuit.*

The Address of the Subscribers, members of the GRAND JURY, *in answer to the honourable Judge* IREDELL'S *Charge.*

WE are sensible of the importance of the subjects discussed in the charge delivered to us, and we most sincerely wish that all our fellow citizens were impressed with the duties, which it inculcates. We participate in the eulogies bestowed on the conduct of the *Executive*, and hope the patriotic exertions of our fellow citizens to support the laws on the occasion you mention, will ever ensure them the gratitude and esteem of their country.

We hope the disgraceful insurrection which called forth the energies of the friends to order and good government will only be remembered as a warning to others of the folly and danger of such unavailing and ruinous attempts. It has however been attended with good consequences, whatever evils might have been contemplated by its authors. It has afforded another proof of the firmness, the wisdom, and benevolence of our much beloved President, in whom our confidence continues to be undiminished.

It has opened the eyes of a once deluded people, and enabled them to see their true interests. Their recent conduct affords us a pleasing and decided confirmation of this sentiment.

Although we had not any official act to perform, on which the subject of treaties came under our view, yet we cannot forbear, as citizens called to a very confidential station, mentioning our sentiments on a subject, which now so much engages the public mind. We mean the several treaties lately made with foreign powers, on the due execution whereof the peace and happiness of our country so materially depend.[1]

Much misconception, and much unfounded alarm existed as to one of these treaties, namely that with Great Britain. But we can from a knowledge of the people, among whom we live, truly say that the subject being now better understood by those, who were alarmed and deceived, has produced a desire in the minds of the great body of the people that this treaty as well as the others may without delay be carried into effect. And we express our own, and we confidently believe the wishes of the great majority of this District, when we hope no impediment may be thrown in its way by our Representatives, so far as their agency is necessary to effectuate its objects.[2] Were this nation in a condition to dictate a compact, one might have been made exactly to our mind—but we believe this treaty is the best which under all circumstances could be obtained. It places great points of controversy, either of which might have produced war, in a train of amicable adjustment;— and, in our opinion, it is one among the many wise and firm measures pursued by our patriotic Chief Magistrate, which have a decided tendency to perpetuate the unexampled prosperity, with which the great Disposer of events has been pleased to bless our dear and happy country.

PETER BROWNE, Foreman.

Jesse Jones,	*Thomas Allibone,*
B. W. Oakford,	*Samuel Howell, jun.*
Isaac Whelen,	*Henry Sheaff,*
Michael Roberts,	*Matthew M'Connell,*
John Fries,	*John Lardner,*
Rich. Downing, jun.	*George Bickham.*

Philadel. April 12, 1796.

(Philadelphia) April 18, 1796. Date and place are those given in the reply.

1. In the months preceding this reply, a number of treaties were formed between the United States and foreign nations: the Jay Treaty, ratified by the United States, August 14, 1795; the Treaty of Peace and Amity with Algiers, signed September 5, 1795; and the Treaty of Friendship, Limits, and Navigation with Spain, signed October 27, 1795. Miller, *Treaties,* 2:245, 275, 318.

2. The grand jury's statement echoes the debate in the House of Representatives on whether to appropriate moneys to execute provisions of the Jay Treaty. The appropriation was finally approved and signed into law on May 6, 1796. *Annals,* 5:426-784, 940-1292; *Stat.,* 1:459.

James Iredell to Hannah Iredell

April 15, 1796   Philadelphia, Pennsylvania

...Our Court began here on Monday, and will last, I suppose, all the month_ ...

ARS (Nc-Ar, Charles E. Johnson Collection). Addressed "Edenton, North Carolina." Postmarked "15 AP."

James Iredell to Hannah Iredell
April 20, 1796   Philadelphia, Pennsylvania

Philadelphia   April 20. 1796.

My dear Hannah,

I was relieved from great anxiety, and made very happy yesterday by receiving together your letters of the 2ᵈ and 9ᵗʰ Instant. Mʳ Anthony had begun to fear no Vessel would soon arrive from Edenton here, and had ordered some things he was to ship himself from New York where there were several _ I was [~~deliberately?~~] deliberating about doing the same thing when I unexpectedly heard yesterday afternoon of a Vessel which was to sail to day, of which Mʳ Anthony had obligingly sent me notice tho' I had not received it. I have been employed ever since in collecting as many of the Things you ordered as I could, some of which I had bespoke before but not all. Chamberlain[1] has unluckily disappointed me about the shoes complaining of his Workmen. I will do all I can to send them by Carpenter[2] who has not yet come. Mʳˢ Powell[3] could not get Russia Sheeting, but has recommended Irish which I sent in its room _ Neither could she get the kind of Pins you wrote for, but has sent others. I have by some accident mislaid the Children's measure, & therefore don't send Helen any shoes now _ But if I can get such as I think will do I will send them by Carpenter _ I send some Needles for Mʳˢ Johnston _ a pair of spectcles for Mʳˢ MᶜKenzie,[4] and a case for you _ I have endeavoured repeatedly to get the Novel of "Woman as she should be",[5] but could not _ A Lady here said she presumed you had no occasion for it.

—I send 2 hats that I hope will please for annie and Helen _ (of the newest fashion) and a hat for James.— The opportunity has been so sudden that I fear some things may have been forgot _ I will examine particularly, and if they be will try to rectify it. Half of this letter I have written in Court _ James Johnston[6] is with me now, and quite well _ So was my Mother on Sunday _ Both send their love to you all _

As many kisses as you please, & my tenderest love to my dear children _ Remember me affectionately to my other Friends, and believe me ever _

Your most affectionate

Ja. Iredell

[postscript illegible because page is torn]

ARS (Nc-Ar, Charles E. Johnson Collection). Addressed "Edenton,   North Carolina." Marked "With 3 Boxes,   & a Hat Box, containing   Things for Family use _ ."

  1. Benjamin Chamberlain, a Philadelphia shoemaker. Thomas Stephens, *Stephens's Philadelphia Directory for 1796* (Philadelphia: W. Woodward, 1796).
  2. John Carpenter, a resident of Philadelphia. Ibid.
  3. Probably Ann Powell, a shopkeeper in Philadelphia. Ibid.

4. Margaret (Cathcart) McKenzie (1754-1823). Wilma Cartwright Spence, comp., *Tombstones and Epitaphs of Northeastern North Carolina* (Baltimore: Gateway Press, 1973), p. 62.

5. Eliza (Phelp) Parsons, *Woman As She Should Be; or, Memoirs of Mrs. Menville,* 4 vols. (London: William Lane, 1793).

6. Son of Samuel Johnston, James Iredell's brother-in-law.

"A Friend to Order"

Aurora

April 23, 1796   Philadelphia, Pennsylvania

In the Daily Advertiser of the 18th inst. I saw an address of some of the members of a grand jury, headed by their foreman, in answer to a charge of judge Iredell.[1] This address carries upon the face of it such extreme presumption, that I feel astonished it has hitherto passed unnoticed. I shall not on this occasion notice the absurdity of the address containing an answer to a subject, which the judge "FORBORE TO MAKE ANY PARTICULAR OBSERVATIONS UPON, AS HE KNEW NO CASE LIKELY TO ARISE UPON WHICH A JUDICIAL CONSIDERATION OF IT WAS REQUISITE." If grand juries make it a point thus to "travel out of the record," and to undertake to express the opinions of the people upon governmental measures, we shall soon see as heterogeneous a compound as was ever exhibited; unless indeed the marshall or prothonotary made it a point to select such grand jurors as would either express his opinions, or the opinions, of those his wishes supported. A question might arise upon the right a grand jury had to give an opinion on a question the national legislature were engaged in discussing. The duties of a grand jury are specific, and it appears a novelty to me, that they should have a right to pronounce upon what measures were proper for the legislature of the union to adopt. If they usurp an authority of this sort, we may next expect they will go a step further, and indite Congress unless they should SUBSTITUTE THE OPINIONS OF A GRAND JURY FOR THEIR CONVICTION!

But while this part of a grand jury were expressing their opinion, they should, at least have confined themselves to the truth, and not have made assertions contradicted by the actual state of things. How, let me ask, could the foreman of that jury, assert that he expressed "THE WISHES OF THE GREAT MAJORITY OF THIS DISTRICT," when he must know, that in the part of the district in which he resides, scarcely a man besides himself can be found of the same sentiment. It is a notorious fact, that the people of the northern liberties are almost to a man opposed to the Treaty, and yet the foreman of a grand jury residing there undertakes to assert, that the great majority of the people are in favour of it! ! The other jurors may have made assertions equally unfounded, this much I am certain of, that the majority of the people, whose opinions they have undertaken to express, abhor the Treaty, and the nation with whom it is made. The SHIFTS to which the Treaty men were driven to procure signers to their petitions, evidences their own opinions of the sense of the people on the Treaty, for instead of candidly telling them their petition was in favour of the Treaty, they proclaimed that it was AGAINST A WAR, and thus seduced many unsuspecting and good citizens to sign in favour of an instrument they detested.

The House of Representatives are not to be duped by the shallow artifices of grand juries, or a few merchants and traders; for even admitting the people of Philadelphia are to a man in favour of the Treaty, is this to influence the national legislature? Are the citizens of Philadelphia to dictate measures to the United States? When the Treaty was under the consideration of the President, and numerous addresses against it were presented from almost all the trading towns on the continent, it was then said by THE FRIENDS OF ORDER, that the TOWNS were not THE PEOPLE of the United States; but now the MERCHANTS AND TRADERS OF PHILADELPHIA alone consider themselves THE PEOPLE, and wish to menace the Representatives into their British measures.[2] These men are friends to the constitution and the constituted authorities as long as they chime with their views; but the moment their will is not to be received as law, every engine is set in motion, to intimidate and to compel an acceptance of their plans. A more nefarious scheme to COERCE the House of Representatives into an execution of the British Treaty was never attempted in any country, then the one hatched in this city, but for the honor of our country it is to be hoped the scheme and its authors will meet that indignation and contempt from the representatives of freemen they so richly merit.

A FRIEND TO ORDER.

(Philadelphia) April 23, 1796. Date and place are those of the newspaper.

1. See Reply of the Grand Jury of the Circuit Court for the District of Pennsylvania, April 12, 1796.

2. On April 20 and 21, 1796, Congress received petitions from "merchants and others of the city of Philadelphia" urging the implementation of the Jay Treaty. *Annals,* 5:1114.

Letter from an Anonymous Correspondent
Aurora
April 25, 1796   Philadelphia, Pennsylvania

The conduct of the grand jury, who published an address to judge Iredell in commendation of the British Treaty,[1] is of a piece with the other proceedings which have been adopted to GULL the people. It is said by one of the Jurors, that THE ADDRESS WAS NOT AGITATED UNTIL THE JURY WAS DISMISSED, AND THAT ALTHO' HE WAS ONE OF THE JURY, HE KNEW NOTHING OF THE ADDRESS 'TILL HE SAW IT IN THE PAPER.[2] Indeed it appears from the face of the thing and the number of signers, that it must have been a SMUGGLED piece of business, much to the discredit of the parties. There is a BARE QUORUM who appear as signers,[3] which adds confirmation to the report, that the thing was a mere TRICK.

Men of intemperate zeal frequently overshoot their object, and in this instance these ORDERLY grand jurors have committed their veracity. They have said that *"from a knowledge of the people among whom they live they can truly say, that there is a desire in the minds of the great body of the people, that the British Treaty should be carried into effect."* Could they have believed this themselves? A subsequent event must make them blush at their presumption, thus to declare things at random. With all the influence of the government, banks, stockjobbers &c. &c. with all the deceptions practised, & falshoods told the whole number of signers in favour of carrying the Treaty into effect amounts to but little more than fifteen hundred when the signers to the address against making appropriations amount already to TWO THOUSAND SIX HUNDRED.[4]

(Philadelphia) April 25, 1796. Date and place are those of the newspaper.

1. See Reply of the Grand Jury of the Circuit Court for the District of Pennsylvania, April 12, 1796.

2. The reply of the grand jury, dated April 12, 1796, came one day before the grand jury was dismissed from court.

3. A number of grand jurors did not answer the venire and were subsequently fined by the court. Thirteen did appear, were impaneled as grand jurors, and eventually signed the reply. There remains some confusion as to the identity of Jesse Jones, who signed the reply but was not listed as a grand juror in the court's minutes. In addition, Thomas Forrest, who was listed as a grand juror, did not sign the reply. Engrossed Minutes, CCD Pennsylvania, RG 21, PPFAR; Reply of the Grand Jury of the Circuit Court for the District of Pennsylvania, April 12, 1796 (q.v.).

4. The *Annals* records petition signatures received from the Philadelphia area on April 20 and 21 totaling roughly 1,692 for the treaty and 2,300 against. *Annals,* 5:1114.

Circuit Court for the District of Connecticut ――――――――――
April 25, 1796 New Haven, Connecticut

On April 25 court opened with Associate Justice Samuel Chase and Judge Richard Law in attendance. Court adjourned on May 4.[1]

1. Docket Book, CCD Connecticut, RG 21, MWalFAR.

Circuit Court for the District of Georgia ――――――――――
April 25, 1796 Savannah, Georgia

Chief Justice Oliver Ellsworth and Judge Nathaniel Pendleton convened court on April 25. The Chief Justice delivered a charge to the grand jury. After completing its business, court adjourned on May 4 to the next term.[1]

1. Minutes, CCD Georgia, RG 21, GEpFAR; Oliver Ellsworth's Charge to the Grand Jury of the Circuit Court for the District of Georgia, April 25, 1796 (q.v.).

Oliver Ellsworth's Charge to the Grand Jury of the Circuit Court for the District of Georgia ——————————————————————

Columbian Museum
April 25, 1796   Savannah, Georgia

Gentlemen of the Grand Jury,

THIS court has cognizance of all offences against the United States, committed within the district of Georgia, or elsewhere, without the jurisdiction of any particular state, by persons afterwards found within this district. After all such offences, you will therefore enquire, and due presentment make.

Your duty may perhaps be deemed unpleasant, but it is too important not to be faithfully performed. To provide in the organization, that reason shall prescribe laws, is of little avail, if passions be left to controul them. Institutions without respect—laws violated with impunity, are to a Republic the symptoms and the seeds of death. No transgression is too small, nor any transgressor too great, for animadversion.

Happily for our laws they are not written in blood, that we should blush to read, or hesitate to execute them. They breath the spirit of a parent; and expect the benefits of correction, not from severity, but from certainty. Reformation is never lost sight of, till depravity becomes, or is presumed to be incorrigible. Imposed as restraints, here are, not by the jealousy of usurpation, nor the capriciousness of insensibility; but as aids to virtue and guards to rights, they have a high claim to be rendered efficient.

Nor is this claim more heightened by the purity of their source, and the mildness of their genius, than by the magnitude of the interests they embrace. The national laws are the national ligatures and vehicles of life. Tho' they pervade a country, as diversified in habits, as it is vast in extent, yet they give to the whole, harmony of interest, and unity of design. They are the means by which it pleases heaven to make of weak and discordant parts, one great people; and to bestow upon them unexampled prosperity. And so long as America shall continue to have one will, organically expressed and enforced, must she continue to rise in opulence and respect. Let then, the man, or combination of men, who, from whatever motive, oppose partial to general will, and would disjoint their country to the sport of fortune, feel their impotence and error.

Admonished by the fate of Republics, which have gone before us, we should profit by their mistakes. Impetuosity in legislation, and instability in execution, are the rocks on which they perished. Against the former, indeed, we hold a security which they were ignorant of, by a representation instead of the aggregate, and by a distribution of the legislative power, to maturing and ballancing bodies, instead of the subjection of it to momentary impulse, and the predominence of faction. Yet from the danger of inexecution, we are not exempt. Strength of virtue, is not alone sufficient; there must be strength of arm, or the experiment is hopeless. Numerous are the vices, and as obstinate the prejudices, and as daring as restless is the ambition, which perpetually hazard the national peace. And they certainly require that to the authority vested in the executive department, there be added liberal confidence, and the unceasing co-operation of all good citizens for its support. Let there then be vigilance—constant vigilance and fidelity for the execution of laws—of laws made by all, and having for their object, the good of all. So let us rear an empire sacred to the rights of man; and commend a government of reason to the nations of the earth.

But, gentlemen, I will not detain you longer from your duty. You may expect in the performance of it, such assistance from Mr. Attorney, and also from the Court, as you may have occasion for, and it shall be proper for them respectively to give. You will please to retire.

(Savannah) April 29, 1796. Date and place are from an introductory paragraph to the charge.

The charge was reprinted by several newspapers: *City Gazette* (Charleston), May 4, 1796; *Georgia Gazette* (Savannah), May 5, 1796; *Minerva* (New York), May 14, 1796; *Gazette of the United States* (Philadelphia), May 18, 1796; *Argus* (New York), May 21, 1796; *Diary* (New York), May 21, 1796; *American Mercury* (Hartford), May 23, 1796; *Connecticut Courant* (Hartford), May 23, 1796; *Connecticut Journal* (New Haven), May 25, 1796; *Federal Orrery* (Boston), May 26, 1796; *State Gazette* (Providence), May 28, 1796; *Rutland Herald* (Rutland, Vermont), June 13, 1796.

Presentment of the Grand Jury of the Circuit Court for the District of Georgia

April 27, 1796   Savannah, Georgia

We the Grand Jury of the Circuit Court for this District, avail ourselves of this opportunity of Expressing our approbation of the last Legislature which sat at Louiseville, for the passing of an act rendering Null and void the act usurped and passed by the Legislature on the Seventh of January 1795 disposing of the western Territory of this State, removing thereby the greatest Grievance this Country laboured under, and that they deserve the thanks of every disinterested Citizen _ [1]

Every Grand Jury throughout this State have complained of that usurped Act, which was intended to deprive the Citizens and their posterity, not only unconstitutionally, but by Bribery and Corruption, of unascertained millions of acres, to enrich a Set of Speculators, the pest of Society, who have long infested this State, and to whom all the Disorder and Confusion in our public affairs may justly be attributed _

We return our Sincere thanks to the Honorable abraham Baldwin a Representative from this State in the Congress of the United States, and highly approve the manner, in which he repelled the Daring attempt of a

Senator from this State to interrupt, that Gentleman in the faithful Discharge of his Duty as a Representative of the people, we are not at a Loss for the Cause of that unwarrantable attack, whatever pretences may have been offered to the public and hope that should any attempt of the kind be again made, the object will be treated with equal Contempt and Disrespect _ [2]

We present as a grievance that the Compensation allowed to Jurors attending Court from any Distance, is not adequate to their necessary Expenses,[3] We admit that the Sum allowed may be Sufficient in the Northern States, but the high price of provisions and Labour in Georgia, is Such, that the money received by the Juror will not pay half his maintenance _ We also recommend that the marshal be authorized immediatly on the Discharge of the Jury to pay whatever Sum may be allowed _ we are happy to inform the Court that no criminal Business or Information have come before us

We thank his Honor the Chief Justice for his Excellent charge and request that it, together with our presentments be published in the next Gazettes _ [4]

Peter Henry Morel foreman (LS)	Audley Maxwell (LS)
John Tebeau (L:S)	Simon Fraser (L:S)
Lewis Turner (L:S)	N: Hudson (L:S)
John Barnard (L:S)	W^m porter (L:S)
Hampton Lillibridge (L:S)	John Shick Junr (L:S)
Robert Greer (L:S)	Levy abrahams (L:S)
Levi Shaftall (L.S)	William Lewden (L:S)

D (GEpFAR, RG 21, CCD Georgia, Minutes).

On June 4, 1796, the *Gazette of the United States* (Philadelphia) printed the deputy marshal's response, previously published in the *Southern Centinel* (Augusta), to the grand jury's address:

"Lest the community should be again deluded by this last effort, you will oblige the friends to good government by inserting the following certificate—from which it will appear, that the foregoing presentments of the Grand Jury of this district, instead of conveying the public opinion respecting *the Louisville Assembly,* and the *private quarrel* between two gentlemen is in fact nothing more than the extrajudicial intemperate and exparte proceedings of a few individuals from three counties only, ten from Chatham, two from Liberty, and two from Effingham county; altho' there are 24 counties in this state, and the three contain not more than one fifteenth of the whole inhabitants.

I do hereby certify that the persons whose names are subscribed to the foregoing presentments reside in the following counties, viz.

Peter H. Morel, Chatham; John Tebau, Lewis Turner, John Barnard, Wilmington Island in Chatham county.

Hampton Lillibridge, Robert Greer, Levi Sheftall, John Shick, Levi Abrahams, William Lewden, city of Savannah, (Chatham.)

Audley Maxwell, Simon Frazer, Liberty county.

Nathaniel Hudson, William Porter, Effingham county.

Certified by me in the Circuit Court of the United States, for the district of Georgia, this 30th April, 1796.

G. F. HULL, D. M. of the District of Georgia."

1. The grand jury is referring to "An Act supplementary to an act, entitled 'An act for appropriating a part of the unlocated territory of this State for the payment of the late State

troops, and for other purposes therein mentioned,' declaring the right of this State to the unappropriated territory thereof, for the protection and support of the frontiers of this State, and for other purposes." The act was declared null and void by an act passed by the Georgia legislature on February 13, 1796. John D. Cushing, comp., *The First Laws of the State of Georgia,* part 2 (Wilmington, Del.: Michael Glazier, 1981), pp. 557, 577.

2. Abraham Baldwin (1754-1807), represented Georgia first as a congressman (1789-1799), and later as a senator (1799-1807). *BDAC.*

The incident referred to by the grand jury involved Baldwin and Senator James Gunn of Georgia. In March 1796 Gunn charged that a letter concerning the sale of Georgia's western lands, known as the Yazoo, had been sent to Baldwin by the Georgia legislature. Gunn, deeply involved in the controversial land sale as director of the Georgia Company, believed the letter would be used against him and demanded to see it. Baldwin claimed that "such a paper as you describe I have not yet seen." Unsatisfied by this response, Gunn challenged Baldwin to a duel. The matter was later settled without a duel being fought. *Annals,* 5:786-98; C. Peter Magrath, *Yazoo: Law and Politics in the New Republic* (New York: W. W. Norton, 1967), p. 8.

3. According to section 3 of the Process and Compensation Act of 1792, jurors were allowed fifty cents per day and five cents per mile travelled; on June 1, 1796, an act was passed allowing additional compensation of fifty cents per day for attendance by jurors, thus raising their compensation to one dollar per day for attendance. The travel allowance remained the same. *Stat.,* 1:276-77, 492.

4. Oliver Bowen, marshal for the district of Georgia, paid ten dollars and twenty-eight cents for the publication of the charge and presentment in the May 5, 1796, issue of the Savannah *Georgia Gazette.* Miscellaneous Treasury Accounts, No. 10161, RG 217, DNA; Clarence S. Brigham, *History and Bibliography of American Newspapers, 1690-1820,* 2 vols. (Worcester, Mass.: American Antiquarian Society, 1947), 1:127.

James Iredell to Hannah Iredell

May 3-4, 1796   Philadelphia, Pennsylvania

[*May 3:*] I am tomorrow to set off for Annapolis. ...

. . .

I am perfectly well, except that I have a little remains of a slight inflammation in my eye. I tried all the expedients I could, consistently with the necessity of my being in Court every day. Yesterday I got blooded, and have felt much relief from it. I shall have glasses to protect me in travelling.

. . .

[*May 4:*] I am just setting off. My Eye is much better, and gives me no pain to day. ... [1]

ARS (Nc-Ar, Charles E. Johnson Collection). Addressed "Edenton." Sent via "Capt. Carpenter."

1. On May 4 Iredell also wrote to his uncle, Thomas Iredell, that "I have been here upon official duty about 3 months, and am just setting off to attend Courts in Maryland and Virginia." James Iredell Association, Edenton, North Carolina.

Circuit Court for the District of Maryland ——————————
May 7, 1796   Annapolis, Maryland

Associate Justice James Iredell and Judge William Paca convened the court on May 7. After court opened, Justice Iredell delivered a charge to the grand jury. Concluding its business in one sitting, the court adjourned to the next term.[1]

1. Minutes, CCD Maryland, RG 21, PPFAR. Charge not found.

Circuit Court for the District of South Carolina ——————————
May 12, 1796   Columbia, South Carolina

The circuit court opened with Chief Justice Oliver Ellsworth and Judge Thomas Bee present. On the following day the court adjourned to the next term.[1]

1. Minutes, CCD South Carolina, RG 21, GEpFAR.

Circuit Court for the District of Vermont ——————————
May 12, 1796   Bennington, Vermont

Associate Justice Samuel Chase and Judge Samuel Hitchcock convened court on May 12. The court adjourned on May 16 to the next term.[1]

1. Circuit Docket, CCD Vermont, RG 21, MWalFAR.

Letter from an Anonymous Correspondent ——————————
Gazette of the United States
May 13, 1796   Augusta, Georgia

[*The correspondent writes of having attended the Georgia circuit court at Savannah.*] The Chief Justice, Mr. Ellsworth, gave great satisfaction as well by judicious determinations of the various business of the court, as by the most punctual attention. I have the highest esteem and respect for him, and therefore could not without great pleasure, see the citizens of that proud city vieing with each other in endeavors to make his stay among them agreeable to him. ...

(Philadelphia) June 6, 1796. Date and place are those of the letter.

James Iredell to Hannah Iredell ——————————
May 16, 1796   Alexandria, Virginia
May 18, 1796   Richmond, Virginia

[*May 16, Alexandria:*] I arrived at Annapolis on the 6 of May. the Court began the day after, and lasted only one hour _ in consequence of which, had there been an immediate opportunity, I should certainly have gone down the Bay, in the hope of having 4 or 5 days at least to spare to spend with you. But no such agreeable opportunity offered. Tho' I passed my time very pleasantly at Annapolis, I returned to Baltimore on the 10th in the hope of meeting your Brother[1] in which I was not disappointed, and here we are together, expecting to go on to Richmond tomorrow. He is quite well, and so am I now, the inflammation in my eye being quite gone tho' the eye is still weak _ ...

[*May 18, Richmond:*] Your Brother and myself are just arrived, and he has already set off for Petersburg to try to go on to Halifax without delay. He has been a little unwell since I wrote before, but not confined, and is now much better. I am quite well _ I wish I could fix a time now for you to send for me, but find it impossible _ God grant I may soon hear of you _ I must put my letter in immediately, for fear of losing the Post _ ...

ARS (NcD, James Iredell Sr. and Jr. Papers). Addressed "Edenton, North Carolina." Postmarked "RICHM'D. May 18, 1796." Iredell appended the letter of May 18 to the one he wrote Hannah on May 16.
1. Samuel Johnston.

Circuit Court for the District of Virginia ——————————————
May 23, 1796   Richmond, Virginia

The Virginia circuit court convened on May 23 with Associate Justice James Iredell and Judge Cyrus Griffin in attendance. After court opened, Iredell delivered a charge to the grand jury. Court adjourned on June 7.[1]

1. Order Book, CCD Virginia, Vi; James Iredell's Charge to the Grand Jury of the Circuit Court for the District of Virginia, May 23, 1796 (q.v.).

James Iredell's Charge to the Grand Jury of the Circuit Court for the District of Virginia ——————————————
May 23, 1796   Richmond, Virginia

Gentlemen of the Grand Jury,
    Among the numerous means put into our power for preserving the public blessings these States so remarkably enjoy, perhaps none are of greater importance, certainly none deserve a more sacred regard, than those which

AD (NcD, James Iredell Sr. and Jr. Papers). Marked on the last page by Iredell: "Copy of a Charge to the   Grand Jury for the District   of Virginia, at Richmond   Delivered (I believe) May 1796."
    The charge was printed in the *Virginia Gazette, and General Advertiser* (Richmond), June 1, 1796; *Philadelphia Gazette,* June 8, 1796; *Federal Gazette* (Baltimore), June 14, 1796; *North-Carolina Minerva* (Fayetteville), June 16, 1796; and *State Gazette of North-Carolina* (Edenton), June 23, 1796.

relate to the Administration of Justice. Liberty without Law is Anarchy; Law without Liberty is Oppression. A due mixture of both can alone make any People at once prosperous and happy.

What may constitute a proper union of both it is ~~perhaps~~ difficult to say in regard to any People, until Experience has given some sanction to Theory. The habits, manners, principles, and propensities differ so much in different Nations that it is impossible that the same kind of System can suit them all _ No People however can rationally desire more than that they should themselves chuse the Government under which they are to live. ~~They h~~ave^There is no no_alternative but ~~between~~ this,[1] no Government at all, or one which owes its birth to Usurpation or Accident.

The People of the United States not only were the first who enjoyed the high distinction of chusing a Government of their own, but in the course of many years experience of War and Peace they have_opportunities to put many principles to the test, and_appreciate their value accordingly. Thus it was found that in time of War, when a vast majority of the People concurred in one common object, being actuated by a common danger, and having one great end only in view, the feeble Articles of Confederation were sufficient to keep them together, to conduct them gloriously through the trying conflict in which they were engaged, and at length terminate it with equal honour and advantage. But when this common object was obtained, when the danger of a foreign Enemy was removed, then soon appeared the influence of selfish and contending Interests, too many forgetting how necessary Union was to preserve what had been with so much difficulty acquired. The consequences we well know. The voice of the Union disregarded, Public Debts not only unpaid but unprovided for, Private as well as Public Credit at a very low ebb, Commerce languishing, Agriculture discouraged, Measures of Disunion every day adopting, an illiberal and malignant Jealousy taking place of a rational and manly Confidence, and the most melancholy symptoms prevailing of a speedy Dissolution of the Union, or a disgraceful and ungovernable Anarchy. The magnitude of the danger alarmed all considerate Men, and by one of the greatest and most disinterested Efforts ever made by public Bodies, each making Voluntary Sacrifices to accomplish a magnanimous Reformation, the present Constitution of the Union was formed and adopted. The consequences which have happened I need not depict. They are felt, if not acknowledged by all _ They have advanced the United States to a degree of prosperity and glory to which no imagination reached before the experiment was made _ They leave scarcely any thing to wish, but that Rashness may not throw away what Wisdom has so nobly procured.

---

1. A crossed-out carat appears beneath the crossed-out interlineation which follows.

All Governments depend more or less upon the confidence and support of the People for whose benefit they do or ought to subsist. But a free Government more especially does so, and the freer the Government the greater such

therefore
Citizen of the U. S.   ~~in our own Country~~
dependence must be. Every ~~In di vi dual therefore,~~ whatever his station or situation may be, has an important responsibility attached to himself. He owes to his Country by all possible and honorable means to promote its prosperity, and to do nothing either negligently or with design to counteract it. Considering himself as a Member of a single Community, which is in itself a

Individual
Member of another in a larger sphere, he should reflect that he is only one
connected with [*phrase inked out*] of others   ~~separate~~ separately   [*phrase inked out*]
~~among~~ a great number whose[2] authority is ₐ equal, and ~~whose~~ each of whose
are   with his own
sentiments ₐ~~are~~ entitled to equal deference ~~with his own~~: that his Individual Interest, when it comes into competition, must yield to that of the State in which he resides; and that the Interest of the State itself, when it stands in competition with that of the United States, must yield to this as a superior
a real & effective union can be founded upon no other basis.
Interest also; since ~~this~~ is ~~the only basis upon which a Union of the whole~~
founded[*word inked out*]
~~can be~~ [accom ₐplished?]. At the same time that he exercises with Zeal, and maintains with firmness, the right of each Individual to express his sentiments on all public concerns, he should endeavour as well as his opportunities will admit to understand them thoroughly, that he may neither be unwaringly misled himself nor unwaringly mislead others. He should seriously meditate on the awful stake which not only himself but Millions of others have in the public prosperity, and make reasonable allowances for the difficulties which will perpetually occur in the management of the concerns of so great a number so as to combine as nearly as possible the interests of the few
render
with the interests of the many, and ~~ma ₐke~~ the whole subservient to the exalted principles of honour and justice. To effect these great objects is indeed no easy task, and he who thinks it so shews either extreme ignorance of the subject, or a vain presumption in his own powers for which no judicious Man will give him any credit. As long as Governments shall subsist, under any form or of any description, various opinions will be entertained upon the subject of political regulations. They embrace a variety of interests all of which cannot equally be promoted, though all ought to be consulted and as much as possible to be reconciled. They respect future contingencies upon which
at best
enable him ~~at best~~ to form ₐ but probable conjectures.
the limited foresight of Man can ₐ~~pronounce with little reasonable assurance.~~ ₐ

2. A crossed-out carat appears here.

~~They are sometimes employed about cases of great exigency which confound the clearest Un-derstandings, and in which no steps, however cautious can be sure to tread with safety.~~ Cases of extraordinary exigency sometimes present themselves which confound the clearest understandings and in which ~~the~~ no steps however cautious can be sure to tread with safety.

~~such~~   ~~regard to~~ in investigating a subject

~~under~~ circumstances like these, in the management of concerns to which so many
The ablest Men, ~~under a state of such complication and uncertainty,~~ will often
intricacies belong,
differ about the proper means of obtaining the same common object. These difficulties occur even if the best dispositions should universally prevail. But that never can be the case in an extensive Country. However numerous the well-disposed may be, there will be always ill-disposed Men ready to take advantage of opportunities to do mischief. They will neglect no means of doing it, where they have any chance of success. Misrepresentations may be easily made which for a time will impose on many who possess the purest intentions, since no Man can judge but according to the information he receives, and if that be erroneous an opinion grounded on it must necessarily be so too. Plausible reports will be raised to catch the credulous, ~~unreason-~~
unwarrantable apprehensions   arrogant ~~hypocritical~~
~~able~~ fears will be suggested to alarm the timid, ~~extrav~~ agant pretensions to Patriotism will be employed to seduce those who revere and practise it. By arts like these much mischief may be effected before the public mind can be thoroughly informed, and the true grounds of public measures rightly understood. It is in this interval alone that a free Government, conscious of its integrity, has any thing to fear. The Government of the United States has passed through several of these trials. Thro' them all Time has removed prejudices which successively had great sway. Reason, when it was allowed a fair scope, has had its full effect on an enlightened, Justice on a virtuous, Candour on a generous People. They have never yet failed, and I trust never will, to bestow their confidence when convinced it has been really deserved. They well know how much is in their power if in any instance it be abused, but they will not suffer Men to be condemned unheard, because they have been thought
prevailed upon
worthy of their highest confidence, nor will they be ~~persu~~ aded, under any temporary delusion, to abandon a Government of their own choice, and which has constantly risen in their estimation after every attempt to discredit it.

I make these observations, Gentlemen, because it is the glory of a free Government, and I doubt not is the first wish of our own, to rely upon the good opinion and affections of the People as the firmest basis of its Power: because ill grounded Discontent not only preys upon the mind, and diminishes its usefulness in society, but has too natural a tendency to create an indifference, if not an aversion to Government, and from either of these the gradation to actua[l] disobedience is less than seems commonly to be
considered
~~supp~~ osed: because tho' Courts of Justice have authority to punish Disobedience, Yet if they can be in any manner instrumental in rendering the ex-

ercise of such authority unnecessary, they may perform more real services to their Country (and certainly such as are more pleasing to themselves) than by

appearing only in the stern character of Power, and ~~Humanity can never be~~ ~~deemed an improper Associate of~~ Justice: _ I may add perhaps without impropriety, because I am persuaded that the better the measu[re]s of the Government are understood the more they will be approved, and whatever difference of opinion may still remain ~~in regard~~ to the policy of some of them, there will be found upon the most scrutinizing research no reason for supposing that they have not originated in the most upright intentions to promote the welfare of our common Country.

to prevent Crimes
a humane precaution ^ can never be deemed
an improper attribute of Justice *with*
as to

I have heard, Gentlemen, of no offences likely to come before ~~you but~~
[*passage inked out*]   [*word illegible*]
~~such about which no difference of opinion can be entertained as to~~ [*word missing*] ~~injurious consequences of the Crime.~~

you but such as are unquestionably of a very immoral & dangerous nature, & altogether unconnected with ~~Party~~ [*word inked out*] Political Dissentions.

No particulars have come officially to my knowledge, but I have understood that very serious Prosecutions are depending for ^Frauds committed upon the public Mail, which by a special Act of the Congress of the United States are made highly penal; in some instances punishable with death.[3] It would be improper for me to enter into a detail concerning transactions of which I have received no official information, but I think it proper to read to you such parts of the Act as may concern the Prosecutions in question, not doubting that you will proceed in the investigation of the charges with all the attention and care suited to their solemnity and importance.

some species of

(Here read the 16 & 17 Sect _ 3 Vol. p. 48, 49).[4]

If in the course of your enquiry upon these Prosecutions, or any other, you should require any assistance from the Court which can be properly afforded, it shall be most readily given.

3. Sections 16 and 17 of "An Act to establish the Post-office and Post-roads within the United States," May 8, 1794. *Stat.,* 1:360-61.

On May 24, 1796, John Goosley was indicted "for Robbing the public Mails of the United States." He pleaded not guilty and was acquitted by the jury on May 27, 1796. Order Book, CCD Virginia, Vi; *DHSC,* 1:850, 852n.

4. Iredell used as his source *Acts passed at the Third Congress of the United States of America* (Philadelphia: Francis Childs, 1795).

Reply of the Grand Jury of the Circuit Court for the District
of Virginia ———————————————————————————

Virginia Gazette, and General Advertiser
  May 26, 1796   Richmond, Virginia

GENTLEMEN,

WE are convinced of the importance of the observations delivered in your
charge, to men who have the happiness to live under a government of their
choice. It can subsist only in the confidence of the people; and any attempt
to destroy this support, leads directly to its subversion. But we can with
pleasure declare, that the government of the Union, which was called into
existence by the voice of the people, is still the object of their warmest
attachment; that they are sufficiently enlightened to appreciate justly, as well
the blessings it has bestowed, as the calamities it has averted; and clearly to
perceive that their very liberty, peace, and prosperity, can rest on no other
secure foundation.

If various interests agitate the different parts of the Union, as their various
sentiments might lead us to fancy, it is fortunate that their government
compels them at last to harmonize; that dissention evaporates in debate,
instead of engendering hostile feuds; and that while the Senate is convulsed,
the people are tranquil. But instead of deriving this difference of opinion
from opposite and irreconcilable interests, which only our enemies would
delight to mark, we may fairly trace it to local and temporary circumstances,
which the hand of time is gently removing, and anticipate a period, when
the national character, as well as national government, shall be the pride
and boast of every American.

It is to be expected, that the people will watch the conduct of a
government, in which are deposited their hopes of happiness, with a jealous
attention. And this irritable state of the public mind, may sometimes receive,
too favorably, the seeds of distrust and suspicion, which are every where
scattered by industrious malice; a temporary delusion may succeed, which
soon however will yield to the genuine good sense of the people operating
upon fuller and more accurate information.

Our government, as you observe, has more than once experienced these
crises of public opinion; and we trust that instead of suffering by the shock,
it has grown in the public estimation. Conscious of its integrity, it must desire
to be scrutinized by the intelligent and candid, and if it regards its own
preservation, the first objects of its policy should be to diffuse knowledge
among the people, and to cultivate that inflexible virtue, which corresponds
with its institution, and can alone give to it stability.

We shall not fail to bestow on those subjects particularly committed to us, that serious attention which their importance to the interests of society demands.

By the majority of the Grand Jury,

HENRY LEE, *Foreman.*

MAY 26th, 1796.

(Richmond) June 1, 1796. Date and place are those of the reply.

Reply to the Grand Jury of the Circuit Court for the District of Virginia by James Iredell and Cyrus Griffin ────────────

Virginia Gazette, and General Advertiser
May 27, 1796   Richmond, Virginia

To HENRY LEE, ESQ.

SIR,

THE sentiments contained in the address you have done us the honor to present, give us great satisfaction. They breathe a spirit of union and republicanism, which the situation of the United States peculiarly demands, and which appears with peculiar dignity and weight, in those who have so eminently contributed to the establishment of both. Such an example must produce the happiest effects on many, who, though they highly value the liberty and reputation of their country, too slightly estimate the dangers to which they are exposed, when a temper of indiscriminate distrust is substituted for a wise and discreet jealousy, and unavoidable differences of opinion are suffered to rankle into personal animosity and ill will. But we trust, and doubt not, that, as the people of the different states become better acquainted with each other, a great deal of unfortunate prejudice which still prevails, will be done away, and that every day will more strongly cement that union so essential to the prosperity of all.

We have the honor to be,   With the highest respect,   Sir, Your most obedient, and   Most faithful servants,

JA. IREDELL.
C. GRIFFIN.

Richmond, May 27, 1796.

(Richmond) June 1, 1796. Date and place are those of the reply.

Circuit Court for the District of New Hampshire ────────────
May 27, 1796   Portsmouth, New Hampshire

Associate Justice Samuel Chase and Judge John Pickering opened court on May 27. The court adjourned on June 1 to the next term.[1]

1. Records, CCD New Hampshire, RG 21, MWalFAR.

James Iredell to Hannah Iredell
June 1, 1796   Richmond, Virginia

... I am very much afraid that we shall not be able to finish on Saturday though we are making every exertion possible for that purpose. But the business is immense. I now lament that I had not omitted ordering my horses till this Post _ but I hope they will still have to wait for me at most only two days. If I don't arrive by Wednesday morn you may be assured it is owing to the business of the Court. I shall be very impatient for the Post this evening, having no Letter last week but by way of Baltimore. The severity of the inflammation in my Eye which made writing painful to me prevented my being more particular in directing you how to send your letters _ In the affecting Trial we had of the young Man for robbing the Mail we were very near being obliged to examine the Father _ The scene was beyond exception distressing. Nothing saved the young Man's life but that it appeared his evidence was grounded on a promise not to prosecute him, and therefore the Court would not permit the evidence to be given _ And the only thing which avoided the Father's testimony was that it appeared he knew nothing but in consequence of that confession _ [1] ...

ARS (Nc-Ar, Charles E. Johnson Collection). Addressed "Edenton, North Carolina." Postmarked "RICHM'D. June 1 1796."

1. *United States v. Goosley.* See footnote 3 in James Iredell's Charge to the Grand Jury of the Circuit Court for the District of Virginia, May 23, 1796.

Circuit Court for the District of North Carolina
June 1, 1796   Wake Court House, Wake County, North Carolina

Chief Justice Oliver Ellsworth and Judge John Sitgreaves were present to open court. On June 9 the court adjourned to the next term.[1]

1. Minutes, CCD North Carolina, RG 21, GEpFAR.

Circuit Court for the District of Massachusetts
June 7, 1796   Boston, Massachusetts

The circuit court convened with Associate Justice Samuel Chase and Judge John Lowell in attendance. After court opened, Chase delivered "an animated, comprehensive and elegant" charge to the Grand Jury. On June 14 the court adjourned to the next term.[1]

1. Final Records, CCD Massachusetts, RG 21, MWalFAR; *Columbian Centinel* (Boston), June 8, 1796. Charge not found.

Circuit Court for the District of Delaware ———————————
June 8, 1796   New Castle, Delaware

Associate Justice James Wilson and Judge Gunning Bedford, Jr., opened the Delaware circuit court. The docket of the circuit court does not record the court's closing. The "teste" day was June 15.[1]

1. Appearance Docket, CCD Delaware, RG 21, PPFAR. James Iredell had arranged for James Wilson to substitute for him at this court. See James Iredell to Hannah Iredell, March 11, 1796.

Circuit Court for the District of Rhode Island ———————————
June 20, 1796   Newport, Rhode Island

On Monday, June 20, Associate Justice Samuel Chase and Judge Henry Marchant convened the Rhode Island court, and on June 25 they adjourned it.[1]

1. Minutes, CCD Rhode Island, RG 21, MWalFAR.

Supreme Court of the United States—Assignment of Circuits ————
August 6, 1796   Philadelphia, Pennsylvania

We, the Chief Justice and Associate Justices of the Supreme Court of the United States, do hereby appoint the ensuing Circuits to be attended as follows:

The Eastern Circuit	By Judge Cushing.
The Middle Circuit	By Judge Wilson.
The Southern Circuit	By Judge Paterson.

In the Supreme Court of the United States _ August 6th 1796.

Oliv.ʳ Ellsworth
Wᵐ Cushing
James Wilson
Ja. Iredell
Wᵐ Paterson.
Samuel Chase

DS (DNA, RG 267, Records of the Office of the Clerk). Except for the signatures, this document is in the hand of Associate Justice James Iredell.

James Iredell to James Wilson ———————————————————————
  August 20, 1796   Richmond, Virginia

                                                Richmond   August 20th 1796:
Dear Sir,
I arrived here last night, extremely fatigued for want of sleep, but my last
night's rest has compleatly recruited me _ I intended going down the Bay,
had there been an immediate opportunity, but finding only an uncertain one
could not bear to stay. Reflecting upon what you said to me concerning my
eventual attendance at this Court next November,[1] I think it proper to state
more particularly circumstances which have occurred to me than I could then.
A Suit in Equity of great importance, and upon which a large sum of money
is depending, which came on last November before Judge Griffin and myself.
An issue had been directed by Judge Blair and Judge Griffin, which was
tried before us last November, and a Verdict found in it to a large amount.
After the trial of the Issue, it occurred to me for reasons that I stated that
it was an Issue which could not be made up at law. Judge Griffin was of a
different opinion, so that there could be no Decree. The difference of opinion
continued at last Term _ which necessarily occasioned another continuance.
There is no prospect of our ever agreeing, and a further delay for the same
cause might occasion great injury, and certainly would much discontent _ [2]
In addition to this reason of a public nature, let me add, _ that I have not
been at home 6 weeks since the 18th of January _ that being now to return
in the midst of our sickly season I expect not to enjoy one hour of unmixed
satisfaction until it is over, which can't be counted upon until the beginning
of November _ thus to attend this Court, as the distance of 160 miles which
                                      set off
I should have to travel back again before I ~~should have to go~~ to Philadelphia
would break in upon almost the only remnant of truly valuable time in point
of happiness, should my Family's escape from the season be ever so fortunate,
which I could rely upon during the interval allowed me, and preceding a
new absence of 5 or 6 months at least. Not only my personal enjoyments
                                  interrupted,
would thus be distressingly ~~broken in upon,~~ but a considerable additional
expence incurred, and all attention to my little private property, which
requires some consideration, rendered in a manner impossible. I state these
circumstances thus particularly, as I am anxious to shew you how unwilling
I am to decline any request of yours without the strongest reasons to urge
me.
    I never expect to hear in a letter from you how you or your Family are _
But I assure you I shall always be solicitous to know, and shall feel real
satisfaction in hearing favourable accounts, whenever I have an opportunity
of knowing. You will oblige me in presenting my very respectful Compliments
to Mrs Wilson, Miss Emily,[3] and your Sons who are capable of receiving them.

The youngest has my wishes equally for his happiness, as he possesses no small share of my admiration.[4]

I am ever,   Dear Sir,   with great respect and attachment,   Your faithful and   obedient Servant

Ja. Iredell

ADfS (Nc-Ar, Charles E. Johnson Collection). Marked "Substance of a letter to Judge Wilson."

1. Apparently, after Wilson was assigned the Middle Circuit, he asked Iredell to attend the Circuit Court for the district of Virginia in his place. No circuit court was held the fall term of 1796, because no Supreme Court justice appeared.

2. The case to which Iredell refers is *Braxton v. Ware, Executor of Jones*, an equity case concerning a tobacco sale by the firm of Farrell & Jones. On November 27, 1795, a jury at the Circuit Court for the district of Virginia returned a verdict in the amount of $6426 in favor of the plaintiff in this case. Two weeks later the court continued the suit until the next term, stating that "any point in the same is to be considered as open for future discussion." The case was next heard in the spring of 1797, when both parties agreed to its dismissal. Order Book, November 27, 1795, December 12, 1795, May 24, 1797, CCD Virginia, Vi.

To resolve tie votes in a circuit court, section 2 of the Judiciary Act of 1793 provided that the case was to be continued to the next session. If two judges still disagreed at the second hearing, with a different Supreme Court justice present and the district judge adhering to his previous opinion, judgment would be rendered according to the opinion of the Supreme Court justice. The act, however, did not anticipate a continuing disagreement between the district judge and the same Supreme Court justice. Having presided at the two previous sessions of the circuit court (fall 1795 and spring 1796), Iredell realized that *Braxton v. Ware* could not be decided until another justice sat at the Virginia court. *Stat.,* 1:334.

3. Emily Wilson (b. ca. 1783), second daughter of James and Rachel Wilson. Smith, *James Wilson,* pp. 210-11.

4. James Wilson had four sons: William (b. 1774); Bird (1777-1859); James, Jr. (b. 1779); and Charles (b. 1786). A fifth son, Henry (b. May 1796), died in infancy. Smith, *James Wilson,* pp. 59, 97, 140, 210-11, 380; *DAB* entry for Bird Wilson; Harry C. Green and Mary W. Green, *The Pioneer Mothers of America,* 3 vols. (New York: G. P. Putnam's Sons, 1912), 3:206.

Circuit Court for the District of New York ————————————
September 5, 1796   New York, New York

Associate Justice William Cushing and Judge John Laurance opened the New York circuit court. A charge was delivered to the grand jury on September 5, and the court adjourned on September 9.[1]

1. Minutes, CCD New York, RG 21, NjBaFAR. Charge not found.

Circuit Court for the District of Connecticut ————————————
September 26, 1796   Hartford, Connecticut

On Monday, September 26, the circuit court commenced its session with Associate Justice William Cushing and Judge Richard Law in attendance. The following day the court adjourned to the next term.[1]

1. Docket Book, CCD Connecticut, RG 21, MWalFAR.

First View of the Coast of Virginia, March 3ᵈ 1796 by Benjamin Henry Latrobe (1764-1820). Pen and ink and watercolor on paper, 1796. Courtesy Maryland Historical Society, Baltimore. Benjamin Henry Latrobe Papers. Especially when traveling to and from the Southern Circuit, the justices preferred sailing by ships such as the one depicted in this scene, rather than taking the more arduous overland route by horse and carriage.

John Young Noel to William Paterson
October 3, 1796   New York, New York

...I wrote you Yesterday Eveng by Captn Anthony, to inform that the ship Carolina, Captn Lusher, is advertized for sailing on the 6th Instant _ That her Accomdations are good _ she is under the Direction of Danl Ludlow & Co: _ To whom you had better write, if you find it convenient to go in her _ ...

ARS (NjR, William Paterson Papers). Originally addressed "Brunswick," and marked "By Mr Perrine." Brunswick was then crossed out and the following inserted after Paterson's name: "now at Savanna." In the same hand, the letter is marked "To the Care of John Y: Noel Esqr."

John Young Noel, former solicitor general of Georgia, was a practicing attorney and mayor of Savannah. Richard A. Harrison, *Princetonians: A Biographical Dictionary,* vol. 3, *1776-1783* (Princeton: Princeton University Press, 1981), pp. 196-98.

Circuit Court for the District of New Jersey
October 3, 1796   Trenton, New Jersey

Associate Justice James Wilson and Judge Robert Morris convened court on Monday, October 3. Wilson delivered a charge to the grand jury, and the court, having no business, adjourned to the following term.[1]

1. Minutes, CCD New Jersey, RG 21, NjBaFAR. Charge not found.

William Paterson to Euphemia Paterson
October 10, 1796   Charleston, South Carolina

Charleston,   10th Octbr, 1796.

My dear Affa,

We have just arrived. Our passage has been remarkably quick; we run from the capes of Delaware to this place in sixty eight hours. The wind was as favourable as could blow, being N. E., and was strong and steady. Charleston is as healthy at present as is usual at this season of the year. The sickness, that prevailed some weeks ago, has entirely disappeared; and indeed the accounts you had of it were much exaggerated. Being fatigued with the voyage, and bereft of sleep for two nights past, I have not delivered any letters, or been out of my lodging; and have just taken up the pen to inform you of my safe arrival, as I knew your anxiety respecting me to be great.

My tenderest love to Cornelia and Billy; I hope, that they will be careful to improve in every useful and elegant accomplishment. My best respects to all friends.

May every species of happiness await you my beloved Euphemia is the fervent prayer of   Your

Wm Paterson

ARS (NjR, William Paterson Papers). Addressed "New Brunswick,   New Jersey." Postmarked by hand, "Ch.ton Oct. 11."

Circuit Court for the District of Pennsylvania
October 11, 1796   Philadelphia, Pennsylvania

Court was convened by Associate Justice James Wilson and Judge Richard Peters on October 11.[1] The court adjourned on October 15 to the next term.[2]

1. The holding of a circuit court at York, Pennsylvania, was eliminated with passage of "An Act to repeal so much of an act intituled 'An act to establish the judicial courts of the United States,' as directs that

alternate sessions of the Circuit Court for the district of Pennsylvania shall be holden at Yorktown; and for other purposes," May 12, 1796. *Stat.*, 1:463.

2. Engrossed Minutes, CCD Pennsylvania, RG 21, PPFAR.

Circuit Court for the District of Massachusetts
October 12, 1796   Boston, Massachusetts

The Massachusetts court commenced its session with Associate Justice William Cushing and Judge John Lowell in attendance. On October 15 the court adjourned to the next term.[1]

1. Final Records, CCD Massachusetts, RG 21, MWalFAR.

Circuit Court for the District of New Hampshire
October 24, 1796   Exeter, New Hampshire

Court was opened by Associate Justice William Cushing and Judge John Pickering. It met again the following day before adjourning to the next term.[1]

1. Records, CCD New Hampshire, RG 21, MWalFAR.

Circuit Court for the District of South Carolina
October 25, 1796   Charleston, South Carolina

Associate Justice William Paterson and Judge Thomas Bee opened court on October 25. After completing its business, court adjourned October 29 to the next term.[1]

1. Minutes, CCD South Carolina, RG 21, GEpFAR.

Circuit Court for the District of Delaware
October 27, 1796   Dover, Delaware

Judge Gunning Bedford, Jr., attended court, but the docket records neither the presence of Associate Justice James Wilson nor the date of the court's adjournment. The "teste" day was October 29.[1]

1. Appearance Docket, CCD Delaware, RG 21, PPFAR.

Henry William De Saussure to William Paterson
October 30, 1796   [Charleston, South Carolina]

sunday morning. 30⸴ oct:

Dear sir.

I was disappointed of the pleasure of seeing you last Evening when I Called to bid you adieu & to wish you a pleasant Journey. This morning I am on

A Scene in the Theatre Charleston by Charles Fraser (1782-1860). Watercolor on paper, ca. 1796. Courtesy South Carolina Historical Society, Charleston. Estate of Maud Winthrop Gibbon. The building in the left foreground is the county courthouse, which housed the state and federal courts. In the right foreground is St. Michael's Church, where in 1795 John Rutledge gave his famous speech in opposition to the Jay Treaty.

the wing, & Can only hastily sketch Your rout from Augusta to North Carolina. On leaving Augusta you may either go to Cambridge, (in this state) wch is 50 miles, thro' a good well settled Country and thence proceed through our hilly Country, thro a well Settled Country, all the way into North Carolina _ I have been so partially on this road that I cannot give any particulars of it _ But the Country is a fine one, & abundant _ the chief objection, is that If a rainy season comes on The rivers rise very high, & are Impassable _ The rout w^{h} I pursued last, was from Columbia to Charlotte in N. C. _ On this rout, your stages will be as follows. From Augusta to the Ridge _ 30 miles of good road, & decent accomodation at the ridge. From the Ridge to Granby _ 45 _ thro' a thinly settled Country, but a good road _ and some accomodations all the way _

      From Granby to Columbia.   3 Miles _
      From Columbia to Camden _   35 _ Miles _

From Camden to Rugeley's Mill.	12 Miles
From R. Mills to George Millers _	10 Miles _ only tolerable.
Thence to Hanging rock	6 _ no accomod:
Thence to Berbeley's	12 _
Thence to Boyd's	6. plentiful _
Thence to Crawford's	2 _
Thence to M:[Koys]	22 _
Thence to Charlotte (Mr Cooks)	8 _ Excellent.
Thence to Col. smiths	14 _ good.
to Phifers	6. tolerable
to savages	10. tolerable
to salisbury _ Yarborough's	10. good

to Salisbury

I rather think the rout from Charlotte ̬is too high for you, and that you must strike out a road from Charlotte obliquely thro' the Country _

Whatever rout you take, & wherever they lead you, I sincerely hope, health & happiness will attend you.

I am D: sir   With great respect   and regard   Your Most ob serv.ᵗ

Henry W^m DeSaussure

ARS (NjR, William Paterson Papers). Addressed "Broad street." Place determined from content of letter.

Edward Rutledge to Henry Middleton Rutledge ──────────────────

November 1, 1796   [Charleston, South Carolina]

...The Circuit Court has sat for a Week, _ Judge Patterson presided, he is a good Lawyer, & possesses sound Judgment. Taking time by the fore lock, he arrived eight or ten days before the sitting of the Court, which afforded us Leisure, & opportunity, to shew him the Civilities of our City. He received them in great abundance; & appear'd highly delighted. He dined twice with us, & would have dined more frequently, but for his numerous Engagements.
. . .

ARS (PHi, Dreer Collection). Place determined from content of letter.

Henry Middleton Rutledge (1775-1844), son of Edward Rutledge. Mabel L. Webber, comp., "Dr. John Rutledge and His Descendants," *South Carolina Historical and Genealogical Magazine* 31 (January 1930): 24.

William Paterson to Euphemia Paterson ──────────────────────

November 5, 1796   Augusta, Georgia

...The court lasted about a week at Charleston. I left that place on tuesday last, and arrived here yesterday. The distance is one hundred and fifty miles

View of Mulberry (House and Street) by Thomas Coram (1756-1811). Oil on paper, ca. 1800. Courtesy Carolina Art Association, Gibbes Art Gallery, Charleston, South Carolina. This South Carolina plantation scene was typical of those observed by the justices during their many days of travel on the back roads of the Southern Circuit.

View of Cooper River at Mulberry by Thomas Coram (1756-1811). Oil on paper, ca. 1800. Courtesy Carolina Art Association, Gibbes Art Gallery, Charleston, South Carolina. The many rivers and streams in South Carolina, which often flooded the roads during heavy rains, were traveled by sailboat in the coastal regions.

through pines and over sand. At Charleston I purchased a sulkey,[1] two horses, &c which was a deviation from my original intention of buying horses at this place; but I could not hire a carriage to take me up. The gentlemen of Charleston are extremely attentive, hospitable, and polite to strangers; indeed more so than any place I have ever been in. Although there is a diversity of sentiment among them as to political matters, yet it never interrupts their intercourse, or disturbs their social happiness. Men of all political parties mingle together, and are indiscriminately invited to their tables, where much conviviality reigns, and where they are studious to please. Charleston, from its situation, will be a large commercial city; for it engrosses nearly all the trade of South Carolina, and draws, besides, a considerable trade from the adjacent states of Georgia and North Carolina. About ⅛ᵗʰ of the town was destroyed by the late fires; the ravages of which will, however, be scarcely perceived in the course of a few years.[2] They are busily employed in building up, but unfortunately the new houses are generally composed of timber. The streets, except two, are very narrow, rather alleys than streets; and therefore it is probable, that the greater part of the city will sooner or later be destroyed by fire. It is in contemplation to procure a law at the next session of the legislature to compel persons to build of brick or stone in future _ The late sickness, in the course of six weeks, carried off a number of people; by the return it appears, that 439 white persons fell victims to it; no account was kept of the death of the negroes, but of these you may safely reckon 361, which will make the whole loss 800 _ Charleston is now very healthy _

The present weather resembles our finest weather in the beginning of June. The season has been remarkably dry; and the people in many places are waiting for rain in order to plough for their winter grain, in which they include oats. The crops of every kind have been abundant. ...

ARS (NjR, William Paterson Papers).
1. A light two-wheeled carriage, seating one person. *OED*.
2. A large fire swept through the city of Charleston on June 13, 1796. *City Gazette* (Charleston), June 14, 1796.

Circuit Court for the District of Maryland ——————————
November 7, 1796　　Easton, Maryland

Associate Justice James Wilson and Judge William Paca were present to open court on November 7. The court met again the following day before adjourning to the next term.[1]

1. Minutes, CCD Maryland, RG 21, PPFAR.

A View of Charles Town by Thomas Leitch (dates unknown). Oil on canvas, 1774. Courtesy Museum of Early Southern Decorative Arts, Winston-Salem, North Carolina.

Circuit Court for the District of Vermont ——————————————
November 7, 1796   Rutland, Vermont

On November 7 the circuit court was convened by Associate Justice William Cushing and Judge Samuel Hitchcock.[1] Having concluded its business in one sitting, the court adjourned to the next term.[2]

1. This was the first time a fall session was held in Vermont. The session was added by "An Act altering the Sessions of the Circuit Courts in the Districts of Vermont and Rhode Island; and for other purposes," May 27, 1796. The Vermont circuit court would henceforth meet at Rutland in the fall and at Windsor in the spring. *Stat.*, 1:475.
2. Circuit Docket, CCD Vermont, RG 21, MWalFAR.

Circuit Court for the District of Georgia ——————————————
November 8, 1796   Augusta, Georgia

The Georgia circuit court commenced its session on November 8 with Associate Justice William Paterson and Judge Joseph Clay, Jr., in attendance. The court adjourned November 16 to the next term.[1]

Savannah-born Joseph Clay, Jr. (1764-1811), graduated from the College of New Jersey and studied law in Williamsburg under George Wythe. Clay rose to prominence as a lawyer in Georgia, playing an influential role in 1795 in revising the Georgia Constitution and later in drafting that state's constitution of 1798. In September 1796 Clay was given a recess appointment as United States judge for the district of Georgia, an appointment later made permanent by renomination on December 21, 1796, and Senate confirmation on December 27. Following the reorganization of the court system by the Judiciary Act of 1801, Clay was nominated in February of that year to be a judge on the Circuit Court for the Fifth Circuit. Although the Senate confirmed the appointment, he declined the position and then resigned his district judgeship in May 1801. Clay joined the Baptist Church in Savannah, where he was ordained in 1804, and subsequently moved to Boston, where he became pastor of the First Baptist Church.[2]

1. Minutes, CCD Georgia, RG 21, GEpFAR.
2. *DAB; SEJ,* 1:216-17, 218, 383, 385, 401; 30 F. Cas. 1367-68; *Stat.,* 2:89.

Circuit Court for the District of Rhode Island ——————————————
November 19, 1796   Providence, Rhode Island

On November 19 Judge Benjamin Bourne attended court but was unable to open it because of the absence of Associate Justice William Cushing.[1] On Monday, November 21, however, court was convened by Cushing and Bourne. Court adjourned on November 25.[2]

Judge Benjamin Bourne (1755-1808), a native of Bristol, Rhode Island, graduated from Harvard College in 1775. After service during the Revolution, Bourne read law with James K. Varnum and opened a law office in Providence. He was a justice of the Inferior Court of Common Pleas (1782); justice of the Superior Court (1784);

Benjamin Bourne by an unknown artist. Reverse painted silhouette, date unknown. Courtesy Mary Thurber Clark.

and a justice of the peace (1785-1789). Bourne also served as a representative in the state assembly and encouraged Rhode Island's ratification of the Constitution. A representative to Congress from 1790 to 1796, Bourne was given a recess appointment as United States judge for the district of Rhode Island in October 1796, an appointment made permanent by the Senate on December 22, 1796. In February 1801 Bourne was appointed one of the judges of the Circuit Court for the First Circuit under the Judiciary Act of 1801. That position was abolished by the Repeal Act of 1802, and Bourne returned to private practice.[3]

1. The date for holding the fall circuit court had been changed from November 7 to November 19 by passage of "An Act altering the Sessions of the Circuit Courts in the Districts of Vermont and Rhode Island; and for other purposes," May 27, 1796. *Stat.*, 1:475.

2. Minutes, CCD Rhode Island, RG 21, MWalFAR.
3. Helen Bourne Joy Lee, *The Bourne Genealogy* (Chester, Conn.: Pequot Press, 1972), pp. 59-61; *DAB; BDAC;* John C. Fitzpatrick, ed., *The Writings of George Washington from the Original Manuscript Sources, 1745-1799,* 39 vols. (Washington, D.C.: Government Printing Office, 1931-1944), 35:241, 244; *SEJ,* 1:216-17, 217, 381-83.

Circuit Court for the District of Virginia ———————————
November 22, 1796   Richmond, Virginia

Only David Meade Randolph,[1] the marshal of the district, was present at court on November 22. No judge attended this term, and Randolph adjourned the court on November 26.[2]

1. David Meade Randolph (1760-1830) of Presque Isle, Virginia, was appointed marshal for the district of Virginia in October 1791. *PTJ,* 22:219-20; *PGW, Diary,* 6:111; *SEJ,* 1:86, 88.
2. Order Book, CCD Virginia, Vi. Associate Justice James Wilson had been assigned the Middle Circuit this term and had tried to get James Iredell to take his place. Iredell declined in a letter to Wilson on August 20, 1796 (q.v.).

William Paterson to Euphemia Paterson ———————————
November 28, 1796   Raleigh, North Carolina

Raleigh, Monday,
28th Novr 1796.

My dear Affa —

On Saturday I reached this place, which is about 300 miles from Augusta. I am afraid, that the business will detain me near three weeks, which will throw me into winter on my way home. The court will open on wednesday. Raleigh is the seat of government in North Carolina, and has been built up in the course of a few years. The town is small, containing about 30 houses, and the legislature, consisting of about 200 members, are now in session, which renders it difficult to procure accommodations. From Raleigh to New Brunswick will count 520 miles —

At Wilmington, a town on the sea-board in this state, the yellow fever has been more malignant and mortal than any place I have heard of in the United States. It contains about 1,000 inhabitants; all left the town, that could conveniently do so; of those that remained at least one fourth were carried off by the disorder.

My love to Cornelia and Billy, and compliments to all friends. With wishes the most pure and fervent for your health and happiness

I remain your

Wm Paterson.

Mrs Paterson.

ARS (NjR, William Paterson Papers). Paterson appended the letter of November 28 to the one he wrote Euphemia on November 5.

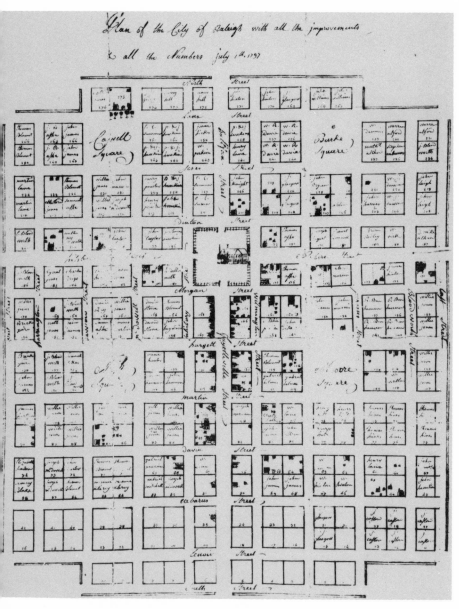

Plan of the City of Raleigh Pen and ink on paper, 1797. Courtesy Library of the University of North Carolina, Chapel Hill. Southern Historical Collection. The county courthouse, located on Fayetteville Street in the center of the block bounded by Davie and Martin Streets, was first used by the circuit court in June 1797.

Circuit Court for the District of North Carolina ⸺⸺⸺⸺⸺⸺
November 30, 1796   Wake Court House, Wake County, North Carolina

On November 30 court was opened by Associate Justice William Paterson and Judge John Sitgreaves. After completing its business the court adjourned December 3.[1]

1. Minutes, CCD North Carolina, RG 21, GEpFAR.

Spring and Fall Circuits 1797

The justices of the Supreme Court began their eighth year of circuit riding in an atmosphere of political turmoil. In the press, in broadsides, and in political cartoons, Federalists and Republicans were engaging in a rancorous debate over politics, government, and foreign affairs. Each side accused the other of betraying the ideals of the Revolution. "[T]he contests of that day were contests of principle," Thomas Jefferson recalled, "between the advocates of republican, and those of kingly government."[1]

The specter of war dominated much of American politics in 1797, due in large part to the ongoing deterioration of relations between France and the United States that began with ratification of the Jay Treaty. Events early in the new year offered no prospect of an improvement. The American minister to France, James Monroe, had been one of the few American officials to display sympathy for the French. Monroe's behavior, however, became too partisan for the administration, and it ordered his recall in December 1796. Outraged by this slight, the French refused to accredit the new American minister, Charles Cotesworth Pinckney, and ordered him out of France in late January 1797. Meanwhile, French ships increased their seizures of American vessels and cargoes. By March relations had become so strained that President John Adams, in office for only three weeks, called a special session of Congress for May 15, 1797. "The great theme of every man's inquiries," Fisher Ames declared, "is, are we going to war with France."[2]

The idea of war was anathema to Republicans. France, they proclaimed, would always be a beacon of liberty in a world of autocracy. Even the bloody Reign of Terror had failed to cool their ardor. Throughout the year, Republicans blasted Federalist calls for war with France. One withering criticism issued from the pen of Samuel Jordan Cabell, a Republican representative from Virginia. "*What! war* with *France? Impossible!*" Cabell thundered in a January 12, 1797, circular letter to his constituents. "[L]iberty and republicanism loudly forbid it—virtue, wisdom, and policy deprecate it—nay, even the very heavens themselves would feel indignant at the apostacy and denounce it."[3] Cabell also blasted the recent election of President John Adams. The

---

1. Thomas Jefferson, February 4, 1818. Ford, *Works of Jefferson*, 1:167. The quotation is taken from a group of papers commonly referred to as Jefferson's "Anas." For an essay and interpretation of the history of this collection of papers, see *PTJ*, 22:33-38.

2. William B. Allen, ed., *Works of Fisher Ames*, 2 vols. (Indianapolis: Liberty Classics, 1983), 2:1245; Samuel Flagg Bemis, *A Diplomatic History of the United States*, 3d ed. (New York: Henry Holt, 1950), pp. 111-14; Marvin Zahniser, *Charles Cotesworth Pinckney: Founding Father* (Chapel Hill: University of North Carolina Press, 1967), pp. 140-46; *Annals*, 7:50. Later in 1797, in an effort to repair the growing rift between France and the United States, President Adams appointed a special commission consisting of Pinckney, John Marshall, and Elbridge Gerry to secure a treaty of commerce and amity with France. The delegation would become embroiled in what is known as the XYZ affair, which is discussed in the introduction to "Spring and Fall Circuits 1798."

3. Noble E. Cunningham, Jr., ed., *Circular Letters of Congressmen to Their Constituents, 1789-1829*, 3 vols. (Chapel Hill: University of North Carolina Press, 1978), 1:69.

outcome, he declared, was enough to make "the patriotism of 76 and republicanism ... sicken—... O the depravity of the times!" he lamented. "O the corruption of the manners!"[4]

Cabell's missive raised Federalist ire. In a charge to a Virginia grand jury in May, Justice James Iredell warned of the need to protect "weak men" from being confused by political dissent, and reminded jury members that "any public officer, who has misbehaved, is liable to trial, punishment and disgrace."[5] Iredell added, however, that he knew of no specific actions that might be presented by the grand jury. The jury thought differently though, and issued a presentment denouncing "as a real evil the circular Letters of several members of the late Congress," particularly those of Cabell.[6]

The presentment unleashed a torrent of criticism from Republicans who claimed that Iredell had prompted the grand jury. "Our Congressional district is fermenting under the presentment of their representative by the Grand jury," Thomas Jefferson wrote to his friend John Francis Mercer.[7] For John Clopton, a Republican representative from Virginia, the presentment was "a dangerous encroachment on the liberty of opinion" that could "establish an alarming ascendancy in the judiciary over the popular branch of the legislature."[8]

The charges did not go unchallenged. Iredell denied ever seeing Cabell's circular, and Calohill Mennis, a member of the Richmond grand jury, claimed that he had planned to have Cabell presented well before hearing Iredell's charge.[9] Meanwhile, supporters rallied behind Iredell. At a dinner honoring North Carolina Congressman William Barry Grove on August 9, residents of Fayetteville toasted the embattled justice: "Judge Iredell—may the scales and sword of justice, never be influenced by a *Cabal*."[10]

Jefferson continued to view the presentment as a violation of the rights of free speech. Denouncing it as "a great crime, wicked in its purpose, and mortal in its consequences," the vice president drafted a petition that called upon the Virginia House of Delegates to impeach and punish the members of the grand jury.[11] In a letter to James Monroe, he complained that the presentment infringed on the "right of free correspondence" between the people and their elected representatives. "[I]t is not the breach of mr Cabell's privilege which we mean to punish," Jefferson declared. "[I]t is the wrong done to the citizens of our district."[12]

Although the Virginia House of Delegates did pass a resolution criticizing the presentment as "a violation of the fundamental principles of representation ... an usurpation of power ... and a subjection of the natural right of speaking and writing freely,"

4. Ibid., p. 70.

5. Iredell's charge to the Virginia grand jury was the same one he delivered earlier on the circuit in Maryland. See James Iredell's Charge to the Grand Jury of the Circuit Court for the District of Maryland, May 8, 1797.

6. See Presentment of the Grand Jury of the Circuit Court for the District of Virginia, May 22, 1797.

7. Ford, *Works of Jefferson*, 8:338.

8. Cunningham, *Circular Letters*, 1:96.

9. Letter of James Iredell, June 21, 1797, and Calohill Mennis to Samuel Jordan Cabell, June 15, 1797 (qq.v.).

10. *Gazette of the United States* (Philadelphia), August 28, 1797.

11. Ford, *Works of Jefferson*, 8:322-31.

12. Thomas Jefferson to James Monroe, September 7, 1797, James Monroe Papers, DLC.

no action was taken against the members of the grand jury. No prosecution was ever brought against Cabell either.[13]

The justices' perennial grievances about circuit riding continued in 1797, as did their efforts to reform it. References in their letters suggest the justices may have drafted the Circuit Court Act of 1797.[14] The act, passed on March 3, revised and streamlined the order of circuit riding in the Eastern, Middle, and Southern Circuits, but Congress struck a key provision from the justices' version of the bill.

That provision concerned the date and place for holding the spring session of the Delaware circuit court. In their draft bill, the justices planned to have Congress repeal that part of the District and Circuit Court Act of 1794 governing the date of the spring circuit court and reinstate the date first established by the Judiciary Act of 1789. They reasoned that the current sequence of riding circuit—New Jersey, Pennsylvania, Maryland, Virginia, and Delaware—was inconvenient to justices who lived in the south because they were required to ride north again to convene the Delaware court; there was also too long an interval between the Pennsylvania and Maryland court sessions. Instead, they proposed changing the date of the Delaware circuit court from June (after the Virginia court) to April (after the Pennsylvania court). The justices also wanted all of the circuit court sessions held at Wilmington, rather than alternately between New Castle and Dover, because of the greater volume of cases at Wilmington. Even after this provision in their draft bill was eliminated, the justices persisted in trying to effect the change, petitioning the president, Congress, and the governor of Delaware. Ultimately, the justices' petition to change the date of the Delaware court session was killed by the Senate, and the House refused to relocate the Delaware court from New Castle to Wilmington.[15]

The justices' problems with circuit riding paled in comparison to James Wilson's burgeoning financial woes. In the 1780s and '90s, Wilson had speculated extensively in undeveloped land in New York, Pennsylvania, Virginia, Kentucky, North Carolina, South Carolina, and Georgia.[16] By the mid-1790s, however, he and other speculators began defaulting on their loans. "Ruin is staring in ye faces of most of ye Land Speculators," warned Edward Burd of Philadelphia. "The Day of reckoning is at hand, and no prospect of disposing of their Lands."[17]

Wilson left Philadelphia during the summer of 1797 and failed to appear at the August term of the Supreme Court. "All the Judges are here but Wilson who unfortunately is in a manner absconding from his creditors," Iredell wrote to his wife Hannah on August 11. "What a situation."[18]

13. *Federal Gazette* (Baltimore), January 19, 1798. Jefferson drafted another petition in 1798, but state representatives set it aside to deal with the outcry over the Alien and Sedition Acts. Adrienne Koch and Harry Ammon, "The Virginia and Kentucky Resolutions: An Episode in Jefferson's and Madison's Defense of Civil Liberties," *William and Mary Quarterly*, 3d ser. 5 (April 1948): 152-54.

14. In a letter to James Iredell, Justice Chase commented that Congress had altered the Eastern and Southern Circuits "as We proposed." Samuel Chase to James Iredell, March 12, 1797 (q.v.).

15. Samuel Chase to James Iredell, March 12, 1797; Justices of the Supreme Court to John Adams, August 15, 1797; and Justices of the Supreme Court to Gunning Bedford, August 15, 1797 (qq.v.). See also Appendix B under "An Act concerning the Circuit Courts of the United States," March 3, 1797.

16. Charles Page Smith, *James Wilson: Founding Father, 1742-1798* (Chapel Hill: University of North Carolina Press, 1956), pp. 159-168, 382; Geoffrey Seed, *James Wilson* (Millwood, N.Y.: KTO Press, 1978), p. 161.

17. Edward Burd to Jasper Yeates, August 4, 1796, Lewis Burd Walker, ed., *The Burd Papers: Selections from Letters Written by Edward Burd, 1763-1828,* (Pottsville, Pa.: Standard Publishing, 1899), pp. 191-92.

18. *DHSC*, 1:290, 856.

Wilson's luck ran out in early September when two of his creditors, Simon Gratz and Isaac Hopper, caught up with him in Burlington, New Jersey and had him arrested and jailed.[19] The spectacle of one of America's premier jurists in prison for debt flabbergasted observers. "What shall we come to?" Thomas Shippen confided to his diary on September 3, 1797. "One of the highest Court in the United States, one of the 6 Judges in a Jersey Gaol!"[20]

After his release from prison, Wilson headed to North Carolina and Georgia to assess his property holdings and to attempt to reorganize his finances.[21] But his problems would persist. "The prospect before him is very gloomy," noted a prescient James Gibson. "[I]t is impossible at present to foretell the final issue."[22] Wilson's complicated financial affairs would leave the Supreme Court bereft of his presence into the spring and summer of 1798.

19. *James Wilson ads. Simon Gratz*, Docket #14913, and *Isaac Hopper v. James Wilson*, Docket #18293, Judiciary Records, Supreme Court, New Jersey State Archives, Trenton, New Jersey. The editors wish to thank Bette Barker of the New Jersey State Archives for her help in locating these documents.

20. Diary of Thomas Shippen, Shippen Family Papers, DLC. Wilson may even have been jailed in Philadelphia as early as September 1796. In a letter to Pierce Butler dated March 22, 1797, James Gibson, a Philadelphia attorney, noted that Wilson had been "in custody under an execution" in September 1796, and was "actually within the Prison." In December 1796, Congressman Chauncey Goodrich wrote his brother-in-law, Oliver Wolcott, Sr., " 'tis said that Judge Wilson has been to gaol and is out on bail." Goodrich, however, said he could not confirm the rumor. James Gibson to Pierce Butler, March 22, 1797, Pierce Butler Papers, PHi; George Gibbs, *Memoirs of the Administrations of Washington and John Adams, Edited from the Papers of Oliver Wolcott, Secretary of the Treasury*, 2 vols. (New York: W. Van Norden, 1846), 1:410.

21. James Wilson to Bird Wilson, December 17, 1797, and James Wilson to Joseph Thomas, December 17, 1797 (qq.v.).

22. James Gibson to Pierce Butler, March 22, 1797, Pierce Butler Papers, PHi.

Jeremiah Smith to William Plumer ———————————————————

February 13, 1797   Philadelphia, Pennsylvania

... M[r] Cushing told me last evening he imagined he would (M[r] E[1]) be assigned to the eastern Circuit _ In that Case you will have the pleasure of an acquaintance _ It is however doubtful whether M[r] Iredell or he will be the man. ...

ARS (Nh, Plumer Papers).

Jeremiah Smith (1759-1842) represented New Hampshire in Congress. In July 1797 Smith resigned his congressional seat for an appointment as United States attorney for the district of New Hampshire, a position he held until February 1801. *DAB; SEJ*, 1:249, 381, 383.

William Plumer (1759-1850), a lawyer and speaker of the New Hampshire House of Representatives (June-December 1797), was a resident of Epping, New Hampshire. *DAB; Laws of New Hampshire*, vol. 6, *1792-1801* (Concord, N.H.: Evans Printing, 1917), p. 390.

1. Chief Justice Oliver Ellsworth.

James Iredell to Hannah Iredell ————————————————————————

February 17, 1797   Philadelphia, Pennsylvania

... The middle Circuit is assigned to me _ The Eastern to M[r] ~~Chase~~ Elsworth _ The Southern to M[r] Chase. If you were only within 200 miles of me I could have spent some time at home on the vacation between the Courts. As it is, it would be silly to attempt it.[1] ...

ARS (Nc-Ar, Charles E. Johnson Collection). Addressed "Edenton, North Carolina." Postmarked "17   F[E?]."

1. A week earlier, Iredell had written that "The Circuits are not yet fixed, but I have great reason to hope I shall go the middle one." James Iredell to Hannah Iredell, February 9, 1797, Charles E. Johnson Collection, Nc-Ar.

Samuel Chase to James Iredell
March 7, 1797   Baltimore, Maryland

Baltimore.   7th March 1797.

My Dear Sir

I got Home safe in three Days, but the Cold I caught in Philadelphia has confined Me until a few Days ago. I see in the Papers that a law has passed respecting the Circuit Courts. I hope it was not materially altered.[1] I wish you would send Me a Copy._ I intend to embark from this City, for Savannah, about the first of next Month, but I suppose the Passage may be preformed, without Accident, in 14 Days. I shall be glad to receive Directions as to the Road, which will be governed by the new Law. If the Court is to be held at Charles Town I imagine I must come by Water from Savannah, but if at Columbia, by Land. in Columbia I shall want the Road to it from Savannah, & from Columbia to Raleigh. If in Charles Town then the Road from thence to Raleigh, & thence Home. I am anxious to see the Law. I shall also be obliged to you for the Names of the Judges, Marshalls, Clerks, and District Attornies, in Georgia, South, & North Carolina

I request you to accept my best Wishes for your Health and Happiness, and to believe, that I am Dear Sir,

With very great Respect & Esteem   Your Affectionate & Obed! Serv!

Samuel Chase

What will a pair of good Horses cost in Charles Town?

ARS (PHi, Gratz Collection). Addressed to Iredell "at   Mrs Yorke's North Front   near Arch Street _."

1. Chase is referring to the Circuit Court Act of 1797. For details of the passage of this act and its provisions, see introduction to "Spring and Fall Circuits 1797."

William Paterson to James Iredell
March 7, 1797   New Brunswick, New Jersey

... I acknowledge the receipt of your letter of the 4th of this month;[1] and am sorry, that any alterations have taken place in the bill concerning the circuit-courts. I wish it had passed in its original shape; but that not being the case we must make the best of it we can.[2] It is certainly right, that we should be accommodating to each other; for in this way we shall facilitate our official duty, and render its burden more supportable. I shall with much pleasure attend the court at Newcastle in your stead; but being ignorant of the day on which it is to be held, you will be pleased to ascertain the time, and inform me of it. If convenient, I shall be happy to see you with us for a few days before the opening of the court at Trenton. I returned from Philad.ᵃ with a bad cold, of which I am not yet entirely rid.

. . .

I have written to Judge Chase,[3] and inclosed the necessary route and directions. . . .

ARS (Nc-Ar, Charles E. Johnson Collection). Addressed to Iredell "At M.ʳˢ Yorke's N.° 62 North Second Street. Philad.ᵃ."
    1. Letter not found.
    2. For details of the provisions of the Circuit Court Act of 1797, see introduction to "Spring and Fall Circuits 1797."
    3. Letter not found.

Samuel Chase to James Iredell ————————————————————————
March 12, 1797   Baltimore, Maryland

                                          Baltimore.   12ᵗʰ March 1797 _
My Dear Sir
    Your very polite and friendly letters of the 3ʳᵈ, & 9ᵗʰ Instant,[1] are duly received; and I am greatly obliged to You for them. I intend to embark
                                      of next
from this City, about the first ₐMonth, for Savannah, which will allow 20 Days for the Passage; will this be Time enough, or will less be sufficient? I have been advised to come from Savannah to Charles Town, by Water. What is your Opinion? I take a Carriage with Me to Savannah, and, as at present advised, I propose to bring it with Me, by Water, to Charles Town; if I come by land I must purchase Horses at Savannah. which woud advise? _ if by Water ought I not (if in my Power) to ship my Carriage from there to Charles Town, to wait Me there? _ Can good Horses be purchased as reasonably at Charles Town as in Savannah; & what will probably be the Price of a proper Pair? _ As I am to go from Charles Town to Raleigh I wish to know if there is a line of Stages between those Places, and also from Raleigh to Peters burgh, or any other Place in Virginia, where a line is established to Maryland. I wish, if possible, to avoid the taking a Carriage, and the Purchasing of Horses. the trouble and Expence will be great, and I expect to be [word illegible] in Horses. I imagine the Road from Savannah to Charles Town is good, and no Way difficult to find _ is there no line of

Stages between those places? _ If You could procure Me ~~the~~ Directions of the Road from Charles Town to Raleigh I should be compleatly furnished, as Brother Paterson has been so obliging as to send Me the Road from Raleigh to Peters burgh. I believe there is a line of Stages from this City to Charles Town, but I beg You will enquire, & inform Me, for fear I should be disappointed in a Vessell from home. You can also learn how many Days it will take to go from this Place to Charles Town in the Stage. I give You a great Deal of trouble, but hope You will excuse Me. I fear the Journey, and am axious for Information _

The Law is some Improvement of the old System. the Eastern and Southern Circuits are as We proposed. the Arrangement of the Middle Circuit is certainly objectionable, & very inconvenient to Me, and most Oppressive on You, without any possible benefit to the public.[2] the Objection, that the Times of Holding the State Courts of Delaware had been altered to accord with the federal Courts as at present fixed, might have been very easily obviated by Commencing the proposed Change in the Circuit Courts of Delaware, in March 1798; before which time the State Legislature might regulate their State Courts. _ but why alternate the Circuit Courts between New Castle & Dover, especially the latter? why not stationary at Wilmington. there is little Business at either New Castle or Dover; and private Suits might be tried with Convenience to the Parties at Wilmington. I hope the Judges will memorialise on this Subject at August, & if We do I expect We shall succeed.[3] I wish that Baltimore only had been fixed in this State, because it would conduce to the Convenience of Jurors & Suitors, and the Dispatch of legal Business, none of which originates at Annapolis, & if the Court must sit there I wish it had been in the Fall of the Year. _ will the Law be forwarded to Georgia, South and North Carolina. if not Done the Juries will not be summoned. will You send Copies to the Judges.?

I wish You a pleasan[t cir]cuit, and a safe Return to Your Family and Friends and I remain, Dear Sir,

Your Affectionate & Obed.ͭ Serv.ͭ

Samuel Chase

ARS (NcD, James Iredell Sr. and Jr. Papers). Addressed to Iredell at "M.ͬˢ Yo[rke's] north Front Street   near Arch Street   Philadelphia." Postmarked "BALT-MAR-12."

1. Letters not found.
2. See introduction to "Spring and Fall Circuits 1797."
3. For a discussion of the justices' objections to the time of holding the circuit court in Delaware, see introduction to "Spring and Fall Circuits 1797."

James Iredell to Hannah Iredell ────────────────────
March 18, 1797   Philadelphia, Pennsylvania

... I shall probably not leave this City till early in May.[1] The Delaware Court which is within my Circuit, not being till after that in Virginia, I should have been greatly distressed had not Judge Paterson most obligingly, at my request, agreed to attend it for me. ...

ARS (Nc-Ar, Charles E. Johnson Collection).
   1. On March 17 Iredell had written to his wife that "Though I shall be absent a few days in Jersey I shall not leave this City for Maryland till the beginning of May." Charles E. Johnson Collection, Nc-Ar.

James Iredell to Hannah Iredell ────────────────────
March 29, 1797   Philadelphia, Pennsylvania

... The Court is to begin at Trenton next Saturday, and in this City on the 11 April, where I expect to be detained till the beginning of May. ...

ARS (Nc-Ar, Charles E. Johnson Collection). Addressed "Edenton, North Carolina." Postmarked "29 MR."

Circuit Court for the District of New Jersey ────────────────────
April 1, 1797   Trenton, New Jersey

Associate Justice James Iredell attended court on April 1, but adjourned it because the district judge, the federal marshal, and the jury were not present.[1] On Monday, April 3, the court opened despite the absence of the district judge, and Iredell delivered a charge to the grand jury. The court adjourned on April 4.[2]

   1. The date for holding the court was changed from April 2 to April 1 with passage of the Circuit Court Act of 1797. *Stat.*, 1:517.
   2. Minutes, CCD New Jersey, RG 21, NjBaFAR. Charge not found.

Circuit Court for the District of New York ────────────────────
April 1, 1797   New York, New York

On April 1 court convened with Chief Justice Oliver Ellsworth and Judge Robert Troup in attendance.[1] After the opening of the court, Ellsworth delivered a charge to the grand jury. The court adjourned on April 8 to the following term.[2]

Judge Robert Troup (1757-1832), a graduate of King's College, read law first with Thomas Smith of Haverstraw, New York and later with future Chief Justice John Jay. During the Revolution, Troup served as a lieutenant colonel in the Continental Army and then as secretary of the Board of War (1778-1779) and Board of Treasury (1779-1780). After the war, Troup completed his law studies under the tutelage of

Portrait of Colonel Robert Troup by Ralph Earl (1751-1801). Oil on canvas, 1786. Private collection.

another future Supreme Court justice, William Paterson, and opened a practice in Albany and New York City. At the time of his nomination as United States judge for the district of New York, Troup was the clerk of the federal district and circuit courts for New York. The Senate confirmed Troup's appointment on December 10, 1796, and he served as a federal judge until his resignation in late March or early April 1798.[3]

1. The Circuit Court Act of 1797 had changed the date of the spring circuit court from April 5 to April 1. *Stat.*, 1:517.
2. Minutes, CCD New York, RG 21, NjBaFAR; Oliver Ellsworth's Charge to the Grand Jury of the Circuit Court for the District of New York, April 1, 1797 (q.v.).
3. *DAB; PAH*, 20:381; 21:366; *SEJ*, 1:215, 269.

Oliver Ellsworth's Charge to the Grand Jury of the Circuit Court for the District of New York

April 1, 1797   New York, New York

Gentlemen of the Grand Jury _

Placed as guardians of the laws, you have in trust the government itself. A government, let me remark, entitled to affection, as well as support. _ A government legitimate in its origin, free in its principles, and tested by effects eminently benificent. If we look upon as it is, the pelladium of American liberty, and ground of national hope; our solicitude for its preservation will increase with the dangers to which it is exposed.

That fondness for novelty, and extravagant anticipation of good, which aided the government at its outset;[1] must, from an eight years experiment of what any government on earth could realize, have given way to disgust, & the project of some new theory.

Less to have been expected is the baleful influence of those elements of disorganization, & tenets of impiety, which have been propogated with a zeal that would have done honor to a better cause. Of the discipled many it is manifest, that, unhinged & imperious, the mind revolts at every institution which can preserve order or protect right; while the heart, demorallized, becomes insensible to social & civil obligations. _ So radically[2] hostile to free government, are the impassioned, & the impious![3]

It is further observable, that ~~the~~ evils which annoy us, by ^a^ disingenuous ascription to causes that have had no[4] agency in producing them, are made extensively the means of seduction.

With concern I add, that whatever of disaffection has[5] sprung from these sources, or the common incidents of government, or from untowardness[6] of temper, a spirit of party has not failed to cherish, to ripen, and to marshal. _ A spirit alas! which circumspection has been incompetent to prevent; and which mischief seems incompetent to satisfy. While it estranges[7] honest men, poisons the sources of public confidence, and palsies the hand of administration; it opens a door to foreign influence, that "destroying angel of republics."

If from these indications within, we derive an argument for vigilance & firmness in the execution of laws, how much is it strengthned by the convulsing aspect of ~~forreign~~ exterior affairs? Whether allured by caresses, or impelled by violence,[8] the object still is to seperate the people from the government. _ Yes the avowed object is to seperate the people from the government; and of course to prepare them by sedition[9] & rebellion, for a new order of things _ We trust in god that forreign government is not to prevail here; but without m~~ore~~ᴬ support & energy given to our own, our trust is ~~bu~~ᴬt presumption _

[Above "m~~ore~~": prompt] [Below line: mere]

You will now gentlemen, retire for consideration. You will diligently enquire after all offences cognizable by this court, and due presentment make. _ Should it be necessary, Mʳ Attorney will assist you with forms, or the court with further directions _ [10]

AD (CtHi, Ernest Law Papers). Date and place determined by comparing the text of the manuscript with newspaper printings of the charge Ellsworth delivered to the grand jury of the Circuit Court for the district of New York on April 1, 1797.

A cover sheet to this charge identifies it as "A charge of Chief Justice Ellsworth, while on the Supreme Court of the United States, delivered to a Grand Jury in North Carolina. Presented to the Conᵗ Historical Society by Wᵐ W Ellsworth July 17ᵗʰ 1841. The charge is in the hand writing of Judge Ellsworth." The cover sheet was written by William Wolcott Ellsworth (1791-1868), Oliver Ellsworth's son, but the editors believe that he erred in claiming that this charge was delivered at the North Carolina circuit court. Oliver Ellsworth rode the Southern Circuit only twice in his career as chief justice: in the spring of 1796 and of 1799. Oliver Ellsworth's Charge to the Grand Jury for the District of Georgia, April 25, 1796 (q.v.), does not parallel this manuscript. As it was common for justices to deliver the same charge at all courts on a circuit, it is likely that Ellsworth delivered a version of the Georgia charge at the North and South Carolina courts in 1796. Also, a passage in this manuscript refers to the "eight years experiment" of the federal government which would place the manuscript charge closer to the spring 1797 circuit than to the spring 1796 circuit. We wish to acknowledge the contribution of Kathryn Preyer in dating this document.

The charge to the New York grand jury was published in the *Argus* (New York), April 6, 1797; *Diary* (New York), April 6, 1797; *Claypoole's American Daily Advertiser* (Philadelphia), April 11, 1797; *Porcupine's Gazette* (Philadelphia), April 11, 1797; *New World* (Philadelphia), April 12, 1797; *Columbian Centinel* (Boston), April 15, 1797; *Connecticut Courant* (Hartford), April 17, 1797; *American Mercury* (Hartford), April 17, 1797; *Federal Gazette* (Baltimore), April 18, 1797; *Gale's Independent Gazetteer* (Philadelphia), April 21, 1797; *Virginia Argus* (Richmond), April 21, 1797; *United States Chronicle* (Providence), April 27, 1797; *Oracle of the Day* (Portsmouth, New Hampshire), April 27, 1797; *Rutland Herald* (Rutland, Vermont), May 1, 1797; and *North-Carolina Minerva* (Fayetteville), May 13, 1797.

Ellsworth also delivered this charge to the grand jury of the Circuit Court for the district of New Hampshire on May 19, 1797. The *Oracle of the Day* (Portsmouth), May 20, 1797, noted that the New Hampshire charge was the same as the one delivered at New York and already had been published in its April 27, 1797 edition. On June 16, 1797, Ellsworth delivered this same charge to the grand jury of the Circuit Court for the district of Rhode Island. The charge was published in the *Newport Mercury* (Newport, Rhode Island), June 27, 1797. Substantive differences between the manuscript and newspaper printings are noted.

1. Printed as "overset" in *Porcupine's Gazette* (Philadelphia), April 11, 1797; *New World* (Philadelphia), April 12, 1797; *Columbian Centinel* (Boston), April 15, 1797; and *Oracle of the Day* (Portsmouth, New Hampshire), April 27, 1797.

2. In *Claypoole's American Daily Advertiser* (Philadelphia), April 11, 1797, "readily."

3. In the *New World* (Philadelphia), April 12, 1797, and *American Mercury* (Hartford), April 17, 1797, appears as "imperious."

4. *Porcupine's Gazette* (Philadelphia), April 11, 1797, prints "an."

5. In *Claypoole's American Daily Advertiser* (Philadelphia), April 11, 1797, the phrase reads "whenever a disaffection had."

6. In the *North-Carolina Minerva* (Fayetteville), May 13, 1797, "outwardness."

7. In the *Argus* (New York), April 6, 1797; *Diary* (New York), April 6, 1797; *Claypoole's American Daily Advertiser* (Philadelphia), April 11, 1797; *Porcupine's Gazette* (Philadelphia), April 11, 1797; *New World* (Philadelphia), April 12, 1797; *Columbian Centinel* (Boston), April 15, 1797; *American Mercury* (Hartford), April 17, 1797; *Federal Gazette* (Baltimore), April 18, 1797; *Gale's Independent Gazetteer* (Philadelphia), April 21, 1797; *Virginia Argus* (Richmond), April 21, 1797; *Oracle of the Day* (Portsmouth, New Hampshire), April 27, 1797; and *North-Carolina Minerva* (Fayetteville), May 13, 1797, appears as "changes."

8. In the *Columbian Centinel* (Boston), April 15, 1797, and *Oracle of the Day* (Portsmouth, New Hampshire), April 27, 1797, "vigilance."

9. In the *New World* (Philadelphia), April 12, 1797, "seduction."

10. The *Newport Mercury* (Newport, Rhode Island), June 27, 1797, printing of the Rhode Island charge omits the last sentence.

James Iredell to Oliver Ellsworth
April 10, 1797   Philadelphia, Pennsylvania

Philadelphia   April 10th 1797.

Dear Sir,

I called at your lodgings the morning that you left the City, but unfortunately was too late to have the pleasure of seeing you. I wished very much to have delivered you a receipt I had prepared, and of which the above substantially is a Copy, with a variation as to the dates.[1] At Trenton only two Cases were to be decided, one by the Court, and the other by a Jury, both involving the great question as to Interest on British Debts. The Jury Case came on first, and was strenuously argued.[2] I was alone, and after time taken to consider charged the Jury (assigning my reasons particularly) in favour of the full Interest, but after being out two hours they found contrary to my direction. It was the case of a Bond to which Payment was pleaded, and upon which it seems it has been always usual for the Jury, not only in the State but the Circuit Courts in Jersey, instead of finding payment or no payment or a partial one specially, to assess the sum due _ A Rule returnable next Term to shew Cause why a new Trial should not be had was moved for and granted. Had the question come on immediately I should undoubtedly have ordered a new Trial. I gave Judgment however in the case where I was not controuled by a Jury according to my own sentiments, without deference to the Jury opinion which had over-ruled mine.[3]

I sincerely hope you have found all your Family well. On my return from Trenton I met the melancholy account of the death of an Uncle which has affected me very much.[4]

I am,   Dear Sir,   with great respect,   Your faithful and   obedient Servant

Ja. Iredell

ARS (PP, Hampton L. Carson Collection). Addressed "near   Harford   Connecticut." Postmarked "11   AP."

1. Receipt missing from letter.

2. *John Reid v. Daniel Covenhaven and George Taylor.* Minutes, April 1797 term, CCD New Jersey, RG 21, NjBaFAR.

3. *John Reid v. Executors of William Halstead.* Minutes, April 1797 term, CCD New Jersey, RG 21, NjBaFAR.

4. Thomas Iredell (d. 1796), a Jamaican planter and uncle of James Iredell, disinherited James for taking an oath of allegiance to America and left the bulk of his estate to Arthur Iredell, James Iredell's younger brother. *PJI*, 1:30n, 36n, 280; 2:423, 458-59.

Argus

April 11, 1797   New York, New York

The late charge to the Grand Jury, by the Chief Justice of the United States, has been cried up as a master piece in its way.[1]—For my part I like neither his politics nor his religion. They have a strong tincture of transatlantic prejudices, by means of which Europe has for ages past been kept in Chains. It has been the policy of Kings and Priests to stifle all enquiry; as their dominion is founded upon and preserved only by ignorance. Thus a free and manly investigation of public measures is stigmatized by the harsh epithets of "sedition and rebellion." The arcana of government must be studiously veiled from vulgar eyes. This sanctum sanctorum must remain forever shut against the swinish multitude, who must be taught to view it from a distance with stupid awe and reverence. "Sedition and Rebellion!" Sounds truly greeting and discordant to the ear of a republican. It is a language only fit to be spoken by tyrants to slaves.

But why conjure up these foul fiends *now*, when all parties seem heartily disposed to place due confidence in the integrity and ability of the *present* administration.

But what call of duty or necessity does our good Chief Justice obey, when he turns preacher and inveighs against impiety? Does he wish to revive again at this enlightened period, and among too the "most enlightened people in the world," the old confederacy between church and state?—What clause of the constitution gives the federal judiciary cognizance respecting religious tenets? Is it any part of the duty of a Federal Grand Jury to make *"diligent enquiry,"* whether the writer of this is Jew, Turk, or Christian?

By the "tenets of impiety, which have been propagated with so much zeal," I suppose, is meant Tom Paine's Age of Reason, which has spread so far and wide.[2] But what have government to do with theological disputes? In the name of peace, in the name of "social and civil," and let me add, religious toleration, let us leave these polemical champions to fight their own battles. Is the Chief Justice of the United States *seriously* shocked at the freedom of Paine's strictures against the religion he professes? Then let him fairly and manfully enter the lists against him. Let him sternly arrain him at the bar of Reason. In this court, when alone, his "offences are cognizable;" let him "diligently enquire," "and due presentment make." Here, if he shall be found guilty, he may be *safely* convicted and condemned, without endangering the peace and order of society.

But above all, is this a proper season, or, indeed, is it fitting at any season, for a Chief Justice of the United States to join the hue and cry of a party against the French nation or against any nation. Certainly a judicial officer wanders most egregiously from the line of his duty, when, in a charge to a Grand Jury, he undertakes to arraign, in terms the most opprobrious, the conduct of a great and powerful nation. It is a business with which Judges and Jurymen, as such, ought not to concern themselves.

Is the American character really so dull and stupid, so meek and spiritless, so devoid of iracibility and passion, as to make it necessary that the trump of war should be sounded from the seats of justice? How ardent must be the wish of a certain party for a war with France, when means so indecorous are resorted to.

(New York) April 11, 1797. Date and place are those of the newspaper.

1. See Oliver Ellsworth's Charge to the Grand Jury of the Circuit Court for the District of New York, April 1, 1797.

2. Thomas Paine (1737-1809), a revolutionary pamphleteer, published his two-part *Age of Reason* in 1794 and 1796. The pamphlet, which argued that the basic tenets of Christianity were incompatible with reason and insisted that science, not biblical scripture, was the source of "true theology," was sharply criticized as the work of an infidel and atheist. *DAB;* Eric Foner, *Tom Paine and Revolutionary America* (New York: Oxford University Press, 1976), pp. 245-49.

Circuit Court for the District of Pennsylvania ―――――――――――

April 11, 1797   Philadelphia, Pennsylvania

Associate Justice James Iredell and Judge Richard Peters convened court, and Iredell delivered a charge to the grand jury. On April 29 the court adjourned to the next term.[1]

1. Engrossed Minutes, CCD Pennsylvania, RG 21, PPFAR; James Iredell's Charge to the Grand Jury of the Circuit Court for the District of Pennsylvania, April 11, 1797 (q.v.).

James Iredell's Charge to the Grand Jury of the Circuit Court for the
District of Pennsylvania ———————————————————
Philadelphia Gazette
   April 11, 1797   Philadelphia, Pennsylvania

GENTLEMEN OF THE GRAND JURY,
   Though occasions like the present so frequently occur, yet so great is the
importance of the high trust reposed in you, that it never ought to be entered
upon without the most serious reflection on the duties it enjoins. The
administration of justice is in every particular deeply interesting to the
community; but, when it affects the life or liberty of any individual, by
inflexible laws, which either endanger the safety or promote the security of
all, it is a subject upon which no man can be indifferent, much less those to
whom that administration is entrusted. A sense of duty in a well disposed
mind, would, indeed, induce an equal endeavour to do justice in a single
case which could be productive of neither good nor evil as an example, and,
were the person who was the object of it no otherwise to be regarded, than
as an individual accused of a crime of which it remained to be proved that
he was guilty. An individual so circumstanced would, in the eyes of God
and man, be an object of consideration entitled to all the attention we could
bestow upon a fellow creature claiming the common rights of man, to be
deemed innocent until clear proof could be adduced against him. But, happy
is that country, where the security of each individual depends, not on a strict
and undeviating regard to justice alone, arising from a principle of moral
duty, which the passions of men are too apt to controul or weaken; but
where the security of each depends on the security of all, and no man can
do an act of injustice to another, however indifferent or even obnoxious to
him, without exposing himself, his family, or his friends to a danger of the
like injustice on some future occasion. The ties of interest thus co-operating
with the ties of duty cannot but have a most powerful effect.
   Whatever may be the condition of other countries, the situation of our
own has long been such that we must all stand or fall together. We have no
men distinguished by any exclusive political advantages from the rest of their
fellow-citizens; no one man, who possesses any political power, but such as
is held by the delegation of his fellow-citizens, and in trust for the whole of
which he himself is a part; none who will not feel the benefit of good laws,

(Philadelphia) April 17, 1797. Date and place are given in an introductory paragraph to the charge.
Readings in brackets taken from other printings of the charge.
   A number of newspapers reprinted Iredell's charge: *Federal Gazette* (Baltimore), April 19, 1797;
Claypoole's American Daily Advertiser (Philadelphia), April 20, 1797; *Gale's Independent Gazetteer*
(Philadelphia), April 21, 1797; *New World* (Philadelphia), April 21, 1797; *American Mercury*
(Hartford), May 1, 1797; *Pennsylvania Herald* (York), May 3, 1797. Substantive differences be-
tween printings are noted below.

and the mischief of bad ones. There is no office to which a competent responsibility is not annexed. We have thus every security against partial oppression, which can be provided by the laws of any community.

If ever any government was entitled to confidence, and the laws of any government to a cheerful and ready obedience, the government of the United States, and the laws enacted under their authority, surely are. In every stage of their progress, the people of these states have not only been nominally, but in reality the origin of all power. Representatives of the people in each state have established or sanctioned the governments of the several states, some of which have been since with equal solemnity and deliberation altered. Representatives of the people in each state have established the government of the United States, and this has been done by the unanimous concurrence of all the states in the union. These several solemn acts have, in every instance, taken place without tumult, or confusion, deliberately, voluntarily, uninfluenced by the artifices, unawed by the coercion of any foreign power, and owing their whole force and efficacy to the genuine good sense, moderation, patriotism and discerning foresight of the people themselves. The world had never before seen such an example, and certainly no people could undergo such various important and critical changes, with greater order, and a stricter degree of justice, than have uniformly characterised these illustrious scenes. Experience has justified the wisdom of their institutions. They have been found not only highly conducive to public prosperity, but the strongest support of individual and private justice. The political liberty and independence of our country have not only hitherto been preserved inviolate (God grant they may ever remain so!) but individual and personal liberty have been sacredly protected. The humblest condition is secure where no offence has been committed. The greatest cannot shield an oppressor from punishment.

Such, however, is the lot of man, so incessantly are exertions necessary to preserve as well as to acquire any good whatever, much more any lasting political good, that an indolent enjoyment of it is never permitted with impunity. Vice will ever be at war with virtue, and the selfish part of mankind constantly opposed to the generous and distinterested. An immediate good, though of the slightest kind, will often be preferred to the most important which is a little distant. Private interests will be magnified: Public ones, though unavoidably comprehending the latter, regarded as of comparative insignificance; and the prevailing indifference of scattered members of the community endanger not only the prosperity, but the safety of the whole. To counteract these tendencies, laws are necessary, compelling bad members of the community to do their share of the duty of the whole; providing not only for immediate, but guarding against remote dangers; consulting as much as possible the interest of each, but when necessary, without scruple,[1] making

---

1. The *Pennsylvania Herald* (York), May 3, 1797, omits "without scruple."

a lesser good subservient to a greater; and combining, in one general system, every practicable means of promoting the public welfare consistently with the personal safety, interest and happiness of each individual entitled to partake of it.

The laws of the United States, as contradistinguished from those of each state in the Union, have one characteristical mark of distinction. Every thing that concerns one state alone, is governed by the laws of that state. Every thing that concerns the United States, is governed by the laws of the United States. This principle no one can deny to be proper; but as the concerns of a single state are more simple and obvious than those of the union at large, they are apt to create a stronger attachment, and to be viewed with less jealousy than those of the other, as if one state could long be safe, much less prosperous, without a connexion with the rest in those great points upon which their common interest and safety unquestionably depend.

All the objects of the Union are undoubtedly of great importance, but none certainly are so critical as the relation of this country to foreign powers. The true desire of all men who love their country, and understand its real interest, must be to be upon friendly terms with all of them—to perform our duty faithfully to each whether arising from the law of nations generally, or any special treaties or conventions in particular, cordially to wish the success of liberty, justice and virtue, when struggling with oppression in any shape, or upon any pretences whatsoever, but to regard as our first duty the maintenance of the independence,[2] the defence of the honour, the pursuit of the interest of our own country, whose rights[3] we are, by the most sacred ties, bound to preserve, and whose interests (as is the case also with every other country) we are alone competent to decide upon. Not only history, but experience, must have convinced us, what erroneous ideas independent nations are apt to entertain of each other—How incompetent therefore they are for the most part, to judge of each other's situation and consequently that it is no less the dictate of prudence and wisdom, than of duty, to forbear any active interference with what does not particularly concern us, upon an idle conjecture of remote and imaginary contingencies, which are constantly eluding the foresight of the most sagacious of men. Nevertheless, as ambition is constantly active[,] as the rulers of nations are not always actuated by patriotism and duty alone, but in disregard of their real interest will frequently aim at the gratification of injurious and destructive passions, to the prejudice of the rest of mankind. A principle of self defence requires, that each government should be perpetually on its guard against the machinations of others and at the same time that [it] sacredly regard[s] the rights of other nations[,] be prepared to resist all attacks, and resent [all] insults committed

2. The *Pennsylvania Herald* (York), May 3, 1797, omits "the maintenance of the independence."

3. The *Pennsylvania Herald* (York), May 3, 1797, omits this word.

against its own. To [do] this with a proper mixture of temper and firmness, to preserve real independence without pride, to conciliate without meanness, and by a prudent forbearance, where forbearance is practicable, to leave an opening for[4] an honourable reparation where reparation can be made if any injury is committed, is a duty which all nations owe not only to the pe[ace] and happiness of their own country, but to mankind at large, which have had their origin in pride[5] or ambition alone without regard to any thing but the dictates of violent, impetuous passions, kept under no restraint, governed by no principle, and indulged without any remorse.

The constitution of our country fortunately guards us against wars of such a description, since our government can voluntarily[6] engage in no war, nor permit any act of hostility, but by the authority of the congress of the United States, who are so constituted as to form a most powerful check on the temporary ambitious delusion which at certain times unaccountably actuates even a people generally temperate and wise. Standing therefore for the most part upon the defensive, we stand upon fairer[7] ground than most other nations, and may have the satisfaction to hope, that if the peace of our country should be unhappily interrupted, it will be by the misguided ambition or unqualified injustice of some other government, and not provoked by any unwarranted hostilities of our own.

The congress of the United States having alone the authority to declare war, or permit any act of hostility, it is evident that until they exercise this authority, it is the duty of the citizens of the United States to forbear any hostile act to any power whatever. When any injury is sustained it will be proper to prefer a complaint to the government, which will undoubtedly bestow every possible attention to it; but what other proceedings the case may require must be left to the respective branches of the government, to whose discretion the proper remedy is confided. There can be no reason to doubt that every means will be pursued for relief which the nature of the case requires, and the condition and circumstances of our country admit of.

As there was reason to fear, early in the present unfortunate contest in

4. The *Pennsylvania Herald* (York), May 3, 1797, omits "an opening for."

5. On April 18, 1797, the *Philadelphia Gazette* published a correction to its printing of Iredell's charge, noting that "for 'mankind at large, which have had their origin in pride,' &c. read, 'mankind at large, *who have suffered incalculable evils from wars*, which have had their origin in pride,' &c." The *Federal Gazette* (Baltimore), April 19, 1797; *Claypoole's American Daily Advertiser* (Philadelphia), April 20, 1797; *Gale's Independent Gazetteer* (Philadelphia), April 21, 1797; *New World* (Philadelphia), April 21, 1797; *American Mercury* (Hartford), May 1, 1797; and *Pennsylvania Herald* (York), May 3, 1797, printed the charge with the corrected passage.

6. In the *Federal Gazette* (Baltimore), April 19, 1797, *New World* (Philadelphia), April 21, 1797, "warrantably."

7. Appears in the *Federal Gazette* (Baltimore), April 19, 1797; *Claypoole's American Daily Advertiser* (Philadelphia), April 20, 1797; *Gale's Independent Gazetteer* (Philadelphia), April 21, 1797; *New World* (Philadelphia), April 21, 1797; *American Mercury* (Hartford), May 1, 1797; and *Pennsylvania Herald* (York), May 3, 1797, as "safer."

Europe, that some of the citizens of the United States, unacquainted with the law of nations, and therefore ignorant of the duties incumbent upon them in a case altogether new to our country, or impelled by an unprincipled love of plunder, might dishonor the character of the government, and endanger the public peace, by giving hostile assistance to some one of the powers at war, a proclamation was issued by the president, informing all of the duties incumbent upon them in this important case, and of the consequences that would follow a disregard of them.[8] The object in effect was, to preserve that peace which the president was bound upon every tie of honor and duty to maintain inviolate to the utmost of his power, until congress thought proper (if they deemed it expedient at all) to authorise any species of hostility; to maintain, in short, due obedience to the laws of the country then actually in being. This proclamation, which for a time was the subject of an absurd clamour, of which most of the promoters seem at present to be heartily ashamed, had the decided approbation of both houses of congress, and the policy of it (which they alone could alter) they have persevered in to the present hour, notwithstanding all the artifices used to shake them from a purpose so essential to the country's welfare. But as it was highly expedient to enforce the observance of duties so important in their nature, and which too general a disposition had been shewn to disregard, the legislature thought proper, by an express law, to detail a series of prohibitions, which, though existing in effect,[9] might otherwise be the subject of doubt and controversy, and to substitute a precise and positive direction as to punishments for one too vague and indefinite to be regarded with equal confidence and respect. This law was passed in the year 1794 for a limited time, and at the last session was re-enacted with a further limitation.[10] As temptations may yet occur for its violation, and our legal condition is still the same as when the law was originally passed, and lately reinforced, and must remain so until congress shall think proper to alter it, I will read you its several provisions, recommending them earnestly to your attention as of the highest moment to be exactly observed.

(Here the provisions in the act were read.)

The observations I have made relative to circumstances at the present time are so highly important, that I thought them deserving of your attention, in preference to any other. It is full time that any men who have been deluded by inconsiderate foreign attachments of any kind, and in the fervor of their

---

8. The Neutrality Proclamation was issued April 22, 1793. *ASP, Foreign Relations,* 1:140.

9. In *Claypoole's American Daily Advertiser* (Philadelphia), April 20, 1797; *Gale's Independent Gazetteer* (Philadelphia), April 21, 1797; *New World* (Philadelphia), April 21, 1797; and *American Mercury* (Hartford), May 1, 1797, the phrase used is: "though existing in effect before." In the *Federal Gazette* (Baltimore), April 19, 1797, this phrase reads: "which I thought existing in effect before."

10. The Neutrality Act of 1794, passed on June 5, 1794, was continued for two more years on March 2, 1797, by the Neutrality Continuation Act of 1797. *Stat.,* 1:381, 497.

zeal lost sight of their own country, should seriously reflect on the duties they owe to it, and the great stake entrusted to them, as well as the rest of their countrymen, to preserve. God forbid that it ever should be said of the[11] United States that, after having succeeded in one of the noblest and most difficult contests ever maintained by men; after procuring unexampled freedom with a degree of order and justice unparalleled in the history of the world; after having peaceably submitted to irregular and imperfect governments of their own formation, though under many disadvantages both of a private and public nature; after establishing new ones calculated to remedy former defects, and undergoing this change, as well as all the former, with a moderation and order, surprising even to themselves, and which had never been supposed practicable before; after experiencing the most happy effects—effects exceeding her most sanguine expectations, from the last change (calculated to perpetuate their freedom and happiness, I trust for ages to come;) that in the wantonness of success, instead of preserving with vigilance what had been with so much difficulty and such extraordinary marks of providence acquired, they lost it all by an infatuated disregard of the most formidable danger to which their situation can never[12] expose them, that of foreign influence blindly yielded to by some, and supinely unattended to by others, until a fatal catastrophe involved them in one common ruin, a deplorable example of the vanity, presumption and folly of mankind! May God in his mercy preserve us from this ruinous and disgraceful fate, and on the contrary enable this country, in addition to other illustrious examples it has had the glory to exhibit, to present the spectacle of a people, who knowing what freedom is, and wishing and respecting independence in others, knowing how to preserve it themselves, and at all hazards will defend it against all attacks, whether covert or open, from without as from within, whatever force may annoy, whatever temptations may assail it!

11. At this point *Claypoole's American Daily Advertiser* (Philadelphia), April 20, 1797; *Gale's Independent Gazetteer* (Philadelphia), April 21, 1797; and the *Pennsylvania Herald* (York), May 3, 1797, also have "citizens of the."

12. In the *Federal Gazette* (Baltimore), April 19, 1797; *Claypoole's American Daily Advertiser* (Philadelphia), April 20, 1797; *Gale's Independent Gazetteer* (Philadelphia), April 21, 1797; *New World* (Philadelphia), April 21, 1797; *American Mercury* (Hartford), May 1, 1797; and *Pennsylvania Herald* (York), May 3, 1797, "ever."

Reply of the Grand Jury of the Circuit Court for the District of Pennsylvania

Philadelphia Gazette

April 11, 1797   Philadelphia, Pennsylvania

The grand inquest have listened to the charge, this day delivered by the court, with much pleasure; the sentiments therein contained are perfectly congenial with their own, and, they think, with the interests, honour, and happiness of the United States. Thus impressed, they take the liberty of requesting a copy, for the purpose of making it known to the public through the medium of the press.

J. COPPERTHWAIT, F.M.

April 11, 1797.

(Philadelphia) April 17, 1797. Date is that of the reply; place is determined by the location of the circuit court.

Circuit Court for the District of Connecticut
April 13, 1797   New Haven, Connecticut

On April 13 Chief Justice Oliver Ellsworth and Judge Richard Law opened the Connecticut circuit court,[1] after which a charge was delivered to the grand jury. The court adjourned on April 21.[2]

1. The date of the spring court had been changed from April 25 to April 13 by the Circuit Court Act of 1797. *Stat.*, 1:517.
2. Docket Book, CCD Connecticut, RG 21, MWalFAR. Charge not found.

James Iredell to Hannah Iredell
April 14, 1797   Philadelphia, Pennsylvania

...Our Court here began last Tuesday_ and will continue [*letters inked out*] probably through next week_ perhaps longer_ But I shall not leave this for Maryland till early in May, the Court beginning at Annapolis on the 7th Upon the 28th of this month, be so good as to direct to me at Annapolis. Upon the 5th of May to Baltimore. And afterwards to Richmond. You see I name the Post Days as a matter of course_ Tho' I believe I named Friday instead of Saturday. ...

ALS (Nc-Ar, Charles E. Johnson Collection).

Abigail Adams to John Adams
April 17, 1797   Quincy, Massachusetts

...I have just been reading chief Justice Elsworths Charge to the Grand jury at New York! did the good gentleman never write before? can it be genuine? the language is stiffer than his person, I find it difficult to pick out his meaning in many Sentences, I am Sorry it was ever publishd_ ...

ARS (MHi, Adams Manuscript Trust). Addressed "Philadelphia." Postmarked "1[9] A[P] BOST[ON]."
    Abigail (Smith) Adams (1744-1818), wife of John Adams. *DAB*.

Circuit Court for the District of Georgia ————————————
April 20, 1797   Augusta, Georgia

Court convened on April 20 with Associate Justice Samuel Chase and Judge Joseph Clay, Jr., in attendance.[1] The court adjourned on May 2.[2]

1. The Circuit Court Act of 1797 changed the date of the commencement of the court's session from April 25 to April 20. *Stat.*, 1:517-18.
2. Minutes, CCD Georgia, RG 21, GEpFAR.

James Iredell to Hannah Iredell ————————————————
April 21, 1797   Philadelphia, Pennsylvania

... I had fully intended writing to M[r] Tredwell and my Brother, as well as you, this post, but as I am to prepare a very important Opinion to be delivered this morning in Court by which I am to dismiss (as a single Judge, M[r] Peters being a party) 68 Ejectments, and the property of great value, it is utterly impossible, and they must excuse me.[1] ... Will you be so good as to get M[r] Tredwell to ask Wills[2] to publish the inclosed Sentiments of the Grand Jury and my Charge?[3] The President spoke to me in very flattering terms on the occasion.

Early the week after next I intend to set off for Maryland. ...

ARS (NcD, James Iredell Sr. and Jr. Papers). Addressed "Edenton, North Carolina." Postmarked "21   AP."
1. On April 21 James Iredell dismissed a total of seventy ejectment suits brought by the lessee of Solomon Maxfield (Maxwell), a Delaware resident, against Aaron Levy, David Evans, John McClure and Mathias Hollenbark, which had been brought to try title to land on Little Sugar Creek in Pennsylvania. Iredell ruled that the diversity jurisdiction had been fraudulently invoked by the real purchaser of the lands, Samuel Wallis, a Pennsylvania resident, solely for the purpose of gaining access to federal court, and that, therefore, the suits should be dismissed. Richard Peters, along with Timothy Pickering and Samuel Hodgson, claimed to be the rightful owners of the lands along Little Sugar Creek and were in the process of applying to the state of Pennsylvania to have their land patents signed by the governor. Although Maxfield's attorney, Joseph Thomas, made mention of an appeal to the United States Supreme Court for a writ of mandamus to the circuit court for the district of Pennsylvania to compel a jury trial, no such motion was ever made. Richard Peters, Timothy Pickering, and Samuel Hodgson to the Board of Property for the State of Pennsylvania, June 14, 1797, General Correspondence 1687-1882, Office of the Secretary of the Land Office, RG 17, PHarH; Engrossed Minutes, April 21, 1797, CCD Pennsylvania, RG 21, PPFAR; Joseph Thomas to the Board of Property for the State of Pennsylvania, June 10, 1797, General Correspondence 1687-1882, Office of the Secretary of the Land Office, RG 17, PHarH.
2. Henry Wills, publisher of the *State Gazette of North-Carolina* at Edenton. Brigham, *American Newspapers*, 2:760.
3. See James Iredell's Charge to the Grand Jury of the Circuit Court for the District of Pennsylvania, April 11, 1797; and Reply of the Grand Jury of the Circuit Court for the District of Pennsylvania, April 11, 1797.

John Adams to Abigail Adams

April 24, 1797   Philadelphia, Pennsylvania

... You and Such petit Maitres and Maitresses as you, are forever criticising the Periods and Diction of Such great Men as Presidents and Chief Justices. _ [1] Do you think their Minds are taken up with Such Trifles. there is Solid [keen?], deep sense in that Morsel of Elsworths _ You ought to be punished for wishing it not published. ...

ALS (MHi, Adams Manuscript Trust).
   1. See Abigail Adams to John Adams, April 17, 1797.

James Iredell to Hannah Iredell

April 28, 1797   Philadelphia, Pennsylvania

... Our Court is still sitting, owing to unexpected business,[1] but I imagine we shall break up to day. We were in Court yesterday from 10 till halfpast 8, with an interval only of half an hour. I preserve my health remarkably well. I propose leaving Town for Maryland on Wednesday next. ...

ARS (Nc-Ar, Charles E. Johnson Collection). Addressed "Edenton, North Carolina." Postmarked "28   AP."
   1. On April 28 the circuit court heard arguments on the habeas corpus petition of Francis Villato, who had been arrested and charged with treason for serving aboard a French privateer. The prisoner was discharged after both Iredell and Peters held that he was not a naturalized American citizen and therefore could not be charged with treason. *United States v. Villato, Dallas,* 2:370; James Iredell's notes on the Circuit Court for the district of Pennsylvania, under date of April 28, 1797, James Iredell Papers, Southern Historical Collection, NcU.

Circuit Court for the District of Vermont

May 1, 1797   Windsor, Vermont

Chief Justice Oliver Ellsworth convened the circuit court on May 1.[1] The court adjourned on that day to the following term.[2]

   1. With passage of the Circuit Court Act of 1797, the commencement date of the court was moved from May 12 to May 1. *Stat.,* 1:517.
   2. Circuit Docket, CCD Vermont, RG 21, MWalFAR.

James Iredell to Hannah Iredell

May 4, 1797   Baltimore, Maryland

... I arrived here two or three hours ago in perfect health, and am to go to Annapolis tomorrow. I was relieved from great anxiety on Tuesday by receiving your letters of the 15th and 22 April. Thank God that you were all then so well. I had barely time to get the things you wrote for last, but I did in the best manner I could _ I left in Mr Anthony's care the following Articles, as nearly as I can enumerate them _

> 1 Barrel Brown Sugar
> 100^lb Loaf Sugar
> 4 lb Tea (2lb. of each kind)
> 1 Barrel Madeira Wine.
> 1 Box Medicines
>   Garden seeds (in the Medicine Box)
> 3 pair Shoes
> 1 p^r black silk   ⎫
> 1 black Fan (I am afraid not a proper one) ⎬ for you[1]
> Some black ribbon   & black buckles   ⎭
> 5 yards Gingham   ⎫
> 6¾ yards clouded Muslin   ⎬ Annie and Helen
> 1 Dress, made by Miss Mease   For Annie
> 1 Doll, dressed by Miss [Sprugel?],   For Helen
> 1½ yard clouded Muslin _   For Peggy Tredwell
>   Ribbons
> 1 p^t Silk_∧_ For our own Girls, Peggy Tredwell, Jenny Hosmer,
>   and Fanny & Helen Johnston, if enough.
> 25 yards Linen _ & Cambrick _ (To have ruffles only to the bosom)
> 1 Box Raisins.
> 1 Box almonds
> 2 Cheeses _ 1 North Wiltshire _ 1 New England _
> Casimer[2] &c. to make Cloaths for James
> 2 doz green handled Knives & Forks
> 2 doz Wine Glasses
> 33¾ [word illegible] Gauze
> 4 wash basins
> 2 large Brooms
> 1 flesh brush
> 2 large scrubbing brushes
> 6 Chamber Pots.

I just perceive one or two articles omitted. I will try to get them by writing to Philadelphia. It was too late to get James a Book. I meant to get some Books for him & his Sisters, but really found my Cash run low. Tell Helen I could not get her a make believe Boy in the whole City I could much more easily have got her a sure enough one . . .

ARS (Nc-Ar, Charles E. Johnson Collection). Addressed "Edenton, North Carolina." Postmarked "BALT MAY 7."

1. James Iredell's uncle, Thomas Iredell, died in Jamaica in September 1796. Elsewhere in his letter of May 4 Iredell notes that although he will not receive anything from his uncle's

estate, "If agreeable to you I would rather wish you should wear mourning, as I do, lest it should be thought I slighted his memory as he left me no legacy."

2. "A thin fine twilled woollen cloth used for men's clothes." *OED* under Cassimere.

Circuit Court for the District of South Carolina
May 6, 1797   Charleston, South Carolina

Court was opened by Associate Justice Samuel Chase and Judge Thomas Bee on May 6 in Charleston.[1] Chase delivered a charge to the grand jury on May 9, and court adjourned on May 16.[2]

1. The date for holding court had been changed from May 12 to May 6 by the Circuit Court Act of 1797. The act also provided that the circuit court be held only in Charleston, eliminating Columbia from the circuit. *Stat.*, 1:517-18.
2. Minutes, CCD South Carolina, RG 21, GEpFAR. Charge not found.

Circuit Court for the District of Maryland
May 8, 1797   Annapolis, Maryland

Only Associate Justice James Iredell attended court on Monday, May 8. After he opened court, Iredell delivered a charge to the grand jury. The court adjourned the following day to the next term.[1]

1. Minutes, CCD Maryland, RG 21, PPFAR; James Iredell's Charge to the Grand Jury of the Circuit Court for the District of Maryland, May 8, 1797 (q.v.).

James Iredell's Charge to the Grand Jury of the Circuit Court for the District of Maryland
Maryland Gazette
May 8, 1797   Annapolis, Maryland

Gentlemen of the Grand Jury.

THE frequent returns of courts of justice necessarily[1] occasion us to reflect on the origin from which they flow. However painful such review may be to some nations, to us it can afford nothing but satisfaction and gratitude. We trace the origin of ours as well as of every other authority to the purest source from which any authority can be derived, the spontaneous but

(Annapolis) May 18, 1797. Date and place are given in an introductory paragraph to the charge.

An extract of the charge was published by the *Federal Gazette* (Baltimore), May 22, 1797.

On May 22, 1797, Iredell delivered virtually the same charge to the Circuit Court for the district of Virginia. That charge was printed in the *Virginia Independent Chronicle* (Richmond), May 24, 1797. Substantive differences between the Maryland and Virginia charges are noted below.

1. The *Virginia Independent Chronicle* (Richmond), May 24, 1797, printed "naturally."

deliberate grant of the people themselves for whose benefit it is established. Liberty, to a considerable degree, had subsisted in other ages and other countries, but such an exercise of it as this (notwithstanding the fanciful opinion of some ingenious writers) probably first took place in our own. The attempt was noble, and the success hitherto has been beyond all expectation. Whether its blessings are to be preserved or lost, must in no small degree depend on the conduct of the people themselves.

If they wish for good laws, they must choose able and disinterested men to make them. If they wish for officers adequate to their stations in the other departments of government, it is in their power directly or indirectly to secure them by a discreet and judicious exercise of the choice with which they are invested. If in any particular their confidence should be abused, a plain and adequate remedy is provided. After a stated interval their legislators may be changed. Without any delay, but such as the occasion must require, any public officer, who has misbehaved, is liable to trial, punishment and disgrace. To this may be added, what probably is not the weakest restraint, the general odium that must attend a manifest departure from duty in an important public employment.

The people at large having these securities for the faithful discharge of offices of public trust, it is fit that those whom they select as their officers should have some security on their part. It is not to be presumed that men, chosen as they are, should be remarkably deficient either in ability or integrity, and therefore they have a right to expect that their conduct should not immediately be condemned, merely because some persons are ready to find fault with it. The task they have to perform is of no common magnitude both as to difficulty and importance. If in the small concerns of private life few men can conduct themselves with strict regularity and exactness, and unexpected difficulties will disconcert even the most orderly and discreet, can we conceive the path perfectly plain and obvious for the government of millions of men, who, though possessing one common and united interest, have an infinite variety of private views tending to divert them from the great object of union, even if their understandings and dispositions were perfectly alike? But if to this we add the various degrees of their understanding, their different means of improvement and information, the delusive and dangerous passions by which many are guided, the activity of bad citizens, the supineness of good, until some critical alarm alike actuates both to a struggle which may endanger the government at the moment when its utmost energies are necessary, we cannot wonder at the diversity of opinion which prevails in respect to most public measures, nor at the consequences which follow from rival sentiments, too apt to disturb the temper even of the best minds, but which unavoidably give a full scope to the passions of weak, arrogant, or unprincipled men, who either make no allowances for difficulties which weak minds never perceive, or from an excess of vanity and presumption, suppose none can surmount them but themselves, or with views too base to be avowed, hesitate not to gratify malignant propensities of their own,[2] without the slightest independent regard to the honour, the interest, or even the safety of their country. Such causes most often produce great agitation in any country, but must operate with increased and dangerous vigour in one, like our own, composed of many powerful states, to a great degree independent of each other, having either real or imaginary differences of local interests, and with little other effectual cement to bind them together, but a sense of foreign external danger, which, with respect to many, will be apt to operate but too weakly until it has increased to a magnitude which astonishes and confounds them.

Considerations like these are calculated to impress upon the mind that salutary caution with which all public measures ought to be examined. If it be a point of duty or justice, we need inquire no further. Policy is out of the question: The duty must be performed—justice must be satisfied at all risks. Men would be forever unjust, and morality would be a name, if exceptions were once admitted upon any principle whatever to a strict observance of it. If a subject of policy is in question, nothing affords greater room for real differences of opinion. The wisest men, with the best motives, have been always divided upon such questions, and always will be—because nothing is more fallible than human judgment, when it extends its views into a futurity for the greatest part so impenetrably hid from the sight of man. All political measures must be grounded on such views, and consequently must partake of the imperfection of the grounds on which they are adopted. Diffidence, therefore, as to any point of policy, is becoming the ablest men, and in reality they are, for the most part, the best disposed to entertain it. Some mode of decision, however, must take place. Can we desire a better than that it should be such a decision as the people themselves have deliberately thought best adapted to the case? It is indeed, as well as all other political subjects, a natural and proper object of their review: for their own sake, that review ought to be conducted with temper and moderation.[3] Before they condemn any one measure, where some measure was necessary, they ought to be very sure that a better could be adopted. None can ever be adopted without some inconveniencies—Few, perhaps, without some advantages. It is the part of wisdom to weigh one against the other, and decide in favour of that measure where the advantages are greatest, the inconveniencies fewest. Any other mode of considering great questions of public policy is idle and insignificant. If after all, any individual disapproves of the voice of his country, what does duty and common modesty require of him? To be perfectly confident he is right in his opinion, and those

---

2. In the *Virginia Independent Chronicle* (Richmond), May 24, 1797, this reads "malignant or groveling purposes of their own."

3. In the *Virginia Independent Chronicle* (Richmond), May 24, 1797, "lest they should themselves suffer by a precipitate and erroneous judgment" was added to this sentence.

intrusted, to decide are wrong! Who is the man entitled to so arrogant an estimation of his own abilities? Is he rashly to determine that the measure has been adopted from some dishonest motive? What right has any one man to charge another with dishonesty without proof? Let him prove and punish if he can—If he can do neither, but will throw out calumny at random,[4] he must stand in the view of his fellow-citizens as a slanderer, and incur the suspicion that his readiness to suspect others of dishonourable intentions, has probably arisen from something in the texture of his own mind which led him to ascribe worthless motives as the most natural inducement of action. The part surely for every man who loves his country, but who disapproves of any public authoritative decision, is to submit to it with diffidence and respect, considering the many chances there are that his own opinion may be really wrong, though he cannot perceive it to be so; that whether it be or not he does not live in a despotic government where any one man's opinion, not even his own, is to decide for all others; and that the very basis of all republican governments in particular, is, the submission of a minority to the majority, where a majority are constitutionally authorised to decide. For a man to call himself a republican without entertaining this sentiment, is folly. To be one, without acting upon it, is impossible.

Since, therefore, the plainest dictates of duty, and the principles of republicanism itself, which in their due application ennoble the human mind, though nothing can more disgrace it than the abuse of them, require of us all to obey the laws of our country, it is incumbent on us to take care that an obligation so important be not rendered merely nominal, but that every individual shall perform his share of the common trust, or answer for his neglect of it. Many instances of neglect or indifference towards it, which may have great effects on the happiness of his country, are of a nature not punishable by human laws, and the punishment of them, therefore, must be left to the conscience of the individual, and the reproach which a violation of the rules of morality, though unaccompanied by any human sanction, seldom fails to draw upon it. There are, however, others of so serious a nature, and so directly tending either to destroy or injure the society at large, that laws are provided by it for their punishment; and without such laws, and a due execution of them, no society could subsist, for an idea that all men will support voluntarily any government, however excellent, or cheerfully obey any laws, however wise, is ridiculous. But as it is of great moment to establish some laws containing penal sanctions, so it is also of the highest importance that the execution of these should be provided for in such a manner, as to secure as much as possible the conviction only of the guilty, leaving innocence nothing to fear. The mode of prosecution so long adopted

---

4. The *Virginia Independent Chronicle* (Richmond), May 24, 1797, prints "but will indulge in atrocious calumny."

in our country probably contains this security in its utmost extent; accusation by one jury—trial by another—the trial being altogether public—witnesses adduced face to face—the prisoner under no restraint but from mere confinement—challenges to a considerable number in all capital cases to set aside jurors even for momentary dislike—the jury not being a permanent, but an occasional body, liable to be affected[5] either as members of the community, or as individuals who may be subjected to a similar prosecution, by their own precedents—All these circumstances probably provide as great a security for innocence as is compatible with avoiding a total immunity for guilt. With us, happily, this is no theoretic speculation: None of us can remember a time when these privileges were not in a great degree familiar to us; so familiar indeed, that knowing scarcely any thing of oppressive prosecutions, but from the history of other countries, we are too apt to undervalue this inestimable blessing in our own.

To you, gentlemen, are committed prosecutions for offences against the United States. The object is the preservation of a union, without which undoubtedly we should not now be enjoying the rights of an independent people, and without the support of which it is in vain to think we can continue to enjoy them. This country has great energies for defence, and by supporting each other might defy the world. But if we disunite, if we suffer differences of opinion to corrode into enmity, jealousy to rankle into distrust, weak men to delude by their folly, abandoned men to disturb the order of society by their crimes, we must expect nothing but a fate as ruinous as it would be disgraceful, that of inviting some foreign nation to foment and take advantage of our internal discords, first making us the dupe and then the prey of an ambition we excited by our divisions, and to which those divisions if continued, must inevitably give success. So critical and peculiar is our situation, that nothing can save us from this as well as every other external danger, but constant vigilance to guard against even the most distant approaches of it, and being at all times ready to provide adequate means of defence. Our government is so formed, that that vigilance can always be exerted, and those means when necessary be drawn forth. To rely upon these is not only our indispensable duty, but the only chance of securing that union of spirit and exertion without which in a moment of danger no efforts can be of any avail. For 21 years that union has preserved us through multiplied dangers, and more than once rescued us from impending ruin. I trust it will still display itself with its wonted efficacy, and that no threats, no artifices, no devotion to names without meaning, or professions without sincerity, will be capable of weakening, by any impression on a sensible people, a cement essential to their existence.

I have troubled you with this address, gentlemen, on account of the

---

5. In the *Virginia Independent Chronicle* (Richmond), May 24, 1797, "associated."

extreme importance of the matter of it at the present moment.[6] The sentiments have flowed warmly from my heart, and I flatter myself are not uncongenial to your own. The present situation of our country is such as to require the exertion of all good men to support and save it. I enter into no particulars, as the legislature of the United States are on the point of meeting, and for whose decision every worthy citizen must wait with solicitude and respect.[7] In the mean-time it is of the utmost consequence that every man should sacredly obey the laws of the country actually in being. They cannot be altered, nor the observance of them in any instance dispensed with, without the authority of the congress of the United States, in any exigence, however great, in any situation, however alarming. There is no occasion to doubt, but that the whole proceedings of that most respectable body, will be conducted with a degree of temper and firmness, suited to the important and trying situation which called them together, and that the great object of all their deliberations will be, if possible, to preserve the peace, at the same time that they maintain inviolably, the honour, the interest, and the independence of their country.

6. In the *Virginia Independent Chronicle* (Richmond), May 24, 1797, this sentence was omitted and the following put in its place: "I deliver this general address, not knowing of any particular offences likely to come before you."

7. On March 25, 1797, President Adams issued a proclamation calling for Congress to meet in special session on May 15 to consider the deteriorating relationship of the United States with France. See introduction to "Spring and Fall Circuits 1797."

James Iredell to Hannah Iredell

May 12, 1797   Annapolis, Maryland

...I have been here now just a week, and am to leave Annapolis to morrow, expecting to be in Richmond on Friday next. Our Court here lasted only two days. My health is very good, and I have passed my time here as agreeably as I could expect in so declining a place. The Governor[1] and M.[r] Carroll's[2] Family in particular have been very attentive to me...

ARS (NcD, James Iredell Sr. and Jr. Papers). Addressed "Edenton, North Carolina." Postmarked by hand "Annapolis May 12."

1. John Hoskins Stone (ca. 1750-1804), governor of Maryland from November 20, 1794, to November 13, 1797. Frank F. White, Jr., *The Governors of Maryland, 1777-1970*, publication no. 15 (Annapolis: Hall of Records Commission, 1970), pp. 33-36.

2. Charles Carroll of Carrollton, whom Iredell had first met while riding circuit in the spring of 1791. James Iredell to Hannah Iredell, May 9, 1791, *DHSC,* 2:162.

John Hoskins Stone by Rembrandt Peale (1778-1860). Oil on canvas, 1797-1798. Courtesy Anglo-American Art Museum, Baton Rouge, Louisiana. Gift of an Anonymous Donor.

Oliver Ellsworth to Oliver Wolcott, Jr. ————————————————————

May 14, 1797   Springfield, Massachusetts

ed
... Since leaving Philadelphia, I have attend₍courts in New York, Connecticut & Vermont, and been in the western parts of Massachusetts & New Hampshire; and found every where an increased & increasing attachment to the government; and I have no doubt that any measure which, in the present crisis, it may judge expedient to adopt, will have general acquiescence & support from this quarter of the Union. ...

ARS (CtHi, Oliver Wolcott Jr. Papers). Addressed "Philadelphia."

Circuit Court for the District of New Hampshire ————————————

May 19, 1797   Portsmouth, New Hampshire

On May 19[1] Chief Justice Oliver Ellsworth and Judge John Pickering convened the court, and Ellsworth delivered a charge to the grand jury. The court met again the following day before adjourning to the next term.[2]

   1. The date for holding court had been changed from May 27 to May 19 by the Circuit Court Act of 1797. *Stat.*, 1:517.
   2. Records, CCD New Hampshire, RG 21, MWalFAR; Oliver Ellsworth's Charge to the Grand Jury of the Circuit Court for the District of New Hampshire, May 19, 1797 (q.v.).

Oliver Ellsworth's Charge to the Grand Jury of the Circuit Court for the District of New Hampshire ————————————————————

May 19, 1797   Portsmouth, New Hampshire

[*According to a report in the May 20, 1797, issue of the* Oracle of the Day *(Portsmouth, New Hampshire), on May 19, 1797, Chief Justice Ellsworth delivered "a charge to the Grand Jury, in the form published in our paper of 27th ult." On April 27, 1797, the newspaper had printed a copy of a charge that Ellsworth had delivered to a grand jury in New York on April 1, 1797. For the text of that charge, see Oliver Ellsworth's Charge to the Grand Jury of the Circuit Court for the District of New York, published above under date of April 1, 1797.*]

Circuit Court for the District of Virginia ————————————————

May 22, 1797   Richmond, Virginia

Court was convened by Associate Justice James Iredell and Judge Cyrus Griffin, and Iredell delivered a charge to the grand jury. The court adjourned on June 7 to the following term.[1]

1. Order Book, CCD Virginia, Vi; James Iredell's Charge to the Grand Jury of the Circuit Court for the District of Virginia, May 22, 1797 (q.v.).

James Iredell's Charge to the Grand Jury of the Circuit Court for the District of Virginia
May 22, 1797   Richmond, Virginia

[*On May 22, 1797, Iredell delivered to the grand jury in Virginia the same charge he gave at the Maryland circuit court on May 8. For the text of that charge, see James Iredell's Charge to the Grand Jury of the Circuit Court for the District of Maryland, published above under date of May 8, 1797.*]

Presentment of the Grand Jury of the Circuit Court for the District of Virginia
May 22, 1797   Richmond, Virginia

John Blair foreman,[1] Thomas Griffin Peachy, Otway Byrd, Thomas Thompson, Corbin Griffin, Richard Randolph, John Gibson, John Mc Crea, Thomas Newton, Edward Hack Manley, Robert Pollard, Joseph Selden, Robert Burton, Andrew Donald, Calohill Minnis, Thomas Tinsley and William Vannerson were sworn the grand Inquest for the body of this District who having received their charge ̭ returned with the following Presentment, "We of the grand Jury of the United States for the District of Virginia, present as a real evil the circular Letters of several members of the late Congress, and particularly Letters with the Signature of Samuel J: Cabell, endeavoring at a time of real public danger, to disseminate unfounded calumnies against the happy Government of the United States, and thereby to separate the people therefrom, and to encrease or produce a foreign influence ruinous to the peace, happiness and independence of these United States." on which they were discharged.[2]

D (Vi, CCD Virginia, Order Book).
1. Former Associate Justice John Blair. See letters from "Scaevola" to James Iredell, June 11, 1797, and "Timothy Tickle" to Samuel Jordan Cabell, July 5, 1797, where mention is made of there having been a judge on the bench and a judge in the jury room; and Peregrine Fitzhugh to Thomas Jefferson, June 20, 1797.
2. For background on the controversy involving Virginia Congressman Samuel Jordan Cabell, see introduction to "Spring and Fall Circuits 1797."

James Iredell to Hannah Iredell

May 25, 1797   Richmond, Virginia

... Though I arrived here on Friday last it was too late to write by the Post, which I suppose arrived yesterday in Edenton. ...

... You will find by a Presentment of our Grand Jury composed of many of the most respectable Men in the State a temper highly suitable to our present situation. There is such an immensity of business to do here that I cannot even conjecture when I can get away. For a great deal of it I am to thank Judge Wilson who suffered the Court last Term to be entirely lost by his non-attendance. I expect to be detained at least a fortnight or 3 weeks, for I am resolved to leave no neglect chargeable on me, anxious as I am beyond expression to be with you and our dear Children. ...

ARS (Nc-Ar, Charles E. Johnson Collection). Addressed "Edenton, North Carolina." Postmarked "RICHMOND, *May* 24 1797." We do not know why the postmark reads May 24 while the letter is dated May 25.

Oliver Ellsworth to Oliver Wolcott, Jr.

May 29, 1797   Boston, Massachusetts

                                                              Boston   May 29. 1797
Dear Sir,

Since writing you from Springfield, I have attended Court at Portsmouth; and have now been some days at this place._ The President's speech is well received, and if well answered by both Houses, as we expect, will do much good at home & abroad._ I repeat, that neither Congress or the Executive, need hesitate about any proper measures from an apprehension that public opinion & spirit will not support them. There is still however that diversity of opinion among the best of men as to the measures expedient to be taken, that I can give no useful information on that point, and perhaps went too far in the conjecture I hazzarded in my former Letter._ [1]

Truly your's

                                                              Oliv Ellsworth

Mr Wolcott

ARS (CtHi, Oliver Wolcott Jr. Papers). Addressed "Philadelphia." Postmarked "30   MA BOSTON."

1. A reference to the continuing deterioration of relations with France, which had prompted President Adams to call a special session of Congress. In a letter to Wolcott written on May 14, Ellsworth had mentioned the possibility of imposing an embargo against France while sending a special envoy to Paris to negotiate a resolution of differences between the two countries. Oliver Wolcott Jr. Papers, CtHi. See also introduction to "Spring and Fall Circuits 1797."

Letter of Samuel Jordan Cabell ——————————————————
Aurora
  May 31, 1797   Philadelphia, Pennsylvania

                                        Philadelphia,   May 31, 1797.
Fellow Citizens,
  THE charge of Judge Iredell to the jury at Richmond, and the consequent
presentment of myself and others[1]—I have lately read with every sentiment
of indignation which could be inspired in the bosom of a free man: If my
countrymen do not feel the same resentment it must be because they have
forgotten those sentiments so favourable to the freedom of opinion which a
few years ago we fought and bled for. The judiciary institutions of the United
States are valuable only as they tend to preserve the public peace and
individual rights, by a regular and just execution of the laws:—If no law has
been violated, there can be no business for the federal judiciary, and it is as
yet a feature of liberty we enjoy, that no law has made it culpable to entertain
or to express our opinions either in matters of religion or politics; It has,
however been a regular practice of the federal judges, to make political
discourses to the grand jurors throughout the United States: They have
become a band of political preachers, instead of a sage body to administer
the law:—They do not complain of violations of any law and point out the
true course of redress, but they complain of opinions which they seem to
think tend to defeat their system of politics; the next thing I suppose will
be, their system of religion. They seem to be making use of their power
and influence both personally and officially to control the freedom of
individual opinion, and these things excite a suspicion that if they are
continued, the time will come, when men of different political and religious
sentiments from the judges, will not find that easy access to justice which
those of different opinions may expect. Besides the impropriety of these
kind of charges to jurors as they are a departure from the immediate province
of the judges—they shew a political influence over the judges by the
executive, which is calculated to do irretrievable harm. Judge Iredell's charge
at Richmond not only countenances these remarks, but will give rise to the
most serious train of reflections, that can engage the mind of any man devoted
to the freedom of opinion.—The jury who acted under this charge, appear
by their presentment to have considered it as an authority for censuring the
independence of private opinion. They have presented as a real evil the
circular letters of several members of Congress, without name, and particularly
mine by name, because they disseminate unfounded calumnies against the
government, tending to separate the people from it, and increase or produce
a foreign influence. If these letters contained calumnies that were illegal—If
they produced, or increased a foreign influence in our country contrary to
law, the authors were fit subjects for a presentment and for punishment.
The omission to present the authors as culprits, and confining presentment

to the opinions contained in the letters, afford the most unanswerable proof that these letters were not the evidences of any illegal act; if they were, neither the court or jury seem to have understood the proper manner of doing their duty; if they were not they have judicially animadverted upon the freedom of opinion, with a view either to suppress it, or to counteract its beneficial effects. At a distance from my constituents, charged with their best interests, and bound to give them such information relative to their public concerns, as I possessed, I never before knew it was criminal to execute this duty. If I have written falsely with a view to deceive my countrymen, why did not this enlightened jury state the facts which I have misrepresented? I could then have acquitted myself by the proofs I possess; but when they attack my political opinions, which are but the result of facts, they do but oppose opinion to opinion. If they can draw better conclusions from all necessary evidence relative to the points upon which I have spoken than myself, they should have presented to you that course of reasoning by which they were satisfied, and thus by addressing themselves to your judgments have satisfied you in opposition to the opinions which I have given; but this would not have answered their purpose. They were armed with an awful power, and a naked presentment succeeding a political charge from the bench was better calculated to overawe than a manly course of argument. I need not say to my fellow citizens, that I love my country and will support its government, upon the principles of a freeman:—I do not believe any branch of its administrators is infallible, and whenever they appear to me to incroach on the principles which are necessary to support our freedom and independence, I will continue to act the part of a watchful centinel at the post where you have placed me; a charge that I was attempting by my letters to produce, or increase a foreign influence destructive of my country's interest, seems to be but the result of an act too often and too successfully used by those who are meditating the object they proscribe, while by alarms they are diminishing the affection of the public towards a nation they dread, they are but secretly making way for a new attachment towards a nation they love; and in proportion as they can succeed in the first view, they are sure in the course of human events of obtaining their wishes in the latter view. Look at the names of the grand jury who have made this unexampled presentment although you will find some native Americans who have been attached to the independence of their country, you will readily perceive what they mean by foreign influence: I, like you, my fellow citizens, can have no views of this sort. I have felt, and I still do feel, an attachment for the French nation: They assisted my country to establish its independence, and they aided us in securing peace: They have formed a republic on the overthrow of monarchy and tyranny; I therefore feel interested in their favour: I look with a friendly eye on their faults, but I admire their heroism and military prowess. Still if that nation or any other on earth, shall invade the independence and freedom of my country, I shall view the attempt as an independent American.

It is British influence that we have most to dread. In proportion as our commerce and intercourse with England has become more necessary to them, by the events in Europe, a stronger desire has been manifested to stop our intercourse with France and engage it in favour of Great Britain. Whenever our commerce has turned in favour of France, England has oppressed it; whenever it has turned in favour of England, France has oppressed it. Our commerce has become a subject of contest between these two nations: It is injured and opprest by both. England was appeased for a moment by Mr. Jay's treaty: As a neutral nation we are bound to place France on the same footing: But the occasion has offered a favourable opportunity to England to irritate us with France, and France with us, with a view to establish an incurable quarrel, the consequence of which must be a complete monopoly of us and our interests by Great Britain.—In this view it is that alarms are spread about French influence; for if a quarrel can be insured between France and America, no moral truth can be more true, than this political one, that the United States will be thrown into an alliance offensive and defensive with Great Britain. My wishes and my determinations have always been to maintain the neutrality of the United States, and regardless of the interest of other nations to keep free from connecting our national fortunes with those of any European power.—For these things and for these endeavours my opinions have been held up by a grand jury at Richmond as derogatory to the happiness and peace of my country: You my fellow citizens will view this attempt to influence opinion with the indignation it deserves, and I promise you most sincerely it shall not intimidate me from pursuing the same means of informing you which has incurred the censure of this political court and jury.

I am with every sentiment of respect, my Fellow Citizens, your faithful servant,

SAM: J. CABELL.

Those printers who are friends to freedom of opinion, and especially such as may have published the charge and presentment alluded to are requested to give the above a place in their papers.

(Philadelphia) June 6, 1797. Date and place are those of the letter.

1. See Presentment of the Grand Jury of the Circuit Court for the District of Virginia, May 22, 1797.

James Iredell to Hannah Iredell ———————————————————————
May 31, 1797   Richmond, Virginia

... I continue extremely well, and am in Court every day from ten till 4 or 5, and a great deal of business has been already done, but a vast deal still remains to do, for Judge Wilson did not attend here at all last fall _ and I have the business of both Courts to do. I am resolved however to leave nothing undone, which makes my stay here very uncertain, and I have too much reason to fear at present that we cannot finish until Saturday the 10th of June, in which case I cannot be in Suffolk until Tuesday the 13th. I shall however use every effort in my power to finish, if possible sooner, and therefore venture to request you will let Hannibal[1] meet me with the Horses at Suffolk on Saturday the 10th, but the chance of my getting there on that day is so much against me that I must earnestly request you not to expect me until the Wednesday following, when I hope with confidence I may have the happiness of seeing you _ God grant I may find you and my dear Children, and all my Friends in good health _ ! ... The business of this Court is of such immense consequence both to Individuals and the Public that I never could justify leaving any of it unfinished, and I am sure, anxious as I doubt not you are to see me _ you would rather see me on Wednesday with my mind at ease than on Sunday in the paltry condition of a Man who had sacrificed his public duty to his private feelings. ...

ARS (Nc-Ar, Charles E. Johnson Collection). Addressed "Edenton, North Carolina." Postmarked "[R]ICHMOND, *May* 31 1797."
    1. Presumably a slave belonging to James Iredell.

Circuit Court for the District of Massachusetts ——————

June 1, 1797   Boston, Massachusetts

On June 1 Chief Justice Oliver Ellsworth and Judge John Lowell opened court, and Ellsworth delivered a "pertinent, patriotic and elegant Charge" to the grand jury.[1] On June 13 the court adjourned to the next term.[2]

    1. *Massachusetts Mercury* (Boston), June 2, 1797. The *Daily Advertiser* (Philadelphia), June 12, 1797, described Ellsworth's charge as "a pertinent display of profound judicial knowledge and political rectitude." Charge not found. The date of the convening of the court had been moved from June 7 to June 1 by the Circuit Court Act of 1797. *Stat.*, 1:517.
    2. Final Records, CCD Massachusetts, RG 21, MWalFAR

Circuit Court for the District of North Carolina ——————

June 1, 1797   Raleigh, North Carolina

Judge John Sitgreaves opened court but then adjourned it to the following term, because Associate Justice Samuel Chase was unable to attend. The minutes note that Sitgreaves had been "inform'd by Letter from ~~Judge~~ Samuel Chace Esqʳ one of the Justices of the Supreme Court to whom was assigned the Holding of this Term, that he was unable to attend."[1]

    1. Minutes, CCD North Carolina, RG 21, GEpFAR. Letter from Samuel Chase not found. For some comments on why Chase missed court, see the *North-Carolina Journal* under date of June 1, 1797; "Vox Populi," *Aurora* under date of June 6, 1797; and "Holt" to Samuel Chase, *Porcupine's Gazette* under date of June 15, 1797.

This was to have been the first meeting of the circuit court at the new courthouse in Raleigh, in accordance with the Circuit Court Act of 1793. *Stat.*, 1:335.

Letter from an Anonymous Correspondent ——————————
Aurora
June 1, 1797   Virginia

No doubt you have seen or heard of the presentment made by the grand jury in the federal court of this state respecting the circular letters written by several members of Congress particularly one by Sam. Cabell, Esqr. This presentment, I think the most extraordinary step that aristocracy has ever yet taken, and their cloven foot is now more conspicuous than it ever has been.[1] I am glad they are so bold; for sure I am, the most blind among us must now see the intentions of the enemies of liberty and equality.

(Philadelphia) June 8, 1797. Date and place are those of the letter.

1. Benjamin Henry Latrobe, an architect living in Richmond and a frequent observer at court, noted "aristocratic" tendencies of a different sort when, on June 1, 1797, he attended the circuit court referred to in the text. Latrobe sketched a courtroom scene that included, at the extreme right, a presiding judge—presumably James Iredell, who attended court alone that day—wearing a robe and wig, and George Wray, a customs collector, sporting a gown and fur collar and carrying a staff with a metal tip, called a tipstaff. Wray may have been acting as marshal or deputy marshal and would have used the tipstaff to signal the arrival of the judges. At the fall term in Richmond, Ephraim Kirby, a lawyer from Connecticut, also took note of the finery worn by those attending court and commented to his wife that he felt embarrassed about his coat. Latrobe, however, observed that such finery was unusual in American courts. Edward C. Carter et al., eds., *Latrobe's View of America, 1795-1820: Selections from the Watercolors and Sketches* (New Haven: Yale University Press, 1985), pp. 124-25; Order Book, May 26 and June 1, 1797, CCD Virginia, Vi; *DAB* under Ephraim Kirby; Ephraim Kirby to Ruth Kirby, November 30 and December 1, 1797, Ephraim Kirby Papers, A-Ar; Edward C. Carter et al., eds., *The Virginia Journals of Benjamin Henry Latrobe, 1795-1798*, 2 vols. (New Haven: Yale University Press, 1977), 1:129. See illustration "Remains of good old fashions, exhibited in the Foederal Court Richmond June 1ˢᵗ 1797."

North-Carolina Journal ——————————————————
June 1, 1797   Raleigh, North Carolina

The Circuit Court of the United States for the district of North-Carolina, was opened here this day by the district Judge, John Sitgreaves, Esq. who after making the necessary orders respecting the venire for the next term, informed the gentlemen of the bar and the jurors, that Mr. Chase, whose duty it was to hold this court, would not attend, owing to some difficulty in procuring horses to effect the journey from Charleston; that it would therefore be useless to continue the court or detain the jury—the jury were then dismissed and the court adjourned to the next term.

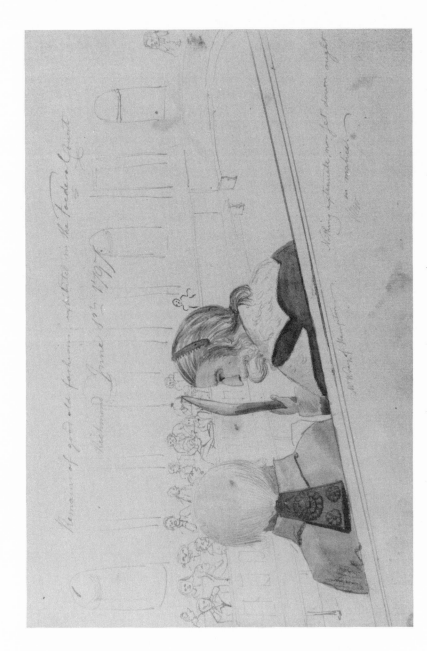

Remains of good old fashions, exhibited in the Foederal Court Richmond June 1ˢᵗ 1797 by Benjamin Henry Latrobe (1764-1820). Pencil, pen and ink, and watercolor on paper, 1797. Courtesy Maryland Historical Society, Baltimore. Benjamin Henry Latrobe Papers.

As many persons were attending from Virginia, South-Carolina, and some even from Georgia, this accident produced considerable disappointment, and his Honour, Judge Chase, has been severely censured—his excuse for nonattendance appeared too light and trifling for such gross negligence, and the allegation that he could not procure horses to bring him on from Georgetown, was reckoned wonderful indeed![1]

(Halifax, North Carolina) June 12, 1797. Date and place are those of the headline.

1. Under a Raleigh headline dated June 1, another article noted the failure of the North Carolina circuit court. "This disappointment has taken place by the accident of Mr. Chase's horse falling sick somewhere in South Carolina, upon which his honor returned to Charleston. This excuse appearing to be very frivolous, and the circumstance of his not being able to procure another horse in that part of the country not being believed, his non-attendance has excited great disgust and indignation." *City Gazette* (Charleston), June 30, 1797.

Henry Tazewell to [John Page?]

June 3, 1797   Philadelphia, Pennsylvania

...I have lately seen in the Richmond paper a presentment of a Grand Jury signed by M[r] Blair ag[t] some circular Letters from this place, particularly Colo Cabell's _ Is it possible that this act can be viewed in Virg[a] without abhorrence, and indignation _ If the writers had violated the Laws, the Court and Jury knew that the Culprits and not their opinions were the fit subjects for animadversion _ Having presented the Letters and not the writers, they shew that the writers were no further censureable than for their political opinions _ Thus have a Court and Jury erected themselves into a tribunal of political Censors _ The standard of truth is their own opinion _ whether such a tribunal be a government M̶a̶c̶h̶i̶n̶e̶ engine, or a rod over Government, it becomes equally dangerous _ and the habit which the federal Judges have been in of giving political charges _ compared with this presentment is enough to open the Eyes of the public to their danger _ Religious opinions must be made to bend next to the views of the Executive _ I am sorry M[r] Blair's o̶p̶i̶n̶ name appears to this presentment.[1] Some others of the Jury I am not astonished at. They should however remember that the inventor of the Guilotine in France was the first Victim _ You know that in the Eastern states m̶u̶c̶h̶ ̶p̶a̶i̶n̶s̶ an opinion has been inculcated that the Virginians were a divided people. That their principles were unfriendly to order and every kind of governmental restraint _ This evidence of the truth of that opinion seems to have been given in concert with those who invented it. I have therefore no hesitation in determining that those who made the presentment are not only inimical to the freedom of opinion, but desireous to destroy the liberties of their Country _ [2] ...

ALS (DLC, Miscellaneous Manuscripts Collection). The identification of John Page as the possible recipient of this letter results from a comparison of this letter with other correspondence between

Tazewell and Page in the Miscellaneous Manuscripts Collection, DLC. Unprinted passages in this letter also suggest a familiarity with Congress and the issues before it consistent with writing a former colleague and political ally.

On the following day, June 4, 1797, Tazewell wrote a letter almost identical to this one to James Madison. James Madison Papers, DLC.

Henry Tazewell (1753-1799), senator from Virginia from 1794 until his death. *BDAC.*

John Page (1743-1808), a representative from Virginia from 1789 to March 1797. *DAB.*

1. Others also expressed surprise at former Associate Justice John Blair's presence on the grand jury. In a letter to the *Aurora,* one correspondent remarked: "Before I quit this subject, pardon me while I express my astonishment, and lament to see Mr. Blair the foreman of this extraordinary jury. The venerable age of that man (I wish his late conduct did not make it improper that I should say more of him) would have inspired the hope, that, as he is just taking leave of the world—has indeed already pretended to depart from it, he would have permitted himself to be glided down the current of life without again encountering its turbulency. But, unfortunately for the human race, there is a period when infancy resumes its reign." "A Virginian," *Aurora,* (Philadelphia), June 21, 1797.

2. John Page expressed a similar dissatisfaction with the Cabell affair. "What think you of the late Presentment? I confess I feel almost disposed to impeach the Judge & his Gr^d Jury _ !!!" John Page to St. George Tucker, June 14, 1797, Tucker-Coleman Papers, ViW.

Thomas Jefferson to Peregrine Fitzhugh ——————————————

June 4, 1797   Philadelphia, Pennsylvania

... the proceedings in the federal [court?] of Virginia to overawe the communications between the people & their representatives incite great indignation. probably a great fermentation will be produced by it in that State. indeed it is the common cause of the confederacy as it is one of their courts which has taken the step. the charges of the federal judges have for a considerable time been inviting the Grand juries to become inquisitors on the freedom of speech, of writing & of principle of their fellow citizens. perhaps the grand juries in the other states as well as in that of Virginia may think it incumbent in their next presentment to enter a petition against
                                                                              even
this perversion of their institution from a legal to a political engine, & ^[*word inked out*] to present those concerned in it. _ ...

APcS (DLC, Thomas Jefferson Papers).

At the time this letter was written, Thomas Jefferson was vice president of the United States.

Peregrine Fitzhugh (1759-1811), a resident of Washington County, Maryland, corresponded with Jefferson on political and agricultural matters. Daughters of the American Revolution, *DAR Patriot Index,* 3 vols. (Washington, D.C.: n.p., 1966-1986), 1:239; Thomas J. C. Williams, *A History of Washington County Maryland* (1906; reprint ed., Baltimore: Regional Publishing, 1968), p. 140; Dumas Malone, *Jefferson and His Time,* vol. 3, *Jefferson and the Ordeal of Liberty* (Boston: Little, Brown, 1962), p. 320.

"Vox Populi" ————————————————————————————————————

Aurora

June 6, 1797   Wilmington, North Carolina

MR. HALL,[1]

You are directed to make it known to our representatives in Congress, through the medium of your Gazette, that the people of this state are very much irritated at the conduct of the federal judiciary, towards them, that the most thinking part of us never approved of that aukward ill-organized judicial system; but that as sincere friends to the federal government, we have hitherto borne the inconvenience and injury arising from the neglect of the judges. We cannot forget, that in common with the rest of our fellow-citizens, we pay these men for their services—we do not say they are our servants, but we say they shall not be our masters—And we require our representatives to state to that authority which has the power of redress, that in this state we have lost four courts from the non attendance of the circuit judge; that at three of these courts jurors, suitors, witnesses, and lawyers have attended from distant parts of the country; that the lawyers now refuse further attendance on their suits, without further compensation; and that they conceive themselves *particularly* ill treated.

We desire, sir, that you will supply each of our members at Congress, with a copy of this letter; perhaps they have not forgot their native state so much, but that they will with us feel that honourable pride, becoming freemen, and in our behalf firmly seek redress.[2]

The excuse made by the last judge appointed to this circuit, we think is adding insult to injury—he attended at Georgia and South Carolina; on his way to this state, one of his horses, he says, gave out, and prevented his coming on. It is known that South Carolina and our state abound with horses, and it is also known that judges prefer the ease of proceeding from Charleston to their respective places of abode by water, to doing their duty to their country.

VOX POPULI

At this time judge Iredell is attending his duty in Virginia, and has never permitted his own ease or convenience to interfere with his public duties.

(Philadelphia) July 1, 1797. Date and place are those of the letter.

1. Allmand Hall was the publisher of *Hall's Wilmington Gazette*. Brigham, *American Newspapers,* 2:781.

2. To remedy the failure of the court "a bill for reviving and continuing suits and process in the circuit court for the District of North Carolina" was introduced in the House of Representatives on June 30, 1797, by Thomas Blount of North Carolina; it was enacted on July 5, 1797. *HRJ,* 3:59; *Stat.,* 1:526.

"Scaevola" to James Iredell ————————————————————————
Daily Advertiser
June 11, 1797   Richmond, Virginia

To James Iredell, one of the associate judges of the supreme court of the United States.

SIR,

That our federal judiciary is wisely constituted, every one will admit. But the best institution may be perverted—the most perfect theory distorted in its practice. While judges administer the law, they answer the end of their appointment. But when they are degraded into the engines of an executive, they deviate widely from what their duty should prescribe. When a charge to the grand inquest of a state breathes the spirit of peace and decorum, it is salutary—but when it is merely a political invective, calculated to irritate and inflame, it is a bane instead of a blessing to society. A judge should confine himself in his charge, to offences against the existing laws of the country. He should neither descant on the general politics of, nor indulge in the political vagaries which his own heated imagination may suggest. He should neither approve the tenets of one party, nor inveigh against the principles of another. He should neither commend the wisdom of an administration, nor mark the virulence of its opponents. Above all, he should be very vigilant, lest he impresses on the public mind that he fosters in his own bosom all the acrimony of a partizan.

What induces you to suppose, sir, you are an emissary sent round the United States to inculcate certain principles in politics? Is there any law of congress which confers on you the powers of a political missionary: or have you, according to the diplomatic regimen, secret instructions to disseminate such principles? That your address is inflammatory, is apparent from its language and its sentiments. Under the assumed garb of moderation, you endeavour to incite the jury to make a presentment responsive to the address.—To make them accessories, is proscribing political opinions to which you are hostile. That this was your intention, is a fair construction of your charge. The effect which that charge produced, equally demonstrates the malignity of the motive. That presentment is an overt act of treason against the good sense of Virginia. To that treason you are an accessory, if not a principal. There is one principle that is inculcated in your charge which I really had esteemed exploded from this country. You endeavour to prescribe to the people of this state the manner in which they shall discuss public measures; you endeavour to regulate the degree of heat which shall enter into those discussions.—You offer yourself as a political thermometer for the use of the Virginians! But I fear, sir, that the mercury of your political composition, will never rise to the temperature of manliness. In delivering a political charge, you exceeded the powers of a judge—you usurped an authority not delegated to you by the laws or constitution of your country.

And now let me ask you, sir, what must be your sensations, when you see your charge inserted in every ministerial paper through the United States, as subservient to the views of a party? What must be the impression of the world on your judicial consistency? At the moment when you recommended to the jury a vigilance against infractions of the law, you violated it yourself: like most empty declaimers, you ran into the very vice you were inveighing against.—Your charge is, on your own principles, more exceptionable than the letter of mr. Cabell. He had at least a semblance of justification. It was a communication between the representative and his constituent. Your presentment says he exceeded, not usurped, authority. But what is your anathema? It has not the shadow of right for its basis. Had the jury acted consistently, they should have presented your charge as a greater nuisance than the letter of colonel Cabell.

Having thus cursorily analyzed the charge itself, let me advert to the presentment, which may be considered as the offspring of that charge—and the child will be found to exceed the malignancy even of its parent. And let me again observe, sir, what may be the vices discoverable in that presentment is imputable, in some measure, to yourself—since your address invited such an answer. The heinous sin imputed to mr. Cabell, was his representing to his constituents, that the administration of our government was defective; or (if you please, sir), depraved.—This our immaculate jury term seditious. This is an indefinite expression. If the jury consider that the expression of sentiments relative to the executive, when those sentiments reflect on its wisdom or integrity is sedition, they are unsupported by the laws of the United States. And I defy these hunters after sedition, these panders of the executive, to shew that the expression of such sentiments is criminal. I defy them to demonstrate it, though asserted by a judge on the bench, and a judge in the jury room. But the jury considers the practice of writing, generally, as contrary to law. In a free government, the people possess every power which is not abridged by express ordinance. Let the jury shew in this instance, the law which prohibits this species of intercourse between a representative and his constituent—Is it to be found in the constitution or laws of the union? I have searched both critically, but have found no clause in either which prohibits it. The inference is then, that it is a right which a member of congress unequivocally possesses.—The jury are guilty of the same incongruity with the judge. While they censure an usurpation of power in a representative, they are guilty of a greater as a grand jury. This presentment is a violent attack upon the liberty of America—upon immunities which are the palladium of our civil rights, it profanes the freedom of political intercourse, and attempts covertly to annihilate the liberty of the press. But I have too much reliance on the good sense of Virginia, not to hope that such lawless attempts will only reflect an odium upon the authors of them. Attacks on liberty must be nipt in the bud, or they will be eventually successful. You have the honour, sir, to be the first judge who has made an attack upon our rights, and I trust you will be the first to feel the punishment which public opinion can inflict.

The obloquy which was attached to the memory of a Jefferies,[1] was a sufficient torture for his crimes. But what justification can you give for your conduct after the address was delivered into court? Your inconsistency was more glaring than before. If the conduct for which mr. Cabell was presented was criminal, the court should have directed a prosecution; if it was no offence, the court should have informed the jury that they had exceeded their powers both to rescue a man who was innocent, and prevent future juries from falling into the same error: by not directing the attorney for the United States to prosecute, you tacitly admitted that the presentment was improper[;] by not informing the jury that it was illegal, you evinced that you had not candour sufficient to do justice to an innocent man.—Thus you discovered you were actuated by party motives. In using this explicit language, sir, delicacy is not wounded—you shewed no respect for colonel Cabell's feelings—you deserve none for your own.

It was not personal consideration for you which prevented these strictures from appearing, during the sitting of the court, it was an unwillingness to reflect disgrace on the tribunals of my country.

Virginia has been honoured by your presence for many successive circuits; in requital for the hospitality you have received, you have endeavoured to curtail her rights. It only remains for her to wish, that your future travels may take a different direction. Whether your conduct has not deservedly elicited such a wish, is left for the awful tribunal of public opinion to decide.

SCÆVOLA.

Richmond, June 11, 1797.

(Philadelphia) June 28, 1797. Date and place are those of the letter. The headline notes that this is "FROM THE VIRGINIA GAZETTE."

1. George Jeffreys (1648-1689), appointed lord chief justice of England in 1683 by Charles II, became infamous for his vigorous application of the death penalty, particularily to anti-Stuart rebels at the "Bloody Assizes" of 1685. *DNB.*

Circuit Court for the District of Rhode Island ——————————————
June 15, 1797   Newport, Rhode Island

On June 15[1] Judge Benjamin Bourne attended court but adjourned it to the next day because there was no quorum. The following day Chief Justice Oliver Ellsworth and Bourne opened court, and Ellsworth delivered an "excellant" charge to the grand jury. On June 24 the court adjourned to the next term.[2]

1. The Circuit Court Act of 1797 had changed the date of the court from June 19 to June 15. *Stat.*, 1:517.

2. Minutes, CCD Rhode Island, RG 21, MWalFAR; *Newport Mercury* (Newport), June 20, 1797; Oliver Ellsworth's Charge to the Grand Jury of the Circuit Court for the District of Rhode Island, June 16, 1797 (q.v.).

"Holt" to Samuel Chase ————————————————————————
Porcupine's Gazette
June 15, 1797   New Bern, North Carolina

To the Hon. SAMUEL CHASE,

SIR,

By not attending at Raleigh, for the purpose of holding the circuit court there, on the first of June instant, you have offended, and injured more persons, than you can ever hope to please or to benefit, by any action of your future life. It was unfortunate that the docket was crowded with causes, and the town with people; it was unfortunate that besides a multitude of jurors, witnesses, and suitors, compelled (some of them from great distances) to attend the court, numbers were allured by the reputation of your great talents, and thronged to the place in expectation of beholding an eloquent speaker, and an able judge. It was also unfortunate that some of your predecessors had omited to hold courts in this state; that these omissions had subjected the business to great confusion, as well as delay, and had brought the federal judiciary into disgrace with the citizens. It certainly behooved you in riding the southern circuit, not to neglect North Carolina without some weighty reason, some necessity which there was no way to avoid, or difficulty, which could not possibly be surmounted. From a man of your known ability, it was natural to expect no frivolous plea, or childish justification; and accordingly your friends were happy to find that nothing less than the illness of your horse was alledged to have prevented you from attending to your duty. Your horse? Good God, Sir! Where were you? Is there a wild uninhabited country, in which no horses are to be found, within the jurisdiction of a federal judge? The fact should instantly be stated to Congress; the power of the United States should be exerted, and a caravan assembled on the borders of the desert to conduct the next judge of his circuit. The stream of federal justice must not be obstructed for want of a horse.

I am sorry however to inform you, that in weighing your excuses, and estimating the credibility of your assertion, the people here, unmindful of the dignity of the judge, seem strangely disposed to consider you in the dubious capacity of a traveller; and their faith consists accordingly of much astonishment and little belief. To overcome this prejudice, and indeed for the safety of future travellers, you ought to publish a map, containing an accurate designation of the spot, where you were shipwrecked, and where, after desisting from the further prosecution of your voyage, you were necessitated to be taken in tow, and carried back in distress into Charleston. To move the public compassion, you should by no means omit to draw up in the most impressive language, a narrative of the fatigues you suffered, and the perils to which you were exposed, in penetrating that savage country, to the distance of no less than sixty miles, under innumerable difficulties, and with a sick horse.

The people of this state, sir, are of a restless and inquisitive disposition; not apt to receive without scrutiny, and information, however high its authority, in regard to public affairs; easily provoked by the neglect of their business, and not easily pacified by a smooth apology; the weakness of which, they have more readiness and sagacity in detecting, than you seem to have calculated upon. They are totally free from a slavish veneration for power, and are far from allowing that any rank or reputation can exempt a man from the most scrupulous discharge of the duties of his station: I submit it to you, sir, whether your justification would not be more satisfactory to such a people, if very large additions were made to the weight and to the probability of the facts, which you have alledged.

The impracticability of procuring a horse in any part of the United States, is treated here as a supposition the most wild and extravagant, and altogether inadmissible. It is also confidently asserted, that if you at all proposed the purchase of a horse, you must have voluntarily declined it, on account of some objection to the price, or colour, or other circumstance of equal importance. We do not pretend to know whether you are partial to a bay or a sorrel, but it is a subject of universal regret, that a horse having short ears, or a long head, or three white feet, should prevent the sitting of the Federal Court. Some have insinuated that it was the presentiment of a long and dreary journey in this hot season, that produced the sickness of your horse; and that even you were so sensibly affected by the same cause, that you could not avoid preferring a pleasant passage by water from Charleston to Baltimore.

There is certainly a difference between the efforts of ancient and modern patriotism, and a reader of Roman history would probably smile to hear it recorded of a Cato, or a Brutus, that if he could have procured a proper horse, for the purpose, he would have maintained the liberties of his country.

However, sir, I am one of those few who are disposed to do justice to your character, and am ready to admit, that with the aid of a good draft horse you would have performed glorious and astonishing things. Envy shall suppress no circumstance, which may benefit your fame. Posterity shall know that you loved your country, and made great exertions to purchase a gelding for your carriage; that you had an incredible zeal to serve the United States, and went within three hundred miles of the place to which your duty called you. The world shall also be informed, that out of pure patriotism, you proceeded from Charleston to Georgetown, and then back from Georgetown to Charleston.

HOLT.

(Philadelphia) June 29, 1797. Date and place are those of the headline.

Calohill Mennis to Samuel Jordan Cabell ————————————————
Virginia Gazette, and General Advertiser
June 15, 1797   Richmond, Virginia

SOLDIER's REST, *Bedford county,*
June the 15*th,* 1797.

To Col. SAM: J: CABELL.

SIR,

HAVING seen your furious letter of the 31st of [May, addressed to your fellow citizens, in which you express so much resentment and indignation against the presentment of the federal grand jury; and having had the honor (whatever you may think of it) of being one of that body myself, I was prompted by an inclination, which I could not easily resist, of taking some little notice of that extraordinary epistle; though I was well persuaded at the same]¹ time, that treating it with a contemptuous silence would have been the most efficacious method of consigning so flimsy and pitiful a production to its merited oblivion.

I by no means intend to enter into a political discussion with you, relative to the propriety or legality of the presentment which you complain of with so much acrimony; but just simply to observe, that it is owing to such worthies as you are, and to those turbulent and inflammatory productions, which you, and those of your political complexion, are the authors of, that the French have conceived the opinion, that the people of the United States are in opposition to their government, and that in the event of a rupture between the two Republics, a considerable part of our countrymen would declare in their favor; and also to observe, that it is from their viewing us as thus politically circumstanced, that they have dared to insult us in a manner that stands unrivalled in the annals of the proudest and haughtiest monarchies.

You ought, I humbly conceive, Sir, as a lover of your country, and as a member of the general legislature, to whom your constituents have entrusted a portion of their happiness, to have employed every means (especially as we have but too many reasons to apprehend entering into a war) in uniting your fellow-citizens together in the defence of their common country, their lives, their liberty, and all that can be dear to them as men. But instead of promoting so necessary and salutary an end, and one so much to be wished for by every worthy and virtuous American, you have been industriously employed in taking every step that appeared to you as most likely to counteract it, both by attempting to render the government odious in the eyes of the people, and by endeavouring to alienate their confidence and affection from that great and good man, who administered it, and also by representing his successor as inimical to the interests and cause of the French nation, and consequently hostile to the general principles of republicanism.

Surely such conduct tends not only to create a foreign influence among us, but likewise to invite the French to make war upon us, with every assurance of meeting with the approbation and good wishes of a considerable proportion of our countrymen. Viewing you then in this light, and as guilty of those charges, is there any man in his sober senses, who has discernment enough to distinguish between the incendiary and the firm, but peaceful lover of his country, who does not abhor you as a traitor? Your patriotism (if it is not an abuse of terms to call it so) and your writings border on the wild and incoherent ravings of a madman—and you rather resemble the fury Electo, scattering the seeds of jealousy, insurrection, and confusion, over this happy land, than the able statesman, or the wise and beneficent legislator. It was for those reasons, Sir, and not from a desire of lessening the independence of private opinion, as you affect to believe, that I determined before I set off from home, to have you presented if I possibly could: and I found that every member of the grand-jury, with whom I had any conversation on the subject, exactly coincided with me in sentiment, that you were a fit and proper object to come under the cognizance of a Federal Grand-Jury; consequently, the inference, that the presentment was the result of the charge, which was delivered by the judge, is entirely founded in error. I will tell you more, Mr. Cabell—there was not one dissentient opinion among the whole of the jury; and that it was owing to the tenderness of one of the only two foreigners who served on it, the word *unanimous* was not inserted in the presentment. I will also tell you another thing, sir, that you must not think of imposing upon the good sense and discernment of Americans by the tinsel glare of virtue and patriotism, with which you in vain attempt to blind them. The veil, believe me, is too thinly spread to conceal you; and such conduct as you pursue, serves but the more to expose you to obloquy and contempt. You accuse us of dreading the French nation; but I am of opinion, that were this charge founded in truth, we should have avoided your censure; and that to have acted consistently with our fears, we should never have presented you for loving them better than your own country, and for being so abject and mean, as to be ready, upon all occasions, to sacrifice the dignity of American to appease their wrath. Your vanity and presumption, Colonel Cabell, have ever induced you to over-rate your importance, and to boast of performing what you have never achieved; for all those who were best acquainted with you in the army, know, that to the empty vapourings of the gasconade, you by no means unitted the firmness of the hero.

I am,   Sir,   Your obt. servt.

CALOHILL MENNIS.

(Richmond) July 5, 1797. Date and place are those of the letter.

Calohill Mennis (ca. 1745-1812) served as a captain in the Virginia Continental Line during the Revolution and was captured at Charleston in 1780. Mennis was exchanged in 1781 and continued to serve until the end of the war. *DAR Patriot Index,* 1:463; E. M. Sanchez-Saavedra, comp., *A Guide to Virginia Military Organizations in the American Revolution, 1774-1787* (Richmond: Virginia State Library, 1978), p. 54; Daughters of the American Revolution, *Lineage Book,* 144 vols. (Harrisburg, Pa., 1895; and Washington, D.C., 1896-1935, n.p., 1895-1935), vol. 5 (1898), p. 254; John H. Gwathmey, *Historical Register of Virginians in the Revolution: 1775-1783* (1938; reprint ed., Baltimore: Genealogical Publishing, 1973), p. 552.

    1. The text in brackets is transcribed from the *Gazette of the United States* (Philadelphia), July 17, 1797, because the print is obscured in the *Virginia Gazette, and General Advertiser.*

Daily Advertiser
June 15, 1797   Wilmington, North Carolina

We are sorry to hear that the packet in which judge Chase took his passage home, from South-Carolina, is taken by Le Grouper a French privateer, off the Long Bay.[1]

(Philadelphia) June 27, 1797. Date and place are those of the headline.

    1. This story was a hoax; see James Iredell to Hannah Iredell, August 3, 1797.

Oliver Ellsworth's Charge to the Grand Jury of the Circuit Court for the District of Rhode Island
June 16, 1797   Newport, Rhode Island

[*On June 16, 1797, Ellsworth delivered to the Rhode Island grand jury the same charge that he had given at the New York circuit court on April 1, 1797. For that charge, see Oliver Ellsworth's Charge to the Grand Jury of the Circuit Court for the District of New York, published above under date of April 1, 1797.*]

Letter from an Anonymous Correspondent
Philadelphia Gazette
June 16, 1797   Richmond, Virginia

... A sufficient number of judges to constitute a general court not meeting early in this term,[1] it is presumed, was the reason why there was no grand jury; after the court had proceeded for some time to business, the names of those who had been summoned were called over, and not enough appearing, to afford a prospect of a jury, those who did attend were discharged by the court. You are authorised to say, had there been jurors enough to have proceeded on business, the following would have been offered by one of that body, and that those who did appear, were unanimous in agreeing to it.

... *Ignorance* has ever been considered the high and certain road to slavery; *Information,* as the first object and very basis of all *free governments*: ought not the latter, therefore, to be encouraged and made as extensive as possible?

Every attack upon information we consider as wounding the vitals of republicanism, and restraining enquiries, on which all that is dear to man may rest. When judges and juries, whose province is rigid justice under the law, quit that solid ground for the wide field of opinion, they may thereby become political engines in the hands of a designing man, so as ultimately to work our ruin, instead of being solemn tribunals of justice, governed by known and established laws, on which our security alone can depend; ought not freemen then to be tremblingly alive, and most seriously alarmed, at every attempt to shake this rock of liberty? If members of Congress, in fact ourselves, for they are our representatives, are not to think, or if they do, not to express their thoughts, where is liberty? If indeed the act or the expression of the representative is contrary to the sentiments of his constituents, they happily have a safe remedy always at hand, he can shortly after be turned out. To endeavour then to fix a stigma on those representatives who give their real sentiments on matters of the greatest importance to our welfare, and particularly in the instance alluded to, when the people have re-elected the same person, after the supposed offences had been committed, made known, and publicly commented on, is not only a daring attack upon the liberty of the individual, but on the whole district of which he is a member, and of the society at large. Open war is a dreadful thing; but secret machinations, which lead to such dangerous consequences, are, we think, infinitely more alarming: we are, therefore, sorry to say, that a late presentment before the circuit court of the United States, by John Blair & others, on the subject of communications from representatives in congress to their constituents, although it may not have been the effect of any dark design, yet we conceive it fraught with the dangerous tendency to a subversion of liberty; and although, as we have already said, we condemn the interference of judges and juries on political subjects, yet it having been already alarmingly practised, we consider it a bounden duty, to express thus publicly our disapprobation of such conduct; we shall forbear to comment further on the judge or the jury . . .

(Philadelphia) June 26, 1797. Date and place are those of the letter. The headline indicates this was reprinted from the *Virginia Argus* (Richmond).

1. The reference is to the Virginia General Court.

Peregrine Fitzhugh to Thomas Jefferson

June 20, 1797   "Cottage," Washington County, Maryland

. . . I had read with a mixture of indignation & Contempt the proceedings of the Grand Jury of the Federal Court of Virginia. The aristocratic Party have for time past manifested a disposition to encroach on the liberty of the Yeomen of this Country but they have hitherto proceeded with great tenderness and caution. They have however got more bold and in this last attempt have laid their ax at the root of the Tree for whenever it shall be recognized as a constitutional doctrine that every Man is to be branded as an enemy to his Country who shall dare to speak or write with freedom on Men & measures the said Fabric which has been erected at so great an expence of blood & Treasure will be erased and the freedom and independence of their United States vanish like mists before the morning Sun I shall not fail to use my endeavors to impress the federal grand Jurors which may be summoned to the next Term with the propriety of entering protestations against such proceedings _ I have lately heard that the I am told that the People of your State have shown a proper spirit on the occasion & that the Grand Jury thought it prudent to acknowledge that they had err'd and to express their Sorrow for having done so _ this if true is the only atonement they could make and may serve as a caution to future Grand Juries _ I was surprized to find the name of Blair who had generally been esteemed a man of Virtue and Talents at the head of the list of those transgressors of justice _ ...

ARS (DLC, Thomas Jefferson Papers).

Letter of James Iredell ————————————————————————————
Virginia Gazette, and General Advertiser
June 21, 1797   Edenton, North Carolina

TO THE PUBLIC.

HAVING seen with great surprise in some of the public newspapers an attack upon my judicial character, signed with the name of Mr. CABELL,[1] a member of Congress, I think it proper to take some notice of it, on account of a mistake in point of fact which he seems to have committed. From the tenor of his observations, any one would conclude that I wrote the charge he condemns with a view to draw forth a censure upon him or some other member of Congress who had written circular letters to their constituents. The truth is, I never knew that Mr. Cabell had written any circular letter at all, until I heard the presentment read in court, nor have I seen the letter alluded to to this hour. I had indeed seen printed letters of one or two other members of Congress from the same state, but had them not in my thoughts when I prepared that charge, which I wrote deliberately in Philadelphia, in order to be delivered in Maryland and Virginia. The same charge was delivered substantially in both states, and without a view to any particular person. With regard to the sentiments of that charge, I am ready on all proper occasions to vindicate every word of it, as well as the propriety of delivering such a charge on such an occasion. In the mean time, I have a right to expect, that if the charge be censured, it shall be censured for what it really contains, and not for what exists merely in the imagination of the censurer. I have no hesitation in saying that if it has the tendency Mr. Cabell ascribes to it, it does, in my opinion, deserve a severer censure than any he has bestowed upon it.

The conduct of the court after the presentment has incurred Mr. Cabell's censure. It is difficult to say what can escape it if the conduct of the court on that occasion cannot. They knew not such a presentment was in contemplation. It was brought into court the same day the charge was delivered, and without any adjournment having taken place, and agreeably to the usual practice, I presume, in Virginia, (though different from that in some other states) was read by the clerk without even being seen by the court. None of the circular letters which were the object of the presentment was produced to the court, nor in possession of the judges. The jury were asked if they had any business to require their attention longer, or if they wished to stay to consider of any. They answered in the negative. The attorney for the United States was asked if he wished them to be detained longer. He declared he knew of no occasion for it. They were then discharged. Were the court to chatechise the jury for their censure of a publication which they themselves had never seen? or to direct a prosecution upon a publication without knowing the contents of it? Ought they in any instance indeed to direct a prosecution in the presence of the attorney, within whose particular department it lies, and when no occasion calls for their immediate interposition? Were they to interfere unnecessarily, they might justly be charged with becoming parties to a prosecution and incapacitating themselves from the impartial conduct of judges afterwards. Whatever might be the intention of the jury, which was composed of very respectable men, it has been a frequent practice in some of the southern states for grand juries to present what they considered as grievances though they could not be the foundation of a criminal prosecution in the court. I have known such presentments containing very heavy charges against the government itself. It never occurred to me to be proper to suppress a practice which I found established, whether the exercise of it was agreeable to my private sentiments or not; and I incline to think, had the grand jury at Richmond, instead of presenting those circular letters, presented any obnoxious act of the government, and the court by an exertion of power had arbitrarily suppressed the presentment, it would have been the subject of a very virulent—and possibly a very just—invective, by some of those persons who have no scruple in condemning the court for not interfering with this.

With regard to the illiberal epithets Mr. Cabell has bestowed, not only on me, but on the other judges of the supreme court, I leave him in full possession of all the credit he can derive from the use of them. I defy him or any man to shew, that in the exercise of my judicial character, I have been ever influenced in the slightest degree by any man either in or out of

office, and I assure him I shall be as little influenced by this new mode of
attack by a member of congress as I can be by any other.

JAMES IREDELL.

Edenton, North-Carolina, }
   June 21st, 1797.   }

*Those Printers who published Mr. Cabell's observations, are requested to publish
the above.*

(Richmond) July 5, 1797. Date and place are those of the letter. This letter also was printed in
broadside form. North Carolina Collection, NcU.
  1. See Letter of Samuel Jordan Cabell, May 31, 1797.

"Marius" to "Jugurtha" ————————————————————
Virginia Gazette, and General Advertiser
June 24, 1797   Richmond, Virginia

Richmond, June 24, 1797.

TO JUGURTHA;—

SIR,

THE zeal which you have displayed in favor of the contested rights of
judges and juries, makes me tremble for the fate of my little production,
while writing it. But I flatter myself that it will escape their animadversion,
not only because it cannot "excite civil discord," but, also, because it is not
of a gigantic magnitude. It is intended for the instruction of the incautious,
and not for the information of the generality of our countrymen, of whose
understandings I entertain too high an opinion, to imagine that they can be
deluded even by the insidious wiles of a Jugurtha.[1]

I shall, with you, decline a censure or a defence of Mr. Cabell's address,
and shall in the course of a few remarks, confine myself to the proposition,
to which your reasoning is reduceable—"That if, upon the supposed principle
of doing right, Mr. Cabell addressed his constituents to obviate or remove
any erroneous opinions, the jury, upon the same principle, were not
blameable for censuring those addresses, to obviate the consequences to be
apprehended from the futility of his logic, or the glare of his language." It
appears to me strange that you should conceive Mr. Cabell guilty of an
indecency, in taking offence at the censure of those who think he has done
wrong, because you cannot but perceive that a man, who acts from a wish
to do right, may, from the same conscious rectitude of his intentions, feel
himself wounded by the acrimonious reflections of those, who deprecate his
conduct. To the judgment of his constituents he would not have hesitated
to submit it; but he doubts, and I doubt with him, whether a judicial body

of men have a right to brand with infamy, the expression of his political sentiments.

I hope you will not impute it to ignorance, when I say, that I never before heard, that jurors are conservators of morals, in the sense in which you are understood—if they are, they have been very negligent, as a number of offences (if they may be so termed) of the nature at present in dispute, have escaped their notice. I have always understood, that a jury is to determine whether the laws have been violated, and if so, to apply the remedy it has ordained. If they possessed any thing more than this power, they would punish (which is not the case) a number of offences against moral law, which the positive law does not reach. If they do not punish them because they are without their jurisdiction, neither can they take cognizance of political opinions, which the law has not expressly placed within it. When they go farther than this, they exceed the line of their duty, and assume a species of legislative power by inflicting a punishment upon persons obnoxious to them, according to their own vague notions of right and wrong. For certainly it must be a punishment of a very disagreeable nature, to be held up by twenty four men, as an object of derision or detestation to the other members of the community. You tell us, that as the people have, individually, a right to censure the opinions of an individual, the same right attaches itself to a collection of individuals—I thought you knew that the right of judging individually and judicially, are different—individuals having delegated their judicial power to a select body of men—they transferred it, because they were incapable of exercising it themselves collectively. But there was danger in trusting it in the hands of a few, without express rules to confine it; and every power not expressly delegated, is retained. Indeed, sir, that contended for, is built on a precarious foundation, since it is difficult to suppose that the legislature, which has been so cautious to prevent crimes of very trivial turpitude, should have neglected to give (expressly) authority to restrain political opinions, had they conceived it necessary.—In whatever manner certain opinions or actions, may be amenable to the law, I have not yet learned, that the former, disapprobative of the measures of government, or its administration, are subject to the same severity. Probably, sir, a predilection for the English law, and the decisions of their courts, has led you astray; but permit me to remind you, that our freedom flows not from so impure a source.

The consequences that would result from an admission of your principle itself, are, I think, sufficiently forcible to warrant a conclusion against you. If opinions that are not punishable by law, are subject to the animadversion of a grand jury, I would ask, if equal benefits would not flow from the influence of those expressed by respectable individuals in their private capacities; or whether they would not think themselves equally bound, in that case, to propagate those that are just, among the people, as when they compose a grand jury. On the other hand, if they are liable to be damned by a jury—the abilities and skill of a judge, may have great influence with a jury, and a juridical opinion may have great weight with the people. The opinions of the jurors being by themselves considered as incontrovertible—inconsonant to those they are to judge, and they bound down to no settled rule of deciding in that particular, the latter are condemned, and thus a way is, at least, paved, for obstructing the discussion of ministerial proceedings. Far be it from me to impeach the integrity of our judges or jurors—I assert the possibility of their abusing such a trust. In short, I believe no reflecting mind which considers how peculiarly careful the government of this country has been to preserve from the least degree of restraint, the freedom of opinion, on civil or religious subjects, can approve of an attempt to vest this power in a body of men, who, under pretence of repressing those inimical to public advantage, may damp the ardor that may animate a virtuous agent of the public, to express his sentiments for the benefit of his constituents.

Perhaps, sir, it will with some, be a matter of surprise, that so much time should have been expended upon a question so simple: But ingenuity can dim the lustre of the brightest truth, and yours has been instrumental in effecting that end on the present occasion—Yet, whenever arts of that description are used to confuse our minds, they shall be opposed by the efforts (however feeble they may be) of

MARIUS.

(Richmond) July 5, 1797. Date and place are those of the letter.
   1. We have been unable to locate a copy of the article by "Jugurtha."

"A Virginian" ————————————————————————————————
Columbian Centinel
June 24, 1797   Boston, Massachusetts

THE writer of this is a *Virginian*, and is as free as the honourable citizen *Cabal*, who has had the audacity to charge the Federal Court with impurity; and (what is more unnatural) the Grand Federal Jury of his own State, with the same infamous crime. Freedom of opinion is certainly an inherent privilege.—So is freedom of action.—But murder is to be punished by death. And although Grand Jurors are not lawmakers, yet they are its guardians, and it is their peculiar province to stop sedition—to quell, in short, all those vile Jacobinical publications, that have so strong a tendency to separate the government from the people, and thereby promote their favorite aim, viz. A CIVIL WAR. It is not foreign influence, that sways some Members of Congress—indeed it is domestic.—Some of my countrymen hate government, because it is just, and compels them to pay those abominable things, called *British Debts*. I shall, however, be just to my country, and say that, to use modern language, *Le Citoyen Cabal*, does not *speak* the sentiments of *Virginia*;

and that nine tenths of those who owe *British Debts*, have endeavoured to pay.

A VIRGINIAN,

Who will give his name, with the same freedom, as he does his sentiments, to those who may have a right to inquire for it.

(Boston) June 24, 1797. Date and place are those of the newspaper.

Gazette of the United States ————————————————————————

June 24, 1797   Fayetteville, North Carolina

Our intelligence announced in the last Wilmington paper, of the capture of Judge Chase, by the French privateer Le Grouper,[1] gives the friends of the federal judiciary in this state much concern.

It is well known this gentleman was lately called to a seat on the bench of the Supreme court of the U. States by reason of his law knowledge, his transcendent virtues and great discretion: his loss therefore, may be severely felt by deprivation of such judicial assistance.

But in another view, it may be deeply deplored, when it is considered that the practice of the French corsairs on our coasts, is to send their booty to the island of Guadalope for condemnation; should the Judge Chase fall into the unsparing hands of Victor Hugues; he might as property belonging to the United States, be deemed contraband, and as such, adjudged good prize[2]—As the Judges of Guadaloupe are said not to be enough to execute their duty in condemnation of American captures, (so numerous are they there) it may therefore be apprehended, Victor, from his supreme authority, may add Chase to the number of his Judges: If so, from that man's rapid progress towards the federal judgment seat in this state,—North-Carolina may tremblingly await the intimation of his decrees in another tribunal.

(Philadelphia) July 5, 1797. Date and place are those of the headline.

1. See the *Daily Advertiser* under date of June 15, 1797. This story was a hoax; see James Iredell to Hannah Iredell, August 3, 1797.

2. Victor Hugues, special agent of the French government in the French West Indies, had issued on February 1, 1797, a decree authorizing the capture of all neutral vessels bound for the British-occupied Windward and Leeward Islands. Such vessels would then be taken into French ports, "declared good prize, and ... sold for the benefit of the captors." *PAH,* 21:488n; 20:553-54n.

William Richardson Davie to James Iredell ————————————————

June 25, 1797   Halifax, North Carolina

...I received your letter from Richmond[1] covering your excellent charge delivered to the Grand Jury of that District, for which you will please to accept of my Thanks: I have often occasion to regret that the few men with whom my heart has formed attachments are scattered over the Earth by business and accident; and that the vagabond-life of a Lawyer, of which I am now heartily sick, deprives me even of the satisfaction of a regular correspondence; and I look forward with some anxiety to that period when this last inconvenience will be done away —

On my return to this place on monday last I received the Virginia Gazette containing the publications occasioned by your charge and the presentment of the Grand Jury of that District; this solemn evidence of a change of the public sentiment has given a serious alarm to the whole faction, and they will now move heaven and Earth to secure themselves from merited odium, and draw back the public mind into the sphere of French influence; where to the great misfortune of this Country it had been a long time stationary.

It will hardly be denied in this Country that all measures, whether of public or private men which have a direct tendency to destroy or disturb the Peace, good Government, or happiness of the Community are strictly within the inquest of a Grand Jury, and of course proper objects for a Judge's charge, and surely the greatest evil with which we were threatened at the present alarming crises was the disorganising effect of the correspondence of certain members of Congress, the baneful effects of which are visible in every part of the Southern States. ...

ARS (NcD, James Iredell Sr. and Jr. Papers). Addressed "Edenton." Sent "By Mʳ Amis."
1. Letter not found.

Circuit Court for the District of Delaware ——————————————
June 27, 1797   New Castle, Delaware

On June 27[1] court was opened by Associate Justice William Paterson and Judge Gunning Bedford, Jr. The docket of the circuit court does not note the court's closing. The "teste" day was June 27.[2]

1. The Circuit Court Act of 1797 had changed the day for holding court in Delaware from the second Monday in June to June 27. *Stat.*, 1:517.
2. Appearance Docket, CCD Delaware, RG 21, PPFAR.

"A Friend to Juries" to Samuel Jordan Cabell ——————————————
Virginia Gazette, and General Advertiser
June 30, 1797   Albemarle County, Virginia

SIR,
ADMIRING your attachment to the cause of liberty as I do, I cannot but lament, that the means you have adopted for its promotion, are not as

(Richmond) July 5, 1797. Date and place are those of the letter. Readings supplied in brackets where document is damaged.

promising of success, as both the object and intention deserve. That your intentions are pure, I never had a doubt. But unfortunately, those who are the greatest advocates for the freedom and exercise of opinion themselves, are of late, the greatest enemies, in reality, to that freedom of opinion in others, when it happens to differ from their own. Thus while you are supporting the freedom of opinion as it applies to yourself, you are endeavouring to sap the foundation of that same freedom in others; and that too in the most dangerous part to the community at large.

Your right, as an individual, to entertain whatever sentiment your judgment may dictate to you to be right, is not more valuable to yourself, than the maintenance of your independence, as a representative, in divulging those sentiments, is of consequence to your fellow-citizens at large. But neither the freedom of individual thought, nor the independence of representative expression, can be more valuable to either, than the protection and preservation of the judiciary, on whose freedom and independence, not only those, but all our other rights depend.

How far the judges are warranted to go, or what is the exact rule by which they ought to be governed in their charges, I will not undertake to say; nor do I believe it can be possibly shewn. That it is as much their duty however, to recommend temperance and good order in society, as it is to point out the actual offences against the laws, I have not the smallest doubt. How they are to do either, and yet avoid political topics, is what you and a few other late writers, who are entitled to all the honor of the discovery, can best point out. In order to have fixed the exact point to which the judges have a right to go in their charges to grand juries, you should have told us by what rule we might distinguish a political from a legal charge. The actual offences against the laws, you admit, are properly within their reach. The punishment of these offences, and the means of arriving at that punishment, I had ever thought, were a part of the political œconomy of the state. The judiciary itself is a part of the government of America, recognized by the Constitution, which is the written and only guide to all the different departments of that government. That the principles of that government can be too well understood, or those who are appointed to administer it, to whatever branch they may belong, can too often point out the reciprocal duties of the people and the government towards each other, is, I confess, what I never expected to hear from as warm an admirer of free government as yourself. Your own letters, as a member of one of the branches of that government, I make no doubt, were intended to explain to your constituents what *you* conceived to be the true doctrines of political happiness for them to embrace. In this I have as little doubt, you conceived you were discharging your duty. Why then may the judge, who is a member of another branch of the government, not explain to the grand-jury, what *he* conceives to be the obligation of the citizen to the government, and the government to the citizen? This I take it was the judge's object in the observations he made to the grand-jury at Richmond, of which you complain so much.

But your charge against the judge is far from being the most serious part of your complaint. In calling upon the indignation of the people to support you in the freedom of *your* opinions, you have made a direct attack on the freedom of the people themselves. Who, Sir, were the jury who made the presentment? a part of the free and independent people of America. Who had a right to controul *their* opinions? Not a power upon this earth certainly. As individuals they had as much right to enjoy their opinions as any other citizens. By becoming jurors they could not be abridged in those privileges. But if the offence was not punishable in any other way than by a naked presentment, you conclude, that the judge ought to have silenced the presentment. This, Sir, is an error, I am sure, which proceeded from your not being much accustomed to courts and juries, and not a wilful mistatement to deceive your countrymen. It is well known to every one the least conversant in these things, that there are offences which cannot be and never are punished in any other way. And it is obvious to any one who will reflect a moment on the nature of the punishment, that it is beyond the reach of any power of controul, short of that of the jurors themselves. It is the punishment of censure, which consists in the bare publication of a disapprobation of opinion. That publication must be made before the judge or any one else, besides the jurors can know the contents of the presentment. If then the law had given the judge the power of erasing the presentment, it must have given him the powers of Lethe[1] also, to have extended the benefit to a suspension of the punishment. But the judge had neither of those powers; and the jury might have presented his own charge, and he must, like yourself, have submitted to the punishment.

In the liberty of their opinions and the subject of their presentments, juries have no other limitation than the observance of their oath. They are sworn to present every irregular and disorderly, as well as illegal and criminal act, that comes within their knowledge. How then, if they conceived your letters were calculated to produce disorders in the society by inflaming the people, were they to avoid presenting them, and yet answer that neglect to their own consciences and the community whose peace and welfare they were thus bound to protect? Here, and here only then, they differed in their quality as jurors from their other quality as private citizens. The one has a right to conceal his opinions; the other is bound to declare them to his country. This you say *you* were bound to do from similar obligations as a member of Congress. You and the jury then stand upon precisely the same ground in point of official duty; as well as in the right to enjoy your opinions as private

---

1. In Greek mythology, a river in Hades whose water caused forgetfulness in those who drank it. *OED.*

citizens. But in some other respects, the jury will have the advantage, I should suppose, in the appeal that has been made to the public in the case.

This attack which has been made upon juries, who have ever been considered the greatest and best guardians of *all* our rights, calls for the most serious and attentive consideration of the people! Can there possibly be a more alarming attempt to overawe the freedom of opinion? If members of our Federal Legislature, will, at this early period of their existence, attempt to abridge this sacred institution in *its* rights, to serve their own ambitious or party views, what may we expect will be their regard for the *people's* rights at a more advanced period?—In England indeed the judges have sometimes attempted to prescribe the duty of juries. But never, in that corrupt country even, have the representatives of the people yet called upon the *people* themselves to direct that *their* conduct should be held sacred and above enquiry. Reflect, Sir, but a moment, on the consequences of such a precedent, and your own intentions in making the appeal, I am sure, will be at variance immediately with its obvious tendency!

I know the zeal and openess of your disposition. May I not be permitted then, to believe, that your name and the occasion, have been made use of by men, more designing than yourself, to answer *their* political views? I know not those suspected of being the substantial authors of the design. But if I may judge of the sentiments it is meant to exalt above the enquiry and animadversions of the people, from some of the literary labours of certain members in Congress, I think, I may venture to predict, without assuming to myself more sagacity than belongs to every citizen who pretends to look at all into his future prospects of political happiness, that the preservation of the independence of juries will be of infinitely more consequence towards the support of the real liberties of our country, than all the light that will ever be reflected from their letters; and, that if any are to be abridged in the freedom of opinions, by the *indignation* of the people, it had, at least, as well be, a few of those letter-writing politicians in Congress, as our juries, who are, in fact, the people themselves, in their original, and not their secondary or representative shape.

But, Sir, neither is necessary. You and those gentlemen too, have a right to think and write for *one-another* whatever you please; and the people, either in their individual or collective capacities, have a right to judge of your sentiments. Whether this inquest of the people over the body of this state have judged right or wrong, is not for me or any one else but themselves to determine. Perhaps if I had been one of them, my opinion might have differed from those who made the presentment, in the means of correcting the evil it was meant to remedy. But if a majority of the jurors thought the presentment necessary, as I make no doubt they did, there can be no question about their right to make it.

Give me leave to set you right in another particular respecting the jury, which strikes at once, at the reputation of the court, the marshal, and the jury, who are all too honest, I am sure to merit such a censure. You insinuate that the jury was packed, and that of foreigners, to answer the particular purpose of supporting certain party politics. This, Sir, was an ungenerous insinuation to be made at random; and (as it only could have been made from a sight of the panel, at such a distance from the spot where they were impannelled) I am sure was done without giving yourself time to reflect, that there are many people often of the same name. I have enquired into the actual persons of the jurors, and know them all except two. These might have been foreigners for ought I know. The rest were native Americans, taken from very different parts of the state, as they ought to have been. And one of them, who, I will venture to presume, you concluded from the name, was an inhabitant of Richmond, was a citizen of Campbell, or Bedford county, and opposed to the presentment, I will hazard an assertion which, I doubt not [you] will find to be correct on further examina[tion.]

[Permit me?] now to close those observations, which have been designedly delayed until you returned from Congress, with assuring you, that I am personally, your friend. Many considerations combine to make me so. And it has often been a subject of regret, that the difference of opinion in politics, had separated so far from me in his public pursuits, a man, who had been among my most early and intimate associates in private life: who, believe me, upon every other ground, possesses still the affections of—a real constituent, and—

A FRIEND TO JURIES.

Albemarle, June 30, '97.

Daily Advertiser ───
July 1, 1797   Philadelphia, Pennsylvania

We learn, that the state of South-Carolina is in very great want of horses; otherwise the learned judge Chase could certainly have got one for his carriage. The state is said, however, to have some tolerable oxen. Doctor Sparman penetrated the immense mountains behind the Cape of Good-Hope in a waggon drawn by ten or twelve oxen.[1] But our judge had no formidable mountains to cross—a cart with one horse would have drawn him. Many a good journey has been accomplished upon a jack ass, and even upon foot. There have been repeated examples of this kind of negligence on the part of the bench.

(Philadelphia) July 1, 1797. Date and place are those of the newspaper.

1. Anders Sparrman (1748-1820), a Swedish physician and naturalist, explored the interior of South Africa in 1775 and 1776. He recounted his journeys in *A Voyage to the Cape of Good Hope,* an English translation of which was published in London in 1786. *Dictionary of South African Biography* (Johannesburg: National Council for Social Research, 1968).

Samuel Johnston by an unknown artist. Oil on canvas, date unknown. Courtesy James Iredell Association, Edenton, North Carolina.

Samuel Johnston to James Iredell ————————————————
  July 5, 1797 Williamston, North Carolina

...I have read Mr Cabels very illiberal and unprovoked attack upon you and your answer than which nothing could be more proper, if it was proper to give it any answer at all. I am very sensible of the difficulty with which a man of warm feelings and conscious integrity submits to bear, without a reply illiberal and unmeritted Censure; yet I am not certain but that it is more suitable to the dignity of one placed in a very high and respectable department of State, to consider himself bound to answer only when called upon constitutionally before a proper Tribunal; otherwise it may happen that too much of that time ^and attention which he owes to the duties of his Office will be wasted in answering the petulant attacks of every vain or wicked man who takes it into his head that he has a Talent for writing; it is besides very difficult to say how a contest of this kind is to be decided, for after innumerable replications and rejoinders fresh matter will continually arise to keep it perpetually alive. As to Mr Cabel's putting his name to his publication, I do not consider that that circumstance entitles him to more respect than if he had written under a fictitious signature, it is an evidence rather of his confidence than his Candor _. ...

ARS (Nc-Ar, Charles E. Johnson Collection). Addressed "Edenton."

"Timothy Tickle" to Samuel Jordan Cabell

Virginia Gazette, and General Advertiser
July 5, 1797   Richmond, Virginia

SIR,

I HAVE often heard of people's being condemned without *judge* or *jury*—but I am sure you cannot say this has been your case. Your letters have been seen, read, and fairly judged of by all America; and even your best friends and meanest relations have condemned them. A court and jury, you say, have passed sentence upon them. You may, therefore, fairly be said to have been tried by your peers. After all this, common prudence ought to have dictated to you to have committed yourself no further: But like one who has suffered all the disgrace of condemnation, a reprieve has been of no other service to you, than to prepare you the better for the prosecution of your favorite practice. We must, therefore, try you again for this new offence of *letter-borrowing*.

I will not, however, make the charge of *borrowing* this last rag of knowledge from the letter-manufactory of Philadelphia, the only charge against you, but will try the thing on its real merits as if it was actually your own.

The charge then now turns upon a discantation on the duty of courts and juries, and their right to intermeddle with the freedom and independence of *your* thoughts. Without a quibble, we might fairly try this last production, before any court and jury, with out intermeddling, much, with the freedom

(Richmond) July 5, 1797. Date and place are those of the newspaper. Readings supplied in brackets where paper is torn.

and *Independence* of *your* thoughts, if the general conjecture be true, of that *independence* consisting chiefly in the right of substituting the thoughts and sentiments of others for your own. But as you are the first in America who has had the honor of objecting to the trial by court and jury, I will leave the *freedom* and *independence* of your borrowing the *thoughts* of others, which is but a mere personal thing, to the true enjoyment of those *independent* considerations, and examine into your objections to the court and jury mentioned in your address, which indeed are of some consequence to the real liberties of this country.

Unfortunately for some of those who bow down, with the most constant and loud professions of love and admiration, to the goddess of liberty, they view the lovely medal on but one side only. They are friends to the "liberty and independence of thought" only, while that liberty and independence of thought consists in adopting the thoughts of others, and turning them particularly to their use, this appears to be wholly the amount of your idea of the liberty and independence of thought—which you appear to have borrowed, with many other excellent things, from that favourite republic, which is now rambling all over the world with its destructive armies, and *compelling* all the nations it can to be *free—but upon their own terms.*

One of the terms upon which they have *compelled* some nations to be *free*, is, that they subscribe to governments similar to their own. One of the excellent traits of their government, I believe, at the time when they set Holland *free*, and it is pretty much the practice still, was the happy nack which the *democrats* had of dispensing with the little ceremonies and formalities of *courts* and *juries* in the trial of the *aristocrats*. Those tribunals, might, perhaps, have exercised some "liberty and independence of thought," as well as the *democrats*, and thereby have stopped the effusion of so much innocent—such horrid sluices of infant and female blood.

You, sir, it is well known, have laboured as far as your feeble efforts could effect it, to prevail on the people of this country to make no resistance—or rather, to join those bloody monsters in case they should invade your country; and you have now subscribed your name to another inflammatory address, calculated to render the institution of courts and juries unpopular, if it is calculated to do any thing, in order to make way for those noble consequences which flowed from the want of them in France, whose principles you so much adore, and have thus attempted to introduce here.

The judges of the federal court you arraign for becoming a band of political preachers (as you are pleased to call them) and going about with unwarrantable sermons to support the government of the United States. This appears to be the substance of the charge against them. Admitting it in its fullest latitude then, to what does the charge amount?— The insinuation goes to shew that they have nothing to do with politics. In the name of common sense, what is the judiciary, who are the judges of this country? Are they not a branch of the American government, bound to support that government, as well as every other branch of it, both by the nature of their relationship with the government and their oath? What is the government they are thus bound to support, what the laws of that government, which your adopted address seems to admit is their duty to expound to do justice between individuals, if they are not a part of the political arrangements of this country? How then are the judges possibly to avoid political discussions, and giving their political opinions between the government and individuals, and yet do their duty?—Suppose the government, or rather a part of the government, was to attempt to abridge you in any of your rights—For instance, to impress you as a seaman, or pretend to enlist you as a soldier, to fight against the French, would you not then think that the judiciary should interfere? And what would that interference be, but one of the greatest political questions that could arise between an individual and a state? Why not then, when the injury is attempted to be reversed from the individual to the state, suffer the judge to interpose a little political advice?

You (or rather the person who writes for you) seems to admit, that if you had done any thing criminal, the judge was right. That is admitting, I suppose, that a judge, though he be a federal judge, has a right to give it in charge to a jury, as their duty, to present all felonies, such as treason, murder, and all other capitol offences—but, that every thing that falls below the dignity of any other punishment, but a bare presentment of a jury, is not cognizable in that way. You should have remembered, in the first place, that you were not the proper judge of the degree of your own guilt. And in the second place, it is a fact, well known to every one who has ever been a juryman in any part of America, that there are certain offences which cannot be punished in any other way, but by the censure of "naked presentment." Admitting it to be the right of a judge then, to enter into a history of the rise and progress of juries, which certainly cannot be told over too often to the real lovers of liberty, and to enter into an explanation of their duty in the presentment of actual offences against the laws, which are certainly a *political* grievance, I see not how your letters, which had been condemned as a political petty-larceny by every hangman in the state, were possibly to escape!

But, Sir, admitting every thing that is said in that paper against the judge to be right, though in fact he said nothing about you, your letters, or any one else in his charge, how is, what is there said of the jury, to be reconciled to that love which you pretend to have for the "freedom and independence of thought?"

The jury by whom that presentment was made, was composed of the free and independent citizens of Virginia, who were as much entitled to think and act for themselves as any other citizens of America—the members of congress themselves even not excepted. Unless it can be proved, then, that the jury was packed (which you dare not assert) they are no more chargeable with having acted wrong, for having exercised *their* "freedom and independence of thought," than you yourself were intitled to prefer *your* *own* "freedom and independence of thought," to the borrowing of the genius of a Madison in the composition of the letters they presented. And whoever is acquainted with the jury, and will* look over the pannel, as you have invited them, will as clearly see, that there was no more of the influence of an Iredell in the presentment, than there was the genius of a Madison in the letters. Here then you and the jury stand upon exactly equal ground with respect to the "freedom and independence of thought," which is the mighty and important burthen of this last political ditty.

But how do you stand in this last attempt, with respect to the actual means of securing the liberties and independence of your country?—Juries, altho' I believe we are indebted to that wretched place, Great-Britain, for their institution (and this is one of the reasons, perhaps, why you hate the exercise of their power so much) have ever been considered the great palladium of American, as well as British liberty. Which do you really think would be best, then, for the people to join you in your "INDIGNATION" to awe those useful institutions from the exercise of *their* "freedom and independence of thought," or suffer them to go on without reproach, as they think necessary and right, to expose the follies of a few little letter-writing politicians in Congress?

It might indeed be a valuable thing to those gentlemen who have no other means of supporting their popularity, to establish the doctrine of their conduct's being held sacred and above enquiry, while in Congress. But after an attempt to destroy that inestimable "freedom and independence of thought" which ought always to be attached to courts and juries, to make way for that kind of sacredness in the Representative branch of the government, what would the people have to expect? Could they be surprised to see that branch attempt to erect itself into any thing, which the same love of popularity, that suggested the first attempt might invite them to in a more promising degree? It is to the preservation of the independence of the judiciary, I had always thought, that we were to look for the salvation of liberty. While you are standing as a *centinel* then, over the "freedom and independence of the *valuable* thoughts" of Messrs. Claiborne, Clopton, New, and yourself, I shall stand as an humble advocate for the RIGHTS OF JURIES, and a constant

---

*I have complied with your request in looking over the names of the grand jury, who you insinuate were all foreigners but a few—I know them all, I think; except two—These may be foreigners for ought I know—The rest are native Americans, and I will venture to say as valuable citizens as yourself, though not members of congress; and if you will be at the trouble of looking over their names again, yourself, I think you may expect to hear from some of them in a different way, than through the newspapers, for your dark and false insinuations against them.

exposer of the many follies and improprieties which such writers are endeavouring to impose on the people in their own favour.

For after all that has been said about the court and jury's "overawing the freedom of thought," can there possibly be a more alarming attempt, than for the members of the legislature, to call up the terror of the people, to overawe the courts and juries in *their* favor?—Really, Sir, this last attempt, which cannot be repeated too often, or shewn in too many different shapes, if possible, exceeds the first, in which you endeavoured to prevail on the people to join the French *against themselves*. But fortunately, both attempts are equally absurd; and the execution nothing more than a ridicule of the design. Whenever I look into one of your letters as a mere matter of curiosity, as I seldom do for any thing else, I feel an almost irresistable inclination to laugh. But when I turn my reflections from that source of meriment, to the district you represent, I feel an involuntary propensity to weep. For, if it be true, that there is a design to increase the powers of the Union, whether it be by the *aristocratic* or *democratic* exertions of its members, what (alas!) must be the chance of *that* district for its due share in the distribution of those powers?—For Heaven sake then, if you have no delicacy and tenderness for yourself, have some small compassion for the poor unfortunate district you represent, at least; and write no more for the press.

The people send you to Congress, as I have once told you before, Sir, to do their business; and not to employ all your time in writing letters. They wish to hear from you, as other districts do from their representatives, in the exercise of your duty, through the debates, and not through the channel of those badly-letter-composed-common-place-party sayings, which they get in all the news-papers, at least a week, before they do through those ponderous bales from your letter-copartnery. It would answer the valuable end of shewing them what was really the "free and independent thoughts" of their own representative—and would furnish the means of a more fair and just appreciation of those real thoughts which I promise you shall never be neglected, by your friend and real constituent—

TIMOTHY TICKLE.

P.S. I will not be so wanting in candor however, as to conceal from you, that, notwithstanding your many errors and party-violence, there are two or three in this part of the world who think with you; nor will I be so ungenerous as to keep from you the "free and independent opinions" of one of those friends, which you are entitled to, in aid of some others which have already been published in your favor. It is a letter picked up in the road, supposed to have been droped by the post on its way to you. I have directed the printer to publish it in all its valuable originality of "freedom of thought," false grammer and bad spelling; as it would be wrong, you know, to interfere with your friends liberty and right to disgrace themselves. I have only subjoined a few notes of my own by way of explanation. The very first line of the letter shews the relationship which your correspondent claims.

---

to cousin sammy *caball* by the post boy.

dear cousin,

i take up my pen to inform you that your last pisle has come to hand. you dont think how the risticats that you tokt so much about grind at the presentement of the guree against you. but for my part it made me right mad. the court and some of the guree you no are men of larning, and I hate your men of larning, and they dont like us you may depend upon it cousin *caball*. but I like you for that reson. for a representive ot to be a representive you no. he ot to represent what he is intended to represent. and how wood a man of larning be a good representation of a magouetee of your *colleges*.[*][1] what better cood be expected then from a court where there was a gudge upon the bench and a gudge in the guree room. every boddy must no that thay wood be shore to go rong. and contrary to law. i dont like that same fiddral court at tall. you no it was them that made your good old f—in—law pay a large old brittish debt which ruined him. and them dets you no ot not to be pade. what did you and we pore millissee men fite so d—d hard for last war if our best frends and deerest relashons are to be ruinned at last to pay these old brittish marchunts acconts. i o one myself. and i never will pay it as long as i can get such good fellows as you and some of your supporters to stand by me and cry down the fiddral court and gurees. in short i think all our courts and gurees have too much power, thay ot not to be suffered to think as thay plese. cant you get a law paced in congris that if thay think and act contrary to law that all thay doo shall go for nothing. i think with the *ass siistance* of my cousin *jiles* and some of the rest of our french functionarrities† you might have it done. and then you might right and say what you please you no, and the guree would have no right to think about it. but ant it strange that you congris men will let one of the gudges from ireland come over here and act as a gudge and a preacher too both at once. i suppose if this same ireland gudge or gudge [*word missing*] gudges of the law all the weke and then pre[aches] about religion of sundays as you say he must be p[ade] for both. and i raly think as one of your friends does who has ritten in the papers about it. and says he has bin treeted very

---

* Simon here means constituents I suppose. But his own word will do full as well.

† I suppose Simon means by this a word which I observe Mr. Giles has just received from the French mint, which coins a great many delightful words as well as principles for this country's coxcombs, apes and pedants.

1. No asterisk appears in this printing of "Simon Simple's" letter; its placement is taken from a reprint in the *Gazette of the United States* (Philadelphia), July 13, 1797.

hospitally in vurginnee, that our good bacun and collards that he eats so much off when he rides here so fur upon one off his long towers just to present your litters which he sees is to do so much good to this cuntry against his is pay anuf for his empty irish guts. this was a good hit in your frend dont you think it was to tell him how he was treeted in your cuntry where he had treated you so ill. and therefore that he did not desirve any better than to be told off it. igad i think he was up with him for his presentment. wont he now. upon the hole. that is to say. by the by. as i has herde some of your common fox say. who say a word and then give you a nother of the same sort to explane it you no. it is true what you have sade in your last fine pise. vedelesit to wit. that no moral *truth* can be more *true* than that palitikal truth that is true. or something like that. tantenount there four every thing that you have sade must be twice true. etsetteree and so fourth. i forgot to tell you that‡ alias morris and tempore the taylor are determined to be your enemies at the next lection. and i raly beleve from what I have heard they will do you a grate deal off harm. i advise you therefore when you right again only rite to your friends. and tell um to clear away your *litters* off ove thare hobs and jams after they have red um for feer some more of these larned men may come in and afterwards git on the gurees. but above all. stick to your sentry box as you have promised. and continue to hollow and make all the racket you can and as you say you will against the government cousin *caball* and you shall ever have the vate and interest of your sincere frend and near relation.

simon simple.

notty binny. give my kind love and sarvis to cousin jiles. unkle claburn. *brother* clapton. daddy newcurnul *sparker.* and all frends and good fellows. granny diner who dancd with you so much at the last lection and got you so many votes thanks you for your last kind and loving pisle. no more at present, but all is well and hope this will find you in same citeation.

S. S.

‡ He takes *alias* and *mores* for Elias Morris, some constituent of his cousin's, I suppose. And no wonder that poor Simon should be run into such an error by his cousin's learning, when we are told that one of his ablest advocates on being asked the meaning of *O tempora! O mores!* after pausing a little and considering that much was said in that letter about speculations, bankruptcies, &c. and reflecting at the same time on the lowness of certain notes, said, that it was an advice to be temperate in Morris's notes. In short it is impossible to number the various translations and uses that have been made of these celebrated words, or to measure the demand that these letters have been in, and still are. The Duke of Cumberland's love-letters never were in higher demand, nor more deservedly.

[Notty binny, as Simon says—I have taken the liberty of marking some of Simon's words to be printed in Italics. Indeed some of his friends names, as he has spelt them, deserve to be written in letters of gold.]

T—— T——.

James Iredell to Hannah Iredell ————————————————————
    August 3, 1797   Baltimore, Maryland

... Mͬ͟ Chase is safe at home ... I have just left his house _ The story of his capture was a mere fabrication, but I believe real disappointments alone prevented his reaching Raleigh.[1] He has mentioned particulars which satisfy me. ...

ARS (Nc-Ar, Charles E. Johnson Collection). Addressed "Edenton, North Carolina." Postmarked "BALT-AUG [3?]."
    1. See reports of Samuel Chase's capture by privateers in the *Daily Advertiser* under date of June 15, 1797; and *Gazette of the United States* under date of June 24, 1797.

Justices of the Supreme Court to John Adams ————————————————
    August 15, 1797   Philadelphia, Pennsylvania

                                                    Philadelphia,   Augͭ͟ 15͟ᵗͪ 1797.
Sir
    We take the liberty of representing to you, that a very inconvenient change took place in June 1794, in altering the time of holding the Circuit Court for Delaware from the 27͟ᵗͪ of April to the 27͟ᵗͪ of June.[1] Upon the former arrangement the Judge attended the Courts belonging to the Middle Circuit in the following regular succession, viz. New Jersey, Pennsylvania, Delaware, Maryland and Virginia. Since the above alteration there is an unnecessary interval between the times of holding the Courts of Pennsylvania and Maryland (neither of which has been altered) and any judge appointed to that Circuit who lives to the Southward of Delaware would be put to great inconvenience in being obliged to return immediately from Virginia to Delaware to hold a Court there, which we presume, with equal convenience to the public, might be held in the former course. We therefore request the favor of you, Sir, to lay this letter before the Congress at the next session,[2] in the hope, that they will be pleased to alter the existing law by restoring the former time of holding the spring session of Delaware, viz. 27͟ᵗͪ April instead of the 27͟ᵗͪ of June, the time now appointed. We think it proper to add, that to avoid any inconvenience to the State of Delaware, we have written a letter to the Governor of that State, informing him of the͟ intention to make this application.[3]

We have the honor to be,   With the greatest respect,   Sir,   Your most obedient and most humble   servants.

> Oliv̄: Ellsworth
> Wᵐ Cushing
> Ja. Iredell
> Wᵐ Paterson.
> Samuel Chase.

RS (DNA, RG 59, Miscellaneous Letters); C (DNA, RG 46). Except for the signatures, the version published here is in the h?nd of Supreme Court clerk Jacob Wagner. The copy indicates that this representation was addressed to President John Adams. James Wilson's signature does not appear on the representation because he was not present at the August 1797 term of the Court. DHSC, 1:290n.

1. For further information on changes in the time of holding the spring Delaware circuit court and the justices' objections, see introduction to "Spring and Fall Circuits 1797."

2. The president sent the justices' representation to Congress on December 13, 1797. SLJ, 2:415; HRJ, 3:103.

3. See Justices of the Supreme Court to Gunning Bedford, August 15, 1797.

Justices of the Supreme Court to Gunning Bedford ———
August 15, 1797   Philadelphia, Pennsylvania

Philadelphia   August 15ᵗʰ 1797.

Sir,

Upon the first arrangement of the Circuit Courts by Congress[1] the Courts in the middle Circuit were held in the following Order _ New Jersey, Pennsylvania, Delaware, Maryland, and Virginia _ beginning with the first, and ending with the last: And the Circuit Court for the District of Delaware was held in the Spring on the 27ᵗʰ of April, immediately following that for the District of Pennsylvania which was, and is still held on the 11ᵗʰ of April. In June 1794 an Act of Congress made an alteration as to the Circuit Court for Delaware, by directing the Court which was formerly to have been held on the 27ᵗʰ of April to be held on the   of June;[2] and at the same time no alteration was made in the times of holding the other Courts upon the same Circuit, so that a considerable interval of time was in a manner lost, and those Judges who lived to the Southward of Virginia ₍were₎ put to the extreme hardship of returning from Virginia to Delaware to hold a Court there, instead of spending a few weeks in a short vacation with their Families, or subjecting some other Judge to the inconvenience of extra-duty in addition to a share oppressive enough under any circumstances. The alteration was made without the knowledge of any of the Judges but one that such an alteration was intended.[3] As however the alteration has subsisted for some time, and we understand the times of holding some of the State Courts have been accomodated to it, we did not wish that any change should take place, even by restoring the former time which we think will be proper to be done, so as to produce an immediate inconvenience to the business of the State Courts. We therefore, Sir, now take the liberty to inform You that it is our intention to apply to the Congress at their next Session to restore the former time, and we flatter ourselves this early notice will enable the State to take such measures in regard to the times of holding the State Courts which may interfere with the proposed time of holding the Circuit Court, as may obviate all inconveniences which would otherwise subsist.[4]

We have the honour to be, with great respect, Sir, Your most obedient and most humble Servants

> Oliv̄: Ellsworth
> W͞ᵐ Cushing
> Ja. Iredell
> W͞ᵐ Paterson.
> Samuel Chase

RS (PHi, Gratz Collection). Except for the signatures, the letter is in the hand of Associate Justice James Iredell. Addressed to "His Excellency The Governor of the State of Delaware, Newcastle, Delaware." Postmarked "16 AV." James Wilson's signature does not appear on this letter because he was not present at the August 1797 term of the Court. *DHSC,* 1:290n.

Gunning Bedford (1742-1797), a cousin of Judge Gunning Bedford, Jr., was governor of Delaware from January 1796 to September 30, 1797. *BDAC.*

1. Judiciary Act of 1789, sections 4 and 5. *Stat.,* 1:74-75.

2. Section 2 of the District and Circuit Court Act of 1794 provided that the court be held on the second Monday of June. *Stat.,* 1:395.

3. On January 12, 1798, Samuel Chase wrote to John Rutledge, Jr., (q.v.), that only Associate Justice James Wilson had been informed of the proposed change.

4. For further information on the justices' objections to the change in the date of the commencement of the spring Delaware circuit court, see introduction to "Spring and Fall Circuits 1797."

James Iredell to Hannah Iredell ─────────────────────────────

August 16, 1797   Philadelphia, Pennsylvania

... I propose leaving this City tomorrow or next day. Your Friends in general here are well_ Some few Persons have lately died of a Fever at the south end of the Town which has created a little alarm, and by some is supposed to be the yellow Fever, tho' I was told last evening Dᴿ Rush[1] had said it was only a Fever to which at this season the City has been for many years accustomed _ I am to go no Circuit this Fall. I spent Sunday with my Mother _ She was remarkably well. ...

ARS (Nc-Ar, Charles E. Johnson Collection). Addressed "Edenton, North Carolina."

1. Benjamin Rush (1745-1813), a prominent Philadelphia physician. *DAB.*

Circuit Court for the District of New York ———————————
September 1, 1797   New York, New York

On September 1[1] Associate Justice William Cushing and Judge Robert Troup opened court, and a charge was delivered to the grand jury. The court adjourned on September 5 to the following term.[2]

1. The Circuit Court Act of 1797 changed the date for holding court in New York from September 5 to September 1. *Stat.,* 1:517.
2. Minutes, CCD New York, RG 21, NjBaFAR. Charge not found.

James Wilson to Bird Wilson ———————————
September 6, 1797   Burlington, New Jersey

Burlington 6th Septr 1797

Dear Bird

An Express from Mr Wallis[1] gives me an Opportunity of expressing my extreme Astonishment at your not coming here before this Time. At all
                                                    to Morrow Morning at latest.
Events set out as soon as you possibly can upon receiving this Letter; ∧ .
Another Process has been executed, which will require about 300 D^{rs} or Bail to the Amount of 600 D^{rs} to discharge it. Mention this to Mr Thomas.[2] Bring with you some Shirts and Stockings _ I want them exceedingly _ as also Money as much as possible, without which I cannot leave this Place.[3]

Yours affectionately

James Wilson

B. Wilson Esq

ARS (PHi, James Wilson Papers).
Bird Wilson had been admitted to the Philadelphia bar in March 1797. *MBBP,* p. 324.
1. Samuel Wallis (1730-1798), of Lycoming County, Pennsylvania, was a land speculator and business partner of James Wilson. John F. Meginness, *History of Lycoming County, Pennsylvania* (Chicago: Brown, Runk, 1892), pp. 66-80.
2. Joseph Thomas, Wilson's lawyer in Philadelphia. Smith, *James Wilson,* p. 383.
3. Wilson needed the money to get out of the Burlington jail. For Wilson's financial problems and jailing, see introduction to "Spring and Fall Circuits 1797."

Circuit Court for the District of Connecticut ———————————
September 18, 1797   Hartford, Connecticut

Associate Justice William Cushing and Judge Richard Law opened the fall session of the circuit court on Monday, September 18.[1] The court adjourned on September 25.[2]

1. The Circuit Court Act of 1797 changed the date for holding court in Connecticut from September 25 to September 17. *Stat.,* 1:517.

2. Docket Book, CCD Connecticut, RG 21, MWalFAR.

Circuit Court for the District of New Jersey ——————————————
October 2, 1797   Trenton, New Jersey

On Monday, October 2,[1] Associate Justice William Paterson convened court and delivered a charge to the grand jury. The court adjourned the same day to the following term.[2]

1. The date of the court was changed from October 2 to October 1 by the Circuit Court Act of 1797. *Stat.,* 1:517.

2. Minutes, CCD New Jersey, RG 21, NjBaFAR. We have been unable to identify the specific charge given. For undated Paterson grand jury charges, see Appendix A.

Circuit Court for the District of Vermont ——————————————
October 3, 1797   Rutland, Vermont

Associate Justice William Cushing and Judge Samuel Hitchcock opened court on October 3.[1] The court adjourned on October 7 to the next term.[2]

1. The date for holding the Vermont court was moved from November 7 to October 3 by the Circuit Court Act of 1797. *Stat.,* 1:517.

2. Circuit and Rough Dockets, CCD Vermont, RG 21, MWalFAR.

Circuit Court for the District of Pennsylvania ——————————————
October 11, 1797   Philadelphia, Pennsylvania

During the late summer and early fall of 1797 a yellow fever epidemic swept Philadelphia. No judges attended court on opening day, October 11, so the marshal of the district adjourned it. He did the same from day to day until October 14 when, as no judges had yet appeared, he adjourned the court until the next term.[1]

1. James Mease, *The Picture of Philadelphia* (1811; reprint ed., New York: Arno Press, 1970), p. 37; Engrossed Minutes, CCD Pennsylvania, RG 21, PPFAR.

Circuit Court for the District of Massachusetts ——————————————
October 20, 1797   Boston, Massachusetts

On October 20[1] court opened with Associate Justice William Cushing and Judge John Lowell in attendance. The court adjourned on October 30.[2]

1. The Circuit Court Act of 1797 changed the date for holding court from October 12 to October 20. *Stat.,* 1:517.

2. Final Records, CCD Massachusetts, RG 21, MWalFAR.

Circuit Court for the District of South Carolina ———————

October 25, 1797   Charleston, South Carolina

Associate Justice James Wilson and Judge Thomas Bee convened the court on October 25. James Wilson delivered a charge to the grand jury after court was opened. On October 28 the court adjourned to the following term.[1]

1. Minutes, CCD South Carolina, RG 21, GEpFAR. Charge not found.

Circuit Court for the District of Delaware ———————

October 27, 1797   Dover, Delaware

On October 27 Associate Justice William Paterson and Judge Gunning Bedford, Jr., opened court. The docket of the circuit court does not note the court's closing. The "teste" day was October 28.[1]

1. Appearance Docket, CCD Delaware, RG 21, PPFAR.

State House, Dover, Delaware, built 1788-1792, restored 1972-1976 to its appearance ca. 1815. Photograph 1987. The federal courts in the 1790s did not have their own courthouses, but rather used the main government building in each town. In Dover this would have been the State House.

Courtroom in the State House, Dover, Delaware, built 1788-1792, restored 1972-1976 to its appearance ca. 1815. Photograph 1987. The judges sat at the elevated table at the far end of the room, with the clerk at the small table in front of them. The lawyers worked at the large table in the middle of the room; the jurors heard testimony from the wings. When the petit jury was present it was located on the left, and when the grand jury was in session, it sat on the right. The defendant occupied the prisoner's dock in the front, where two staffs with metal tips, called tipstaves, flanked him on either side. The tips were painted white on one side and red on the other and would be turned white side out to signal innocent and red to signal guilty.

Circuit Court for the District of New Hampshire ————————
November 2, 1797   Exeter, New Hampshire

Associate Justice William Cushing and Judge John Pickering convened the New Hampshire circuit court on November 2.[1] On November 4 the court adjourned to the following term.[2]

1. The date for holding court had been changed from October 24 to November 2 by the Circuit Court Act of 1797. *Stat.,* 1:517.
2. Records, CCD New Hampshire, RG 21, MWalFAR.

Circuit Court for the District of Maryland ————————————
November 7, 1797   Baltimore, Maryland

On November 7 court commenced in Baltimore[1] with Associate Justice William Paterson and Judge William Paca in attendance. Court was adjourned on November 11 to the following term.[2]

1. The Circuit Court Act of 1797 changed the place for holding the fall circuit court from Easton to Baltimore. *Stat.,* 1:517.
2. Minutes, CCD Maryland, RG 21, PPFAR.

Circuit Court for the District of Georgia ————————————
November 8, 1797   Augusta, Georgia

Court opened with Associate Justice James Wilson and Judge Joseph Clay, Jr., in attendance. On November 17 the court adjourned to the following term.[1]

1. Minutes, CCD Georgia, RG 21, GEpFAR.

Circuit Court for the District of Rhode Island ————————
November 15, 1797   Providence, Rhode Island

On November 15[1] court was convened by Associate Justice William Cushing and Judge Benjamin Bourne and was adjourned on November 22.[2]

1. The Circuit Court Act of 1797 changed the date of the fall court from November 19 to November 15. *Stat.,* 1:517.
2. Minutes, CCD Rhode Island, RG 21, MWalFAR.

Circuit Court for the District of Virginia ————————————
November 22, 1797   Richmond, Virginia

On November 22 Associate Justice William Paterson and Judge Cyrus Griffin opened court. A charge was delivered to the grand jury on the same day. The court adjourned on December 4.[1]

Providence from Across the Cove by Alvan Fisher (1792-1863). Oil on canvas, 1818. Courtesy Rhode Island Historical Society, Providence.

1. Order Book, CCD Virginia, Vi. We have been unable to identify the specific charge given. For undated Paterson grand jury charges, see Appendix A.

James Iredell to Hannah Iredell
November 29, 1797   "Hermitage," Martin County, North Carolina

...I propose going as far as Sam. Williams's[1] tomorrow on my way to Halifax _ Capt. Collins[2] is to send off from Raleigh on Friday morning if Wilson does not arrive on Thursday, and I probably shall wait the arrival of his Servant all day on Saturday. If he does not arrive, or I hear Wilson is at Raleigh, I shall set off immediately on my return.[3] ...

ARS (Nc-Ar, Charles E. Johnson Collection). Addressed "Edenton."

1. Possibly Samuel Williams, the brother of Elizabeth (Williams) Johnston (d. 1789), who was married to Hannah Iredell's brother, John Johnston (1735-1791). Williams probably lived near the Roanoke River, in either Bertie or Halifax County. *PJI*, 1:137; "Abstract of Bertie County Wills," *North Carolina Historical and Genealogical Register* 2 (July 1901): 3.

2. Josiah Collins, Sr., (1734-1819), a wealthy North Carolina merchant and long-time acquaintance of James Iredell's. *Carolina Centinel* (New Bern), May 22, 1819; Spence, *Tombstones and Epitaphs of Northeastern North Carolina*, p. 56; Alice Barnwell Keith, William H. Masterson, and David T. Morgan, eds., *The John Gray Blount Papers, 1764-1833* 4 vols. (Raleigh: State Department of Archives and History, 1952-1982), 1:177; *MJI*, 2:52n, 303, 430.

3. Iredell wrote to his wife the next day that, "I am just setting off for [Halifax?] Allowing all Saturday to hear from Raleigh I can't expect at any rate to set out on my return till Sunday, if I find no necessity for going to Raleigh which God forbid _ I am now quite well _ " (James Iredell to Hannah Iredell, November 30, 1797, Charles E. Johnson Collection, Nc-Ar).

In the spring of 1797 no court had been held at Raleigh because of the absence of Associate Justice Samuel Chase. Iredell may have feared that either James Wilson's pressing financial affairs or a lengthy circuit court session in Georgia would prevent Wilson from reaching Raleigh in time to hold the North Carolina circuit court. For further information about James Wilson's financial difficulties, see introduction to "Spring and Fall Circuits 1797."

Circuit Court for the District of North Carolina
November 30, 1797   Raleigh, North Carolina

Associate Justice James Wilson and Judge John Sitgreaves convened the court. On December 8 the court adjourned to the following term.[1]

1. Minutes, CCD North Carolina, RG 21, GEpFAR.

William Paterson to James Iredell
December 3, 1797   Richmond, Virginia

Richmond,   3 Decem[r], 1797.

Dear Sir,

Your obliging letter of the 24th of last month I rec[d] a few days ago,[1] and was highly gratified by being informed, that you and your family have been favored with a better state of health than usual. Without health all other earthly pleasures lose much of their relish. My family were well when I left home, and continued so, when I heard of them last, which was about three weeks ago.

We heard of Judge Wilson being at Ch⁵ton; but I did not know of his having gone by the way of Edenton till the receipt of your letter. I was happy to find, that you were going to Halifax, in order to be near Raleigh, lest any thing should prevent the attendance of Judge Wilson.² This was a very proper measure. The court here will rise to-morrow or next day; there were 200 causes at issue, of which we have dispatched about 170. I shall continue here till all the trials are gone through, and the lawyers have nothing more to do.

Your observations on the explosion in France are such as must be approved of by every wise and good man.³

I desire to be remembered most respectfully to Mʳˢ Iredell, Govʳ Johnston, and all my friends your way.

Your's most sincerely.

Wᵐ Paterson.

Honᵇˡᵉ
    Mʳ Iredell.

ARS (NcD, James Iredell Sr. and Jr. Papers). Addressed "Edenton. North Carolina." Postmarked "RICHMOND, Dec. 5 1797."
    1. Letter not found.
    2. See James Iredell to Hannah Iredell, November 29, 1797.
    3. Probably a reference to the coup d'etat of 18 Fructidor (September 4, 1797). *The New Columbia Encyclopedia,* ed. William H. Harris and Judith S. Levey (New York: Columbia University Press, 1975), under Fructidor.

James Wilson to Bird Wilson ────────────────────────────────
December 17, 1797   Raleigh, North Carolina

Raleigh   17ᵗʰ Decemʳ 1797.
    Dear Bird

From Mʳˢ Wilson you will learn the Cause of my long Silence. It is indeed surprising that you have not written to me. A singl[e] Reflexion must have sugge[s]ted to you that any thing I could write to you either concerning Mʳ Butler or a Company at Lancaster,¹ must have depended very much on the Result of your Interview with Mʳ [Coxe?];² and your promise to write to me as soon as possible afterwards. And yet to this Day I have not heard a single Syllable from you. You might have known from the Laws of the United States ‿ and, I think I particularly told you at the red Lion ‿ the Times and Places of holding the Circuit Courts. I could give you no more particular Information; for I did not myself know how long each Court would last.

I expect that, immediately on the Receipt of this, you will se[t] out to meet me at Edenton. [To?] Mrs Wilson I refer you on this Point. I need not tell you to bring with you all the Money that shall be possible. I have many Things to say to you, which cannot be communicated by Letter. I am Yours affectionately

James Wilson

Bird Wilson Esq.

ARS (PHi, James Wilson Papers). Addressed "Market Street N° 274 Philadelphia." Postmarked "Raleigh   17 Decmr." Readings supplied in brackets where document is damaged or where reading is conjectural.

Along the margin of this letter, Wilson wrote: "Copy the Letter for Mr Thomas, and then deliver it: I consider it as for you both." See James Wilson to Joseph Thomas, December 17, 1797.

1. We have been unable to determine the identity of "a Company at Lancaster."

2. Probably Tench Coxe (1755-1824), commissioner of the revenue from 1792 until December 1797 and a prominent Philadelphia merchant. Before leaving Philadelphia, James Wilson had given Bird Wilson a power of attorney to enter into various land transactions. One plan, which is located in the Tench Coxe Papers at the Historical Society of Pennsylvania and is dated October 4, 1797, was to sell or mortgage lands in Pennsylvania worth $1,200,000. Although such a transaction never took place between Tench Coxe and James Wilson, Coxe did agree to lend Wilson $16,500, secured by 1,000 acres of Pennsylvania lands. Copy of power of attorney from James Wilson to Bird Wilson, September 21, 1797, Tench Coxe Papers, PHi; James Wilson's Proposals, October 4, 1797, Tench Coxe Papers, PHi; Tench Coxe to William Buckley, Samuel W. Fisher, and John Hall, July 30, 1799, Tench Coxe Papers, PHi.

James Wilson to Joseph Thomas ————————————————
December 17, 1797   Raleigh, North Carolina

Raleigh 17th Decem^r 1797

Dear Sir

In your letter of the 24th of October last,[1] which I had the pleasure of receiving at Augusta, you promised to write me fully by the next Post But that next Post has not yet arrived. Agreeably to what you authorise me to do I have drawn on you two bills payable at sight _ one for fifty, the other for one hundred dollars. In a few days I shall probably draw for somewhat more.

So little time is allowed here between the coming in & the going out of the Post, that I cannot now give you a particular account of the Purchases I made in this State and in Georgia so far as I have received information concerning them I can only say, in general, that the information hitherto has been favorable in a degree much exceeding my most sanguine hopes. In this State I am now procuring the most minute account of the Situation, title, & quality of every particular tract which I purchased. To prosecute this object is essential both here and in Georgia. But in order to prosecute it I must pass the winter in those States. This I have determined to do.

But in order to accomplish & secure every object money as well as information is necessary. You can have no conception of what importance it is to me to have some funds. Twenty thousand dollars would I believe secure every thing: Ten thousand would secure a great deal. Even the Whole of those sums would not be necessary to be transmitted here in Cash or Bankbills. One third part would suffice: And an unexceptionable Authority to draw bills on Philad^a for the residue payable in two and three months will answer every purpose. How much, & whether any thing can be done in this matter, you can best tell. I can only repeat you can have no conception of what importance it would be. Without funds much must be lost

Remember me, in the best Manner to Mrs Thomas[2] Write to me fully by Bird. With much regard I am

    dear Sir   your's sincerely

James Wilson

C (PHi, James Wilson Papers). Probably in the hand of Bird Wilson. See source note to James Wilson to Bird Wilson, December 17, 1797.

1. Letter not found.

2. Probably Rebecca (Cottman) Thomas. University of Pennsylvania, *Biographical Catalogue of the Matriculates,* p. 24.

Spring and Fall Circuits 1798

The year 1798 was a turbulent one, marked by a growing tension between the United States and France that led to a wave of nationalism and xenophobia. This national mood gave rise to four pieces of legislation, known collectively as the Alien and Sedition Acts, that were aimed at quieting political dissent and at reducing or eliminating the influence of foreign nationals who were thought to be fueling it. Although the various acts relating to aliens did not give rise to much litigation, a total of fifteen indictments for seditious libel were brought under the Sedition Act before it expired in 1801, resulting in ten convictions.[1]

A major impetus for these events was the revelation in early April that agents of French Foreign Minister Talleyrand—given the pseudonyms X, Y and Z—had solicited a $250,000 bribe from three American envoys who were in France attempting to negotiate an end to French harassment of American shipping. The envoys indignantly rebuffed the French overture with the words, "No, no, not a sixpence," which became a popular catch-phrase in a slightly different form: "Millions for defense, but not a cent for tribute!"[2] On April 13, shortly after the Philadelphia *Aurora* published dispatches from the American envoys, Senator James Ross of Pennsylvania wrote that Philadelphia "is aroused by the publication of the dispatches and instructions, addresses are preparing by all parties except the red hot leaders of Jacobism, who appear to be in a great measure deserted by their usual adherents."[3]

In the words of Fisher Ames, the XYZ affair "really electrified all classes," and the previously unpopular President John Adams found himself and his administration buoyed on a wave of enthusiastic patriotism.[4] Suspicion of the French led to suspicion of domestic opposition to the administration and to accusations that the Republicans were in league with the French. Anti-French—and anti-Republican—"addresses" such as those from grand juries in Pennsylvania and Maryland poured into the president's office, and he was kept so busy replying to them that his wife began to fear for his health.[5] Supreme Court justices, in the course of their circuit riding duties, found occasion to remark on the deepening political division in the country. Justice Iredell observed to North and South Carolina grand juries that "[t]he present situation of our country is alarming to a very great degree," and Associate Justice William Cushing,

---

1. Miller, *Federalist Era*, p. 235; Goebel, *Antecedents and Beginnings to 1801*, p. 637-38. James M. Smith states that fourteen indictments were found under the Sedition Act. James M. Smith, *Freedom's Fetters: The Alien and Sedition Laws and American Civil Liberties* (Ithaca, N.Y.: Cornell University Press, 1956), p. 185.

2. Miller, *Federalist Era*, p. 235; Smith, *Freedom's Fetters*, pp. 4, 8.

3. James Ross to George Stevenson, April 13, 1798, Ross-Woods Correspondence, PPiHi.

4. Smith, *Freedom's Fetters*, pp. 7-8.

5. Address of the Grand Jury of the Circuit Court for the District of Pennsylvania to John Adams, April 13, 1798; Reply to the Grand Jury of the Circuit Court for the District of Pennsylvania by John Adams, April 14, 1798; Address of the Grand Jury of the Circuit Court for the District of Maryland to John Adams, May 8, 1798; Reply to the Grand Jury of the Circuit Court for the District of Maryland by John Adams, May 18, 1798 (qq.v.); Miller, *Federalist Era*, p. 213.

according to a newspaper report, commented to a Rhode Island grand jury on "the dangerous Tendency of jacobin Principles."[6]

While Federalists in Congress made preparations for an expected war with France, they also took steps against the perceived domestic threat. In June and July of 1798 they secured the passage of the Alien and Sedition Acts, which limited freedom of speech and of the press and curtailed the liberty of resident foreigners. The first of these pieces of legislation was a naturalization act, passed on June 18, which increased the term of probationary residence for immigrants from five years to fourteen years and required them to register with a federal officer.[7] Although by its terms the act was directed at foreigners, its underlying targets were the Republicans, much of whose support was drawn from naturalized citizens.[8]

In late June and early July, two more pieces of anti-alien legislation were enacted—the Alien Act of 1798, and the Alien Enemies Act of 1798.[9] Both acts gave the president broad authority to deport aliens, the first in time of peace and the second in time of war. Because no war was declared during the life of the Alien Enemies Act of 1798, it never went into effect. The Alien Act of 1798, although in effect for two years, was never enforced. Its presence on the books, however, prompted a number of French resident aliens to return to their native land, and several foreign-born Republican journalists were moved to become citizens.[10] Secretary of State Timothy Pickering kept a close watch on the political activities of aliens, suggesting a conference between William Rawle, the United States attorney for the district of Pennsylvania, and Richard Peters, United States judge for the district of Pennsylvania, when both men had written him separately to report their suspicions of foreigners.[11] Some well-connected aliens fared better: Pickering wrote to the Marquis de Clugny that after receiving "information" from Associate Justice James Iredell, he was sure that the Marquis and his family were "not the dangerous aliens to whom the Act of Congress [in?] question was intended to apply."[12]

The last and most important of the acts passed by Congress was the one familiarly known as the Sedition Act of 1798, whose second section made it a crime to "write, print, utter or publish ... any false, scandalous and malicious writing or writings against the government of the United States, or either house of the Congress of the United States, or the President of the United States, with intent to defame" them or bring them into contempt or disrepute.[13] The prescribed punishment was a fine of up to two thousand dollars and imprisonment for up to two years. Although clearly uncon-

---

6. James Iredell's Charge to the Grand Jury of the Circuit Court for the District of South Carolina, May 7, 1798; *Newport Mercury* (Newport, Rhode Island), June 19, 1798 (qq.v.).

7. "An Act supplementary to and to amend the act, intituled 'An act to establish an uniform rule of naturalization; and to repeal the act heretofore passed on that subject,'" *Stat.*, 1:566; Miller, *Federalist Era*, p. 230.

8. Smith, *Freedom's Fetters*, p. 22.

9. *Stat.*, 1:570, 577. For congressional debate on this legislation, see *Annals*, 8:1785-96, 1896-97, 1792-2030.

10. Smith, *Freedom's Fetters*, p. 159; Miller, *Federalist Era*, p. 230.

11. Smith, *Freedom's Fetters*, pp. 163-64; Richard Peters to Timothy Pickering, August 24, 1798, Pickering Papers, MHi. Requesting a copy of the recently passed Alien Act of 1798, Peters reported to Pickering, "There are some Rascals posted near me both Aliens & infamous Citizens, that I want to handle if I can do it legally ... If I can get a full Account of the Alien Scoundrels I will send it to you. One of them is an English Democrat the worst, if possible, of all."

12. Timothy Pickering to Marquis de Clugny, August 8, 1798, Domestic Letters, RG 59, DNA.

13. *Stat.*, 1:596. For congressional debate on this statute, see *SLJ*, 2:516, 518-20, 524-28; *Annals*, 8:2093-2114, 2133-72.

stitutional under modern precedents, the Sedition Act was actually less harsh than the common law. The statute specifically made truth a defense to the libel charge, whereas the old common law standard had been, "the greater the truth, the greater the libel." In addition, the act required proof of intent to defame, and the jury was to "have a right to determine the law and the fact, under the direction of the court." Under the common law, the jury's role had been limited to deciding the fact of publication and the meaning of the statement at issue (often referred to as the innuendo); the judge then decided whether there had been a libel as a matter of law.[14]

Federalists defended the constitutionality of the Sedition Act by arguing that it codified—indeed weakened—the common law. The Constitution, Federalists said, granted the federal government jurisdiction over all common law crimes, including seditious libel.[15] Furthermore, the First Amendment's guarantee of freedom of speech and of the press, they claimed, meant only freedom from prior restraint; subsequent punishment for "false, scandalous and malicious" writings was not prohibited.[16]

These arguments were echoed by Chief Justice Oliver Ellsworth in a letter to Timothy Pickering. "[T]he Sedition act does not create an offence," he wrote, "but rather, by permitting the truth of a libel to be given in justification, causes that, in some cases, not to be an offence which was one before; nor does it devise a new mode of punishment, but restricts the power which previously existed, to fine & imprison." On the First Amendment point, Ellsworth continued, "who will say that negating the right to publish Slander & Sedition, is 'abridging the freedom of speech & of the press,' of a right which ever belonged to it? Or will shew us how Congress, if prohibited to authorise punishment for speaking in any case, could authorise it for perjury, of which nobody has yet doubted?"[17]

Other Supreme Court justices found occasion to endorse the Sedition Act in grand jury charges given during 1798. William Paterson in Vermont and William Cushing in Virginia alerted grand juries to the existence of the act and impressed upon them the seriousness of the crimes at which it was directed.[18] Abigail Adams thought so highly of Justice Cushing's charge that she wrote to the president urging its publication along with copies of the act.[19]

Justice Paterson's charge had even more concrete results. On October 5, two days after he charged the grand jury that offences under the Sedition Act "demand instant and full investigation" because they "strike at the being of our political establishment,"[20] the grand jury returned an indictment—the first under the Sedition Act—

14. Miller, *Federalist Era*, p. 231; Smith, *Freedom's Fetters*, p. 129; *Stat.*, 1:597; *Annals*, 8:2135-38, 2168.

15. *Annals*, 8:2145-47; 9:2989; 10:917, 948-50. For a discussion of the debate over the existence of a federal common law of crime, see introduction to "Spring and Fall Circuits 1799."

16. *Annals*, 8:2147-48, 2167-68; 9:2988-89; 10:968-71; Smith, *Freedom's Fetters*, pp. 132-36; Miller, *Federalist Era*, pp. 232-33.

17. Oliver Ellsworth to Timothy Pickering, December 12, 1798, Timothy Pickering Papers, MHi. In another letter to Pickering, Judge Richard Peters was similarly dismissive of the impact of the Sedition Act: "I think it gives the judiciary very little if any Power they did not before possess." Richard Peters to Timothy Pickering, August 24, 1798, Timothy Pickering Papers, MHi.

18. William Paterson's Charge to the Grand Jury of the Circuit Court for the District of Vermont, [October 3, 1798]; William Cushing's Charge to the Grand Jury of the Circuit Court for the District of Virginia, November 23, 1798 (qq.v.).

19. Abigail Adams to John Adams, December 21, 1798 (q.v.).

20. See William Paterson's Charge to the Grand Jury of the Circuit Court for the District of Vermont, [October 3, 1798].

against Matthew Lyon, an outspoken and rambunctious Republican congressman from Vermont. The indictment contained three counts. The first was based on a letter to the editor of a Vermont newspaper, written before the passage of the act, in which Lyon had accused "the Executive" of engaging in a "continual grasp for power" and exhibiting "an unbounded thirst for ridiculous pomp, foolish adulation, and selfish avarice." The second and third counts were based on Lyon's publication of a letter written from France by Joel Barlow, the poet and French sympathizer, criticizing American policy towards that country. Specifically, Barlow cited a "bullying speech" by President Adams, followed by a "stupid answer" from the Senate.[21]

Lyon's trial began in Rutland on Monday, October 9, before Justice Paterson and District Judge Samuel Hitchcock. Acting pro se, Lyon argued, first, that the court lacked jurisdiction because the Sedition Act was unconstitutional, at least as applied to writings composed before its passage; second, that he had not acted with the requisite "bad intent;" and third, that the contents of the writings were true.[22] He called no witnesses on the first two points, but in support of his third argument he asked Justice Paterson, then on the bench, whether he had not frequently "dined with the President, and observed his ridiculous pomp and parade?" Apparently unperturbed by this unorthodox procedure, Justice Paterson "replied, that he had sometimes, though rarely, dined with the President, but that he had never seen any pomp or parade; he had seen, on the contrary, a great deal of plainness and simplicity." The defendant followed up by asking whether Paterson "had not seen at the President's more pomp and servants there, than at the tavern at Rutland?" This time the justice did not answer.[23]

Paterson instructed the jury that they were not to pass on the constitutionality of the Sedition Act, whose validity could not be disputed until it was "declared null and void by a tribunal competent for the purpose."[24] After an hour's deliberation, the jury returned a verdict of guilty. Before sentencing the following day, Lyon informed the court of his sorry financial condition. Unmoved, Justice Paterson remarked that Lyon, as a congressman, must have been well acquainted with the act and the evils at which it was directed: "Your position," he told the defendant, "so far from making the case one which might slip with a nominal fine through the hands of the court, would make impunity conspicuous should such a fine alone be imposed." He then sentenced Lyon to four months imprisonment and imposed a fine of one thousand dollars. Lyon was transported to jail at Vergennes, from which he wrote a widely published letter complaining of his treatment. Despite his imprisonment, in December he was reelected

21. Wharton, State Trials, pp. 333-34; DAB under Joel Barlow; Connecticut Courant (Hartford), November 5, 1798.

22. Wharton, State Trials, p. 335; Smith, Freedom's Fetters, pp. 226-27, 233. In Paterson's notes of the trial, he summarized Lyon's arguments as being, "1. Innocence. 2. Unconstitutionality. 3. Publication after the law." U. States v. M. Lyon, Notes, Vermont, [October 1798], Hampton Carson Papers, PHi.

23. South-Carolina State-Gazette (Charleston), November 7, 1798; Wharton, State Trials, p. 335.

24. Wharton, State Trials, p. 336. According to the Philadelphia Aurora, this instruction contradicted one that Paterson had given in another case a mere three days earlier. That case involved a challenge to a Vermont statute authorizing the confiscation of glebe lands previously reserved for the support of the Church of England. In the glebe lands case, according to the Aurora, Paterson charged the jury that "if legislatures assumed to themselves the power to enact unconstitutional laws they ought not to be binding upon juries; and that courts and juries were the proper bodies to decide on the constitutionality of laws." Aurora (Philadelphia), November 9, 1798; Goebel, Antecedents and Beginnings to 1801, pp. 591-92.

to his seat in Congress by a healthy margin—a vote that was interpreted by some as an expression of protest against the Sedition Act.[25]

Matthew Lyon was the most notorious of the victims of the Sedition Act, but other indictments were returned against prominent Republicans during the course of the year. Two of these were brought under the common law of seditious libel before the Sedition Act had even been passed. Benjamin Franklin Bache, Benjamin Franklin's grandson and editor of the Philadelphia *Aurora*, was arrested on June 26, 1798, and charged with "libelling the President & the Executive Government, in a manner tending to excite sedition, and opposition to the laws, by sundry publications and re-publications." Before he could be brought to trial, however, he died, victim of one of Philadelphia's dreaded outbreaks of yellow fever.[26] Also indicted under the common law was John Daly Burk, Irish-born editor of the New York *Time Piece*. Like Bache, Burk never stood trial. With the assistance of Aaron Burr, he negotiated an agreement with the government under which he would return to Ireland in exchange for a dismissal of the case against him. Instead of leaving, however, Burk went into hiding under an assumed name in Virginia until the Alien and Sedition Acts had expired.[27]

Although most trials under the Sedition Act took place in 1799 and 1800, a number of indictments were returned in 1798. On October 23—two weeks after Matthew Lyon's trial—William Paterson and District Judge John Lowell presided over the arraignment in Boston of Thomas Adams, editor of the fiercely Republican *Independent Chronicle*. Adams died before he could be brought to trial.[28] On a more comic note, three men were indicted in New Jersey after one of them—apparently somewhat inebriated—was heard to remark, during a sixteen-gun salute to the visiting president, that "he did not care if they fired thro' " the Chief Executive's posterior. All three ultimately pleaded guilty and were fined.[29]

The Alien and Sedition Acts served as rallying points for the Republican opposition. Republican journalists inveighed against them, to the extent that the strictures of the law would allow them to.[30] In the south, particularly in Virginia and Kentucky, public meetings adopted resolutions expressing their opposition to the new laws.[31] In November and December, respectively, the Kentucky and Virginia legislatures passed resolutions directed against the Alien and Sedition Acts and invited their sister states to join their protest. Although these resolutions were introduced and championed by members of the two state legislatures, their real authors were Thomas Jefferson, then

25. Wharton, *State Trials*, pp. 336-37; *Independent Chronicle* (Boston), November 22, 1798; Smith, *Freedom's Fetters*, pp. 237-41; *Argus* (New York), January 2, 1799; *Aurora* (Philadelphia) February 21, 1799; Miller, *Federalist Era*, p. 236.

26. Smith, *Freedom's Fetters*, pp. 200, 203. In a letter to Rufus King, Timothy Pickering wrote on August 29, 1798: "The Yellow fever has again driven us from Philadelphia: the public offices are removed to this place [*Trenton*]. The fever is more malignant than in any former year: upwards of eighty persons, chiefly adults, died in the 48 hours from the 25ᵗʰ to the 27ᵗʰ instant." Miscellaneous Duplicate Consular and Diplomatic Despatches (1796-1854), RG 59, DNA. Bache, however, remained in Philadelphia, where he caught the yellow fever in September. Smith, *Freedom's Fetters*, p. 203.

27. Smith, *Freedom's Fetters*, pp. 204-20.

28. Ibid., pp. 247-57; *Connecticut Courant*, October 29, 1798.

29. Smith, *Freedom's Fetters*, pp. 270-71.

30. *Aurora* (Philadelphia), July 17 and 21, 1798, for example.

31. *Aurora* (Philadelphia), November 7, 1798; Koch and Ammon, "The Virginia and Kentucky Resolutions," p. 156.

vice president of the United States, and his fellow Republican James Madison. The Kentucky resolutions, drafted by Jefferson, were the more radical of the two, declaring that since the Union was merely a compact among the states, each state retained the right "to judge for itself, as well of infractions [*of the compact*] as of the mode of redress." Although effective in uniting Republicans, the Kentucky and Virginia resolutions failed to attract support from any other states, and several state legislatures passed resolutions specifically rejecting the view that a state was competent to decide the constitutionality of federal legislation.[32]

Earlier in the year, however, the states had won an important victory in the ratification of the Eleventh Amendment, which provided that federal jurisdiction "shall not be construed to extend to any suit in law or equity commenced or prosecuted against one of the United States by citizens of another State." Three fourths of the states having adopted the amendment, President Adams declared it to be a part of the Constitution on January 8. At the February term the Supreme Court dismissed a number of pending suits that were now prohibited by the amendment.[33]

While these events were taking place on the national stage, one member of the Supreme Court was experiencing a personal crisis. Associate Justice James Wilson had been in financial difficulty since the fall of 1796, but in 1798 his affairs came to a head. In the fall of 1797 Wilson took the opportunity of riding the Southern Circuit to flee farther away from his creditors and to attend to his southern investments. He never returned home. By February 1798 he was in Edenton, North Carolina, reportedly too ill to travel.[34] But even in Edenton, where he was joined by his wife, Hannah, Wilson was not safe from his creditors. As early as February 16, Pierce Butler, to whom Wilson was indebted in the amount of $197,000, was threatening to sue Wilson in North Carolina. Butler offered to give Wilson two or three years to pay off the debt, provided that Wilson gave him a security interest in his Pennsylvania lands. But, alternately optimistic and self-pitying, Wilson would neither divide up his lands and surrender them to his creditors nor convey them to trustees.[35]

Meanwhile, Wilson's health was deteriorating, and he and Hannah were leading a hand-to-mouth existence in Edenton. In July, he was attempting to recover from what may have been malaria—"an intermiting fever," Hannah called it. In early August Wilson had sufficient strength to send off a letter to his son Bird in Philadelphia, upbraiding him for not sending information concerning the creditors' reaction to a plan Wilson had proposed. "The time is opening, in which, I think, Something very effectual may be done," he wrote hopefully. But a few weeks later he contracted "a violent nervous fever" and became delirious. Hannah stayed by his side for three days and three nights,

32. Koch and Ammon, "The Virginia and Kentucky Resolutions," pp. 147-62; *Virginia Gazette, and General Advertiser* (Richmond), November 22, 1799; *Federalist* (Trenton), January 28, 1799; *Companion* (Newport, Rhode Island), February 23, 1799.

33. *Message from the President of the United States, accompanying a Report from the Secretary of State, and Copies of Acts of the Legislatures of the States of Connecticut, Maryland, and Virginia, ratifying the amendment proposed by Congress, concerning the Suability of States* (Philadelphia: William Ross, 1798), Congressional Collection, DLC; *DHSC*, 1:305.

34. Minutes, November 8, 1797, CCD Georgia, RG 21, GEpFAR; *DHSC*, 1:858-59.

35. [Thomas Blount] to [John Gray Blount], February 16, 1798; James Wilson to Bird Wilson, April 21, 1798; Pierce Butler to Samuel Wallis, June 14, 1798 (qq.v.); Pierce Butler to William Slade, May 24, 1798 (James Wilson Papers, PHi).

at last leaving him on the evening of August 21 when she "could not bear the scene any longer." A few hours later, he was dead.[36]

News of Wilson's death spread quickly and was widely reported.[37] On August 25, Iredell—who had arrived in Edenton from Philadelphia the very night Wilson died—wrote to Timothy Pickering informing him of what had occurred and urging that a successor be appointed as soon as possible, as Wilson had been scheduled to ride the Southern Circuit that fall. Pickering passed this information on to the president, who was ready to appoint either John Marshall, one of the envoys involved in the XYZ affair, or Bushrod Washington, a nephew of George Washington. Given Marshall's greater age and experience (Washington was only 36), he was the preferred candidate. But Pickering was doubtful that Marshall, then enjoying a lucrative legal practice, would give it up for the low wages and difficult life of a Supreme Court justice. Pickering proved right, at least for the time being. Washington gladly accepted the commission and set off on the Southern Circuit.[38]

36. Hannah Wilson to Bird Wilson, June 23, 1798; Hannah Wilson to Bird Wilson, July 28, 1798; James Wilson to Bird Wilson, August 4, 1798; Hannah Wilson to Bird Wilson, September 1, 1798 (qq.v.); Smith, *James Wilson,* p. 387.
37. *DHSC,* 1:864.
38. James Iredell to Timothy Pickering, August 25, 1798 (q.v.); *DHSC,* 1:861, 53, 126-28, 130, 131, 132, 133.

Samuel Chase to John Rutledge, Jr. ─────────────────────────
January 12, 1798   Baltimore, Maryland

Baltimore   12th Jany 1798. _

Dear Sir/

I observe in the News Papers, that the application of the Judges of the Supreme Court to appoint the time of holding the Spring Circuit Court in the State of Delaware, to be on the 27th day of April, instead of the 27th day of June, has been referred to a select Committee;[1] and that a Remonstrance against this application of the Judges, has been presented by the Chancellor, & Sundry Citizens of the Delaware State._ I cannot conceive the grounds on which opposition is given to so reasonable a request of the Judges.

By the ~~act~~ Act "to establish the Judicial Courts of the United States," ch. 20, Sect. 5. (passed 24th Septem^r 1789) the thirteen States were erected into Districts; and thirteen Districts divided into three Circuits; called the Eastern,

middle, and Southern; a Circuit Court, was appointed to be held in each District; and the Spring Circuit Court, for the State of Delaware, was appointed to be held at New Castle, on the 27th day of April._ This arrangement was proper, and Convenient to the Judges, and so remained, until, by the Act "Making certain alterations &c," ch. 64, sect. 2 (passed the 9th June 1794) the day was changed from the 27th of April, to the second Monday in June.

                                             1792,
By the Act of the 13ᵗʰ² of April‸ch. 21, the Judges of the Supreme Court were authorized to determine the Circuits they, respectively, should attend; but their attendance was to be by Rotation.

By the Act of the 2ⁿᵈ March 1793, ch. 22, only one Judge of the Supreme Court was required to attend the Circuit Court.

By the Act of the 3ᵈ March 1797, ch. 81,³ The middle Circuit (which is composed of five States, from New Jersey, to Virginia, inclusive) was
                                                                                be
appointed to commence at Trenton on the 1ˢᵗ day of April; and to‸held in Philadelphia on the 11ᵗʰ of April; in Annapolis, on the 7ᵗʰ of May; in Richmond, on the 22ⁿᵈ of May; and at New Castle, on the 27ᵗʰ of June. _ The same objection applies to the holding of the Circuit Court, for Delaware, at New Castle; on the 27ᵗʰ June, by this Act; as on the second Monday, in June, by the Act of June 1794.

When the Act, of 9ᵗʰ June 1794, passed only Judge Wilson was informed of the proposed alteration of the first Law (of Septᵣ 1789), and he made no objection to the change; but he did not advert to the [letters inked out] great hardship thereby imposed on his brethren, who lived South of the State of
                e
Delaware. _ That alteration from April, to June, was probably made to suit the arrangement of the times of holding the Delaware State Courts.⁴

It is incontrovertible, that the administration of Justice, by the Federal Government, does not require, that the Circuit Court, for the State of Delaware, should be held in the month of June, in preference to the month of April. _ An attention to one fact alone will shew the very great burthen imposed on one of the Judges Mʳ Iredell lives at Edenton, in North Carolina. When he is appointed to attend the Middle Circuit, he holds the Circuit Court for New Jersey, at Trenton, on 1ˢᵗ of April; and, at Philadelphia, on the 11ᵗʰ of the same month; he then passes through the State of Delaware (by Annapolis) to hold the Court, on 22ⁿᵈ of May, at Richmond, in Virginia, (267 miles.); from thence he must return, the same distance, to hold his Circuit Court, on 27ᵗʰ June, at New Castle, in Delaware; and thus he is compelled to travel 534 miles more, than he would do, if he held the Court at New Castle, on 27ᵗʰ April (as proposed by the Judges) on his way from Philadelphia to Richmond. _ The only mode to relieve Judge Iredell from this burthen is by some of his brethren holding the Court, at New Castle, in his place. This lays him under an obligation, which is always attended with some inconvenience; and will sometimes, from unavoidable Circumstances, be declined. _ A permanent system should not impose such hardship on any officer of Government, when the Interest of the public does not require it.

It may be said that Congress by thus frequently altering the times of holding the Circuit Court, in the State of Delaware, puts the Legislature of that State to the inconvenience of altering the time of holding its State Court. _

I have been informed that the Change from April to June, was at the desire of one of the Senators of that State.[5]

I believe the principal reason, for making the meetings of the State Courts to suit the time of holding the Federal Court, is for the Convenience, and benefit of the Lawyers.

The Judges wrote to the Governor of Delaware, and informed him of their intended application, for the proposed alteration, in order that the Legislature of that State might alter its State Court to suit the Federal Court, if they thought proper.[6]

If Congress will delay their decision, on the application of the Judges, and the Remonstrance against it, until the first week in February, the Judges will be then in Philadelphia; and can give information on the subject; and make their remarks (if they think proper) on the Remonstrance.

I am Sir,   with great respect,   y.r Most Obed.t Serv.t

Samuel Chase

The Honorable
   John Rutledge Jun.r.
      in Congress.

RS (NcU, Southern Historical Collection, John Rutledge Papers). Probably in the hand of Chase's son, Thomas, with interlineations in the hand of Samuel Chase.

On the address cover of this letter, John Rutledge, Jr., noted the following names: "Bayard Kittera   Dennis." These were the three members of the select committee appointed to consider the justices' application: James A. Bayard, representative from Delaware; John Wilkes Kittera, representative from Pennsylvania; and John Dennis, representative from Maryland. *HRJ*, 3:118; *BDAC*.

1. See Justices of the Supreme Court to John Adams, August 15, 1797. For details of the controversy over changes in the time of holding the Delaware spring court and the justices' representation, see introduction to "Spring and Fall Circuits 1797."

2. A crossed-out caret appears after "13.th."

3. The citation should be to chapter 27 of the acts of the second session of the Fourth Congress. *Stat.*, 1:517.

4. The dates for holding the state courts were established by an act passed on June 14, 1793, and amended on February 7, 1794. By those acts the spring courts occupied most of the months of April and May. John D. Cushing, comp., *The First Laws of the State of Delaware*, 2 vols. (Wilmington, Del.: Michael Glazier, 1981), 2:1088, 1191; *Stat.*, 1:395.

5. The senator was John Vining (1758-1802). On March 28, 1794, Vining gave notice that he would introduce a bill to alter the date of the spring circuit court in Delaware. Although no such bill was introduced, Vining was appointed to the committee considering a House bill changing the dates of certain courts. The committee changed the date of holding the spring Delaware circuit court from April 27 to the second Monday in June. *BDAC; SLJ*, 2:58, 103; Committee Reports and Papers, June 6, 1794, House Bills, RG 46, DNA.

6. See Justices of the Supreme Court to Gunning Bedford, August 15, 1797.

James Iredell to Hannah Iredell ————————————————————

February 5 and 8, 1798   Philadelphia, Pennsylvania

[*February 5, 1798: Arriving in Philadelphia on February 2,*] I alighted out of
the Stage to enquire for Mrs Wilson, and found her and all his Family at his
House in Market Street. She was very well, but extremely affected in seeing
me, and finding Mr Wilson was not coming, she burst into tears.[1] His Family
generally are well. ...

[*February 8, 1798:*] Mrs Wilson at present thinks of returning with me, which
I suppose will be soon after the rising of this Court, for I take it for granted
I shall go the Southern Circuit.[2] ...

ARS (Nc-Ar, Charles E. Johnson Collection). Addressed "Edenton, North Carolina."
Postmarked "8   FE."
    1. Wilson had remained in North Carolina after riding the fall 1797 Southern Circuit for
reasons variously ascribed to illness or his increasingly difficult financial situation. See introduction
to "Spring and Fall Circuits 1798."
    2. Hannah Wilson did accompany James Iredell to Edenton. *DHSC,* 1:858.

[Thomas Blount] to [John Gray Blount] ————————————————

February 16, 1798   Philadelphia, Pennsylvania

... Major Butler who holds Judge Wilson's paper to a very considerable
amount as collateral Security for the debt due him from William Blount &
                    has
David Allison,[1] [*letter inked out*] determined to sue his Judgeship in Carolina
& hold his body in custody, if he can get hold on it, at all hazards until he
gives him satisfactory security _ and he ha[s] upon my advice, which I found
it impossible to avoid giving, determined to impower William Slade,[2] of
Edenton, where he understands the Judge now is, to commence & carry on
the suit.[3] Should Mr Slade shew any reluctance to undertaking the Business,
I wish you to give him all necessary encouragement for the major's motive
is certainly friendly to Wm Blount & he will pledge himself to indemnify his
agent. My reason for wishing Mr S. to undertake the business is to prevent
an application to your or Jacob,[4] w^h in the event of his refusal will I fear be
made. Mr Butler's power of Attorney to Mr Slade & the papers on which
suit is to be brought will go from me, under cover to Capt Collins, the day
after Tomorrow by Judge Iredell _ [5] this mode of conveyance is adopted for
the sake of secresy which in the opinion of Major B. is highly necessary _
& I shall request Capt Collins to sound Mr S. & know whether he is willing
to engage in the Business before he communicates to him the substance of
it _ In case Mr Slade should refuse to act, can you recommended to Major
Butler through me, any person that will act[?] if you can, you will greatly
oblige him.[6] ...

AR[S?] (Nc-Ar, John Gray Blount Papers). Readings supplied in brackets where document is torn or where reading is conjectural. The conclusion of this letter is missing. Sender and recipient identified in the *John Gray Blount Papers*, 3:208.

Thomas Blount (1759-1812) represented North Carolina in the House of Representatives. Thomas was also part of a business partnership with his brothers John Gray Blount and William Blount. *DAB;* Keith, Masterson, and Morgan, *John Gray Blount Papers*, 1:xxii.

John Gray Blount (1752-1833), Thomas Blount's brother, was a merchant and landowner in Washington, North Carolina. William S. Powell, ed., *Dictionary of North Carolina Biography*, vol. 1 (Chapel Hill: University of North Carolina Press, 1979), p. 179; Keith, Masterson, and Morgan, *John Gray Blount Papers*, 1:xxi-xxiv.

1. David Allison (d. 1798), a land speculator from North Carolina and Tennessee, was working in Philadelphia as an agent for the sale of western lands. Keith, Masterson, and Morgan, *John Gray Blount Papers*, 2:197n; 3:xiii-xiv, 255. Pierce Butler had received Wilson's bond for $174,000 dollars from Allison and Blount "in part payment for the Salvadore Tract." Thomas Blount to [John Gray Blount], February 26, 1798, John Gray Blount Papers, Nc-Ar.

2. William Slade (d. 1813), a lawyer in Edenton, North Carolina. Carrie L. Broughton, comp., *Marriage and Death Notices from Raleigh Register and North Carolina Gazette, 1799-1825* (Baltimore: Genealogical Publishing, 1966), p. 148; Keith, Masterson, and Morgan, *John Gray Blount Papers*, 3:417n.

3. For details of Butler's legal pursuit of Wilson, see introduction to "Spring and Fall Circuits 1798."

4. Jacob Blount (1760-1801) of Edenton, North Carolina, was also a brother of William and John Gray Blount. Keith, Masterson, and Morgan, *John Gray Blount Papers*, 1:xxvii-xxviii; Powell, *Dictionary of North Carolina Biography*, p. 178. On March 8 Jacob Blount commented to John Gray Blount about the proposed suit against Wilson, "In my opinion it is bad policy to sue him he having no property that can be got hold of, will I fear be so Iritated that he never will pay it if able, he appear much distressed in mind now and is unwell and if he is sued not being able to procure security will probably make a finish of him and the debt finally lost." John Gray Blount Papers, Nc-Ar.

5. A year earlier Pierce Butler had asked Iredell to carry important papers concerning his financial affairs and had even asked his advice on how to proceed against William Blount. There is no evidence, however, that James Iredell had any knowledge of the significance for James Wilson of the documents he was to carry to Captain Josiah Collins, an old friend of Iredell's and a relative of the Blounts. Pierce Butler to James Iredell, September 28, 1797, and Pierce Butler to James Iredell, November 7, 1797, Pierce Butler Letterbook, PHi; *MJI*, 2:52, 303, 430; Keith, Masterson, and Morgan, *John Gray Blount Papers*, 1:177.

6. On February 26 Thomas Blount wrote another letter to John Gray Blount detailing the plans for the suit against Wilson and emphasizing, "If the Judge should be sued as he certainly will if Mʳ Slade acts as Major B. has directed him, I beseech you not to be his security, even for his appearance on the next day, on any account whatever, for his son & his lawyer have both told Major B. that he has no real Estate any where that is not encumbered with at least one Mortgage, & if you rely on his honor, or trust him in any thing, he will certainly deceive you _ let him go to goal _ it will be for W. B.'s benefit, as then he will probably come forward by his attorney here & make Major B. secure according to his promise _ but otherwise he certainly will not. _ I have written a Letter of caution on this subject to Jacob [*Blount*] for his Mʳ Collin's benefit & requested him to write to you which I hardly thought necessary." John Gray Blount Papers, Nc-Ar.

Circuit Court for the District of New Jersey ————————————
April 2, 1798   Trenton, New Jersey

Associate Justice Samuel Chase and Judge Robert Morris opened the New Jersey circuit court on April 2. After court convened, Samuel Chase delivered a charge to the grand jury. The court adjourned on April 9 to the next term.[1]

 1. Minutes, CCD New Jersey, RG 21, NjBaFAR. Charge not found.

Circuit Court for the District of New York ————————————
April 2, 1798   New York, New York

On Monday, April 2, Associate Justice William Paterson and Judge Robert Troup opened court, and a charge was delivered to the grand jury. The court adjourned on April 6 to the next term.[1]

 1. Minutes, CCD New York, RG 21, NjBaFAR. We have been unable to identify the specific charge given. For undated Paterson grand jury charges, see Appendix A.

James Iredell to Hannah Iredell ————————————
April 5, 1798   "Hermitage," Martin County, North Carolina

... In almost any other house but your Brother's[1] I should have been inexpressibly mortified at being shut up 3 days on my Journey. It has been raining incessantly since Monday afternoon, and though it has looked something like clearing up to day it seems still doubtful. I hope to get away to morrow, and to have time by diligence to make up for this delay. The waters must be every where so full that I think it very probable I should not have gained much had I been beyond Tarborough when the bad weather began _ It would be a great relief to me if I could hear from you before I proceed _ I have my health very well _ I have not only read "Edward"[2] here, but "Man as he is not"[3] with which I am nearly as much pleased _ I inclose letters for Mrs Tredwell and the Children, besides Letters to you and Judge Wilson ... Presenting best respects to the Judge and Mrs Wilson. I shall be very anxious to hear about them ...

ARS (Nc-Ar, Charles E. Johnson Collection). Addressed "Edenton."
 1. Samuel Johnston.
 2. John Moore, *Edward. Various Views of Human Nature, taken from life and manners, chiefly in England* (Mount Pleasant, N.Y.: W. Durell, 1798).
 3. [Robert Bage], *Hermsprong; or, Man as he is not,* 3 vols. (London: Minerva Press, 1796).

William Paterson to Euphemia Paterson ————————————————————
    April 7, 1798   New York, New York

... We had a very pleasant ride on saturday; the road so good, that we reached
Pawlis hook in time to dine. ... I propose to set out for New Haven on
monday or tuesday next in the stage or packet. I am informed, that we shall
have a great deal of business to go through in Connecticut, which will prevent
me from returning as soon as I wish. ...

ARS (NjR, William Paterson Papers). Addressed "New Brunswick."

James Iredell to Hannah Iredell ————————————————————————
    April 10, 1798   Williamston, North Carolina

... You will doubtless be surprised to receive a letter from me of this date
from this place, which was owing to the impossibility of my crossing Tar
River at Tarborough _ or proceeding on in any other direction. I left M[r]
Johnston's with very little hope on Saturday, but resolved to make every
effort in my power to get on. I proceeded accordingly, with a letter to Col[o]
Mayo[1] to assist me on the road if necessary. I soon was informed that all
the bridges had been broken up, but that he had been prep repairing two
that morning, and I reached his house (about 18 miles from here) without
any difficulty. He told me he suspected the Bridges on a great swamp called
Coneta[2] had been broke up, but recommended me to call on a M[r] Pippin[3]
on this side of it and request his advice and assistance _ I had proceeded
several miles when Col[o] Mayo overtook me in order that he might speak to
M[r] Pippin himself. We found the Bridges were gone, but he thought with
the aid of two Negroes whom he lent me I might get through safely, and
they both assured me, after passing that swamp, there was no obstacle to
my passing safely to the banks of the River, for though I should have to go
through a good deal of water none of it was deep. We got through the swamp
with some difficulty, having in some places to plunge through very deep
holes where the bridges had been. I then thought all my difficulties over,
and proceeded on in high spirits _ I [found over?] the water in one or two
swamps much deeper than I expected, and began to be a little alarmed at
my situation. Still however I went on, having full confidence in the
information I had received. At length, when I suppose we had got within
about a mile of the River, we entered a very long Swamp that had a most
formidable appearance. I directed Hannibal who was before to proceed with
great caution, and if he found the water grew very deep to stop. He did,
and I directed him to return immediately _ and I afterwards discovered that
in two minutes he would have been in swimming water _ In that Swamp it
was swimming water for 40 yards _ and in another a little beyond for 100 _

I then found myself in a very disagreeable situation: It was impossible to return without the two Negroes I had parted with, and I knew of no house near where I could go to, and the night was advancing fast_ After going back a little distance I saw a house not very far off on my left, to which I went_ and there fortunately I found a most obliging Man and his Wife, a Mr and Mrs Ford,[4] who had lately removed from the neighbourhood of Halifax_ People apparently poor, but their kindness and hospitality affecting to a great degree. The River was then higher than it had been known for 20 years, and was then rising. If it fell, Mr Ford told me it would be two or three days before the swamps would be passable without swimming, and I saw no possibility of crossing with my Chair and Horses without great risque & delay, and had every reason to believe it would be impossible for some time to travel in any road beyond Tarborough. I then enquired if I could take any other road_ even the road to Halifax_ but found insurmountable obstacles in any. Calculating the time I had to spare, I was convinced there was not the slightest probability of my getting to Savannah in time, and being in a poor and private house where I could not prevail on the Family to receive any thing from me, nor there being a single Tavern between that and this which was the only road passable at all_ I at length with inexpressible reluctance gave up the attempt to reach Savannah, and after informing the District Judge of my situation by a letter[5] to be sent from Tarborough I resolved to return here, which I did the same day, Mr Ford lending me two Negroes to assist me as before through the dangerous swamp of Coneta_ I arrived at Mr McKenzie's,[6] where I now am, having called at your Brother's,[7] and finding they were gone, early in the afternoon. I cannot, after a review of my conduct, strictly blame myself, for could I have proceeded at the time I intended, or even within 3 or 4 days of it, I had plenty of time, and the extraordinary disappointments I have met with were entirely unlooked for, nor had I any reason to expect such. If I had I undoubtedly would have set off much earlier. I am here shut up on every side_ but hope soon to be able to travel conveniently enough, and I propose going on gradually to Charleston where probably I shall arrive some days before the Court is to meet. Could I travel in any road towards the sound I might possibly spend 2 or 3 days with you, which God knows would make me very happy_ but I should be afraid to indulge myself, for it would never do to lose another Court by a regard to my own indulgence, whatever command of time I might be supposed to possess._ My health in general has been good, and I doubt not will be perfectly so if I can go on without many more disappointments. . .

ARS (Nc-Ar, Charles E. Johnson Collection).

1. Mayo was a common family name in this area of North Carolina. It is possible that this is Nathan Mayo (1742-1811), who served as an officer in the Revolution and later as a member of the North Carolina House of Commons (1777-1779), and resided near the Coneghta Swamp

Warrenton, North Carolina by Miss Somerville (dates unknown). Oil on canvas, ca. 1805. Courtesy Warren County Historical Society, Warrenton, North Carolina.

in Edgecombe County. *DAR Lineage Book,* 96:42; U.S., Department of Commerce and Labor, Bureau of the Census, *Heads of Families at the First Census of the United States Taken in the Year 1790: North Carolina* (1908; reprint ed., Salt Lake City: Accelerated Indexing Systems, 1978).

2. The "Coneghta Pocoson" or swamp was located east of Tarborough, Edgecombe County, North Carolina. Henry Mouzon et al., *An accurate map of North and South Carolina* (Paris: Le Rouge, 1777).

3. The identity of this person cannot be ascertained.

4. Identities not ascertained.

5. Letter to Joseph Clay, Jr., not found.

6. William McKenzie.

7. Samuel Johnston.

Circuit Court for the District of Pennsylvania
April 11, 1798   Philadelphia, Pennsylvania

Associate Justice Samuel Chase and Judge Richard Peters opened court on April 11 and adjourned it on April 20.[1] According to a newspaper article signed "One of the Traverse Jury," Samuel Chase delivered a charge to the grand jury on April 12.[2]

1. Engrossed Minutes, CCD Pennsylvania, RG 21, PPFAR.
2. See below under date of April 18, 1798. Charge not found.

Circuit Court for the District of Connecticut
April 13, 1798   New Haven, Connecticut

Associate Justice William Paterson and Judge Richard Law convened the court at the state house, and Paterson delivered a charge to the grand jury. On April 18 the court adjourned.[1]

1. Docket Book, CCD Connecticut, RG 21, MWalFAR. We have been unable to identify the specific charge given. For undated Paterson grand jury charges, see Appendix A.

Address of the Grand Jury of the Circuit Court for the District of Pennsylvania to John Adams
Claypoole's American Daily Advertiser
April 13, 1798   Philadelphia, Pennsylvania

The GRAND INQUEST of the United States, for the district of Pennsylvania, to the PRESIDENT of the United States.

SIR,

THE disclosures which you have made of the instructions given to our Envoys to France, and the dispatches received from them, evidence a strong determination to promote and preserve a good understanding with the French

Republic, provided it could be accomplished without affecting our national character and the independence of the United States.[1] We wanted no fresh proof of your attachment to your country, nor your unremitted attention to the duties of your high and responsible situation. We are well convinced that the conduct of our government to all nations has been just and honourable, and we wish to express in the strongest terms our confidence in it.

It is true, Sir, that there are some characters in the United States who call themselves Americans, and who, with patriotism on their lips, and professions of regard for the Constitution of our country, are endeavouring to poison the minds of the well meaning citizens and to withdraw from the government the support of the people. Their measures are hostile to the happiness of this country, and they are the instruments of disorganization and sedition; many of whom are probably employed by that nation, whose rulers seek the destruction of America, and the tendency of whose system is to exterminate from the world every moral and religious principle.

Yet, Sir, we hesitate not to declare it as our firm belief, notwithstanding the opinion of the enemies of America, that the great mass of our fellow citizens approve of your administration, and are determined to support it. With unanimity among the people and with the rectitude of our government, we trust in God we have nothing to fear. These sentiments and these expressions the Grand Inquest of the United States for the district of Pennsylvania have taken the liberty to present to you, and feel themselves happy in adding that although their body is composed of citizens from different parts of the state, yet an unanimity has prevailed in making this communication.

They beg leave to offer their warmest wishes for the welfare of the United States and the happiness of their Chief Magistrate.

JOHN LARDNER, Foreman.

Philad. April 13, 1798.

(Philadelphia) April 16, 1798. Date and place are those of the address.

1. A reference to the publication of correspondence from the special envoys to France (Charles Cotesworth Pinckney, Elbridge Gerry, and John Marshall) to Secretary of State Timothy Pickering, and what became known as the XYZ affair. At the request of the House of Representatives, President Adams had transmitted the letters to Congress on April 3, 1798. The letters described the French attempt, through agents designated "X, Y," and "Z," to solicit a bribe from the envoys as a prerequisite for treaty negotiations. The correspondence was made public by members of the House of Representatives on April 6, 1798. *ASP, Foreign Relations,* 2:153-68; *Annals,* 8:1377-80. For further information on the XYZ affair, see introduction to "Spring and Fall Circuits 1798."

Reply to the Grand Jury of the Circuit Court for the District of
Pennsylvania by John Adams ————————————————————————
Claypoole's American Daily Advertiser
April 14, 1798   Philadelphia, Pennsylvania

To the Grand Inquest of the United States for the District of Pennsylvania

Gentlemen,

I thank you for this address—Your approbation of the part I have taken
in an interesting negociation gives me great pleasure; but the conviction you
express, that the conduct of our government to all nations has been just
and honorable, affords me the highest satisfaction. A nation which is conscious
of having done no wrong to others, even when suffering for a course of
years, under the provocation of a series of insults, depredations and cruelties,
may appeal to God, with a humble trust in his blessing, and to the world, in
a full assurance of obtaining its confidence.

If there are perverse characters who call themselves Americans, I am well
assured there have been greater numbers merely erroneous, deceived by
partial information, and transported by too ardent a zeal.

For myself I have never entertained a doubt that the great mass of our
fellow citizens would support an administration which has nothing in view
but impartial justice to all nations, and the character, independence and
prosperity of the country; nor have I ever dispaired of a unanimity of the
people in such sentiments, and in pursuit of these objects—and with you I
humbly, but firmly trust in God, we have nothing to fear.

Under a constitution like ours, the intelligence and integrity of juries, in
the legal support of the government, are essential to the preservation of its
existence.—With their impartial countenance and faithful exertions, it can
scarcely fail to answer the ends of its institution, by confirming the safety,
securing the honor, promoting the prosperity, and I will add, establishing
the power and advancing the glory of the nation.

While I join with you in your warmest wishes for the welfare of the United
States, I beg leave to assure you of mine, for the happiness of the Grand
Inquest of Pennsylvania.

Signed, JOHN ADAMS.

United States, April 14.

(Philadelphia) April 16, 1798. Date is that of the reply. Place determined from other Adams
correspondence; information courtesy of Celeste Walker, Adams Papers project.

Oliver Ellsworth to William Cushing
April 15, 1798 Windsor, Connecticut

... I propose venturing to Vermont & New Hampshire. Brother Patterson has releived me from New York & this State; and I hope it will not be inconvenient for you to take the courts at Boston & Newport. You will allow me to furnish a little money for your expenses, as it may never be in my power to repay you in kind.

I left pending before the Senate, on the 23^{d} of March, a judiciary bill with a prospect of its making some progress this Session & being an early subject for the next. It goes to releive us from circuit riding, to form five new districts & two associate district Judges for the circuit Courts. Mr Sedgwick, who remained the most strenuous for their insertion, agreed that the new districts should be stricken out if, upon discussion, they should appear to embarrass the bill.[1]

...

P.S. A letter from Mr Tracy rec^{d} this moment says The Judiciary will probably get thro' the Senate before the Session ends the other business prevents much attention to it at present_ ...

ARS (MHi, Cushing Family Papers, 1650-1840). Addressed "Scituate." The postscript appears after Ellsworth's signature.

1. "A bill to alter and amend the act, entitled 'An act to establish the judicial courts of the United States,' " had its first reading in the Senate on March 19, 1798. The bill provided for a second district judge for the states of New York, Pennsylvania, Virginia, North Carolina, and South Carolina. A second district court was created for each of these states by dividing them into two districts, an eastern and a western one, except for New York, which was divided into a northern and a southern district. All districts except Maine, Kentucky, Tennessee, and the western district of Pennsylvania were organized into five circuits, with two courts to be held annually in each district by a panel of the district judges, any two of whom would constitute a quorum. The district court for western Pennsylvania, like the district court for Kentucky, was given the original jurisdiction that ordinarily would be exercised by a circuit court, with an appellate jurisdiction to be exercised by the circuit court for the eastern district of Pennsylvania. On April 25 the Senate voted to postpone further consideration of the bill, but it was never taken up again. *SLJ*, 2:457, 463, 474, 479. A printed copy of the original Senate bill is in MiU-C. Because of the bill's importance to understanding the development of the Judiciary Act of 1801, it will be treated more fully in volume 4 of the *DHSC*.

The possibility of revision was also of interest to others in the judicial system. On April 8, 1798, Rhode Island district judge Benjamin Bourne had written to Massachusetts senator Theodore Sedgwick: "I have seen a Bill pending before Congress which contemplates a new arrangement of the Judiciary. something of the same nature was talked of some years ago. is it probable that the organisation contemplated by the Bill will be agreed to?" Sedgwick I Papers, MHi.

James Iredell to Hannah Iredell
April 17, 1798 Williamston, North Carolina

... I hope you received a letter wherein I informed you of the reasons which inevitably compelled me to relinquish my Journey to Savannah and return here, having found it impossible to proceed owing to the height of the waters in every direction.[1] In one of the waters of Tar River, within a mile of Tarborough, Hannibal and myself were very near being drowned, having entered a Swamp which we afterwards understood had 40 yards swimming water. I expected to have gone much sooner, but the waters continued high many days longer than was expected, and since I heard of the inoculation at Edenton _ I have been inexpressibly anxious to hear from thence. We have heard of the condition of the Town in general, but not of our particular Friends. A hope of receiving a letter by tomorrow's post may possibly detain me till the day after. My health has been in general good, but I have had a little complaint in my bowels from which Cream Tartar and one day's abstinence perfectly recovered me _ ... I shall write you frequently on the road, if I think a letter will reach you. I shall certainly have plenty of time, not being obliged to be in Charleston before the 6th of May tho' I will if possible! ...

ARS (Nc-Ar, Charles E. Johnson Collection). Addressed "Edenton."
  1. See James Iredell to Hannah Iredell, April 10, 1798.

"One of the Traverse Jury"
Commercial Advertiser
April 18, 1798   New York, New York

While enemies from without, and traitors from within, are devising the extirpation of our most sacred rights, and robbing us of our property and inestimable privileges—It is a most pleasing circumstance, to find our Executive and Judiciary Departments, supported by able, prudent and firm men.

It was with the highest satisfaction that I heard, and I wish I could recapitulate, the masterly, seasonable, and animated address of Judge CHASE, delivered to the Grand Jury of the United States, for the District of Pennsylvania, on the 12th inst. With a masterly pencil, he delineated the features of our excellent constitution, the security it afforded to our liberties, the protection of innocence, and the detection and punishment of guilt.— The trial by jury was noted as an impregnable barrier of freedom and independence.

It was with the greatest propriety remarked that the downfall of the trial by jury, had ever been the certain harbinger of despotism. The cases of the Northern Powers of Europe were mentioned, as awful lessons for our instruction.

The explanation of the oath taken by every grand jury man, was certainly the most important part; and every man worthy of the name, will consider it as an inestimable loss to himself, the public, and posterity, if such an able, and seasonable production, on that solemn subject, shall remain shut up in the portfolio of the ingenious and judicious author. When I repeat a concluding sentence it may give some idea of the general import "do to others the same, as you wish that they in a like case should do to you." It is with regret that I mention my inability to repeat what I most earnestly wish to be indelibly impressed on the heart of every juror.

One of the Traverse Jury.

(New York) April 18, 1798. Date and place are those of the newspaper. The headline indicates this article was reprinted from the Philadelphia *Gazette of the United States.*

Aurora
April 19, 1798   Philadelphia, Pennsylvania

An address has been presented by a grand Jury of the district court of the United States to the president, signed *John Lardner,* containing an approbation through thick and thin of executive measures, and a reprobation of the conduct of those, who do not see perfection in the proceedings of the administration.[1] To give an importance to this address, they state, that they are convened from different parts of the state. This may be all true; but they neglected to inform the public, for whom this address was designed, that they are the creatures of the Marshal of the district, and that the marshall is the creature of the President.[2] The address must then be viewed as an address of the President to himself. Whether such a grand jury was selected for *party purposes* is not mentioned, and can only be conjectured from the stile of their production. We have already seen judges appointed by the President turn preachers of certain political opinions, and now we see Grand Juries converted into party apostles. That progress in improvements is certainly highly commendable, which shews judges administering politics instead of law and grand juries echoing the doctrines of an officer of the government instead of watching over the rights of the citizen!

(Philadelphia) April 19, 1798. Date and place are those of the newspaper.
   1. The address was from the circuit court rather than the district court. See Address of the Grand Jury of the Circuit Court for the District of Pennsylvania to John Adams, April 13, 1798.
   2. Section 29 of the Judiciary Act of 1789 provided that the jurors in United States courts "be designated by lot or otherwise in each State respectively according to the mode of forming juries therein now practised, so far as the laws of the same shall render such designation practicable by the courts or marshals of the United States." *Stat.,* 1:88. The marshal of the district carried out the summoning and selection of jurors.

James Iredell to Hannah Iredell
April 20, 1798   Tarborough, North Carolina

... I wrote you two letters from M^r McKenzie's,[1] which I left this morning ... I found the road bad enough to day, tho' none of it dangerous. I am

advised to go by Raleigh, which I intend to do. My health, thank God, is
very good _ ...

ARS (Nc-Ar, Charles E. Johnson Collection). Addressed "Edenton."
  1. See James Iredell to Hannah Iredell, April 10 and April 17, 1798.

Circuit Court for the District of Georgia
April 20, 1798   Savannah, Georgia

The circuit court for this term did not meet because of the absence of Supreme
Court Justice James Iredell. The marshal of the district, however, did attend and
adjourned the court from day to day until April 25, when Judge Joseph Clay, Jr.,
appeared and adjourned court to the next term.[1]

  1. Minutes, CCD Georgia, RG 21, GEpFAR. See James Iredell to Hannah Iredell, April 10, 1798, for
Iredell's explanation of why he missed this court session.

James Wilson to Bird Wilson
April 21, 1798   Edenton, North Carolina

Edenton   21st April 1798

Dear Bird

  Mr Thomas's Letter and yours on the same Sheet ~~I hav~~ and dated the 29th
of the last Month I have received.[1] He and you will consider this as an
Answer to both. The Draught which Mr Thomas has been good enough to
authorise upon him, cannot be negociated here, as there is no Command of
Money at present: I will try what can be done at Norfolk. A Suit by Major
Butler has been brought against me here.[2] This will necessarily detain me
till it can be arranged; though I believe it important that I should return to
the Northward as soon as possible. He proposes, by his Attorney,[3] that, "if
I will give him Security on Lands in Pennsylvania, he will give me two Years
longer [*letters inked out*] nay three to pay him." You know I have wished to
bring this Matter to a Settlement; and, indeed, did not know but that it had
taken Place[.] Let it be done if possible, and as soon as possible. I have
                        been informed   probably
since I came to the Southward,ₐthat Major Butlerₐhas from Govr Blount,
Mr Allison or both, other Security for this Debt, which you know was
originally none of mine.[4] If this be the Case, I think it would be Nothing
more than reasonable that he should by proper Instruments, give me the
Benefit of that other Security upon my paying this Debt, and upon his being
       any
paidₐother Demands which he may have against those Gentlemen or either
of them. Will you make this Proposal to him? Upon this Subject I shall

as I expect more Information.[5]

write farther by next Post$_\wedge$. Do not [omit?] to write to me. Remember me to the Family and to M^r and Mrs Thomas.

I am   Yours affectionately

James Wilson

ARS (PHi, James Wilson Papers). Addressed "High Street N° 274   Philadelphia."

1. Letter not found.

2. We have been unable to determine how far Butler had pressed his legal claim against Wilson by the time Wilson wrote this letter. On April 10 the clerk of the North Carolina Superior Court for the district of Edenton had issued a writ of debt against James Wilson, returnable October 6, 1798. The undertaking to prosecute was in the form of an endorsement by William Slade and Jacob Blount. There is no endorsement of service by the sheriff, and, aside from the writ itself, there is no mention of *Butler v. Wilson* in the records of the Superior Court for the district of Edenton. It may be that the case does not appear in these records because James Wilson died before the date of return of the writ. *Butler v. Wilson,* Edenton District Superior Court Records 1798, Nc-Ar. We are indebted to George Stevenson of the North Carolina State Archives for information regarding *Butler v. Wilson.*

3. William Slade.

4. Butler held Wilson's paper as collateral security for a debt due him from William Blount and David Allison. See [Thomas Blount] to [John Gray Blount], February 16, 1798.

5. On April 28 and May 5 Wilson wrote to Bird intimations of a plan by which to salvage his fortunes. James Wilson to Bird Wilson, April 28, 1798, Dreer Collection, PHi; James Wilson to Bird Wilson, May 5, 1798, James Wilson Papers, PHi. Finally, on May 12 Wilson set out his plan in a lengthy letter to Joseph Thomas (q.v.).

James Iredell to Hannah Iredell ──────────────────────────

May 1, 1798   Camden, South Carolina

... I arrived here about an hour ago, in perfect health, tho' after a disagreeable Journey from Fayette Ville, the weather having been very uncomfortable, and the roads the worst I ever knew them. This day has been so dull a one that it has not inspired me with a proper tune for May morning, tho' I have thought about it. I am now within 120 miles of Charleston, and have reason to believe the roads before me are very good, as they have had no freshes, and much less rain here than to the Northward ── Hannibal is very well, and has behaved with great propriety ── and my horses have performed excellently. I am very anxious to reach Charleston in hopes to receive some letters from you ── My anxiety is inexpressibly great. I am told our old Friend Mrs Chesnut (Miss Mary Cox that was)[1] is in Town, and well, and propose waiting on her in the afternoon ──. A Family on the road at whose house I staid the other night, and where I have frequently been, had heard so circumstantial an account of my death some time ago that they took me for a Brother of mine, and it was with some difficulty I could convince them their information was ill founded ── but the satisfaction they expressed in

finding it was not affected me a good deal. I was overtaken at the house where I staid last night by an itinerent Methodist Preacher who appears to be a very worthy good Man, but extremely weak. We travelled here together. He and hundreds more are employed by the Society to go constantly about preaching, for which he receives his travelling expences, and 64 Dollars a year to fund him in every thing else. They are all, I find, under regular discipline, and receive precise orders, and are governed by certain rules agreed upon at a stated Meeting of the Society which is usually held at Baltimore. Bishop Coke and Asbury act in conjunction as Wesley acted singly before.[2] Such a Society under artful Men might do a great deal of mischief. He seems to be a good Government Man, which I hope is the fashion of the Society.
. . .

ARS (Nc-Ar, Charles E. Johnson Collection). Addressed "Edenton, North Carolina." Postmarked "Cam.S.C.May 3."
    1. Mary (Cox) Chesnut (ca. 1775-1864), daughter of John Cox of Philadelphia. In 1796 she married James Chesnut (1773-1866), a large plantation owner and resident of Camden, South Carolina. Thomas J. Kirkland and Robert M. Kennedy, *Historic Camden* (Columbia, S.C.: State Company, 1905), pp. 369-70.
    2. In 1784 John Wesley (1703-1791), founder of the Methodist Church in England, ordained Thomas Coke (1747-1814) and Francis Asbury (1745-1816) superintendents (later styled bishop) of the Methodist Episcopal Church in America. *DAB* under Thomas Coke and Francis Asbury; *New Columbia Encyclopedia* under Methodism and under John Wesley.

Circuit Court for the District of Vermont

May 1, 1798   Windsor, Vermont

Chief Justice Oliver Ellsworth and Judge Samuel Hitchcock opened court on May 1 and adjourned court on May 7.[1]

    1. Circuit Docket, CCD Vermont, RG 21, MWalFAR.

James Iredell to Hannah Iredell

May 5, 1798   Charleston, South Carolina

. . . I arrived here perfectly well, tho' after a disagreeable Journey, yesterday afternoon. . . . I have much satisfaction in finding that there is not much business to do here. I begin to receive the usual civilities of this agreeable place. Mr Edward Rutledge called on me, and left an invitation to dine with him to day, and I have another for Thursday next _ I hope not to be detained here above ten days, which will enable me to have an easy ride to Raleigh. My Horses held out exceedingly well, and Hannibal answers every purpose I could wish for. I just begin this letter now, expecting to add to it before a Post can carry it away.[1] . . .

ARS (Nc-Ar, Charles E. Johnson Collection). Addressed "Edenton, North Carolina." Postmarked "MAY 8."

1. For a continuation of this letter, see James Iredell to Hannah Iredell, May 8, 1798.

City Gazette ————————————————————————————————————
May 5, 1798   Augusta, Georgia

We learn by a gentleman just from Savannah, that there has been a failure in the meeting of the circuit federal court for that district. The judge did not attend, or send any letter or message to inform the district judge, why he could not come. On the fifth day, the jury were paid for their attendance, and discharged. This failure has been a serious disappointment to the numerous suitors in that court, some of whom attended from foreign countries and distant states.[1]

(Charleston) May 15, 1798. Date and place are those of the headline.

1. For an explanation of the failure of the court, see James Iredell to Hannah Iredell, April 10, 1798.

Circuit Court for the District of Maryland ————————————
May 7, 1798   Annapolis, Maryland

Judge William Paca was present at court but adjourned it from day to day, because no Supreme Court justice attended. On May 9 court was adjourned to the next term.[1]

1. Minutes, CCD Maryland, RG 21, PPFAR.

Circuit Court for the District of South Carolina ———————
May 7, 1798   Charleston, South Carolina

Associate Justice James Iredell and Judge Thomas Bee opened court on Monday, May 7. Iredell delivered a charge to the grand jury on the same day. On May 12 the court adjourned to the next term.[1]

1. Minutes, CCD South Carolina, RG 21, GEpFAR; James Iredell's Charge to the Grand Jury of the Circuit Court for the District of South Carolina, May 7, 1798 (q.v.).

James Iredell's Charge to the Grand Jury of the Circuit Court for the
District of South Carolina ————————————————————
City Gazette
May 7, 1798   Charleston, South Carolina

Gentlemen of the Grand Jury,

THE duty you are now called upon to perform, is to present offences
committed against the United States. These may be distributed, in a general
point of view, into the following classes.

1. Offences against the United States, as one of the nations of the world.

2. Offences against the United States, as having the sole care of all concerns
with foreign powers.

3. Offences against the United States, relative to their connections among
themselves.

Under the first head, are comprised such offences as are deemed to be
committed against the universal law of society, and the punishment of which
does not belong to one nation more than another, because committed out
of the limits of any; such, for instance, are the crimes of murder or piracy
committed on the high seas. These crimes are so atrocious in their nature,
and would be so terrible in their consequences, if they were to be committed
with impunity, that all nations concur in punishing them: but as the right
belongs equally to all, each hath an equal right, if it can apprehend the
offender, and procure sufficient testimony to apprehend and bring him to
trial. And as this is an object of great national concern, and might give rise
to abuses for which one nation would be accountable to another, it belongs
to the United States, to whom all national concerns in which the different
states are interested are entrusted.

The two remaining classes of offences more immediately relate to the
principal objects for which the government of the United States was formed.
These are well expressed in the dignified introductory words to the
constitution itself, where the objects of it are declared to be: "To form a
more perfect union, establish justice, insure domestic tranquility, provide
for the common defence, promote the general welfare, and secure the
blessings of liberty to ourselves and our posterity."

The attainment of these important purposes required common counsels,
united strength and inflexible principles, from which no deviation should be
permitted, where private morality and public faith could not without perfidy
admit of any. Not only the objects are among the noblest that ever were
deliberately provided for by any nation, but the government itself is so
constituted, as to secure the highest probability that they will be in fact the
leading objects of its pursuit. This, however, will not prevent great clamour
and discontent. A virtuous conduct will ever be hated by vicious men, justice

by the unjust, impartiality by those who, from sinister motives, wish partial measures to be pursued; and men with the best intentions are liable to be deceived by artful intentional misrepresentation. Some measures too, however proper they may in reality be, will sometimes appear so doubtful in their nature, and so uncertain in their consequences, that men of equal understandings, and hearts and intentions equally uncorrupt, will differ in opinion; and in proportion to the importance of the measures, will differ with zeal concerning them. All these are unavoidable consequences of difficult situations, which are to be provided for with so limited a foresight as the ablest of mankind possess.

There is no expedient to prevent that anarchy which all such causes would lead to, but by enabling, by regular and constitutional authority, a delegated number, as the nature of each case may require, to direct the conduct of the whole. Those who know the value of regularity and order, and have a proper abhorrence of confusion, well knowing it is the most dangerous enemy even to liberty itself, will readily submit to such a decision, in each case, as the constitution sanctions, however different it may be from their own private opinion, and with whatever confidence they may believe their own opinion to be right. In many cases, most men, whose vanity does not destroy all distrust in themselves, and all respect for others, will suppose it possible at least that they may themselves be mistaken, as well as other men, and therefore will exercise some caution, lest, with unpardonable arrogance, as well as want of duty, they counteract the execution of measures as judicious as they are obligatory. It is however necessary, whatever may be the conduct or motives of individuals, that laws, when constitutionally made, should be obeyed. The safety and interest of the whole, are not to be sacrificed to the caprice, the want of patriotism, or deliberate disaffection of a few. Every law, therefore, must have some sanction annexed to it, which ought to be more or less rigorous, as the nature of the case requires. Some of these sanctions are merely fines and penalties, for which prosecutions of a civil nature are carried on. In others, the punishment goes beyond these, and then the offence partakes of the nature of a crime presentable by a grand jury; and, after trial and conviction, by another jury, punishable as the law has particularly prescribed.

Besides offences of this description, which are solely in violation of the duty incumbent on us all to obey the laws of our country, there are others of a kind immoral in their own nature, presentable by a grand jury of the United States, if committed within a place in their district, under the jurisdiction of the United States, and not of any particular state: such as murder or larceny within any fort, arsenal, dock-yard or magazine, under the exclusive jurisdiction of the United States. So also are other crimes, if committed in the course of an execution of an authority of the United States: such as perjury in any suit depending in one of their courts. I specify these merely as examples, not thinking an exact enumeration of each kind to be at present material. From these instances, you may form a judgement of the whole.

With respect to the manner in which your inquiries are to be conducted, a very few observations will be sufficient. You are, among other things, directed to keep secret your own counsel and that of the United States. This has been considered by some as an arbitrary regulation, and injurious to the person accused. It appears to me, however,[1] to be founded in the strongest principles of reason and justice. If any person knew of an important prosecution depending against him, he might make his escape, and thus elude it altogether, in a case possibly of great moment to the public. At the same time, considering all circumstances, this course of proceeding is more favorable to the person accused himself, than if he was permitted to know of the prosecution and defend himself before the grand jury, because, in that case, he would appear with greater disadvantage before the jury who were to pronounce finally on his fate. They would be naturally biassed in favor of a decision already given by another jury, perhaps of a greater number than their own, at least in all probability equally enlightened and upright as themselves, and bound by the most sacred obligations of religion and justice, equally with themselves, to decide impartially between the public and him. In that case, too, there could be no room for the suggestion, that they found on probable evidence only, from the consideration that another jury was to convict or acquit him; for though that would be a very good argument when the evidence only on one side could be received, it could be of no weight if there had been an opportunity of hearing both.

It may also be observed, that the person accused, though he may suffer unjustly by a false accusation, has in the present method every chance for escaping, not only punishment, but odium, which an innocent man can wish for. He has in the first instance to rely on the integrity and discernment of the grand jury, who, when partial evidence alone is given, will naturally scrutinize it with great particularity. Though they may deem, and I suppose ought to deem, probable evidence sufficient, they will think the probability should not be a light one, but amounting nearly to a moral certainty, admitting the evidence to be true; because, if not absolutely false, evidence on one side is apt to give a colour to facts, which opposite evidence can do away. If, however, the grand jury should be deceived by evidence too probable to be rejected, yet when the defence is heard, if the person accused can entirely take off its force, no imputation can be either on him or the grand jury: much less can any lie on either, if direct perjury has been committed. So that it can rarely happen to any man, entirely innocent, that his acquittal by the jury who is finally to try him does not restore his reputation, as well as secure his safety.

You certainly are not confined to prosecutions commenced by the attorney of the United States, or to such evidence as he may lay before you. But if you are possessed of information which he is not, it will be safest to consult with him, and avail of his legal assistance, without which your best intentions might be frustrated. Upon this subject, I think it only necessary to add, that twelve at least should agree upon finding any bill.

The present situation of our country is alarming to a very great degree. But it is only alarming for want of that spirit of union which alone procured us peace and independence, and without which it is impossible to preserve either, or save ourselves from ruin and contempt. We have a government formed and calculated to cherish, and with the best intentions to promote it. But in vain are all the efforts of the government, if the people do not co-operate, each in his several station, in its support. They have every blessing to preserve by it, and every danger to dread from supineness or indifference. May they be sensible in time of the great crisis which requires their exertions! and by that manliness, virtue, and intrepidity, which have so often saved their country when on the verge of ruin, extricate it with equal honour and success from its present difficulties! The late illustrious example in this city, cannot but highly contribute to so desirable an event.[2]

(Charleston) May 8, 1798. Date and place are from an introductory paragraph to the charge.

On June 1, 1798, Iredell delivered this charge to the grand jury at the Circuit Court for the district of North Carolina. The charge at the North Carolina circuit court was printed by the *State Gazette of North-Carolina* (Edenton), July 4, 1798; *Claypoole's American Daily Advertiser* (Philadelphia), August 8, 1798; the *Philadelphia Gazette,* August 8, 1798; and the *Federal Gazette* (Baltimore), August 10, 1798. An extract of the North Carolina charge appeared in *Russell's Gazette* (Boston), August 16, 1798; *South-Carolina State-Gazette* (Charleston), September 21, 1798; and the *Commercial Advertiser* (New York), October 12, 1798. Substantive differences between the South Carolina and the North Carolina charges are noted.

1. Printings of the North Carolina charge published in the *State Gazette of North-Carolina* (Edenton), July 4, 1798; *Claypoole's American Daily Advertiser* (Philadelphia), August 8, 1798; *Philadelphia Gazette,* August 8, 1798; and *Federal Gazette* (Baltimore), August 10, 1798, contain the following parenthetical statement: "(for which I have the sanction of very high authority)." Iredell may be referring to John Hawles, *The Grand-Jury-Man's Oath and Office Explained; and the Rights of English-Men Asserted. A Dialogue between a Barrister at Law, and A Grand-Jury-Man* (London: printed for Langley Curtis, 1680), pp. 4, 5-6.

2. The last sentence of this paragraph was omitted from the North Carolina charge. For the event to which Iredell refers, see James Iredell to Hannah Iredell, May 8, 1798.

Reply of the Grand Jury of the Circuit Court for the District of South Carolina

City Gazette

May 7, 1798   Charleston, South Carolina

THE Grand Jury of the Federal District of South-Carolina, for the present term, return their thanks to his honor, Judge Iredell, for the excellent charge he has delivered to them, and request he would please to furnish the clerk of the court with a copy for publication; they conceiving that, at this period, it may tend to continue that harmony which they now find so happily existing in this District.

JOHN EDWARDS, Foreman.

(Charleston) May 8, 1798. Although the reply of the grand jury is not dated, the minutes of the circuit court indicate it was given on the same day as the charge, May 7, 1798. Minutes, CCD South Carolina, RG 21, GEpFAR.

Address of the Grand Jury of the Circuit Court for the District of Maryland to John Adams

Federal Gazette

May 8, 1798   Annapolis, Maryland

To the PRESIDENT *of the* UNITED STATES.

Sir,

We, the undersigned jurors attending the circuit court of the United States for the district of Maryland, think it our duty to address you on the alarming situation into which our public affairs have been brought by the unconciliating spirit, ambition and rapacity of those who now govern the republic of France.

At the first dawn of the revolution in that country, we fondly hoped that a new era was opening upon mankind, when liberty, justice and humanity, would take the place of slavery, rapine and cruelty, which had too long disgraced the world. Allured by this delusive phantom, many of us long excused the errors, and apologised for the crimes of that ill-fated people.

But at length our eyes are opened, when we see them aiming deadly blows at the small remains of republicanism in Europe, and menacing us also with destruction, the only people on earth who have ever shewn them sincere friendship, and who have nothing to reproach ourselves with as to them, but too fond, too blind an attachment. On a calm retrospect of the conduct of your illustrious predecessor, and a view of the measures which have been pursued during your administration with regard to that nation, we can perceive nothing which ought to have offended, nothing unattempted that could have averted the calamity with which we are threatened, unless we had chosen to have become their ally in a war foreign to our interests, and probably fatal to our independence.

Anxious as we always have been, and still are, to avoid war, yet we are persuaded that there is one evil greater and more dreadful, national degradation, the certain harbinger of slavery. Accept then, sir, our assurances, as in some measure representing our district, that you will find us animated with the spirit of freemen, and determined at all hazards to defend the rights and independence of our country, and if there be any of a different sentiment, as hath been presumptuously asserted, they will be found few indeed.

John Campbell,	William C. Brent,
Richard Forrest,	Charles Wallace,
Isaac Pollock,	James Williams,
Charles Carroll, jun.	Alexander Green,
John Galloway,	Samuel Bayle,
Denton Jaques,	William Dallam,
George Kennedy,	Randolp B Latimer,
Patrick Murdock,	Samuel Robertson,
Evan Gwinn,	Thomas Nowland,
William Lee,	J. J. Bugh,
Samuel C. Hall,	John R. Key.

Annapolis, May 8th, 1798.

(Baltimore) May 24, 1798. Date and place are those of the address.

James Iredell to Hannah Iredell
May 8, 1798   Charleston, South Carolina

...Our Court began yesterday, and there is so little business to do that I have no doubt I shall leave this City early next week. I receive great civilities here, having dined out yesterday, and still having 3 dinners ahead _ A very large & respectable Meeting here on Saturday last passed unanimous and strong resolutions in support of Government, and an address to the President and Congress, and opened a subscription which it is supposed will amount to 20000 Dollars for an additional sum to that granted by Congress for fortifying the harbour _ French Privateers are every day off the Bar, and not only taken Vessels, but some of the Men have landed, and taken provisions against the will of the [word inked out] Owners for which they have in one or two instances paid less than the value _. One or two Spanish Privateers have also begun to plunder, and one the other day had the insolence to fire on a Vessel in the Harbour of S̲ᵗ Mary's in Georgia. The Grand Jury did me the honour to thank me for my Charge, and it is published this day at their request.[1] I have not yet seen M̲ʳ Izard,[2] but intend waiting ₍on him₎. He is unfortunately in a very dangerous way with a Palsey which has almost deprived him of the use of one side. I am told M̲ʳ John Rutledge is quite recovered _ [3] He was from home when I arrived, but called on me yesterday evening, when I was unluckily from home. ... I probably may be at Raleigh 3 or 4 days before the Court is to meet _ My health is very good. What happiness would it give me to hear that was the case with you and our dear Children, and Friends in general _ May God Almighty grant it. ... Give my best respects to M̲ʳ and M̲ʳˢ Wilson, and my other Friends You know I wish to be remembered to. Tell M̲ʳˢ Wilson I frequently remember her admonition about exclamation and swearing, and am sure I have improved by it, but the vile roads I had to pass sometimes unavoidably made me transgress. ...

. . .

I am in Judge Wilson's old Lodgings _ Mrs Smith's.[4]

ARS (Nc-Ar, Charles E. Johnson Collection). Addressed "Edenton, North Carolina." Postmarked "MAY 8." On May 5, 1798, James Iredell had begun a letter to Hannah (q.v.). Three days later, he continued the letter and dated the new passage May 8.

1. See James Iredell's Charge to the Grand Jury of the Circuit Court for the District of South Carolina, May 7, 1798.

2. Former United States Senator Ralph Izard (1742-1804), resided on an estate near Charleston, South Carolina. In 1797 he suffered a paralytic stroke which left him an invalid for the remainder of his life. *DAB.*

3. John Rutledge, former chief justice of the United States, reputedly suffered bouts of insanity in the fall of 1795 and may also have been physically debilitated. *DHSC,* 1:100, 811-21; *Aurora* (q.v. under date of December 1, 1795).

4. Mrs. Smith seems to have operated a boarding house on Charleston's Broad Street. See source note to Elihu Hall Bay to James Iredell, May 13, 1798. This sentence was added as a postscript after Iredell's signature.

James Iredell to Hannah Iredell ————————————————
   May 11-12, 1798   Charleston, South Carolina

[*May 11:*] Our Court will probably end to day certainly tomorrow, and I intend to leave Town on Monday. I continue to receive the greatest civilities _ I have dined only once at my lodgings, and have engagements for every day I am to stay. Mr John Rutledge was out of town when I came, but immediately on his return waited on me, and he has repeatedly pressed me to stay at his house, which however I have declined as I had previously engaged lodgings. I have not yet seen Mr Izard, but intend to call on him if I can to day. I have a number of kind invitations from many Gentlemen to take their houses on my return _. I have accepted of three, so that I shall not move very rapidly for the first three or four days, and as I shall not be directly on the Post Road don't be surprised at your not receiving a letter from me for one Post _ I intend to return by Camden and Fayette Ville, and hope by moderate Journies to reach Raleigh 2 or 3 days before the Court is to meet. Mr Rutledge is perfectly recovered, and in such high spirits that he and another Gentleman and myself outsat all the rest of the Company at a Friend's house till near 11 o'clock _ He remarked with surprise, that I never swore, which seems to be an equal proof of my former sin and present reformation. He himself and most of the Gentlemen here swear a good deal _. I am glad to hear that Judge Wilson and his Wife are well, but am still a little uneasy about that Writ.[1] Be pleased to present my best respects particularly to them ...

[*May 12:*] Our Court ended this morning, and I still intend leaving Town on Monday morning, having been engaged for several days to dine with an agreeable Family that day, about 7 miles from here. Though I was in Court yesterday from 10 till near 8 I am perfectly well. The weather is so cold today, the Thermometer is at 68. The other day it was at 85. I have just come from sitting an hour with M᷊ Izard. He and M᷊ʳˢ Izard[2] seemed very glad to see me. The palsey affliction under which he labours is too visible. His face is a good deal affected by it _ But his understanding seems perfectly good. ... I am to dine to day with M᷊ J. Rutledge, who has invited a number of other Gentlemen _ This week, I am told, is the first time he has broke from his retirement. ...

ARS (Nc-Ar, Charles E. Johnson Collection). Addressed "Edenton, North Carolina." Postmarked "C MAY 15."

1. Iredell is referring to the writ of debt issued against Wilson by Pierce Butler in the North Carolina Superior Court. See note to James Wilson to Bird Wilson, April 21, 1798.

2. Alice (De Lancey) Izard (ca. 1745-1832). *South Carolina Genealogies*, 5 vols. (Spartanburg, S.C.: Reprint Co., 1983), 2:428.

James Wilson to Joseph Thomas ————————————————————
May 12, 1798   Edenton, North Carolina

Edenton   12th May 1798
Dear Sir
    I sit down to write to you upon a subject, which, for some time past has occupied, as it merited, my most serious and deliberate attention.[1] Whether I shall be able to express my sentiments in the manner, in which I wish to express them, I cannot say; but the will must be taken for the deed.—You urge me to return; and Bird, in a letter to Mrs. Wilson,[2] informs her, that, in a letter from you to me "you tell me, that something considerable may be done in my favour if I return" On this <u>particular</u> point I find nothing in your letter. Many reasons, some respecting my health, concur in forming a strong wish for my return. But against my return at present there are insuperable objections; some respecting Major Butler, others respecting the general conduct of my creditors. If they will agree, that, on terms of the best security for them, I shall have it fully in my power to make every personal and intellectual effort for their interest and my own, I will—for I wish to—return whenever the arrangements necessary here shall be made.
    In the letter before mentioned, Bird says that contrary to your former opinion, you now think it proper, that I should make a conveyance to Trustees in general trust. I confess myself not a little surprised at this change. Ask the oldest, the most experienced, and the most judicious of your friends, whether, in every instance, such a measure, where a large or even considerable

property was in question, universal dissatisfaction and disappointment did not prevail among all—but the Assignees? This measure, as I view it, would effectually preclude me from doing fair and equal justice. It would lay the field open for a system of iniquitous speculation, which, I have too much reason to think, has been already contemplated and commenced by some who are, and by some who are not, my creditors, with an avidity cruel, treacherous and insatiable. The consequence, would be a loss, heavy and unmerited, in some instances; and in others, advantages disproportionate, or totally without just claim. To avoid such consequences, I have submitted, and, if necessary, will submit to every personal indignity and persecution. I have been hunted—I may be hunted—like a wild beast: I have suffered much—I may suffer essentially in my health and otherwise: But as, at present, I consider the subject, the last extremity shall never compel my signature to an act, which would exclude me from performing the duty, and feeling the pleasure, of doing full and effectual justice to all.—I dare, with the most undismayed confidence, appeal to my conduct for evidence the most unequivocal, that my principles and views are upright and honourable. The keenest periods of distress—and you well know their keenness—have not driven me to raise money by methods, ruinous to those, to whom I am indebted: Nor have certain sentiments of the most tender kind, seduced me to withdraw a single foot of my property from what I deem the sacred fund for discharging all that I owe. From this conduct I mean never to deviate. If my creditors will agree, that I may act, unmolested on these Principles; and will appoint a person, of whom both they and I shall approve, to be confidential on both sides; I will engage to communicate to such person, the sales as they shall be made, and not to appropriate a shilling of the Proceeds without his knowledge and consent. Into any immediate contract, which may be thought efficient for securing the execution of such engagements and of the great object in view, I will enter with pleasure. My wish is, merely, to have every fair opportunity given me to make the most vigourous exertions for the benefit of all that are interested. From many circumstances I think there is reason to believe that the season is approaching when such exertions may be crowned with the most abundant success. Perhaps some may suggest that I have not been so active as I might have been about my affairs. My life has not been a life of idleness or indolence. But there are times, when nothing, not ruinous, can be done. Such times I have unfortunately experienced. Besides, you know well how many useless and hurtful impediments have been thrown in my way. You can vouch for the many steps I have taken, and for the full powers which I have given others that everything possible might be done for relief. This is not the first era of my life, in which I have encountered difficulties; and, I hope, on this, as on a former occasion, I shall be able to surmount those difficulties with safety to all, and advantage to many, who are interested in the situation of my affairs. My resources, if they can be brought fairly into operation, are proportionately greater now than they were at the period, to which I allude. Nothing that may be thought advisable, on this, or on the other side of the Atlantic, shall be left unattempted. With the strongest sentiments of regard, I am

Dear Sir   Sincerely yours

James Wilson

P.S. You may easily conceive how anxious I shall be till I hear from you.[3]

Tr (PCarlD, Founder's Box). Typewritten document.

1. On May 5 Wilson had written to Bird Wilson that he intended to transmit a plan for arranging his financial affairs to Bird and Joseph Thomas "by the next Post" (James Wilson Papers, PHi).

2. Letter not found.

3. On May 24 Pierce Butler wrote to William Slade that two days earlier Bird Wilson had visited him and read aloud part of the above letter, at which point Butler had responded: "I repeated to this young man what I had Often told him & his father, my wish to avoid proceeding to extremity, and my disposition to contribute to soften his sorrows _ I reminded him of my repeated Offers, _ he made his bow _ on parting I told him, I should not wait longer than this day, to receive proposals, and If none were made to me, I should write to you to let the Law have its opperation, I have not heard from him since, I am therefore In duty to myself and Children, tho reluctantly constrained to request that you will let the Law have its Opperation, his debt to me including the interest due is now $197000 or more, tho the Principal Of two of the bonds will not be due till the first of Next February _ I have again offered his son to extend the time of payment, two & three years provided they secure it to me, I have no wish to possess his lands nor the most distant inclination to Speculate on his ruin. I should therefore hope he did not mean to do me the injustice of including or Classing me among his malignant Creditors" (James Wilson Papers, PHi). What actions William Slade took as a result of this letter are unclear. See Pierce Butler to Samuel Wallis, June 14, 1798.

Elihu Hall Bay to James Iredell
May 13, 1798 [Charleston, South Carolina]

Dr Sir _

Inclosed, I send you the Directions of the Road to Cheraw Court House,[1] by the way of Le neau's Ferry, together with a Line to Mr Dollard,[2] who lives about 3 Miles above the Point, where you will fall in with the main Ge° Town Road. _ I w^d advise you by all means, to stay a day w^h him, and rest y^r horses. _ you will feel y^r self perfectly at home there _ ~~After~~ Wishing you a pleasant Jouney _ give me leave to assure you, I am w^h very sincere Respect and Esteem   Dr Sir   Y^r M° Obd^t Hb^e Servt

E: H: Bay
13 May 1798 _

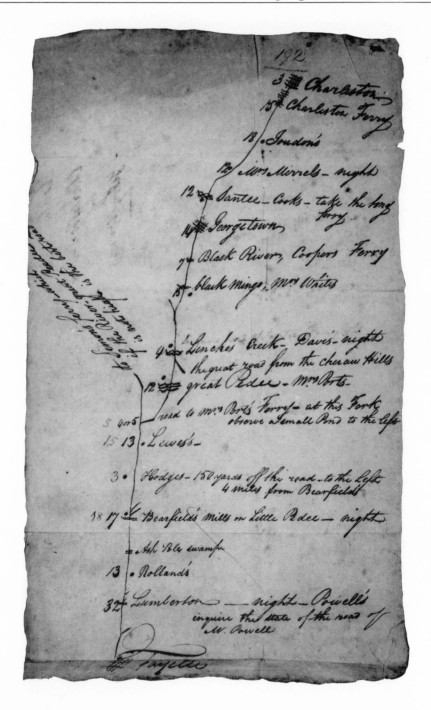

Route from Charleston, South Carolina to Fayetteville, North Carolina. Courtesy North Carolina Division of Archives and History, Raleigh. Charles E. Johnson Collection. Endorsed "Route to Charleston by Georgetown."

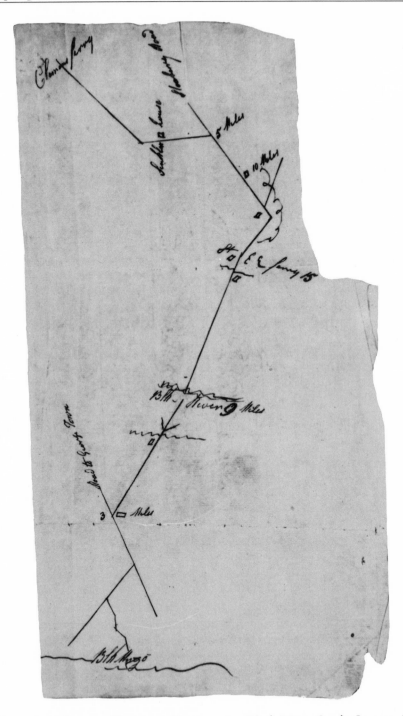

Route from Clements Ferry (near Charleston) to Black Mingo Creek. Courtesy North Carolina Division of Archives and History, Raleigh. Charles E. Johnson Collection. The above map shows a shortcut further inland from the more coastal route shown on the facing page.

The honb[l] Judge Iredell _

[*Enclosure 1:*]

Iredell's
Directions for Judge ∧~~Iredale's~~ Route to
Cheraw Co[t] House on Pedee River _

I w[d] advise you to cross Santee River at Le neau's Ferry. _
To Le neau's Ferry, there are two ways. 1st either to cross Cooper River at
Clements's Ferry, 6 Miles above the City, and then up through S[t] Thomas's
Parish, to Bonneau's Ferry on the East Branch of Cooper River. _ ~~and and~~
then 4 Miles further up ~~the Road~~ you fall in with the Road which leads
from Strawberry Ferry to Le'neau's _ [3] or
~~or~~ 2[dly] to go directly up the Camden Road to the 23 Mile House, and then
take a Right hand Road 6 Miles to Strawberry Ferry, at once   from whence
you go directly to Le neau's. ~~at once~~
I think I sh[d] prefer the latter way, tho the Road is not so good; as you
will be less embarrassed with Ferries _

From Le neau's _ proceed up to what is called Potatoe Ferry, on Black
River. _ then to the Meeting <u>House on the Ge[o] Town Road</u>, which leads
up to Cheraws. _

You will fall into the Ge[o] Town Road about 3 Miles below M[r] Dollard[s],
which you will find an excellent Stage, and where you will meet w[h] ~~mu~~ much
genuine hospitality. (I have given a Letter to him) ~~M[r] Dollard knows the~~
from M Dollard[s], y[r] next good Stage will be at Witherspoons Ferry, ~~over~~
over Lynch's Creek _

From Linch's Creek, it is one day's Journey to Black Creek; _ Road
excellent where there is a very good house. _ from Black Creek to Cheraw
Court House on the long Bluff ~~Pee~~ Pedee is 20 Miles. good Road

to find out M[r] Dollard's House _

after you fall into the Ge[o] Town Road and go ab[t] 2 Miles the Road fork
take the Right hand one _ and ab[t] ¾[th] of a Mile you'l ~~obt~~ observe a large
House and Plantation to y[r] Right _ that is M[r] Dollards. _

To Strawberry Ferry _	32
Leneau's Ferry _	25
Black River Ferry _	18
Dollard's _	12 or 15[4]

[*Enclosure 2:*]

D[r] Sir _
This will be handed to you by Judge Iredell, of the Federal Bench, _ whose
acquaintance, you will be proud of. _ He is on his way to Fayetville N[o]
Carolina, _ I know y[r] Hospitality, _ and I know I need say no more on the

Subject. _ My Compt⁵ to Mrs Dollard⁵ and believe that I ever am Dr Sir Fr^d and very Obd^t Hb^e Servt

E: H: Bay

13 May 1798

Patrick Dollard Esqr

Elihu Hall Bay to James Iredell: ARS (NcD, James Iredell Sr. and Jr. Papers). Addressed to Iredell "at Mrs Smith's Br^d Street." Enclosure 1: AD (Nc-Ar, Charles E. Johnson Collection). On the verso of these directions, Bay wrote: "Directions for Judge Iredell." Enclosure 2: ALS (Nc-Ar, Charles E. Johnson Collection). On the verso of the letter of introduction Bay wrote: "Patrick Dollard Esqr near Black Mingo Ferry_ Fav^d by the Honbl: Judge Iredell."

Elihu Hall Bay (1754-1838), associate judge of the Court of Sessions and Common Pleas of South Carolina, was a resident of Charleston, South Carolina. John Belton O'Neall, *Biographical Sketches of the Bench and Bar of South Carolina,* 2 vols. (1859; reprint ed., Spartanburg, S.C.: Reprint Co., 1975), 1:53-65.

1. Iredell was traveling to the circuit court in Raleigh, North Carolina, but did not use the directions offered by Elihu Bay.

2. Patrick Dollard (ca. 1746-1800) had represented Prince Frederick Parish in the South Carolina ratifying convention and operated a tavern in that parish. Jeannie Hayward Register, comp., "Marriage and Death Notices from the *City Gazette,*" *South Carolina Historical and Genealogical Magazine* 26 (April 1925): 128-29; George C. Rogers, Jr., *The History of Georgetown County, South Carolina* (Columbia: University of South Carolina Press, 1970), p. 169-70; Richard N. Cote, ed., *Dictionary of South Carolina,* vol. 1 (Easley, S.C.: Southern Historical Press, 1985), p. 92.

3. James Iredell had a map of the road from Clements Ferry to Black Mingo Creek, but we do not know if he received it at the same time as the directions from Elihu Hall Bay. The map shows the same roads and some of the same landmarks and represents a more direct route than the coastal road through Georgetown. See illustrations "Route from Charleston, South Carolina to Fayetteville, North Carolina" and "Route from Clements Ferry (near Charleston) to Black Mingo Creek."

4. The mileage notations are in the hand of James Iredell. A second route suggested at some point to James Iredell was to take the coastal road through Georgetown, which intersected the road from Leneau's Ferry a few miles north of Potato Ferry on the Black River. See illustrations "Route from Charleston, South Carolina to Fayetteville, North Carolina" and "Route from Clements Ferry (near Charleston) to Black Mingo Creek."

5. Ann Dollard, wife of Patrick Dollard. Ronald Vern Jackson and Gary Ronald Teeples, eds., *South Carolina 1800 Census* 2nd ed. (Bountiful, Utah: Accelerated Indexing System, 1975).

Reply to the Grand Jury of the Circuit Court for the District of Maryland by John Adams ————————————

Federal Gazette

May 18, 1798   Philadelphia, Pennsylvania

ANSWER

To the Jurors attending the Circuit Court of the United States for the district of Maryland.

Gentlemen

I THANK you for this address. The French revolution was a phenomenon, so unusual in the modern history of the world (although the changes of dynastic's were common in the great empires of antiquity) and held up to our view in the amiable light of reformation and regeneration, while its deformities were carefully concealed from the public in America, that it is not surprising, that a new æra was thought by many to be opening upon mankind. It is now apparent to all men, that slavery, rapine and cruelty, have been augmented and multiplied, instead of being succeeded by liberty, justice and humanity.

I rejoice that your eyes are at length opened; the deadly blows aimed at the small remains of republicanism in Europe, and the menaces of destruction against us, who have nothing to reproach ourselves with, but too fond, too blind an attachment, cannot fail to alarm every candid mind.

The satisfaction you express in the conduct of the executive authority of this country towards France, is very acceptable. Many strong indications have escaped, from time to time, for several years, that nothing would satisfy the French rulers short of our becoming their ally in a war, foreign to our interest, and fatal to our independence, by becoming tributary to their ambitious views of universal domination, by sea and land, and to the rapacious avarice of influential individuals.

This national degredation, the certain harbinger of slavery, or rather slavery itself, is certainly an evil greater, and more dreadful than war.

Your determination, at all hazards, to defend the rights and independence of your country, shews you to be animated with the spirit of freemen, and does you great honor.

JOHN ADAMS.

Philadelphia, May 18, 1798.

(Baltimore) May 24, 1798. Date and place are those of the reply.

James Iredell to Hannah Iredell ———————————————————————
May 18-19, 1798   Stateburg, South Carolina

[*May 18:*] I am thus far on my return in perfect health, having broke away with great difficulty from the agreeable hospitality of Charleston, and the road I have passed from it. I left Charleston on Monday, and spent a delightful day at Mʳ Roger Smith's,[1] only about 7 miles from Charleston upon Ashley River, and by far the handsomest place I have seen in the whole State. This Gentleman is married to a Sister of Mʳ Rutledge's,[2] and has a very large and agreeable Family. Mʳ Rutledge came out with [me], and we had other Company from Town specially invited. Mʳ Rutledge has lived so much in retirement that tho' very fond of his Sister and the whole Family they had not seen him for a long time, and it was truly affecting to see their meeting and how happy they all seemed to be. M.ʳ Rutledge himself was in the highest spirits the whole day, and prolonged his stay as long as he could. I staid there that night, and the next morning went to M.ʳ Bee's[3] (about 12 miles) where I passed the remainder of the day, receiving every possible degree of kindness. I was at two private houses afterwards, but came along with great rapidity. I hope by easy stages to reach Fayette by Wednesday next _ I was very much tempted to stay another day in Charleston, in the hope of getting letters from you, but the weather was so fine that I thought, as my business was done, it would be inexcusable to neglect it. I have directed any letters that may arrive for me to be forwarded to Fayette Ville God grant the accounts may continue favourable _ The last I had, thank God, was very much so in deed _ . The distinction and kindness I met with in Charleston exceeded, if possible, what I experienced before. I dined only one day at my Lodgings, and considering that M.ʳ Rutledge had lived totally reclus[e?] before my arrival, his attention, his friendship, I could almost say his affection to me, was conspicuous in a remarkable degree. I saw frequently your old acquaintance, M.ʳˢ Eveleigh that was, now M.ʳˢ Edward Rutledge _ [4] They both look as young as ever I saw them, and are supposed by their acquaintances to be extremely happy with each other _ He had courted her before either was married, being then a young Man without fortune her Father would not consent to the match. M.ʳ Izard's handsome Daughter,[5] whom you saw in Philadelphia, is soon to be married to a young Gentleman of the name of Deas[6] with whom I am not acquainted.

[*May 19:*] I went yesterday afternoon to see our old Friend M.ʳˢ M.ᶜNair[7] who lives within two miles from this place. She seemed very happy to see me, and much obliged to [me?] for coming. ... She wished me very much to stay all night, but that I had not prepared for _ I am detained h[er]e by rain to day. ... Present my best respects to M.ʳ and M.ʳˢ Wilson. I am still uneasy about that Writ. You may tell M.ʳˢ Wilson that I have nearly effected my reformation as to swearing and exclaiming, and if I can do it thoroughly shall owe her unspeakable obligations for the friendly frankness with which she corrected those failings. ...

ARS (Nc-Ar, Charles E. Johnson Collection). Addressed "Edenton, North Carolina." Postmarked by hand "Stateburgh May 20ᵗʰ." Iredell noted that Stateburg was located "22 miles from Camden."

1. Roger Smith (1745-1805). Webber, "Dr. John Rutledge and His Descendants," p. 13.

2. Mary (Rutledge) Smith (1747-1832), sister of former Chief Justice John Rutledge, was the wife of Roger Smith. Webber, "Dr. John Rutledge and His Descendants," p. 13.

3. Judge Thomas Bee.

4. Mary (Shubrick) (Everleigh) Rutledge (1753-1837) was the second wife of Edward Rutledge, brother of John Rutledge. Webber, "Dr. John Rutledge and His Descendants," p. 14.

5. Anne Izard (1779-1863). *South Carolina Genealogies*, 2:429.

Rose Hill Plantation by an unknown artist. Oil on canvas, ca. 1810-1830. Courtesy Charleston Museum, Charleston, South Carolina.

6. William Allen Deas (1764-ca. 1820), an attorney, was a member of the South Carolina House of Representatives. He and Anne Izard were married on November 2, 1798. Emily B. Reynolds and Joan R. Faunt, comps., *Biographical Directory of the Senate of the State of South Carolina, 1776-1964* (Columbia: South Carolina Archives Department, 1964), p. 204; Brent H. Holcomb, *South Carolina Marriages, 1688-1799* (Baltimore: Genealogical Publishing, 1980), p. 61.

7. Elizabeth McNair, wife of John McNair, a Claremont County, South Carolina cotton mill owner. Jackson and Teeples, *South Carolina 1800 Census;* U.S., Department of Commerce and Labor, Bureau of the Census, *Heads of Families at the First Census of the United States Taken in the Year 1790: South Carolina* (1908; reprint ed., Bountiful, Utah: Accelerated Indexing Systems, 1978); Anne King Gregorie, *History of Sumter County* (Sumter, S.C.: Library Board of Sumter County, 1954), p. 108.

Circuit Court for the District of New Hampshire
May 19, 1798   Portsmouth, New Hampshire

On May 19 Chief Justice Oliver Ellsworth and Judge John Pickering convened court. After the opening, Ellsworth delivered to the grand jury "a very excellant Charge, which united the multum in parvo,[1] to an eminent degree." On May 22 the court adjourned to the next term.[2]

1. "Much in little." Hugh P. Jones, *Dictionary of Foreign Phrases and Classical Quotations* (1908; reprint ed., Boston: Longwood Press, 1977), p. 72.
2. Records, CCD New Hampshire, RG 21, MWalFAR; *Oracle of the Day* (Portsmouth), May 26, 1798. Charge not found. Another newspaper described Ellsworth's charge as "short but very comprehensive and pathetic." *New-Hampshire Gazette* (Portsmouth), May 22, 1798.

Circuit Court for the District of Virginia
May 22, 1798   Richmond, Virginia

The order book of the circuit court contains no record of a spring term.[1]

1. Order Book, CCD Virginia, Vi.

Circuit Court for the District of Massachusetts
June 1, 1798   Boston, Massachusetts

On June 1 Associate Justice William Cushing and Judge John Lowell opened court. The court adjourned on June 8.[1]

1. Final Records, CCD Massachusetts, RG 21, MWalFAR.

Circuit Court for the District of North Carolina
June 1, 1798   Raleigh, North Carolina

On June 1 the circuit court commenced its session with Associate Justice James Iredell and Judge John Sitgreaves in attendance. Iredell delivered a charge to the grand jury. On June 9 the court adjourned to the next term.[1]

1. Minutes, CCD North Carolina, RG 21, GEpFAR; James Iredell's Charge to the Grand Jury of the Circuit Court for the District of North Carolina, June 1, 1798 (q.v.).

James Iredell's Charge to the Grand Jury of the Circuit Court for the District of North Carolina
June 1, 1798   Raleigh, North Carolina

[*On June 1, 1798, Iredell delivered a charge to the grand jury in North Carolina described by the* State Gazette of North-Carolina *(Edenton), July 4, 1798, as being* "the same charge which was in substance delivered to the Grand Jury of the United States for the District of South-Carolina, in the Circuit Court held at Charleston, May 7, 1798." *For the text of the charge, see James Iredell's Charge to the Grand Jury of the Circuit Court for the District of South Carolina, published above under date of May 7, 1798.*]

Reply of the Grand Jury of the Circuit Court for the District of North Carolina
State Gazette of North-Carolina
June 4, 1798   Raleigh, North Carolina

CIRCUIT COURT, *June term,* 1798.
In Grand Jury, 4th June, 1798.
Resolved, as the unanimous opinion of the Grand jury, That their thanks are justly due to his Honour *Judge Iredell,* for his excellent charge delivered to them at this term, and for his considerate conduct in not wishing to detain them here to their manifest inconvenience at this important season of the year, longer than was absolutely necessary for the business of the court.

(Signed)

THEOPHILUS HUNTER, *Foreman.*

(Edenton) July 4, 1798. Date and place are those given in the reply.

Pierce Butler to Samuel Wallis
June 14, 1798   Philadelphia, Pennsylvania

Philadelphia   June the 14th 1798.
Sam! Wallace Esq!
Sir
M! Allison declines agreeing to the proposal unless accompanied by terms so highly injurious to me, as to merit nothing more than a hearing.[1] Reflecting on the proposed negociation between You and myself, I am irresistibly forced

to draw this conclusion, that if You, who know so much of Judge Wilson's affairs, can doubt of obtaining security for $51,000, in such a way as to free Yourself from responsibility, there must on Your mind be little expectation of geting security for $500,000, the amt. of our joint claim. Call to mind the circumstance that gave rise to the negociation between You and myself, vidz.ᵗ, Your declaration, that from deeds and papers in Your possession, from Your intimate knowledge of Judge Wilson's affairs, You believed You coud secure the whole or if not the whole, the greater part of Judge Wilson's debt to both of us; "woud then Mr Butler give $10,000 for securing his demand?" the answer was yes; but the advancement, not only the advancement but the presentation of $10,000 on a ground, the stability of even one fifth of which You hesitate to acknowledge as firm; is not, ought not, to be expected. What I require as the smallest return for my $10,000 is, that if Judge Wilson is taken out of gaol, I shall have decidedly secured to me $51,000, being the moiety of what he is committed for; and even in that event I make myself responsible to Mr Allison for the whole sum for which the Judge is commited; yet this responsibility I am willing to take on myself, provided You engage to be responsible to me, that in case You take Judge Wilson out of gaol, at least $51,000 of my demand shall be secured; and for the better ascertaining of which, that same paper which secures, on certain conditions the refunding of the whole or part of the $10,000, shall be made liable, and the original lodged either with Mr Rawl[2] or myself. On this condition I am willing to go forward.[3] The more I view the measure of my sending an agent, the more I am persuaded of the futility of such a step, not to mention the unreasonable delay consequent thereon.

I remain   Sir   Yr Most Obedᵗ

P. B.

Lb (PHi, Pierce Butler Letterbook); R[S?] (Private collection of the Samuel Wallis Papers deposited on microfilm at PHi).

1. See introduction to "Spring and Fall Circuits 1798" for information on David Allison's debt to Pierce Butler.

2. William Rawle (1759-1836), United States attorney for the district of Pennsylvania, was apparently retained by Pierce Butler to handle some of his legal affairs. Most United States attorneys had to rely on private clients to supplement their incomes, because their only compensation from the government was in the form of fees for handling specific cases. *DAB; Stat.,* 1:92-93; Goebel, *Antecedents and Beginnings to 1801,* pp. 612-13.

3. It seems clear from the text above and other evidence that Butler thought James Wilson was at least temporarily in jail in Edenton, pursuant to Butler's instructions to William Slade to "let the Law have its Opperation." See note to James Wilson to Joseph Thomas, May 12, 1798. On June 18, in response to Samuel Wallis's intervention on Wilson's behalf, Butler executed a power of attorney enabling Wallis to arrange for Wilson's "release and discharge ... the said James Wilson being now in confinement at Edenton." Smith, *James Wilson,* p. 386.

On the basis of this evidence, the editors stated in volume one of this series that James Wilson had been imprisoned while in Edenton. *DHSC,* 1:48, 859n. However, an exhaustive search for the power of attorney, cited by Smith as being in the private collection of James Alan Montgomery, Jr., has been unsuccessful. Also, since the publication of that volume, new evidence has come to light indicating that Wilson probably avoided going to jail by giving his word that he would remain in Edenton pending the resolution of Butler's claim against him. On or before September 6, however, Butler apparently became aware that Wilson had in fact never been jailed in Edenton. On that day Butler wrote a letter to James Gibson concerning Wilson's death, in which he remarked, "I feel a degree of satisfaction that I prohibited his being put in gaol; he was on parole only" (Pierce Butler Letterbook, PHi). This conclusion is buttressed by the fact that no prosecution bond or bail bond has been found. We are indebted to George Stevenson of the North Carolina State Archives for information regarding *Butler v. Wilson*. See note to James Wilson to Bird Wilson, April 21, 1798.

Circuit Court for the District of Rhode Island
June 15, 1798   Newport, Rhode Island

Associate Justice William Cushing and Judge Benjamin Bourne opened court on June 15. On the first day, William Cushing "delivered a pertinent, lengthy, and well adapted charge to the Grand Jury." The court adjourned on June 23.[1]

1. Minutes, CCD Rhode Island, RG 21, MWalFAR; *Argus* (New York), June 26, 1798. Charge not found but see *Newport Mercury* under date of June 19, 1798.

James Iredell to Timothy Pickering
June 16, 1798   Edenton, North Carolina

... I very unfortunately was prevented reaching Savannah by one of the greatest floods of rain ever known in this State which met me on my Journey, and rendered it impossible for me to proceed any considerable distance, all the bridges almost being broke up in every direction, and the obstacles such as could not be surmounted for several days. I made every effort in my power, and was nearly drowned in the attempt, but obliged at length absolutely to desist. ...

ARS (MHi, Timothy Pickering Papers). Addressed "Philadelphia."
Secretary of State Timothy Pickering (1745-1829). *DAB.*

Newport Mercury
June 19, 1798   Newport, Rhode Island

On Friday last the Circuit Court of the United States for this District, convened in this Town—The Hon. Judge CUSHING addressed the Grand Jury in a Charge of considerable Length. he remarked with great Energy and Perspecuity on the alarming political Situation of the United States, and commented in a forcible Manner on the dangerous Tendency of jacobin Principles, and the Necessity of giving our Confidence and Support to our own Government.

(Newport, Rhode Island) June 19, 1798. Date and place are those of the newspaper.

Hannah Wilson to Bird Wilson ——————————————————
June 23, 1798   Edenton, North Carolina

... Your papa and myself were disapointed my dear Bird in not receiving any letters by the two last Posts, I expected to have had one from Polly. I know that she is not so averse to writing as you are. I begin to feel quite home sick, but when we shall leave Edenton I do not know, I think if I was
once at home, that I should ^be^ content never to leave it again, we are at a very great expence here, and if your pap does not attend the Supreme Court, I feel afraid of the consequence; It was a most unfortunate thing his leaving Philadelphia, however, Mr Thomas advised for the best. I dare say something would have been done by this time but the longer it is put off the, more-exasperated the Creditors will be and the more difficult he will find it to
come ^to^ any settlement I am afraid he will ^not^ give up his property. he says what advantage has Mr Greenleaf[1] by doing it. his property sold for one third of the value, and he still in confinement, what reason do the Creditors give for ^him^
keeping still confined? I still think it would be but justice for your papa to give up every thing, if he can not settle any other way, I am sure he would feel much happier but it is a subject that he never wishes to her mentioned. he says that he knows his own affairs best, remember my dear Bird I write
in confi^de^nce to you. By accident your papa discovered that his desk was broke open, [*letter inked out*] I was mentioning some quills that he had bought. your papa said that he had some goose quills which he had from Hamburgh. I told him that I had found three bunches which he did not know he had he said that he he had put them in the de[sk] he asked me if any one had got a false key. I told him that it was obliged to be open for some papers that M^r^ T[2] wanted. but that you would take very good care every thing, you must put the locks in good order. I hope to hear by the next letter that you have got a house somewhere, or other, and not subject to the ill temper of Mr Leaper[3] any longer. Your papa has drawn an order on you payable on the fourth july. do not let any thing prevent you from paying it it was money that was paid for our lodgings, I believe it is an ~~order~~ a bill I do not know wether there is any difference _ [4]

... Mr Iredell returned last week, ... Your papa is waiting to hear from you before he writes. Is Mr Morris still confined? ther is a report here that he has taken to drink, have you heard any thing of it?[5] ...

ARS (PHi, James A. Montgomery Collection, Bird Wilson Correspondence). Addressed "High Street N° 274   Philadelphia."

1. James Greenleaf (1765-1843), a Bostonian active in business ventures in New York City and Philadelphia, became heavily and disastrously involved in land speculation along with Robert Morris and John Nicholson. Mary-Jo Kline, ed., *Political Correspondence and Public Papers of Aaron Burr*, 2 vols. (Princeton: Princeton University Press, 1983), 1:289-90; *PAH*, 18:298n.

2. Probably Joseph Thomas.

3. Thomas Leiper (1745-1825), a wealthy tobacco manufacturer, owned the house on the corner of 8th and Market in Philadelphia that was rented by the Wilsons. *DAR Lineage Book,* 99:64; Smith, *James Wilson,* p. 365.

4. The Wilsons' lodgings at Horniblow Tavern in Edenton were not paid for prior to Wilson's death. See James Iredell to Bird Wilson, September 1, 1798.

5. Robert Morris was imprisoned for debt on February 15, 1798, as a result of the overextension of his speculation in real estate. He remained there for more than three years, finally winning release in 1801 under the federal bankruptcy law. *PAH,* 18:295; *DAB.*

Circuit Court for the District of Delaware

June 27, 1798   Newcastle, Delaware

The docket records the presence of Judge Gunning Bedford, Jr., on June 27, 1798. That day "the ^Court Met according to Law, when on Account of the Non-Attendance, of a Circuit Judge, the Court was adjourned, untill the 28th when It met & was adjouned for the Cause afs^d to the third of July 1798, when It was finally adjourned ^ to the Time & Place appointed by Law."[1]

1. Appearance Docket, CCD Delaware, RG 21, PPFAR.

Letter from a Member of Congress from Virginia to His Constituents

Aurora

June 30, 1798   Philadelphia, Pennsylvania

...The *judiciary*, within a few years, have so far stepped out of their ordinary course of business, as to embrace almost every important topic of political controversy in their charges to Grand Juries, and a responsive Grand Jury in our own state has aimed its first blow at the privileges of the house of representatives;[1] so that it is not difficult to discern, to what party judiciary influence attaches. ...

(Philadelphia) June 30, 1798. Date and place are those of the newspaper. The identity of the congressman is unknown.

1. See Presentment by the Grand Jury of the Circuit Court for the District of Virginia, May 22, 1797.

John Young Noel to William Paterson

July 20, 1798   Savannah, Georgia

...The failure of a Circ^t Court for this District last Spring was a very serious Disappointm^t indeed _ The Business prepared on both the Law & Equity Dockets was much greater & more important than we have ever before had _

J. Irdell must be more in Favor with the News = Paper Scribblers than J. Chase _ by his escaping the Censure which was bestowed on M.ʳ Chase, for I do not think his Excuse was by any means ᴧas M.ʳ Chase's for the Default in North Car.ª _ ¹ ...

ARS (NjR, William Paterson Papers). Addressed "Philadelphia."

1. For James Iredell's explanation of why he was unable to attend the Circuit Court for the district of Georgia in April 1798, see James Iredell to Hannah Iredell, April 10, 1798. For comments on Samuel Chase's failure to appear at the spring 1797 court in North Carolina, see the *North-Carolina Journal* under date of June 1, 1797; "Vox Populi," *Aurora* under date of June 6, 1797; and "Holt" to Samuel Chase, *Porcupine's Gazette* under date of June 15, 1797.

Hannah Wilson to Bird Wilson ————————————————————
July 28, 1798   Edenton, North Carolina

Edenton   28ᵗʰ July

I write my dear Bird at your papas request[;] he wishes you to make an apology to M.ʳ Iredell for his not writing him, but he is too weak to attempt it, though he is much better, he has sat up three hours to day, he has had a violent attack, that it will be some days before he recovers his strength, and the weather is very warm; I suppose that M.ʳ Iredell has told you that it is an intermiting fever which is very common to here, he has not had a return of the fever since monday. h[e] takes bark constantly; weakness is his chief complaint now. I have kept my health very well. my friends advise me to be very carefull as the sickly season is coming on. but I think I shall be proof against it. I am obliged to leave off every minute to wipe the perspiration from my face and hands.

I am very happy to here there is a prospect of James¹ being being placed in a Store, as he has so short a time to serve I was afraid he would find it difficult.

M.ʳ Iredell has by this, told you what will surprise you, as much as it did me, that your papa has requested the Southern Circuit, what he means to do with me, (as I cannot [for me to?] go with him, as I have no cloaths, if it was otherwise convenient), I know not, a single Chair & horses will cost three hundred dollars. he certainly never could think of buying a Carriage, his cloaths are all going to peices, he has not had any thing since he left home, which is fifteen months, it would take 60 dollars at least to furnish ᴧhim with what would be necessary to go so long a Circuit. besides the expences of the journey, your papa has never got a new hat, which was very shabby when you saw it, you may think what tis now. He intended to write you fully, and M.ʳ Iredell if he had been well enough. he will open his mind to you but not to me, but it is a subgect that I have done speaking upon, as we think so differently.

write me what people say to our not coming home, you need not be afraid of distressing me, as I can hear nothing worse than I expect.[2] Have you much business? is the matter determined with Leaaper? write me very particularly, Ask Polly if she will put up your papa callico dressing gown, and a pair of slippers that I had made at Bethlehem, and send them to M[r] Iredell, and ask him to put them up with his things, that he is going to send by water. they are both in my closet I believe, I want them to walk in the country in, as I mean to walk before breakfast, my pen is bad, your papa is asleep and I have no one to mend it. I expect a long letter from Polly & Emily[3] by M[r] I, remember me to him. M[r] & M[rs] Thomas, D[r] Whites family,[4] and love to Polly Emily & James

write me by M[r] I if you have received this, as I should not like to have it miscarry _ your papa has just waked and desires his love

H W

ARS (PHi, James A. Montgomery Collection, Bird Wilson Correspondence). Addressed "N°
274 High Street   Philadelphia."
    1. James Wilson, Jr.
    2. On July 28 Samuel Johnston wrote to James Iredell of his deep concern for Hannah Wilson and his hope that Wilson would resign rather than be convicted or impeached. *DHSC*, 1:859.
    3. Mary Wilson, known as "Polly," and Emily Wilson.
    4. Bishop William White (1748-1836), a doctor of divinity, the Protestant Episcopal bishop of Pennsylvania, and rector of Christ Church in Philadelphia. *DAB*.

James Wilson to Bird Wilson ————————————————————————
    August 4, 1798   Edenton, North Carolina

                                        Edenton,   4th August 1798
Dear Bird:
    Yours of the 5th of last Month I received;[1] and, as Mrs. Wilson wrote you, waited to hear from you before I sent another Letter. You "know not what Information I can expect from you." Before the 24th of May last you received a long, and, to me, not an unimportant Letter.[2] Mr. Thomas, in a short Letter, acknowledged the Receipt of it;[3] and twice assures me that I shall hear from him fully by the then next Mail. I have never since heard from him—and do you really think that I had no Right to expect any Information from you in Consequence of that Letter? Was it shown to any or to whom of the Creditors? Was any—or what Answer was given to it— or by whom? Was any Alteration suggested—or by whom? Is it likely that nearly the whole or Majority of the Creditors will accede to that or a similar Plan? These, and many others, are Articles of Information of some Moment to me. Concerning none of them have I received a single Syllable from you. Some certainly might have been obtained, or, at least, attempted in my Absence as well as in my Presence. Mr. Iredell will return soon after this

will reach you. That will be a good opportunity of writing to me fully and particularly upon every Subject. The Time is opening, in which, I think, Something very effectual may be done.

I enclose to you a Copy of Major Butler's Letter to his Attorney, dated the very Day on which you wrote to me.[4] You see how he represents Matters concerning your Proposals. I doubt not your Veracity; but hope you will have everyThing cleared up, as it is now in your Power, about that Business. I am much better, but still weak. Remember Mrs. Wilson and me to all the Family. Show this Letter to Mr. Thomas and deliver the enclosed immediately to Mr. Iredell.[5] Believe me to be

Yours affectionately

James Wilson

B. Wilson, Esq

Tr (PSC-Hi, Konkle Manuscripts). Typewritten document.
  1. Letter not found.
  2. See James Wilson to Joseph Thomas, May 12, 1798.
  3. Letter not found.
  4. No letter from Pierce Butler to William Slade, dated July 5, 1798 (the date of Bird's letter mentioned in the opening sentence above), has been found. The only known letter from Pierce Butler to William Slade fitting Wilson's description is that of May 24, 1798. A copy of that letter, which is in the James Wilson Papers at PHi, was enclosed in a note from William Slade to James Wilson written on July 22, 1798 (James Wilson Papers, PHi). See note to James Wilson to Joseph Thomas, May 12, 1798.
  5. Enclosure not found.

James Iredell to Hannah Iredell

August 6, 1798   Philadelphia, Pennsylvania

... A most astonishing discovery of a private nature was made here on Saturday just after my arrival. Mr Thomas, Judge Wilson's Attorn[ey] and who had been universally thought a very honest Man (tho' some suspicions[, however, h]ave been entertained of him lately) absconded, after having defrauded [among others] some his most intimate Friends, by taking up money on faced checks on the [bank] _ It is now supposed he has done it for a long time, but that he contrived to repay the money before the checks were presented _ The Frauds are supposed to amount to upwards of 60000 Dollars. There is not the smallest doubt as to the fact, and the whole City is greatly agitated by it. His poor Wife,[1] who is a very amiable Woman far advanced in her pregnancy, dropped down senseless and remained in that condition for an hour on Officers of Justice coming to search for him. Before he went away he assigned all his effects to Mr Edward Tilghman[2] and others. I am afraid this must unavoidably add to Judge Wilson's distresses, tho' as yet I

know [*word illegible*]ₐno particulars. One of his Friends I expect will write a letter
accompanying this. It is an event as surprising as it was affecting. Until lately,
tho' a most violent Partisan, he was thought so able and honest a lawyer
that both Parties indiscriminately employed him, and it is supposed his
practice at one time amounted to £3000. a year. Judge Wilson's Family are
all well. Miss Wilson[3] has obligingly offered to get the hats you wished
for _ ...

ARS (Nc-Ar, Charles E. Johnson Collection). Addressed "Edenton, North Carolina." James
Iredell's letter is damaged; readings in brackets come from *MJI*, 2:533.
   1. Rebecca (Cottman) Thomas.
   2. Edward Tilghman (1751-1815), a prominent Philadelphia lawyer. *DAB*.
   3. Probably Mary (Polly) Wilson.

Special Session of the Circuit Court for the District of Pennsylvania —
   August 6, 1798   Philadelphia, Pennsylvania

On August 6 Associate Justice Samuel Chase and Judge Richard Peters opened a
special session of the Pennsylvania circuit court. The court adjourned the following
day.[1]

   1. Engrossed Minutes, CCD Pennsylvania, RG 21, PPFAR.
   We have been unable to establish why a special session of the Pennsylvania circuit court was held.

William Cushing to Charles Cushing ————————————————————
   August 14, 1798   Newark, New Jersey

[*Associate Justice Cushing notes that, following the adjournment of the Supreme
Court in Philadelphia because of a yellow fever epidemic, he and his wife*] left
the city, meaning to go on as ₐfar Eastward as Middletown,[1] to spend the time
there till About the 20ᵗʰ September when I must return to Trenton by the
first of October to hold the first Court of the fall Circuit Assigned me, being
the middle circuit, which carries me no further Southward than Virginia.
The Southern Circuit is assigned again to Judge Wilson at his request;[2] the
Eastern to Judge Patterson. ...

ARS (MHi, William Cushing Papers). Addressed "Boston." Postmarked "AUG 16."
   1. Middletown, Connecticut.
   2. See Hannah Wilson to Bird Wilson, July 28, 1798.

William Cushing attributed to James Sharples (ca. 1751-1811). Pastel on paper, ca. 1796-1797. Courtesy Independence National Historical Park, Philadelphia.

James Iredell to Timothy Pickering ——————————————————————
August 25, 1798   Edenton, North Carolina

                                        Edenton, N. C.   Aug. 25. 1798
Dear Sir,
   It is with the truest concern I inform you of the unfortunate death of my
Friend Judge Wilson, one of the Judges of the S. C. of the U. S., which
~~unfortunately~~ happened here on the night of the 21 _ Inst _ I take the liberty
~~here~~ to mention that it is of great consequence this vacancy should be
supplied as early as it can be found convenient, as the ensuing Southern
Circuit was assigned to Judge Wilson, in which business of the utmost
consequence is depending: Tho' I should be disposed cheerfully to make
great personal sacrifices for the public Interest, yet having been from home
~~the~~ almost the whole of the present year, & as I must leave it early possibly
on an absence of many months the beginning of the next, it does not appear
practicable to me notwithstanding my utmost wishes ~~to engage~~ to attend in
S°. C. upon the next Circuit, and there would be a manifest impropriety, if
it can be avoided, in my attending in this State, as there are some suits of
                                        Defendant
great weight and consequence in which I am a ~~Party~~ as an Exōr, which have
been long depending, and I think [*word inked out*] unreasonably delayed
hitherto, and it might be extended with the utmost prejudice to the Plaintiffs
if any further delay should take place.[1] As I shall feel much anxiety on this
subject, you will particularly oblige me if you will take the trouble to inform
                                              in regard to
me when the President has supplied this vacancy, and also ~~of~~ ˄ the probability
                      fill in
that the Gentleman appointed to ~~succeed~~ ˄ ~~Judge Wilson~~ will be able to attend
the S. Circuit this fall _ [2]
   I have the honor to be, &c _

The hon. T. Pickering Esq.

ADf (NcD, James Iredell Sr. and Jr. Papers). Marked "Substance of a Letter to Mʳ Pickering,
Secretary of State."
   1. Despite James Iredell's concerns, *Smith v. Smith Executors* and *Phenias Bond v. Executors of
Hews and Smith* were not heard until June 1799. Minutes, June 11, 1799, CCD North Carolina,
RG 21, GEpFAR.
   2. Secretary of State Pickering forwarded this letter to President Adams on September 6.
On September 13, Adams informed Pickering that "The Reasons urged by Judge Iredell for an
early Appointment of a Successor, are important." A temporary commission was made out for
Bushrod Washington on September 29, 1798; the Senate confirmed the appointment on
December 20, 1798. *DHSC*, 1:126-27, 132-35.

James Iredell to Bird Wilson ——————————————————————
    September 1, 1798   Edenton, North Carolina

...I took the liberty last week of confiding to Bishop White a most
melancholy task, the necessity for which none of your Friends could deplore
more than I did.[1] I knew of no Person so likely to execute it with all the
delicacy and tenderness the mournful occasion required, though I well knew
the severe trial to which I exposed his sensibility. I inclose you now a letter
from M.ʳˢ Wilson.[2] Her sufferings, tho' uncommonly severe, and accompanied
with incessant watching and fatigue and want of rest, have however fortunately
not deeply injured her health. She is now nearly in as good health as ever,
and I hope soon will find it entirely restored to her. She has been so good
as to consent to stay at our house, and you may be assured of every possible
care and attention being shewn her. Her intention is, as soon as she
conveniently can, to go to her Mother, but to be first for some little Time
in Philadelphia. Could she conveniently get there I think it would be highly
imprudent in her, on account of her health, to quit this Climate sooner than
the middle of October, from the risque she would run of being sick on the
road. If she could be satisfied to stay till towards the latter end of December,
she would confer a great obligation on M.ʳˢ Iredell and myself, and I could
at that time with perfect convenience attend her myself to Philadelphia.[3]
Whenever the time arrives when M.ʳˢ Iredell must part with her she will regret
it most painfully. Never was any Lady more respected and esteemed in any
place than she has been universally here, nor did any ever experience truer
sympathy in misfortune. What she underwent for some days previous to the
unfortunate event of anxiety, [trouble?], and distress, I believe no language
could paint. I saw only a small part of it myself, but have received a most
affecting account of it from others.

    I take the liberty to inform you the amount of the sums due here, so far
as I have been able to learn them, and which I believe are all except what is
due to the Doctors. Their accounts I will endeavour to obtain and forward
next week. Those I know are as follow, viz.

	Dollars	Cents
To M.ʳ John Horniblow[4] (at whose house M.ʳ and M.ʳˢ Wilson staid) £422..7..10. N.º Carolina Currency equal to about	845	
To sundry Persons for Funeral Expences £21..2..3 _ equal to about	42	25

. . .

    M.ʳˢ Wilson knows not if there was any Will, and thinks there was none. I
mentioned to her, that considering the complicated concerns of the Estate,
and your being so well acquainted with them, it appeared to me adviseable
                                        on M.ʳ Wilson's Estate
that if she had any preferable right to administer to her she had better

relinquish it in your favour ⎯. She has authorised me to inform you, that she relinquishes any right she may have in this respect to you, but she does not at present consent to yield it in favour of any other Person ⎯ You will of course at a convenient time inform her of her rights and prospects. ...

ARS (PHi, James A. Montgomery Collection, Bird Wilson Correspondence). Addressed "Bird Wilson, Esqʳ (The Postmaster is requested, if a favorable opportunity offers, to convey this to Bishop White, with a letter sent before for him if still in the Post Office) Philadelphia." The text in parentheses and the word "Philadelphia" were crossed out and replaced with "To the Care of Gen: Nichols Pottsgrove."

1. Letter not found. Because of his close friendship with the Wilson family, Bishop William White was asked to break the news of Wilson's death to the family. On September 8 White wrote back to Iredell that he had contacted Wilson's daughters, who had closed the house in Philadelphia because of the yellow fever epidemic, and that he had sent Iredell's letter to Bird Wilson. William White to James Iredell, September 8, 1798, Charles E. Johnson Collection, Nc-Ar. Iredell responded on November 10 thanking White for his help and apprising him of Hannah Wilson's situation in Edenton. James Wilson Papers, PHi.

2. See Hannah Wilson to Bird Wilson, September 1, 1798.

3. Hannah Wilson remained in Edenton throughout the fall of 1798 as a guest of the Iredells. She spent time recuperating from the ordeal of Wilson's last months and corresponding with Bird about the many problems of administering James Wilson's estate. She decided to accept Iredell's offer to accompany him northward for the opening of the Supreme Court and therefore did not return to Philadelphia until February 1799. James Iredell and Bird Wilson corresponded throughout the fall about Hannah Wilson and about James Wilson's seriously encumbered estate. Iredell continued to take an active interest in the members of the Wilson family, and as late as July 1799 he was still trying to help them with their precarious financial situation. Hannah Wilson to Bird Wilson, November 10, 1798 (Founder's Box, PCarlD); James Iredell to Hannah Iredell, January 18, 22, and 24, and February 28, 1799 (Charles E. Johnson Collection, Nc-Ar); James Iredell to Bird Wilson, September 24, 1798 (Founder's Box, PCarlD); Bird Wilson to James Iredell, October 22, 1798 (Charles E. Johnson Collection, Nc-Ar); James Iredell to Bird Wilson, November 10, 1798 (James Wilson Papers, PHi); and James Iredell to John Gray Blount, July 3, 1799 (John Gray Blount Papers, Nc-Ar).

4. John Horniblow (d. 1799), an Edenton innkeeper. Sarah M. Lemmon, ed., *The Pettigrew Papers*, vol. 2, *1819-1843* (Raleigh: North Carolina Department of Cultural Resources, Division of Archives and History, 1988), p. 19n; "Benedict Arnold in Edenton, N.C., March 2, 1774, as Master of the Brig Harriet and John," *North Carolina Historical and Genealogical Register* 3 (April 1903): 299.

Hannah Wilson to Bird Wilson ⎯⎯⎯⎯⎯⎯⎯⎯⎯⎯⎯⎯⎯⎯⎯⎯
September 1, 1798   Edenton, North Carolina

Edenton Sep 1ˢᵗ

The shock my dear Bird which you must all have felt by the death of your Dear papa, affects me sensibly; the seperation is a severe trial of my fortitude, but if it was not for you children, I think I should feel resigned, to know that his suffering is at an end, but when I think of your situation, it seems too much, but I hope my dear, Bird you will exert yourself, remember you are the only one they have to look up to, and think how much happier your papa is, it would be from a selfish motive if we wished

his return, his mind had been in such a state for the last six months, harassed and perplexed, that it was more than he could possibly bear, and brought on a violent nervous fever   I never knew of his arrest till since his death, and now can account for many things he said in his delirium,[1] I cannot be thankful enough that I did not leave Edenton with Judge Iredell, I never should have forgiven myself if I had left him. when he was sensible he took so much ‸in seeing me by him, and requested me not to leave him, but that
                 pleasure
was not five minutes at a time, I had not my cloaths ‸, for three days and
                                                             off
nights, nor left him till the evening of his death, when I could not bear the scene any longer, I am astonished at myself when I think of what I have gone through, they told me he died easy. I have the sattisfaction to know that every thing was done that could be, there is a very excellent Physician here. Mr Iredell did not arrive till the evening of your papas death, and he was saved the painful intelligence of Mr Thomass villany,[2] but his cruelty to you in taking the two hundred dollars was worse than all the rest when he knew it was all your support.

Mr Iredell has been kind beyond every thing (his family were all very ill at the time) he has watched by me night and day, what with the fatigue and anxiety of mind). I was very low when I came here, but I am now much better, and I hope shortly my health will be quite restored, remember me affectionately to them all, I shall be very anxious to know what you determine upon. I shall return to Boston. once more my dear Bird let me intreat you to exert your usual fortitude; this has been a most painful task, but I hope in future I shall write with more composure, but shall always be

Your affectionate mother

H Wilson

Mr Iredell writes to you at my request—

ARS (PHi, James Wilson Papers). Addressed "274 High Street   Philadelphia."

1. It seems likely that Hannah Wilson is referring to James Wilson's knowledge of the writ for his arrest procured by William Slade at the request of Pierce Butler as a preliminary step in the suit Butler contemplated against Wilson. Slade, contrary to Butler's original instructions, had accepted Wilson's word that he would remain in Edenton until the October term of the Edenton Superior Court, when the formal legal proceedings in the suit would begin. It is possible, however, that the fear of arrest and jailing hung over Wilson's head throughout the spring and summer of 1798, and that he may have made statements relating to that fear in his delirium. See James Wilson to Bird Wilson, April 21, 1798, and note to Pierce Butler to Samuel Wallis, June 14, 1798.

2. See James Iredell to Hannah Iredell, August 6, 1798.

John Sloss Hobart attributed to James Sharples (ca. 1751-1811). Pastel on paper, ca. 1795-1802. Courtesy Independence National Historical Park, Philadelphia.

Circuit Court for the District of New York ——————————
September 1, 1798   New York, New York

Associate Justice William Paterson and Judge John Sloss Hobart attended the opening of court on September 1. The court met again on Monday, September 3, before adjourning to the next term.[1]

Judge John Sloss Hobart (1738-1805), a native of Fairfield, Connecticut, graduated from Yale College in 1757, moved to New York, and opened a law practice. During the Revolution, he served on the Committee of Correspondence (1774), as a delegate to the Provincial Congress (1775-1777), and as a member of the Council of Safety (1777). He also attended the New York state ratifying convention at Poughkeepsie (1788). Hobart sat as a justice of the New York Supreme Court from 1777 to 1798. In January 1798 he was elected to fill a vacancy in the United States Senate but resigned his seat when President Adams appointed him United States judge for the district of New York on April 11. Hobart held that position until his death in 1805.[2]

1. Minutes, CCD New York, RG 21, NjBaFAR.
2. *BDAC; DAB; SEJ,* 1:269.

Circuit Court for the District of Connecticut ——————————
September 17, 1798   Hartford, Connecticut

Chief Justice Oliver Ellsworth and Judge Richard Law opened court on September 17, and a charge was delivered to the grand jury. The court adjourned on September 24.[1]

1. Docket Book, CCD Connecticut, RG 21, MWalFAR. Charge not found.

William Paterson to Euphemia Paterson ——————————
September 24, 1798   Albany, New York

... We reached this place very early on Saturday; and should have been here on friday, if business had not detained Capt.ⁿ Thomson for three hours at New York. These were precious hours, the wind being fair and strong. As it was we have no reason to complain of our passage. To-day I dine with Gen.ˡ Schuyler, to morrow with the L.ᵗ Gov.ʳ,[1] and the next day with M.ʳ Taylor;[2] on Thursday I propose to set out for Rutland, where I expect to be by Saturday night.

It is very sickly at and about Saratoga, but remarkably healthy here and at
                                          there
Ballstown springs, where ᵣis at present and has been during the summer a considerable concourse of strangers. ...

ARS (NjR, William Paterson Papers). Addressed "New Brunswicke."
1. Stephen Van Rensselaer (1764-1839), lieutenant governor of New York from 1795 to 1801. *DAB.*
2. John Tayler (1742-1829) was a judge of the Albany County Court of Common Pleas (1797-1803). Gorham A. Worth, *Random Recollections of Albany, from 1800 to 1808,* 3d ed. (Albany: J. Munsell, 1866), p. 69n; *PAH,* 26:113n.

Circuit Court for the District of New Jersey ———————————
October 1, 1798   Trenton, New Jersey

On October 1 Judge Robert Morris opened court but adjourned it to the next day because a Supreme Court justice was not present. On October 2 the court convened with Associate Justice William Cushing and Judge Morris in attendance, and a charge was delivered to the grand jury. The court adjourned on October 3.[1]

1. Minutes, CCD New Jersey, RG 21, NjBaFAR. Charge not found.

Circuit Court for the District of Vermont ———————————————
October 3, 1798   Rutland, Vermont

Associate Justice William Paterson and Judge Samuel Hitchcock opened court on October 3. Paterson followed the opening with a charge to the grand jury. The court adjourned on October 9 to the next session.[1]

1. Circuit Docket, CCD Vermont, RG 21, MWalFAR; William Paterson's Charge to the Grand Jury of the Circuit Court for the District of Vermont, [October 3, 1798] (q.v.).

William Paterson's Charge to the Grand Jury of the Circuit Court for the District of Vermont ———————————————
[October 3, 1798]   Rutland, Vermont

Gentlemen of the grand jury.

The office, into which you have been sworn, is of the utmost importance to the good order, peace, and prosperity of the government under which we live. Offences of an indictable nature create distrust, excite terror, and disturb the public tranquility. Their example too is contagious and alarming, especially if suffered to pass without legal and speedy animadversion. For the security, then, of government, and the uninterrupted enjoyment of our civil liberties and rights, it became necessary, that crimes should be enquired into, and their perpetrators denounced by some competent authority. The experience and wisdom of ages have not[1] been able to establish any institution so adequate for this purpose as that of grand juries. The more we contemplate their formation and nature, their powers and duties, the higher they rise in celebrity and esteem. They are indeed the best preservative of civil liberty and order, and essentially necessary for the support of good government. As they are the medium, through which offences receive judicial discussion and reproof, it may with truth be observed, that the justice and safety of the nation are, in criminal matters, committed to their care. They must present before courts can punish. To the exercise of this high office, you are, gentlemen, called upon by the laws of your country. These laws prescribe your duty; and direct to the investigation and presentment of every offence, which may have been perpetrated, in this district, against the United States. No offender, whatever may be his condition, can hope to elude the vigilance, and to avert the justice of a tribunal, whose duty and interest happily coincide for the detection and punishment of crimes, and whose authority descends to the lowest, and reaches to the highest character in social life. Hence it[2] follows, that the proper exercise of your function protects the innocent, and brings forward the guilty for conviction, allays the fears of the good and chastens the outrageous spirit of the bad, checks vice, promotes virtue, preserves order, and vindicates the violated supremacy of the laws.

To enter into an enumeration of all the crimes of an indictable nature would be an unnecessary expense of time. Permit me, however, to mention two species of offences, which, under the existing circumstances of the United States, merit your particular attention. The one is, the forgery of the bills or notes emitted by the bank of the United States; which, besides its moral turpitude and fraud, has a direct and powerful tendency to impair the credit, and impede the currency of that species of circulating medium. The other class of offences, worthy of your notice, is unlawful combinations and conspiracies, seditious practices, and false, scandalous, and malicious writings, publications, and libels against the government of the United States. Transgressions of this description became so frequent, dangerous, and alarming, as at length to attract the attention of Congress, who, at a late session, passed an act relative to them. The law is entitled, "An act in addition to the act, intituled, An act for the punishment of certain crimes against the United States," and runs in the following words. Here read the act _ [3]

Approved _ July 14, 1798.

Gentlemen,

The offences specified in this act are of a serious nature, and, when perpetrated, demand instant and full investigation. Unlawful combinations, conspiracies, riots, and insurrections strike at the being of our political establishment. They need no comment. Written or printed detraction, calumny, and lies are odious and destructive vices in private, and still more so, in public life. They are deliberate acts, perpetrated with a view to wound and do injury; and besides, their duration is longer, and their circulation more extensive than verbal obloquy and scandal. The man, who is guilty of publishing false, defamatory, and malicious writings or libels against the government of his country, its measures, and its constituted authorities, must, if not callous to the dictates of the moral sense, stand self-condemned. He sins against light; for he must be sensible, that such publications are contrary to clear and known duty. In such case, nothing short of idiocy can operate as an excuse. They destroy confidence, excite distrust, disseminate discord and the elements of disorganization, alienate the affections of the people from their government, disturb the peace of society, and endanger our political union and existence.[4] No government, indeed, can long subsist, where offenders of this kind are suffered to spread their poison with impunity. An aggravating ingredient in the composition of the crimes described in this act is, that they are levelled against the people themselves. For the constitution, government, and constituted authorities of the United States are emphatically the creation and work of the people, emanating from their authority, and declarative of their will. To support them is our primary duty _ to attempt their destruction is an offence of deep malignity. Observance of the laws and obedience to legal authority are the great bulwark of public liberty, which, however, free states find difficult to maintain; because their salutary restraint sits uneasy on turbulent spirits,[5] and is mistaken for slavish subjection by the rude and ill informed part of the community, who delight in irregularity, sedition, and licentiousness as symptoms of freedom, and indications of republican spirit. Ah licentiousness! thou bane of republics, and more to be dreaded than hosts of external foes. The truth is, that libellous publications and seditious practices are inconsistent with genuine freedom, and subversive of good government. They tend to anarchy, and anarchy always terminates in despotism. May we avoid these evils by a cheerful and constant observance of the laws, and obedience to legal authority, in which civil liberty consists. The result will be order, union, peace, and happiness among ourselves, and the transmission of our constitution, government, and rights, pure and entire, to our posterity.

May the God of Heaven enable us all to discharge our official, relative, and social duties, with diligence, fidelity, and honest zeal!

AD (NjR, William Paterson Papers); ADf (NjR, William Paterson Papers). Date and place derived from newspaper account of charge. See *Porcupine's Gazette* under date of October 8, 1798.
  1. In draft, "The wisdom of ages has not."
  2. Here the draft appears to be missing a leaf. The next page of the draft begins with the text of section 4 of the Sedition Act of 1798. The two versions resume a parallel text where the phrase "Approved _ July 14, 1798" appears.
  3. Sedition Act of 1798. *Stat.,* 1:596.
  4. The draft omits "union and."
  5. The draft manuscript ends here.

Reply of the Grand Jury of the Circuit Court for the District
of Vermont ————————————————————————————
Rutland Herald
   October 5, 1798   Rutland, Vermont

To the Hon. WILLIAM PATERSON, *judge of the Circuit Court of the United States.*

THE Grand Jurors, within and for the body of the District of Vermont, beg leave to express their unanimous sentiments of gratitude and thanks for the solemn, momentous and invaluable charge delivered them by the Hon. Judge at the opening of this session. The pure principles of justice and government, contained in this charge, accord with the sentiments of our most deliberate moments. Had we wanted further proof, our enquiries would have furnished the most glaring testimonials. We lament for our District, that our liberties, in some instances, are abused to licentiousness, and we solemnly feel what the Hon. Judge has so powerfully expressed, that licentiousness more endangers the liberties and independence of a free Government than hosts of invading foes.

We desire to carry with us to our houses the words of the charge we so gratefully received, and deem it our duty to express to the Judge that in our opinions, the general good of this District seems to require that this charge be made public; we therefore, unanimously and earnestly request a copy of the charge, that the same may be published by press. We pray for the public and private happiness of your honor, and may Almighty God continue wisdom and virtue in our government; righteousness in our Judges; to our country independence, without faction, and liberty without licentiousness.

(Signed.) ELI COGGSWELL, Foreman.

Rutland, 5th Oct. 1798.

(Rutland) October 15, 1798. Date and place are those of the reply.

In its printing of the grand jury's reply on October 27, 1798, the New York *Daily Advertiser* observed that it "will afford real satisfaction to every friend of his country. It breathes a considerate, yet manly spirit; and the approbationary manner in which they speak of the Charge of their truly respectable Judge, we have not the smallest doubt was, on his part, fully merited."

Reply to the Grand Jury of the Circuit Court for the District of Vermont by William Paterson
Rutland Herald
[ca. October 5], 1798   Rutland, Vermont

GENTLEMEN,

YOUR note, expressed in the most affectionate and polite terms, I have this moment received. My charges are made for the Grand Jury, and not for the public; and therefore I have laid it down as an invariable rule of conduct, never to give a copy of any of them for publication. I hope, that you will be pleased to accept of this as an excuse for not complying with your request. It gives me unfeigned pleasure, that my address to you has met with your approbation.

With wishes the most pure and fervent for your health and happiness, and for the prosperity of the state of Vermont, I am Gentlemen, Your obedient humble servant.

WM. PATERSON.

(Rutland) October 15, 1798. Date and place are derived from the grand jury's reply.

Hannah Cushing to Abigail Adams ——————————————
    October 8, 1798   Maidenhead, New Jersey

... We have been roving to & from, since we had the pleasure of meeting you. We reached Philadelphia the 5th of August & left it the 9th; Court sitting only three days as the alarm of the prevailing fever had in that time become general.[1] We returned to Middletown & passed the time with our Friends till the 22nd of Sept when we departed for Trenton, where Mr Cushings Circuit begins; as the middle one falls to his lott. To avoid N York we crossed White plains to Dobb's ferry, which is 26 miles above the City; & after staying there two nights without being able to cross, the wind continuing very high we went up 20 miles further to Kings ferry at Verplanks point where the river is not so wide & the boats better & after waiting there also two ~~nigh~~ nights we safely passed the ferry, rejoicing as though we had been released from prison. ... The inhabitants on the other side appear'd to be as ignorant of the Country on this, as I am of that beyond the Atlantick. Four miles from the ferry we came through the Clove, a notch of a small Mountain, & then had a good road through a fine cultivated country inhabited by ~~Dutch~~ Dutch people residing in stone houses one story high. They ride in open waggons. We met 19, containing whole families, going to meeting at Tappawn a small village 18 miles below Kings ferry. Thirteen miles further down is Hackensack, a hansome town near the head of the river of the same name. Thirteen more carry us in a straight, level, pleasant way, bordering on the extensive meadow of the Hackensack, to Newark. From Middletown here the inhabitants of N York were scattered & we some time times found it difficult to be accommodated. Trenton is crouded with the Citizens of Philadelphia so much ~~so~~ that we have taken up our residence here for some days. ... Court sat only two days. The Grand Jury found three inditements for seditious words. One person only was taken who pleaded guilty, for saying some what like this_ that if the French came he would join them & fight for a shilling a day, & would deliver up any that were inimical to them _ & for D——g the P—— &c. For which he was fined but forty dollars, being very poor.[2] Judge Paterson is on the Eastern Circuit & is now at Vermont. What will become of the Southern I know not, as that was assigned to poor Judge Wilson. We hope however that Judge Iredel will attend the Court in N Carolina at least. ... We expect to leave Trenton by the 19th for Dover in the State of Deleware, where the Court is to sit the 27th. From thence to Baltimore & lastly to Richmond; pleasing ourselves with ᴀthe idea of passing a day or two with our good Genl & Mrs Washington on our way. ...

ARS (MHi, Adams Manuscript Trust). Hannah Cushing wrote this from "Hendricksons," a tavern in Maidenhead (now Lawrenceville), New Jersey, located six miles north of Trenton. Francis B. Lee, *Genealogical and Personal Memorial of Mercer County,* 2 vols. (New York: Lewis Publishing,

View of a Manor House on the Harlem River, New York by William Groombridge (1748-1811). Oil on canvas, 1793. Courtesy Terra Museum of American Art, Chicago. Daniel J. Terra Collection.

Hannah (Phillips) Cushing attributed to James Sharples (ca. 1751-1811). Pastel on paper, ca. 1795-1802. Courtesy Independence National Historical Park, Philadelphia.

1907), 2:522; Donald H. Tyler, *Old Lawrenceville: Early Houses and People* (n.p.: by the author, 1965), pp. 9-10.

1. In the fall of 1798, an epidemic of yellow fever swept through many eastern cities, including Philadelphia and New York. Carroll and Ashworth, *George Washington*, p. 543; Richard G. Miller, "The Federal City, 1783-1800," in *Philadelphia: A 300-Year History*, ed. Russell F. Weigley (New York: W. W. Norton, 1982), p. 197; John Duffy, "An Account of the Epidemic Fevers that Prevailed in the City of New York from 1791 to 1822," *New-York Historical Society Quarterly* 50 (October 1966): 343-48.

2. Indictments for "seditious words" were brought against Lespenard Colie, Brown Clark, and Luther Baldwin. The only one of the three to appear in court this term, Lespenard Colie, retracted a not guilty plea and was fined forty dollars. Minutes, October 3, 1798, CCD New Jersey, RG 21, NjBaFAR. See introduction to "Spring and Fall Circuits 1798," *Federalist,* under date of April 8, 1799, and Bushrod Washington to James Iredell, October 20, 1799.

Porcupine's Gazette —————————————————————————
    October 8, 1798   Rutland, Vermont

On Wednesday last the Circuit Court was opened in this town. The Honorable Judge *Paterson* gave an excellent charge to the Grand Jury, recommending, among other things, a careful attention to the dangerous practice of counterfeiting the bank notes of the United States, and to the seditious attempts of disaffected persons to disturb the government. We do not remember ever to have heard a more candid, useful, or judicious charge given in any court of justice: And we much regret that it is not in our power to favour the public with a copy of this very valuable production.

(Philadelphia) October 20, 1798. Date and place are those of the headline.
This article originally appeared in the October 8, 1798, edition of the *Rutland Herald.*

Circuit Court for the District of Pennsylvania —————————————
    October 11, 1798   Philadelphia, Pennsylvania

The marshal of the district attended court on the appointed opening day, but the absence of both the district judge and a Supreme Court justice on that and successive days caused him, on October 15, to adjourn the court to the next term.[1]

1. Engrossed Minutes, CCD Pennsylvania, RG 21, PPFAR. No court was held this session because of the yellow fever epidemic in Philadelphia and the near evacuation of the city. William Cushing, who would have presided at the Pennsylvania circuit court, remained in Maidenhead, New Jersey. See Hannah Cushing to Abigail Adams, October 8, 1798.

Bushrod Washington to George Washington —————————————
    October 19, 1798   Richmond, Virginia

... I am Just preparing to go upon the Southern Circuit, & shall if possible leave this place tomorrow. ...

ARS (DLC, George Washington Papers). Addressed "Mount Vernon Fairfax County." Postmarked "RICHMOND, OCT. [19?] 1798."

Circuit Court for the District of Massachusetts ─────────
October 20, 1798   Boston, Massachusetts

Associate Justice William Paterson and Judge John Lowell opened court on October 20, and, according to one Boston newspaper, William Paterson delivered "an animated and judicious Charge" to the grand jury. The court adjourned on October 29 to the next term.[1]

1. Final Records, CCD Massachusetts, RG 21, MWalFAR; *Russell's Gazette* (Boston), October 22, 1798. For another account of the charge, see the *Massachusetts Mercury* (Boston), October 23, 1798. We have been unable to identify the specific charge given. For undated Paterson grand jury charges, see Appendix A.

Massachusetts Mercury ──────────────────────────────
October 23, 1798   Boston, Massachusetts

On Saturday the Circuit Court of the U. S. opened in this town. Judge PATTERSON delivered the Charge to the Jury. It was an elegant display of Jurisprudential and Political Science, and was received with general admiration.

(Boston) October 23, 1798. Date and place are those of the newspaper.

George Washington to Bushrod Washington ──────────
October 24, 1798   Mount Vernon, Fairfax County, Virginia

[*Acknowledging Bushrod Washington's letter of October 19 (q.v.), George Washington writes:*] I only regret that Judge Wilson had it not in his power to have postponed his exist[1] (which I am persuaded he was not indisposed to do) to a later period. _ ...

I wish your Circuit may be pleasant and honorable to you, and that you may return safe to your family & friends. _ The Season is propitious for a Southern tour, and I hope your attention to the duties of your present Office will give satisfaction. _ Of <u>some</u> of the Judges who have gone that Circuit their has been heavy Complaints _ ...

ARS (ViMtV). Addressed to Bushrod Washington "In the Southern Circuit." Postmarked by hand "Alex 26 Oct'."

1. Presumably, Washington meant to write "exit."

Circuit Court for the District of South Carolina ——————————
October 25, 1798   Charleston, South Carolina

Judge Thomas Bee was present to open court, but the absence of a Supreme Court justice caused him to adjourn the court to the following day. He continued to adjourn court from day to day until November 3, when he adjourned court to the next term.[1]

1. Minutes, CCD South Carolina, RG 21, GEpFAR. Associate Justice Bushrod Washington explained his failure to attend the South Carolina court in a letter to James Iredell on December 5, 1798 (q.v.).

Circuit Court for the District of Delaware ——————————
October 27, 1798   Dover, Delaware

On October 27 Associate Justice William Cushing and Judge Gunning Bedford, Jr., opened court, after which Cushing delivered a charge to the grand jury. The docket of the circuit court does not record the court's closing. The "teste" day was November 1.[1]

1. Appearance Docket, CCD Delaware, RG 21, PPFAR; *Gazette of the United States* (q.v. under date of November 2, 1798). Charge not found.

James Iredell to William Cushing ——————————
October 28, 1798   Edenton, North Carolina

... According to your request I applied to Mrs Gilbert[1] at Richmond on my return to secure lodgings for you and Mrs Cushing at her house, and she promised to do so. I flatter myself you will find them as agreeable as at so public a time could be expected. Our unfortunate Friend Judge Wilson died the very night of my arrival from Philadelphia (the 21 August) and was speechless when I arrived. He had been for sometime in ill health, but his last illness was but of a few days duration, and his death was undoubtedly owing to the extreme agony of his mind. ... I have been much concerned in not hearing of an appointment to supply his place, as it was of great moment the Southern Circuit should not fall through _ . I informed Mr Pickering of the vacancy as early as possible, and at the same time of the impracticability of my attending it, which I would have done if I could rather than it should have fallen through. _ [2] ...

ARS (MHi, Cushing Family Papers, 1650-1840). Addressed "Baltimore, Maryland." Marked as "Recommended to the   care of the Honorable   Judge Chase."

1. This may have been the proprietress of Mrs. Gilbert's Coffee House. Earle Lutz, *A Richmond Album* (Richmond: Garrett & Massie, 1937), p. 112; Samuel Mordecai, *Richmond in By-Gone Days* (1856; reprint ed., New York: Arno Press, 1975), p. 45.

2. See James Iredell to Timothy Pickering, August 25, 1798.

Circuit Court for the District of New Hampshire ——————————
November 2, 1798   Exeter, New Hampshire

Associate Justice William Paterson and Judge John Pickering opened court on November 2. The court met again the following day before adjourning to the next term.[1]

1. Records, CCD New Hampshire, RG 21, MWalFAR.

Gazette of the United States ————————————————————
November 2, 1798   Dover, Delaware

Tuesday last the 30th of October, the anniversary of the birth of our illustrious President JOHN ADAMS, was celebrated in a manner worthy of the memorable occasion, and highly indicative of the patriotic spirit of our citizens. A very large company of Gentlemen, partook of an elegant dinner prepared for the purpose at captain Furbee's tavern, to which Judge Cushing, and Judge Bedford (the Circuit Court of the United States being then in session) and the honorable James A. Bayard[1] were invited. After dinner the following toasts were drank:—

   . . .
   4. The Judiciary—the pillars of society and government.
   . . .

VOLUNTEERS.
The Judges being absent.
Judge Cushing—may his charge to the grand jury be the creed of Federalists. . . .

(Philadelphia) November 7, 1798. Date and place are those of the headline.
1. James Ashton Bayard (1767-1815), a Delaware attorney, served in Congress from 1797 to 1803. *BDAC.*

Circuit Court for the District of Maryland ——————————————
November 7, 1798   Baltimore, Maryland

Associate Justice William Cushing convened court and delivered a charge to the grand jury. On the next day the court met again and then adjourned to the following term.[1]

1. Minutes, CCD Maryland, RG 21, PPFAR; Reply of the Grand Jury of the Circuit Court for the District of Maryland, November 7, 1798 (q.v.). Charge not found.

Reply of the Grand Jury of the Circuit Court for the District of Maryland ——————————————————————
November 7, 1798   Baltimore, Maryland

State of Maryland   City of Baltimore
November 7 1798

Sir

We the grand Jury, for the United States, of the district of Maryland, highly approving the charge delivered by you, this day, to them, and being fully impressed, with the propriety of diffusing the important truths, and the virtuous sentiments therein contained, do earnestly request of you, a copy thereof, with permission that the same, may be published _ .

J H Stone Foreman
City of Annapolis
Thomas Lee   Annarund[el]
Rob.ᵗ [Benoir?] ⎫
John Smith Brookes ⎬ P. G. County
Thoˢ Lansdale ⎭
William Potts ⎫
Jaˢ Smith ⎬ Frederick County
David Shriver ⎭
David Lynn   Allegʸ Cotʸ
David Stewart ⎫
Moor Falls ⎬ City of Baltimore
R. B. Latimer ⎭
Harry D. Gough ⎫
Robᵗ Lyon ⎬ Baltimore County
D. Carroll ⎭
John Cox   Harford County

D (MHi, William Cushing Papers).

Circuit Court for the District of Georgia ——————————————————
November 8, 1798   Augusta, Georgia

Neither the district judge nor a Supreme Court justice attended court on November 8, so the marshal adjourned the court to the following day. On November 9 Associate Justice Bushrod Washington and Judge Joseph Clay, Jr., arrived to open court. The court met until November 17, when it adjourned to the following term.[1]

1. Minutes, CCD Georgia, RG 21, GEpFAR.

William Cushing to James Iredell ──────────────
November 9, 1798   Baltimore, Maryland

...I received your favor of the 28th last, and am obliged by your attention in bespeaking us lodgings at Mrs. Gilbert's. We heartily sympathize with you in your trouble of indisposition in your family; and with Mrs. Wilson in her greater troubles. Hers will be mitigated by your kindness. Mrs. Cushing joins me in sincere regards to you and Mrs. Iredell, Gov. and Mrs. Johnston, Mrs. Wilson, and Mrs. Iredell. We arrived on Monday the 5th, and purpose setting out to-morrow for Richmond. The Court here was short, sat but two days— no civil business—a short trial for stealing a bank-bill out of a letter by a letter-carrier in the city. The proof failed in two material points—no proof of his receiving the letter, nor of any money being in the letter.[1]

...

You have heard that Mr. Bushrod Washington is appointed to the bench, and I am told he has gone on for the Southern Circuit, and hope it is so.

From Philadelphia we went the 9th August, and spent a month at Middletown, Connecticut, and then came on, passing King's ferry, forty-six miles above the city of New York, and in short, cautiously went as much out of the way of infectious places as we could. I hope the weather and frost will soon put an end to that ravaging disorder. ...

Pr (Printed in *MJI*, 2:539-40).
1. *United States v. Isaac Smith Isaacs.* Minutes, November 8, 1798, CCD Maryland, RG 21, PPFAR.

Circuit Court for the District of Rhode Island ──────────
November 15, 1798   Providence, Rhode Island

Chief Justice Oliver Ellsworth and Judge Benjamin Bourne convened court on November 15 and on November 21 adjourned it to the following term.[1]

1. Minutes, CCD Rhode Island, RG 21, MWalFAR.

Circuit Court for the District of Virginia ──────────────
November 22, 1798   Richmond, Virginia

Associate Justice William Cushing opened court on November 22 and delivered a charge to the grand jury on November 23. The court adjourned on December 15.[1]

1. Order Book, CCD Virginia, Vi; William Cushing's Charge to the Grand Jury of the Circuit Court for the District of Virginia, November 23, 1798 (q.v.).

William Cushing's Charge to the Grand Jury of the Circuit Court for
the District of Virginia ⎯⎯⎯⎯⎯⎯⎯⎯⎯⎯⎯⎯⎯⎯⎯⎯⎯
Federal Gazette
November 23, 1798   Richmond, Virginia

Gentlemen of the Grand Jury,
YOUR important duty and ours, respect the support of GOVERNMENT,
by which are secured to US the enjoyment of all our rights and privileges,
with whatever we hold most dear and valuable in life.

The PEOPLE of this country, from the beginning, being generally educated
in principles and habits of virtue; used to regular, orderly government; sensible
of its absolute importance to the peace and happiness of society; having fought
and bled, and spent their treasure to settle their liberties upon a solid basis;
having deliberately formed their own constitutions, so balanced as they
conceived best to guard against despotism on the ONE hand, and licentious
anarchy on the OTHER; having clearly seen the absolute necessity of a close
union of these states, to their security and independence; and established a
constitution accordingly, upon the same free model with all the state
governments—these weighty considerations bearing upon the minds of all
considerate men, of all good citizens, they will ever hold themselves sacredly
bound to maintain to their utmost, and perpetuate those fundamental barriers
to liberty and property—those supports to virtue and piety, against all
combinations of foreign influence and intrigue, of internal anarchy and discord,
misrepresentation, calumny and falsehood, operating from POLITICAL,
ambitious and selfish purposes—against all impious attemps to root out of
men's minds every trace of christian and natural religion, with all sense of a
Deity and moral obligation—Of ALL which evil workings we have seen too
many and lamentable specimens in America within a few years past.

As to the federal union or general government; it may give us a particular
striking view of its importance, by only turning our minds to the consequences
& the probable situation which these states might have been involved in,
had they remained separate and disconnected, during the fierce struggles and
convulsions that have been taking place in Europe: When we find the whole
power of the union, with all its energy has been competent (but with

(Baltimore) December 6, 1798. Date and place are taken from an introductory paragraph to the
charge. The paragraph notes that the charge was published at the request of the grand jury.

The charge was reprinted in the *City Gazette* (Charleston), December 10, 1798; *Russell's Gazette* (Boston), December 27, 1798; *New-Hampshire Gazette* (Portsmouth), January 2, 1799; and
the *Providence Journal* (Rhode Island), January 9, 1799. Substantive differences among the printings are noted.

In printing Cushing's charge, *Russell's Gazette* (Boston), December 27, 1798, noted that: "If
such publications are generally made and read, the public, or any considerable portion of them,
cannot remain long deceived about the *alien* and *sedition laws*, the *projects* of *France*, the *duplicity*
of her *advocates*, or the *danger* of our *situation*."

difficulty) to preserve the peace and tranquility of this country; amid the clamors of faction, the unaccountable rage of PRETENDED PATRIOTS to subvert the government and general interest of this country, by subjugating all to the political will and pleasure a foreign ONE; slandering all REAL PATRIOTS with whom the constitution and the people have entrusted the management of their affairs; extending their unceasing torrent of calumnies even to the character of the great and good WASHINGTON, who has spent a painful and laborious, but successful life, in war and peace, in virtuous and noble actions, in calm, wise, intrepid, dignified conduct—and in glorious atchievements for his country, and for the cause of *real liberty*; who LIKE AN ANGEL OF DELIVERANCE, now again appears to command our armies.[1] Continuing the same shameless indecencies and abuse towards his able and inflexibly PATRIOTIC SUCCESSOR, whose unshaken independent spirit of liberty, and eminent displays of genius in the most useful services to his country in the most critical crimes,[2] for above 30 years, in America and in Europe, are well known to ALL who are acquainted with the history of their own times.

How is it possible for any free government to stand the shock of such perpetual, inveterate, malicious, hostile attacks?

I will tell you—It is only by the people being *inquisitive, knowing*, and *alive* to their own interests; by their being *wiser, honester* and more *patriotic*, than those who abuse and would mislead them.

As light and knowledge increase to the people, deception vanishes; hence it is that *democratic societies*, set up to pull down *free republics*, are now scarcely known or heard of.

And, yet the same evil spirit continues to operate in the unbounded licentiousness of some presses, by the grossest misrepresentations of public men; and almost every measure taken for the safety of the country.

Those who have so long advocated the cause of a foreign nation against their own, with as much zeal as if under large pay for their services, to seduce this people out of their neutrality and plunge us into the wars of Europe; on a sudden, would have imposed this other extreme absurdity upon their country—that a simple preparation for defence against the most flagrant attacks upon property, amounts to a *declaration of war*.

There has been an unprovoked war upon property, for above five years past, to the amount of many MILLIONS, by estimation, besides five or six more by violation of contracts, under which, widows and orphans and others

---

1. On July 2, 1798, President Adams had nominated George Washington "Lieutenant General and Commander in Chief of all the armies raised, or to be raised, in the United States." The Senate confirmed the nomination the next day, and on July 13 Washington accepted the appointment. *SEJ*, 1:284, 291-92.

2. In the *City Gazette* (Charleston), December 10, 1798; *Russell's Gazette* (Boston), December 27, 1798; *New-Hampshire Gazette* (Portsmouth), January 2, 1799; and *Providence Journal* (Rhode Island), January 9, 1799, "times."

are now suffering, throughout the United States; in direct infringement of the rights of mankind, and of solemn treaty.[3]

These hostilities commenced near a year and an half prior to the British treaty;[4] that great pretext and apology (with some) for violating all principles of right and justice.

Though that was only an exercise of the right of a free and independent nation, to adjust their own differences, amicably, by negociation, rather than rush, in the first instance, upon the uncertainty of sword and battle; at the same time expressly reserving the rights of all other nations, uninfringed.

The clamor so much labored to be raised against that measure, by the opposers of neutrality, was clearly owing to this—that it tended to defeat the great object which they had so invariably and intemperately pursued from Mr. Genet's arrival; the embarking us in the war (at all hazards,) on the side of France.

There is somewhat so abhorrent to justice, that one can hardly find a name for it—*that* while our envoy, or envoys, have been humbly waiting and attending in a foreign country for a year and an half, with full powers to settle all difficulties upon the most liberal principles, and have been rejected or kept at a distance, treated with contempt, unheard, unreceived by the government; that very time has been improved to encrease hostilities to so extensive and almost universal devastation of our commerce; so that, (as our able and faithful envoys declare in their late memorial at Paris)—*"The property of American citizens has been taken to a much larger amount than would have been possible in a state of actual war."*[5] All which, and much more, appears from the dispatches, instructions, and other publications, which have been lately exhibited to the world.

Instead of making reparations for injuries and insults, she additionally demands large tribute, as of a conquered nation, and large douceurs for the private pockets of her ministers.

The most likely way to prevent war is by being prepared for self defence.

The right to defend property at sea, that great high way of nations, is the same as at land.

Tamely to give up ONE, is but an invitation to avarice and ambition to demand the OTHER.

As to foreign commerce, that source of wealth, so interesting to the farmer, the merchant, the seaman, to manufacturers, tradesmen, and mechanics of various sorts; so important to the support of government; so likely, if uninterrupted, to afford revenues sufficient, or nearly so, without the aid of other

---

3. The Treaty of Amity and Commerce (1778) between the United States and France. Miller, *Treaties*, 2:3.

4. The Jay Treaty. Miller, *Treaties*, 2:245.

5. Charles Cotesworth Pinckney, John Marshall, and Elbridge Gerry to the French Minister of Foreign Affairs, Charles Maurice Talleyrand, January 17, 1798. *ASP, Foreign Relations*, 2:181.

duties or taxes. In what manner this great object can or ought to be defended, with our country in general, at *any* and *at all* points:—*Our only* safety is in leaving such power and discretion where the constitution has lodged them—to our representatives in congress assembled—whose time, talents and studies are devoted to such great national objects; for whose propriety of conduct we have all the security the nature of things admit; their integrity and ability; their liableness to the same consequences of war: their sensiblity to the same blessings of peace, with any of us their constituents.

And, though individuals have an undoubted right to express their opinion upon public matters, in a decent manner: Yet, that it should oblige congress to act against their own sense and judgment of things, I believe no mortal will pretend.

As such a supposition would tend to utter anarchy, confusion, and the dissolution of all government.

A charge against America, long dwelt upon by the unceasing opposers of our government, has been, that France being a free republic, fighting for liberty at land, and for the freedom of the seas; America had ungratefully refused to join her; thereby risquing the extinction and the loss of all liberty.

'Tis true, when that revolution began, America rejoiced—in hope of seeing real liberty spread far and wide, and established upon a substantial, unmoveable basis: but, nine years melancholy experience and observation present a very different prospect and state of things.

The first three years (which were not without their multiplied troubles and commotions) were spent principally in tearing up the old foundations and erecting a new system, called a limited monarchy; to which all orders of state solemnly swore fidelity, in the field of MARS—in the midst of 600,000 spectators.[6]

In a little more than two years, the same constitution so solemnly established, was completely overturned by the aid of some of the same men who introduced it, by means of a formidable insurrection, attended with the slaughter of multitudes of citizens in the streets of Paris, on the famous 10th August, 1792.[7]

In less than a month followed the horrid massacres of September in the prisons of Paris, of above a 1000 citizens, untried and uncondemned of any crime; perpetrated by a band of hired assassins—deliberately carried on night and day for four days together—unchecked by any authority—though done

6. A mass oath to support the revolution was taken at the Fête de la Fédération, held at the Champ-de-Mars in Paris on July 14, 1790. *New Columbia Encyclopedia* under Champs-de-Mars; Leo Gershoy, *The French Revolution and Napoleon* (New York: Appleton-Century-Crofts, 1933), p. 139.

7. A reference to the insurrection in Paris which established the revolutionary government of the Commune of Paris. Under the Commune the monarchy was suspended, the King and Queen arrested, and the Constitution of 1791 forgotten. *New Columbia Encyclopedia* under French Revolution; Gershoy, *The French Revolution and Napoleon*, pp. 212-17.

under the very eye of the national assembly; in whom was supposed to center all power—executive, legislative and judicial.

No justice of the nation has ever reached a single one of those assassins, to this day; on the contrary, some persons who had the virtue and courage to solicit an inquiry into the villainy, were obliged to meet the same adverse fate, in order to intimidate from all further attempts to discover or punish the authors of those horrid butcheries.

The same dreadful and barbarous example was immediately followed in other great cities, by sacrificing all the prisoners who were committed on party or political suspicions; while, unauthorized, they liberated from jail all who were imprisoned for robbery, theft, or any other crimes against the old standing laws of the country.

The whole bloody reign of Robespierre[8] and his accomplices, which followed in 1792, 1793 and 1794, when above 400,000 people were under imprisonment *at one time*, upon mere suspicions; when 400,000 of all classes of citizens, *men, women*, and *children*, were obliged to submit to the guillotine, to drowning, or to some violent death, without trial, without evidence of crime; many sacrificed merely for their wealth, acquired by industry; when the christian religion was banished, and men dared not assemble together the first day of the week to worship their Creator; when a member in convention could rise and announce himself an atheist, with public applauses—this certainly was not a time of *true liberty*, but the reign of wild anarchy, terror and cruelty.

And yet, at the very time, these horrors were committing, and all principles of humanity were continuing to be outraged beyond example, we had a set of men in this country and a set of servile newspapers constantly employed in celebrating and extolling that same unhappy man, *Robespierre*, as the great patron and defender, of liberty.

Astonishing insult and imposition upon the good people of these states! What has been the state of things since that period?

Their last constitution of 1795, after providing many articles in favor of liberty and free elections, proceeds to establish several other articles, which are the bane of all liberty, and directly tend to subvert the whole—furnishing the usual weapons, by which liberty is overturned at a blow, a standing army in time of peace to maintain internal government—and a power to put an entire restraint upon the freedom of the press.

What the practice has been under this constitution, the notable events of the 4th of September 1797, among others, will inform; when part of Buon-

---

8. Maximilien Robespierre (1758-1794), leader of the Jacobins during the French Revolution. Along with others, Robespierre directed the Committee of Public Safety in its campaign to eradicate suspected enemies of the Revolution. This campaign, the "Reign of Terror," lasted from 1793 to 1794 and claimed the lives of thousands before it was halted by the Convention on July 27, 1794 (the Thermidorian Reaction). Robespierre was arrested, tried, and put to the guillotine the next day. *New Columbia Encyclopedia* under Robespierre and Reign of Terror.

aparte's army of veterans, under orders from the directory surrounded the legislative body, at 4 o'clock in the morning—seizing above 50 of its principal members, with two of the directory and compelling an instant decree of banishment against them and a number of public officers to a distant country; (a number of whom had certainly publicly advocated peace and amity and a more friendly conduct towards America; *which probably was their greatest crime*;) also nullifying above 140 elections of the people, in an instant; all in violation of the most useful important articles of their constitution—*without trial*—without liberty of defence—without evidence offered of any crime—arresting and punishing without trial above 30 printers, and subjecting the press to the entire control of government.

Where then is French liberty?

What becomes of the boasted, free republican constitution upon paper, before an immense army in the hands of the directory?

Again, what has been the treatment of other nations?

Belgium, a neighboring province, was entered by an army, Nov. 1792, as friends, under a solemn decree of convention, promising full security to property, public and private, and a right unmolested to form and enjoy their own government.

The next month passed, another decree directly the reverse; ordering general Demourier[9] to seize all the public property of Belgium, with the treasure in churches, to the use of the republic. This order appeared so unprincipled and outrageous, that Demourier refused to execute it: and it was, in fact, executed by other agents, inferior jacobin officers, who are said to have embezzled, in the collection, a large share to their own private use.

And, to complete the scene of treachery—instead of being suffered to form their own government, (according to promise) the Belgians were intimidated and compelled, at the point of the sword, to pray and petition to be annexed to France.

Another army entered Holland, being easily let in, by the aid of the patriots, so called, in hopes of having their liberties better secured, according to promises, understood to be held out by decrees of the convention.

And now Holland is groaning under tribute, after advancing immense sums upon requisition, with a foreign army in its bowels, dictating and controling all its councils and operations, and causing decrees of banishment against uncomplying, refractory members of the Dutch convention, after the example of the 4th of September, at Paris.

Venice sold to a foreign power.

Great part of Italy revolutionized into nominal republics, and enslaved to its conquerors.

---

9. Charles François Dumouriez (1739-1823), commander of the French army during the early years of the revolution. *New Columbia Encyclopedia.*

The Pope,[10] called Anticrist,[11] whose spiritual romantic power over nations had been declining for ages, and had become reduced, nearly to a nullity, forcibly thrust out of his small remaining territory; but succeeded by another antechrist, composed of atheism, military despotism, and the prostration of all principle, civil, moral, and religious.

Query—Whether the people can be gainers by such a change?

Spain, now trembling for the mischiefs which she dreads from her antient ally.

Portugal, also in danger, being too near and too small to expect to escape the all devouring grasp of the *republic.*

The small but virtuous and respectable republic of Geneva: which had, for centuries, produced some of the greatest men in learning and in arts: whose liberties the most powerful monarchs of France had respected, and left untouched; now, without provocation, overturned in blood compelled by a course of the villest treacheries and seditious practices: aided by an army, to renounce its independence, & lose itself in the great despotic *republic.*

Those innocents, whom kings, in their pride, had spared, have been wantonly and without mercy sacrificed, by haughty pretended republicans.

Thus, also, has fallen in the fatal snare, the too credulous, though brave people of Switzerland, who had maintained their independence in the mountains towards 500 years, and had lived, perhaps, the most easy and happy of any people on the continent of Europe, till lately they were surprised, trepanned and fraternized out of their liberties.

America, the first to acknowledge the *republic,* and conducting with all possible friendship consistent with the rules of neutrality, threatened with like vengeance, and a similar fate.

All this does not bear any of the marks of fighting for liberty at land, or for the freedom of the seas, but for the absolute dominion of both, and for a general domination over all countries.

We certainly wish for peace and amity with all nations, but not for subjection to any.

Whatever nation should gain the full mastery, both at land and sea, the probable consequence and counterpart would be general vassalage and subjugation.

It must, therefore, be the dictate of self-preservation and sound policy to keep up a balance of power among nations, as much as may be by all lawful and prudent means.

Thus, are we unfortunate enough to see despotism only changing its form—

10. Pius VI (1717-1799), pope from 1775 to 1799. *New Columbia Encyclopedia.*

11. In the *City Gazette* (Charleston), December 10, 1798; *Russell's Gazette* (Boston), December 27, 1798; *New-Hampshire Gazette* (Portsmouth), January 2, 1799; and *Providence Journal* (Rhode Island), January 9, 1799, "Antichrist."

the people changing masters;—and, under the specious pretences and allure-
ments of *liberty* and *equaily*, and *republics one and indivisible*, we only see the
people of many of the smaller nations of Europe subjected, under a foreign
power, to the strong irresistable arm of a cruel settled military tyranny.[12]

It is important here to remark, and seriously consider, that all those sub-
jugated nations, who are now paying large exactions to foreign armies for
keeping them in subjection, did not come to their fate, *so much by the* power
of arms, *as* by their imprudent listening to artful incendiary intrigues, to false,
flattering promises of fraternity and protection held out to allure all people
to revolt from their governments; thus duping them to their own destruction,
making the people the voluntary instruments of their own misery.

This horrible plot against the rights of nations and of mankind, and against
all religion and virtue, order and decency, carried on by French ministers,
emissaries and philosophers, and what is worse and more astonishing, abetted
by a party of our own countrymen, is now pretty generally seen through, and
has roused the spirit of free Americans to a sense of their danger and to some
preparation to prevent the fatal explosion of it upon themselves.

Thank heaven—America is not in very great danger of revolutionizing, at
present, unless by force of arms, and a superior overbearing power operating
in the heart of the country; *for this* plain reason—that the fellow citizens of
America, all now stand upon an equal footing, in point of property, and of
civil and religious rights—as *government society* and the *nature* of things admit;
we have chosen our own governments and constitutions; our elections under
no governmental military control; that we live under the *only free republics*, of
any extent, that exist upon earth; the only ones that do or can maintain civil
government without the aid of a standing army—kept in pay for that purpose.

Under the smiles of heaven, through the prudence and patriotism of our
representatives, America has been wonderfully preserved in peace—while many
nations of Europe, for a course of above six years, have been shaken to the
center by discord, wars and convulsions.

Many, through blood, seeking for liberty; while the blessing, like a phantom, flies before them, and continually eludes their *grasp.*

What is the result of all?

That in this alarming crisis, all parties and patriots firmly unite and persev-
ere in support of their own *government, constitution, liberties* and *independence,*
and of all necessary measures adopted and to be adopted for the general safety.

And God grant that all national differences may soon be accommodated;
and the *blessings of peace—substantial liberty,* and *stable government,* be the portion of *all* nations!

Gentlemen, I must put you in mind of the special duty of your office at

12. In the *City Gazette* (Charleston), December 10, 1798, this phrase reads: "to the strong
and cruel arm of a settled military tyranny."

this time—to make diligent enquiry and true presentment of offences against the *United State*, according to law; where in you will be duly assisted by the attorney for the government and by the court, if necessary.

I shall mention particularly, a law which has been much misrepresented, a late law against an old offence, against what must be deemed a dangerous offence in all societies & under all forms of government, viz. combinations or conspiracies to raise insurrections against government, or to obstruct the operation of the laws made by proper authority; *subjecting* offenders to fine and imprisonment; also printing and publishing false, scandalous and malicious writings against the government, with intent to stir up sedition or insurrection—or resistance to the laws—or to encourage any hostile designs of any foreign nation against the United States, their people or government; offenders of this kind are also subjected to fine and imprisonment, and justly— for every one must see, that an unbounded, unchecked *licence*, or rather *licentiousness*, in this way, would put it in the power of bad and discontented men— nay, of the worst men in a community, to overturn the freest government in the world, by dealing out under false, fictitious *signatures*, a continued course of falsehood, misrepresentation, deception and imposition upon the public.[13]

What but this with the artful, inflammatory and impudent publications of the democratic societies, set up by Mr. Genet to overthrow the federal union, [and to subject this people to the entire controull of France][14] what but this, encouraged and produced the insurrection at Pittsburg? which cost the United States a million and an half of money to suppress: an insurrection raised, under the groundless pretext of opposing an arbitrary law about a small matter *of excise;* a law in its foundation expressly warranted by the constitution:— *Taxes, duties, imposts and excises* being the necessary means explicitly lodged in the hands of congress, by the constitution, for the support of government, for the common defence and for the general welfare.[15]

What but this, so long deceived many good people in America, with respect to the internal state and designs of France; representing her, as exhibiting a perfect pattern of true liberty, and wishing to communicate it to all the world; when, in fact, according to their own histories, written by the revolutionists themselves, such as Brissot,[16] Louvet[17] and others, and by the records and reports in the national convention itself, a course of cruelties, tyrannies and perpetual violations of all principles of liberty and property, was

---

13. Sedition Act of 1798. *Stat.,* 1:596.

14. Brackets appear in newspaper.

15. A reference to the tax on distilled spirits and the 1794 Whiskey Rebellion in western Pennsylvania. See introduction to "Spring and Fall Circuits 1794" in volume 2 of the *DHSC*.

16. Jacques Pierre Brissot de Warville (1754-1793), French revolutionary and journalist. *New Columbia Encyclopedia*.

17. Jean Baptiste Louvet de Couvray (1760-1797), French literary figure and politician. *New Encyclopædia Britannica*, 15th ed.

more extensive and atrocious than was, perhaps, ever known under any monarchy.

What but this has deceived even the rulers of France, for a time at least; making them believe, that their diplomatic skill had had its full effect in setting the people of America at war with their own government, and making them ready to join France in overturning it. And yet some printers have cried out, that by this law they are abridged the liberty of the press.

But certainly not; unless the liberty of the press comprehends a right to print and propagate scandalous and malicious falsehoods, to the injury of the public; which no man of virtue[18] or modesty will pretend, any more than that liberty of action admits of committing murder, theft or any other crime.

The law provides a full and sufficient guard to innocence, by allowing the party accused, a fair trial by a jury of his country and to acquit himself entirely, only by proving the truth of his own assertions.

Thus is this important point of the liberty of the press, placed upon the only just and equitable foundation; SAFE to the innocent and the patriot, by allowing them to publish any truths they please—essential to the preservation of any free government—only forbidding malicious lies and slander, which no man possessed of any principle of virtue or honesty, would indulge himself in.

Different in this from the law of England, which admits not the privilege of proving the truth of the words written upon an indictment for a libel; and more different still from the practice in France, where a citizen may be arrested at the pleasure of the directory, for publishing any thing disagreeable, *however true*, and SENT without trial beyond seas into banishment, perhaps 4000 miles distant from his native country, his FAMILY and his ESTATE.[19]

As to the alien law;[20] it is a little strange, that any American should be found to complain of *that* which touches not the rights of any individual free citizen; but only provides for the safety of all (in case of war or threatened invasion) by the removal of dangerous alien enemies, who may be plotting secret mischief in the midst of us, & cooperating with the enemy without—in order to invade or subjugate our country.

Objections are made to the constitutionality of these laws.

But can any reasonable man suppose, that a government, instituted for the protection of all the states and all the citizens, with full powers to do every

18. In the *City Gazette* (Charleston), December 10, 1798, "wealth."

19. Nearly nine years prior to delivering this charge, William Cushing and John Adams discussed "the Subject of libels & liberty of the press" as it applied to their native Massachusetts. William Cushing to John Adams, February 18, 1789, William Cushing Papers, MHi; John Adams to William Cushing, March 7, 1789, William Cushing Papers, MHi.

20. Cushing is referring to the Alien Enemies Act of 1798. *Stat.,* 1:577. Another act respecting aliens was in force at the time of this charge, the Alien Act of 1798, which gave the President the power to deport dangerous aliens although a state of war did not exist and invasion was not threatened. Ibid., 1:570.

thing necessary for that important end, has no power to protect itself by laws to prevent crimes which tend directly to its overthrow and destruction?

Can it be imagined, that the supreme authority of a government, which is vested with the important powers of war and of the common defence against public enemies, and of protecting each and all the states against invasions, and is expressly authorised, by the constitution, to make all laws necessary and proper to carry those powers into execution, has no power to remove alien enemies—to remove *aliens* who belong to, and owe allegiance to, a foreign state, that is waging war with us; that is invading, or upon the point of invading, our country by an hostile army?

But it is suggested, that aliens cannot be touched in such case without the intervention of a jury, because it is provided (in the 7th article of the amendments to the constitution) that "*no person shall* be held to answer for a capital or other infamous crime, but upon a presentment or indictment of a grand jury; or be deprived of life, liberty or property, *without due process of law*"— and in the 8th article of amendments, that the accused shall have a trial by jury.[21]

There is no doubt, but that any alien permitted to reside among us, committing any crime against the municipal laws of the country, is to be tried in the common way, by jury. But that no way touches the present case.

There is no crime of that sort charged.

The grand question is—Whether the supreme authority has not a right, with ample powers, in case of the country being invaded, or about to be invaded by a hostile nation, to remove aliens who are subjects or citizens of, and owe allegiance to such hostile nation, and who may be extremely likely to join its standard; and to prescribe the modes of removal with all its circumstances and conditions, as congress cannot do it in person?

Surely these articles of amendments never intended to take away the powers before granted, to defend the country against invasions, and "to make all necessary and proper laws for that purpose.

Nearly as well might it be said, in case an hostile army was to land on our coast, that we must summon juries to try the soldiers of that army, before we could proceed to abridge them of their liberty.

No; the only constitutional mode, in such case, is to proceed, directly, with sword and bayonet.

So as to aliens of such hostile nation, not actually in arms, to remove them

---

21. Cushing is referring to the Fifth and Sixth Amendments. His citations to the Bill of Rights differ numerically from modern ordering, because he was using Zephaniah Swift's edition of the United States session laws. That edition, also known as Folwell's edition, prints the text of the twelve amendments proposed by Congress to the states in 1789, with an endnote stating that the first two articles were not ratified. Zephaniah Swift, ed., *The Laws of the United States of America,* 3 vols. (Philadelphia: Richard Folwell, 1796), 3:454-57; Clarence E. Carter, "Zephaniah Swift and the Folwell Edition of the Laws of the United States," *American Historical Review* 39 (1934): 689-95.

from a situation to injure us; and this, by the essential rights of war and self-defence.

What possible motive can any persons have for their great zeal and anxiety to get rid of these wholesome and necessary laws, unless they imagine it will give them a more easy task to overturn the government and constitution of the United States; unless they mean to pave the way to a more easy invasion and conquest of this country, by some foreign power?

Gentlemen

Let us all be faithful in discharging, not only our special duties of office, but, generally, all those of men and citizens, of patriots and christians, and thereby endeavor to secure the blessing of Heaven upon ourselves, and upon our country.

Federal Gazette ──
November 26, 1798   Richmond, Virginia

...On Friday a lengthy charge was delivered by judge Cushing, who presided, to a most respectable and intelligent grand jury, which had been selected from every part of the state. We have not been able to obtain a copy of the charge, but we are told it was fraught with *political* intelligence, and that it contained a succinct detail of the causes which have produced the present awful crisis. When we can be so fortunate as to obtain it, we shall lay it before our readers as the highest authority. Taking it for granted, that it must have been given in charge to the grand jury, to notice all crimes against the United States, and all violations of its *existing laws*, what a triumph must it be to every Virginian to see the issue of the grand jury's enquiry! NOT A SINGLE PRESENTMENT! ...

(Baltimore) November 30, 1798. Date and place are those of the headline.

Circuit Court for the District of North Carolina ──────────────────
November 30, 1798   Raleigh, North Carolina

Associate Justice Bushrod Washington and Judge John Sitgreaves opened court. On December 5 the court was adjourned to the following term.[1]

1. Minutes, CCD North Carolina, RG 21, GEpFAR.

Bushrod Washington to James Iredell ──────────────────────────
December 5, 1798   Raleigh, North Carolina

...When I left Richmond, I meditated a visit to you, not knowing but that Edenton was contiguous to the rout which I should have to take. But when

I reached Petersburg, and entered into consultation with those who very kindly undertook to direct the course of my Journey, I found that it would be impracticable to reach Augusta in time for the Court, unless I pursued a more direct road than that which led through your town. I was consequently obliged to abandon my first intention, and this I did with considerable regret.

I left home within five days After I recieved my commission, and yet it was not possible for me to reach Charleston in time to hold the Court there, in consequence of which I went at once to Augusta. ...

ARS (Nc-Ar, Charles E. Johnson Collection). Addressed "Edenton."

Aurora
December 10, 1798   Philadelphia, Pennsylvania

Among the many forms and usages which we have borrowed from the English institutions, that of a presidential speech is one of the most unfortunate—evil, or error, like crocodiles and other destructive animals, by some unaccountable principle in the natural economy, possess a disposition and capacity to multiply their species, to an inordinate extent.

Thus an annual speech of 60 lines from a *British king* has given birth to an annual speech of from 3 to 600 by an American *president*, 1000 from a *state governor*, and from 2000 to 6000 from a *federal judge*?

. . .

The excess to which this style and abuse of *speechifying* has been carried, particularly by the members of our judiciary establishment, whose duty belongs but to the law, reflects not a little discredit on our jurisprudence, and on those who encourage and practise it. ...

(Philadelphia) December 10, 1798. Date and place are those of the newspaper.

Abigail Adams to John Adams
December 21, 1798   Quincy, Massachusetts

... I would move to have as many coppies of Judge Cushings late Charge to the grand jury,[1] publishd and anexed to the Laws, as there are coppies of the Laws printed, to a candid mind I should think it would be equally usefull _ [2] ...

ARS (MHi, Adams Manuscript Trust). Addressed "Philadelphia."
    1. Abigail Adams is referring to William Cushing's charge to the grand jury at the Circuit Court for the district of Virginia, delivered on November 23, 1798 (q.v.).
    2. On January 18, 1799, Abigail Adams wrote to John Adams that she "got his Charge publishd in our papers." Although we cannot ascertain to which newspaper Abigail Adams refers, William Cushing's charge was published by at least one Massachusetts paper: *Russell's Gazette* (Boston), December 27, 1798.

Spring and Fall Circuits 1799

Like 1798, 1799 was a year of domestic political tension. Virginia, always a hotbed of Republican fervor, began to arm itself, and some Federalists feared civil war. In Pennsylvania popular opposition to a federal property tax escalated into what some perceived as an insurrection, and a number of its leaders were indicted and tried for treason. In addition, the continuing enforcement of the Sedition Act and the actions of some Federalist judges led to a heated debate over the existence of a federal common law of crimes.

The so-called "Fries Rebellion" in eastern Pennsylvania was the most dramatic event of the year. The rebels' ire focused on the direct tax acts passed by Congress in 1798.[1] Despite its progressive nature, the tax caused great indignation in the counties of Northampton, Bucks, and Montgomery, where some assessors were prevented from carrying out their tasks by threats and intimidation. By early March 1799 the federal marshal for Pennsylvania, William Nichols, had arrested a number of protesters in Northampton County and was holding them at Bethlehem. There, a large mob—led by John Fries, an itinerant auctioneer—confronted Nichols and demanded the release of his prisoners. Nichols, who had assembled a much smaller *posse comitatus* of his own, yielded to the demand.[2]

Although resistance largely died down after this incident, President Adams sent federal volunteer troops and Pennsylvania state militia to make arrests.[3] This action may have been prompted by a communication from Nichols to Secretary of State Timothy Pickering, which concluded that "the laws of the United States cannot be executed by the officers of the Government throughout the county of Northampton, without military aid; the people are determined to resist; they calculate largely on their strength in this State, and the aid they will have from the neighbouring States, and particularly that of Virginia."[4] Others, too, saw the Fries Rebellion as a harbinger of widespread insurrection. Robert Lenox, writing to James Iredell just a few weeks before the latter would preside over Fries's trial for treason, observed, "I hope the Pro-

---

1. The federal property tax was imposed through two acts: "An Act to provide for the valuation of Lands and Dwelling-Houses, and the enumeration of Slaves within the United States" (July 9, 1798), detailing the process for assessing private property, and "An Act to lay and collect a direct tax within the United States" (July 14, 1798), setting each state's apportionment. *Stat.,* 1:580, 597.

2. For accounts of the Fries Rebellion, see Miller, *Federalist Era,* pp. 247-48; Carroll and Ashworth, *George Washington,* pp. 574-75; *PAH,* 22:532n; Dwight F. Henderson, "Treason, Sedition, and Fries' Rebellion," *American Journal of Legal History* 14 (1970): 308-17. See the *DAB* for a sketch of John Fries (ca. 1750-1818).

3. The use of federal troops was authorized by "An Act giving eventual authority to the President of the United States to augment the Army" (March 2, 1799). *Stat.,* 1:725. The authority to call out state militia was granted by "An Act to provide for calling forth the Militia to execute the laws of the Union, suppress insurrections, and repel invasions; and to repeal the Act now in force for those purposes" (February 28, 1795) *Stat.,* 1:424. That act also required the president to issue a proclamation ordering the insurgents to disperse, which Adams did on March 12, 1799. *ASP, Miscellaneous,* pp. 187-88. Letters from the secretary of war calling out the state militia and the federal volunteer force are published in *ASP, Miscellaneous,* pp. 188-89.

4. William Nichols to Timothy Pickering, March 11, 1799, *ASP, Miscellaneous,* p. 186.

moters [*of the rebellion*] will Continue to resist till they put it fairly in the Power of Government to make Examples of them; for rest assured these are all so many Means formed to feel the Pulse of the Country & Preparatory to the Grand fete when the Great Leaders are to appear."[5]

While the troops were still in the field making arrests, the federal circuit court met in Philadelphia. On April 11, Justice Iredell—sitting alone for a week while District Judge Richard Peters issued warrants and took examinations in the southeastern counties—delivered a charge to the grand jury that specifically adverted to the Fries Rebellion. Iredell advised the jury that if the insurgents had acted "with a general view to obstruct the execution of" the tax act, any forcible opposition to it constituted "levying war," and therefore was treason within the meaning of the Constitution.[6] On April 22, the grand jury indicted John Fries for treason, and his trial began on April 30.[7]

The arguments at trial hinged on the legal definition of treason. The prosecution argued that the Constitution, by borrowing the words "levying war" from a statute of Edward III,[8] had incorporated the expansive English common law definition of the phrase. Echoing Iredell's grand jury charge, the prosecutors—Samuel Sitgreaves and United States attorney William Rawle—stated that forcible opposition to the execution of a single statute was sufficient to support a conviction for treason, relying on precedents established during the Whiskey Rebellion of 1794. Fries's defense counsel, Alexander James Dallas, William Lewis, and William Ewing, countered that the English gloss on the words "levying war" was not binding in the United States. The "plain natural meaning" of levying war was the taking up of arms "with a view to put an end to [*the government's*] existence," and this definition was clearly inapplicable to Fries's actions. The defense also contended that, even if the English definition were adopted, Fries's acts amounted only to riot or to a violation of the Sedition Act, but not to treason.[9]

Iredell's charge to the petit jury essentially endorsed the prosecution's position. Declaring that the Whiskey Rebellion precedents were binding, he observed that "opposition by force to one law, is of the same nature as opposition to all the laws; the offence is levying war against the government."[10] Not surprisingly, the jury returned a unanimous verdict of guilty after deliberating for about three hours.[11] Fries's conviction was a source of satisfaction to the Adams administration and its supporters. Secretary of State Pickering, writing to the president, commented that the conviction was "anxiously expected by the real friends to the order and tranquillity of the country, and to the stability of its government. Among such men I have heard of but one opinion, that an *example* or *examples* of *conviction* and *punishment* of such high handed

---

5. Robert Lenox to James Iredell, March 20, 1799, James Iredell Sr. and Jr. Papers, NcD.
6. See James Iredell's Charge to the Grand Jury for the District of Philadelphia, April 11, 1799.
7. Engrossed Minutes, April 22 and 30, 1799, CCD Pennsylvania, RG 21, PPFAR. For accounts of Fries's trial, see Wharton, *State Trials*, pp. 458-609; and Stephen B. Presser, "A Tale of Two Judges: Richard Peters, Samuel Chase, and the Broken Promise of Federalist Jurisprudence," *Northwestern University Law Review* 73 (1978-1979): 83-88.
8. 25 Ed. 3, c. 2.
9. Wharton, *State Trials*, pp. 491-92, 537-39, 555, 558-59, 567-68, 570-71, 574-75, 579-81.
10. Ibid., p. 591.
11. Ibid., p. 598.

offenders were *essential*, to *ensure future obedience to the laws*, or *the exertions of our best citizens to suppress future insurrections.*"[12]

Iredell, however, felt some sympathy for Fries, who seemed genuinely contrite and surprised that his actions could be interpreted as treasonable; the justice wrote to his wife that he dreaded the task of pronouncing sentence.[13] As it turned out, Iredell was spared the task: the day after the jury returned its verdict, Fries's attorneys moved for a new trial on the ground that one of the jurors, after he had been summoned, had declared that Fries "ought to be hung." Iredell found it his duty "to vote for a new trial . . . , as the fact appears too clear to be controverted." Peters reluctantly agreed.[14]

Fries's second trial was scheduled for October, when Justice Bushrod Washington was to preside with Judge Peters. Because of a yellow fever epidemic, the marshal, William Nichols, adjourned the court from Philadelphia to Norristown. Before Fries's case came up, however, it was discovered that Nichols's commission had expired and had not been properly renewed. His action in adjourning the court to Norristown and all subsequent acts of the court were therefore void. Accordingly, Fries's trial had to be postponed until April of 1800.[15]

If the Fries Rebellion caused some to view Pennsylvania as "the Land of Treason," Virginia had become "the land of Sedition."[16] In the aftermath of the Kentucky and Virginia Resolutions, [17] a bill was introduced in the Virginia legislature providing that any person arrested for a violation of the Alien and Sedition Acts could be set at liberty by a state judge. Although the bill did not pass, alarmed Federalists, including James Iredell, saw this as a decisive step towards civil war. Even more disturbing, rumors circulated that Virginia was arming its militia and constructing an armory at Richmond. Virginians claimed that these preparations were aimed at the French and the Indians, but others concluded that Virginia was preparing for a confrontation with federal troops.[18]

Indictments under the Sedition Act of 1798 continued to be returned in 1799 as government officials redoubled their efforts to silence Republican critics. The principal target that year was neither a newspaper editor nor a political leader, but a laborer and itinerant political speaker named David Brown.

Brown stumped Massachusetts in 1798 and 1799, inveighing against the Sedition Act and against Federalist officeholders who accumulated wealth at the expense of "the laboring part of the community."[19] In the fall of 1798, Brown came to Dedham, where he denounced "the sins and enormities of the government," and blasted what he considered the misbegotten wealth of the town's leading citizen, former Federalist

---

12. Timothy Pickering to John Adams, May 10, 1799, Charles Francis Adams, *The Works of John Adams*, 10 vols. (Boston: Little, Brown, 1850-1856), 8:644.

13. Wharton, *State Trials*, pp. 550-51; James Iredell to Hannah Iredell, May 11, 1799 (q.v.).

14. Wharton, *State Trials*, pp. 598-609.

15. Bushrod Washington to James Iredell, October 20, 1799 (q.v.). For details of Fries's second trial and subsequent pardon, see introduction to "Spring and Fall Circuits 1800."

16. Samuel Johnston to James Iredell, May 25, 1799, Charles E. Johnson Collection, Nc-Ar.

17. For information on the Virginia and Kentucky Resolutions, see introduction to "Spring and Fall Circuits 1798."

18. John C. Miller, *Crisis in Freedom: The Alien and Sedition Acts* (Boston: Little, Brown: 1951), pp. 173-75; William Heth to Alexander Hamilton, January 18, 1799, *PAH*, 22:423; Miller, *Federalist Era*, p. 241.

19. Smith, *Freedom's Fetters*, pp. 258-59. For his sketch on Brown, Smith acknowledges Frank M. Anderson's "The Enforcement of the Alien and Sedition Laws," *Proceedings of the American Historical Society* (December 1912), pp. 122-25.

Representative Fisher Ames. Such pronouncements outraged Ames, who described Brown as "a vagabond ragged fellow" who promoted "lies" and "wickedness."[20] A warrant for Brown's arrest was sworn, but the "wandering apostle of sedition"[21] disappeared before it could be served. Soon afterwards, Dedham residents erected a liberty pole capped by a sign that read: "No Stamp Act, No Sedition, No Alien Bills, No Land Tax; downfall to the Tyrants of America, peace and retirement to the President, Long Live the Vice-President and the Minority." Irate Federalists blamed Brown and renewed their quest to capture him.[22]

Brown was finally arrested in Andover in March 1799 and indicted at the June circuit court in Boston for seditious writings and his alleged involvement in the liberty pole affair. Benjamin Fairbanks, a wealthy Dedham farmer and friend of Fisher Ames, was also indicted for sedition for his part in the liberty pole affair.[23]

At his trial Brown first pleaded not guilty, then recanted and entered a guilty plea. After accepting his plea, Samuel Chase, the presiding judge, admonished him for "the vicious industry with which he had circulated and inculcated his disorganizing doctrines,"[24] and sentenced him to eighteen months in prison and a fine of $400—the harshest sentence ever imposed under the Sedition Act. Fairbanks fared better: after a contrite confession and a speech on his behalf by Fisher Ames, Chase sentenced him to serve six hours in prison and to pay a five dollar fine and the costs of prosecution.[25]

The continued enforcement of the Sedition Act intensified debate over an issue that had emerged sporadically since the early 1790s: the existence of federal common law. Federalists defended the constitutionality of the Sedition Act of 1798 on the ground that it was merely a liberalization of the common law of seditious libel. This, in turn, led Republicans like those in the Virginia legislature to challenge federal jurisdiction over common law crimes. The assertion of such jurisdiction, the Virginia legislature warned in a report authored by James Madison, "opens at once the hideous volumes of penal law, and turns loose upon us the utmost invention of insatiable malice and ambition, which, in all ages, have debauched morals, depressed liberty, shackled religion, supported despotism, and deluged the scaffold with blood."[26] One year later, the state assembly instructed Virginia's senators to "oppose the passing of any law founded on or recognizing the principle lately advanced, that the common law of England is in force under the government of the United States."[27]

The extent to which Federalist judges and legislators believed that federal courts had common law jurisdiction remains a subject of debate among scholars. According to some students of the period, Federalist judges adopted the view that a general

---

20. Fisher Ames to Christopher Gore, December 18, 1798, Allen, *Works of Fisher Ames*, 2:1303.

21. *Independent Chronicle* (Boston), June 20, 1799.

22. Smith, *Freedom's Fetters*, pp. 259-60. Liberty poles dated at least as far back as the Revolution, when—according to one Republican newspaper defending Brown's actions—"a flag-staff surmounted with the American standard was called a Liberty Pole and was approved and cherished by Government." Smith, *Freedom's Fetters*, p. 262.

23. Final Records, June 1799 term, CCD Massachusetts, RG 21, MWalFAR. For the trial of Brown and Fairbanks, see Smith, *Freedom's Fetters*, pp. 265-68.

24. *Independent Chronicle* (Boston), June 17, 1799.

25. Final Records, June 1799 term, CCD Massachusetts, RG 21, MWalFAR; Smith, *Freedom's Fetters*, pp. 269, 265-66.

26. "Address of the General Assembly to the People of the Commonwealth of Virginia," January 23, 1799, Gaillard Hunt, ed., *The Writings of James Madison*, 9 vols. (New York: G.P. Putnam's Sons, 1900-1910), 6:337.

27. *Daily Advertiser* (New York), January 22, 1800, supplement.

common law jurisdiction inhered in the federal government as an essential attribute of sovereignty. Others argue that most judges merely believed that the law of nations had been implicitly incorporated into federal law.[28] It is clear, however, that with the exception of Samuel Chase,[29] no federal judge in this period actually *denied* the existence of a general federal common law jurisdiction. And in 1799 Chief Justice Oliver Ellsworth explicitly endorsed it.

In a charge to the grand jury for the district of South Carolina, Ellsworth stated that the scope of the grand jury's inquiry extended beyond statutory offenses and acts contravening the law of nations to include "acts manifestly subversive of the national government." It was not necessary to "particularize" such acts, he told the jury, because they were defined by the common law, which had been brought by the colonists from England and which had "attach[ed]" upon the United States at the time of "the formation of the national compact."[30]

Ellsworth's assertion of federal common law jurisdiction prompted at least one spirited rebuttal.[31] But at the September sitting of the Circuit Court for the district of Connecticut, Ellsworth translated his words into action. One Isaac Williams had been indicted for accepting a commission from France to commit acts of hostility against Britain in violation of Article 21 of the Jay Treaty. Williams's defense was that at the time he accepted the commission he had already become a naturalized citizen of France and was therefore not bound by the treaty.[32] Ellsworth flatly rejected this defense, holding that "[t]he common law of this country remains the same as it was before the Revolution," and that under the common law a citizen could not expatriate himself without the consent of the government. "The present question is to be decided by two great principles," he declared; "one is, that all the members of civil community are bound to each other by compact. The other is, that one of the parties to this compact cannot dissolve it by his own act."[33]

Williams prompted further heated responses from Republican writers, who interpreted the decision as holding that "the English common law, untouched, unimproved, unaltered, is the rule by which the federal judges are to dispense justice."[34]

28. Presser, "A Tale of Two Judges," pp. 46-72; Stewart Jay, "Origins of Federal Common Law: Part One," University of Pennsylvania Law Review 133 (June 1985): 1003-116; Stewart Jay, "Origins of Federal Common Law: Part Two," *University of Pennsylvania Law Review* 133 (July 1985): 1231-333; Kathryn Preyer, "Jurisdiction to Punish: Federal Authority, Federalism and the Common Law of Crimes in the Early Republic," *Law and History Review* 4 (Fall 1986): 223-65.

29. The confusion over the issue is evident from *United States v. Worrall* (1798), which arose from an attempt to bribe the commissioner of the revenue, Tench Coxe. Before the prosecution was brought, William Paterson observed to Coxe that since no federal statute prohibited such a bribery attempt, "if an offence, it must be so on common law principles." But at Worrall's trial, Samuel Chase declared from the bench that an indictment based solely on the common law could not be maintained in federal court. District Judge Richard Peters, also presiding at the trial, disagreed, and an unusual compromise was worked out under which Worrall was convicted but his sentence was mitigated. By 1799, Chase had apparently abandoned his heretical views in this regard, presiding over a common law prosecution that ended in conviction. William Paterson to Tench Coxe, October 16, 1797, Tench Coxe Papers, PHi; Presser, "A Tale of Two Judges," p. 69. But see Preyer, "Jurisdiction to Punish," pp. 234-36.

30. Oliver Ellsworth's Charge to the Grand Jury of the Circuit Court for the District of South Carolina, May 7, 1799 (q.v.).

31. See "Citizen" to Oliver Ellsworth, *Virginia Argus* under date of August 9, 1799.

32. Miller, *Treaties*, 2:260-61; Wharton, *State Trials*, pp. 652-53.

33. Wharton, *State Trials*, p. 653.

34. "Aristogiton," *Argus* (New York), November 2, 1799; *Mirror of the Times* (Wilmington), September 13, 1800.

The Republican position was that while each state had adopted whatever part of the English common law it chose to, the United States as a whole had never done so—and, some argued, did not have the power to do so. They maintained that the federal government, being a government of limited powers, did not have the authority to assert jurisdiction over the whole range of common law subjects; such authority belonged exclusively to the states under the Constitution.[35]

While the debate over the reception of the common law raged, some—like John Marshall, who became chief justice of the United States in 1801—dismissed it as much ado about nothing. No one was arguing that the Constitution had adopted the common law of England as the common law of the United States, he wrote to a friend, and in *Williams* the common law that was applied was "not [*that*] of England, but of our own country."[36] In any event, the debate was not ultimately resolved until 1812, when the Supreme Court ruled in *United States v. Hudson and Goodwin* that there was no federal common law of crimes.[37]

In addition to embroiling himself in the controversy over the existence of federal common law, Chief Justice Ellsworth also found himself pressed into diplomatic service. With relations with France improving, President Adams determined that the time had come to hazard another diplomatic mission there in the wake of the disastrous XYZ affair.[38] In February, Adams asked Ellsworth to serve as one of three ministers plenipotentiary, along with William Vans Murray and William Richardson Davie, and Ellsworth reluctantly agreed. The diplomatic overture was not popular with Ellsworth's Federalist friends, who attempted unsuccessfully to persuade him not to go. As it turned out, because of a coup in France that reconstituted the Directory, the envoys' departure was postponed until November. While they were at sea, Napoleon overthrew the Directory and made himself First Consul, further complicating the situation. The mission was unable to reach an agreement with France until late in 1800, and not until 1801 did the United States and France sign a convention bringing the quasi-war between the two countries to an end. And while Ellsworth remained in Europe, the Supreme Court functioned without a chief justice.[39]

Towards the close of the year 1799 the Supreme Court suffered another blow—the death of Associate Justice James Iredell. Too sick to attend the August session of the Supreme Court, Iredell may have been exhausted by his circuit riding duties the previous spring, when he presided at the nine-day trial of John Fries. Although he seemed to have recovered his health by September, the following month Iredell succumbed to a short illness and died on October 20 at his home in Edenton. In December 1799, Alfred Moore, another North Carolinian, was appointed to fill the vacancy left by Iredell's death.[40]

35. "Aristogiton," *Argus* (New York), November 2, 1799; "Report on the Resolutions," Hunt, *Writings of James Madison*, 6:372-82; Jay, "Origins of Federal Common Law: Part One," pp. 1086-89; *Annals*, 10:413-14.
36. John Marshall to St. George Tucker, November 27, 1800, John Marshall Collection, DLC.
37. *United States v. Hudson and Goodwin*, 11 U.S. (7 Cranch) 32 (1812).
38. For details of the XYZ affair, see introduction to "Spring and Fall Circuits 1798."
39. *DAB* entry for Oliver Ellsworth; Brown, *Oliver Ellsworth*, pp. 273-281; Miller, *Federalist Era*, p. 246. Although the mission to France was something of a diplomatic success, it proved disastrous to Ellsworth personally. The voyage to Europe had been difficult, and Ellsworth's health was permanently broken. In October, 1800, he submitted his resignation from the Supreme Court by letter and remained on the continent until 1801 in an unsuccessful attempt to regain his strength. On his return to the United States he retired to his estate in Connecticut, where he died on November 26, 1807. *DHSC*, 1:118, 123, 900.
40. *DHSC*, 1:876-79, 140-43.

James Iredell to Samuel Johnston ─────────────────────────
February 28, 1799   Philadelphia, Pennsylvania

[*Following the February 1799 meeting of the Court, Iredell was uncertain whether*
Ellsworth would be riding circuit because of his appointment as envoy to France.]
Whether he still intends to go to the Southward I have not heard him say.
There were 6 Negatives to him in the Senate on account of his being Chief
Justice, and I by no means like the practice of taking a Man from the exercise
of one duty to perform another _ [1] ...

ARS (NcU, Southern Historical Collection, Hayes Collection). Addressed "near Williamston,
North Carolina." Postmarked "PHI   28   FE."
   1. In a letter to Hannah Iredell on March 7, Iredell noted that "Our Chief Justice set off for
Georgia by land yesterday morning." Charles E. Johnson Collection, Nc-Ar.

James Iredell to Hannah Iredell ──────────────────────────
March 14, 1799   Philadelphia, Pennsylvania

... I shall have business enough at the Court here, for an Insurrection has
begun in Northampton County (that in which Bethlehem is) on account of
the Land Tax Act _ .[1] A Body of armed Men, between 80 and 100, in military
[array?], forming one troop of Horse and two Companies of Foot, rescued
from the Marshall 23 Prisoners he had taken. Very active civil and military
measures are taking, and I don't doubt it can be easily suppressed, and some
of the Insurgents punished _ . I have lately had my health perfectly well.
...

ARS (Nc-Ar, Charles E. Johnson Collection). Addressed "Williamston,   North Carolina." Marked
"To the care of Samuel Johnston Esq." Postmarked "PHI   14   MR."
   1. Fries's Rebellion. For a discussion of this uprising, see introduction to "Spring and Fall
Circuits 1799."

Samuel Chase to William Paterson ─────────────────────────
March 17, 1799   Baltimore, Maryland

                                                      Balt[r]   17 March 1799 _
My dear Sir.
   I have been unwell, for the last Eight Week, five of which I have been
confined to my Bed-Chamber, and three to my Bed. this Day fortnight I
left my Bed-Chamber, but am so very weak and low, that I have no Hope
of being able to travel so as to reach New York by the first day of next
~~Month~~ Month. my Lungs are so very weak that I could bear the Motion of
any Carriage for a few Miles, and a Relapse would be fatal. under these

Falls of the Schuylkill by James Peller Malcom (1767-1815). Watercolor on paper, ca. 1792. Courtesy H. Richard Dietrich, Jr., Philadelphia. Photograph by Will Brown.

Circumstances I am to solicit the favor of You to hold the Court for Me in New York. _ This will afford Me ten Days longer, and if possible I will be at New Haven on the 13th of april. If I find it impracticable I must submit to the unmerited abuse which fall on Me   I wish that Congress had given the Judges of the District Power to try all Cases originating in the Circuit Court. I beg the favor of a line in answer to this Request. and I am Dear Sir

with great Respect & Esteem   Your affectionate and   Obed^t Servt

Samuel Chase

ARS (NHi, Miscellaneous Manuscripts C). Addressed "New-Brunswick New-Jersey." Postmarked "BALT MAR 17."

On March 17, in a letter to James Iredell, Chase wrote that his health was poor, and that he was asking Paterson to attend for him at the circuit court in New York. Chase further noted that he would try to attend at Connecticut and in the rest of the courts of the Eastern Circuit if he recovered his health. James Iredell Sr. and Jr. Papers, NcD.

William Paterson to Samuel Chase ————————————————
March 20, 1799   New Brunswick, New Jersey

New Brunswick,
20th March, 1799

Dear Sir,

Your letter of the 17th instant has just come to hand. Previous arrangements & engagements, to say nothing of indisposition, put it out of my power to attend the circ[t] court at New York agreeably to your request. I am glad to hear of your recovery, and sincerely wish, that you may be speedily reinstated in your health. I entreat you to ᴧa call ~~upon me~~ on your way eastward. I returned from Philad[a] with a severe cold and sore throat, of which I have not yet got the better. I continue under the doctor's hands. This is one of my physic-days _ For a few days past I have also been afflicted with the piles. These circumstances are mentioned to shew you the state of my health.[1]

I am, dear sir, with   great respect,   Y[r] ob. hb. ser[t]

W[m] Paterson.

The Hon[ble]
M[r] Chase _

ADfS (NHi, Miscellaneous Manuscripts C). This draft was written at the bottom of the letter, dated March 17, 1799 (q.v.), that Paterson received from Samuel Chase.

1. The text in smaller print was added by Paterson after he had completed the letter.

Richard Peters to James Iredell ————————————————
March [22], 1799   [Philadelphia, Pennsylvania]

Dear Sir

I ask your Pardon for not sending your Charge earlier which my Engagements this Afternoon prevented.

I must beg of you to leave out the Words in the last Page but one beginning with "But if the Intention &c to the End of the Paragraph.[1] I know this may be set up as a Defence & I would not like an Opinion to be anticipated. It would embarrass us to give a previous Opinion & as I now view the Subject I think it would tend to defeat all the Prosecutions for Treason. I cannot see the Distinction as you do in its Extent & should be sorry to differ with you on a Point thought so clear as to be delivered in a deliberate Charge.

With sincere Esteem   your obed Serv[t]

Richard Peters

Friday Evening

Judge Iredel

ARS (NcD, James Iredell Sr. and Jr. Papers). The dating of this letter is conjectural. At the bottom of the letter, Peters wrote "Friday Evening"; Iredell endorsed the letter "March 26. 1799." March 26, however, was a Tuesday, not a Friday. Possibly, Iredell endorsed the letter with the date he received it (although this was not his practice), and Peters sent it to Iredell the preceding Friday. Although Peters did not note where he wrote this from, he was probably in Philadelphia. Wharton, *State Trials*, p. 465n.

1. Iredell did not remove this from his charge. See note 33 to James Iredell's Charge to the Grand Jury of the Circuit Court for the District of Pennsylvania, April 11, 1799.

Circuit Court for the District of New Jersey ──────────────
April 1, 1799   Trenton, New Jersey

Associate Justice James Iredell and Judge Robert Morris opened court on April 1 but adjourned it shortly thereafter because the marshal was absent.[1] The following day Iredell delivered a charge to the grand jury after which the court was adjourned to the next term.[2]

1. According to Iredell's own notes, he adjourned the court on opening day because the marshal had summoned the jurors to appear on April 2. Notes on the "New Jersey Circuit Court, April Term 1799," vol. 16, James Iredell Papers, Southern Historical Collection, NcU.
2. Minutes, CCD New Jersey, RG 21, NjBaFAR. Charge not found, but described in the Reply of the Grand Jury of the Circuit Court for the District of New Jersey, April 2, 1799, and in the *Federalist* (Trenton), under date of April 8, 1799 (qq.v.).

Circuit Court for the District of New York ──────────────
April 1, 1799   New York, New York

Judge John Sloss Hobart opened court, but the court lacked a quorum to do business because a Supreme Court justice was not present. Hobart continued to adjourn the court from day to day until April 4, when he adjourned it to the next term.[1]

1. Minutes, CCD New York, RG 21, NjBaFAR. Samuel Chase was unable to attend court because of illness. See Samuel Chase to William Paterson, March 17, 1799.

Reply of the Grand Jury of the Circuit Court for the District of New Jersey ──────────────
Federalist
April 2, 1799   Trenton, New Jersey

"RESOLVED, (with only *one* dissenting voice) *That this Grand Jury do entirely approve of the observations and sentiments contained in the charge of the court, as well as of the* ALIEN *and* SEDITION *acts particularly noticed therein, which, in our opinion, the late and present critical situation of our country rendered indispensable."*

By order of the Grand Jury,
BENJAMIN SMITH, *Foreman.*

(Trenton) April 8, 1799. Date and place are derived from the minutes of the circuit court.

James Iredell to Hannah Iredell ————————————
April 4, 1799   Philadelphia, Pennsylvania

... I returned from Trenton to day in perfect health. ... I am able to tell you nothing new of any of your Friends in Town, as I have not yet been out of the house since I arrived. Mrs Wilson was well when I left town on Saturday last _ I have not heard from her since. I luckily got just about the quantity of Gingham's you wanted of Mrs Powell. I was detained all day at Trenton yesterday by an uncommon high wind. We made an ineffectual attempt with 7 Hands, and to day crossed with some difficulty and not without a little alarm. The Horse from this City marched against the Insurgents this morning. ...

ARS (NcD, James Iredell Sr. and Jr. Papers). Addressed "Williamston,   North Carolina." Marked "To the care of Samuel Johnston, Esq." Postmarked "PHI   4   AP."

City Gazette ————————————————————————
April 8, 1799   Charleston, South Carolina

The Chief Justice of the United States, arrived in this city on Friday last, on his way to hold the Circuit Court of the United States in the state of Georgia.

(Charleston) April 8, 1799. Date and place are those of the headline.

Federalist ————————————————————————————
April 8, 1799   Trenton, New Jersey

On Tuesday last the CIRCUIT COURT of the United States, for the district of New-Jersey, commenced its session in this city.[1]
JUDGE IREDELL delivered to the GRAND JURY a truly patriotic CHARGE. After some general reflections, on the relative situation between the United States and France, the learned Judge went into a defence of the ALIEN and SEDITION laws, and proved them, it is believed to the satisfaction of every *unprejudiced* mind, to be perfectly consistent with the principles of the

Members of the City Troop and other Philadelphia soldiery by Pavel Petrovich Svinin (1787-1839). Watercolor on paper, ca. 1811-1813. Courtesy Metropolitan Museum of Art, New York. Rogers Fund, 1942.

constitution, and to be founded on the wisest maxims of policy. The Judge concluded with calling the attention of the Grand Jury to the present situation of the country, and with remarks on the mild and virtuous administration of the government.[2]

. . .

☞ It is happy for the United States, that they have judges so conspicuous for wisdom, and venerable for integrity! It is the province of the judiciary to decide on the *constitutionality* of the laws. If the alien and sedition acts so much complained of, are inconsistent with the principles of the constitution, the federal courts will undoubtedly declare so: but the opinions of Congress. It is absurd to say, the judges are the creatures of the President, and the mere tools of faction; they are the most independent officers of the government, and are equally remarkable for deep understanding, and incorruptible integrity.

At this court *Luther Baldwin* and *Brown Clark*, of the county of Essex, were brought in upon process, and charged upon two several indictments, found at the last session, for *seditious expressions* against the government of the United States. They traversed the indictments, but declaring themselves not ready for trial, were bound over to the next session.

☞ It is deemed proper to state, that these indictments are at the *Common Law,* and not upon the *Sedition Act,* as has been falsely stated in some of the Jacobin prints.[3]

(Trenton) April 8, 1799. Date and place are those of the newspaper.

1. The court first met on Monday, April 1, 1799. See Circuit Court for the District of New Jersey, April 1, 1799.

2. At this point the *Federalist* printed the response of the grand jury. See Reply of the Grand Jury of the Circuit Court for the District of New Jersey, April 2, 1799.

3. See introduction to "Spring and Fall Circuits 1798" and "Spring and Fall Circuits 1799."

James Iredell to Hannah Iredell

April 11, 1799   Philadelphia, Pennsylvania

... Our Court here is to begin today, and there is an immensity of business both civil and criminal. We expect to try some of the Insurgents. Some are committed for Treason _ There is a respectable Force now among them, taking up some of them every day. I expect to sit alone for about a week, Judge Peters having gone into the Country to take examinations, and issue Warrants &c. I heard from my Mother yesterday. She was very well. So are your Friends in Town in general. ... I saw Mrs Wilson the day before yesterday. She desired her love to you and the Children _ I hope George Blair has got to Edenton before this time. I long to hear from him. I am sure you must want money, and wish you would draw for some. As you desired me to name a sum I mentioned 300 Dollars in particular, but without meaning to limit you; only for any sum beyond that I should wish for a little previous notice. I hope the things I sent have arrived safely. Inform me freely of any others you want _ Tell James I have got some Battledores[1] for him _ that is, I don't mean for his own use, but that of the Family _ But I mention him, as he asked for them particularly. I thank the dear little Fellow for

Statehouse and Congress Hall by James Peller Malcom (1767-1815). Watercolor on paper, ca. 1791. Courtesy H. Richard Dietrich, Jr., Philadelphia. Photograph by Will Brown. The center building is the State House and the partially completed building on the left is the City Hall of Philadelphia. Beginning in 1791, the circuit court and the Supreme Court moved from the State House to City Hall.

continuing to write to me. I am afraid it will not be in my power now to acknowledge his letter, tho' do tell him I am much obliged to him for it. Why will not Annie write me a single line? One line, to tell me she loves me, would give me great pleasure _ Does my little Helen ever speak of me? ... If you have any immediate opportunity, I wish you would send me my spectacles, one of the glasses of which is broke, and the 6 last Volumes of Gibbon. I shall be here till early in May. ...

ARS (Nc-Ar, Charles E. Johnson Collection). Addressed "Edenton, North Carolina." Postmarked "PHI 11 AP."
    1. "An instrument like a small racket used in playing with a shuttlecock." *OED.*

Circuit Court for the District of Pennsylvania ─────────────
April 11, 1799   Philadelphia, Pennsylvania

Associate Justice James Iredell convened the court; Judge Richard Peters, "absent from the City on official Business," did not attend court until April 19. After court opened Iredell delivered a charge to the grand jury. Iredell adjourned the court on May 18 to the next term.[1]

    1. Engrossed Minutes, CCD Pennsylvania, RG 21, PPFAR; James Iredell's Charge to the Grand Jury of the Circuit Court for the District of Pennsylvania, April 11, 1799 (q.v.).

James Iredell's Charge to the Grand Jury of the Circuit Court for the District of Pennsylvania ─────────────
Claypoole's American Daily Advertiser
April 11, 1799   Philadelphia, Pennsylvania

Gentlemen of the Grand Jury,
    THE important duties you are now called upon to fulfil, naturally increase with the increasing difficulties of our country.—But however great those difficulties may be, I am persuaded you will meet them with a firm and

(Philadelphia) May 16 and 17, 1799. Date and place are those given in an introductory paragraph. The newspaper also notes that the charge was published "at the request of the Grand Jury."
    Other newspapers also published Iredell's charge: *Commercial Advertiser* (New York), May 18 and 20, 1799; *Aurora* (Philadelphia), May 23, 28, and 30, 1799; *Independent Chronicle* (Boston), May 27, 30, and June 3, 1799. The Charleston *South-Carolina State-Gazette* printed the charge in two installments, but we have only been able to find the second half in its issue of June 14, 1799. An extract of the charge was printed in the *Daily Advertiser* (New York), May 21, 1799, and the *South-Carolina State-Gazette* (Charleston), June 4, 1799.
    On May 17, 1799, the day before it began printing the charge, the New York *Commercial Advertiser* published the following notice: "A long but sensible and pertinent Charge from Judge IREDELL to the Grand Jury of the United States for the district of Pennsylvania, delivered in April, appears in a Philadelphia paper. Altho this Charge would occupy a large portion of our paper for two days, and necessarily exclude much other matter, we shall nevertheless endeavor to lay it before our readers."

intrepid step, resolved, so far as you are concerned, that no dishonor or calamity (if any such should await us) shall be ascribable to a weak or partial administration of justice.

If ever any people had reason to be thankful for a long and happy enjoyment of peace, liberty and safety, the people of these states surely have. While every other country almost has been convulsed with foreign or domestic war, and some of the finest countries on the globe have been the scene of every species of vice and disorder, where no life was safe, no property was secure, no innocence had protection, and nothing but the basest crimes gave any chance for momentary preservation; no citizen of the United States could truly say that in his own country any oppression had been permitted with impunity, or that he had any grievance to complain of, but that he was required to obey those laws which his own representatives had made, and under a government which the people themselves had chosen. Yet in the midst of this envied situation, we have heard the government as grossly abused as if it had been guilty of the vilest tyranny, as if common sense or common virtue had fled from our country, and those pure principles of republicanism, which have so strongly characterized its councils, could only be found in the happy soil of France, where the sacred fire is preserved by five Directors on ordinary occasions, and three on extraordinary ones—who, with the aid of a Republican army, secure its purity from violation by the Legislative representatives of the people.—The external conduct of that government is upon a par with its internal.—Liberty, like the religion of Mahomet, is propagated by the sword. Nations are not only compelled to be free, but to be free on the French model, and placed under French guardianship. French arsenals are the repository of their arms, French treasuries of their money, the city of Paris of their curiosities; and they are honored with the constant support of French enterprizes in any other part of the world. Such is the progress of a power which began by declarations that it abhorred all conquests for itself, and sought no other felicity but to emancipate the world from tyrants, and leave each nation free to chuse a government of its own. Those who take no warning by such an awful example, may have deeply to lament the consequences of neglecting it.

The situation in which we now stand with that country is peculiarly critical. Conscious of giving no real cause of offence, but irritated with injuries, and full of resentment for insults; desirous of peace, if it can be preserved with honor and safety, but disdaining a security equally fallacious and ignominious at the expence of either; still holding the rejected Olive Branch in one hand, but a sword in the other—we now remain in a sort of middle path between peace and war, where one false step may lead to the most ruinous consequences, and nothing can be safely relied on but unceasing vigilance, and persevering firmness in what we think right, leaving the event to heaven, which seldom suffers the destruction of nations, without some capital fault of their own.

Among other measures of defence and precaution which the exigency of the crisis, and the magnitude of the danger, suggested to those to whom the people have entrusted all authority in such cases, were certain acts of the legislature of the United States, not only highly important in themselves, but deserving of the most particular attention, on account of the great discontent which has been excited against them, and especially as some of the state legislatures have publicly pronounced them to be in violation of the constitution of the United States.[1] I deem it my duty, therefore, on this occasion to state to you the nature of those laws, which have been grossly misrepresented, and to deliver my deliberate opinion as a Judge, in regard to the objections arising from the constitution.

The acts to which I refer you will readily suppose to be what are commonly called the Alien and Sedition acts. I shall speak of each separately, so far as no common circumstances belonging to them may make a joint discussion proper.

I. *The Alien Laws*, there being two.[2]

To these Laws, in particular, it has been objected,

1. That an Alien ought not to be removed on suspicion, but on proof of some crime.

2. That an Alien coming into the country on the faith of an act stipulating that in a certain time, and on certain conditions, he may become a citizen, to remove him in an arbitrary manner before that time; wou'd be a breach of public faith.

3. That it is inconsistent with the following clause in the constitution. (Art. I. sec. 9.)[3]

"The migration or importation of such persons as any of the states now existing shall think proper to admit, shall not be prohibited by the Congress prior to the year one thousand eight hundred and eight; but a tax or duty may be imposed on such importation, not exceeding ten dollars for each person."

With regard to the first objection, viz. "That an alien ought not to be removed on suspicion, but on proof of some crime." It is believed that it never was suggested in any other country, that *aliens* had a right to go into a foreign country, and stay at their will and pleasure without any leave from the government. The law of nations undoubtedly is, that when an alien goes into a foreign country, he goes under either an express or implied safe-conduct. In most countries in Europe, I believe, an express passport is

---

1. A reference to the Virginia and Kentucky Resolutions. Jonathan Elliot, ed., *The Debates in the Several State Conventions, on the Adoption of the Federal Constitution, as Recommended by the General Convention at Philadelphia, in 1787*, 2d ed., 5 vols. (Philadelphia: J. B. Lippincott, 1876), 4:528, 540.

2. The Alien Act of 1798, and the Alien Enemies Act of 1798. *Stat.*, 1:570, 577.

3. The *Independent Chronicle* (Boston), May 27, 1799, misprints this as section 6 of the Constitution. For examples of this argument, see *Annals*, 8:1978-79, 2009-10.

necessary for strangers. Where greater liberality is observed, yet it is always understood that the government may order away any alien whose stay is deemed incompatible with the safety of the country. Nothing is more common than to order away, on the eve of a war, all aliens or subjects of the nation with whom the war is to take place. Why is that done, but that it is deemed unsafe to retain in the country men whose prepossessions are naturally so strong in favour of the enemy that it may be apprehended they will either join in arms, or do mischief by intrigue, in his favour? How many such instances took place at the beginning of the war with Great-Britain, no body then objecting to the authority of the measure, and the expediency of it being alone in contemplation! In cases like this, it is ridiculous to talk of a crime, because perhaps the only crime that a man can then be charged with, is his being born in another country, and having a strong attachment to it. He is not punished for a crime that he has committed, but deprived of the power of committing one hereafter to which even a sense of patriotism may tempt a warm and misguided mind. Nobody who has ever heard of Major Andre,[4] that possesses any liberality of mind, but must believe that he did what he thought right at the time, tho' in my opinion it was a conduct in no manner justifiable. Yet how fatal might his success have proved! If men, therefore, of good characters, and held in universal estimation for integrity, can be tempted when a great object is in view, to violate the strict duties of morality, what may be expected from others who have neither character nor virtue, but stand ready to yield to temptations of any kind? The opportunities during a war of making use of men of such a description are so numerous and so dangerous, that no prudent nation would ever trust to the possible good behaviour of many of them. Indeed most of those who oppose this law seem to admit that as to *alien enemies* the interposition may be proper, but they contend it is improper before a war actually takes place to exercise such an authority, and that as to *neutral aliens* it is totally inadmissible. To be sure the two latter instances are not quite so plain, but the objection I am considering belongs equally to them all, for if an alien cannot be removed but on conviction of a crime, then an alien enemy ought not to be removed but on conviction of treason, or some other crime shewing the necessity of it. If, however, we are not blind to what is evident to all the rest of the world, equal danger may be apprehended from the citizens of a hostile power, before war actually declared as after, perhaps more, because less suspicion is entertained; and some citizens of a neutral power are equally dangerous with the others. What has given France possession of the Netherlands, Geneva, Switzerland and almost all Italy, and enables her to domineer over so many other countries, lately powerful and completely independent, but that her arts have preceded her arms, the smooth words

---

4. Major John André (1751-1780), a British officer captured and hanged as a spy for his involvement in the treason of Benedict Arnold. *New Columbia Encyclopedia*.

of amity, peace, and universal love, by seducing weak minds, have led to an unbounded confidence which has ended in their destruction, and they have now to deplore the infatuation which led them to court a fraternal embrace from a bosom in which a dagger was concealed! In how many countries, alien friends as to us, dependent upon them, are there warm partisans not nominally French citizens, but compleatly illuminated with French principles, electrified with French enthusiasm; and ready for any sort of revolutionary mischief! Are we to be guarded against the former and exposed to the latter? No, gentlemen. If with such examples before their eyes, congress had either confined their precaution to a war in form, or to citizens of France only, losing all sense of danger to their country in a regard to nominal distinctions, they would probably justly have deserved the charge of neglecting their country's safety in one of its most essential points, and hereafter the very men who are now clamorous against them for exercising a judicious foresight, might too late have had reason to charge them, (as many former infatuated governments in Europe may now fairly be charged by their miserable deluded fellow-citizens) as the authors of their country's ruin. But those who object to this law seem to pay little regard to considerations of this kind, and to entertain no other fear but that the President may exercise this authority for the mere purpose of abusing it. There is no end to arguments or suspicions of this kind. If this power is proper it must be exercised by some body. If from the nature of it it could be exercised by so numerous a body as congress, yet as congress are not constantly sitting it ought not to be exercised by them alone. If they are not to exercise it, who so fit as the president? What interest can he have in abusing such an authority? But on this occasion, as on others of the like kind, gentlemen think it sufficient to shew, not that a power is likely to be abused (which is all that can be prudently guarded against), but that it possibly may, and therefore to guard against the possibility of an abuse of power the power is not at all to be exercised. The argument would be just as good against his acknowledged powers, as any others that the legislature may occasionally confide to him. Suppose he should refuse to nominate to any office? or to command the army or navy? or should assign frivolous reasons against every law so that no law could be passed but with the concurrence of two thirds of both houses! Suppose congress should raise an army without necessity, lay taxes where there was no occasion for money, declare war from mere caprice, lay wanton and oppressive restraints on commerce, or in a time of imminent danger trifle with the safety of their country, to gain a momentary breath of popularity at the hazard of their country's ruin! All this they *may* do. Does any man of candour, who does not believe every thing they do wrong, apprehend that any of these things will be done? They have the *power* to do them, because the authority to pass very important and necessary acts of legislation on all those subjects, and in regard to which discretion must be left, unavoidably implies that as it may be exercised in a right manner, it may, if no principle prevent it, be exercised in a wrong one. If the state legislatures should combine to choose no more senators, they may abolish the constitution without the danger of committing treason. If to prevent a house of representatives being in existence, they should keep no law in being for a similar branch of their own, deeming the abolition of the government of the United States cheaply purchased by such a sacrifice, they may do this. They have the same power over the election of a president and vice-president. What is the security against abuse in any of these cases? None, but the precautions taken to procure a proper choice, which, if well exercised, will at least secure the public against a wanton abuse of power, tho' nothing can secure them absolutely against the common frailty of men, or the possibility of bad men, if accidently invested with power, carrying it into a dangerous extreme.[5] We must trust some persons, and as well as we can submit to any collateral evil which may arise from a provision for a great and indispensable good that can only be obtained thro' the medium of human imperfection. At the same time it may be observed, that in the case of the president or any executive or judicial officer wantonly abusing his trust, he is liable to impeachment, and there are frequent opportunities of changing the members of the legislature if their conduct is not acceptable to their constituents.

The clause in the constitution, declaring that the trial of all crimes, except by impeachment, shall be by jury,[6] can never in reason be extended[7] to amount to a permission of perpetual residence of all sorts of foreigners unless convicted of some crime, but is evidently calculated for the security of any citizen, a party to the instrument or even of a foreigner if resident in the country, who when charged with the commission of a crime against the municipal laws for which he is liable to punishment, can be tried for it in no other manner.

The second objection is, "That an alien coming into the country, on the faith of an act stipulating that in a certain time and on certain conditions he may become a citizen, to remove him in an arbitrary manner before that time would be a breach of public faith."

With regard to this, it may be observed, that undoubtedly the faith of government ought under all circumstances, and in all possible situations, to be preserved sacred. If, therefore, in virtue of this law, all aliens from any part of the world had a right to come here, stay the probationary time, and become citizens, the act in question could not be justified, unless it could be shewn that a real (not a pretended) over-ruling public necessity, to which

5. In the *Aurora* (Philadelphia), May 23, 1799, this sentence reads: "None, but the precautions taken to procure a proper choice, which, if well exercised, will at least secure them against the common frailty of men, or the possibility of bad men, if accidently invested with power, carrying it into a dangerous extreme."

6. Article III, section 2.

7. In the *Aurora* (Philadelphia), May 23, 1799, and *Independent Chronicle* (Boston), May 30, 1799, "expected."

all inchoate acts of legislation must forever be subject, occasioned a partial repeal of it. But there are certain conditions, without which no alien can ever be admitted, if he stay ever so long; and one is, that during a limited time (two years in the case of aliens then resident; five in the case of aliens arriving after) *he has behaved as a man of a good moral character, attached to the principles of the constitution of the United States, and well disposed to the good order and happiness of the same.*[8] If his conduct be different,[9] he is no object of the naturalization law at all, and consequently no implied compact was made with him. If his conduct be conformable to that description, he is no object of the alien law to which the objection is applied, because he is not a person whom the President is empowered to remove, for such a person could not be deemed dangerous to the peace and safety of the United States, nor could there be reasonable grounds to suspect such a man of being concerned in any treasonable or secret machinations against the government, in which cases alone the removal of any alien friend is authorized. Besides, any alien coming to this country must or ought to know, that this being an independent nation, it has all the rights concerning the removal of aliens which belong by the law of nations to any other; that while he remains in the country in the character of an alien, he can claim no other privilege than such as an alien is entitled to, and consequently, whatever risque he may incur in that capacity, is incurred voluntarily, with the hope that in due time by his unexceptionable conduct, he may become a citizen of the United States. As there is no end to the ingenuity of man, it has been suggested that such a person, if not a citizen, is a denizen, and therefore cannot be removed as an alien. A denizen in those laws from which we derive our own, means a person who has received letters of denization from the king, and under the royal government such a power might undoubtedly have been exercised. This power of denization is a kind of partial naturalization, giving some, but not all the privileges of a natural-born subject. He may take lands by purchase or devise, but cannot inherit. The issue of a denizen born *before* denization can not inherit; but if born *after* may, the ancestor having been able to communicate to him inheritable blood. But this power of the crown was thought so formidable, that it is expressly provided by act of parliament, that no denizen can be a member of the Privy Council, or of either House of Parliament, or have any office of trust civil or military, or be capable of any grant of lands from the crown.[10] Upon the dissolution of the royal

---

8. Iredell quotes from section 1 of "An Act to establish an uniform rule of Naturalization; and to repeal the act heretofore passed on that subject," passed on January 29, 1795. Parts of that act had been amended by "An Act supplementary to and to amend the act, intituled 'An act to establish an uniform rule of naturalization; and to repeal the act heretofore passed on that subject,'" passed on June 18, 1798. That act required a fourteen-year residency. *Stat.,* 1:414, 566.

9. In the *Aurora* (Philadelphia), May 23, 1799, "conformable."

10. 12 & 13 Will. 3, c. 2, s. 3.

government, the whole authority of naturalization, either whole or partial, belonged to the several states, and this power the people of the states have since devolved on the Congress of the United States. Denization therefore (in the sense here used) is a term unknown in our law, since the right was not derived from any general legislative authority, but from a special prerogative of the crown, to which parliamentary restrictions afterwards were applied. So much so, that if an act of Parliament had passed, giving certain rights to an alien with restrictions exactly similar to those of a denizen, I imagine he would not have been called a denizen, because the royal authority was not the source from which his rights were derived. As to acts of naturalization themselves, they are liable in England, by an express law, to certain limitations, one of which is, that the person naturalized is incapable of being a member of the privy council, or either house of parliament, or of holding offices or grants from the crown.[11] Yet I never heard, nor do believe that such a person was ever called a denizen; for which, as there is no foundation in precedent, or in the constitution of the United States, I presume it is a distinction without solidity. Fixed principles of law cannot be grounded on the airy imagination of man.

The third objection is, "That it is inconsistent with the following clause in the constitution, viz.

"The migration or importation of such persons as any of the states now existing shall think proper to admit, shall not be prohibited by the congress prior to the year one thousand eight hundred and eight, but a tax or duty may be imposed on said importation not exceeding ten dollars for each person."

I am not satisfied, as to this objection, that it is sufficient to over-rule it, to say the words do not express the real meaning, either of those who formed the constitution, or those who established it, although I do verily believe in my own mind, that the article was intended only for slaves, and the clause was expressed in its present manner to accommodate different gentlemen, some of whom could not bear the name *slaves*, and others had no objection[12] to it. But, though this probably is the real truth, yet, if in attempting to compromise, they have unguardedly used expressions that go beyond their meaning, and there is nothing but private history to elucidate it, I shall deem it absolutely necessary to confine myself to the written instrument. Other reasons may make the point doubtful, but at present I am inclined to think it must be admitted; that congress, prior to the year 1808, cannot prohibit the migration of free persons to a particular state, existing at the time of the constitution, which such state shall, by law, agree to receive. The states then existing, therefore, till 1808 may (we will say) admit the migration of persons to their own states, without any prohibitory act of congress.—This they may

11. Idem.
12. In the *Independent Chronicle* (Boston), May 30, 1799, "had objections."

do upon principles of general policy, and in consistence with all their other duties. The states are expressly prohibited from entering into an engagement or contract with another state, or engaging in war, unless actually invaded, or in such imminent danger, as will not admit of delay. The avenues to foreign connection being thus carefully closed, it will scarcely be contended, that in the case of a war, a state could, either directly or indirectly, permit the migration of enemies. If they did, the United States could certainly without any impeachment of the general right of allowing migration, in virtue of their authority to repel invasion, prevent the arrival of such. And as such invasion may be attempted without a formal war, and congress have an express right to *protect* against invasion, as well as to *repel* it, I presume congress would also have authority to prevent the arrival of any enemies, coming in the disguise of friends, to invade their country. But, admitting the right to permit migration in its full force, the persons migrating on their authority must be subject to the laws of the country, which consist not only of those of the particular state, but of the United States. While aliens, therefore, they must remain in the character of aliens; and, of course, upon the principles I have mentioned, be subject to a power of removal, in certain cases recognized in the law of nations; nor can they cease to be in this situation, until they become citizens of the United States; in which case they must obey the laws of the union as well as of the particular state they reside in. But, gentlemen argue as if because the states had a right to permit migration the migrants were under a sort of special protection of the state admitting it, lest the United States, merely to disappoint the purpose of migration, should exercise an arbitrary authority of removal without any cause at all. It would be just as consistent to say, that if such migrant was charged with a murder on the high seas, or in any fort or arsenal of the United States, he should not be tried for it in a court of the United States, lest the court and juries, out of ill will to the state, should combine to procure his conviction and punishment, in all events, to defeat the state law. The two powers may undoubtedly be made compatible, if the legislatures of the particular states, and the government of the United States do their duty, without which presumption, not an authority given by the constitution can exist. They surely are more compatible than the collateral powers of taxation, which, under each government, go to an unlimited extent; but the very nature of which forbids any other limitation than a sense of moral right and justice. If we scepticize in the manner of some gentlemen on this subject, suppose each legislature should tax to the amount of 19*s* in the pound. Each has the power; but is such an exercise of it more apprehended than we apprehend an earthquake to swallow us all up, at this very moment? All systems of government, suppose they are to be administered by men of common sense and common honesty. In our country, as all ultimately depends on the voice of the people, they have it in their power, and it is to be presumed they generally will chuse men of this description: but, if they will not, the case to be sure is without remedy. If they chuse fools, they will have foolish laws. If they chuse knaves, they will have knavish ones. But this can never be the case until they are generally fools or knaves themselves, which, thank God, is not likely ever to become the character of the American people.

HAVING[13] said what I thought material as to the alien laws, upon the subject of the particular objections to them, I now proceed to discuss the objections which have been made to what is called the sedition act,[14] one of which equally applies to the alien laws as well as to this. But I think it proper previously to read the law itself.

The objections (so far as I have heard them) to this act are as follow:

1. (And this applies to the alien law also) That there is no specific power given to pass an act of this description, though in the particular specific powers given there is authority conveyed as to other offences specially named.

2. That this law is not warranted by a clause in the constitution, conveying legislative authority, which, after designating particular objects, adds:

"And to make all laws which shall be necessary and proper for carrying into execution the foregoing powers, and all other powers vested by this constitution in the government of the United States, or in any department or officer thereof"[15]—Because it is not necessary and proper to pass any such law in order to cary into execution any of those powers.

3. That admitting the former positions are not maintainable, yet the exercise of this authority is incompatible with the following amendment to the constitution, viz.

"Congress shall make no law respecting an establishment of religion, or prohibiting the full exercise thereof; or abridging the freedom of speech, or of the press, or the right of the people peaceably to assemble, and to petition the government for a redress of grievances."[16]

With regard to the first objection, I readily acknowledge, that soon after the constitution was proposed, and when I had taken a much more superficial view of it than I was sensible of at the time, I did think congress could not provide for the punishment of any crimes but such as are specifically designated in the particular powers enumerated. I delivered that opinion in the convention of North Carolina, in the year 1788, with a perfect conviction, at the time, that it was well founded.[17] But I have since been convinced it was an erroneous opinion, and my reasons for changing it, I shall state to you as clearly as I am able.

---

13. The *South-Carolina State-Gazette* (Charleston), June 14, 1799, begins printing its second installment of the charge here.

14. Sedition Act of 1798. *Stat.,* 1:596.

15. Article I, section 8.

16. First Amendment.

17. See Iredell's speech to the North Carolina ratifying convention in Hillsborough on July 30, 1788, in Elliot, *Debates in the Several State Conventions, on the Adoption of the Federal Constitution,* 4:218-23.

It is in vain to make any law unless some sanction be annexed to it, to prevent or punish its violation. A law without it might be equivalent to a good moral sermon, but bad members of society would be as little influenced by one as the other. It is, therefore, necessary and proper, for instance, under the constitution of the United States, to secure the effect of all laws which impose a duty on some particular persons, by providing some penalty or punishment if they disobey. The authority to provide such is conveyed by the following general words in the constitution, at the end of the objects of legislation particularly specified: "To make all laws which shall be necessary and proper for carrying into execution the foregoing powers, and all other powers vested by this constitution in the government of the United States, or in any department or officer thereof." A penalty alone would not in every case be sufficient, for the offender might be rich and disregard it, or poor, though a wilful offender, and unable to pay it. A fine, therefore, will not always answer the purpose, but imprisonment must be in many cases added, though a wise and humane legislature will always dispense with this, where the importance of the case does not require it. But if it does, from the very nature of the punishment, it becomes a *criminal*, and not a *civil* offence; the grand jury must indict, before the offender can be convicted.

This general position may be illustrated by a variety of instances under the penal code of the United States, which have, I believe, never been objected to as unconstitutional, though there have never been wanting penetrating and discerning members who were ready enough to take exceptions where they found any plausible ground for them. I shall enumerate a few.

In the act entitled, an act for the punishment of certain crimes against the United States (vol. 1. Swift's edition, p. 100.[18]) among other crimes specified, are the following.

Murder or larceny in a fort belonging to the United States. Misprision of felony committed in any place under the sole and exclusive jurisdiction of the United Sttates. Stealing or falsifying a record of any court of the United States. Perjury in any court of the United States. Bribing a judge of the United States. Obstructing the execution of any kind of process issuing from a court of the United States.[19]

In the collection act, 1 vol. p. 237, it is provided, that in all cases where an oath is by that act required from a master or other person having command of a ship or vessel, or from an owner or assignee of goods, wares and merchandize, his or her factor or agent, if the person so swearing shall swear falsely, such person shall, on indictment and conviction thereof, be punished by fine or imprisonment, or both, in the discretion of the court, before whom

---

18. Iredell's statute citations here and elsewhere in the charge were taken from Zephaniah Swift, ed., *The Laws of the United States of America,* 3 vols. (Philadelphia: Richard Folwell, 1796).
19. Sections 3, 6, 15, 16, 18, 21, and 22 of the Crimes Act of 1790. *Stat.,* 1:112.

such conviction shall be had, so as the fine shall not exceed one thousand dollars, and the term of imprisonment shall not exceed twelve months.[20]

In the act laying duties on distilled spirits, (vol. i. p. 324) in the 39th section it is provided as follows:

"If any supervisor, or other officer of inspection, in any criminal prosecution against them, shall be convicted of oppression or extortion in the execution of his office, he shall be fined not exceeding five hundred dollars, or imprisoned not exceeding six months, or both, at the discretion of the court; and shall also forfeit his office."[21]

These instances deserve great consideration; because I believe no candid man will deny that these provisions were constitutional exercises of authority, within the scope of the general authority conveyed, tho' not specially named as objects which it should be competent for Congress to provide for. And they certainly derive weight from the consideration, that the principle of them (which I believe was the case) was never objected to, tho' the expediency of some of the provisions may have been.

In further illustration of this subject, I shall state a case which was determined in this Court—The United States against *Worrell*, published in Mr. *Dallas*'s Reports, p. 384.[22] Where there was an indictment against the defendant for attempting to bribe Mr. *Coxe*, the Commissioner of the Revenue. The defendant was found guilty, and afterwards a motion was made in arrest of judgment, assigning, together with some technical objections, this general one, that the Court had no cognizance of the offence, because no act[23] of Congress had passed creating the offence and prescribing the punishment, but it was solely on the foot of the common law. The very able and ingenious gentleman who is the reporter of that case, and was the defendant's Counsel in it, in the course of his argument, makes the following observations, part of which are remarkably striking and pertinent to my present subject: "In relation to crimes and punishments, the objects of the delegated power of the United States are enumerated and fixed. Congress may provide for the punishment of counterfeiting the securities and current coin of the United States; and may define and punish piracies and felonies committed on the high seas, and offences against the law of nations. Art. i. § 8. And so, likewise, *Congress may make all laws which shall be necessary and proper for carrying into execution the powers of the General Government.* But here is no reference to a common law authority: Every power is matter of definite and positive grant; and the very powers that are granted cannot take effect until they are

---

20. Section 66 of the Collection Act of 1790. *Stat.*, 1:175-76.

21. Excise Act of 1791. *Stat.*, 1:208.

22. *United States v. Worrall* was decided at the April 1798 term of the Circuit Court for the district of Pennsylvania and is reported in *Dallas*, 2:384.

23. In the *Independent Chronicle* (Boston), May 30, 1799, "effect."

exercised through the medium of a law. Congress had *undoubtedly* a power to make a law, which should render it criminal to offer a bribe to the Commissioner of the Revenue; but not having made the law, the crime is not recognized by the Federal code, Constitutional or Legislative; and consequently, it is not a subject on which the Judicial authority of the Union can operate."[24] So far the observations of the defendant's Counsel. Judge *Chase*, who on that occasion differed from Judge *Peters*, as to the common law jurisdiction of the Court, held, that under the 8th section of the first article, which I am now considering, although bribery is not among the crimes and offences specially mentioned, it is certainly included in that general provision; and Congress might have passed a law on the subject, which would have given the Court cognizance of the offence. Judge Peters was of opinion, that the defendant was punishable at common law; but that it was competent for Congress to pass a Legislative act on the subject.

I conclude, therefore, that the first objection is not maintainable.

With regard to the second objection, which is, That this law is not warranted by that clause in the Constitution authorising Congress to pass all laws which shall be necessary and proper for carrying into execution the powers specially enumerated, and all other powers vested by the Constitution in the Government of the United States, or in any department or officer thereof; because it is not necessary and proper to pass any such law in order to carry into execution any of those powers, it is to be observed, that from the very nature of the power it is and must be discretionary. What is necessary and proper in regard to any particular subject, cannot, before an occasion arises, be logically defined, but must depend upon various extensive views of a case which no human foresight can reach. What is necessary and proper in a time of confusion and general disorder, would not perhaps be necessary and proper in a time of tranquillity and order. These are considerations of policy, not questions of law, and upon which the Legislature is bound to decide according to its real opinion of the necessity and propriety of any act particularly in contemplation. It is, however, alledged, that the necessity and propriety of passing collateral laws for the support of others is confined to cases where the powers are delegated, and does not extend to cases which have a reference to general danger only. The words are general, "for carrying into execution the special powers previously enumerated, and all other powers vested by the Constitution in the Government of the United States, or any department or officer thereof." If therefore there be any thing necessary and proper for carrying into execution any or all of those powers, I presume that may be constitutionally enacted. Two objects are aimed at by every rational Government, more especially by free ones. 1. That the people may understand the laws, and voluntarily obey them. 2. That if this be not done by any individual, he shall be compelled to obey them, or punished for disobedience. The

24. *Dallas*, 2:391.

first object is undoubtedly the most momentous, for as the legitimate object of every Government is the happiness of the people committed to its care, nothing can tend more to promote this than that by a voluntary obedience to the laws of the country, they should render punishments unnecessary. This can never be the case in any country but a country of slaves, where gross misrepresentation prevails, and any large body of the people can be induced to believe that laws are made either without authority or for the purpose of oppression. Ask the great body of the people who were deluded into an insurrection in the western parts of Pennsylvania, what gave rise to it?[25] They will not hesitate to say, that the Government had been vilely misrepresented, and made to appear to them in a character directly the reverse of what they deserved. In consequence of such misrepresentations, a civil war had nearly desolated our country, and a certain expence of near two millions of dollars was actually incurred, which might be deemed the price of libels, and among other causes made necessary a judicious and moderate land tax, which no man denies to be constitutional, but is now made the pretext of another insurrection.[26] The Liberty of the Press is indeed valuable. Long may it preserve its lustre! It has converted barbarous nations into civilized ones, taught Science to rear its head, enlarged the capacity, increased the comforts of private life, and, leading the banners of Freedom, has extended her sway where her very name was unknown. But as every human blessing is attended with imperfection, as what produces by a right use the greatest good, is productive of the greatest evil in its abuse, so this, one of the greatest blessings ever bestowed by Providence on his creatures, is capable of producing the greatest good or the greatest mischief. A pen in the hands of an able and virtuous man, may enlighten a whole nation, and by observations of real wisdom, grounded on pure morality, may lead it to the path of honour and happiness. The same pen in the hands of a man equally able, but with vices as great as the other's virtues, may, by arts of sophistry easily attainable, and inflaming the passions of weak minds, delude many into opinions the most dangerous, and conduct them to actions the most criminal. Men who are at a distance from the source of information[27] must rely almost altogether on the accounts they receive from others. If their accounts are founded in truth, their heads or hearts must be to blame if they think or act wrongly. But if their accounts are false, the best head and the best heart cannot be proof against their influence; nor is it possible to calculate the combined effect of innumerable artifices, either by di-

25. The Whiskey Rebellion in 1794.

26. The federal property tax was imposed through two acts: "An Act to provide for the valuation of Lands and Dwelling-Houses, and the enumeration of Slaves within the United States" (July 9, 1798), detailing the process for assessing private property, and "An Act to lay and collect a direct tax within the United States" (July 14, 1798), setting each state's apportionment. *Stat.,* 1:580, 597. For information on the opposition to the tax, known as the Fries Rebellion, see introduction to "Spring and Fall Circuits 1799."

27. In the *Independent Chronicle* (Boston), June 3, 1799, "contagion."

rect falsehood, or invidious insinuations, told day by day, upon minds both able and virtuous. Such being unquestionably the case, can it be tolerated in any civilized society that any should be permitted with impunity to tell falsehoods to the people, with an express intention to deceive them, and lead them into discontent, if not into insurrection, which is so apt to follow? It is believed no Government in the world ever was without such a power. It is unquestionably possessed by all the State Governments, and probably has been exercised in all of them: sure I am it has in some. If necessary and proper for them, why not equally so, at least, for the Government of the United States, naturally an object of more jealousy and alarm, because it has greater concerns to provide for? Combinations to defeat a particular law are admitted to be punishable. Falsehoods in order to produce such combinations, I should presume, would come within the same principle, as being the first step to the mischief intended to be prevented; and if such falsehoods with regard to one particular law are dangerous, and therefore ought not to be permitted without punishment, why should such which are intended to destroy confidence in Government altogether, and thus induce disobedience to every act of it? It is said, libels may be rightly punishable in Monarchies, but there is not the same necessity in a Republic. The necessity in the latter case, I conceive greater, because in a Republic more is dependent on the good opinion of the people for its support, as they are directly or indirectly the origin of all authority, which of course must receive its bias from them. Take away from a Republic the confidence of the people, and the whole fabric crumbles into dust.

I have only to add, under this head, that in order to obviate any probable ill use of this large discretionary power, the Constitution and certain Amendments to it, have prohibited in express words the exercise of some particular authorities which otherwise might be supposed to be comprehended within them. Of this nature is the prohibitory clause relating to the present object which I am to consider under the next objection.

3.[28] That objection is, That the act is in violation of this Amendment of the Constitution. (3d vol. Swift's Edition, p. 455. Article 3d.[29])

"Congress shall make no law respecting an establishment of religion, or prohibiting the free exercise thereof; or abridging the freedom of speech, or of the press; or the right of the people peaceably to assemble, and to petition the Government for a redress of grievances."

The question then is,

Whether this law has abridged the Freedom of the Press.

28. In the *Independent Chronicle* (Boston), June 3, 1799, "4."

29. Iredell means the First Amendment. His citations to the Bill of Rights differ from modern numbering because he was using Swift's edition of United States laws. This edition (also referred to as Folwell's edition) prints the text of the original twelve amendments as proposed to the states in 1789 with an endnote stating that the first two articles were not ratified. Swift, *Laws of the United States of America*, 3:454-7; Carter, "Zephaniah Swift and the Folwell Edition of the Laws of the United States," pp. 689-95.

Here is a remarkable difference in expressions as to the different objects in the same clause. They are to make no law *respecting* an establishment of religion, or prohibiting the free exercise thereof; or *abridging* the freedom of speech, or of the press. When as to one object they entirely prohibit any act whatever, and as to another object only limit the exercise of the power, they must in reason be supposed to mean different things. I presume, therefore, that Congress may make a law *respecting* the press, provided the law be such as not to *abridge its freedom*. What might be deemed the Freedom of the Press, if it had been a new subject, and never before in discussion, might indeed admit of some controversy. But so far as precedent, habit, laws and practices are concerned, there can scarcely be a more definite meaning than that which all these have affixed to the term in question.

We derive our principles of law originally from England. There the press, I believe, is as free as in any country of the world, and so it has been for near a century. The definition of it is, in my opinion, no where more happily or justly expressed than by the great Author of the Commentaries on the Laws of England,[30] which book deserves more particular regard on this occasion, because for near 30 years it has been the manual of almost every student of law in the United States, and its uncommon excellence has also introduced it into the libraries, and often to the favourite reading of private gentlemen; so that his views of the subject could scarcely be unknown to those who framed the Amendment to the Constitution, and if they were not, unless his explanation had been satisfactory, I presume the Amendment would have been more particularly worded, to guard against any possible mistake. His explanation is as follows:

"The Liberty of the Press is indeed essential to the nature of a free state: And this consists in laying no *previous* restraints upon publications, and not in freedom from censure for criminal matter when published. Every freeman has an undoubted right to lay what sentiments he pleases before the public; to forbid this, is to destroy the freedom of the press: but if he publishes what is improper, mischievous, or illegal, he must take the consequence of his own temerity. To subject the press to the restrictive power of a Licenser, as was formerly done, both before and since the revolution, is to subject all freedom of sentiment to the prejudices of one man, and make him the arbitrary and infallible judge of all controversial points in learning, religion, and government. But to punish (as the law does at present) any dangerous or offensive writings, which, when published, shall on a fair and impartial trial be adjudged of a pernicious tendency, is necessary for the preservation of peace and good order, of government and religion, the only solid foundations of civil liberty. Thus the will of individuals is still left free; the abuse only of that free will is the object of legal punishment. Neither is any restraint hereby laid upon freedom of thought or enquiry: liberty of private sentiment is still

30. William Blackstone.

left; the disseminating, or making public, of bad sentiments, destructive of the ends of society, is the crime which society corrects. A man (says a fine writer on this subject) may be allowed to keep poisons in his closet, but not publickly to vend them as cordials. And to this we may add, that the only plausible argument heretofore used for the restraining the just freedom of the press, "that it was necessary to prevent the daily abuse of it," will entirely lose its force when it is shewn (by a reasonable exercise of the laws) that the press cannot be abused to any bad purpose, without incurring a suitable punishment: whereas it never can be used to any good one, when under the control of an Inspector. So true will it be found, that to censure the licentiousness, is to maintain the liberty of the press." 4 Black. Com. 151.[31]

It is believed, that in every state in the union the common law principles concerning libels apply; and in some of the states words similar to the words of the amendment are used in the constitution itself, or a contemporary bill of rights of equal authority, without ever being supposed to exclude any law being passed on the subject. So that there is the strongest proof that can be of a universal concurrence in America on this point, that the freedom of the press does not require that libellers shall be protected from punishment.

But in some respects the act of congress is much more restrictive than the principles of the common law, or than perhaps the principles of any state in the union. For under the law of the United States the truth of the matter may be given in evidence, which at common law in criminal prosecutions was held not to be admissible; and the punishment of fine and imprisonment, which at common law was discretionary, is limited in point of severity, tho' not of lenity. It is to be observed too, that by the express words of the act both malice and falshood must combine in the publication, with the seditious intent particularly described. So that if the writing be false, yet not malicious, or malicious, and not false, no conviction can take place. This therefore fully provides for any publication arising from inadvertency, mistake, false confidence, or any thing short of a wilful and atrocious falshood. And none surely will contend that the publication of such a falshood is among the indefeasible rights of men, for that would be to make the freedom of liars greater than that of men of truth and integrity.

I have now said all I thought material on these important subjects. There is another upon which it is painful to speak, but the notoriety as well as the official certainty of the fact, and the importance of the danger make it indispensable. Such incessant calumnies have been poured against the government for supposed breaches of the constitution, that an insurrection has lately began for a cause where no breach of the constitution is or can be pretended. The grievance is the land tax act, an act which the public exigencies rendered unavoidable, and is framed with particular anxiety to avoid its falling oppres-

31. 4 Bl. *Comm.* *151-53.

sively on the poor, and in effect the greatest part of it must fall on rich people only. Yet arms have been taken to oppose its execution: officers have been insulted: the authority of the law resisted: and the government of the United States treated with the utmost defiance and contempt. Not being thoroughly informed of all particulars, I cannot now say within what class of offences these crimes are comprehended. But as some of the offenders are committed for treason, and many certainly have been guilty of combinations to resist the laws of the United States, I think it proper to point your attention particularly to those subjects. The provisions in regard to the former, so far as they may at present be deemed material or instructive, are as follow:

(Here the passages referred to were read.)[32]

The only species of treason likely to come before you is that of levying war against the United States. There have been various opinions, and different determinations on the import of those words. But I think I am warranted in saying, that if in the case of the insurgents who may come under your consideration the intention was to prevent by force of arms the execution of any act of the congress of the United States altogether (as for instance the land tax act, the object of their opposition) any forcible opposition calculated to carry that intention into effect was a levying of war against the United States, and of course an act of treason. But if the intention was, merely to defeat its operation in a particular instance, or through the agency of a particular officer, from some private or personal motive, though a high offence may have been committed, it did not amount to the crime of treason. The particular motive must however be the sole ingredient in the case, for if combined with a general view to obstruct the execution of the act, the offence must be deemed treason.[33]

With regard to the number of witnesses in treason, I am of opinion that two are necessary on the indictment as well as upon the trial in court. The provision in the constitution, that the two witnesses must be to the same overt-act (or actual deed constituting the treasonable offence) was in consequence of a construction which had prevailed in England, that though two witnesses were required to prove an act of treason, yet if one witness proved one act, and another witness another act of the same species of treason, (as for instance that of levying war) it was sufficient; a decision which has always appeared to me contrary to the true intention of the law which made two witnesses necessary—this provision being, as I conceived, intended to guard against fictitious charges of treason, which an unprincipled government might be

---

32. Treason is defined in Article III, section 3 of the Constitution and in section 1 of the Crimes Act of 1790. *Stat.*, 1:112.

33. Richard Peters, United States judge for the district of Pennsylvania, had previously asked Iredell to omit the last two sentences of this paragraph from the charge. See Richard Peters to James Iredell, March [22], 1799.

tempted to support and encourage, even at the expense of perjury, a thing much more difficult to be effected by two witnesses than one.[34]

An act of Congress which I have already read to you (that commonly called the sedition act) has specially provided in the manner you have heard, against combinations to defeat the execution of the laws. The combinations punishable under this act must be distinguished from such as in themselves amount to treason, which is unalterably fixed by the constitution itself. Any combinations, therefore, which before the passing of this act, would have amounted to treason, still constitute the same crime. To give the act in question a different construction, would do away altogether the crime of treason as committed by levying war, because no war can be levied without a combination for some of the purposes stated in the act, which must necessarily constitute a part though not the whole of the offence.

Long, gentlemen, as I have detained you, for which the great importance of the occasion, I trust, is a just apology, it will be useful to recollect, that ever since the first formation of the present government, every act which any extraordinary difficulty has occasioned, has been uniformly opposed before its adoption, and every art practised to make the people discontented after it; without any allowance for the necessity which dictated them, some seem to have taken it for granted that credit could be obtained without justice, money without taxes, and the honor and safety of the United States only preserved by a disgraceful foreign dependence. But, notwithstanding all the efforts made to vilify and undermine the government, it has uniformly rose in the esteem and confidence of the people. Time has disproved arrogant predictions; a true knowledge of the principles and conduct of the government has rectified many gross misrepresentations; credit has risen from its ashes; the country has been found full of resources, which have been drawn without oppression, and faithfully applied to the purposes to which they were appropriated; justice is impartially administered; and the only crime which is fairly imputable is, that the minority have not been suffered to govern the majority, to which they had as little pretension upon the ground of superiority of talents, patriotism, or general probity, as upon the principles of republicanism, the perpetual theme of their declamation. If you suffer this government to be destroyed, what chance have you for any other? A scene of the most dreadful confusion must ensue. Anarchy will ride triumphant, and all lovers of order, decency, truth and justice be trampled under foot. May that God whose peculiar providence seems often to have interposed to save these United

---

34. Article III, section 3 of the Constitution requires two witnesses to the same overt act for a conviction of treason. For the British provisions regarding treason that Iredell discusses, see William Hawkins, *A Treatise of the Pleas of the Crown,* in 2 books., 4th ed. (London: E. Richardson and C. Lintot, 1762), 2:258, 428; John Kelyng, *A Report of Divers Cases in Pleas of the Crown, Adjudged and Determined; In the Reign of the late King Charles II* (London: printed for Isaac Cleave, 1708), p. 9; and Thomas Raymond, *Reports of Divers Special Cases Adjudged in the Courts of King's Bench, Common Pleas, and Exchequer* 2d ed. (London: Henry Lintot, 1743), pp. 407, 408.

States from destruction, preserve us from this worst of all evils! And may the inhabitants of this happy country deserve his care and protection by a conduct best calculated to obtain them!

Circuit Court for the District of Connecticut
April 13, 1799   New Haven, Connecticut

No circuit court was held this term because a Supreme Court justice failed to appear. Judge Richard Law did attend court on April 13 and successive days until April 17, when he adjourned it to the next term.[1]

1. Docket Book, CCD Connecticut, RG 21, MWalFAR. Associate Justice Samuel Chase was unable to attend court because of illness. See Samuel Chase to James Iredell, April 28, 1799.

James Iredell to Hannah Iredell
April 18, 1799   Philadelphia, Pennsylvania

... I am perfectly well, but now much engaged in business. The Insurrection is for the present overcome, and the Prosecutions will soon commence _. I wish you would address your next letter to me here, and at the same time write a short line to Annapolis. It is possible (tho' I don't think it probable) that these Trials may make it of more consequence to me to stay here and conclude them, than to hold the Court at Annapolis, about which if necessary I shall consult all Parties concerned _ ...

ARS (Nc-Ar, Charles E. Johnson Collection). Addressed "Edenton, North Carolina." Postmarked "PHI   18   AP."

Circuit Court for the District of Georgia
April 20, 1799   Savannah, Georgia

The Georgia circuit court was opened on April 20 by Chief Justice Oliver Ellsworth and Judge Joseph Clay, Jr. On May 2 the court adjourned to the following term.[1]

1. Minutes, CCD Georgia, RG 21, GEpFAR.
On April 16, 1799, the Savannah *Columbian Museum* noted: "On Saturday last arrived in this City from Charleston, the Hon. OLIVER ELLSWORTH, Esq. Chief Justice of the United States."

James Iredell to William Paterson
April 24, 1799   Philadelphia, Pennsylvania

Philadelphia   April 24 1799.

[My De]ar Sir,
    The criminal business of this Court has unavoidably been so long delayed that tho' some Persons stand indicted for Treason it is not expected any

Trial can come on before Monday next.[1] I am under the necessity of leaving this City the latter end of next week in order to attend the Court at Annapolis. Though no Man can regret more than I do the uncommon extra duty you have had to perform, and for a part of it am under the greatest personal obligation to you, yet it has occurred to M[r] Peters and myself that it may be attended with the utmost benefit to the Public if you could without too much inconvenience assist us on this extraordinary occasion, one of the most important which may perhaps ever offer in our Country, and upon the [true] improvement of which may depend the tranquillity, if not the safety of this Country, for many years to come _ Be so good as to inform us [if] we may hope to see you _. I have heard nothing lately of M[r] Chase. I shall be very happy in any opportunity of repaying your kindness to me by saving you trouble on any Circuit of yours.

I beg the favour of you to present my respectful Compliments to M[rs] and Miss Paterson,[2] and am ever,

My dear Sir, with very great respect, Your faithful and obedient Servant

Ja Iredell.

ALS (NHi, Slavery Manuscripts).

1. The grand jury returned true bills for treason against John Fries and ten others for their part in the Northampton Rebellion. Only Fries was tried at the April 1799 term. Engrossed Minutes, April 22-May 17, 1799, CCD Pennsylvania, RG 21, PPFAR.

2. Cornelia Paterson (1780-1844), daughter of William and Cornelia (Bell) Paterson. Gertrude Sceery Wood, *William Paterson of New Jersey, 1745-1806* (Fair Lawn, N.J.: Fair Lawn Press, 1933), pp. 38, 200.

Richard Peters to William Paterson
April 24, 1799   Philadelphia, Pennsylvania

My dear Sir

In a personal Interview I could better inform you than by Letter of the extreme & indispensible Necessity there is for your Presence here. With you I should feel strong _ but being unfortunately too sympathetic I partake of the Feebleness of those I associate with _ For Godsake if you can come to us _ do it. I fear some Arrangement with M[r] Chace may be in the Way _ but there is no Service of an elimosinary Nature which ought not to give Way to the pressing Occasion which has induced me to prevail on M[r] I. to ask your Assistance.[1] I look upon the Issue of the present Trials to be a Crisis in the Affairs of this unfortunate State _ twice disgraced by infamous Insurrection.[2] A ridiculous or weak Turn [*letters inked out*] given to the Business we have now before us will give Strength & Spirit to the Party, forever on the Watch for such Events. This will not be confined to our Limits but will spread like a Flame to all the combustible Matter too generally dispersed in other Quarters.

With sincere Affection   I am truly yours

Richard Peters

On Monday the first Treason Trial begins & in the Fate of that the whole may be involved _

In Court _ Philad^a 24th Ap^l 1799

Judge Patterson _

ARS (PPIn). Addressed "New Brunswick   Jersey." Marked "To be forwarded   to Judge P. if not   at Home _ ." Postmarked "PHI   24   AP."

Written on the back of Peters's letter is the following note to Paterson from Edward Tilghman, a prominent Philadelphia attorney: "Fully expecting to see you in consequence of the within & Mr I^s Invitation to you, permit me to request that you will take up your Quarters with me _ You shall be perfectly at home _ "

1. See James Iredell to William Paterson, April 24, 1799.
2. The Whiskey Rebellion of 1794 and the Fries Rebellion of 1799.

James Iredell to Hannah Iredell

April 25, 1799   Philadelphia, Pennsylvania

... Though our Court has been constantly employed whenever there was business to do, and several Bills have been found for Treason, none of the Trials can come on before Monday next. As I believe Mr Chase has been detained by indisposition from going on to the Eastward, I have written to him to see if he can attend at Annapolis for me,[1] so as to enable me to finish all the business here at this Term _ Otherwise, I am afraid, a special Court will be unavoidable. But I shall at all events be at Richmond on the 22^d May, and I hope at home about the middle of June _ The Insurrection is completely suppressed, and the Troops returned I suppose there are at least 200 People attending the Court here on that account _ ...

ARS (Nc-Ar, Charles E. Johnson Collection). Addressed "Edenton, North Carolina." Postmarked "PHI   25   AP."

1. Letter not found, but see Samuel Chase to James Iredell, April 28, 1799.

William Paterson to James Iredell

April 27, 1799   New Brunswick, New Jersey

New Brunswick,
27th April, 1799.

Dear Sir,

Your letter reached me yesterday.[1] My state of health is by no means good. It requires nursing and attention. A severe cold, which I took on my return from Philad^a, and a sore throat, the consequence of it, laid me up for some time, and obliged me to keep pretty much in the house. I have also had an attack of the piles. Of these disorders I have at length got the better; but I am apprehensive, that fatigue and hard duty would cause a return of them. My situation is particular in another respect. At the request of the legislature I undertook to revise the laws of this State, or rather to form them anew. The work is nearly completed. I have promised, that the residue should be ready by their adjourned session, which will commence the 15ᵗʰ of next month.[2] My attendance at Philadᵃ will interfere with this business, and retard its execution. This, however, is but a secondary consideration.

Permit me to observe, that it appears to me, that you should continue at Philadᵃ till the criminals are tried. The judge, who commences the business, should close it. The Maryland court is of little importance; it is questionable, whether there will be so much as one argument or trial in that district the ensuing term. Clear it is, that the business in Maryland sinks into nothing when put in competition with the nature and magnitude of the causes, which demand your attention at Philadᵃ _ Let the Maryland court be adjourned by the marshal.[3] You will be able to dispatch all or most of the business at Philadᵃ and be in season to attend the court at Richmond.

If I was well and with you, I could be of no service.   Your's sincerely.

Wᵐ Paterson.

Be pleased to shew this letter to Judge Peters.

Judge Iredell.

ARS (NcD, James Iredell Sr. and Jr. Papers). Addressed to Iredell "now at   Philadᵉ."

1. See James Iredell to William Paterson, April 24, 1799.

2. In 1792 Paterson was asked by the New Jersey legislature to collect and revise the laws of that state to produce a uniform code. Paterson continued this work throughout the 1790s, submitting revised statutes for enactment by the state legislature. The entire revision was not completed and published until 1800. John E. O'Connor, *William Paterson: Lawyer and Statesman, 1745-1806* (New Brunswick, N.J.: Rutgers University Press, 1979), pp. 202-22; *Laws of the State of New Jersey* (Newark: N. Day, 1800).

3. The marshal was empowered to adjourn court by the Adjournment Act of 1794. *Stat.,* 1:369.

Samuel Chase to James Iredell ─────────────────────────────
April 28, 1799   Baltimore, Maryland

Baltʳ   28 April 1799.

Dear Sir/

I wrote You on the 16ᵗʰ of last Month, that I had given over all Hopes of going to New York, and it was out of my Power to attend at Connecticut or Vermont.[1] I have been recovering for the last Month, and intend to set off this Day week for New Hampshire. my Complaint is virtually removed, and my Strength greatly restored, Yet I fear the fatigue will bring on some one of my Complaints. I would with great Pleasure attend for You at

Annapolis, if I did not intend to set off on this Day week. _ [2] Judge Paca is now in Harford, and I expect him at my House tomorrow. I have seen Mʳ Hollingsworth,[3] he says there is no Business for the Grand-Jury. if this should be the Case I imagine, if You desire it M Paca will discharge them, & then

no Inconvenience can attend your not being at Annapolis ~~on~~ ^before^ fryday week. _

week ^if^ You are here on Thursday Week, You can go down in the Stage on fryday week _ Mʳ Moore the Clerk of the Court told my Son[4] that there was not one action for trial _ Mʳ Hollingsworth told Me that he had two Causes for trial. _ I am confident Mʳ Paca will adjourn the Court for four Days _ I expect to see You before You leave Philadelphia. _ I really think that it is so great Consequence to the public that the trials should be finished by You, that I think the Business (if any) in this District should give Way to it. after I converse with Judge Paca you shall hear again from Me or from him.

Accept my best Wishes   Your affectionate &   Most obedᵗ Servᵗ

Samuel Chase

ARS (NcD, James Iredell Sr. and Jr. Papers). Addressed to Iredell "at Mrˢ Yorks.   North. 2ᵈ Street   Philadelphia."

1. The letter referred to was written on March 17, not March 16. See note to Samuel Chase to William Paterson, March 17, 1799.

2. For Iredell's request that Chase substitute for him at the Maryland circuit court, see James Iredell to Hannah Iredell, April 25, 1799.

3. Zebulon Hollingsworth (1762-1824), United States attorney for the district of Maryland. [Joseph A. Stewart], *Descendants of Valentine Hollingsworth, Sr.* (Louisville: John P. Morton, 1925), p. 30; *SEJ*, 1:125-26.

4. Either Samuel Chase, Jr. (1773-1841) or Thomas Chase (1774-1826). Edward C. Papenfuse et al., *A Biographical Dictionary of the Maryland Legislature, 1635-1789*, 1 vol. to date (Baltimore: Johns Hopkins University Press, 1979), entry for Samuel Chase.

Circuit Court for the District of Vermont

May 1, 1799   Windsor, Vermont

Judge Samuel Hitchcock was present to open court, but the absence of Justice Samuel Chase forced him to adjourn the court from "day to day ... for the space of four days," after which he adjourned it to the next term.[1]

1. Circuit Docket, CCD Vermont, RG 21, MWalFAR. Chase was unable to attend court because of illness. See Samuel Chase to James Iredell, April 28, 1799.

James Iredell to Hannah Iredell

May 2, 1799   Philadelphia, Pennsylvania

... The trial of one of the Prisoners for Treason, after an ineffectual attempt to get a special Court in the county, commenced yesterday.[1] There is such an immense number of Witnesses to examine, and the Arguments of Counsel will be so long, that it was found absolutely impossible to Conclude it at one sitting, and perhaps it will yet continue two or three days, tho' we shall probably sit ten hours every day, as we did yesterday. The Jury in the mean time are kept constantly together under an Officer, and sleep in one room. My health is perfectly good, tho' a little fatigued by business. M[r] Paterson is too unwell to come here, and M[r] Chase being just going to the Eastward cannot attend for me at Annapolis, but as there is little or nothing to do there, and the business here of the utmost magnitude, they advise me, as well as Judge Peters, that I ought by all means to give the business here the preference. If the District Judge of Maryland, to whom I have written,[2] concurs in that opinion, I shall probably remain here till about the 14th James Johnston is still here, and perfectly well, and grows in my esteem and affection every day. He had determined to go to Princeton a day or two ago, but has been tempted so far to stay for this trial, which he attends constantly, and tho' there is a prodigious crowd I have procured him a very good seat next to the Clerk who is very obliging to him. ...

ARS (Nc-Ar, Charles E. Johnson Collection). Addressed "Edenton,   North Carolina."
    1. The motion to move the trial of John Fries from Philadelphia to Northampton County, Pennsylvania, was refused by the court on April 30, 1799. Wharton, *State Trials*, pp. 482-89.
    2. Letter to Judge William Paca not found.

William Paca to James Iredell

May 3, 1799   Baltimore, Maryland

Dear Sir

    I came to Town last Night and found your Letter at my friend M[r] Chase's.[1]

    We have only two Causes in our Circuit Court which stand for Trial and it is very doubtful whether the Parties in either Case will be ready. [I] hear of no Business for the Grand Jury[.]

    I think it of much more Consequence to the welfare of the United States that you should remain in Philadelphia to complete the criminal Business in which you are now engaged than to leave it unfinished to attend the Court at Annapolis: I shall therefore dismiss the Juries on the meeting of the Court and after adjourning for the [Day?] Time the Law prescribes from Day to Day adjourn the Court to the Court in Course[2]

    I am dear Sir   Y[r] ob. Humb. S[t]

                                                                    W[m] Paca

Bal. Town.
[d]3 _ May 1799.

ARS (NcD, James Iredell Sr. and Jr. Papers). Addressed to Iredell "at M[rs] Yorks   North 2[d] Street   Philadelphia." Postmarked "[BALT] MAY 2."

1. Letter not found, but see James Iredell to Hannah Iredell, May 2, 1799.

2. By the Adjournment Act of 1794 a circuit court could adjourn to the next term if no Supreme Court justice appeared within four days after its scheduled opening. *Stat.*, 1:369.

South-Carolina State-Gazette

May 6, 1799   Charleston, South Carolina

☞ *The Federal Circuit Court of the United States of America will sit this day at 11 o'clock in the forenoon. All Jurors, Witnesses and others concerned, are required to be punctual in their attendance at the court room.*

May 6.

(Charleston) May 6, 1799. Date and place are those of the newspaper.

Circuit Court for the District of South Carolina

May 6, 1799   Charleston, South Carolina

Judge Thomas Bee attended court, but Chief Justice Oliver Ellsworth's absence caused Bee to adjourn it to the following day. On May 7, the court was opened by Ellsworth and Bee, after which Ellsworth delivered a charge to the grand jury. The court adjourned on May 15.[1]

1. Minutes, CCD South Carolina, RG 21, GEpFAR; Oliver Ellsworth's Charge to the Grand Jury of the Circuit Court for the District of South Carolina, May 7, 1799 (q.v.).

The *City Gazette* (Charleston), May 7, 1799, noted that "The Chief Justice of the United States arrived in town yesterday, from Georgia; the Circuit Court of the United States will be held this day, in the Court-House, at eleven o'clock."

Oliver Ellsworth's Charge to the Grand Jury of the Circuit Court for the District of South Carolina

City Gazette

May 7, 1799   Charleston, South Carolina

Gentlemen of the Grand Jury,

THE matters of delinquincy to which your inquiry and presentments will extend, are, all offences against the United States, committed within the district of South-Carolina; or upon the high seas, by persons found here. Those offences are *chiefly* defined in the statutes, with which you are presumed to be acquainted: the residue are, either acts contravening the law of nations, cases which you will rarely meet with; or they are acts manifestly subversive of the national government, or of some of its powers specified in the constitution. I say *manifestly* subversive, to exclude acts of doubtful tendency, and confine criminality to clearness and certainty.

An offence *consists* in transgressing the sovereign will, whether that will be expressed, or obviously implied. Conduct therefore, clearly *destructive* of a government, or its powers, which the people have ordained to *exist*, must be criminal. It is not necessary to particularize the acts falling within this description, because they are readily perceived, and are ascertained by known and established rules; I mean the maxims and principles of the common law of our land. This law, as brought from the country of our ancestors, with here and there an accommodating exception, in nature of local customs, was the law of every part of the union at the formation of the national compact; and did, of course, *attach* upon or apply to it, for the purposes of exposition and enforcement. It is true, that the parties, acting in their sovereign capacity, might have discontinued that law, with respect to their new relations, and the duties thence arising, and have left them to arbitrary decisions: but that they *intended* a discontinuance so contrary to usage in similar cases, and so pregnant with mischief, is certainly not to be *presumed*; and is a supposition irreconcilable with those frequent references in the constitution, to[1] the common law, as a living code.

By the rules then, of a known law, matured by the reason of ages, and which Americans have ever been tenacious of as a birth-right, you will decide what acts are *misdemeanors*, on the ground of their opposing the existence of the national government, or the efficient exercise of its legitimate powers.

Such, gentlemen, very briefly, is the written and the unwritten law, which you will regard; and, by an impartial and faithful application, cause to be respected.

Although an indictment is but an accusation, leaving to the party the right of a traverse; yet it affects too nearly his fame and his liberty, to be founded on *suspicion*; and much less on *preposession*. If juries, instead of being a shield from oppression, would not become the *instruments* of it, let them look, not to the *opinions* of men, but their *actions*; and weigh them, not in the scales of *passion*, or of *party*, but in a *legal* balance—a balance which is undeceptive— which vibrates not with popular opinion; and which flatters not the pride of birth, or encroachments of power.

It is not, however, the whole design of your institution, to save the innocent: a less pleasing, but not a less essential part, is, to bring the guilty to punishment.

Punishment, it is said, of the Supreme Being, "is his *strange* work;"[2] and it certainly is so of every human being, who retains his social impressions. But 'till *avarice* and *ambition*, shall cease to progress with society, or become capable of a nobler restraint than *fear*, *penal* justice will be salutary, And we shall continue to admire that organization of inquests for its *certainty*, which combines with means of information and motives of arraignment, independency of condition and weight of character.

Unmoved by misconception of the severity of laws, you will also, I trust, be unembarrassed with the *policy* of them. Whether they are wise or not, are to be sure, questions of responsiblity with those who *enact* them: tho' frequently dependent so much on a knowledge of the past and of the future, as well as of the present; so much on opinion, in reconciling domestic interests; and so little on calculation, in managing those which are foreign, as not to be easily decided. Admitting, however, that the purity and the patriotism of our legislators, still leave them liable to err; it does not impair, at all, the obligation of the citizen to obey, or of the magistrate to execute. 'Till they overleap the constitution, which, guarded as they are by revisionary checks, and dependent as they are on public confidence, is not to be expected; and, certainly, not believed to have *happened,* while a saving construction remains: 'Till then, the laws they prescribe are *sacred,* and should be *resistless.* Neither the judicial, or executive department, can, for a moment, refuse them effect. It violates, together with their oaths, that distribution of power, without which civil liberty amounts to little, and republican hopes to *nothing.* It is, under our constitution, a *mutiny* of authorities; and, in our condition, a mutiny is a *tempest!*

To this sketch of your duty, gentlemen, it cannot be necessary to add persuasion. You *feel* that you have a *country,* and believe there is a *God.*

(Charleston) May 15, 1799. Date and place are determined from the headline.

The charge was also printed by the *Daily Advertiser* (New York), May 29, 1799; *Claypoole's American Daily Advertiser* (Philadelphia), May 31, 1799; *Philadelphia Gazette,* June 4, 1799; *American* (Baltimore), June 5, 1799; *Federal Gazette* (Baltimore), June 10, 1799; *Independent Chronicle* (Boston), June 13, 1799; *Farmer's Weekly Museum* (Walpole, New Hampshire), June 17, 1799; *Newport Mercury* (Newport, Rhode Island), June 18, 1799; *Columbian Centinel* (Boston), July 7, 1799; *Virginia Argus* (Richmond), August 9, 1799.

1. In the Baltimore *American,* June 5, 1799, "of."

2. Probably a reference to Isaiah 28:21. We are indebted to William R. Casto for his help in finding the source of this quotation.

Reply of the Grand Jury of the Circuit Court for the District of South Carolina

City Gazette

May 7, 1799   Charleston, South Carolina

The Grand Jury of the Federal Circuit Court for the district aforesaid, held at the city of Charleston for said district, on the seventh day of May, Anno Domini 1799, beg leave to return their acknowlegements to his honor the Chief Justice of the United States of America, for his excellent charge, and request the same may be published; at the same time inform him, they have no presentments to make.

James Gregorie, Foreman.

David Cruger,	*Daniel Hart,*
Daniel Hall,	*Hugh Patterson,*
William Doughty,	*Benjamin Russell,*
Thomas Bradford,	*John Lewis Poyas,*
Edwin Gairdner,	*John Reid,*
John Barron,	*James Grierson,*
William Tunno,	*Thomas Martin.*
Robert Flemming,	

(Charleston) May 15, 1799. Date and place are those given in the reply.

Circuit Court for the District of Maryland ——————————————
May 7, 1799   Annapolis, Maryland

On May 7 Judge William Paca attended court, but the absence of Justice James Iredell forced him to adjourn it to the next day. Paca continued to adjourn the court on the successive days required by law until May 10, when he adjourned court to the next term.[1]

1. Minutes, CCD Maryland, RG 21, PPFAR; William Paca to James Iredell, May 3, 1799 (q.v.). Associate Justice James Iredell was unable to attend this court because of the trials of the Northampton insurgents at the Circuit Court for the district of Philadelphia.

Charles Lee to John Adams ——————————————
May 10, 1799   Philadelphia, Pennsylvania

                                               Philadelphia   10 may 1799
Sir
The trial of Fries for high treason which was commenced on monday the 6th instant and which from that period has alone occupied the court was concluded yesterday at 10 oclock at night. The prisoner had the assistance of able counsel Dallas Lewis and Ewing and after a fair & patient trial before an impartial court has by an unexceptionable jury been found guilty.

During the trial of the prisoner I was not present in court, not wishing to hear a part and not having leisure to hear the whole. I am informed that Justice Iredell and Judge Peters concurred in the sentiments which each expressed in a charge to the jury, and that the verdict meets their approbation.

The circuit court of Virginia to which Justice Iredell is necessary is by law to commence its session on the 22d, but may be adjourned by the marshall in case of the non attendance of the circuit Justice for four days successively thereafter.

As many witnesses are attending here, ~~and~~ in prosecutions against several persons now in gaol under the charge of high treason, I was this morning informed by Mr Iredell he should remain here as long as possible consistent with holding the court in Virginia which will permit him to remain here till the 18th The court in Maryland fails of course.

It will not be practicable to finish the criminal business in so short a period as abovementioned, and consequently I presume a special adjourned court will be held here in the month of the July.

I have the honor to be with perfect respect   Sir your most obedient servant

Charles Lee

ARS (MHi, Adams Manuscript Trust).
   Charles Lee (1758-1815), attorney general of the United States. *DAB*.

James Iredell to Hannah Iredell ————————————————————
   May 11, 1799   Philadelphia, Pennsylvania

... I have unexpectedly heard of an opportunity to Edenton to day, and have scarcely a moment to write by it. The extraordinary fatigue I underwent made my head ache a little yesterday, tho' it did not prevent my attending the Court, but as we adjourned early I am quite refreshed to day, and the indisposition of the Attorney for the District allows me a kind of holiday which will prove a great relief. The Man tried for High Treason, after a trial of nine days, was convicted of it. Nothing could be more affecting than the circumstances. The Jury went out about 8 o'clock, and at their request we adjourned to ten. Though we were punctual to a moment, the Court was so full that we could scarcely get through to our seats. The Jury soon after were announced, and after the Clerk put the usual question whether he was guilty or not guilty, the Foreman after a most solemn pause, and in a very affecting tone of voice, pronounced him guilty, which had evidently a most solemn effect on every Person present. Though Mr Peters and myself were clear that such ought to be the Verdict, we both felt a great deal when it was actually pronounced _ . I could not bear to look on the poor Man, but I am told he fainted away. He behaved through the whole of his trial with great modesty and propriety. He now lies in the deepest distress prostrate on the Earth, but acknowledges the fairness of his trial, and the justice of the Verdict. I dread the task I have to perform in pronouncing sentence on him. _ Having been strong advised to remain here as long as I possibly can for the sake of these trials, I have written to the District Judge and the Marshall to adjourn the Court at Richmond from day to day till the 25th, when if I am alive and well I shall certainly be there, and possibly a day or two sooner.[1] Six Trials for Treason, and many for Misdemeanors still remain. I expect one more of the former, but as the points of law are all
by ˄ settled I hope it will not be very long.

James Iredell by Charles Balthazar Julien Févret de Saint-Mémin
(1770-1852). Engraving, 1799.
Courtesy National Portrait Gallery, Smithsonian Institution. Gift
of Mr. and Mrs. Paul Mellon,
1974.

There is a very ingenious Man here who takes a large Picture, and gives a
miniature Print and twelve Copies for 25 Dollars, and as many more copies
as are desired at a dollar a dozen _ .[2] I have been tempted to avail of the
opportunity to oblige (as I hope it will do) some of my Friends, and now
send the large Picture and 16 small ones. ...

ARS (Nc-Ar, Charles E. Johnson Collection). Addressed "Edenton,   North Carolina."
    1. Letters to Judge Cyrus Griffin and Marshal David Meade Randolph not found.
    2. Charles Balthazar Julien Févret de Saint-Mémin (1770-1852), French-born artist and
engraver, who perfected the technique of miniature portrait engraving. *DAB*. See his miniature
of James Iredell reproduced above.

Federal Gazette ──
    May 14, 1799   Norfolk, Virginia

    Judge Iredell, who has presided at the circuit court in Philadelphia, was
by appointment to have commenced the session at Richmond on the 22d
inst.—but he wrote to the marshal of Virginia to adjourn the court from
day to day (which he is authorised to do for 3 days) until he arrives and to
give notice that no person need attend until the 25th.

(Baltimore) May 23, 1799. Date and place are those of the headline.

Philadelphia Gazette ————————————————————————————————
May 15, 1799   Philadelphia, Pennsylvania

[*After reporting on the lengthy trial of six of the people involved in Fries's Rebellion, this article notes that*] it is probable no other cause will come on this term, as Judge Iredell has signified his absolute engagement to attend court in Virginia, so that he must go on Saturday next. ...

(Philadelphia) May 15, 1799. Date and place are those of the headline.

Reply of the Grand Jury of the Circuit Court for the District of Pennsylvania ————————————————————————

Claypoole's American Daily Advertiser
May 15, 1799   Philadelphia, Pennsylvania

Philadelphia,   May 15th, 1799.

SIR,

THE Grand Jury of the Circuit court of the District of Pennsylvania, have heard with great satisfaction, the Charge delivered to them, on the opening of the Court.[1]

At a time like the present, when false philosophy and the most dangerous and wicked principles are spreading with rapidity, under the imposing garb of Liberty, over the fairest countries of the Old World—they are convinced, that the publication of a Charge, fraught with such clear and just observations on the nature and operation of the constitution and laws of the United States, will be highly beneficial to the citizens thereof.

With these sentiments strongly impressed on their minds, they unanimously request, that a Copy of the said Charge may be delivered to them, for publication; especially for the information of those, who are too easily led by the misrepresentations of evil disposed persons, into the commission of crimes, ruinous to themselves, and against the peace and dignity of the United States.

ISAAC WHARTON, Foreman,
J. ROSS,
EDWARD PENNINGTON,
PHILIP NICKLIN,
JOSEPH PARKER NORRIS,
BENJ. W. MORRIS,
THOMAS M. WILLING,
ROBERT RALSTON,
JOHN CRAIG,
SAMUEL COATES,

DAVID H. CONYNGHAM,
JOHN PEROT,
JAMES C. FISHER,
DANIEL SMITH,
GIDEON HILL WELLS,
Wm. MONTGOMERY,
W. BUCKLEY.

Honorable
Judge IREDELL.

(Philadelphia) May 17, 1799. Date and place are those of the reply.
    1. See James Iredell's Charge to the Grand Jury of the Circuit Court for the District of
Pennsylvania, April 11, 1799.

Reply to the Grand Jury of the Circuit Court for the District of
Pennsylvania by James Iredell ────────────────────────
Claypoole's American Daily Advertiser
    May 15, 1799   Philadelphia, Pennsylvania

*To the Gentlemen of the Grand Jury of the United States, for the district of
Pennsylvania.*
Gentlemen,
    I receive with great sensibility the honour of this address, from gentlemen
whom I personally respect so much. Believing, as I have long done, that the
constitution and laws of the United States afford the highest degree of rational
liberty which the world ever saw, or of which perhaps mankind are capable,
I have seen with astonishment and regret, attempts made in the pursuit of
visionary chimeras, to subvert or undermine so glorious a fabric, equally
constructed for public and private security. It cannot but be extremely pleasing
to me, that the sentiments on this subject I delivered in my charge, should
meet with your entire approbation; and as you are pleased to suppose the
publication of them may be of some service in correcting erroneous opinions,
I readily consent to it, considering your sanction of them as giving them an
additional value, which will increase the hope of their producing a good effect.

                                                            Ja. IREDELL.

Philadelphia,   May 15th, 1799.

(Philadelphia) May 17, 1799. Date and place are those of the reply.

James Iredell to Hannah Iredell ─────────────────────────
May 16, 1799   Philadelphia, Pennsylvania

...My stay here does not arise from the difficulty of tearing myself from Philadelphia, but from the immense weight and importance of the criminal business of this Court, the greatest part of which I must yet leave undone. It has oppressed me beyond measure, tho' my health is tolerably good. The other day when Fries was brought up to receive his sentence his Counsel moved for a new Trial, which has occasioned an additional delay of more than two days. I hope it will be finished to day.[1] I expect to leave Town on Saturday. I have bought Muslin enough to make you two Gowns, and shall send the Coffee you desire. The Muslin Mrs Wilson chose. She seemed very well pleased with your letter, and I think it was very well written. I thank my dear Annie for hers, and regret I cannot now answer it, but it is impossible, as my head is entirely taken up with Law points which require all my attention. ...

ARS (Nc-Ar, Charles E. Johnson Collection). Addressed "Edenton, North Carolina." Postmarked "PHI 6 MY."
    1. Fries's counsel moved for a new trial on May 14; on May 17 the court ordered that a new trial be granted. Wharton, *State Trials*, pp. 598-609.

Claypoole's American Daily Advertiser ─────────────────────
May 18, 1799   Philadelphia, Pennsylvania

[*After recounting the decision of the judges of the Circuit Court for the district of Pennsylvania to grant John Fries a new trial on procedural grounds, this article notes:*] The persons convicted of conspiracy, rescue and obstruction of process, will receive their sentence this morning. After which, it is expected the Court will adjourn, as Judge IREDELL is obliged to leave town on Monday morning to attend his duty in Virginia.

(Philadelphia) May 18, 1799. Date and place are those of the headline.

Samuel Johnston to James Iredell ──────────────────────────
May 18, 1799   Williamston, North Carolina

...I declined writing to you by the three last Posts not knowing, with certainty, at what place to address you, in the interim I have been favored with three of your letters, for which I am very much your debtor.
    . . .
    I think your determination to continue the Court at Philadelphia till you got thro the business of the insurrection was judicious, should any of them

be convicted who might, in any sense, be considered as leaders or first movers in the business, it would be well to [*word inked out*] suffer the law to take it's course in a few instances, a little severity at this time would not be amiss, in order to convince the populace that Government was not to be trifled with, how ever lightly or contemptuously their Demagogues may have taught them to consider it. ...

ARS (Nc-Ar, Charles E. Johnson Collection). Addressed "Richmond   Virginia."

James Iredell to Hannah Iredell —————————————————————————
    May 19, 1799   Philadelphia, Pennsylvania

... The Business of the Court was so protracted that it was utterly impossible for me to get away yesterday. I am to go tomorrow. Evidence at length was produced so irrefragable of one of the Jurors having made strong prejudiced declarations against Fries previous to his Trial that contrary to my wishes, bias, and inclination I was at length compelled to vote for his having a new Trial, and Judge Peters with some hesitation acquiesced. Five others were yesterday sentenced to Fine and Imprisonment. Though I have suffered infinite fatigue, my health was much less affected than could be expected. I am now quite well _. ...

ARS (Nc-Ar, Charles E. Johnson Collection). Addressed "Edenton,   North Carolina."

Aurora ——
    May 20, 1799   Philadelphia, Pennsylvania

Judge Iredell has commenced lectures upon men and things; instead of confining himself, as it is his duty, to say what the law is, and to point out the path in which Jurors ought to walk, he enters into political disquisitions, advances opinions extraneous to his functions, and exhibits himself a disciple of party; Is it fit that a Judge, who ought to be the most pure, the most impartial, and the most dispassionate of men, should enter into the politics of the day while in the administration of his august functions?[1] Can justice be fairly dispensed by a Judge, who permits the sensations of party to intrude themselves upon him? It is well known that party feelings often throw an improper bias upon the most upright minds, would it not then be more becoming for a Judge to abstain from political disquisitions, that like Cæsar's wife he might not only be pure but unsuspected?

    The Grand Jury *well selected* and as well calculated to echo the sentiments of any Judge say something about "*false philosophy*," and the most *dangerous* and *wicked principles* which are spreading with rapidity, under the imposing garb of liberty, over the fairest countries of the world"[2]—if any thing can be termed *false philosophy* it must be the perversion of judicial functions to political or party purposes, and if dangerous and wicked principles exist they must exist where the different departments of a government combine to support (not check) each other at the expence of the people. In the fashionable language of *federalism*, liberty means arbitrary power, hence the Irish are *free*, and are abused for wishing to rid themselves of their *liberty*. *Venice* and *Rome* too were *free*, and hence the moanings of the *federalists* over the departed liberty of those two States—the liberty which is now enjoyed in *Ireland*, and was lately enjoyed in *Rome* and *Venice*, is no doubt wished to be transferred to the United States, out of pure love for the people, and hence the lamentations of some Judges and Jurors over the fate of *republicanized* Europe!

(Philadelphia) May 20, 1799. Date and place are those of the headline.

1. See James Iredell's Charge to the Grand Jury of the Circuit Court for the District of Pennsylvania, April 11, 1799.

2. See Reply of the Grand Jury of the Circuit Court for the District of Pennsylvania, May 15, 1799.

Circuit Court for the District of New Hampshire ———————
May 20, 1799   Portsmouth, New Hampshire

On Monday, May 20, Associate Justice Samuel Chase and Judge John Pickering convened the court and on May 22 adjourned it to the next term.[1]

1. Records, CCD New Hampshire, RG 21, MWalFAR.

Circuit Court for the District of Virginia ———————
May 22, 1799   Richmond, Virginia

The circuit court for the district of Virginia was scheduled to begin its session on May 22, but Associate Justice James Iredell did not appear until May 25.[1] He delivered a charge to the grand jury and held court alone until June 1, when Judge Cyrus Griffin joined him. The court adjourned on June 7 to the following term.[2]

1. In a letter to Hannah Iredell, on May 11 (q.v.), Iredell stated that he had written to the district judge for Virginia and informed him that no one need attend court until May 25.

On May 21, 1799, the *Virginia Gazette, and General Advertiser* (Richmond), carried a notice from the Virginia marshal, dated May 17, 1799, advising jurors "that the necessary detention of his honour Judge Iredel, at the circuit court now sitting in Philadelphia, on important criminal business, will occasion the circuit court, which commences in this city on Wednesday next, to adjourn from day to day till the judge arrives. It is therefore recommended that jurors and others may not attend the same sooner than Saturday the 25th."

2. Order Book, CCD Virginia, Vi. Charge not found.

North-Carolina Minerva ——————————————————————————
May 28, 1799   Raleigh, North Carolina

The Circuit Court of the United States commences on Saturday next the first of June—and from the arrival on Sunday last of the Honourable Judge Ellsworth, we are led to believe he is to preside.

As the district of North Carolina has been latterly deprived of Courts by the indisposition of the Judges, &c. so as to prevent their reaching Raleigh, we have thought proper to mention the arrival of the Chief Justice of the United States, that the citizens of this and other states having business, may not apprehend danger of being disappointed by similar casualties.[1]

(Raleigh) May 28, 1799. Date and place are those of the headline.

1. There had been three recent instances of Supreme Court justices missing a session of the Circuit Court for the district of North Carolina. Associate Justice John Blair and Chief Justice John Rutledge did not attend the spring and fall 1795 terms respectively because of illness, and Samuel Chase never appeared in the spring of 1797 because of transportation problems.

Circuit Court for the District of Massachusetts ——————————
June 1, 1799   Boston, Massachusetts

On June 1 Associate Justice Samuel Chase and Judge John Lowell convened court. On Monday, June 3, *Russell's Gazette* (Boston) reported on the opening of the court and noted that Samuel Chase was to deliver a charge "at 11 o'clock, this day." The court adjourned on June 11.[1]

1. Final Records, CCD Massachusetts, RG 21, MWalFAR. Charge not found.

Circuit Court for the District of North Carolina ——————————
June 1, 1799   Raleigh, North Carolina

Court was opened by Chief Justice Oliver Ellsworth and Judge John Sitgreaves. The court met until June 11, when it adjourned to the next term.[1]

1. Minutes, CCD North Carolina, RG 21, GEpFAR.

James Iredell to Hannah Iredell ————————————————————
June 5, 1799   Richmond, Virginia

...I continue quite well, tho' every day much fatigued by the immensity of business here. The Chancery Court being unfortunately sitting, we cannot go into Court till eleven, but we remain there usually till 5 or 6. There is still a great deal to be done, and I shall exert myself to the utmost in order to finish on Saturday, in which case I hope to have the happiness of embracing you on Wednesday. If I should be unfortunately disappointed, you may be assured it is altogether owing to an unavoidable delay of business. ...

ARS (Nc-Ar, Charles E. Johnson Collection). Addressed "Edenton, North Carolina." Postmarked "R'D June 4." We cannot account for the discrepancy between the date of Iredell's letter and the postmark.

Oliver Ellsworth to James Iredell
June 10, 1799   Raleigh, North Carolina

... I thank you very sincerely for your letter from Richmond,[1] & for the great pleasure I had in reading your luminous & pointed charge. That you left a great deal of business undone at Philadelphia, was doubtless a publick misfortune, but it was a still greater that it became necessary to undo what had been done.[2] ...

ARS (NcD, James Iredell Sr. and Jr. Papers). Addressed "Edenton."
    1. Letter not found.
    2. A reference to the need to retry John Fries because a member of the jury had expressed a predisposition to convict.

Circuit Court for the District of Rhode Island
June 15, 1799   Newport, Rhode Island

On June 15 the circuit court commenced its session with Associate Justice Samuel Chase and Judge Benjamin Bourne in attendance. Chase delivered a charge to the grand jury on the same day. The court sat until June 19, when it adjourned to the next term.[1]

    1. Minutes, CCD Rhode Island, RG 21, MWalFAR. Charge not found, but see *Newport Mercury* (Newport, Rhode Island), under date of June 18.

William Richardson Davie to James Iredell
June 17, 1799   Halifax, North Carolina

... I would have written to you while you was in Virginia, but the length of the trials at Philadelphia seem'd to render it doubtful here whether you would be able to hold that Court, and I supposed it too late when I received your letter. It was a very fortunate circumstance in our present situation, that the insurrection in Pensylvania had made so little progress and so few proselytes; more examples than one of the energy of the laws [w]ould have been indispensable had there Treasonable designs taken a wider spread, and thus the last scene of every rebellion becomes the most afflictive to humanity. I am greatly obliged to you for the copy of your charge, it is extremely well written, and the times called for every sentiment it contained. ...

ARS (NcD, James Iredell Sr. and Jr. Papers). Addressed "Edenton N⁰ Carolina." Reading supplied in brackets where document is torn.

"Citizen" to James Iredell ——————————————
Independent Chronicle
June 17, 1799   Boston, Massachusetts

To JUDGE IREDELL.

Sir,

THOUGH you have discovered great talents, candour, and sincerity of heart, in your Charge to the Grand Jury for the United States: yet I have not the pleasure of viewing all the subjects on which you treat in the same light.[1] I therefore, with a republican freedom, take the liberty of addressing to yourself and the public, the objections that appeared to me on reading your able Charge.

I agree with you, that we should be thankful for the long continuance of Peace we have enjoyed. But as you go on with the portrait of our happy situation, and contrasting our situation with other countries, you say, no citizen of the United States, had any other grievance to complain of, but that he was required to obey those laws which his own representatives had made, and under a government which the people themselves had chosen; as although representatives of his own, or a government of his own choosing could not do wrong, nor make laws that should operate as grievances. In this, sir, I cannot agree with you, though the election of our representatives is an highly valuable right, yet that their being of our own choice should make them more perfect, I do not believe. That great imperfection exists in our General Government, as well as all others, is evident from disagreement. Supposing a motion was made in our House of Representatives, and they should be equally divided; I conceive that it would be a mathematical certainty, that one half would be wrong: and it appears from the same principle, that it is more likely that the whole would be wrong than right, as there is a certainty that half would be wrong, but no certainty that any part were right. It is supposed by the Constitution, that grievances may exist, by saying the people shall have a right to petition for a redress of grievances.—If a law should be made under these circumstances of imperfection, involving the most important consequences, that was in itself erroneous, (which from the above principle

(Boston) June 17, 1799. Date and place are those of the newspaper.

1. See James Iredell's Charge to the Grand Jury of the Circuit Court for the District of Pennsylvania, April 11, 1799 (q.v.).

appears more likely than otherwise) and should be conceived so by a majority of the people of the U. States: what would be the remedy? I am sensible the common answer is, neglect electing the same again; but how many cases are there in which that will not answer the purpose? a declaration of war, for one; the time for which our representatives are elected, is sufficient under many circumstances to decide the fate of the nation: when the fortune of war has determined the point, will putting the government into other hands recall what has passed? I conceive not. There is another remedy often mentioned, that we have a right to petition government for a redress of grievances: admitting we should petition for a redress of certain acts that were considered grievances, is there a probability that they would repeal them as long as they thought otherwise? If they should it would be very extraordinary: but that would not answer in case of a declaration of war—the nation or nations that are offended must be consulted.

After finishing your picture of other countries, you say, certain laws of this country have been grossly misrepresented; I cannot say they have not, but several of the objections you mention to have been made, appear to me unanswerable. First, that an alien ought not to be removed on suspicion, but on proof of some crime. You say it is believed that it never was suggested in any other country, that aliens had a right to go into a foreign country and stay at their will and pleasure, without any leave from the government. I think it may be asked, is there any country like this in situation, frame of government, laws, manners, and customs: I must needs say I know of none: If not, I cannot see any force in the argument. Many things that would be deemed necessary in a monarchy would be highly censurable in a republic, and what would be necessary in one republic, would not be in another, from their different circumstances.

We were once an appendage to Britain, but declaring ourselves independent, we took upon us the right of governing ourselves agreeable to the dictates of reason; without being dependent for a constitution, statutes, or common laws, upon any nation. You further ask, how many instances of such removals took place at the commencement of the war with Britain, and that no objection was then made to the authority, the expediency only was in question. I should think you would recollect, sir, that the restriction of authority that we are now talking of was not in being at that time; the Constitution that should now be the regulater of our General Government, I believe was not thought of at that time. With respect to the expediency, it appears necessary you should prove that it was expedient at that time, to make evidence of the expediency now. You say, likewise, that in cases like this, it is rediculous to talk of a crime, because perhaps the only crime that a man can be charged with, is his being born in another country: and having a strong attachment to it. If this is a crime, I believe you will find but few aliens but what are criminals. If this is the protest, why not with greater propriety remove all aliens indiscriminately. Though I think it more proper, yet I do not think even this expedient: for if all the aliens in the United States were removed to other countries, it would remove a considerable proportion of the population, and make enemies to our government and people that otherwise would be our friends.

But in treating further of the expediency of the measure, and describing the dangers our country is exposed to, and enumerating many examples; you say, those who object to this law, seem to pay no regard to considerations of this kind, and to entertain no other fear but that the President may exercise this authority for the mere purpose of abusing it; and that there is no end to such arguments: and if this power is proper, it must be exercised by some body. In the latter part of this clause I agree with you, that if the power is proper, it must be exercised by some body. But that it is as proper for an highly important power to be entrusted to one man, as several, I do not believe: neither can I see why an argument of this kind would not apply very well in favour of a monarchy; for I cannot see any difference between this, and saying a republican and representative government is cumbersome, unwieldy, and destitute of energy; of course better to place all power in the hands of one man: and to every one that should object, ask him what interest he could have in abusing his authority? and that even a numerous body of men may abuse their authority. But does it follow from that, that there is no more danger of an important power being abused by one man, than a numerous body of men? if it does, it is conclusive in favour of a monarchical government. But I believe a principle of this kind, would not be generally received.—With respect to the constitutionality of the law, you say, that the clause in the Constitution declaring that all crimes, except by impeachment, shall be tried by jury, can never, in reason, be expected to amount to a perpetual residence of all sorts of foreigners, unless convicted of some crime; but is evidently calculated for the security of a citizen: but, sir, the dictates of reason (as they appear to different people) being so changeable and uncertain, according to the various circumstances and feelings of different persons, (that is co-existent with the frailties of human nature) we have entered into a general compact, of general principles, that we have acknowledged to be reason: and if we are to digress into an endless train of reasonings upon those principles, and reason them all away, or to something else; and where the expression *all* is used, to say only a *part* in reason is meant, I cannot see the use of the compact. We have acknowledged it to be reasonable to guard against the frailties of man. That the executive and judiciary powers should be kept separate.

The accused Alien may offer evidence in his behalf, but who but the supreme Executive is to be judge of the force and applicability of the evidence.

With respect to the third objection you mention to have been made, that it is provided by the Constitution that Congress shall not prohibit the migration or importation of such persons as any of the states saw fit to admit prior to the year 1808, I agree with you, and that we should take it as it stands: though I believe with you, that nothing was meant by it but slaves. But I cannot see clearly, that because the General and State governments are vested with powers, that if exerted to their greatest extent, would prove highly dangerous, that no power that could be vested would be dangerous: if so, we might give them unlimited powers without any particular constitutions.

After completing your observations on the Alien Laws, you begin with the Sedition Act; saying, there is one objection made that is common to both Alien and Sedition Laws: that there is no specific power given to pass an act of this description, and that in the vestment of general powers to make laws for carrying into execution the particularized. In this, sir, I should agree with you, that Congress have power to make such laws if they should deem it necessary, if there had not been an amendment to the Constitution. In the 3d article of the amendment to the Constitution, there is the following clause.

Congress shall make no law respecting an establishment of religion, or prohibiting the free exercise thereof; or abridging the freedom of speech, or of the press, or the right of the people peaceably to assemble, and petition government for redress of grievances.[2]

It appears from this amendment, that the people of the United States were aware of the danger that might arise from the changability of man, to such an highly important right as *the freedom of the Press*, from making this express prohibition (as it appears to me) against Congress making any law respecting the *Press*.

Though you say, there is a remarkable difference in expressions as to the different objects in the same clause, as to one object they entirely prohibit any act whatever, and as to another object, only limit the exercise of the power. I cannot see in what the difference consists, neither have you made any explanation, which would have been highly important, if a conclusive explanation of the difference could have been made. You say, they are to make no law respecting an establishment of religion, and why respecting the *Press*, when reference is made to the first part of the clause, by the referatory word *or*.

As for the expediency you say but little, though you conclude that none will contend that it is among the indefeasible rights of men to publish falshood, and I believe as few will contend that it is among the indefeasible rights of a government, to make unconstitutional laws, or laws founded on false principles, and why not one as likely as the other to take place. You acknowledge that all originally depends on the people, and that we shall not

---

2. Actually a reference to the First Amendment. Contemporary printings of the Constitution often included the first two articles of amendment, which were not ratified by the states. Swift, *Laws of the United States of America,* 3:454-57.

have bad representatives, nor bad laws, until the people are in general bad themselves. Then if the people and government are mutually dependent on each other for truth and virtue, why should not the government trust to the people, to determine of truth for themselves, as well as the people trust the government with the exercise of such a power. I must conclude, Sir, with hoping if yourself or the public, should think I have taken more freedom than is consistent with Republicanism, you will pardon a well-meaning

CITIZEN.

Farmer's Weekly Museum —————————————————————————————
June 17, 1799   Walpole, New Hampshire

Among the more vigorous productions of the American pen, may be justly enumerated the various charges, delivered by the Judges of the United States, at the opening of their respective courts. In these useful addresses to the jury, we not only discern sound legal information, conveyed in a style at once popular and condensed, but much political and constitutional knowledge. The Chief Justice of the United States has the high power of giving men much and most essential information, in a style the very model of closeness and dignity. His charge, in the first page of this paper, is an illustrious example.[1] Forcible, nervous,[2] well arranged, and compact—it is "like the last embattling of a Roman legion."

(Walpole, New Hampshire) June 17, 1799. Date and place are those of the headline.
   1. A reference to Oliver Ellsworth's Charge to the Grand Jury of the Circuit Court for the District of South Carolina, May 7, 1799 (q.v.).
   2. "Vigorous, powerful, forcible." *OED.*

Newport Mercury —————————————————————————————————————
June 18, 1799   Newport, Rhode Island

The Circuit Court of the United States, for the District of Rhode-Island, convened in this Town on Saturday last, and a Charge was delivered by the Hon. Judge CHASE, in which was displayed all the Energy, Patriotism, and sound legal Knowledge, for which the learned Judge is so eminently distinguished.

(Newport, Rhode Island) June 18, 1799. Date and place are those of the headline.

Circuit Court for the District of Delaware ————————————
June 27, 1799   New Castle, Delaware

Associate Justice William Paterson and Judge Gunning Bedford, Jr., opened court on June 27. The docket of the circuit court does not record the court's closing. The "teste" day was June 29.[1]

1. Appearance Docket, CCD Delaware, RG 21, PPFAR.

Aurora ————————————————————————
July 25, 1799   Philadelphia, Pennsylvania

[*The* Aurora *reprints an* Albany Register *report of a Fourth of July celebration in Hartford, Connecticut at which a toast was drunk to Alexander Addison, a Pennsylvania state judge.*[1] *The report notes Addison's conversion to federalism at the time of the Whiskey Rebellion in 1794 and continues:*] his honour has been as flaming a *federalist*, as he was before a *democrat*; and his subsequent harrangues from the bench have partaken more or less of that political gall which super-eminently distinguishes the harangues of those federal judges who hold their offices of the President of the United States. To this remark, Judge Elsworth, we believe, forms an honarable exception. ...

(Philadelphia) July 25, 1799. Date and place are those of the newspaper.
1. Alexander Addison (1759-1807), judge of Pennsylvania's fifth judicial district. *The Biographical Encyclopædia of Pennsylvania of the Nineteenth Century* (Philadelphia: Galaxy Publishing, 1874), p. 637; Russell J. Ferguson, *Early Western Pennsylvania Politics* (Pittsburgh: University of Pittsburgh Press, 1938), p. 115.

"Citizen" to Oliver Ellsworth ————————————————
Virginia Argus
August 9, 1799   Richmond, Virginia

To OLIVER ELSWORTH, Esq.
Chief Justice of the United States.

SIR,
  Your charge to the grand jury for the district of South Carolina, proves you to be a man superior to most of your brethren.[1] That you are mistaken in some of your principles I verily believe and will endeavor to shew in the subsequent part of these observations; but before I attempt to do this, I will declare that I ascribe to you nothing but an error in opinion. Greatly to

(Richmond) August 9, 1799. Date and place are those of the newspaper. The headline indicates that this was reprinted from the Richmond *Examiner*.
1. See Oliver Ellsworth's Charge to the Grand Jury of the Circuit Court for the District of South Carolina, May 7, 1799.

your honor you have avoided an interference with political subjects; you
have not imitated the too frequent example of disgracing the bench of justice,
by passionate and indecent invectives against your fellow citizens, and against
foreigners; and above all you have not violated that sacred principle of our
constitution which separates the three great departments of government, by
an interference as a judge with legislative and executive affairs: it is true
that no complaint has been made by the other departments of this improper
conduct; this can only be accounted for by the judges having given their
utmost support to all the measures adopted by them. Let the state of things
be reversed, which is not a very improbable event; as the judges hold their
places by a more permanent tenure, than any other officers of the
government, and those who now believe that they derive advantage from
these unconstitutional acts would find that they had sacrificed a principle to
a particular object. Such an interference of the judges violates that distribution
of power without which you properly say, 'civil liberty amounts to little,
and republican hopes to nothing.' The following extract from your charge
does you the utmost honor as a judge, and as a man; and intitles you to the
thanks and esteem of your countrymen: 'Although an indictment is but an
accusation, leaving to the party the right of a traverse; yet it affects too nearly
his fame and his liberty, to be founded on suspicion; and much less on
prepossession. If juries, instead of being a shield from oppression, would
not become the instruments of it, let them look not to the opinions of men,
but their actions: and weigh them, not in the scales of passion, or of party,
but in a legal balance—a balance which is undeceptive—which vibrates not
with popular opinion; and which flatters not the pride of birth, or
encroachments of power.'—Having with sincerity expressed an approbation
of part of your charge, permit me with equal frankness to examine those
parts of it which appear exceptionable. You say 'an offence consists in
transgressing the sovereign will, whether that will be expressed, or obviously
implied. Conduct therefore, clearly destructive of a government, or its powers,
which the people have ordained to exist, must be criminal. It is not necessary
to particularize the acts falling within this description, because they are readily
perceived, and are ascertained by known and established rules; I mean the
maxims and principles of the common law of our land'—This doctrine
embraces such an immense scope, that it is difficult at one view to perceive
its extent and operation. If any subject ever merited the most serious attention
of the people of America, this does; as it involves every thing most valuable
to man; life, liberty, and property are all at stake. The question which presents
itself at the threshold of this inquiry, is whether the common law of England
be the law of the United States. You say that "this law as brought from the
country of our ancestors, with here and there an accommodating exception,
in nature of local customs, was the law of every part of the union at the
formation of the national compact; and did, of course, attach upon us or
apply to it, for the purpose of exposition or enforcement." That each state

had a modification of what is called the common law I admit; but that there is a common law of the United States, I deny, and challenge any man to shew it; even if there had been such a law, it would not now be the law, unless its adoption had been authorized by the convention. This opinion is supported by the authority of the conventions, who framed the state constitutions; as they thought it necessary to adopt their former codes; so that it does not necessarily "attach," as it neither previously existed, nor if it had, would it have continued law, unless it had been reinacted. If the common law for each state, is the law of the United States, upon the ground of prior existence, so are the state laws; for they are not of less authority for being written. If the federal courts have authority under one, they have under the other; and have jurisdiction of every subject in common with the state courts. The written and unwritten laws of each state, form an intire code. Neither is complete without the other. By what course of reasoning it can be shewn, that a part of the laws of the states are the laws of the United States, I cannot conceive. By adopting the laws of the states, you are involved in this dilemma; you must decide that some acts are crimes in one state, that are innocent in others, and that the law of the United States, is not uniform in its penalties. If the common law did not "attach upon us," we could only have got it by adoption, but I cannot find any part of the constitution that justifies such a conclusion; on the contrary, great pains seem to have been taken to ascertain what should be considered as the law of the U.S. In the 3d art. sec. 2d, the constitution declares that "the judicial power shall extend to all cases, in law and equity, arising under this constitution; the laws of the United States, and treaties made, or which shall be made, under their authority.' In the 6th article it is declared, that "this constitution and the laws of the United States, which shall be made in pursuance thereof and all treaties made, or which shall be made, under the authority of the United States, shall be the supreme law of the land;" thereby most explicitly excluding the idea of any thing else being law, but the constitution, laws made in pursuance thereof, and treaties made or to be made. Indeed I have not been able to find the words *common law* in any part of the original constitution; it is true they occur in the IXth amendment, but they are there used to narrow the jurisdiction of the federal court.[2] By the constitution, as originally formed, the supreme court had appellate jurisdiction, both as to law and fact; under this judicial power, it was feared that the use of juries would be destroyed, to prevent which, it is provided in the IXth amendment, that "in suits at common law, where the value in controversy shall exceed twenty dollars, the right of trial by jury shall be preserved, and no fact tried by a jury, shall be otherwise reexamined, in any court of the United States, than according

---

2. Actually a reference to the Seventh Amendment. Contemporary printings of the Constitution often included the first two articles of amendment which were not ratified by the states. Swift, *The Laws of the United States of America*, 3:454-57.

to the rules of the common law;" the words common law are here used to distinguish the case meant to be provided for from chancery cases. It would be singular indeed, if this clause of the constitution, which was evidently intended to abridge the power of the federal court should by a forced and false construction be made to extend it.

You say, "it is true that the parties acting in their sovereign capacity, might have discontinued that law, with respect to the new regulations, and the duties thence arising, and have left them to arbitrary decisions: but that they intended a discontinuance so contrary to usage in similar cases, and so pregnant with mischief, is not to be presumed; and is a supposition irreconcileable with these frequent references in the constitution to the common law, as a living code.'—It by no means follows that without the common law, the decisions of the courts would be arbitrary, as it is the duty of congress to prescribe a rule of conduct for their courts. To what you allude, when you speak of the frequent references in the constitution, to the common law, I cannot conceive, as the words *common law* are not to be found in the constitution, except in the solitary instance that I have mentioned. You are equally unintelligible, when you speak of a discontinuance not being intended; if your words have any meaning, it must be, that there was at the adoption of the constitution, a common or an unwritten law of the United States, for it would be ridiculous to suppose that any thing that never existed could be discontinued.

Before this government was formed, the confederation was the only compact between the states; that instrument neither adopted the common law, nor authorised congress to do it, and I will assert, that it was never believed or suggested, that it was done by either the old or the existing government, until very lately. The state conventions adopted the common law with great caution. They adopted it as modified by themselves, and subject to future alterations by the ordinary legislatures; but if it can be established that the common law was adopted by the constitution, it can only be altered in the same manner that the constitution can; and for the change of the most trifling municipal regulation a convention must be called, or the other mode prescribed by the constitution pursued, which is attended with such difficulties as to render it next to an impossibility to succeed. If not withstanding everything that has been said upon this subject, it should be decided that there is an unwritten law in the United States, I should be glad to be informed what that law is? It is known that what is called the common law, was not the same in any two of the states, when the constitution was formed: if the common law "attached" I beg leave to be informed whether it is the law as it is in force in England, at the present, or any past period? Or whether it is the law of any particular state? The unwritten law is the basis of all our laws; by it our property is regulated and secured. The criminal laws are a part of the common law, improved in many of the states by particular statutes. In Virginia for instance, we know how our property will be distributed, if a man dies without a will; we know for what actions a man is subject to punishment, but we do not know what the laws of England, or the laws of the other states are. It is of the utmost importance, that we should be informed if the aristocratic principle of primogeniture is to be restored, and if the bloody penal code of England, is to be in force in this country. If the common law of England, "attached upon us," it must have been the intire code, in that case, the mischiefs that I have depicted, will be found to be real, and not imaginary. There can be no pretence that the common law has been adopted by congress. Such an act would transcend their power, and there is not a sufficient degree of insinuation, to induce a belief that congress may, by connecting a vast variety of laws, adopt a system, when they could not adopt the parts separately. Neither the code being "English," nor that of our ancestors, would reconcile me to a violation of our constitution, or the sacrifice of our liberties. It is a sufficient mortification to me, that my ancestors were the victims of priestcraft, and kingcraft. Their being so, would only increase my abhorrence of every thing which has that tendency.

Until I read your charge I never knew that the common law of England was considered by the people of America, after their independence, as their birthright. In England every part of the common law is subject to be changed by act of Parliament, and so in every State in America what remains of that system may be changed by the ordinary legislature. In this country we do not believe that we hold our birth rights by the courtesy of any man or set of men; we know that both the federal and state constitutions forbid them to be touched by unhallowed hands. Among the most important of our birth rights we consider the right of self government; which secures us from the operation of laws to which we have not by our representatives given our assent; alike excluding the laws of the Romans, the English, the Turks, and of every other nation.

Of equal importance we estimate our religious freedom, the freedom of the press, and of speech. These with some others we consider as our birth rights but we are far from considering them as rights peculiar to us. We believe them to be the rights of man, the best gift of our all bountiful creator. Be assured sir, that the people of the United States will not consent to be governed by laws that no man can say when or by whom they were adopted, or what they are. It has long been feared that the government of the United States tended to a consolidation, and consolidation would generate monarchy. Nothing can so soon produce the first as the establishment of the doctrine, that the common law of England, is the law of the United States: it renders the state governments useless burthens; it gives the Federal government and its courts jurisdiction over every subject that has heretofore been supposed to belong to the States; instead of the general government being instituted for particular purposes, it embraces every subject to which a government can apply, and instead of being confined to the important purposes of securing union, regulating commerce, providing for the general defence, and supporting our relations with foreign nations, the whole range of legislation and jurisprudence is within its omnipotent grasp, in consequence of which the people of America may find, when it is too late to apply a remedy, that they have been cheated out of that liberty which they gained by their gallantry in the field, by the wiles and intrigue of designing men. The contemporaneous writings in defence of the constitution, and the speeches of the conventions that adopted it, prove under what impressions, and for what purposes, the general government was formed. Compare the opinions of that day with those of this, and it would appear that they were different instruments. I am not conscious of having any partiality to the State governments, I feel as much interest in the one, as the other, and should be as much opposed to encroachments by the state governments, as I am to an infringement of the state powers by the general government. These observations are submitted to you by a man who is not a lawyer, and who knows himself incompetent to do justice to the cause he has espoused, but one who anxiously wishes the happiness and prosperity of his country, and whose fondest hope is to remain a free

CITIZEN.

William Paterson to William Cushing ──────────────────
    August 17, 1799   New Brunswick, New Jersey

... The eastern circuit is assigned to you of course; and I shall with pleasure attend the court for you at New York. I hope, that this letter will find you fully reinstated in your health. ...

ARS (MHi, Cushing Family Papers, 1650-1840). Addressed "Scituate   Massachusetts."

Bushrod Washington to James Iredell ──────────────────
    August 20, 1799   Alexandria, Virginia

... Upon my arrival at Baltimore about the first of the month, I heard from Judge Chace, with great concern that you were too much indisposed to attend the supreme Court. The fatigue to which you had been exposed during the Circuit was well calculated to produce this consequence, and you would have acted imprudently I think to venture upon so long a Journey in your then state of health. It will afford me very sincere pleasure to hear of your recovery.

    ...

    Being allotted to the middle Circuit, I shall have to retry the many perplexing cases which engaged so much of your time at Philadelphia in the Spring. I can easily foresee that the trials will be rather lengthened than curtailed, unless the same Judge presides who was present at the former trials. To avoid unecessary prolixity so far as may consist with perfect Justice to both sides, I could wish if possible to be made acquainted with the Circumstances attending the insurgent cases; (particularly that of Fries) the mode in which the trials were conducted, & the points made & decided. This may in many instances prevent unecessary discussions, & may aid in the better understanding of such as are important. If you can without much inconvenience forward to me at Philadelphia an abstract from your notes relative to those cases it will much oblige me.[1] I shall be at that place about the 20th of September on my way to Trenton; should your letter arrive after I have gone through, I will direct it to be forwarded to me. ...

ARS (Nc-Ar, Charles E. Johnson Collection). Addressed "Edenton   North Carolina." Postmarked "A[LE]X. Vᵃ AUG   26."

1. Iredell's notes of the Fries trial at the April 1799 term of the Pennsylvania circuit court cover nearly two hundred pages of volumes 15 and 16 of the James Iredell Papers, Southern Historical Collection, NcU. He probably used these notes to compile the account of the Fries trial that Washington acknowledged receiving on October 20. Bushrod Washington to James Iredell, October 20, 1799 (q.v.).

Oliver Ellsworth to William Cushing
August 24, 1799   Windsor, Connecticut

... The assignment you requested was readily agreed to; and Brother Patterson will releive you from New York. I should also with great pleasure take the Court at Hartford, but being called upon to prepare for a speedy embarkation for France, I dare not undertake it.[1] ...

ARS (MHi, Cushing Family Papers, 1650-1840). Addressed "Scituate   near Boston." Postmarked "HARTFORD   AUG.   27."

1. Ellsworth did not depart for France until November 3, 1799, and so was able to hold the circuit court at Hartford in September.

Circuit Court for the District of New York
September 2, 1799   New York, New York

On Monday, September 2, Associate Justice William Paterson and Judge John Sloss Hobart convened court, and Paterson delivered a charge to the grand jury. The court adjourned on September 6.

1. Minutes, CCD New York, RG 21, NjBaFAR. We have been unable to identify the specific charge given. For undated Paterson grand jury charges, see Appendix A.

View of the City and Harbour of New York taken from Mount Pitt, The Seat of John R. Livingston, Esq. by Charles Balthazar Julien Févret de Saint-Mémin (1770-1852). Etching, 1794. Courtesy New York Public Library, Astor, Lenox and Tilden Foundations, New York. I. N. Phelps Stokes Collection, Miriam & Ira D. Wallach Division of Art, Prints & Photographs Division.

Robert Troup to Rufus King

September 2, 1799   New York, New York

...Judge Hobart is now here with Judge Paterson holdig our circuit Court_ Both are well_ Paterson is the most popular & respected of all the supreme Court Judges_ He gave us yesterday[1] an elegant charge ag.[t] riots, insurrections, & lies against the Government & its officers _ ...

ARS (NHi, Rufus King Papers).

1. The reference to a charge having been delivered "yesterday" calls into question Troup's dating of this letter since the previous day fell on a Sunday, and the circuit court for New York began on Monday, September 2. Troup may have begun this sixteen-page letter on September 2 and completed it the following day so that the reference to "yesterday" would be correct.

Oliver Ellsworth to Richard Law

September 4, 1799   Windsor, Connecticut

Windsor   Sep[r] 4 _ 1799.

Dear Sir,

I have been favoured with your letter of the 2d of Aug.[tl] and have been two days this week at Hartford, and beleive a court might at present be holden there with as much safety as in any town in the State.[2] Should appearances however change, so as to render that place, in my opinion, at all unsafe, I will endeavour to give you the earliest notice of it. Judge Cushing I expect will attend with you, but should he by any means fail, I must supply his place.

I am, dear Sir, with much esteem,   your obed.[t] humble Servant

Oliv. Ellsworth

Hon.[bl] Judge Law

Tr (CtHi, Ernest Law Papers). Marked by the transcriber as an "ALS." Addressed "New London."

1. Letter not found.

2. Although yellow fever was present in Hartford, the city "at large, continues healthy, considering the fears which necessarily spring from such a desolating distemper" and "there are fewer people sick in town, than has been known, at this season, for many years." *Connecticut Courant* (Hartford), August 26 and September 2, 1799.

Philadelphia Gazette ————————————————————————————

September 10, 1799   Philadelphia, Pennsylvania

United States; ⎱
District of Pennsylvania. ⎰ *ss*

To the Marshal of the Pennsylvania District of the United States.

WHEREAS in my opinion a contagious sickness in the city of Philadelphia, renders it hazardous to hold the next stated Session of the Circuit Court of the United States, in and for the Pennsylvania District of the middle Circuit of the said city, the place appointed by law at which to hold the stated Session of the said Court—These are by virtue of the powers and authorities vested in me,[1] RICHARD PETERS. Judge of the Pennsylvania District of the United States, in the name and by authority of the United States, to order and direct you to adjourn the Session of the said Circuit Court, directed to be held at Philadelphia, on the eleventh day of October next, to Norris Town, in the county of Montgomery in the same District, being a convenient place within the same for holding the said Court; and you are to make publication hereof in one or more public papers printed at the said city, that the said Court is adjourned as it is hereby directed to be; and you are accordingly to adjourn the said Court to the said place hereby appointed from the time you shall receive this order to the said eleventh day of October next, the time by law prescribed for commencing the said Session.

(L.S.) Given under my hand and seal at Belmont in the said district this sixth day of September in the year of our Lord 1799 and in the twenty-fourth year of the Independence of the United States.

RICHARD PETERS.

WHEREFORE I, the said Marshal, by virtue of the powers vested in me by the above order and directions from the honorable Richard Peters, Esquire, judge of the Pennsylvania district of the United States, and in the name and by the authority of the United States, do adjourn the session of the Circuit court of the said United States, which was to have been held at Philadelphia, on the eleventh day of October next, to the courthouse in NORRIS TOWN in the county of *Montgomery* in the same district, there to meet on the said eleventh day of October next at ten o'clock in the forenoon of the same day of which all persons bound by Recognizance or have otherwise to do thereat are desired and required to take notice and give their attendance accordingly.

William Nichols, Marshal.[2]

Marshal's, Office at Philadel- ⎱
phia. 7, September, 1799. ⎰

(Philadelphia) September 10, 1799. Date and place are those of the newspaper.

1. The authority for moving the court was granted by section 7 of "An Act respecting Quarantines and Health Laws," February 25, 1799. *Stat.*, 1:621.

2. William Nichols (1754-1804) was first appointed to a four-year term as United States marshal for the district of Pennsylvania on June 25, 1795. He was renominated on June 26, 1799. Emma St. Clair Whitney, *Michael Hillegas and His Descendants* (Pottsville, Pa.: privately printed, 1891), p. 37; *SEJ*, 1:189, 325.

William Cushing to Richard Law

September 13, 1799   Scituate, Massachusetts

Scituate   Sepr 13. 1799

Dear Sir,

I find myself so unwell, in consequence of bad colds, caught by riding in all the coldest weather of last winter & in some storms; with an obstruction in my breast (and being under the Doctor's hands) that I shall not be able to attend Hartford, which is next Tuesday: this is the more unfortunate, as I understand the court failed last spring.

I did expect from the encouragement given me by the Chief Justice that he would have been able to attend for me; but, evening before last, I received from him informing that he could not, by reason of his being called upon to prepare for a Speedy embarkation for France.[1]

I was the rather emboldened to ask the favor of the Chief Justice, as I had taken two courts for him, last year in the time of his indisposition.

But smaller matters must give way to greater. With much regard & esteem, I am yours affectionately

Wm Cushing

Tr (CtHi, Ernest Law Papers). Marked by the transcriber as an "ALS." Addressed "Hartford Connecticut."

1. See Oliver Ellsworth to William Cushing, August 24, 1799.

Circuit Court for the District of Connecticut

September 17, 1799   Hartford, Connecticut

Judge Richard Law attended court on September 17, but the absence of a Supreme Court justice caused him to adjourn the court to the next day. On September 18, the court was opened by Chief Justice Oliver Ellsworth and Judge Law. The court met until September 26 and adjourned to the following term.[1]

1. Docket Book, CCD Connecticut, RG 21, MWalFAR.

Recollection of Mr Ellsworth by William Vans Murray (1760-1803). Pencil on paper, ca. 1800. Courtesy Library of Congress. William Vans Murray Papers.

Oliver Ellsworth to John Adams ——————————
    September 18, 1799   Hartford, Connecticut

The President of the United States

Sir,

If the present convulsion in France, and the sumptoms of a greater change at hand, should induce you, as many seem to expect, to postpone for a short time, the mission to that country, I wish for the earliest-notice of it.[1] The Circuit Court here in this State and Vermont, fell thro' last spring from the indisposition of Judge Chase, and must now fall thro' again from the indisposition of Judge Cushing, unless I attend them. I am begining the Court here, and should proceed on to Vermont, if I was sure of not being called on in the mean time to embark _ It is, Sir, my duty to obey, not advise, I do not therefore, offer my own opinion, and have only to hope that you will not disapprove of the method I take to learn the spediest intimation of yours.

I have the honor to be,   Sir,   with the highest respect,   your obedient humble servant

                                                      Oliver Ellsworth

Hartford Sepr
    18 1799 _

ARS (MHi, Adams Manuscript Trust).
    Ellsworth mentioned this letter and its contents in two other letters: Oliver Ellsworth to Tim-
othy Pickering, September 19, 1799, Timothy Pickering Papers, MHi; Oliver Ellsworth to Oliver
Wolcott, Jr., September 20, 1799, Oliver Wolcott Jr. Papers, CtHi.
    1. See John Adams to Oliver Ellsworth, September 22, 1799.

John Adams to Oliver Ellsworth ——————————————————
September 22, 1799   Quincy, Massachusetts

... I rec[d] last night your favour of the 18th Judge Cushing called here
Yesterday in his Way to Vermont. This however may not perhaps make any
alteration in your Views.

The Convulsions in France, the Change of the Directory and the
Prognosticks of greater Changes will certainly induce me to postpone, for a
longer or shorter time, the Mission to Paris. I wish you to pursue your Office
of Chief Justice of the United States, without Interruption till you are
requested to embark. ...

ARS (MH-H, bms Am 1583); Lb (MHi, Adams Manuscript Trust). Marked "Chief Justice
Elsworth   at Hartford or Windsor   Connecticutt."

Oliver Ellsworth to Cephus Smith, Jr. ——————————————
September 22, 1799   Hartford, Connecticut

Hartford   Sept[r] 22[d] 1799.

Dear Sir,

Judge Cushing to whom the Eastern Circuit was assigned writes me that
he is sick _ [1] accordingly I am attending Court in his room here _ and I
shall also endeavour to get on to Vermont if he continues unable to go,
provided the President to whom I have wrote upon the Subject ~~will~~ shall
think I can be spared long enough for that Court before he wishes me to
Embark for France _ [2] This is all the information I can give you at present. I
very much wish your Court may not fall thro' again & if you hear nothing
farther from me or M[r] Cushing I think it will be best to adjourn the Court
from day to day for a few days ~~but~~ in expectation ~~after~~ that a Judge may
arrive _

I am Sir   your humb[l] Serv[t]

Oliv. Ellsworth

M[r] Smith

ARS (MB, Ch. C. 11.40 #2). Addressed "Rutland."
    Cephus Smith, Jr. (1760-1815), of Rutland, Vermont, served as clerk of the federal district
and circuits courts in Vermont. Elijah Ellsworth Brownell, *Rutland County Vermont Genealogical*

Gleanings, typescript (Philadelphia, 1942), p. 302; Cephus Smith, Jr., to Jacob Wagner, July 15, 1797, *DHSC,* 1:856.
    1. Letter not found; but see Oliver Ellsworth to William Cushing, August 24, 1799.
    2. See Oliver Ellsworth to John Adams, September 18, 1799.

Oliver Ellsworth to John Adams ————————————————————
    September 26, 1799   Hartford, Connecticut

...I am this moment honored with your letter of the 22[d] and must apologize for my mistake concerning Judge Cushing. When I wrote I had only seen here his letter to Judge Law, in which he said he was "under the Doctor's care & could not attend the Court at Hartford"_ and from thence inferred that he would not go to Vermont.[1] Since then his letter to me,[2] which had got to Windsor & lain there two or three days came to hand, and informed that though he could not attend at Hartford, he hoped to be able to go to Vermont.[3] ...

ARS (MHi, Adams Manuscript Trust).
    1. See William Cushing to Richard Law, September 13, 1799.
    2. Letter not found.
    3. In two letters written on October 1, 1799, Ellsworth mentioned that Cushing would be presiding at the Circuit Court for the district of Vermont. Oliver Ellsworth to Timothy Pickering (Timothy Pickering Papers, MHi); Oliver Ellsworth to Oliver Wolcott, Jr. (Oliver Wolcott Jr. Papers, CtHi).

Circuit Court for the District of New Jersey ————————————
    October 1, 1799   Trenton, New Jersey

Associate Justice Bushrod Washington and Judge Robert Morris opened court on October 1, and Washington delivered a charge to the grand jury. Court adjourned on October 7.[1]

    1. Minutes, CCD New Jersey, RG 21, NjBaFAR. Charge not found.

Circuit Court for the District of Vermont ————————————
    October 3, 1799   Rutland, Vermont

Court convened with Associate Justice William Cushing and Judge Samuel Hitchcock in attendance. Court adjourned on October 11.[1]

    1. Circuit Docket, CCD Vermont, RG 21, MWalFAR.

Circuit Court for the District of Pennsylvania ──────────
October 11, 1799   Norristown, Pennsylvania

Judge Richard Peters attended court in Norristown after publishing the legally required notice of the change in meeting place,[1] but the absence of a Supreme Court justice led him to adjourn the court to the following day. On October 12 court was opened by Associate Justice Bushrod Washington and Judge Peters, and Washington delivered a charge to the grand jury. The court adjourned on October 22.[2]

1. See the *Philadelphia Gazette* under date of September 10, 1799.
2. Engrossed Minutes, CCD Pennsylvania, RG 21, PPFAR. Charge not found.

Aurora ──────────────────────────────────
October 14, 1799   Bristol, Pennsylvania

The Federal District Court[1] held by adjournment at Norristown, Montgmery County, was opened on Friday by *Judge Peters*; the absence of *Judge Washington*, prevented the Court from proceeding to business, the only authority vested in Mr. Peters, being to adjourn the Court, which was done to Saturday morning.

It was supposed that Judge *Washington* met with some accident on the road, which occasioned his absence, as he had set out for Pennsylvania at a very early day—and was expected in the middle of the last week.

(Bristol) October 14, 1799. Date and place are those of the newspaper. Because of the yellow fever epidemic in Philadelphia, the *Aurora* was published in Bristol, approximately twenty miles outside of Philadelphia, from August 30 to October 19, 1799. Brigham, *American Newspapers,* 2:891.
1. This should have read "Circuit Court."

Bushrod Washington to James Iredell ──────────
October 20, 1799   Norristown, Pennsylvania

... Your favor enclosing the residue of the examination in the case of Fries I received upon my arrival at this place, the former having come to hand a few days sooner.[1] I know not how to apologize to you for the trouble you have taken upon this occasion; I certainly should not have made the request which produced it, if I could have formed the slightest idea of the labor to which I was about to expose you. I beg you to accept my warmest thanks, and upon similar occasions or otherwise to command my services.

I had very little to do at Trenton; the Court decided one important case in equity tho not finally, and imposed fines upon two penitent speakers of sedition.[2]

Since the sitting of the Judges at this place about 25 persons indicted for misdemeanors have withdrawn their pleas and submitted. The trials of the treason cases have been delayed for want of Jurymen & witnesses. On Tuesday next I had hoped to enter upon those cases._ I am now overwhelmed with mortification and chagrin at knowing that there is an end to our further proceedings in those as well as other cases. You will be not less astonished than myself at the cause of this extraordinary event. On [*letters inked out*] Friday, the Marshall obtained leave of absence for a day or two, and in the evening of that day the clerk[3] suggested to Mr Peters and Mr Rawle a doubt whether the mar[sh]all's commission which expired in June last had been renewed. An express was immediately sent to him, and his answer upon this subject tho' it does not confirm is far from removing our doubts. Yesterday we dispatched another messenger to Mr. Pickering,[4] and expect this evening to receive the information we want. But should the Commission have been made out in time, it is clear that he has not since qualified thereto by giving a new bond and taking the oath which the law requires to be done before entering upon the duties of his office, and if the exercise of his powers be dependent upon the performance of those things, his acts as marshall are void. If so, the adjournment of the court hither was a void act and all done here is coram non Judice.[5] At all events if a doubt only hangs upon the business, I would not for the Universe proceed in the trials of criminal cases, much less would I pass sentence upon any man. This is our present distressful situation and I have seldom felt myself in a more unpleasant one. Tommorrow we shall come to some decision upon the subject, and that I expect will be to proceed no further. What will become of the many important acts done by this officer since June I know not. I wish he may not be involved in much trouble.

. . .

Should you favor me with a letter, direct to me at Baltimore _ [6]

. . .

The circumstances related in this letter respecting the Marshall may as well be con[fidential at?] least for the [*phrase missing*] [f]all assize [*phrase missing*] our adj. in general terms.[7]

ARS (NcU, Southern Historical Collection, Hayes Collection). Addressed "Edenton   North Carolina." Readings in brackets supplied where letter is torn.

1. Letters not found, but see Bushrod Washington to James Iredell, August 20, 1799.

2. The equity case was *Dunham v. Van Horne*. Minutes, October 2, 1799, CCD New Jersey, RG 21, NjBaFAR. For an account of the sedition trials, *United States v. Clark* and *United States v. Baldwin*, see Smith, *Freedom's Fetters*, pp. 270-74.

3. David Caldwell (1770-1835), clerk of the United States district and circuit courts for Pennsylvania. John H. Campbell, *History of the Friendly Sons of St. Patrick and of the Hibernian Society for the Relief of Emigrants from Ireland: March 17, 1771-March 17, 1892* (Philadelphia: Hibernian Society, 1892), p. 102; *Stat.*, 1:76.

4. The secretary of state at this time, Timothy Pickering, was responsible for affixing the seal of the United States on all civil commissions. *Stat.*, 1:68.

5. "In presence of a person not a judge." *Black's Law Dictionary;* Giles Jacob, comp., *A New*

Law Dictionary, 10th ed., rev. by J. Morgan (London: W. Strahan and W. Woodfall, 1782). The United States marshal for the district of Pennsylvania, William Nichols, had been nominated to a four-year term on June 25, 1795. Nichols was then renominated on June 26, 1799, during a recess of the Senate. *SEJ,* 1:189, 191, 325.

6. Associate Justice James Iredell died at his home in Edenton, North Carolina on the day this letter was written. *DHSC,* 1:877-79.

7. This sentence appears as a postscript in the margin alongside the signature. Text is missing because of damage to the document where the seal was affixed. A microfilm of the document, taken before preservation procedures further obliterated some of this text, exists, and we have transcribed from the film.

Circuit Court for the District of Massachusetts

October 21, 1799   Boston, Massachusetts

On Monday, October 21, the circuit court commenced its session with Associate Justice William Cushing and Judge John Lowell in attendance. The court adjourned on October 26.[1]

1. Final Records, CCD Massachusetts, RG 21, MWalFAR.

Richard Peters to Timothy Pickering

October 23, 1799   "Belmont," Philadelphia County, Pennsylvania

Belmont   23 Oct.ʳ 1799

Dear Sir,

I returned from Norristown yesterday after the blowing up of the Court.[1] We are all too much chagrined to say much about the Circumstances or its Consequences. Most of those you have detailed certainly follow.[2] But we cannot remedy them, nor can even the Legislature remedy them all, tho' it may restore the Court to Activity, from a State of Torpor & temporary Death. If Nichols had not stupidly given more Weight than he ought to a transient Conversation of Mʳ Wolcot's _ [3] if he had known his Duty or his Situation & had mentioned a Syllable of it to me or to you all this unfortunate Business would have been prevented. But so it is & we can't make it better by Lamentation. Nothing can make it much worse. We do not say anything about the true Reason of our breaking up. We assigned as a Reason that we had discovered since the last Adjournment an Error in the Proceedings, which made it too doubtful with us, to go on with the Business; & also that, from the small Number of Jurors attending, the Trials were not likely to proceed; so many of the Citizens of Philadᵃ, of whom there were 26 in the panells, having absented themselves, & declared it was ruinous to them at this Time to be compelled to leave their Business, just getting into Operation, after the Calamity the City had undergone.[4] I bound over the Defendants _ Duane[5] & 2 or 3 more (who had entered into Recognizances in Court _ all void _) excepted, as they had gone off. I also bound over the Witnesses to appear at a stated or special Court, & gave a new Comittment to the Marshall (after he was legally qualified) of all the Prisoners in Gaol. We think it will be absolutely necessary to hold a special Court sometime in January. But we dared not order it, as we did not know whether any Judge of the Supreme Court could attend it. And if this failed also, Matters would appear to the public still worse. Judge Washington could not attend; but he says he will endeavor to arrange it with Judge Patterson, who he expects to see on his Return from Georgia. If he is successful he will write me Time enough to issue the Venire, as this is our only Chance. The Court was adjourned in the usual Form to the next stated Session, to give an Opportunity of further Examination, tho we have no Doubts on the Subject.

The Affairs of this District partake dismally of the Glooms which darken our political Horizon nationally. Your private Information is no Cordial. It seems as if some Demon possessed our great Man_ We shall smart severely before this Devil is cast out. The Appointment was I thought as bad a Measure as could be taken_ but the Mission now is infinitely worse.[6] The british are beginning their Vexations or rather encreasing them. This Mission will afford a Pretext. Enough will be made of all this to give us a stormy Winter. But I am weary of croaking_ Sufficient unto the Day is the Evil thereof _ [7]

Yours affectionately

Richard Peters

The Situation of the City is not yet perfectly safe. Your Neighborhood is not yet clear. There is a Case opposite my House in Walnut Street.

Col Pickering_

ARS (MHi, Timothy Pickering Papers). Marked "(Private)." Belmont was the West Philadelphia country home of the Peters family.

1. For information on the failure of the circuit court at Norristown, see Bushrod Washington to James Iredell, October 20, 1799.

2. Letter from Timothy Pickering to Richard Peters not found. ₁

3. Oliver Wolcott, Jr. (1760-1833), secretary of the treasury. *DAB.*

4. For the third time in as many years Philadelphia suffered a serious epidemic of yellow fever, with over one thousand deaths between August and October 1799. Mease, *Picture of Philadelphia*, pp. 37-38.

5. William Duane (1760-1835), editor of the Philadelphia *Aurora*, had been indicted for seditious libel. *DAB; United States v. Duane*, Engrossed Minutes, October 16, 1799, CCD Pennsylvania, RG 21, PPFAR; Smith, *Freedom's Fetters*, pp. 285-86.

6. Peters is referring to the appointment of Oliver Ellsworth as special envoy to France. See introduction to "Spring and Fall Circuits 1799."

7. Matt. 6:34.

View from Belmont, the Seat of Judge Peters by William Russell Birch (1755-1834). Oil on canvas, ca. 1808. Courtesy Henry Francis du Pont Winterthur Museum, Winterthur, Delaware.

Circuit Court for the District of South Carolina ——————————

October 25, 1799   Charleston, South Carolina

Associate Justice William Paterson and Judge Thomas Bee opened court. On October 29 the court adjourned to the next term.[1]

1. Minutes, CCD South Carolina, RG 21, GEpFAR.

"Thoughts on the Judiciary of the United States" by "Hale" —————— *Argus*

October 25, 1799   New York, New York

... In charges to Federal Grand Juries, instead of the legal subjects of enquiry, we find factious political disquisitions; tedious and disgusting details of the conduct of foreign nations to each other—approbation or censure of the parties which divide America—and extrajudicial anticipations of expected constitutional questions, thereby prejudging without argument, and even without trial, the individuals who may be brought before them. Of this fact the declarations in these charges "that the Alien and Sedition Laws are Constitutional," and the alarming assertion "that the common law of England is the Federal law[1] of the United States as to crimes and punishments," *(a)* (an assertion teeming with the most fatal consequences) are undeniable proofs; and thus the rule *'audi alteram partem,'*[2] deemed sacred in the administration of justice, and which ought to be the motto of every impartial judge, is substantially violated. ...

(a) It is rather unfortunate that this was ardently pressed, in a late charge to a federal grand jury in South Carolina by another chief justice, who had at the time an appointment to a like foreign embassy.—See the charge.[3]

(New York) October 25, 1799. Date and place are those of the newspaper. Headlined "From the EXAMINER," a Richmond, Virginia newspaper.

1. In the newspaper the phrase, "of England is the Federal law," is repeated at this point.
2. "Hear the other side." *Black's Law Dictionary.*
3. Oliver Ellsworth's Charge to the Grand Jury of the Circuit Court for the District of South Carolina, May 7, 1799 (q.v.).

Circuit Court for the District of Delaware ——————————

October 27, 1799   Dover, Delaware

"October 27. 1799. This day being the day, prescribed by Law for the holding of the Circuit Court at Dover, but being on Sunday, was opened on the day following. _ Monday October 28. 1799. The Court was Opened by the Marshall, him and the Clerk being present, but on Account of the Non = Attendance of the Circuit Judge. The Court was Adjourned over by the Marshall until four days Successively, as is by

Law directed. At which time Thursday October 31. 1799. being the last of the four days. _ The court was adjourned over until the time and place prescribed by Law . . . "[1]

1. Appearance Docket, CCD Delaware, RG 21, PPFAR.

"Spectator" ————————————————————————————————

Aurora

October 28, 1799   Philadelphia, Pennsylvania

I send you the following particulars of the proceedings of a court of the United States, held lately at Norristown.

A contagious sickness again occurring in Philadelphia, Judge Peters thought himself authorized by law to remove the Circuit Court, and unfinished business of a former session to Norris Town. Proclamation was made accordingly,[1] and there it was opened the 15th, when Mr. Dallas moved to shew that the court at Norris Town had no jurisdiction over indictments found at Philadelphia, and that the district judge had no farther power by the quarantine and health law, passed 25th of February last, than to remove the prisoners for safe keeping in case of contagion.[2] The motion was ably supported by Mr. Dallas, and opposed by Mr. Rawle, attorney for the district. The court finally determined that it had cognizance of the indictments at Norris Town, and that the trials should proceed there "even if it sat till Christmas."

In conformity with this decision Jacob Eyerman (the minister) was tried and found guilty, as were about 22 others for misdemeanours upon their own submission. The trial of Fries, which was intended to precede the rest, was postponed for a few days on account of the sudden indisposition of Mr. Dallas, one of his council.

On Friday the 18th, after doing little business, the court adjourned till Monday, when it did not meet till three in the afternoon, and met but instantly to adjourn to the next morning! *Fries's* trial was announced and expected then to proceed, but then the court met only to bind over the witnesses and prisoners *even those who had been tried, as well as those who had been accused,* to appear at the next circuit court in Philadelphia.

Thus sir, an anxious multitude of jurors, witnesses, and citizens waited a session of twelve days to see, to hear, and to do—nothing more. The reason for this extraordinary adjournment remains an impenetrable secret excepting with the judges, &c.[3] One dollar twenty five cents per day, each and mileage, was the allowance paid to an immense number of jurors and witnesses, besides the expence of removal, and the common court expences.[4]

SPECTATOR.

(Philadelphia) October 28, 1799. Date and place are those of the newspaper.

1. See Judge Richard Peters's order as published by the *Philadelphia Gazette* under date of September 10, 1799.

2. "An Act respecting Quarantines and Health Laws," was passed on February 25, 1799. *Stat.,* 1:619.

3. See Bushrod Washington to James Iredell, October 20, 1799, and Richard Peters to Timothy Pickering, October 23, 1799, where the adjournment is discussed.

4. The rate for jurors and witnesses was set by section 6 of the Compensation Act of 1799. *Stat.,* 1:626.

Massachusetts Mercury ————————————————————————————————
November 1, 1799   Boston, Massachusetts

The Proceedings of the Circuit Court at Norristown, *(Pen.)* are nullified by the discovery of a flaw in the notification of removal from *Philadelphia*.

(Boston) November 1, 1799. Date and place are those of the headline.

Circuit Court for the District of New Hampshire ————————————
November 2, 1799   Exeter, New Hampshire

The circuit court was convened on November 2 by Associate Justice William Cushing and adjourned later that same day.[1]

1. Records, CCD New Hampshire, RG 21, MWalFAR.

Aurora ——
November 4, 1799   Philadelphia, Pennsylvania

... The bench has been made an instrument of party and the open addresses of Judges, the vehicles of party tenets, to the disgrace of justice and the dishonour of the legal purity of the bench; the season is now coming when these judicial trumpeters of faction were about to blow a blast—but the frustration of these *British stratagems* has cut short the *blast!*

(Philadelphia) November 4, 1799. Date and place are those of the newspaper.

William Paterson to Euphemia Paterson ————————————————————
November 7, 1799   Augusta, Georgia

... I tarried at Sullivan's island till the day preceding the court, when I passed over to Charleston.[1] The epidemic had almost disappeared when I left Charleston; there being only a few cases among the sea-faring people, and here and there a child laid up of it. It is impossible to give the number of deaths, as the intendant of the city had not rec^d all the returns before I left it. About four weeks ago it began to be sickly at Savannah, where several persons have died. We have had easterly winds, cool weather, and heavy rains, which have contributed to the restoration of public health; but a frost, which, in this country, is a sovereign remedy against all fevers, has not yet made its appearance. It has kept off unusually long. Owing to the yellow fever, which shut up all communication between Charleston and the country, the stage, which had run between the former place and this twice a week, was given up at least for a time, and it is quite uncertain whether it will be set up again. A stage continues to run from Charleston to Savannah, and from Savannah to this place. A covered waggon or coachee cannot be hired at Charleston. They have no such vehicle to let. My route hither was circuitous. I took the stage for Savannah, and stopt about 15 miles from the town, at Spencer's tavern, being one of the best inns in Georgia, where I tarried till the arrival of the Augusta stage. The court here will commence to-morrow, and, the business being heavy, will continue at least two weeks. I reckon upon reaching Charleston about the first of next month, and my stay there will depend upon the sailing of vessels for some of the eastern ports. It will be late in the season, but this inconvenience cannot be avoided, consistently with the discharge of my official duty. Judge Iredell takes the North Carolina court for me.[2] ...

ARS (NjR, William Paterson Papers).

1. Paterson arrived in Charleston on October 15, ten days before the opening of the circuit court, and may have gone to Sullivan's Island to escape the yellow fever. *City Gazette* (Charleston), October 15, 1799.

2. Paterson was not yet aware that Iredell had died on October 20, 1799.

Circuit Court for the District of Maryland ———————
November 7, 1799   Baltimore, Maryland

On November 7 court was opened by Associate Justice Bushrod Washington and Judge James Winchester, after which Washington delivered a charge to the grand jury. The court adjourned on November 12.[1]

A native of Maryland, Judge James Winchester (1772-1806) established a law practice in Baltimore and served in the Maryland General Assembly. On October 31, 1799, Winchester, just twenty-eight years old, was issued a temporary commission as United States judge for the district of Maryland. President Adams sent his nomination to the Senate on December 5, and it was confirmed on December 10, 1799. Winchester served until his death in 1806.[2]

1. Minutes, CCD Maryland, RG 21, PPFAR. Charge not found.

2. Robert William Barnes, comp., *Marriages and Deaths from Baltimore Newspapers, 1796-1816* (Baltimore: Genealogical Publishing, 1978), p. 356; Judicial Conference of the United States, Bicentennial Committee, *Judges of the United States* (Washington, D.C.: Government Printing Office, 1978); "Maryland Politics in 1796—

View of Baltimore from Chapel Hill by Francis Guy (1760-1820). Oil on canvas, ca. 1803. Courtesy Brooklyn Museum, Brooklyn, New York. Gift of George Dobbin Brown.

McHenry Letters," *Publications of the Southern History Association* 9 (1905): 374; *Votes and Proceedings of the House of Delegates of the State of Maryland, 1794* (Annapolis: Frederick Green, 1795), p. 1; Thomas L. Hollowak, *Maryland Genealogies: A Consolidation of Articles from the Maryland Historical Magazine,* 2 vols. (Baltimore: Genealogical Publishing, 1980), 2:482; *SEJ,* 1:325, 327.

American ——————————————————————————————

November 8, 1799   Baltimore, Maryland

Yesterday the Federal District Court was opened in this city.[1] Judge WASHINGTON addressed the Jury, and I[2] am told he exceeded BROOKS[3] in *stupidity*, and HARPER[4] in *malignity*. The chief object of his speech appeared to be aimed against the republicans; he declared in the course of his *spouting*, that "he who did not support the present administration, ought to be deprived of the privileges of an American citizen."—This is charming doctrine, and deserves the deepest consideration. I was not, from a press of business, present at the delivery of the speech, or my patrons should have it in full; but I hope that the judge will publish it at large, for the edification of the American public.

Now I would wish to ask the *sapient* judge what he conceives to be the *"present administration,"* to which we must pay such servile adulation, whether TIMOTHY PICKERING, or Mr. ADAMS; if he avows either, I will engage to *dish him* on his own arguments. For TIMOTHY and JOHN seem to be as widely different from each other, as *little* BROWN[5] and *myself.* TIM appears to be for *war*, and JOHN for peace.

(Baltimore) November 8, 1799. Date and place are those of the newspaper.

1. This reference is to the circuit court, not the district court.
2. Alexander Martin (ca. 1777-1810), publisher of the Baltimore *American.* Brigham, *American Newspapers,* 1:223; A. Rachel Minick, *A History of Printing in Maryland, 1791-1800* (Baltimore: Enoch Pratt Free Library, 1949), p. 73.
3. David Brooks (1756-1838) had served as a representative from New York from March 1797 until March 1799. *BDAC.*
4. Robert Goodloe Harper (1765-1825), a representative from South Carolina and a supporter of the alien and sedition laws. *DAB.*
5. Matthew Brown (ca. 1767-1831) publisher of the Baltimore *Federal Gazette.* Minick, *History of Printing in Maryland,* p. 46; *Federal Gazette* (Baltimore), January 10, 1832.

Circuit Court for the District of Georgia ——————————

November 8, 1799   Augusta, Georgia

Associate Justice William Paterson and Judge Joseph Clay, Jr., opened court. On November 15 the court adjourned to the next term.[1]

1. Minutes, CCD Georgia, RG 21, GEpFAR.

American ——————————————————————————————————

November 9, 1799   Baltimore, Maryland

Public anxiety was much excited yesterday, in consequence of a report that I[1] had been arrested under the *odious* SEDITION LAW, and for a libel against Judge WASHINGTON.[2] I, therefore, to alleviate the feelings of my friends, declare that such a report is without foundation. As to incurring the penalties of the Sedition Law, I have never, *in my own compositions*, made any assertion, but such as I CAN PROVE. And as to *libelling* Judge Washington, when such fellows as *Porcupine* and *Fenno*,[3] are allowed with impunity, to insult the chief Magistrate of the Union; to calumniate our happy Constitution, and to openly advance the most diabolical principles of monarchy, I am sure that the worshipful Judge cannot find a *libel* in any thing which I published yesterday.

(Baltimore) November 9, 1799. Date and place are those of the newspaper.
    1. Alexander Martin.
    2. See the Baltimore *American,* under date of November 8, 1799.
    3. William Cobbett (1763-1835) published *Porcupine's Gazette* (Philadelphia) and John Ward Fenno (1778-1802) published the *Gazette of the United States* (Philadelphia). *Daily Gazette* (New York), March 8, 1802; *DAB.*

Federal Gazette ————————————————————————————

November 9, 1799   Baltimore, Maryland

The Federal Court for the district of Maryland, commenced at the court house, in this city, on Thursday. Judges WASHINGTON and WINCHESTER presided. The jury was selected from among the most respectable characters of the state, who were addressed in a charge from Judge Washington, replete with wisdom, and characteristic of the knowledge, uprightness, and independence of the American bench. We should be happy in having it in our power to gratify the public with a perusal of its contents; but this we are sorry to say cannot be done, as application was made to that effect yesterday, by the grand jury, but the request, for certain reasons which the judge gave them, was not complied.

(Baltimore) November 9, 1799. Date and place are those of the newspaper.

American ——————————————————————————————————

November 11, 1799   Baltimore, Maryland

☞ When it is proved that President ADAMS is *infalliable*;—when it is proved that TIMOTHY PICKERING is attached to the *true* interest and honor of his country;—and when it is proved that the BENCH and the PULPIT have not frequently been converted into engines, or their *occupiers* into more *machines*, to diffuse the two first absurd doctrines; then it would be requisite that I should make an apology for doing that justice, which, as an editor and a gentleman, an *unintential misstatement* renders incumbent on me. The observations on the speech of Judge WASHINGTON, which appeared in my paper of Friday last, were hastily sketched from heresay;—On the representation *which was made to me*, of its tenor, I not only felt a *pleasure*, but thought I executed a *duty*, in the severity of my remarks.[1] And was I not now fully convinced that I had been *misinformed*, I would not retract a single sentence.

In the conduct of this paper, I have, and *will continue to*, lash with the utmost severity, any attempt to diffuse the anti-republican doctrine of *passive obedience and non-resistance*. But I shall always feel more happiness, in bestowing *praise* where it is due, than in censuring, even where it is merited. I therefore hope, that those of my customers who may have read the paragraph in question, will attribute it to my misinformation, and not to an *intentional* wish to injure the feelings of the judge or his friends, or bestow undeserved censure.

These declarations I have made *voluntarily*; not from having received any *threats*, or a dread of *any thing whatever*, but the imputation of having censured where it was not due.

Whatever *I* have said relative to the Federal Judge's Speech, I hope is now done away, but there is one *stigma* on it that never can be removed— LITTLE BROWN[2] has *praised it!*

(Baltimore) November 11, 1799. Date and place are those of the newspaper.

1. See the Baltimore *American* under date of November 8, 1799.

2. The Baltimore *Federal Gazette,* printed by Matthew Brown, commented on Bushrod Washington's charge in its issue of November 9, 1799 (q.v.).

Circuit Court for the District of Rhode Island ————————————
November 15, 1799   Providence, Rhode Island

Associate Justice William Cushing and Judge Benjamin Bourne convened court on November 15 and adjourned it on November 20.[1]

1. Minutes, CCD Rhode Island, RG 21, MWalFAR.

Circuit Court for the District of Virginia ————————————
November 22, 1799   Richmond, Virginia

Associate Justice Bushrod Washington opened court on November 22 and delivered a charge to the grand jury. Judge Cyrus Griffin joined the court the next day. On December 7 court adjourned.[1]

1. Order Book, CCD Virginia, Vi. Charge not found.

Circuit Court for the District of North Carolina ——————————
November 30, 1799   Raleigh, North Carolina

Associate Justice William Paterson opened the North Carolina circuit court and delivered a charge to the grand jury on November 30. The court adjourned on December 4.[1]

1. Minutes, CCD North Carolina, RG 21, GEpFAR. Charge reported in the *Raleigh Register*, December 3, 1799 (q.v.). We have been unable to identify the specific charge given. For undated Paterson grand jury charges, see Appendix A.

Raleigh Register ——————————————————————
December 3, 1799   Raleigh, North Carolina

On Saturday Judge Patterson, one of the Associate Justices of the United States, opened the Circuit Court of this District, in this city. The Grand Jury being impanelled, the Judge delivered his charge to them, which was a neat and well-written composition, and was pronounced with great propriety and emphasis. It commenced by pointing out the duties, and by describing the importance of the office, of Grand Jurors. It would be unnecessary, he said, to speak to them of all the indictable offences of which they had cognizance; but he would particularly mention two; the first was the crime of counterfeiting the notes of the Bank of the United States; the other was, offences committed under the Sedition Act, which act he read; and dwelt for some time on the heinous nature and ruinous effects of crimes of this latter description.

Having finished his charge, the Judge wished to have immediately proceeded to the trial of causes; but the gentlemen of the bar informing him it was not customary to proceed to trials on the first day of the Court, after expressing his disapprobation of the custom; and saying that the Circuit Court, in future, would proceed to the trial of causes on the first day of the Court, he adjourned to Monday at ten o'clock.

Yesterday the court commenced the trial of the causes entered on the docquet.

(Raleigh) December 3, 1799. Date and place are those of the headline.

Spring and Fall Circuits 1800

The year 1800 began with the addition of a new justice to the Supreme Court: Alfred Moore of North Carolina, who had been appointed in December 1799 to fill the vacancy left by the death of James Iredell. Before the year was over the Court also had a new home. By December the seat of government had been moved from Philadelphia to the still-unfinished federal city on the Potomac River, where the Supreme Court was allotted a small basement room in the Capitol.[1]

But the year was dominated by the imposing figure of Associate Justice Samuel Chase, who, from April to June, "roamed the Middle Circuit stamping out sedition wherever he could."[2] William Paterson presided over a seditious libel trial in Vermont that resulted in conviction for a supporter of imprisoned Congressman Matthew Lyon, but it was Chase who became the focus of Republican ire for his zealous—at times overzealous—enforcement of the Sedition Act of 1798. The events of this circuit later became the basis of seven of eight articles of impeachment brought against Chase in 1804, of which he was ultimately acquitted.[3]

Chase was an impulsive, quick-tempered man who did not hesitate to speak his mind. An Anti-Federalist in the 1780s, Chase moved slowly but steadily into the Federalist camp and soon shared that party's hostility to criticism of its administration. In 1796, two years before the passage of the Sedition Act, Chase was already expressing views he would echo in statements he delivered from the bench in 1800: "a free Press is the Support of Liberty and a Republican Goṽ," he wrote to a friend, "but a licentious press is the bane of freedom, and the Peril of Society, and will do more to destroy real liberty than any other Instrument in the Hands of knaves & fools."[4]

Chase's tour of duty this year began in Philadelphia, where, sitting with Judge Richard Peters, he presided over the sedition trial of the Republican journalist Thomas Cooper and the second treason trial of John Fries, leader of the Fries Rebellion.[5] Cooper was an English-born radical whose writings had offended Federalists and whom they undoubtedly would have preferred behind bars during the presidential campaign of 1800. In April Cooper was indicted by a federal grand jury on the basis of a handbill he had written the previous November, in which—in the course of defending himself against an attack on his integrity—he sharply criticized the policies of President Adams. Although Chase's conduct of Cooper's trial did not form the basis of any of the articles of impeachment later leveled against him, Chase made a number of questionable rulings that were hostile to the defense, and his charge to the trial jury sounded like an argument for the prosecution. One of Cooper's allegedly libellous statements ac-

---

1. *DHSC,* 1:139; Miller, *Federalist Era,* pp. 254, 275.
2. James Haw et al., *Stormy Patriot: The Life of Samuel Chase* (Baltimore: Maryland Historical Society, 1980) p. 197.
3. Miller, *Crisis in Freedom,* pp. 123-25; *Trial of Samuel Chase,* 2 vols (Washington, D.C.: printed for Samuel H. Smith, 1805), 1:5-8. For details of Lyon's trial, see introduction to "Spring and Fall Circuits 1798."
4. Samuel Chase to James McHenry, December 4, 1796, James McHenry Papers, DLC.
5. For details of the Fries Rebellion and Fries's first trial, see introduction to "Spring and Fall Circuits 1799."

cused Adams of having reduced the nation's credit "so low as to borrow money at eight per cent in time of peace." In reviewing this aspect of the case for the jury, Chase protested that the country was indeed in the midst of hostilities with France and exclaimed, "I cannot suppress my feelings at this gross attack upon the President. . . . The traverser . . . has published an untruth, knowing it to be an untruth."[6]

Chase refused to let Cooper subpoena the president, whose testimony Cooper maintained was crucial to his defense, and he refused to postpone the trial to allow Cooper to obtain authenticated copies of Adams's writings. Chase also placed the burden of proof squarely on the defendant: "the traverser in his defense must prove every charge he has made to be true; he must prove it to the marrow. If he asserts three things, and proves but one, he fails; if he proves but two, he fails in his defence, for he must prove the whole of his assertions to be true." This instruction virtually assured a conviction, and indeed the jury returned a verdict of guilty. At sentencing, Chase voiced his suspicion that any fine imposed by the court would actually be paid by Cooper's party; this was too much even for Judge Peters, who remarked, "I think we have nothing to do with parties; we are only to consider the subject before us." The Republican press commented in disgust that Chase had "conducted himself as if he had been a Lawyer, with a fee of five hundred guineas in his pocket, employed against the prisoner."[7]

Chase's subsequent conduct at the second trial of John Fries stirred opponents of the government to even greater heights of indignation. Chase was aware that Fries's counsel, Alexander James Dallas and William Lewis, would make the same argument they had made at Fries's first trial the previous year: that Fries's forcible resistance to a single law of the United States did not amount to treason. Before the trial even began, Chase issued an opinion that squarely held against them on that point. Seeing their defense crumble, Dallas and Lewis announced that they could not proceed when the court had prejudged the legal issues. Chase offered to withdraw the opinion, but the defense attorneys were adamant. When Fries refused to have other counsel appointed for him, Chase declared, "Then we will be your counsel; and, by the blessing of God, do you as much justice, as those who were assigned to you." Opinions differed as to how solicitous the court was of Fries's interests, but in any event the defendant was convicted and sentenced to death. Before pronouncing sentence, Chase addressed the defendant at length on the enormity of his crime and the need for repentance.[8]

At his impeachment trial, Chase pointed out that the substance of his opinion in the Fries case was well supported by precedent. He defended its precipitous delivery as an effort to speed the progress of the trial at a time when the court's docket was extremely crowded. And Fries was not as defenseless as he appeared: he had refused the appointment of counsel on the advice of Dallas and Lewis, whose theory apparently was that such a position would make a presidential pardon more likely. In this they were correct. Against the advice of his cabinet, President Adams issued a pardon in May 1800, and according to one account Fries went on to open a tin-ware store in

---

6. Wharton, *State Trials,* pp. 661n, 672-73; Letter from an Anonymous Correspondent to Meriwether Jones, May 7, 1800 (q.v.); Presser, "A Tale of Two Judges," pp. 93, 96-98.

7. Wharton, *State Trials,* pp. 676, 678-79; *Friend of the People* (Richmond), July 5, 1800.

8. *Trial of Samuel Chase,* 1:140, 156; Wharton, *State Trials,* pp. 624n, 637-41; Presser, "A Tale of Two Judges," pp. 88-93.

Philadelphia, "where, profiting by the custom his notoriety drew to him, he acquired a respectable fortune, and a respectable character."[9] But Chase's conduct promoted a wave of abuse and vilification that lasted throughout the year. The Republican press declared that Chase's definition of treason was "a construction subversive of the rights of free citizens," adding, "forever cursed be that tyrant who invades these sacred rights." In New York, Chase was compared to the bloodthirsty seventeenth century English chief justice, George Jeffreys, and "toasted" with the words, "May he speedily begin that course of repentence for himself, that he so lately recommended to Fries."[10]

From Philadelphia Chase went on to Annapolis, where, according to one report, he unsuccessfully attempted to have the grand jury indict a Baltimore printer on sedition charges.[11] While Chase was there, his friend Luther Martin, attorney general of Maryland, passed on a copy of a pamphlet called *The Prospect Before Us,* written by a hotheaded Scotsman then living in Virginia named James Thomson Callender. Martin had underlined the parts that he considered libellous. Chase was heard to declare that he would take the pamphlet with him to Richmond, the next stop on his circuit, "as a proper subject for prosecution," adding that "if the commonwealth or its inhabitants were not too depraved to furnish a jury of good and respectable men, he would certainly punish Callender."[12]

The grand jury in Richmond returned an indictment on May 24, and Callender was apprehended several days later. As the first case brought in staunchly Republican Virginia under the Sedition Act, the Callender prosecution aroused enormous public interest, and partisan feeling ran high. Three Virginia attorneys, including the state's attorney general, volunteered their services as defense counsel, and Callender entered a plea of not guilty. The defense began by attempting to obtain a continuance to the fall term in order to assemble material witnesses and documents and prepare their case. Chase denied the motion, but did postpone the trial for six days. Finally, on June 3, the trial began, in a room "thronged with spectators from every quarter."[13]

During the trial, which lasted eight hours, Chase and the defense attorneys wrangled repeatedly. Chase bluntly told the attorneys that their interpretations of the law were wrong and refused to let them argue to the jury the unconstitutionality of the Sedition Act—an argument on which their entire case was based. He refused to dismiss a juryman who admitted that he had read excerpts from *The Prospect Before Us* and believed them to be seditious. He barred the testimony of Callender's sole defense witness because it went to refute only part of one of the charges against Callender rather than the charge as a whole. Finally, as in the Fries trial, the defense attorneys grew so exasperated that they packed up their papers and refused to proceed. After deliberating for two hours, the jury returned a verdict of guilty, and Callender was fined two hundred dollars and sentenced to nine months of imprisonment. Before passing sentence, Chase expounded upon the gravity of Callender's offense and vigorously defended President Adams against his attack.[14]

9. *Trial of Samuel Chase,* 1:33-34, 140; Wharton, *State Trials,* p. 648. The *DAB* says there is no support for this story.

10. *American Citizen* (New York), May 28, 1800; *Aurora* (Philadelphia), May 30, 1800; *Aurora* (Philadelphia), July 14, 1800.

11. *City Gazette* (q.v. under date of June 4, 1800).

12. Haw, *Stormy Patriot,* pp. 202-3; *Trial of Samuel Chase,* 1:193.

13. Haw, *Stormy Patriot,* pp. 203-4; *Universal Gazette* (Philadelphia), June 19, 1800.

14. Haw, *Stormy Patriot,* pp. 203-6; Wharton, *State Trials,* pp. 696-97, 709-12, 718; *Trial of Samuel Chase,* 1:185-87, 199-205; *Connecticut Courant* (Hartford), June 23, 1800.

Chase's last stop was in New Castle, Delaware, where the grand jury, after deliberating for a little while, announced it had found no one to indict and asked to be discharged. Chase refused, remarking that he had heard there was a "most seditious printer" in Wilmington—apparently meaning James Wilson, editor of the *Mirror of the Times*—and directed the district attorney to look into the matter immediately. The next day the district attorney reported that he could find nothing seditious in the paper, and Chase agreed to dismiss the grand jury.[15]

Throughout the spring and summer, newspapers across the country were filled with attacks on Chase, along with a few articles written in his defense. One anonymous observer of the Cooper and Fries trials in Philadelphia detailed what he termed Chase's "arbitrary, high handed and tyrannical" behavior in a letter to the editor of the Philadelphia *Aurora*, leading Chase to threaten a libel action.[16] Most of the criticism centered on Chase's conduct of the Callender trial. Chase's refusal to delay the trial until Callender could assemble his witnesses "must alarm even the most thoughtless and indifferent spectators of public transactions," the *Albany Register* fumed. Another commentator denounced Chase's ruling that the constitutionality of the Sedition Act was for the court, not the jury to decide. Yet another concluded that "it was sufficient punishment for Callender's offence, that he was obliged to remain so long in the fangs of such an ungenerous and relentless judge."[17]

Off the bench, Chase's efforts on behalf of President Adams in the election of 1800 brought him yet more ridicule and denunciation in the opposition press. In August, the Philadelphia *Aurora* mistakenly reported that the Supreme Court lacked a quorum because, among other reasons, Chase was electioneering in Maryland: "What a becoming spectacle to see *Chase* mounted on a stump, with a face like a full moon, vociferating in favor of the present President, and the Supreme Court adjourning from day to day ... until Chase shall have disgorged himself!" "A Republican"—possibly Charles Pinckney—commented in October that "the papers say ... that Judge C_____ ... has been attending public meetings, and making speeches" in support of Adams, and speculated on what chance any critic of the Adams administration would have if brought before Chase on seditious libel charges. An English observer of the American election campaign expressed horror at the sight of a judge of the Supreme Court "mounting the tub at an electioneering meeting of the people ... and there exposing the dignity of the national judiciary, to the coarse gibes and scoffing jokes of every mischievous bystander." Although Chase was the target of most of the abuse, he was not the only Supreme Court justice engaging in partisan activity: Bushrod Washington's letters predicting a Federalist victory in South Carolina—a crucial state in the close presidential race of 1800—were widely circulated in the Federalist press.[18]

Adams lost the election despite Chase's efforts, and the Republican candidates for president and vice-president, Thomas Jefferson and Aaron Burr, tied with seventy-

---

15. Haw, *Stormy Patriot,* pp. 206-7; *Trial of Samuel Chase,* 1:7-8. See also Letter from an Anonymous Correspondent, June 28, 1800, and *Mirror of the Times,* July 4, 1800.

16. See Letter from an Anonymous Correspondent, May 7, 1800; Samuel Chase to Meriwether Jones, May 26, 1800; "A Card to Judge Chase," under date of June 20, 1800; and Samuel Chase to Meriwether Jones, July 1, 1800.

17. *Albany Register* (Albany), June 24, 1800; *American Citizen* (New York), July 1, 1800; *Aurora* (Philadelphia), June 13, 1800.

18. *DHSC,* 1:895; *Aurora* (Philadelphia), October 27, 1800; *Virginia Argus* (Richmond), August 15, 1800; Kline, *Political Correspondence and Public Papers of Aaron Burr,* 1:464-65; Miller, *Federalist Era,* p. 267.

three electoral votes each. This threw the election into the House of Representatives, where, after an apparent deadlock, Jefferson eventually prevailed. The Federalist party was also decisively defeated in the congressional elections. Thus began twenty-four years of uninterrupted Republican domination of the federal government.[19]

As it became evident that the Republicans would win, the *Mirror of the Times* gloated at Chase's predicament: "Naturally proud, imperious, & overbearing—positive in his dogmas—supercilious in his manners—prejudiced in his decisions,—and headstrong in his opinions, what must he feel, when all parties transfer him to eternal contempt, and even the meanest of the mean despise him?" Others, however, saw Chase scheming to stave off defeat: one Republican newspaper identified Chase as a key figure in a conspiracy to retain Federalist control of the government. One element in the plan, the paper reported, was "to carry forward . . . the judiciary bill, which was lost last session, in order to provide in time for such persons as should be found active in promoting this vast *project of usurpation.*"[20]

Although this perceived Federalist conspiracy did not succeed, the judiciary bill did—at least for a while. The Judiciary Act of 1801, passed just a few weeks before the Republicans took office, greatly expanded the jurisdiction of the federal courts and, at last, abolished that bane of a Supreme Court justice's existence, circuit riding. Six new circuit courts and sixteen new circuit judgeships were created, along with the ancillary positions of clerks, United States marshals, and United States attorneys. But Republicans disliked the act and their opposition intensified when the outgoing President Adams hastily filled the new positions with members of his own party—the so-called "Midnight Judges." The fate of the legislation was sealed. In 1802 a Republican-controlled Congress repealed the 1801 act; many Federalist judges were unseated, and the justices of the Supreme Court were forced to resume their rounds. But in one important respect Adams was able to leave his mark on the federal judiciary. In January 1801 he nominated John Marshall, then his secretary of state, for the position of chief justice, filling the vacancy created by the resignation of Oliver Ellsworth in late 1800. During his thirty-four years in that office, Marshall transformed the Supreme Court into a powerful and central institution of government and was instrumental in laying the groundwork of modern constitutional interpretation.[21]

---

19. Noble E. Cunningham, Jr., "The Jeffersonian Republican Party," ed. Arthur M. Schlesinger, Jr., *History of U.S. Political Parties,* 4 vols. (New York: Chelsea House, 1973), 1:259.

20. Miller, *Federalist Era,,* pp. 268-74; *Mirror of the Times* (Wilmington), November 15, 1800; *Gazette of the United States* (Philadelphia), January 10, 1801.

21. George Haskins and Herbert Johnson, *Foundations of Power: John Marshall, 1801-15,* vol. 2 of *The Oliver Wendell Holmes Devise History of the Supreme Court of the United States* (New York: Macmillan, 1981), pp. 107-35; Miller, *Federalist Era,* p. 275; *DHSC,* 1:151-55.

Circuit Court for the District of New Jersey ——————————
April 1, 1800   Trenton, New Jersey

Associate Justice Samuel Chase and Judge Robert Morris opened court on April 1, and Samuel Chase delivered a charge to the grand jury. The court met twice before adjourning on April 3.[1]

1. Minutes, CCD New Jersey, RG 21, NjBaFAR. Charge not found.

Circuit Court for the District of New York ——————————————
April 1, 1800   New York, New York

On April 1 court commenced with Associate Justice Bushrod Washington and Judge John Sloss Hobart in attendance. Washington delivered a charge to the grand jury after the opening of the court. The court adjourned on April 9.[1]

1. Minutes, CCD New York, RG 21, NjBaFAR. Charge not found.

Circuit Court for the District of Pennsylvania ——————————————
April 11, 1800   Philadelphia, Pennsylvania

Associate Justice Samuel Chase and Judge Richard Peters opened court on April 11. Chase delivered a charge to the grand jury the following day. The court adjourned on May 2.[1]

1. Engrossed Minutes, CCD Pennsylvania, RG 21, PPFAR; Samuel Chase's Charge to the Grand Jury of the Circuit Court for the District of Pennsylvania, April 12, 1800 (q.v.).

Samuel Chase's Charge to the Grand Jury of the Circuit Court for the District of Pennsylvania ——————————————
April 12, 1800   Philadelphia, Pennsylvania

Gentlemen of the Grand Jury/
    In the charge, which I heretofore delivered to the Grand Jury of this District,[1] I expressed my opinion that the Federal Constitution was founded on the two pillars of Representation, and Responsibility; and that both these
                                    & fully
were amply ˄secured by the provisions contained in i[t] _ I endeavoured to point out the prominent and striking features of that Constitution; and I did not hesitate to declare, that our national, and State Constitutions are more favorable to Civil and religio[us] liberty, than any other forms of Government, or any system of Laws in the whole world. _ I also attemped to shew the necessity, the utility, and importance of the trial by Jury; and to explain the

D (MdHi, Samuel Chase Charge Book, MS. 2565). In the hand of Samuel Chase's son, Thomas Chase, with most of the interlineations in the hand of Samuel Chase. Date and place determined from evidence in the charge and the circuit court minutes.
    Although this charge is a discrete document and could have been read in its entirety, we do not know how much of it actually was read. Internal evidence also suggests that major portions of the charge were first delivered during the spring 1799 circuit at courts in New Hampshire, Massachusetts and/or Rhode Island.
    1. Chase presided at the April 1798 session of the Pennsylvania circuit court and delivered a charge to the grand jury on April 12. That charge has not been found. See Circuit Court for the District of Pennsylvania, April 11, 1798.

trust, power and duty of Grand Juries; and I [contended] ventu[red] to predict, "That whenever the trial by Jury in Criminal Cases should be substantially altered, or in Civil Cases abolished, in America; that soon after suc[h] event the Liberties of the people would be lost." _

As it appeared to me, that the several branche[s] of the duty required of the Grand Jury were prescribed by the Terms of their Oath, I endeavoured to explain the nature and meaning thereof; and gave my opini[on] that every Grand Jury, before they find an indictment, should expect the same proof, and as satisfactory evidenc[e] of the guilt of the accused as the Petit Jury would require to Justify their verdict against him; and, that if the proof should be doubtful, they should not put the party accused to the expence, and disgrace of a trial before the Petit Jury.

As I consider the trial by Jury of infinite importance, and essentially necessary to the security of the property, liberties, and lives of my fellow-Citizens, I will make some further observations on the subject.

I have often remarked, and esteem it a great public misfortune, that persons in good Circumstances, and of some Education, shew such reluctance to serve on Grand Juries; because such Characters are the most likely to discharge the duties of their office, with integrity, and propriety. They afford a great security to the peace and good order of Government, are a terror to those, who violate the Laws; and an ample security to the innocent. _ The trial by Jury would be more beneficial than it is, if those, who are most capable, and best qualified for the Station, were more ready to execute it. Such men would feel the importance and the weight the Constitution and Laws have given them; and they would firmly maintain their rights. _ In my opinion it is a breach of duty to Society when men of property, and persons of Education, and knowledge, decline serving on Juries, in their turn; unless prevented by some real impediment. Americans are unworthy of the Rights privileges, and the security they enjoy, under their Government and Laws, who will not take a part in those public Duties, that are necessary for their support, protection, & preservation _ If Juries are ignorant of their own rights, or timid in the Execution of those powers, that they are entitled to exercise, the value of this great privilege will be exceedingly diminished.

The petit Jury is of the same utility & importance to the public, as the Grand Jury; but a faithful execution of their trust is attended with more difficulty, and greater labor and fatigue, both of body and mind. The Grand Jury may examine cases before them at their leisure; they may adjourn, seperate, and refresh themselves, and reconsider every case. _ No witnesses but on the part of the United States are to be examined by them; they may have the advice of the Attorney for the District, and also the assistance of the Court; and a majority of them (not less than 12) is sufficient for their Decision, as to the truth of any accusation; or that sufficient testimony is not produced to establish the charge. _ A petit Jury have not the same

opportunity and leisure for enquiry, & decision. Their attention may be
attracted, and diverted by exterior objects. They cannot adjourn, or
                        but from absolute Necessity,
seperate, ∧until they unanimously agree; and in a Capital Case deliver their
open verdict to the Court. In criminal, as well as in Civil Cases, the facts
may be intricate, and the Witnesses numerous, and contradictory. The
examination may be so long, as to distract and confound the attention. _
All verdicts in Criminal Cases (and some general verdicts in Civil Cases)
include legal Consequences, as well as propositions of facts, and in drawing
those Consequences the Jury may mistake, and infer contrary to the Law.
The difficulty and trouble, and often the fatigue, is increased by the unanimity
that the Law requires for their verdict. Their Judgement is liable to be
deceived, or misled by the Oratory, and ingenious arguments of able and
learned Counsel. In Criminal Cases, it is the duty of the Court to assist and
advise the petit Jury on all Questions of Law, and it would betray an improper
suspicion of the Jury to believe, that they would not pay a proper respect
to the opinion of Judges, appointed and qualified to decide the Law, under
the solemn Obligations of Religion, and a regard to their Characters, and
the good opinion of their fellow = Citizens. _ If the Jury in a Criminal Case
should disregard the advice of the Court as to the Law; or find the accused
guilty, contrary to the weight of the Evidence, our Law, with a peculiar
mildness, authorizes the Court to grant a new trial. _ In all Civil Cases (except
only where the Law is so interwoven with the fact, that it cannot be seperated)
the Court are the sole ~~Constitutional~~ Judges of the Law; and the Jury ought
to follow their Direction, at the risque of their verdict being set aside, and
a new trial granted. _ 1 Pᴿ Wmˢ   212. 226.² ⊗

⊗the Exercise of this power by the Coᵗ is no encroachment upon the Jurisdiction of the
Jury nor drawing the ~~Quest~~ Domain of fact from the Jury. 4 Term 654 _ ³

If either party request, and the Court shall direct a special verdict, and the
Jury refuse to find one, the Court will grant a new trial
    It is of the greatest consequence to the administration of Justice, and the
security of property, that the powers of the Court, and of the petit Jury should
be known, and kept distinct and seperate; that the former may determine the
Law; and the latter the fact. It has been contended, that the petit Jury have a
right to determine the Law as well as the fact, in all Cases, Civil as well as
Criminal; but I hold, and have Just delivered a contrary opinion. I am fully
convinced, that the petit Jury have the right to decide the Law, as well as the
fact, in all Criminal Cases (and in that Class I include prosecutions for Li-

2. The citation is located in the margin and is to William Peere Williams, *Reports of Cases Argued and Determined in the High Court of Chancery, and some special Cases Adjudged in the Court
of King's Bench* 2 vols. (London: E. R. Nutt and R. Gosling, 1740), 1:212, 226.
    3. Duberley *against* Gunning (1792). Charles Durnford and Edward East, *Term Reports in the
Court of King's Bench*, 4:654; reprinted in *The English Reports*, 176 vols. (Edinburgh: William
Green & Sons, 1900-1930), 100:1227.

bels.) and consequently to give a general verdict of Guilt or acquittal; and
that the Court have no right to refuse or controul such a verdict; and that
their duty only requires _{them} to assist and advise the Jury, on all questions of Law,
that may occur on the trial of Criminal Cases.[4]

The first political axiom in the formation of our national, as well as our
State Governments, and the only basis upon which they were _{erected} [directed?] is
this, "that a majority of the people have a right to govern;" and this axiom
must be invariably adhered to in the administration of our Governments; or
there will be an end of all order, and all Government. It was not necessary
that the Federal, or State Governments should have been established by universal consent, or by the general voice of the people; but I believe that all
the State Governments, and we all know, that the Federal Government was
adopted and ratified by a very great majority of the Citizens of the several
States. It will not be denied that a considerable number of them refused their
assent to the ratification, without previous amendments, and we know that a
party has since arisen, who wish that the administration of the Government
had been entrusted to other hands; but it cannot be tolerated, that because a
small part of the Community did not concur in the erecting of the Government, or in the persons to administer it, that therefore they are not obliged
to submit to its authority, or to contribute to its support. They enjoy the
benefit of its protection, and the security of the Laws to their persons and
property; and therefore they are bound, in duty, to yield allegiance and submission; and to bear their part of the public Taxes equally with their fellow
Citizens. _ There can be no Government without subordination, which implies submission; and submission in matters of a Civil nature, implies that the
majority minority surrender up their Judgement and will to the Decision of
a majority. Every Citizen in America has engaged to be bound by the Acts
of the majority of his fellow Citizens, signified by their Representatives in
their national and State Legislatures, however repugnant to his own views of
propriety, or even Justice. Private opinion must give way to public Judgement, or there must be an end of Government. No Law can be passed by the
Federal (or any State) Legislature, but by a majority of our Representatives;
and when passed it is binding on the minority and on the whole Community.

But it is said, that Congress have made some Laws, that are unconstitutional; and others that are burthensome and oppressive. It should be remembered, that the members of Congress are chosen either mediately, or and immediately by the peeop people, in the manner, and for the period they
themselves prescribed; and it is their fault if they do not elect men of abilities, and integrity. It should also be remembered, that the members of Congress are, in general, Gentlemen of Landed as well as personal property, and

4. In the margin Chase wrote: "pa. 15." This may have been a reminder to skip to page fifteen
of the charge. An erased signature of Samuel Chase's also appears at this point.

are acquainted with the interests and Circumstances of their Constituents, so far, at least, as they can be the objects of Federal Legislation. They can have no interest in oppressing their fellow Citizens, every Law that is is detrimental to them must prove hurtful to themselves, for they can make no Law that will not affect them equally, in every respect, with their Constituents. The most dissatisfied and factious man in America must acknowledge, that every one of our Citizens (of every rank and station in life) enjoys an equal share of Civil Liberty, an equal protection of Law, and an equal security for his person and property. Every dispassionate and well informed Citizen, will admit, that the Taxes for the support of Government are imposed in as Just and equal a proportion, as the different Circumstances of the Union will permit; and he must be a vain, conceited individual who can think himself as capable to Judge of what is necessary for the support of Government as those whom the nation has chosen, & entrusted for that very purpose. It cannot be credited

that Congress will intentionally violate the $_\wedge$Constitution, contrary to their sacred trust; or wilfully impose ~~but~~ unreasonable and unjust burthens, in which
federal

they must participate. _ But if Congress have, or should from $_\wedge$error in
Inattention, or

Judgement, ~~or want of information~~, pass Laws in violation of the ~~Federal~~
or want of information,

Constitution; or burthensome or oppressive to the people; a peaceable, safe, and ample remedy is provided by the Federal Constitution, ~~and Laws~~. The

people$_\wedge$have established the mode, by which such grievances are to be re-
themselves

dressed; and no other can be adopted without a violation of the Constitution, and the Laws.

If the Federal Legislature should, at any time, pass a Law contrary to the Constitution of the United States, such Law would be void; because that Constitution is the fundamental Law of the United States, and paramount any Act of the Federal Legislature; whose authority is derived from, and delegated by, that Constitution; 2 Dallas   308 Judge   Paterson   sp[5] ~~The Judi~~
which

imposes certain restrictions on the Legislative authority that can only be preserved through the medium of the Courts of Justice. The Judicial power of the United States is co-existent, co-extensive, and co-ordinate with, and altogether independant of, the Legislature & the Executive; and the Judges of the Supreme, and District Courts are bound by their Oath of Office, to regulate their Decisions agreeably to the Constitution. The Judicial power,

therefore, are the only proper and competent authority to decide ~~the Con-~~
whether

~~stitutionality of~~ any Law made by Congress; or any of the State Legislatures$_\wedge$
is contrary to or in Violation of the federal Constitution.

5. This notation appears in the margin and is to Associate Justice William Paterson's opinion in the case of *Vanhorne's Lessee v. Dorrance,* delivered at the April 1795 term of the Circuit Court for the district of Pennsylvania and reported in *Dallas,* 2:308, second paragraph.

If Congress should pass burthensome, or oppressive Laws, the remedy is with their Constituents; from whom they derive their existence, and authority. If any Law is made repugnant to the Sense of a majority of their Constituents, it is in their power to make choice of persons to repeal it; but until it is repealed, it is the Duty of every Citizen to submit to it; and to give up his private Sentiments to the public Will. If a Law burthensome, or even oppressive, in its nature, or execution is to be opposed by force, there can be no Government in this Country. At ev͟ery Session of Congress a Law is passed, which gives offence, and creates a clamour in one part of the Union, and its execution is opposed by force; at another Session another Law is made, equally disagreeable to another part of the Union, and creates similar resistance. If these Laws are immediately to be repealed because of such opposition, every man can see, that such conduct must soon produce a dissolution of the Government; because if the open resistance of a small part of the Community is the effectual means to obtain a repeal of a Law; it will be the height of folly to expect afterwards to see any Law executed.

I wish, Gentlemen, to impress upon you a belief of this political truth, that the Laws are the only security for an impartial administration of Justice, and the protection of your‿Liberty, and property from violence; and that it is the indispensable duty of every Citizen to submit to the Laws, although ever so repugnant to his private opinion; until they are repealed, or declared void, by the Constituted authorities. No man is a good Citizen who intentionally violates the Laws of his Country; and every one is a bad Citizen who opposes by force the execution of the Laws. The man who openly opposes, and the man who secretly advises opposition is equally criminal; and the latter is the most despicable and dangerous character. Patriotism, like religion, is often the cloak for the most wicked actions. The real patriot is the man whose ruling passion is the love of his Country, which consists in due obedience to Government, and its Laws; in a reverence for public Liberty; and a discharge of all social duties. _ The false patriot is the man, who professes himself a friend to Liberty, and yet wilfully misrepresents his Government, and the conduct of its Officers; or, without Just cause, creates distrust and suspicion of the Legislature, or of the Executive, or of the principal Officers of Government; and openly opposes, ~~and~~ secretly foments and encourages opposition to the execution of the Laws. By carefully attending to the actions, and not the professions of men, their principles, and views may be determined. "Ye shall know them by their fruits: A good‿tree cannot bring forth evil fruit, neither can a corrupt tree bring for good fruit."[6] This Rule is equally the Test of political as Religious principles.[7]

---

6. Matt. 7:16, 18.

7. This sentence is in the hand of Samuel Chase.

I have made these observations, Gentlemen, in consequence of the former
        late   this   so happily
and ~~present~~ insurrection in the Common Wealth of Pennsylvania; ~~and I~~
and speedily quelled by the Vigilance and Energy of our Gov.ᵗ; [*word illegible*] and by the zeal,
~~hope you will excuse this digression from the immediate business for which~~
prudence and skill of the General ~~to whom~~ appointed to this Duty
~~you are assembled.~~

You remember, Gentlemen, that you have sworn to present, "not only such
matters and things, as come to your knowledge; but such also, "as shall be
given you in charge." By this engagement to present all such matters and things,
as shall be given you in charge, I understand that, if the Court shall inform
you of any Law of the United States, which makes the doing any act a Crime,
and punishes it as such; and you shall be satisfied from the Evidence before
you, that such act has been committed, that it is your bounden ~~duty~~ and indispensable duty to present the fact; and by whom done. It is my opinion,
that you have no right to decide on the Justice, or the validity of the Law;
and if you should exercise the power, that you would thereby usurp the au-
                                                                    to ~~deter~~ judge
thority entrusted by the Federal Constitution to the Legislature ∧ or ~~Judici-~~
                                                                    Constitutionality.
of the Justice of its laws; and to the judiciary to determine their ∧ ~~Validity~~
~~ary.~~†ᵃ

The Laws ~~punish~~ of Congress punish the highest Crimes and the lowest
offences, against the National Government, but in different Courts.

By the Federal Constitution the Judicial power of the United States was
vested in one supreme Court, and in such other inferior Courts, as Congress
should, from time to time, ordain and establish. Congress by Statute established inferior Courts, called Circuit, and District Courts. 24 Sept.ʳ 1789 c.
20.[8] This Statute gives the Circuit Courts exclusive Jurisdiction of all Crimes
& offences cognizable under the authority of the United States, unless oth-
erways provided by Law; and concurrent Jurisdiction, with the District Courts,
of all Crimes and offences cognizable therein.

†ᵃ[9] I do not think it necessary, Gentlemen, at this time, to enumerate all
the Crimes punishible by the Laws of the Federal Government, because I expect that very few (if any) will be brought before you. The great and Capital
Offences, that are the subject of your enquiry, and within the Jurisdiction of
this Court to punish are, Stat. 30ᵗʰ April 1790 c. 9.[10] 1.ˢᵗ Treason, which consists in two acts only, namely, levying War against the United States; or adhering to their Enemies, giving them aid and comfort. 2.ᵈ Murder, committed
in some place (within the United States) under the sole & exclusive Jurisdic-

8. The citation appears in the margin and refers to the court system created by the Judiciary
Act of 1789, passed September 24, 1789. *Stat.*, 1:73.

9. The daggers may mark the text between them for omission.

10. The citation appears in the margin and is to the Crimes Act of 1790, passed on April 30,
1790. *Stat.*, 1:112.

tion of Congress; as within the District of Columbia, or within any fort, arsenal, Dockyard, or magazine; or on the high Seas, or in any river, haven, bason, or bay, out of the Jurisdiction of any particular State. 3ᵈ Piracy (or robbery, as specified in the Law) or any act of hostility against the United States, or any Citizen thereof, committed by any Citizen, upon the high Seas, under color of any commission from any foreign prince, or State; or on pretence of authority from any person. 4ᵗʰ Robbery, committed upon the high Seas, or in any river, haven, bason, or bay, not within the Jurisdiction of any particular State. 5ᵗʰ Forgery of any Certificate, or other public security, of the United States; or the willingly assisting in such forgery, or passing any forged Certificate, or other public security, of the United States, with intention to defraud and with knowledge of its being counterfeited. 6ᵗʰ Accessaries before the fact, to murder, robbery or other piracy, upon the Seas. There are other Capital Crimes; but to the credit of our Criminal Code they are not numerous. There are a variety of less offences interspersed through the Laws of Congress to which I do not think it necessary even to refer you; because they principally relate to the Revenue and excise Laws; and it will be the duty of the public Officers to give you information of any breaches of those Laws.

The last subject of your Enquiry and to which I require your particular attention, is of any breaches of the Act of Congress, entitled "An Act concerning Aliens," passed 25ᵗʰ June 1798 c. 75. _ [11] or of any breach of the Act of Congress entitled "An Act [in] addition to the Act entitled, An Act for the punishment [of] certain Crimes against the United States," commonly called the Sedition Law; 14ᵗʰ July, 1798. c. 31. _ [12] or of any breach of the Act of Congress entitled, "The Usurpation of Executive authority. "An Act for the punishment of certain Crimes therein specified." _ 30 Jany. 99.[13] which are Usurpations of the Executive Authority of the U.States.

Before I conclude e^tc[14]

Before I dismiss you, Gentlemen, I would observe, that our Common
                              time
Country is, at this Cou^ntry in a very critical and alarming situation. Dangers approach our infant Republic from abroad; and Divisions threaten it from within.

Our rights of Commerce, as a neutral nation, rights recognized and established for ages, by all the Commercial powers of Europe, have been denied. The fair and lawful trade of our Citizens has been, for years, obstructed, and their property on the Seas (to an immense amount) has been seised & condemned as prize in open violation of the Law of Nations, and in contempt of

11. The citation appears in the margin and is to the Alien Act, passed on June 25. *Stat.*, 1:570.

12. The citation appears in the margin and is to the Sedition Act, passed on July 14, 1798. *Stat.*, 1:596.

13. The citation appears in the margin and is to the Crimes Act of 1799, passed on January 30, 1799. *Stat.*, 1:613.

14. This phrase and the preceding sentence are in the hand of Samuel Chase.

a solemn treaty; and in some instances on the most frivolous pretences; The
very arming of our <u>merchant</u> vessels for <u>Defence</u>_∧^{has been} ~~was~~ declared a sufficient
cause for condemnation.

The persons of our fellow Citizens have been frequently insulted and abused;
and in some cases treated_∧^{with} severity and even cruelty. or _ "our fellow_∧^{Citizens} ~~Sub-jects~~ have been subjected to insults, Stripes, Wounds, torture & Imprisonment _ "[15]

Our Federal Government has been grosly insulted and disgraced in the
persons of its ministers. The olive branch has been spurned, and our Ambassadors of peace & friendship rejected with scorn.

A disgraceful <u>tribute</u>, under the name of a <u>Loan</u>, has been demanded, bribes
have been asked, and we have been menaced with the fate of Venice, if we
refuse to comply. From the <u>French</u> Directory we have received <u>all these injuries and insults</u>; and we have been told that we are divided from, and disgusted with, the virtuous characters, to whom we have entrusted the administration of our Government.

Notwithstanding the late appointment of ministers to treat with the French
Republic, I have very little (if any), hope of any sincere and permanent con-
ciliation; at least. I may be allowed to say in the language of our illustrious_∧^{patriotic} and
the determined foe of Vice; the uniform friend of Religion and piety, Morality and Virtue. _
beloved President;_∧ "The most <u>precious</u> interests of the people of the United
States_∧^{says that wise and vigilant Statesman,} are still in <u>Jeopardy</u> by the <u>hostile designs</u>, and <u>insidious</u> Acts of a
<u>foreign nation</u>; as well as_∧^{as} by the dissemination among them of <u>those princi-
ples</u>, subversive of the foundation of all <u>religious</u>, <u>moral</u>, and <u>social</u> obligations, that have produced incalculable mischief & misery in other Coun-
tries."[16]

From this <u>brief</u>, view of the situation of America with respect to France,
permit me, Gentlemen, most earnestly to recommend to you, by the love of
your Country, and a regard to its dearest rights, to exert your <u>utmost</u> endeavours to support your Federal Government, and the present administration thereof; and to maintain inviolate the Union of the States, on which,
under God, your <u>safety</u> depends. Although we may differ in opinion as to
<u>local</u> politics, & <u>particular</u> measures of Government, let us unite to maintain,
at every hazard and danger, its freedom & independence of <u>any foreign</u> power;
let us place a <u>Just</u> confidence in our <u>Legislature and Executive</u>, and use all
the means in our power to protect our Commerce from lawless Depreda-

15. The quotation is in the hand of Samuel Chase.

16. The quotation is from John Adams's March 6, 1799, proclamation for a day of "solemn
humiliation, fasting, and prayer." Martin P. Claussen, gen. ed., *National State Papers of the United
States, 1789-1817*, part II, *Texts of Documents: Administration of John Adams, 1797-1801*, vol. 13
March 1, 1799-November 27, 1799 (Wilmington, Del.: Michael Glazier, 1980), p. 345.

tions, and to preserve the <u>honor</u>, the <u>dignity</u>, and the <u>interest</u> of our Country. Let us prepare our minds to meet, with fortitude and perseverance the events of War, the scourge of Nations; and let us place our <u>whole</u> confidence in the Justice of our Cause; and the protection of the great Rule[r] of the Universe! _ America united has every thing to <u>hope</u>, but divided, w̶i̶t̶ẖ̶o̶u̶t̶ the special interposition of Providence, she has every thing to fear.

I will, Gentlemen, detain you no longer. Be pleased therefore to ᵥyour Chamber & consider such matters as may be brought before you.

Circuit Court for the District of Connecticut ───────────
April 14, 1800   New Haven, Connecticut

On Monday, April 14, the circuit court convened with Associate Justice Bushrod Washington and Judge Richard Law in attendance. The court adjourned on April 18.[1]

1. Docket Book, CCD Connecticut, RG 21, MWalFAR.

Timothy Pickering to William Paterson ───────────
April 21, 1800   Philadelphia, Pennsylvania

Department of State
Philadelphia   April 21. 1800.

Dear Sir,

I have just received the inclosed from Mʳ Rawle.[1] As you perfectly understand the subject, and know the importance of bringing the criminal trials referred to, to a conclusion at this time, and of avoiding a legislative interposition when not [absol?]utely necessary especially toward the close of the session _ [2] [It?] would be improper in me to urge a compliance with the [arrangement?] suggested _ thus you would have the [goodness to?] hold the approaching circuit court in Maryland; whereby Judge Chase will be enabled to finish the Criminal trials in this city.[3]

I am with great   respect, sir   your obᵗ servᵗ

Timothy Pickering

Honble
Judge Paterson

ACS (MHi, Timothy Pickering Papers). Readings in brackets supplied where ink has faded.

1. Enclosure not found.

2. Timothy Pickering is referring to the retrial of John Fries and other Northampton insurgents in the Circuit Court for the district of Pennsylvania. For more information on the Fries case, see "Spring and Fall Circuits 1800."

3. In fact, Justice Chase presided at the circuit court in Maryland. See Circuit Court for the District of Maryland, May 7, 1800.

Alfred Moore by Edward Greene Malbone (1777-1807). Watercolor on ivory, ca. 1805. Courtesy Office of the Curator, Supreme Court of the United States.

Circuit Court for the District of Georgia ————————————
April 21, 1800   Savannah, Georgia

Associate Justice Alfred Moore[1] and Judge Joseph Clay, Jr., opened court April 21 and adjourned it on April 28 to the following term.[2]

1. Alfred Moore had been nominated as associate justice on December 4, 1799, to fill the vacancy created by the death of James Iredell. The Senate confirmed Moore's nomination on December 10. *DHSC*, 1:140.
2. Minutes, CCD Georgia, RG 21, GEpFAR. Charge not found.

Bushrod Washington to William Cushing ————————————
April 22, 1800   New York, New York

New York.   April 22. 1800

Dear Sir

I find that the Judiciary bill is postponed to the next Session, so that we shall have to ride the fall Circuits.[1] Presuming that the Southern Circuit will be extremely disagreable and inconvenient to you, and feeling that it will be not more so to me than the Eastern, which falls to me in the regular course, I propose that we exchange, so as to produce an accomodation to both. Living more contiguous to the Southern Circuit than to the Eastern, it will be in my power to remain a few weeks at home after returning from the Supreme Court in August, which is an inducement, that over-balances the disagreable nature of that Journey. Should this proposition meet your wishes it will afford me great pleasure as well on your account as my own, and I must request a letter from you signifying your pleasure, as it will be necessary for both of us to be prepared when we meet in August. address to me "in Westmoreland County near the + roads Virginia"[2]

With respectful Complts. to Mrs Cushing   I am dear Sir   Y mo. ob. Ser^t

Bushrod Washington

ARS (MHi, Cushing Family Papers, 1650-1840). Addressed "Boston Massachusetts _ ." Postmarked "NEW YORK APR 24."

1. The "bill to provide for the more convenient organization of the courts of the United States," introduced on March 31, 1800, proposed a major reorganization of the federal judicial system, including the elimination of circuit riding. The House of Representatives, however, postponed further consideration of the bill on April 14, 1800. At its next session, new legislation was introduced containing many of the same provisions as the March 1800 bill, and it passed as the Judiciary Act of 1801. *HRJ*, 3:647, 662-63, 743; Congressional Collection, Rare Book Room, DLC; *Stat.*, 2:89. This legislation will receive more complete treatment in volume 4 of the *DHSC*.

2. Cushing's reply not found, but evidently he agreed to the exchange; see Supreme Court of the United States—Assignment of Circuits, August 15, 1800.

Bushrod Washington attributed to Chester Harding (1792-1866). Oil on canvas, ca. 1820-1830. Courtesy Office of the Curator, Supreme Court of the United States.

Julia Ann (Blackburn) Washington attributed to Chester Harding (1792-1866). Oil on canvas, ca. 1820-1830. Courtesy Office of the Curator, Supreme Court of the United States.

View of the North front of Belvidere, Richmond by Benjamin Henry Latrobe (1764-1820). Pencil, pen and ink, and watercolor on paper, ca. 1796-1798. Courtesy Maryland Historical Society, Baltimore. Benjamin Henry Latrobe Papers. Belvidere, on a hill overlooking the James River, was the home of Bushrod Washington from June 1795 until February 1798.

Circuit Court for the District of Vermont

May 1, 1800   Windsor, Vermont

On May 1 court was opened by Associate Justice William Paterson and Judge Samuel Hitchcock. The court adjourned on May 9.[1]

1. Circuit Docket, CCD Vermont, RG 21, MWalFAR.

Philadelphia Gazette

May 3, 1800   Philadelphia, Pennsylvania

[*The* Philadelphia Gazette *first reports on cases that came before the Circuit Court for the district of Pennsylvania during the spring term.*] At the rising of the Court, Judge *CHASE*, when about to leave the bench, observed, that he intended to have said something to the gentlemen of the Bar, and regretted that so many of them had left the Court.

He observed, that this was probably the last time that he should ever preside in this Court; a different arrangement by law, and his own declining health, would prevent his attendance upon any future occasion.[1]

He therefore now thought proper to say, that he parted with deep impressions of the ability, honor and respectability of the *PENNSYLVANIA BAR*. That every one who had observed the business of the Court, must know, that much important matter, civil and criminal, had occured in the present sessions.

That he thought himself bound to pay this tribute of respect and friendship to the Attorney of the District[2] and his Assistant,[3] for the very respectable manner in which they had conducted the prosecutions. He had seldom known any instance of the kind, so perfectly free from any incidental passion, heat or impatience of conduct.

That he also considered the Counsel for the prisoners as having acquitted themselves with ability and propriety.

He wished to be understood, that if any expressions, in the hurry of business, had escaped him, which might have been considered as reflecting upon the conduct of any of the counsel, that he now declared he did not intend to convey any idea of the kind; that he had always been the sincere well wisher of the gentlemen of this Bar, as well in respect to those with whom he had the pleasure to be personally acquainted, as others; and was fully impressed with the ability, integrity and candor which characterised their practice at the bar, and rendered them so useful to the public. He then bid them an affectionate farewell, and turning to Judge Peters, expressed how much he was gratified by the recollection of the general coincidence of sentiment that had subsisted between them, and acknowledged he had derived essential assistance from his Colleague, on subjects of law and business, and much kind and friendly advice on matters of a private nature; and left his best wishes of happiness and prosperity with him and the Bar.

Judge CHASE set out this morning for Annapolis.

(Philadelphia) May 3, 1800, supplement edition. Date and place are those of the newspaper.

1. Chase, despite occasional ill health, remained on the bench until his death in 1811. The legislation referred to is the "bill to provide for the more convenient organization of the courts of the United States." It would have eliminated circuit riding by Supreme Court justices, but further consideration of the bill had been postponed by the House of Representatives on April 14, 1800. Chase apparently believed that the bill would be reintroduced in the next session of Congress. *HRJ*, 3:662-63.

2. William Rawle.

3. Jared Ingersoll (1749-1822), a prominent Philadelphia lawyer and former Pennsylvania attorney general. Ingersoll would succeed William Rawle as the United States attorney for the district of Pennsylvania on May 7, 1800. *DAB;* Wharton, *State Trials*, p. 622; *SEJ*, 1:351-32.

Circuit Court for the District of South Carolina ───────────
May 6, 1800   Charleston, South Carolina

Associate Justice Alfred Moore and Judge Thomas Bee opened court on May 6. The court adjourned on May 9 to the following term.[1]

  1. Minutes, CCD South Carolina, RG 21, GEpFAR.

Circuit Court for the District of Maryland ──────────────
May 7, 1800   Annapolis, Maryland

On May 7 court convened with Associate Justice Samuel Chase and Judge James Winchester in attendance. Chase delivered a charge to the grand jury. The court met until May 16, when it adjourned to the following term.[1]

  1. Minutes, CCD Maryland, RG 21, PPFAR. Charge not found, but see *City Gazette* under date of June 4, 1800.

Letter from an Anonymous Correspondent to Meriwether Jones ───────
Aurora
May 7, 1800   Philadelphia, Pennsylvania

...The judiciary bill will, I believe, sleep for the present session at least. Had twenty nine such judges as Chase been added to the present number, I believe liberty would, in a little time, have been chased out of this country.[1] He has presided in the court which has just terminated its session here.

(Philadelphia) June 10, 1800. Date and place are those of the letter.

The author of this letter probably is Stevens Thomson Mason (1760-1803), senator from Virginia. *DAB*; Stevens Thomson Mason to James Madison, April 23, 1800, James Madison Papers, DLC.

Meriwether Jones (1766-1806), publisher of the Richmond *Examiner*. *PJM*, 3:56n; Brigham, *American Newspapers*, 2:1139.

The *Aurora* published this letter with the following introduction: "The following letter we found sometime since in the Virginia Examiner, but did not think it worth while publishing it, as the public here were already acquainted with the facts, since that period, Judge CHASE has thought it necessary to notice the letter by a publication addressed to the Editor of the Examiner. As it is therefore a matter of justice to the judge, that he should be furnished with the means of addressing the author if he resides in Philadelphia, and that the public should know the whole of the matter between the judge and the writer of the letter, we publish both—We cannot, however, but add a gentle remark of our own—in admiring the generosity of the amiable Judge Chase, in his consenting to let the *truth* be given in justification of the writer, because we must suppose the judge to be either ignorant himself, or that he supposed the writer of the letter ignorant that his consent was not necessary in the case, the laws of Pennsylvania having provided that much already." For Chase's response to this letter, see Samuel Chase to Meriwether Jones, May 26, 1800.

  1. The reference is to "a bill to provide for the more convenient organization of the courts of the United States," introduced in the House of Representatives on March 31, 1800. The bill would have abolished the existing district and circuit court system and established in its place nineteen new districts, each with its own circuit court and circuit court judge. An earlier

I sometimes attended their sittings, and have witnessed the most arbitrary, high handed and tyrannical proceedings and decisions that I believe ever disgraced the judiciary of any country having the least pretensions to freedom. Mr. Thomas Cooper of Northumberland, a gentleman of amiable and irreproachable character, a man of great erudition, and an incomparable writer, having offended the senate by the active part he took in the case of the editor of the Aurora, persecuted by the senate, and the weight of his talents being dreaded at the approaching election of president and vice president, it was determined to crush him.[2]—He had been all the winter in Philadelphia, and every day seen in public, yet no process was taken out against him, until three days before the meeting of the court, on the 11th ultimo. He was indicted for a pretended libel on the president, in a publication of the 2d November last, which was an answer to a very virulent attack made upon him by Fenno, attended with circumstances that reflected no credit on Mr. Adams.[3] Much the greater part of the publication had a referrence to the answers given by Mr. Adams to the addresses presented to him during the[4] memorable war fever of 1798. Mr. Cooper requested to know whether Fenno's paper containing these addresses and answers would be admitted as evidence, observing that it was generally considered as the paper particularly patronized and confided in by the administration, and Fenno was understood to be the printer of the senate. The court declared that these papers would not be admitted as evidence—that Mr. Cooper before he sat down to animadvert upon the conduct or writings of the president, should have been provided with the originals, or such authenticated copies of the documents,

---

version of the bill, introduced on March 11, 1800, and entitled "a bill to provide for the better establishment and regulation of the courts of the United States," would have created twenty-nine districts and an equal number of new circuit court judgeships. This higher number was unacceptable to many in the House, and the bill was quickly sent back to committee for amendment. Congressional Collection, Rare Book Room, DLC; *HRJ*, 3:644-45; *Annals*, 10:646, 648.

2. Thomas Cooper (1759-1839) gained the animosity of Federalist senators for his actions during the Senate's investigation of William Duane, publisher of the Philadelphia *Aurora*. On March 20, 1800, following Duane's publication and criticism of a bill then before the Senate, a committee on privileges (created especially for this incident), ordered that he appear before the Senate and defend printing "false, defamatory, scandalous, and malicious, assertions and pretended information" about that body. Duane tentatively engaged Cooper and Alexander James Dallas as counsel, but both refused to represent him when the Senate restricted how they could conduct Duane's defense. In a letter which Duane made public, Cooper declared, "I will not degrade myself by submitting to appear before the senate with *their gag in my mouth.*" Duane successfully avoided appearing before the Senate. Dumas Malone, *The Public Life of Thomas Cooper, 1783-1839* (New Haven: Yale University Press, 1926), pp. 4, 391; Smith, *Freedom's Fetters*, pp. 288-97; *Annals*, 10:113-15.

3. The attack to which Cooper responded actually appeared in the Reading, Pennsylvania *Weekly Advertiser*, not John Ward Fenno's *Gazette of the United States*. For details on Cooper's seditious libel trial, see Wharton, *State Trials*, pp. 659-81; Smith, *Freedom's Fetters*, pp. 307-33; and Haw, *Stormy Patriot*, pp. 197-99.

4. In newspaper, the phrase "during the" is repeated.

on which he grounded his strictures, as would be unquestionable evidence in a court of justice—and that if he chose to rely on newspaper publications and paragraphs, it must be at his own risque. He then desired time to procure the official papers, which was allowed, but with a remark from the judge, that he knew of no right to demand those papers. Mr. Cooper then wrote to the secretary of state for copies of certain answers to addresses, of which he enclosed a list—Pickering informed him that no such papers were lodged in his office, that they belonged exclusively to the President, and remained with him. Mr. Cooper then wrote to the President, informing him of these circumstances, and requesting that he would suffer the copies to be made out and furnished to him, by his private Secretary Mr. Shaw.[5] The next day having obtained a book containing a collection of these addresses and answers, he sent it by his son to Mr. Shaw, with a note stating that it might save him trouble to collate the originals with the book, and certify the latter to contain true copies. After the youth had been made to wait above half an hour in the entry, Shaw returned to him, with a note to the following purport:— "Mr. Shaw informs Mr. Cooper, that he will receive no information on the subject of addresses or answers from this house."

Thus being denied that information and proof which the court declared to be the only legal evidence, and having been previously refused a subpoena to summon the President, he was forced into the trial, during which every effort was made to embarrass, intimidate, and insult this persecuted man, who defended his own cause without the aid of counsel. To add awe and solemnity to this scene of oppression, all the heads of departments attended. Three of them were placed on the bench, the other took his seat by the jury.[6] The two houses of congress adjourned, and the bench was crowded with many of the high toned members, such as Read, Tracy, Marshall, Lee, T. Pinckney, Rutledge, Griswold, Evans, Harper, &c. &c.[7] On the right hand of Chase sat Timothy Pickering, with the countenance of an inquisitor, evidently taking active interest in the trial. I observed frequent whisperings between him and Chase; and I am informed by those who were earlier in court than myself, that when the jury were called, and some of those who had been struck for the trial did not answer to their names, this accomplished

5. William Smith Shaw (1778-1826), President Adams's secretary and nephew. Stewart Mitchell, ed., *New Letters of Abigail Adams, 1788-1801* (1947; reprint ed., Westport, Conn.: Greenwood Press, 1973), p. 195.

6. A contemporary pamphlet on the trial notes only the attendance of Secretary of State Timothy Pickering, Secretary of War James McHenry, and Secretary of the Navy Benjamin Stoddart. Thomas Cooper, *An Account of the Trial of Thomas Cooper, of Northumberland* (Philadelphia: John Bioren, 1800), p. 24, 64.

7. Senators Jacob Read (1751-1816) of South Carolina and Uriah Tracy of Connecticut; Congressmen John Marshall and Henry Lee of Virginia, Thomas Pinckney and John Rutledge, Jr., of South Carolina, Roger Griswold of Connecticut, Thomas Evans of Virginia, and Robert Goodloe Harper of South Carolina. *BDAC*.

secretary wrote something on a slip of paper, gave it to the judge, who looked at it, and then handed it down to the marshal; he examined it, and proceeded to make up the deficient jurymen.—Whether it was a hint to choose, or to avoid particular characters on the general pannel, from which they were to be drawn, we are left to conjecture, under circumstances so suspicious and disgusting. This however is certain, that in calling over the names of a great number of the jurors, (near an hundred) to see if they were attending the court, none of the few republican names, on the general pannel were called at all.

The judge in the course of the trial, and in his charge to the jury discovered all the zeal and vehemence that might have been expected from a well fee'd lawyer, all the bitterness of a vindictive personal enemy, and all the rudeness and brutality characteristic of Chase: *and little Peters growled in concert.*

Several parts of Chase's charge were so extraordinary, that I took an early opportunity of noting them down. Among other things, he stated that "There were but TWO means by which a republican government could be destroyed—1st. By the introduction of luxury the second (and by far the most certain mean) was the licentiousness of the press"—The judge must have held the understandings of the jury in great contempt, and cared very little about public opinion, to have made this round assertion. It is impossible he could be so ignorant as to believe what he said. History must have informed him that there were many other, and more powerful means of destroying the liberties of a *nation.* At the moment he was thus attempting to impose his dogmas, on the jury, he must have felt himself an instrument to effect this detestable purpose, in a way different from either of those he had mentioned.

He declared that "it was false to say that we were borrowing money at eight per cent. in time of peace. For that though the government had not *declared* war, we are actually at war with France."

He observed that, for "Cooper, (who had shewn himself a man of information and great reading) to assert that we had a standing army, betrayed the most egregious ignorance, or wilful and malicious intention to mislead the public mind. Our army, (he said) were of two descriptions. One part of it was enlisted for five years the other during the continuance of *the war* with France. Would any person pretend to say, that either of these was a standing army? We certainly have no standing army. It is impossible we have a standing army; because by the constitution no appropriations can be made for the support of an army, for a longer period than two years. As congress therefore, make appropriations for the army, every year, and cannot make them for a longer period than two years at a time, there never can be a standing army in this country until the constitution is destroyed."

Behold the logic of a federal court! On the point of justification, he told the jury that Mr. Cooper must prove to them every tittle of what was stated in his publication. It would not be enough to prove that the president had been the cause of bringing about this, that, or the other public evil as asserted by the traverser, or all of them. Nay, though he should also prove that the president had interfered to influence a court of justice to deliver up Jonathan Robbins, *without precedent against law and against mercy*, he would still not support his justification, unless he likewise proved, that Jonathan Robbins was a *native* American citizen; and that he was actually impressed on board a British ship of war.[8] The jury being well selected for the purpose, were taken up to Dunwoody's tavern to consider of their verdict, which did not take them longer than was necessary to prepare and drink their punch, when they returned a verdict of guilty.

The court informed Mr. Cooper, that they would hear any thing he might have to advance in extenuation of his offence, and would wish information as to his pecuniary circumstances. They assigned the Wednesday following to deliver their sentence. Mr. Cooper accordingly attended on that day, at the meeting of the court, Chase asked him if he had any thing to urge in extenuation, and what were his circumstances? However, sir, said he, "there is one circumstance which the court wish to be informed of. You have said sir, in the course of your defence, that this country is divided into two parties. You appear to have attached yourself to one of these parties, and it seems that you write for them, Now it is understood that this party is to pay your fine. If I thought that the fine was to come out of the pockets of the party, I should be laying it to the extent of the law.—But if it could be assured that you were to pay it yourself, I should be regulated by your circumstances, and that of the nature of the offence: the court too, if they saw any kind of contrition or hope that you would not act in the same manner again, might be induced to be moderate. But you seem to think that you have done no wrong.' Cooper then addressed the court, stating the circumstance to be moderate, and that his chief dependence for support was on his practice, from which by confinement, he would of necessity be cut off. He then proceeded to repel the rudeness and indecency with which he was treated in so elegant, manly and dignified a manner, as to interest all who heard him. Even Chase must have felt ashamed of himself; and Peters was quite disconcerted—for he disclaimed Chase's idea of fining a party—said, "He should confine himself to what was before them, and be regulated as to the fine by Mr. Cooper's circumstances—that it made no odds to him, nor did he conceive it was his business to enquire who was to pay it."

---

8. In May 1799 the British minister to the United States had requested that Jonathan Robbins, then in confinement in Charleston, South Carolina, be turned over to British authorities for trial. The British alleged that Robbins was actually Thomas Nash, and that he had committed murder during a mutiny on board the British naval frigate *Hermione*. Nash, the British argued, was therefore subject to the extradition provision of article 27 of the Jay Treaty. For his part, Robbins claimed to be a native of Danbury, Connecticut, who had been pressed onto the British ship from an American merchant vessel and who had played no part in the mutiny. Robbins's subsequent extradition and execution in Jamaica by the British was a source of much anger against the Adams administration. Wharton, *State Trials*, pp. 392-457.

An observation of Cooper's, that "he had never sold himself to any party," appeared to heighten the natural glow in the cheeks of one of his judges.

Chase affecting good nature, said, they would consider of their judgment, and desired Mr. Cooper to retire—observing, that they would let him know when they were ready to give judgment. He desired that a time might be fixed for his attendance. Chase said, "they could not fix a time then, as they had a great deal of business before them. But that it would probably be in a day or two: they would give him notice." He accordingly retired. About dinner time, on the same day, the court, (as if intending to expose him to mortification and to subject him to scoff of sycophants, tories, and tyrants) dispatched a gang of constables in pursuit of him, who, not finding him at his lodgings were hunting him about the city, as if he had been a fugitive. Mr. Cooper having heard in the evening of this unexpected manoeuvre, appeared in court next morning at the hour of meeting, and received his sentence. Which was to pay a fine of 400 dollars, to be imprisoned six months, and after that period, to give bond in the penalty of 1000 dollars, and two securities in 500 each, for his good behaviour, (in other words not to write) for twelve months, and be committed till the sentence should be complied with.

Extraordinary as the above recital may appear to you, it falls short of the conduct of this *extraordinary* court, in the case of Fries, tried and condemned for treason.[9] His offence was precisely that described in the first section of what is commonly called the sedition law; and is punishable by fine and imprisonment.—There had been a trial in this case at the last term, and the verdict set aside. The facts were ascertained and admitted.—The only question was, as to what class of crimes his offence belonged. When brought up for trial, and the jury struck, the court observed, that they had considered of, and made up their opinions, on the question of law, which would arise in the cause. That this opinion they had reduced to writing, That it was founded on reasons unanswerable; and that they should produce authorities in support of it, which could not be controverted, Therefore, they were determined to hear no arguments from counsel, or suffer any authorities to be read in opposition to their decision; which was that there were, and must be, *constructive treasons* under our constitution: and that if the prisoner had committed certain acts, (which were abundantly proved on the former trial, and which were not pretended to be denied) his offence was treason. This decision was read, and four copies made out, one was delivered to the clerk, another to the prosecutor, and one to the counsel for the prisoner, to regulate their conduct; the fourth they declared that they intended to send out with the jury.

Messers. Lewis and Dallas the counsel for Fries, declared that under such

9. For details of the trial of John Fries, see introduction to "Spring and Fall Circuits 1800."

restrictions they would not appear, refused even to read the paper, and withdrew from the defence.

The court were embarassed, and remanded the prisoner to jail. The next morning having discovered the public indignation which their conduct had excited, they expressed a wish to retract what they had done, took back the papers, and requested the counsel to appear and defend their client in any manner they think proper.

This however they declined. Urging that though the papers were taken back, it was not possible to take back the impression which had been made on the minds of the jury. The court then were graciously pleased to say, that they would be counsel for the prisoner, and *with the assistance of God would endeavour to do him justice.* Their endeavours were such as I suppose are exerted by the holy fathers of the inquisition, where they wish to feast their diabolical revenge, by roasting an heretic.

I will give you one among many specimens of their extreme tenderness for a poor ignorant German, whom they had deprived of counsel: a witness was asked by the prosecutor *Did you not hear* the prisoner say, that if an army was sent to enforce the law. they would join the people in opposition to it?" Witness—"Yes, he said, he said, he thought they would join the people against the law." Prosecutor—"*Did you not hear him* say that he wished there would be a war that he might join in it?" Witness—he said that if there was a war he would join in it." Judge Chase—"If there was a war he would join in it?" Witness—He said that if there was a war he would join in it." The judge repeated the words again, with great emphasis, and looked earnestly at the jury the witness answered in the affirmative[.] Then noting it down, he a third time addressed the witness. "You say, sir, that the prisoner declared, that if there was a war he would join in it?" The witness then observed that, "He would not be positive as to the words, but that the amount and substance of the prisoner's declaration was, that *if France or any other foreign nation, would invade this country,* he would turn out and fight *against* them: and would endeavor to get into our army." Thus a patriotic determination to defend his country and its government, was attempted to be distorted into a treasonable intention of resistance; and this by a court who were acting as counsel for the accused, and who promised that *with the assistance of God* they would endeavor to do him justice. I forbear to mention many other disgusting and abominable circumstances, in this trial, to which I was witness.

In this charge, Chase adhered strictly to the extra judicial opinion which he and Peters had made up previous to the case coming before them, and which I have before noticed. He declared that any insurrection, or rising of any set of men, with intent to obstruct or impede the execution of any law, or act of the government whether these were many or few, whether armed or unarmed, whether they acted as a mob, or marched in military array; if any act of violence was committed by any one of the party, it became as to the whole of them *a levying of war against the United States,* within the meaning of the constitution, was TREASON.

Having grown up with the American revolution, and having nearly imbibed, & uniformly acted upon, the principles and opinions of that glorious period, they have become so completely incorporated in my constitution, that they cannot be irradicated or shaken by the most splendid attractions of honors and offices, or the bitterest dose of despotism. You may therefore readily suppose that my blood boiled at such a display of judicial tyranny as I have delineated. Yet this is the tribunal which we are told to look up to for protection, should Congress or the president violate the constitution, or attempt to invade our rights; that we may safely repose ourselves for every thing we hold dear, upon the federal judiciary; a body pure, incorruptable, and completely independent.

Yet we have seen exalted to the bench, a Wilson, a Chase, a Peters, and other names never associated with purity or integrity. We see ambassadors occasionally carved out of these materials with 18,000 dollars additional emolument and their independence by that means completely destroyed.[10] Of the people, and of public opinion, they are indeed independent. But have they not shewn themselves, and may they not always be expected to be subservient to the views of the executive, until some corrective is provided to place them without the influence of the smiles, as well as the frowns of power.

An attempt to guard against this obvious mischief, by disqualifying a judge from holding any other office, was this session, rejected by the senate.[11]
. . .

10. A reference to Chief Justice Oliver Ellsworth, then serving as minister plenipotentiary to France; former Chief Justice John Jay had been minister plenipotentiary to Great Britain (1794-1795). Such envoys were allowed nine thousand dollars per annum with an equal sum for expenses. *Stat.,* 1:128-129, 299, 345, 487, 541.

11. The Senate voted against a bill prohibiting extrajudicial appointments on April 3, 1800. *SLJ,* 3:66; *Annals,* 10:96-102; "A Bill further to amend the act entitled an act to establish the judicial courts of the US," Sen 6A-B1, Bills and Resolutions Originating in the Senate, RG 46, DNA.

William Paterson to Euphemia Paterson ──────────────────

May 19, 1800   Portsmouth, New Hampshire

... The court is to open to-day; but as the clerk[1] has not come in, I cannot say how much business we shall have to go through. In this district the business in the legal line generally has not been much; but it is said to be more at present than at any former period. It is probable, however, that the court will not continue longer than this week; and therefore I hope on Monday next to shape my course homewards.

Overmantel from the Gardiner Gilman house, Exeter, New Hampshire by an unknown artist. Oil on wood panel, ca. 1800. Courtesy Amon Carter Museum, Fort Worth, Texas.

Portsmouth is about 100 miles from Windsor; but the roads being impassable at this time of the year in a direct course, I was obliged to take a circuit of 140 miles to reach this place. As it was, the roads were very bad, over stones, and rocks, and mountains. For one third of the way I did not go more than at the rate of three miles an hour. Though my progress was slow, yet I made out to travel 100 miles in three days, which was what I had allotted to myself when I left home. Vegetation here is not so forward as Windsor; and is much in the same state as it was at Brunswick about the 20th of last month. They have had this way a very rainy season, and a continuation of easterly winds, which have retarded vegetation considerably.

Pr (Printed in *Somerset County Historical Quarterly* 3 (1914), p. 3).

1. Jonathan Steele (1760-1824), clerk of the federal district and circuit courts in New Hampshire. D. Hamilton Hurd, comp., *History of Rockingham and Strafford Counties, New Hampshire, with Biographical Sketches of many of its Pioneers and Prominent Men* (Philadelphia: J. W. Lewis, 1882), pp. 600-601.

Circuit Court for the District of New Hampshire ————————
May 19, 1800 Portsmouth, New Hampshire

On May 19 the spring session of the circuit court commenced; Associate Justice William Paterson presided. According to a Portsmouth newspaper, Justice Paterson delivered a charge to the grand jury after court opened. Court adjourned on May 21.[1]

1. Records, CCD New Hampshire, RG 21, MWalFAR; *United States Oracle* (q.v. under date of May 24, 1800). We have been unable to identify the specific charge given. For undated Paterson grand jury charges, see Appendix A.

"Citizen" ————————————————————————
Massachusetts Mercury
May 20, 1800 Boston, Massachusetts

I Observed a paragraph in your paper which mentions the valedictory address, to the Bar of *Philadelphia*, of that venerable and truly excellent man the honorable Judge CHASE.[1]

This gentleman is really an ornament to the Judicial Bench.—He has completely, in every part of his Judicial character exhibited the marks of a just, impartial and righteous Judge.—No freaks of caprice, no party prejudice, or personal resentment have ever appeared in any of his decisions. Every lenity, consistent with the true character of a Judge, in the impartial execution of his duty, has ever been exercised by him.

When the unfortunate FAIRBANKS, who had been misled by crafty men, and was concerned in a seditious act against government, by erecting the liberty pole in *Dedham*, how did this great and good Judge conduct? He passed the lenient sentence upon FAIRBANKS of two hours' imprisonment—when it was in the power of the Court to have consigned him over to a long confinement and a heavy fine, which would have reduced him and his family to ruin.[2]

What was the effect of the judicious sentence? A remorse of conscience in the culprit which worked a sincere repentance and a thorough reformation in the man; and more effectually checked such unjustifiable conduct, than the severest punishment. For a severe punishment inflicted for a mistaken offence would have created an eternal rancour in the breast of himself, his friends and connections, against the severity of the Judge. But in this instance and in every other, which has come to my knowledge, Judge CHASE has imitated his great master, the RIGHTEOUS JUDGE of the World—who in the midst of judgment remembers mercy.

In the late trials of the unhappy men, now under sentence of death for the greatest crime in community, High Treason, what humanity did he shew them! He did not increase their distress by a brutal treatment;—and after the verdict of the jury was returned, *Guilty*, the Judge addressed them with the kindness of a father, "if you or any one of you can point out any error in the indictment, so that there is ground for you to move an arrest of judgment, sufficient time will be allowed you for that purpose."[3]

In COOPERS trial,[4] he (being a lawyer) defended his own cause. After three hours in his defence—COOPER appeared to be exhausted with fatigue—with what kindness and benignity did this benevolent Judge, say "if you wish for refreshment, take it, for you appear to be exhausted, the Court will patiently wait for you!"

This is the highly respectable, humane and benevolent Judge, who has taken his leave of the Bar; and of whose services and abilities *America* is likely to be deprived.

While I pass this just encomium upon Judge CHASE, I cannot forbear mentioning the respectable Mr. RAWLE the Attorney-General.—In every case he was ready to consent to every indulgence respecting evidence in favour of Prisoners at the Bar.—When he opened the several cases to the juries, he did it candidly. No false colouring or forced construction were put upon the testimony.—No invectives were thrown out against the unfortunate defendants to prejudice the jury; but in every part of his pleadings, the candour of a gentleman and the benevolence of a christian appeared conspicuous.

A very great number of persons attended the trials from day to day, and I never saw such universal solemnity appear on the countenances of the people present as there did on those trials; and they expressed the deepest regret at the danger of loosing the venerable Judge.—I had frequent opportunities, while I tarried at *Philadelphia*, of conversing with gentlemen of the first characters, and of different sentiments in politics, and I never heard one disrespectful word uttered against Judge CHASE, and it appeared that every man had the highest respect for him.

"*Justum et tenacem propositi virum*
Non civium ardor prava jubentium,
Non vultus instantis tyranni
Mente quatit solida."[5]

CITIZEN

(Boston) May 20, 1800. Date and place are those of the newspaper.

1. We have been unable to find the *Massachusetts Mercury* article to which "Citizen" refers, but see the *Philadelphia Gazette* under date of May 3, 1800.

2. For information on the trial of Benjamin Fairbanks, see introduction to "Spring and Fall Circuits 1799."

3. John Fries, Frederick Heany, and John Gettman were sentenced to death on May 2, 1800. They were pardoned by President Adams on May 12, 1800. Engrossed Minutes, May 2, 1800, CCD Pennsylvania, RG 21, PPFAR; Wharton, *State Trials,* p. 641.

4. For the trial of Thomas Cooper, see introduction to "Spring and Fall Circuits 1800."

5. The quotation is from Horace's *Odes.* Translated, it reads:

The man of firm and righteous will,

No rabble, clamorous for the wrong,

No tyrant's brow, whose frown may kill,

Can shake the strength that makes him strong.

Thomas B. Harbottle, *Dictionary of Quotations* (London: Swan Sonnenschein, 1909), p. 118.

Circuit Court for the District of Virginia
May 22, 1800   Richmond, Virginia

Associate Justice Samuel Chase opened court on May 22 and on May 23 delivered a charge to the grand jury, "in a style equally pleasing, pertinent, and impressive— *Suaviter in modo—fortiter in re!*"[1] Judge Cyrus Griffin did not join the court until May 30. The court adjourned on June 4.[2]

1. *Columbian Centinel* (Boston), June 11, 1800. Translated the phrase reads, "Gentle in manner, but resolute in action." Jones, *Dictionary of Foreign Phrases and Classical Quotations,* p. 115.

2. Order Book, CCD Virginia, Vi. Charge not found.

Presentment of the Grand Jury of the Circuit Court for the District of Virginia
May 24, 1800   Richmond, Virginia

We of the Grand Jury Present James Thomson Callender[1] whom we find to have been the publisher of a Book with this Title "The Prospect Before us" which contains several passages tending to defame the Government the President and the Congress of the United States and to bring them into

contempt and disrepute, contrary to An Act of Congress "entitled 'An
            in addition to the Act of Congress entitled An Act
Act for the punishment of certain Crimes against the United States,[2] Where
upon it is Ordered that the United States writ of Capias ad respondendum
do immediately issue commanding the Marshal of this District to bring the
Body of the said James Thomson Callender before this Court now sitting to
Answer the said Presentment

D (Vi, CCD Virginia, Order Book).
    1. For more information on the presentment of James T. Callender, see "Spring and Fall
Circuits 1800."
    2. Sedition Act. *Stat.*, 1:596.

United States Oracle ─────────────────────────────────

May 24, 1800   Portsmouth, New Hampshire

On Monday last the Circuit Court of the United States was opened in
this town. The Hon. Judge PATTERSON presided. After the Jury were
empannelled, the Judge delivered a most elegant and appropriate Charge.—
The *Law* was laid down in a masterly manner: *Politicks* were set in their
true light, by holding up the Jacobins, as the disorganizers of our happy
Country, and the only instruments of introducing discontent and dissatisfaction
among the well-meaning part of the Community:—*Religion & Morality* were
pleasingly inculcated and enforced, as being necessary to good government,
good order and good laws, for "when the righteous are in authority, the
people rejoice."

We are sorry we could not prevail on the Hon. Judge to furnish a copy
of said Charge to adorn the pages of the United States' Oracle.

After the Charge was delivered, the Rev. Mr. ALDEN[1] addressed the
Throne of Grace, in an excellent, well adapted prayer.

(Portsmouth) May 24, 1800. Date and place are those of the headline.
    1. Timothy Alden (1771-1839), assistant pastor of the South Congregational Church of
Portsmouth. *DAB*.

James Monroe to Thomas Jefferson ──────────────────────

May [25], 1800   [Richmond, Virginia]

...Chase harangued the G. Jury in a speech said to be drawn with some
                                        with allusions
art, as it inculcated so[me] popular doctrines w[h] supported by Eastern
calumnies he intended for you. He declared solemnly he wo[d] not allow an
atheist to give testimony in court. You have perhaps seen that the
circumstance of the dinner in Fredbg. being on a sunday is the foundation

for this absurd calumny. The G. Jury of w^h McClurg[1] was for'man presented
law
Calendar under the sedition, & Chase [drew?] the warrant & dispatched the
Marshall instantly in pursuit of him. This was yesterday at 12. since w^h we
have not heard of either.[2] If taken I hope the people will behave with dignity
on the occasion and give no pretext for comments to their discredit. If I co^d
[suppose the journey?] I wo^d take proper steps to aid in bringing him forth;
I mean to prevent any popular meeting to the contrary. will it not be proper
for the Exctive to employ Counsel to defend him, and supporting the law,
give an eclat to a vindication of the principles of the State? ...

ARS (DLC, Thomas Jefferson Papers). Although Monroe dated his letter "Sunday 27. May
1800," that date actually fell on a Tuesday. His reference to the warrant being sworn out
"yesterday" suggests a date of May 25. Endorsed by Jefferson as "rec^d May 25." Place derived
from the location of the state capital. Readings in brackets supplied where letter is torn.
    James Monroe (1758-1831), at the time governor of Virginia. *DAB.*
    1. James McClurg (1746-1823), a Richmond physician, served intermittently as mayor of
Richmond between 1797 and 1804. *PMad.,* 1:296n; *PGW, Diary,* 5:158n.
    2. The warrant was sworn out on May 24. James Callender was arrested in Petersburg, Virginia
and brought into the circuit court on May 27. Smith, *Freedom's Fetters,* p. 345.

Samuel Chase to Meriwether Jones ⸻

Aurora
May 26, 1800   Richmond, Virginia

MR. MERIWETHER JONES.

In your paper styled *"The Examiner"* of Tuesday the 20th of this month,
is published an extract of a letter to you, from a gentleman in Philadelphia,
dated 7th of May 1800;[1] which highly reflects on my character as the *presiding
judge* of the Circuit court of the United States, lately held in the city of
Philadelphia—Be pleased to inform the author of that letter, that I desire,
that he will republish it with his name, (or leave his name with the printer
in some of the newspapers printed in Philadelphia—and I pledge myself to
the public, that I will prove that he is a false, scandalous, wicked, and
malicious *slanderer and caluminator*—For this purpose I will sue him in the
supreme court of the Commonwealth of Pennsylvania, and if he will appear
to the action, I will consent that he may give *the truth* of his publication in
evidence to the jury as his *full justification.*

SAMUEL CHASE.

Richmond, 26th ⎫
    May, 1800. ⎭

    N. B. If any editor of a Newspaper has re-published the above libel on
me, he is requested to print the above note to Mr. Jones.

(Philadelphia) June 10, 1800. Date and place are those of the letter.

1. See Letter from an Anonymous Correspondent to Meriwether Jones, published under date of May 7, 1800.

Circuit Court for the District of Massachusetts
June 2, 1800   Boston, Massachusetts

"The Circuit Court of the United States, which commenced sitting in this town, on the 2d inst. finished term yesterday." Only the attendance of Associate Justice William Cushing was noted.[1]

1. *Columbian Centinel* (Boston), June 11, 1800. The records of the circuit court for this term are missing.

Circuit Court for the District of North Carolina
June 2, 1800   Raleigh, North Carolina

Judge John Sitgreaves attended court on Monday, June 2, but adjourned the court to the next day because of the absence of a Supreme Court justice. On June 3 Associate Justice Alfred Moore and Judge Sitgreaves opened court, after which Moore delivered a brief charge to the grand jury. The court adjourned on June 9 to the following term.[1]

1. Minutes, CCD North Carolina, RG 21, GEpFAR. Charge not found but mentioned in the *Raleigh Register* (Raleigh), June 10, 1800 (q.v.).

Aurora
June 2, 1800   Philadelphia, Pennsylvania

Much surprize was expressed at the suddenness of the departure of *Judge Chase* from this city—but as that Judge shewed himself on Mr. Cooper's case to be *a man of all works,* the thing was supposed to have a meaning in it. It now appears that he is gone to Virginia. *Luther Martin* of *moral memory,* had laid his hands on a work of J. T. Callender, called the *"Prospect before us"*, which has laid naked a volume of public Iniquities of public servants;— the margin of this book *Luther Martin* had ornamented with notes, and put into the hands of *Judge Chase* who set off for *Richmond,* to wreak vengeance on *Callender.* A jury conveniently *packed* by a federal *Marshal* has found a bill under the Sedition law against *Callender,* and *Judge Chase* swears Callender must go into prison, for he cannot get the *official documents* to prove all he has published, though *nobody* doubts a word of what he has stated—as fair calculations.

(Philadelphia) June 2, 1800. Date and place are those of the newspaper.

Aurora ──

June 3, 1800   Philadelphia, Pennsylvania

As it is said of Satan, when cast out of heaven, that "even while falling he blasphemed," so it may now be said of the failing aristocratic party in the United States, knowing their reighn to be short-lived, they appear, by their proscriptions and prosecutions, determined to do all the mischief in their power. Judge CHASE, the *pious* and *religious* Judge Chase, is gone to Virginia, where he says, if a *virtuous* jury can only be collected, he'll punish CALLENDER with a vengeance. The waters of the Susquehanna, have not the virtue of the Jordan, or the Judge would have been cleansed of his aristocratic mania![1]

(Philadelphia) June 3, 1800. Date and place are those of the newspaper. The *Aurora* notes that this was originally printed in the Baltimore *American*.

1. Samuel Chase fell through the ice while crossing the frozen Susquehanna River on his way to attend the February 1800 term of the Supreme Court in Philadelphia. For details, see *DHSC*, 1:887-89.

In a similar vein, the Baltimore *American* noted, "Since Judge CHASE fell into the Susquehanna, a greater number of Shad have been taken from that river than at any preceding season. The fish disgusted at the FEDERAL infection, with which the water has become impregnated, hover to the nets of the fishermen, in preference to existing in an eliment become putrid by cleansing such a mass of aristocracy!" *American* (Baltimore), July 1, 1800.

City Gazette ──

June 4, 1800   Baltimore, Maryland

At the late Circuit Court at Annapolis, in his charge to the Grand Jury, Judge Chase took the freedom to observe, that "except in Pennsylvania and Virginia, one of the most *licentious* presses in the United States was supported in Baltimore." This was an attempt to prepossess the jury, in favour of an indictment which the *sentimental Zeb Hollingsworth* had prepared against the Editor of the American.[1] The indictment was submitted to the grand jury, and although a majority of the gentlemen who composed it, were inimical to the Editor's political sentiments, yet a bill could not be found. One of the principal *counts* in the indictment, was for a publication under the title of "A Bone to Knaw," published in this paper in August last![2] Thus do the hungry cormorants of Aristocracy, search over the musty files of old newspapers, to fine food for the gratification of their distrustful appetites.

(Charleston) June 20, 1800. Date and place are those of the headline.

1. Alexander Martin.

2. "A Bone to Gnaw" was published in the August 27, 1799, issue of the Baltimore *American*. In the article Martin claimed there was a conspiracy between "Federal writers" in the press and government authorities, which "sets up examples of *British* jurisprudence, *British* valor, and *British* laws, as examples worthy of our imitation ... to render us a more easy prey to *British* subjugation."

Raleigh Register ————————————————————————————
June 10, 1800   Raleigh, North Carolina

The Hon. Judge Moore arriving here in the afternoon of Tuesday last, the Circuit Court of the United States for this District proceeded to business on that evening, The Grand Jury being sworn, Judge Moore charged them with their duty; but, instead of expatiating at length on the several objects cognizable in that Court, and insisting on the necessity of carrying the Sedition Law into effect, in particular (as is usual) he barely reminded them of the oath they had taken to execute the trust reposed in them; said there was no necessity for him to take up their time in explaining the nature of their duty, which had been so often explained in that Court, and which they had doubtless frequently seen in the papers from various parts of the country, which would only tend to divert their minds from their proper business, referring them to the Attorney General of the District for legal information.[1]
. . .

(Raleigh) June 10, 1800. Date and place are those of the headline.
   1. Benjamin Woods (d. 1808), appointed United States attorney for the district of North Carolina on February 10, 1795. Keith, Masterson, and Morgan, *John Gray Blount Papers*, 3:14; *SEJ*, 1:172.

Circuit Court for the District of Rhode Island ————————————
June 16, 1800   Newport, Rhode Island

On Monday, June 16, Associate Justice William Cushing and Judge Benjamin Bourne opened the Rhode Island circuit court, and Justice Cushing delivered a "concise and pertinent Charge" to the grand jury. The court adjourned on June 19.[1]

   1. Minutes, CCD Rhode Island, RG 21, MWalFAR; *Newport Mercury* (Newport, Rhode Island), June 17, 1800. Charge not found.

"A Card to Judge Chase" ————————————————————————————
Aurora
June 20, 1800   Richmond, Virginia

The writer of a letter dated at Philadelphia May 7th 1800, of which an extract appeared in the Examiner of the 20th of the same month,[1] though willing to gratify Judge Chase and the *public* by establishing in a court of justice the truth of the allegations contained in that publication, is not disposed to enter into controversy in the federal court, with a *judge* of that court, under the existing practice of packing juries: nor to expose himself to the preposterous doctrine of the *common law*, "that the greater the truth the greater the libel" a doctrine too monstrous to be longer tolerated even

Old Colony House, Newport, Rhode Island. Courtesy Rhode Island Historical Preservation Commission. Photograph by Warren Jagger. Built in 1739 and now restored to its eighteenth-century appearance, Old Colony House was Rhode Island's state house before the Revolution. It contained the first courtroom built in Rhode Island, which was used by the federal courts when they were held in Newport.

in England, but which might be forced down in this country by Mr. Chase and his brethren *of the party colored robe.* Neither has he time or money to squander away upon a character so worthless, by referring the decision to a distant tribunal, where the expences of law suits are extravagantly high. But if Judge Chase believes, or pretends to believe, that injustice has been done him by any thing contained in that letter, the writer is ready to afford ample opportunity for reparation of the supposed injury, by submitting himself to a *civil action* in the highest court of the state in which he resides, where such an action can be brought, and will join issue upon the truth of the publication, provided it shall be agreed that a general commission shall issue to take the depositions of all witnesses, to be read on the trial; and that each party shall give to the other, security to answer the ultimate decision of the cause.

Judge Chase by application to Mr. Jones (the Editor of the Examiner) and subscribing to these terms, may be furnished with the name of the writer, who will cheerfully make the appeal to an impartial jury, or to the public in any other way to decide whether "he is a false, scandalous, wicked and malicious slanderer and calumniator," or Judge Chase AN UNPRINCIPLED tyrant, totally unfit to be intrusted with any power over the lives or liberties of *the free citizens of America*.

(Philadelphia) June 27, 1800. Date and place are those of the headline. The headline also indicates that this article was reprinted from the Richmond *Examiner*.

1. See Letter from an Anonymous Correspondent to Meriwether Jones, May 7, 1800.

Circuit Court for the District of Delaware —————————————

June 27, 1800   New Castle, Delaware

Associate Justice Samuel Chase and Judge Gunning Bedford, Jr., convened court on June 27. After court opened, Chase delivered a charge to the grand jury. The docket does not record the court's closing. The "teste" day was June 28.[1]

1. Appearance Docket, CCD Delaware, RG 21, PPFAR; Letter from an Anonymous Correspondent, June 28, 1800 (q.v.). Charge not found.

Letter from an Anonymous Correspondent —————————————
Aurora

June 28, 1800   New Castle, Delaware

Yesterday the Circuit Court of the United States, was opened in this place, by HIS HONOUR *Judge Chase*. "The Grand Jury after being impanelled, hearing a very learned charge, and spending some time by themselves; returned to the Court, and informed them that they had *no bills* before them, nor any business for the Court, and wished to be discharged. His *Honour!* was much surprized, and intimated that he understood there was *Sedition* somewhere in Wilmington among the Printers, or some where else, and ordered the *Attorney General*[1] *and all the Jury* to go in search of Sedition and return with their report to-morrow, his *orders,* you know, must be complyed with; notwithstanding the Hay-harvest, and Corn, demand the utmost exertions of every man in the comunity; they must all be deserted to *hunt sedition.* When lo! and behold on this day the jury met, and to their honour be it said returned to the court the same answer as yesterday *no business for the court*; not even a presentment against the democratic printer of Wilmington.[2] Do you recollect the name of that Judge whom we read of in English History who performed so many high-handed acts of Justice against the Seditious in Wiltshire and elsewhere of old times—was it Jeffries[3]—or who—it was not Chase, for in *years* he is not old enough.

(Philadelphia) July 1, 1800. Date and place are those of the letter.

1. The United States attorney for the district of Delaware was George Read, Jr. (1765-1836). Anthony Higgins, ed., *New Castle on the Delaware,* Delaware Federal Writers' Project, American Guide Series (1936; reprint ed., New Castle Historical Society, 1973), p. 112.

2. A reference to James Wilson (ca. 1764-1841), publisher of the Wilmington, Delaware *Mirror of the Times. Delaware Gazette* (Wilmington), August 13, 1841; Brigham, *American Newspapers,* 2:1505.

3. George Jeffreys, lord chief justice of England from 1683 to 1685. *DNB.*

Samuel Chase to Meriwether Jones

Aurora

July 1, 1800   Baltimore, Maryland

Mr. Meriwether Jones

By accident I saw a Card directed to me by the writer of a letter dated at Philadelphia 7th of May, 1800, of which an extract was published in your paper styled *"The Examiner,"* on the 20th of the same month.[1] In my note to you, at Richmond, on the 26th of May,[2] I requested you to inform the author of that letter, that I desired he would republish it with his name, (or leave his name with the Printer) in some of the Newspapers printed at Philadelphia; that I would prove him a false, scandalous, wicked, and malicious *slanderer and calumniator*; that for this purpose I would sue him in the Supreme Court of the Commonwealth of Pennsylvania, and that if he would appear in the action I would consent that he might give the truth of his publication in evidence to the jury as his *full justification.* My reason for this proposition was, because the author of this letter had wilfully, and basely, and against his own knowledge, misrepresented my conduct as presiding Judge of the Circuit Court of the United States held in Philadelphia in April last. Any person who will take the trouble to compare the statement of the trial of Mr. Thomas Cooper as published by himself[3] with the statement made by the author of the letter alluded to, will desire no further proof, (if he credits Mr. Cooper) of the base misrepresentation and the barefaced falsehood and calumny of the latter. When any one publishes a libel on a judge, he is liable to prosecution by way of *indictment;*[4] and he is also subject to a civil action. As the facts that took place on the prosecution and trial of Mr. Cooper, and my conduct as one of the Judges, happened in Philadelphia, I therefore proposed to bring a civil action against the author of the libel in the Supreme Court of that Commonwealth and not in the *Federal Court,* as the author of the letter wishes the public to believe. I am a resident of Maryland; the author is *not* a resident of Pennsylvania, but it is believed of Virginia—The author of this letter says—"he is not disposed to enter into controversy in the *Federal Court,* with a Judge of that Court, under the existing practice of packing juries." This observation could only have been made to deceive the public to make them believe that I proposed to sue him in the

Federal (or circuit) court of Pennsylvania and is directly the contrary to the truth; and also for the further purpose of charging the marshal of Pennsylvania with packing juries, in violation of his duty and oath of office. The author of this letter now proposes "that I should sue him in the highest court of the state *in which he resides,* which he does not mention, but I presume is Virginia; and that he will join issue *on the truth of the publication;* and he annexes two conditions, that a general commission shall issue to take the depositions of *all* witnesses, *to be used on the trial*; and that each party give security to answer the ultimate decision of the cause." I shall not sue in Virginia, because of the distance from Baltimore to Richmond, and the expence, and because the facts took place in Philadelphia, and a great number of persons who reside there were present in court, and to whom the facts, stated by the author of the letter, if they ever occured, must be known. I again propose to sue him in the supreme court of Pennsylvania, and if he will appear to the action, I will consent that he may give the *truth* of his publication in evidence to the jury, *as his full justification.* I will also agree to a commission to take the deposition of any witness on interrogatories filed in court, and that such deposition shall be evidence in the same manner, as if the witness was present in court; and I will give security for costs, and he will give special bail to the action as he proposes.

If the author of the letter had only charged me, as a judge, of being 'an *unprincipled tyrant,* totally unfit to be entrusted with any power over the lives or liberties of the free citizens of America,' I should not have taken any notice of such a general accusation. It would have been a matter of *opinion,* but he stated facts that never happened, and opinions which I never delivered. He arraigned my integrity and impartiality as a Judge, "my proceedings and decisions as the most arbitrary, high handed, and tyrannical that ever disgraced the judiciary of any country having the least pretensions to freedom; and he now concludes with calling me "*a worthless fellow.*" This opinion of a person unknown could not have any *possible* weight with people of candor and understanding—If the author was known, his opinion would depend on his reputation for public and private virtue, for veracity and knowledge.—If he possesses all these qualities, I wish for an opportunity on a fair trial before an *impartial court and jury,* to shew him his want of information or error in judgement. If he is, as I suspect, a proud, haughty, and insolent character, heated by party rage, and weak and rash in judgment, regardless of decency and truth, and accustomed to low and vulgar language, no respect will be paid to his wanton and malignant attack on my character.[5]

SAMUEL CHASE.

(Philadelphia) July 22, 1800. Date and place are those of the letter.

The *Aurora* notes that this letter originally appeared in the Richmond *Examiner,* published by Meriwether Jones.

1. See "A Card to Judge Chase," published under date of June 20, 1800.

2. See Samuel Chase to Meriwether Jones, May 26, 1800.

3. Thomas Cooper, *An Account of the Trial of Thomas Cooper, of Northumberland* (Philadelphia: John Bioren, 1800).

4. Sedition Act of 1798. *Stat.,* 1:596.

5. This episode did not result in legal action. Jane S. Elsmere, *Justice Samuel Chase* (Muncie, Indiana: Janevar Publishing, 1980), p. 113.

Mirror of the Times ————————————————————————————————

July 4, 1800   Wilmington, Delaware

On Friday the 27th ultimo, the Circuit Court of the U. S. for the district of Delaware, commenced its sitting at Newcastle—Judge Chase presided. After he had delivered a charge to the Grand-Jury, in which Religion, Morality, and Humanity were inculcated, and the *Liberty of the Press* advocated; and after the Jury, under solemn oath or affirmation, had returned to the Court that they could find no bill, Judge Chase, in the stile of a true . . . . . (*Mem.* not to forget the Sedition Law) to the astonishment of the greater part of those who heard him, propounded the following questions to the Attorney-General and to the Grand-Jury:

Have you found *no bill,* Gentlemen of the Jury!!—Mr. Attorney, have you nothing to prefer to the Grand Jury?

Att. Gen.—I believe not, Sir. No indictable offence has come under my notice.

J. Ch.—Well, but can't you *find something?* Have you no person in this state guilty of libelling the Government of the United States? I am credibly informed, and report says you have a printer who publishes a *very seditious paper* in this state; his name is—but stop—perhaps I may commit myself, and do injustice to the man.—Have you not *two* printers in this state?

Att. Gen.—Yes Sir.

J. Ch.—Very well; one of them is said to be a seditious printer, and *must be* taken notice of. It is part of *my* duty, and it *shall be* attended to. It is *your* business also, Mr. Attorney, to search minutely and constantly into matters of this nature. It is high time, Sir, that the *spirit of sedition* which prevails among many of our printers should be checked. Can you not obtain some of this man's papers by to-morrow, and *enquire,* and *examine,* and *search diligently,* whether he has not libelled the Government of the U. States? It is your duty, Sir, and it *must be done.*—If you *will* enquire, the Court will not discharge the Jury.

Att. Gen.—Certainly, Sir. I conceive it my official duty, and will make it my business to enquire.

J. Ch.—What do you say, Sir?

Att. Gen.—I will enquire, Sir, by to-morrow.

J. Ch.—Very well. Gentlemen of the Jury, the Court cannot discharge you, I believe. Will it be inconvenient for you to attend here to-morrow?

Foreman.[1]—It will be very inconvenient for many of us, who are farmers—may it please your Honor—harvest is at hand, and it is a very busy time.

J. Ch.—*It makes no odds,* the Court will not discharge you, under the present circumstances. You must be in Court, Gentlemen, to-morrow, at 10 o'clock.—*I am determined* to have those seditious printers prosecuted *to the extremity of the law.* The safety and prosperity of the Government depend upon it.

Saturday, June 28.—The Jury attended, and after some little altercation, returned *without finding a bill.*

The above statement was given the Editor by a Gentleman who attended the Court; and, from conversation held with some of the Jury, he is inclined to believe it correct.[2]

(Wilmington) July 4, 1800. Date and place are those of the newspaper.

1. John Hyatt. List of the grand jury summoned to attend the Circuit Court for the district of Delaware in New Castle, June 1800 term. Papers Pertaining to the impeachment proceedings against Samuel Chase, Unbound Records 8th Congress, RG 46, DNA.

2. Chase's conduct at this court formed the basis of one of the articles of impeachment at his trial in 1805. For Chase's recollections and the testimony of others at his Senate trial, see *Annals,* 14:142-44, 227-31, 284-91.

Daily Advertiser ————————————————————————————————
July 9, 1800   New York, New York

On Friday the 27th ult the Circuit Court of the United States for the District of Delaware, commenced its sitting at Newcastle—Judge Chase presiding. A viperous but contemptible paper printed at Wilmington[1] charges this active and patriotic ornament to the American bench, with a conduct which, from our own knowledge of the gentleman, we know to be incompatible with the candor and liberality of his character. It is astonishing what extremes of baseness the malignity of some men's hearts will lead them. If soiling the character of innocence would tend to bleach that of the villain, we should cease to wonder at the industry of these men: but when they know, [and they must inevitably know][2] that the shafts of detraction ultimately recoil on the authors, we are at a loss which most to admire—their perseverance, or their depravity.

(New York) July 9, 1800. Date and place are those of the newspaper.

1. The *Mirror of the Times* published by James Wilson. This may refer to a *Mirror of the Times* article of July 4, 1800 (q.v.).

2. Brackets appear in original.

Aurora ———————————————————————————————————————
July 15, 1800   Philadelphia, Pennsylvania

It is told about town, as from federal authority, that the conduct of Judge Chase during the trial of Callender, excited such general execration among all parties, that during his whole stay in Richmond, no person deigned to invite him to his house.[1]

(Philadelphia) July 15, 1800. Date and place are those of the newspaper. The *Aurora* noted that this article had been reprinted from the Norfolk, Virginia *Epitome of the Times.*

1. After the Virginia circuit court adjourned, Chase left Richmond in the company of John Marshall, who was on his way to Washington as the newly appointed secretary of state. *Virginia Federalist* (Richmond), June 7, 1800; *PJM,* 4:156-58.

Aurora ──

July 17, 1800   Philadelphia, Pennsylvania

There are few men in this country of genuine republican principles who have not been disgusted with the charges which are commonly given to juries by the judges of our federal courts. Instead of confining themselves to an illustration of the law, applying it to those cases on which the jury are to decide, which is all that the duty requires; we find them often spinning out a charge to an enormous length, in defence of some favorite measure of government, with which the *jury,* as such, have no more concern than they have with the edicts of the Grand Turk. These charges are afterwards published in all the papers of a certain stamp, and cried up by the devotees of faction, as master pieces of human wisdom. Thus it is that the bench is perverted into an engine of party. The judges, it is true, *may* be actuated by very laudable motives; but such conduct renders them liable to suspicion, at least with no inconsiderable portion of the community. A judge, however, should not only be *innocent* but *unsuspected.* If the people in general should once begin to suspect the Federal Judges to be under the influence of government, the Federal Courts would no longer be looked upon as the sanctuaries of justice—and the government itself would lose no small share of that respect from the people which is essential to the existence of a republic.

It is much to be regretted, that the foregoing remarks, which have often been made by foreigners as well as our own citizens, are not solely applicable to the federal Bench. The infection is spreading, and has in too many instances seized upon Judges in the state Courts. ...

(Philadelphia) July 17, 1800. Date and place are those of the newspaper. The *Aurora* indicated that this article was reprinted from the *Albany Register.*

Supreme Court of the United States—Assignment of Circuits ─────────

August 15, 1800   Philadelphia, Pennsylvania

Assignment of the circuit courts of the United State for the fall of the year 1800.

Justice William Cushing's one-horse shay. Courtesy Scituate Historical Society, Scituate, Massachusetts.

The eastern circuit to Judge Cushing.
The middle circuit to Judge Paterson.
The southern circuit to Judge Washington.
Given under our hands the 15th day of August, 1800.

Wm Paterson.
Samuel Chase
Alfred Moore
Bushrod Washington

DS (DUSC, Office of the Curator). Except for the signatures, this document is in the hand of Associate Justice William Paterson.

Chief Justice Oliver Ellsworth did not attend court because he was in France as minister plenipotentiary; Associate Justice William Cushing was ill. *DHSC,* 1:325n.

William Cushing to William Gay ————————————————
August 18, 1800   Scituate, Massachusetts

[*Cushing mentions the impending visit of William Gay and his wife.*] M⁽ʳˢ⁾ C.
will doubtless be at home, if I am not & glad to receive you. I am in hopes
Judge Patterson will attend Court for me at Newyork the 1ˢᵗ of September,
in which case I may probably be at home also.[1] I must however be at Hartford
Court the 17ᵗʰ Sepʳ for which I may perhaps set out the 11ᵗʰ _ ...

ARS (NhHi, Hibbard Collection). Addressed "Suffield   Connecticut." Postmarked "BOSTON
25 AV."
   William Gay (1767-1844), an attorney and postmaster of Suffield, Connecticut. His wife,
Elizabeth Richmond (ca. 1769-1837), was a grandniece of William Cushing. Dwight Loomis
and J. Gilbert Calhoun, eds., *The Judicial and Civil History of Connecticut* (Boston: Boston History
Co., 1895), p. 544; Frederick L. Gay, "John Gay, of Dedham, Massachusetts, and some of his
descendants" *New England Historic Genealogical Register* 33 (January 1879): 54; James S. Cushing,
The Genealogy of the Cushing Family (Montreal: Perrault Printing, 1905), p. 90-91; *Suffield Vital
Records,* vol. NB1, p. 225, Barbour Collection, Ct. Information on Elizabeth (Richmond) Gay
courtesy of Richard C. Roberts, Connecticut State Library.
   1. On August 19, 1800, Paterson informed Cushing that the "eastern circuit has been assigned
you, and I shall hold the court at New York agreeably to your request." William Paterson to
William Cushing, August 19, 1800, Robert Treat Paine Papers, MHi.

Letter from an Anonymous Correspondent ———————————
Mirror of the Times
August 27, 1800   Wilmington, Delaware

I have seldom read a publication of a charge from a *court* to a *jury,* in
which I have not met with remarks that however just in their nature, were
not of a kind that I deemed proper for the occasion. In such charges we
often see the judge enter the field of politics instead of confining himself to
his *legal* and *constitutional duty;* this is not only improper from their business
being lost sight of in party zeal, but the jury to whom they address themselves
are inflamed with the sentiments delivered, which they consider as *official,*
and therefore more *authoritative;* and instead of examining the cases brought
before them by the standard of unbiassed truth, such addresses have a
tendency, in my opinion, to regulate their decisions by the scale of party.
These reflections are suggested by reading in your paper of the 4th instant,
an account under the Portsmouth head, of a charge by the Hon. Judge
Patterson, at a circuit court of the United States, to the jury when impanelled:
in which it is said, he not only "laid down the law in a masterly manner,',
[this it was his official duty to do][1] but he went further; "politics were set in
their true light, by holding up the jacobins as the disorganizers of our happy
country, and the only instrument of introducing discontent and disaffection
among the well meaning part of the community."[2] Whatever his opinion might
be, or to whatever class of citizens this was intended to apply, however

numerous they may be, and however dissatisfied they may be, and desirous to change the present administration for another, I think it the more improper, as all party spirit should be banished *on trials* as much as possible. Judge Patterson, I believe, is an able upright Judge; but he has his politics; and the custom that prevails in addresses to juries has probably led him farther in declaiming against the opposite party than he otherwise would, he has not been content with entering the field of politics only, if the said account be true; he also inculcated *religion* and *morality,* both very good things, but neither of them came, in my apprehension, within the business of his office; and perhaps if he entered largely on his clerical functions, he would have to combat as opposite opinions in this country in *religion* as in *politics.* Nor is it only in the charges of judges that I have often felt dissatisfied; juries also frequently travel out of their road; sometimes into that of the *legislature,* and present as grievances matters that are remediable only by law; at other times they get into the path of the *executive* and dictate his duty for him; and at other times they descend to form a club for electioneering purposes: whatever side they may take in all such instances I think it wrong; and it would give me great pleasure to see these things abandoned, and both *judges* and *jury* confine themselves to their duty: and if every department of government will do that, whether *John Adams or Thomas Jefferson are "in authority the people will have cause to rejoice."*

(Wilmington) August 27, 1800. Date and place are those of the newspaper. The headline indicates this article was reprinted from the *Supporter,* a Philadelphia newspaper established on April 4, 1800. Brigham, *American Newspapers,* 2:953.

1. Brackets appear in original.

2. See *United States Oracle* (q.v. under date of May 24, 1800).

Circuit Court for the District of New York ————————————————
September 1, 1800   New York, New York

Associate Justice William Paterson and Judge John Sloss Hobart opened court on September 1, and Paterson delivered a charge to the grand jury. The court adjourned on September 4.[1]

1. Minutes, CCD New York, RG 21, NjBaFAR. We have been unable to identify the specific charge given. For undated Paterson charges, see Appendix A.

Circuit Court for the District of Connecticut ————————————————
September 17, 1800   Hartford, Connecticut

On September 17 court convened with Associate Justice William Cushing and Judge Richard Law in attendance. Cushing delivered a charge to the grand jury after the opening of the court. On September 25 the court adjourned to the next term.[1]

1. Docket Book, CCD Connecticut, RG 21, MWalFAR; *Connecticut Courant* (Hartford), September 29, 1800 (q.v.). Charge not found.

Old State House detail in *Colonel Jeremiah Halsey* attributed to Joseph Steward (1753-1822). Oil on canvas, 1797. Courtesy Connecticut Historical Society, Hartford. After 1796 the circuit court for Connecticut, when in Hartford, met at the then newly completed state house depicted above.

Connecticut Courant ————————————————————————————
September 29, 1800   Hartford, Connecticut

On Thursday last was closed the session of the Circuit Court of the United States, holden for the District of Connecticut, in this town. Judge *Cushing*, in his address to the Grand Jury, pointed out the objects within their cognizance, and illustrated their duty as officers and citizens in a very impressive manner. ...

...

The decisions of the several causes that were tried during the session, manifested the learning and candour which so eminently adorn the venerable Judge who presided in the Court.

(Hartford) September 29, 1800. Date and place are those of the newspaper.

Circuit Court for the District of New Jersey ————————————
October 1, 1800   Trenton, New Jersey

The circuit court opened on October 1, attended by Associate Justice William Paterson and Judge Robert Morris. Justice Paterson delivered a charge to the grand jury, and the court adjourned the same day until the following term.[1]

1. Minutes, CCD New Jersey, RG 21, NjBaFAR. We have been unable to identify the specific charge given. For undated Paterson grand jury charges, see Appendix A.

Circuit Court for the District of Vermont ————————————————
October 3, 1800   Rutland, Vermont

Judge Samuel Hitchcock attended court on October 3, but the absence of a Supreme Court justice caused him to adjourn the court to the next day. On October 4 Associate Justice William Cushing appeared to open court with Judge Hitchcock. The court adjourned on October 11.[1]

1. Circuit Docket, CCD Vermont, RG 21, MWalFAR.

Circuit Court for the District of Pennsylvania ————————————
October 11, 1800   Philadelphia, Pennsylvania

Associate Justice William Paterson and Judge Richard Peters convened court on October 11. On October 16 Paterson delivered a charge to the grand jury. The court adjourned October 23.[1]

1. Engrossed Minutes, CCD Pennsylvania, RG 21, PPFAR. We have been unable to identify the specific charge given. For undated Paterson grand jury charges, see Appendix A.

A View of Philadelphia from the Ferry at Camden, New Jersey by John L. Boqueta de Woiseri (active America, 1797-1815). Watercolor and gouache on paper, ca. 1810. Courtesy New York Public Library, Astor, Lenox and Tilden Foundations, New York. I. N. Phelps Stokes Collection, Miriam & Ira D. Wallach Division of Art, Prints & Photographs Division.

Circuit Court for the District of Massachusetts ——————————
October 20, 1800   Boston, Massachusetts

On October 20 the circuit court opened with Associate Justice William Cushing and Judge John Lowell in attendance. The court adjourned on October 30.[1]

1. Circuit Court Docket, CCD Massachusetts, RG 21, MWalFAR.

Circuit Court for the District of South Carolina ——————————
October 25, 1800   Charleston, South Carolina

Court opened with Associate Justice Bushrod Washington and Judge Thomas Bee in attendance, and Washington delivered a charge to the grand jury. The court adjourned on October 30.[1]

1. Minutes, CCD South Carolina, RG 21, GEpFAR. Charge not found.

Circuit Court for the District of Delaware ——————————
October 27, 1800   Dover, Delaware

Court was convened by Associate Justice William Paterson and Judge Gunning Bedford, Jr. The docket does not record the court's closing, but the last day for which business is recorded is October 28.[1]

1. Appearance Docket, CCD Delaware, RG 21, PPFAR.

Circuit Court for the District of New Hampshire ——————————
November 3, 1800   Exeter, New Hampshire

On Monday, November 3, court was opened by Associate Justice William Cushing. The court met again the following day and adjourned to the following term.[1]

1. Records, CCD New Hampshire, RG 21, MWalFAR.

Circuit Court for the District of Maryland ——————————
November 7, 1800   Baltimore, Maryland

Associate Justice William Paterson and Judge James Winchester convened court on November 7. The court adjourned the following day.[1]

1. Minutes, CCD Maryland, RG 21, PPFAR.

Circuit Court for the District of Georgia ————————————
November 8, 1800   Augusta, Georgia

On November 8 Associate Justice Bushrod Washington and Judge Joseph Clay, Jr., opened court. The court adjourned on November 18.[1]

1. Minutes, CCD Georgia, RG 21, GEpFAR.

Circuit Court for the District of Rhode Island ————————————
November 15, 1800   Providence, Rhode Island

The fall term of the circuit court for Rhode Island commenced on November 15, attended by Associate Justice William Cushing and Judge Benjamin Bourne. The court adjourned on November 24.[1]

1. Minutes, CCD Rhode Island, RG 21, MWalFAR.

William Paterson to Euphemia Paterson ————————————
November 17, 1800   Fredericksburg, Virginia

... I tarried a night and the greater part of the following day at Washington in order to pay my respects to the officers of government, and to visit such of my friends as I could conveniently. ... I called to see M[r] and M[rs] Smith,[1] who live in Jersey street, which is the most populous in the city, and for the elegance of its buildings and the beauty of its prospect is, by way of distinction, called the avenue. It leads from the capitol down to the eastern branch of the Potomack, and it is supposed will become the great scene of commercial business, when Washington shall rival Philad[a] and New York, and be the emporium of the United States. I bowed to the avenue, being the least I could do, and passed along. The president's house is large and elegant, and built for perpetuity. To furnish it any way in style will take at least one hundred thousand dollars. In going through it, I observed to the President, that it would in all probability last as long as the constitution and government of the United States. Our politicians are occupied in enquiries respecting the event of the election of President and Vice-President, which interests and agitates the public mind. What an ocean of time, if I may so phrase it, is wasted in political enquiries and discussions. We are all politicians. A very poor vocation. How much wiser, safer, and better it would be both for the community and ourselves, if most of our people would stay at home, take care of their families, and mind their business; instead of becoming news mongers, and pestering themselves and others about political affairs, of which they know little or nothing.

Gen[l] Marshall[2] informed me, that the business at Richmond would take at least fourteen days, which will throw my return into the winter. I question, whether I shall reach home till Christmas. ...

ARS (NjR, William Paterson Papers). Addressed "New Brunswick, New Jersey." Postmarked "FRED[G V]A NOV 18."

1. Samuel Harrison Smith (1772-1845), publisher of two Washington newspapers: the *National Intelligencer* and the *Universal Gazette.* Margaret (Bayard) Smith (1778-1844) was a prominent Washington hostess. *DAB* entries for Margaret (Bayard) Smith and Samuel Harrison Smith.

2. Former Richmond attorney and Virginia congressman John Marshall was serving as secretary of state. In January 1801 he would become chief justice. *DHSC,* 1:150-51.

Circuit Court for the District of Virginia ————————————————
November 22, 1800   Richmond, Virginia

On November 22 the circuit court was opened by Associate Justice William Paterson, and a charge was delivered to the grand jury. The court adjourned on December 4.[1]

1. Order Book, CCD Virginia, RG 21, Vi. We have been unable to identify the specific charge given. For undated Paterson grand jury charges, see Appendix A.

Circuit Court for the District of North Carolina ————————————
December 1, 1800   Raleigh, North Carolina

Associate Justice Bushrod Washington convened the circuit court for North Carolina on December 1. After court opened, "an elegant and pertinent Charge" was delivered to the grand jury by Justice Washington. The court adjourned on December 6.[1]

1. Minutes, CCD North Carolina, RG 21, GEpFAR; *Virginia Argus* (Richmond), December 12, 1800. Charge not found.

Afterword

The adjournment of the Circuit Court for the district of North Carolina marked the end of circuit riding for the justices of the Supreme Court—or so it seemed. The Judiciary Act of 1801 revised the circuit court system and established a separate tier of circuit court judges who would relieve the justices of the most onerous part of their responsibilities. The new arrangement proved short-lived. In 1802, a Republican-dominated Congress repealed the Judiciary Act of 1801, thereby eliminating the new circuit court judges and returning to the system established by the Judiciary Act of 1789. After a respite that lasted for just three terms, the Supreme Court justices once again rode circuit in the fall of 1802. The circuit riding system designed in 1789 continued in place until 1891. *Stat.,* 2:89, 132, 156; Haskins and Johnson, *Foundations of Power,* pp. 122-26, 163-64; Felix Frankfurter and James M. Landis, *The Business of the Supreme Court* (New York: Macmillan, 1927), pp. 97-101; see introduction to "Spring and Fall Circuits 1800."

APPENDIX A

Undated William Paterson Grand Jury Charges

William Paterson dated none of his grand jury charges. Some of the Paterson charges published in this volume contain specific information that has enabled us to supply dates for them, and we have placed those charges in the text. Others, however, we have been unable to connect to any one of the forty-two circuit courts that Justice Paterson attended between 1793 and 1800.[1] The general nature of the charges makes it difficult to identify when or where they were delivered; accordingly we have published those charges in this appendix in no particular order.

If the ten charges printed here and in the text of volume 3 represent all those that William Paterson wrote (and we cannot be certain of this), then it is clear that he must have delivered the same charge at a number of courts—a practice common to the other justices as well. Furthermore, given their similarity to each other and to the charges published in the text, some or all of these charges may have been drafts that were never delivered.

1. It is clear from the context of these charges that they were written during the early part of his career on the Court and most certainly would not have been composed after 1800.

William Paterson Grand Jury Charge—Number 1 ———————————

Gentlemen of the Grand Jury—

I shall not enter into a particular enumeration of the offences, which are indictable by the laws of the United States. Their penal code is plain and concise, and reduced in its most important points, to written exactitude and precision.[1] But another reason, which supersedes the necessity of a detail, arises from the improbability of any crimes having been committed in this district against the United States. Deeming a description of presentable offences to be at present an unnecessary, as it is always an unpleasing task, permit me to call your attention to preventive justice, which, though connected with penal jurisprudence, is more congenial with the feelings of humanity, and the principles of sound policy, than punishing justice. The best and most effectual method of preventing the commission of crimes is to render the system of education as general and perfect as possible. For supporting good government, cherishing republican principles, and promoting the interests of virtue, and the cause of freedom, schools and seminaries of learning are of primary importance. Knowledge is necessary to our peace, and to our individual as well as social prosperity and happiness. Knowledge refines the manners, exalts the morals, and ameliorates the heart; it inlists the passions on the side of duty, and turns every virtue into a grace. The mind, without literature, is in a rude and dark state, and incapable of high or useful exertions. Even genius, uncultivated, loses half his force; he soars, but with unequal wings. Ages have passed away, generations have rolled on in rapid succession, before civil liberty was ascertained or understood. Seek we the reason? Man was ignorant. Ignorance may be called the mother of slavery as well as of superstition. The mind, when destitute of morals or knowledge, is in a fit state for the reception of every species of falshood and oppression. While overshadowed by ignorance, our mental faculties are unable to discern the subtilties and to resist the fallacies and artful impositions of designing men; but the moment that knowledge begins to break in upon our minds, we think, and judge, and act for ourselves; the film is removed from our eyes; we see things, and discern moral and political sentiments, operations, and characters as they really are, and not through the false and imposing medium of error and deception. Before the torch of science all illusive appearances vanish, like darkness before the dawning of the day. Besides, to act well our part in society, we must know the true interests of the community, in which we live; to perform in a proper manner the various duties incumbent upon us as men and as citizens, we must know what those duties are, what we owe to others, and what is due to ourselves. Knowledge, therefore, by improving the heart and illuminating the understanding, lies at the foundation of social order and happiness. What, indeed, can be expected from uninformed and ignorant minds? They know no country; they have no patriotism. Enough, if they know the spot, on which they were born and rocked; that is their country. Enough, if they know and consult the little interests and narrow politics of the neighbourhood, in which they live and move; that is their patriotism. But of country, which comprehends towns, counties, states, and their numerous and diversified inhabitants and objects[;] which comprehends thousands and millions of men, as well as the earth on which they Live live; and of patriotism, which views those thousands and millions with equal eye, and clasps them all in the same generous embrace; of such a country and of such patriotism, what do they know? Persons, ignorant and uninformed, are easily imposed upon and led astray; they are unable to detect error, or to discern and frustrate hostile but colourable projects and combinations; they have no resources within themselves, and generally repose implicit confidence in others; they are the fit, and, indeed, usual instruments in the hands of artful and aspiring men to serve the purposes of party, and to work out the ruin of a state. Such minds are easily susceptible of the elements of disorganization, and may be induced by subtilty, or transported by passion to pursue the most destructive measures. Zeal they may have in great abundance; but it is a zeal without knowledge, which is dangerous equally in political and religious life. Without mental and moral improvement, neither order, nor civil liberty can be long preserved. Ignorance is freedom's worst foe. Permit me, therefore, gentlemen, to impress upon your minds the importance of diffusing knowledge through the state by the means of proper and well-conducted schools. Believe me, no money is so well bestowed as upon the education of children. They are the hopes of our infant republic. Give them education, give them morals and thus make them useful men and valuable citizens. Remember, that, without morals, there can be no order, and, without knowledge, no genuine liberty.

To a proper system of Education, let me subjoin as the further means of preventing the commission of crimes, an uniform attachment to, and an habitual love and veneration for the ~~laws~~ constitution and laws. This, indeed, ought to be interwoven in the system of a good education. Reverence for the laws is, perhaps, the first political maxim in a republican government. Observance of the laws and obedience to legal authority are the great bulwark of public liberty; which, however, free states find it difficult to maintain; because their restraint sits uneasy upon turbulent spirits, and is mistaken for slavery by the thoughtless and ill-informed part of the community who Delight in irregularity and licentiousness, as sure symptoms of freedom, and certain indications of a manly spirit. The truth is, that civil liberty and order consist in, and depend upon submission to the laws. The constitution and laws contain the articles of our political faith; they point out the path we are to go, and the rule by which we are to walk. They are the work of the people, declarative of their will, and as such ought to be reverenced and obeyed. To fashion our temper, character and conduct, as citizens, by the principles and spirit of the constitution and laws is both our interest and duty; and while we do so, we shall ensure internal order and repose, preserve our civil rights and liberties pure and entire, and be united at home and respected abroad. But why enlarge?

The citizens of this state love the existing constitution of the United States, venerate the general government, and obey the laws; nay more, they are prompt and active in compelling the turbulent and refractory to submit to legal authority. The supremacy of the law they acknowledge; it is the only sovereign they know. These are the brightest virtues that can adorn the republican character. Long may they live, and highly may they be cherished in the bosom of every American _

AD (NjR, William Paterson Papers). Passages in this charge parallel some of the passages in a newspaper essay Paterson wrote under the signature of "Aurelius" during the early months of 1793. Those essays are published in Richard P. McCormick, "Political Essays of William Paterson," *Rutgers University Library Journal* 18 (June 1955), pp. 38-49.

1. Crimes Act of 1790. *Stat.,* 1:112.

William Paterson Grand Jury Charge—Number 2 ——————————

Gentlemen of the Grand Jury,

All free governments originate from the people, and are instituted to protect and secure their property, liberties, and lives, and, in a word, to promote their prosperity and happiness. The more effectually to attain these important ends, the legislative, executive, and judicial authorities have been established by the constitution of the United States, and have, as far as possible, distinct and independent existence. [In] the construction of judicatures, juries compose a capital and distinguished figure; they stand next to the legislature in point of utility, eminence, and importance. The more we contemplate their formation and nature, their powers and duties, the higher they will rise in celebrity and esteem. They are, indeed, the best preservative of civil liberty and order, and essentially necessary for the support of good government. It is a radical and vital principle in the government of the United states, that no person can be affected in his property or life for the commission of any crime, except by the judgment of twenty four good and lawful men; that is, one jury to find the preparatory bill of indictment, and another to pass a verdict upon it.[1] The first of these is denominated the grand inquest or grand jury, principally, perhaps, on account of the plenitude of their power. They are judges both of law and fact; judges upon whose presentment frequently awaits life or death. The due execution of the system of penal jurisprudence depends almost entirely upon the diligence and rectitude, the ability and wisdom of grand juries. The proper exercise of their functions invariably tends to protect the innocent, and to bring forward the guilty for conviction and punishment: and therefore it may truly be said, that the justice of the nation in criminal matters is committed to their discretion and care. These observations apply with peculiar force to the scheme of government formed and adopted by the citizens of the United states. It is a government of laws and not of men; a government, which has freedom for its basis, and the happiness of the people for its object. Crimes perpetrated against such a government ought to be considered as pointed against the well-being, the political existence, and, if I may so phrase it, the majesty of the people themselves. The duties, gentlemen, designated and enjoined upon you by law extend to the investigation and presentment of all offences perpetrated against the United states in this district, or on the high seas by persons in it. To detail these offences would be an unnecessary expence of time. It is sufficient to observe, that the penal code of the United states is simple and concise; the crimes clearly and accurately defined; and the punishment in general duly proportioned to the offence.[2] The court will no longer detain you, gentlemen, from the exercise of your functions; being fully convinced, that you will execute your official duties with impartiality, discernment, and honest zeal.

AD (NjR, William Paterson Papers).
  1. Fifth Amendment and Article III, section 2.
  2. Crimes Act of 1790. *Stat.*, 1:112.

William Paterson Grand Jury Charge—Number 3 ——————

Gentlemen of the Grand Jury.

All free governments originate from the people, and are instituted to protect and secure their property, liberties, and lives, and, in a word, to promote their prosperity and happiness. The more effectually to attain these important ends, the legislative, executive, and judicial authorities have been established by the constitution of the United States, and have, as far as possible, distinct and independent existence. In the construction of judicatures, juries compose a capital and distinguished figure; they stand next to the legislature in point of utility, eminence and importance. The more we contemplate their formation and nature, their powers and duties, the higher they will rise in celebrity and esteem. They are, indeed, the best preservative of civil liberty and order, and essentially necessary for the support of good government. It is a radical and vital principle in the government of the United States, that no person can be affected in his property or life for the commission of any offence; except by the judgment of twenty four good and lawful men; that is, one jury to find the preparatory bill of indictment, and another to pass a verdict upon it _ [1] The first of these is denominated the grand inquest or jury, principally, perhaps, on account of the plenitude of their power. They are judges both of law and fact; judges upon whose presentment frequently awaits life or death _ The due execution of the system of penal jurisprudence depends almost entirely upon the diligence and rectitude, the ability and wisdom of grand juries. The proper exercise of their functions invariably tends to protect the innocent, and to bring forward the guilty for conviction and punishment; and therefore it may truly be said, that the justice of the nation in criminal matters is committed to their discretion and care. These observations apply with peculiar force to the scheme of government framed and adopted by the citizens of the United States. It is a government of laws and not of men; a government, which has freedom for its basis, and the happiness of the people for its object. Crimes perpetrated against such a government ought to be considered as pointed against the well-being, the political existence, and, if I may so phrase it, the majesty of the people themselves. The duties, gentlemen, designated and enjoined upon you by law extend to the investigation and presentment of all offences perpetrated against the United States in this district, or on the high seas by persons in it. To detail these offences would be an unnecessary expence of time. It is sufficient to observe, that the penal code of the United

States is simple and concise; the crimes clearly and accurately defined; and the punishment in general duly proportioned to the offence.[2] Permit me, however, to mention two offences, that, under the existing circumstances of the United States, merit claim particular attention. The one is the forgery of bank bills, which, beside, its moral turpitude and fraud, has a direct and powerful tendency to impair the credit and impede the currency of that species of money.[3] The other offence consists in the violation of neutral principles. The power of declaring war is vested in Congress; and until they exercise that power, and announce hostilities, it becomes us to remain in the line of neutrality and peace.

The court will no longer detain you, gentlemen, from the exercise of your functions; being fully convinced, that you will execute your official duties with impartiality, discernment, and honest zeal _

AD (NjR, William Paterson Papers).
  1. Fifth Amendment and Article III, section 2.
  2. Crimes Act of 1790. *Stat.*, 1:112.
  3. Crimes Act of 1790, section 14. *Stat.*, 1:115.

William Paterson Grand Jury Charge—Number 4

Gentlemen of the grand jury.

All free governments originate from the people, and are instituted to protect and secure their property, liberties, and lives, and, in a word, to promote their prosperity and happiness. The more effectually to attain these important ends, the legislative, executive, and judicial authorities have been established by the constitution of the United States, and have, as far as possible, distinct and independent existence. In the construction of judicatures, juries compose a capital and distinguished figure; they stand next to the legislature in point of utility, eminence, and importance: The more we contemplate their formation and nature, their powers and duties, the higher they rise in celebrity and esteem. They are, indeed, the best preservative of civil liberty and order, and are essentially necessary for the support of good government. It is a radical and vital principle in the government of the United States, that no person can be affected in his property or life for the commission of any offence, except by the judgment of twenty four good and lawful men; that is, one jury to find the preparatory bill of indictment, and another to pass a verdict upon it.[1] The first of these is denominated the grand inquest or jury, principally, perhaps, on account of the plenitude of their power. They are judges both of law and fact; judges upon whose presentment frequently awaits life or death. The due execution of the system of penal jurisprudence depends almost entirely upon the diligence, rectitude, and wisdom of grand juries. The proper exercise of their functions invariably tends to protect the innocent, and to bring forward the guilty for conviction

and punishment; and therefore it may truly be said, that the justice of the nation is, in criminal matters, committed to their discretion and care. These observations apply with peculiar force to the scheme of government formed and adopted by the citizens of the United States. It is a government of laws and not of men; a government, which has freedom for its basis, and the happiness of the people for its object. Crimes perpetrated against such a government ought to be considered as pointed against the well-being, the political existence, and, if I may so phrase it, the majesty of the people themselves. The duties, gentlemen, designated and enjoined upon you by law extend to the investigation and presentment of all offences perpetrated against the United States in this district, or on the high seas by persons in it. To detail these offences would be an unnecessary expense of time. The oath, which you have taken, is an excellent summary of the duties incumbent upon you. It supersedes the necessity of charges in almost every instance. A conscientious observance of the several matters specified in your official oath will ensure a punctual and faithful execution of the trust reposed in you. Permit me, however, to observe, that the penal code of the United States is plain, simple, and concise, and reduced, in the most important points, to written exactitude and precision.[2] Its genius is mild, and happily accords with the spirit of benevolence and humanity, which is a prominent feature in the American character. Under the laws of the United States, we find very few crimes of a capital nature; the greater part of them fall under the denomination of misdemeanors, and are punished by fine and imprisonment. Punishments are in general duly proportioned to their respective crimes; they are graduated upon the scale of justice, attempered by mercy. The degree
is made
of malignity or of danger constitutes the ratio of ~~punishments~~ chastisement. In the present state of our national affairs, the offences, which ought to attrack particular attention, are of a treasonable and seditious nature, and such as violate the law of nations. The latter chiefly refer to our foreign relations, and tend to commit or endanger the neutrality and peace of the United States. The former have a tendency to deprive government of the confidence and affection of the people, to disturb our internal tranquility, and to break in upon and destroy the peace and good order of society. Imbecility, turmoil, and anarchy are the natural consequence of violent feuds, and disorganizing, anti-social principles. Our own country, and, indeed, all free countries, have exhibited signal and melancholy proofs, how prone the people are to be seduced, irritated, and convulsed by the misrepresentations and artifices, the wicked machinations and schemes, or the open and bold attempts and
unprincipled,
enterprizes of factious, designing, and ambitious men. Hence it is, that men raise their voices, and lift their hands against the will of their country. Hence seditious language, writings, and actions. Hence riots, tumults, and insurrections. Order is Heaven's first law. An habitual and cheerful submission

to the laws of our country, and to the powers legally established, is a social duty of primary importance, repeatedly and strongly inculcated and enforced by our holy religion, and, indeed, is the only way to ensure and preserve peace, good order, and national happiness. A disorganizing and tumultuary spirit, ever ready and eager to calumniate and resist legal regulations and acts, is disastrous to civil government, and unavoidably leads to and terminates in political slavery and death. (Seditious persons are common disturbers of public repose, and pests to society; they are bad men and worse citizens. The apostolic rule to ~~min~~ mind our own business, and study to be quiet is an excellent guide in social life. Let us seek peace and be obedient to the laws; let us fear God, respect our government, and honor the constituted authorities of our country. By so doing, we shall perpetuate harmony among ourselves, successfully repel the hostile attempts of foreign nations, promote the prosperity, honor, and dignity of the United States, and transmit our constitution, liberties, and rights pure and entire to our posterity. _)

AD (NjR, William Paterson Papers).
  1. Fifth Amendment and Article III, section 2.
  2. Crimes Act of 1790. *Stat.*, 1:112.

William Paterson Grand Jury Charge—Number 5 ─────────────

  The duties which are designated and enjoined upon you by law extend to the investigation and presentment of all offences perpetrated against the United States [in] this district, or on the high seas by persons in it. To detail these offences would be an unnecessary expence of time. The oath, which you have taken, is an excellent summary of the duties incumbent [upon you. It] supersedes the necessity of charges in almost every instance. A conscientious observance of the several matters specified in your official oath will ensure a punctual and faithful execution of the trust reposed in you. Permit me, however, to observe, that the penal code of the United States is plain, simple, and concise, and reduced, in the most important points, to written exactitude and precision.[1] Its genius is mild, and happily accords with the spirit of benevolence and humanity, which is a prominent feature in the American character. Under the laws of the United States, we find very few crimes of a capital nature; the greater part of them fall [under] the denomination of misdemeanors, and are punished by fine and imprisonment. Punishments are in general duly proportioned to their respective [crimes;] they are graduated upon the scale of justice[, attempered] by mercy. The
                            constitutes
degree of malignity or of ~~great~~ danger is made the ratio of chastisement. In the present state of our national affairs, the offences, which ought to attrack

particular attention, are of a treasonable and seditious nature, and such as violate the law of nations. The latter chiefly refer to our foreign relations, and tend to commit or endanger the neutrality and peace of the United States. Under this description may also be classed offences of a piratical nature; for which the court is informed several persons are now under confinement in this district. Piracy is an alarming and dangerous crime, and, as it merits, will no doubt receive your most close and serious investigation.[2] Treasonable and seditious offences have a tendency to deprive government of the confidence and affection [of the] people, to disturb our internal tranquility, and to break in upon and destroy the peace and good order of society. A republican government, like ours, depends much, if not wholly, upon public opinion, and will work to no good purpose, if public affection be withdrawn from it. It lives in the hearts of the people. Take away their good opinion and affection, and the republic is a body without a soul; the principle of animation is gone; the pulse of life beats no more. Written calumny, detraction, and lies are odious and destructive vices in private, and still more so in public life. They excite a spirit of disobedience, hatred, and disorganization, dangerous to good order, civil liberty, and private property. [Imbecility,] turmoil, and anarchy are the natural consequences of violent feuds, ~~and~~ dissocial principles, and intemperate parties. Our own country, and, indeed, all [free countries,] have exhibited signal and melancholy [proofs,] how prone the people are to be seduced, irritated, and convulsed by the misrepresentations and artifices, the wicked machinations and schemes, or

and enterprizes
the open and bold attempts ^of factious, unprincipled, and ambitious men. Hence it is, that men raise their voices and lift their hands against the will of their country constitutionally promulgated. Hence seditious language, seditious writings, and seditious actions. Hence riots, and tumults, and insurrections. Before popular commotions property, liberty, life, and government are frequently prostrated. For, need I ask, "what spirit rides in such whirlwinds, and directs such storms." "Order is Heaven's first law." An habitual and cheerful submission to the laws of our country and to the powers legally established, is a social duty of primary importance, repeatedly and strongly inculcated and enforced by our holy religion, and, indeed, is the only way to ensure and [preserve] peace, good order, and national happiness. A licentious and tumultuary spirit, ever ready and eager to calumniate and resist legal regulations and acts, is disastrous to civil government, and unavoidably leads to and terminates in political slavery and death. The apostolic direction, to mind our own business and study to be quiet, is an excellent guide in social life. Let us seek peace and be obedient to the laws; let us fear God, respect our government, and honor the constituted authorities of our country. By so doing, we shall perpetuate harmony among ourselves, successfully repel the hostile attempts of foreign nations, promote the prosperity, honor, and dignity of the United States,

and transmit [our constitu]tion, liberties, and rights pure and entire to [our] posterity —

AD (NjR, William Paterson Papers). The document is damaged, and readings taken from other William Paterson charges have been supplied in brackets.
  1. Crimes Act of 1790. *Stat.*, 1:112.
  2. Crimes Act of 1790, sections 8, 9, 12. *Stat.*, 1:113-14, 115.

William Paterson Grand Jury Charge—Number 6

Gentlemen of the Grand Jury

The situation of the U. States is the most happy in the world. In consequence of the moderation and firmness, the political sagacity and rectitude, displayed by the administrators of our government, and of the pacific principles, which they early adopted, and have invariably pursued, we have not been involved in the present European war, which rages with such extensive and destructive fury. War is a dreadful calamity; nothing but a case of extreme necessity should induce any people to engage in it. The evils attendant on a state of war are great and incalculable; to [a] republic, like ours, young, and as it were in [the] cradle, it might be productive of fata[l] effects; clear it is, that it could produce no good. Peace promotes industry, agriculture, manufactures commerce, and good morals; peace cherishes all the benevolent and domestic virtues makes man more friendly to man, and diffuses an air of calmness and benignity over the face of the country. War on the other hand, delights in scenes of violence, devastation, and blood, injures agriculture, destroys commerce, retards population, ruins morals, withers the nerves, and paralyses the growth of a people; war exhausts the resources of a nation, and entails [a] debt of millions on posterity; thousands and tens of thousands fall beneath its stroke, while pestilence and famine often stalk in its rear and close the disastrous scene. God of Heaven! when wilt thou say to the destroying sword, be sheathed, and to the angry nations, be at peace. Happy America! the land of peace and plenty, of rational freedom and social happiness. May no factious nor disorganizing spirits arise within thy peaceful vales to generate and foment internal discord and strife; may insurrection never more rear her crest among us; may neither foes at home nor foes abroad disturb this our rare and high felicity. But may we all as becomes good citizens, lead quiet, regular, and peaceable lives under the guidance and government of the laws. Gentlemen, From our political situation and relations result certain duties with respect to the powers at war, which ought to be observed with fidelity, and performed with punctuality and honor. The U. States are neutral in the present war; they take no part in it; they remain common friends to all the belligerent powers, not favouring the aims of one to the detriment of the others. An exact neutrality must mark their conduct towards the parties at war; if they favor one to the injury of the other, it will be a departure from pacific principles, and indicative of a hostile disposition. It would be a fraudulent neutrality. To this rule there is no exception, but that which arises from the obligation of antecedant treaties, which ought to be religiously observed. All contracts should be held sacred. This principle, so just in itself, applies with peculiar force to treaties which are conventions between sovereigns, or independant states, and have for their object national measures, adjustments, and regulations. To treaties, therefore, inviolability ought to be attached. Besides, in Congress is exclusively vested the power of declaring war, and until they exercise that power, and announce hostilities, it becomes us to remain in the line of neutrality and peace. The station of neutrality, which the U. States have assumed points to a certain course of conduct, which it is incumbent on us invariably to observe. Neutrality implies two things. 1. That we are not to afford succours to any of the belligerent powers, when we are under no obligation to do so, nor voluntarily to furnish them with troops, arms, ammunition, or other articles of direct use in war. 2. In things, which do not respect war, a neutral nation must not refuse to one of the parties, on account of its present quarrel, what it grants to the other. These rules import exact impartiality, and must be strictly observed by neutral nations. A deviation from them denotes an active preference, a favouring of one to the detriment of the other; whereas a neutral must steer an even course, between hostile nations, without leaning in conduct to one side more than to the other. Every active or improper preference is founded upon a predilection for one of the belligerent powers or hatred to the other. If the U. States, for instance, should furnish troops, or ammunition to Great Britain or France, in their present state of hostility to each other, no person would hesitate in pronouncing it to be incompatible with the principles of neutrality. Such supplies would make us confederates and parties in the war. If the United States should knowingly suffer any of the powers at war to equip and fit out privateers within their jurisdiction or territorial limits, it would be considered as an infraction or abandonment of neutral principles. Hence it follows, that if any of our citizens should fit out or aid in fitting out privateers, in [any] of the ports of the United States, to cruize against friendly powers, it would be deemed an offence highly criminal, and justly punishable by the law of nations. The same may be said of a citizen of the United States accepting therein a commission from any foreign nation to act against the enemies of that nation, but who, at the sa[me] time, are our friends. Such acts are repugnant to the principles of neutrality, and dangerous to the peace and happiness of our country, as they have a direct tendency to involve us in disagreeable disputes, and, perhaps, in long and expensive wars. For friendly powers will assuredly resent such hostile conduct, and call upon our government at once to disavow the offence and punish the offender. And yet so ignorant or regardless of duty, so perverse or [prejudice]d, selfish and fond of gain have some [of] our citizens been found, that they have, in direct violation of the principles of neutrality, committed

offences of the foregoing description, and set both law and government at
defiance. Transgressions of this kind became frequent in some parts of the
Union, and at length attracked the notice of Congress, who, in June, 1794,
passed an act declaratory of the law of nations, and enforcing its observance
by vindicatory sanctions.[1] The parts of the act material on the present
occasion, and worthy of your attention, are contained in the first five sections.
They run in the following words. [&c _ ?]

If, therefore, gentlemen, any offenders of the description specified in the
sections just read should come to your knowledge, it will be your duty to
present them. The principles of neutrality, the law of nations, and the laws
of the United States, require, that such transgressors should be proceeded
against and punished according to their respective demerits. The prosperity
and peace of our country depend in a great measure upon grand juries; they
must present before courts can punish. The execution of criminal law, or, in
other words, the justice of the nation, so far as it relates to indictable offences,
is committed to their care. How vast the trust _ I shall close this address,
gentlemen, with re[commen]ding an observance of the principles of
neu[tral]ity, a regard for the constituted authorities, and an habitual obedience
to, and veneration for, the laws of our country. While we pursue this line
of conduct, we shall live in peace at home, and be respected abroad; we
shall cherish a spirit of candor, mutual love and forbearance, and grow more
and more into union; we shall promote good order, justice, social happiness,
and national prosperity; and in a word, gentlemen, as long as we pursue this
line of conduct, we shall maintain the independence, and dignity of the United
States. May the God of Heaven be our protector and guide, and [enab]le us
all to discharge our official, relative, and social duties with diligence, fidelity,
and honest zeal! _

AD (NjR, William Paterson Papers).
    1. Neutrality Act of 1794. *Stat.*, 1:381.

APPENDIX B

Circuit Court Legislation

Volume 4 of *The Documentary History of the Supreme Court of the United States, 1789-1800,* will focus on the major legislation that shaped the development of the federal judicial system from 1789 to 1801. The sixteen statutes discussed below, however, represent attempts by Congress to resolve specific difficulties that the justices of the Supreme Court and others encountered during the first decade of operation of the federal circuit courts. Most of the statutes in this appendix alter the dates and places of holding circuit courts or solve technical problems resulting from the failure to hold a particular court. Some involve such important issues as a mandatory rotation in circuit riding assignments and the transfer of district court jurisdiction to the circuit court because of the incapacity of a district judge. But, unlike the statutes that will appear in the next volume, none constitutes a significant revision of the Judiciary Act of 1789.[1]

There appears to have been a close connection between the introduction of the bills included in this appendix and the justices' concerns about circuit riding. Several draft bills in the records of the United States Senate are in the hand of James Iredell, a fact that suggests he played a direct role in initiating legislation. Iredell's bills focused on the difficulty of traveling the Southern Circuit and on the failure to hold sessions of the North Carolina circuit court in 1795 and 1797. We have printed these drafts as separate documents under the title of the statute as finally passed. Similarly, we have printed an amendment in the hand of Samuel Johnston, senator from North Carolina and Iredell's brother-in-law, that introduced a mandatory rotation of circuit riding assignments into the Circuit Court Act of 1792. An amendment to the printed bill that ultimately became the Circuit Court Act of 1797, concerning the issuing of venires to summon jurors, is also in Iredell's hand.

In the section that follows this introduction, the legislation is presented under the name of the statute as finally passed and in chronological order by date of passage. Each statute is given a narrative history with citations to all of the proceedings in the Senate and House legislative journals, and to the major manuscripts in the Senate and House records at the National Archives. The narrative is followed by the draft bill or amendment, for those instances where such a document still exists in either James Iredell's or Samuel Johnston's hand. Lastly, there is a precis of the statute that details the final version of each section.

---

1. The Judiciary Acts of 1793 and 1801, for example, have provisions that affect the circuit courts, but they have larger implications for the whole judicial system and therefore will be covered in volume 4. Two judiciary bills introduced in the spring of 1798 also deal with circuit riding reform. Because they are important precursors of the Judiciary Act of 1801, we will publish them in volume 4.

We have dated the draft bills and amendments according to the dates they were introduced in the Senate. In so doing we have chosen to rely on the Senate Legislative Journal rather than on the clerk's endorsements that appear on the documents. Where a document is undated, we have relied on information in the Senate Legislative Journal to supply a date in brackets. The Senate Legislative Journal was read and corrected each day in the Senate and represents the most accurate record of Senate proceedings. The significance of the dates used by the clerk cannot always be determined, but they often refer to the date of passage of a bill or the date of acceptance of an amendment. We have included all endorsements by the clerk in the source note to each document.

An Act for giving effect to an Act entituled "An Act to establish the Judicial Courts of the United States," within the State of North Carolina[1]

June 4, 1790

When Congress passed the Judiciary Act of 1789, it created federal courts in the eleven states that had already ratified the Constitution. North Carolina formally approved the Constitution two months after the act was passed and needed special legislation to establish federal courts there.

In January 1790 the Senate appointed a committee to bring in "a bill, in addition to 'An act to establish the judicial courts of the United States.'" The resulting bill provided that the North Carolina district court be held quarterly at New Bern and the circuit court be held twice a year alternately at New Bern and Hillsborough. The committee also established a $1,500 salary for the district judge and added a provision that set the meeting place of the New Hampshire district court at Portsmouth only (eliminating Exeter), after merchants submitted a petition requesting the alteration. The bill, "An Act for giving effect to the Act therein mentioned in respect to the State of North Carolina and to amend the said Act," passed the Senate without further amendment on May 3.[2]

The House passed an amended bill on May 10. The first amendment called for the North Carolina circuit court to be held at New Bern and Salisbury instead of New Bern and Hillsborough. The second struck out the change to Portsmouth as the only place for holding the New Hampshire district court. A third amendment altered the site for the meeting of the Pennsylvania district court from Philadelphia and York to Philadelphia only, and a fourth required that the Kentucky district court be held three rather than four times annually.[3]

The Senate, however, did not agree to the first and second House amendments, so a joint conference committee was formed to work out a compromise. The committee report recommended holding the North Carolina circuit court at New Bern only and the New Hampshire district court at Portsmouth only. Although both houses agreed to the first amendment, the House refused to eliminate Exeter as a place for holding the New Hampshire district court and, therefore, the bill died in conference.[4]

On May 21 Hugh Williamson of North Carolina introduced a new bill in the House that adhered to the joint conference committee recommendation that the North Carolina circuit court be held at New Bern only. Stripped of the provision to hold the New Hampshire district court only at Portsmouth, the new bill passed the House on May 24 and the Senate on May 28.[5]

1. *Stat.*, 1:126.

2. *SLJ*, 1:106, 124, 135, 136, 138, 139, 140, 141, 142, 143; *HRJ*, 1:182, 183-84, 190, 208, 209, 210, 212, 214, 215, 216, 217, 219; *Annals*, 2:1581-82, 1585; Petition of the Merchants and Traders of Portsmouth, New Hampshire, March 11, 1790, Sen 1A-G3, Petitions and Memorials, Resolutions of State Legislatures, and Related Documents, RG 46, DNA; original manuscript bill, reported April 29, 1790, Sen 1A-B1, Bills and Resolutions Originating in the Senate, RG 46, DNA; engrossed bill, passed May 3, 1790, Sen 1A-B4, Bills and Resolutions Originating in the Senate, RG 46, DNA.

3. House amendments, passed May 10, 1790, Sen 1A-B4, Bills and Resolutions Originating in the Senate, RG 46, DNA.

On April 30 the House had appointed a committee to consider bringing in a bill providing for an extra district court session at York, Pennsylvania. The same day the two senators from Pennsylvania, Robert Morris and William Maclay, discussed eliminating York as a place for holding the circuit and district courts and decided to let the House take the lead on this alteration as the original provision for York had been a House amendment to the Judiciary Act of 1789. No bill was ever reported; instead a provision making Philadelphia the sole meeting place was attached to the North Carolina bill. *Pennsylvania Packet* (Philadelphia), May 5, 1790; *HRJ*, 1:206; *FFC, Maclay Diary*, 9:256. For the final disposition of this proposal, see "An Act to Alter the Times for holding the Circuit Courts of the United States in the Districts of South Carolina and Georgia, and providing that the District Court of Pennsylvania shall in future be held at the city of Philadelphia only," under date of August 11, 1790.

In 1789 unsuccessful attempts had been made to have the district court for Pennsylvania hold a session in Carlisle and for the district and circuit courts for Connecticut to meet at Middletown. Daniel Hiester to James Hamilton, September 28, 1789 (PCarlH); William Walter Parsons to Nicholas Gilman, July 23, 1789 (Miscellaneous Manuscripts Collection, NHi); George Phillips to Benjamin Huntington, Jonathan Sturges, and Jonathan Trumbull, July 25, 1789 (Jonathan Trumbull Papers, CtHi).

4. Conference committee report, submitted May 18, 1790, Joint Committee Reports, RG 128, DNA; *DHSC*, 2:80n.

5. *HRJ*, 1:219, 220, 220-21, 227, 233, 234; *SLJ*, 1:144, 146, 147, 148, 150, 151.

PRECIS

Section 1: extends the Judiciary Act of 1789 to North Carolina.

Section 2: appoints one district judge for North Carolina, to hold four court sessions annually at New Bern beginning on Monday, July 5, and thereafter on the first Monday of every third calendar month.

Section 3: annexes the district of North Carolina to the Southern Circuit; establishes a circuit court for North Carolina to be held at New Bern twice a year, on June 18 and November 8.

Section 4: provides a $1,500 annual salary to the district judge for North Carolina.

An act for giving effect to an act intituled "An act to establish the Judicial Courts of the United States," within the State of Rhode Island and Providence Plantations[1]

June 23, 1790

Of the thirteen original states that joined together under the Articles of Confederation, Rhode Island was the last state to ratify the Constitution. A bastion of anti-federalism, the state sent no delegates to the Constitutional Convention in

Philadelphia in 1787, and agreed to call a ratification convention only when the United States Senate passed a bill to boycott the state. On May 29, 1790, Rhode Island ratified the Constitution by a vote of 34-32.[2]

As in North Carolina, special legislation was necessary to establish federal courts in Rhode Island. Accordingly, on June 1, 1790, the House appointed a committee to bring in a bill or bills to give effect to the laws of the United States within the state. Massachusetts representative Theodore Sedgwick reported a bill on June 4 to extend the Judiciary Act of 1789 to Rhode Island, and it passed on June 8. The Senate agreed to the bill on June 14, with one amendment that reduced the salary of the district judge from $1,000 to $800.[3]

1. *Stat.*, 1:128.

2. John P. Kaminski, "'Outcast Rhode Island'—The Absent State," *this Constitution: From Ratification to the Bill of Rights* (Washington, D.C.: Congressional Quarterly, 1988), pp. 49-54.

3. *HRJ*, 1:232, 234, 235, 242, 243, 247, 249; *SLJ*, 1:151, 153, 155, 157, 158, 164, 165; *Annals*, 2:1639-40.

PRECIS

Section 1: extends the Judiciary Act of 1789 to Rhode Island.

Section 2: appoints one district judge for Rhode Island, to hold four court sessions annually beginning the first Monday in August at Newport, and thereafter the first Monday of every third calendar month alternately at Providence and Newport.

Section 3: annexes the district of Rhode Island to the Eastern Circuit; establishes a circuit court for Rhode Island to be held twice a year, on June 4 at Newport and on December 4 at Providence.

Section 4: provides an $800 annual salary to the district judge for Rhode Island.

An Act to alter the Times for holding the Circuit Courts of the United States in the Districts of South Carolina and Georgia, and providing that the District Court of Pennsylvania shall in future be held at the city of Philadelphia only[1]

August 11, 1790

During the early years of the federal court system, the justices of the Supreme Court made numerous attempts to reform the circuit riding system. This bill, written by James Iredell, constitutes their first attempt to develop a legislative remedy for perceived problems.

Iredell, who had just completed the spring Southern Circuit for the first time, concluded that the fall circuit would proceed more smoothly if the Georgia circuit court preceded that of South Carolina, as it did in the spring. Such an alteration would eliminate needless backtracking between South Carolina and Georgia by allowing the justices to begin the fall circuit in Georgia and travel continuously northward to terminate it in North Carolina.

A bill incorporating the change received its first reading in the Senate on August 7, 1790, and passed the following day. After inclusion of a House amendment for holding the district court for Pennsylvania at Philadelphia only, the bill passed both houses on August 9.[2]

1. *Stat.*, 1:184. *DHSC* short title: Circuit and District Court Act of 1790.

2. *SLJ*, 1:204, 205, 206, 207, 207-8, 209; *HRJ*, 1:295, 296, 297; Original Senate Bill, August 7, 1790 (q.v.); engrossed bill, passed August 9, 1790, Sen 1A-B4, Bills and Resolutions Originating in the Senate, RG 46, DNA, printed in *FFC*, 4:218-19. On August 6 William Loughton Smith of South Carolina introduced a motion in the House respecting the circuit courts in South Carolina, but the content of this motion is not known. *Federal Gazette* (Philadelphia), August 10, 1790.

The House had first taken action on the location of the Pennsylvania district court when it appointed a committee to consider bringing in a bill providing for an extra district court session at York. This proposal died in committee. Instead the House included an amendment changing the meeting place of the Pennsylvania district court to Philadelphia only in the first North Carolina judiciary bill, but the bill did not pass. *Pennsylvania Packet* (Philadelphia), May 5, 1790; *HRJ*, 1:206; "An Act for giving effect to an Act entitled 'An Act to establish the Judicial Courts of the United States,' within the State of North Carolina" (q.v. under date of June 4, 1790).

Original Senate Bill, reported August 7, 1790

An Act

A Bi_ll to alter the times for holding the Circuit Courts of The United States in the Districts of South Carolina and Georgia.

Be it Enacted, by the Senate and House of Representatives of the United States of America in Congress assembled, That the Circuit Courts of the United States in the Districts of South Carolina and Georgia shall for the future be held as follows, to wit: In the District of South Carolina on the twenty fifth day of October next at Charleston, and in each succeeding year at Columbia on the twelfth day of May, and in Charleston on the twenty fifth day of October; In the District of Georgia on the fifteenth day of October next at Augusta, and in each succeeding year at Savannah on the twenty fifth day of April, and at Augusta on the fifteenth day of October; except when any of those days shall happen to be Sunday, in which case the Court shall [be] held on the Monday following: And all Process that was returnable under the former law at Charleston on the first day of October next, and at Augusta on the seventeenth day of October, shall now be deemed returnable respectively at Charleston on the twenty fifth day of October next, and at Augusta on the fifteenth day of October next; any thing in the former law to the contrary notwithstanding.

AD (DNA, RG 46, Bills and Resolutions Originating in the Senate, Sen 1A-B1). In the hand of James Iredell. Endorsed "An Act to alter the times for holding the Circuit Courts of the United States in the District of S Carolina & Georgia. August 6th 1790."

PRECIS

Section 1: changes the date of holding the fall circuit court for South Carolina at Charleston to October 25 (the spring court at Columbia remains May 12); changes the date of holding the circuit court for Georgia at Savannah to April 25, and at Augusta to October 15.

Section 2: changes the meeting place of the district court for Pennsylvania to Philadelphia only.

An Act giving effect to the laws of the United States within the state of Vermont[1] ——
March 2, 1791

During the 1780s, Vermont remained in a curious political limbo. Although it had declared itself independent of New York in 1777, Vermont was unrecognized as a state by the Continental and Confederation Congresses. This ambiguity ended on February 18, 1791, when Congress enacted a statute admitting Vermont as the fourteenth state.[2] The House, in conjunction with the act, appointed a committee to bring in a bill or bills to extend all the laws of the United States to the new state. On February 17 Massachusetts representative Theodore Sedgwick reported a bill that provided for the establishment of district and circuit courts. It passed the House on February 21. The Senate agreed to the bill on February 23, with one amendment. The House accepted the amendment the following day.[3]

1. *Stat.*, 1:197.
2. Richard Bernstein, *Are We to Be a Nation? The Making of the Constitution* (Cambridge: Harvard University Press, 1987), pp. 86-87, 271; *Stat.*, 1:191.
3. The Senate amendment concerned customs regulations for the Lake Champlain port of Allburgh. *HRJ*, 1:378, 381, 383, 385, 388, 389, 396, 398, 400; *SLJ*, 1:276-77, 277-78, 278-79, 281, 291, 292, 295, 299.

PRECIS
Section 1: extends the laws of the United States (and specifically the Judiciary Act of 1789) to Vermont.
Section 2: appoints one district judge for Vermont to hold four court sessions annually beginning the first Monday in May at Rutland and meeting the first Monday of every third calendar month thereafter, alternately at Windsor and Rutland.
Section 3: annexes the district of Vermont to the Eastern Circuit; establishes a circuit court for Vermont to be held once a year on June 17 at Bennington.
Section 4: provides an $800 annual salary to the district judge for Vermont.
Section 5: provides for the census to be taken in Vermont.
Section 6: directs that the census begin on April 1 and conclude within five months.
Section 7: provides $200 to the marshal for taking the census; specifies that Collection Act of 1790 will have effect in Vermont.
Section 8: appoints a collector of customs to reside at the only designated port of entry, Allburgh; extends the exemption granted by the Collection Act of 1790 to the district of Louisville (in the Kentucky territory of Virginia), to the Lake Champlain port of Allburgh.

An Act providing compensation for the officers of the Judicial Courts of the United States, and for Jurors and Witnesses, and for other purposes[1] ——
March 3, 1791

One of the shortcomings of the Judiciary Act of 1789 and the Process Act of 1789 was that while provision was made for compensating United States attorneys and the attorney general, neither statute provided compensation to the jurors, witnesses, clerks, and marshals serving in the federal courts. Without a legislative solution to that omission, Associate Justice William Cushing worried that "our Credit & perhaps that of the government may be sinking fast, with the mass of the people."[2]

Efforts to devise a system of compensation began in March 1790, but it was not until February 3, 1791, that the House appointed a committee to bring in a bill or bills making a temporary provision for clerks, marshals, and jurors. The House passed a bill on March 1, and the Senate passed it two days later with amendments to the compensation section.[3]

The act also addressed some of the concerns the justices may have had regarding the order of holding circuit courts. It moved the date of holding each circuit court three or four days later with the exception of Boston, where the schedule was changed by nine days. This allowed the justices an extra week between the Connecticut and Massachusetts circuit courts and reduced by a week the time that separated the Massachusetts and New Hampshire circuit court sessions. Additionally, the business before the circuit court of New York was to be conducted at New York City only, thus eliminating the detour to Albany at the beginning of the fall circuit.[4] Saving travel time may also have been the impetus for the substitution of Richmond for Charlottesville and Williamsburg as the place of business for the circuit court in Virginia.[5]

An additional factor in these changes may have been the volume of cases docketed during the first year of circuit riding. The forty actions on the Connecticut circuit court docket, combined with Jay's memory of the late spring snows that slowed his travel from New Haven to Boston in April 1790, may explain the addition of the extra week between the Connecticut and Massachusetts circuit courts.[6] Albany, Charlottesville, and Williamsburg were probably eliminated as sites for holding the circuit courts because the small amount of business docketed there did not justify the added travel time.[7]

1. *Stat.*, 1:216. *DHSC* short title: Compensation and Circuit Court Act of 1791.

2. *Stat.*, 1:92-93, 93; *DHSC*, 2:140.

3. *HRJ*, 1:286, 289, 369, 375, 376, 384, 385, 389, 395, 396-97, 404, 407, 408; *SLJ*, 1:292-93, 293-94, 303, 307, 310, 312, 314; *Annals*, 2:1862; *FFC*, 5:1141, 1141-42; printed House bill, passed March 1, 1791, and manuscript Senate amendments, passed March 2, 1791, Sen 1A-C1, Bills and Resolutions Originating in the House and Considered in the Senate, RG 46, DNA.

4. It is possible that John Jay and William Cushing believed that some minor adjustments needed to be made after they rode the Eastern Circuit in the spring and fall of 1790. It is also possible that they communicated these concerns to members of Congress, who responded accordingly by passing this act. But a paucity of evidence makes it difficult to show how these concerns came to the attention of Congress or at exactly what point they were introduced into the Compensation and Circuit Court Act of 1791.

5. As early as May 31, 1790, Andrew Moore of Virginia made a motion in the House to bring in a bill for changing some of the places for holding the federal courts in Virginia because they had been found inconvenient. The House, however, tabled the motion. *Pennsylvania Packet* (Philadelphia), June 3, 1790; *Annals*, 2:1626.

6. *DHSC*, 2:160-61, 54.

7. The court had no business at the circuit court openings of May 22, 1790, at Charlottesville and October 4 at Albany. The court met at Williamsburg from November 22 to 26, 1790. *DHSC*, 2:71, 99, 115.

PRECIS

Section 1: sets compensation for the United States attorneys, district court clerks, and Supreme Court clerk for attendance at and travel to and from court; to the mar-

shals for attending court, summoning jurors, serving writs, and miscellaneous expenses; to the grand jurors, petit jurors, and witnesses for attendance at and travel
to and from court. Payment to be retroactive to time of appointment or service.

Section 2: changes the place and date for holding the circuit court for New York to
New York City only on April 5 and October 5; alters the dates of commencement of the other federal circuit courts in the Eastern Circuit: for the fall Connecticut court to October 25 (the spring court remains April 25), for Massachusetts to May 12 and November 12, for New Hampshire to May 24 and November
24, for Rhode Island to June 7 and December 7.

Section 3: changes the meeting place of the circuit court for Virginia to Richmond
only.

Section 4: provides that the act be in force until the end of the next session of Congress.

An Act for altering the times of holding the Circuit Courts, in certain districts of the United States, and for other purposes[1] ——————— April 13, 1792

In the spring of 1792, James Iredell began his fourth tour of the Southern Circuit.
Acutely aware of the rigors of traveling to the far-flung southern courts, he had drafted
a bill to revise the circuit and asked his brother-in-law, Samuel Johnston, to introduce
it in the Senate.[2]

Iredell's draft bill moved the date of the spring circuit court for North Carolina
from June 18 to June 1. The effect of this was to shorten the interval between the
circuit courts in South and North Carolina from thirty-eight to twenty-one days. The
bill also changed the date of the fall circuit court for Georgia at Augusta from October
15 to November 8, which meant that the fall circuit would begin in South Carolina
instead of Georgia (as did the spring circuit). After having made two difficult trips
through the back country of North and South Carolina to reach Augusta, Iredell
concluded that the original plan of the Judiciary Act of 1789—to have Charleston
precede Augusta in the fall circuit—was more convenient.[3] This would allow the
justices to begin the Southern Circuit at one of two ports, Savannah or Charleston.
Since it also had taken over a month for Iredell to reach Augusta in the fall, he
decided to allow more time to travel south by moving the entire circuit two weeks
later, beginning at Charleston on October 25 instead of Augusta on the fifteenth.[4]

After introducing Iredell's bill, Johnston asked for permission to add a clause that
addressed the justice's greatest concern: the establishment of a mandatory rotation
in circuit riding. Weary of riding the long Southern Circuit, Iredell had complained
throughout the spring of 1792 of the need for a more equitable distribution of the
circuit assignments.[5]

Johnston's revised bill also contained amendments that moved the fall schedule of
the Eastern Circuit forward one month, and made permanent the changes made by
the Compensation and Circuit Court Act of 1791 to the spring calendar for the Eastern
Circuit and to the location of the Virginia circuit court.[6] The bill passed the Senate
on March 22. The House passed the bill on April 9 after adding amendments that

changed the date of the district court for Maine. Furthermore, the House added two places at which to hold the district court for North Carolina. The Senate agreed to these changes the following day.[7]

1. *Stat.*, 1:252. *DHSC* short title: Circuit Court Act of 1792.

2. *DHSC*, 2:236-37, 247, 248n; Original Senate Bill, March 20, 1792 (q.v.).

3. Interestingly, it had been Iredell himself who had proposed changing the original order of the circuit courts. See "An Act to alter the Times for holding the Circuit Courts of the United States in the Districts of South Carolina and Georgia, and providing that the District Court of Pennsylvania shall in future be held at the city of Philadelphia only," under date of August 11, 1790.

4. Iredell had left New York for the south on or about September 14, 1790, and after detouring by way of Edenton to transact personal business, had reached Augusta on October 15, 1790. In 1791 the trip had taken an additional two weeks with Iredell leaving Philadelphia on or about September 1 and reaching Augusta on October 13. James Iredell to George Washington, September 20, 1790, George Washington Papers, DLC; *DHSC*, 2:92, 101, 204, 216.

5. *DHSC*, 2:238-39, 246.

6. The amendment that altered the fall schedule of the Eastern Circuit probably was added to allow those justices who lived south of New York City more time to travel home and to be with their families before setting out for the February term of the Supreme Court.

7. *SLJ*, 1:412-13, 413, 414, 423, 424, 425; *HRJ*, 1:352, 362, 364, 544, 546-47, 569, 570-71, 572-73, 575, 577, 579; Motion for Rotation in Circuit Riding (q.v. under date of March 20, 1792); Rotation Amendment, [March 21, 1792] (q.v.); amended bill, passed March 22, 1792, Sen 2A-B1, Bills and Resolutions Originating in the Senate, RG 46, DNA; engrossed bill and House amendments, passed April 9 and 10, 1792, Sen 1A-B4, Bills and Resolutions Originating in the Senate, RG 46, DNA. The addition of Wilmington and Edenton as places at which to hold the district court for North Carolina was the culmination of a two year controversy. *DHSC*, 2:121n.

Original Senate Bill, reported March 20, 1792

An Act to alter the times of holding certain of the Circuit Courts of the United States.

Be it enacted by the Senate and House of Representatives of the United States of America in Congress assembled, That the Circuit Courts of the United States in the Districts of North Carolina and Georgia, shall for the future be held as follows, to wit: In the District of North Carolina on the first day of June, and the thirtieth day of November, at Newbern, in the present and each succeeding year; In the District of Georgia, on the twenty fifth day of April at Savannah, and on the eighth day of November at Augusta, in the present and each succeeding year; except when any of those days shall happen on a Sunday, in which case the Court shall be held on the Monday following.

And be it further enacted, That so much of former Acts as directs different times of holding the said Circuit Courts in the District of North Carolina, and of holding the Circuit Court in the District of Georgia when held at Augusta, be and the same is hereby repealed.

AD (DNA, RG 46, Bills and Resolutions Originating in the Senate, Sen 2A-B1). In the hand of James Iredell. A second copy of this bill is endorsed "Bill respecting Circuit Courts 1ˢᵗ & 2ᵈ Read March 20ᵗʰ 1792. Taken into new draught."

Motion for Rotation in Circuit Riding, introduced [March 20, 1792]

~~To make~~ To bring in a Clause to establish such rotation in the attendance of the
burthen,
Judges at the Circuit Courts as may best apportion the ^duties and not impede the Discharge, of the duties of their office

AD (DNA, RG 46, Bills and Resolutions Originating in the Senate, Sen 2A-B1). In the hand of Samuel Johnston. Endorsed "Motion Judiciary March 21 1792."

Rotation Amendment, reported [March 21, 1792]

And Be it enacted that at each Session of the Supreme Court of the United States or as soon after as may be, the Judges of the Supreme Court attending at such Session shall in writing subscribed with their names (which writing shall be lodged with the Clerk of the Supreme Court and safely kept in his Office) assign to the said Judges respectively the Circuits which they are to attend at the ensuing Sessions of the Circuit Courts; which Assignment shall be made in such a manner that no Judge, unless by his own Consent, shall have assigned to him any Circuit which he hath already attended untill the same hath been afterwards attended by every other of the said Judges

Provided always that if the publick Service or the convenience of the Judges shall at any time, in their Opinion, require a different Arrangement, the same may take place with the consent of any four of the Judges of the Supreme Court

AD (DNA, RG 46, Bills and Resolutions Originating in the Senate, Sen 2A-B1). In the hand of Samuel Johnston. Attached to the amended bill and prefaced: "The Comittee to whom was referred the Act to alter the Times of holding certain of the Circuit Courts of the United States report—the following Amendm⁵." Endorsed "Bill respecting Circuit Courts passed 22ᵈ Mar 92."

PRECIS

Section 1: changes the time of holding some of the circuit courts on the Southern Circuit: for North Carolina to June 1 and November 30; for Georgia at Augusta to November 8.

Section 2: makes permanent changes made by the Compensation and Circuit Court Act of 1791 in the spring calendar for the Eastern Circuit and the place for holding the Virginia circuit court; changes the dates of the fall calendar for the Eastern Circuit to September 5 at New York City, September 25 at Hartford, October 12 at Boston, October 24 at Exeter, November 7 at Providence.

Section 3: mandates a rotation in circuit riding duties so that no justice has to ride the same circuit twice in succession until all the other justices have ridden that circuit, unless, for reasons of public service or convenience, four justices vote otherwise.

Section 4: changes the meeting date of the district court for Maine to the third Tuesday in June.

Section 5: adds Wilmington and Edenton as places where the district court for North Carolina will be held.

An Act to alter the times and places of holding the Circuit Courts, in the Eastern District, and in North Carolina, and for other purposes[1] — March 2, 1793

Attempts to revise the circuit riding system continued in 1793, when Senator Stephen Bradley of Vermont introduced a bill to change the date and place of the circuit court for Vermont from June 17 at Bennington to June 24 alternately at

Bennington and Windsor. An amended bill, passed by the Senate on February 25, included two new sections relating to the circuit court for North Carolina. The first moved the meeting place from New Bern to the Wake Court House and then to the newly constructed state capital of Raleigh. The second overcame any legal difficulties created by the failure to hold the fall 1792 term.[2]

The House soon added amendments revising most of the spring calendar for the Eastern Circuit. As finally passed by both houses on February 28, the act revised the schedule so that after leaving New Haven the justices would travel next to either Windsor or Bennington, and then on to Portsmouth, Boston, and finally Newport.[3]

The changes streamlined the Eastern Circuit by allowing for a single arc of travel—north to Vermont, east to the New Hampshire and Massachusetts coasts, and south to Rhode Island; and for an easy water route back to New York and points south. This was an improvement over the old circuit arrangement which had required a month of extensive travel from Boston to Portsmouth, back to Boston, and then on to Newport, culminating in a rapid ride across Connecticut and Massachusetts to reach Vermont by mid-June. John Jay and William Cushing had found it impossible to keep this schedule in the spring of 1791 and of 1792. In 1791 the amount of business in Newport had delayed Jay from setting off for Bennington until after the day appointed for holding the circuit court for Vermont, while Cushing was too ill to make the long journey at all. In 1792 the Rhode Island court adjourned just three days before the scheduled opening in Vermont, so Jay arrived a week late, with Cushing trailing two days behind him. After Congress mandated a rotation of circuit riding, it was also in the interests of the justices residing south of New York to end their circuit at Newport rather than in the hinterlands of Vermont, where a lengthy boat trip down the Hudson River was the only water route home.[4]

1. *Stat.*, 1:335. DHSC short title: Circuit Court Act of 1793.
2. *SLJ*, 1:477, 482, 493, 499, 501; "An Act for altering the ~~Time and~~ Places of holding the Circuit Courts in the Districts of Vermont, and North Carolina, and for other purposes," amended bill, reported February 23, 1793, Sen 2A-B1, Bills and Resolutions Originating in the Senate, RG 46, DNA.
3. *HRJ*, 1:718, 720, 723, 725, 725-26, 732; "An Act for altering the times and places of holding the Circuit Courts in the Eastern District, and in North Carolina, and for other purposes," engrossed bill, passed February 28, 1793, 1A-B4, Bills and Resolutions Originating in the Senate, RG 46, DNA.
4. *DHSC*, 2:192, 195, 281-82, 282, 286.

PRECIS

Section 1: changes the dates of holding the spring circuit courts on the Eastern Circuit and the meeting place of the circuit court for Vermont: for New York on April 5 (as before); for Connecticut on April 25 (as before); for Vermont on May 12, alternately at Bennington and Windsor; for New Hampshire on May 27; for Massachusetts on June 7; and for Rhode Island on June 19.

Section 2: moves the circuit court for North Carolina from New Bern to the Wake Court House in Wake County, and then to Raleigh once suitable accommodations are built.

Section 3: provides for summoning of jurors to attend the next session of the circuit court for North Carolina and revives all suits and process so as to be proceeded upon at the next session, as if the fall 1792 term had not failed for lack of a quorum.

An Act transferring, for a limited time, the Jurisdiction of the Suits and Offences from the District to the Circuit Court of New Hampshire, and assigning certain Duties in respect to Invalid Pensioners, to the Attorney of the said District[1] ————
April 3, 1794

By 1792, John Sullivan, the United States judge for the district of New Hampshire, had become so chronically ill that he could not carry out his official duties.[2] In December 1793 the House appointed a committee to consider amending the Judiciary Act of 1789 to provide for cases in which a federal judge was incapacitated by sickness or "other disqualifying cause." While no general bill was presented, William Loughton Smith of South Carolina reported a bill on March 6 specifically providing for the transfer of the jurisdiction of the district court for New Hampshire to the circuit court and assigning the invalid pension duties of the district judge to the United States attorney for the district of New Hampshire. On March 21 the Senate considered a similar motion of its own, but ultimately passed the House bill on March 31.[3]

1. *Stat.*, 1:352.
2. *DHSC*, 2:302, 302n.
3. *HRJ*, 2:16, 49, 56, 67, 74, 84, 101, 107, 109, 110, 111; *SLJ*, 2:53, 55, 58, 59, 60, 61; printed bill, passed by the House on March 25, 1794, Sen 3A-C1, Bills and Resolutions Originating in the House and Considered in the Senate, RG 46, DNA; Motion by Mr. Langdon, introduced March 21, 1794, Sen 3A-B3, Bills and Resolutions Originating in the Senate, RG 46, DNA.

PRECIS
Section 1: all actions in the district court for New Hampshire removed to the Circuit Court for the district of New Hampshire.
Section 2: the United States attorney to perform the duties of the district court judge under the Invalid Pensions Act of 1793.
Section 3: provides that the act be in force until the end of the next session of Congress or until a new district judge be appointed.

An Act further to authorize the Adjournment of Circuit Courts[1] ————
May 19, 1794

John Jay's appointment on April 19, 1794, as President Washington's special envoy to Great Britain left unfinished his circuit court duties. For unknown reasons, a plan to redistribute the remaining circuit courts among the five associate justices included no provision for holding the circuit court in Connecticut. When no Supreme Court justice arrived in New Haven to open court the week of April 25, District Judge Richard Law faced the predicament of being unable to adjourn court to the next term. He wrote to Justices Wilson and Paterson and to Senator Oliver Ellsworth of Connecticut, notifying them of the need for a legislative remedy or for the attendance of one of the justices.[2]

On May 12 Ellsworth introduced a bill in the Senate which allowed the district judge or the marshal to adjourn a circuit court to the next term. The Senate passed the bill the following day with one amendment. The House passed the bill on May 14, and the president signed it on May 19.[3]

1. *Stat.*, 1:369. *DHSC* short title: Adjournment Act of 1794.

2. *DHSC*, 2:436-37, 446, 447n, 449, 450, 452-53.

3. *SLJ*, 2:78, 80, 81, 82, 83; *HRJ*, 2:155, 156, 162, 167, 169; engrossed bill, passed by the House, May 14, 1794, Sen 1A-B4, Bills and Resolutions Originating in the Senate, RG 46, DNA.

PRECIS

Provides that the district judge or, in his absence, the marshal may adjourn a circuit court to the next term when no Supreme Court justice arrives within four days of the scheduled date for opening court.

An Act making certain alterations in the act for establishing the Judicial Courts, and altering the time and place of holding certain courts[1]

June 9, 1794

Early in the first session of the Third Congress, the House appointed a committee to recommend changes in the Judiciary Act of 1789. The committee called for provisions to be made for sick or incapacitated federal judges and for reducing the number of marshals attending the Supreme Court. The committee reported two bills: the first applied to the incapacity of the district judge for New Hampshire;[2] the second included a provision requiring only the marshal of the district in which the Supreme Court was sitting to attend that Court. Previously marshals of all districts were supposed to appear at every term of the Court.

The House passed an amended bill on June 4 which included several other provisions applying to the district courts: a new procedure for hearing appraisals of ships and cargo; changes in the dates and places for holding the district courts in Massachusetts, Pennsylvania, Georgia, Delaware, and Kentucky; and a division of the district court for North Carolina into three districts.[3]

The provisions regarding the North Carolina district court received the most attention in the Senate. They were completely rewritten into four sections establishing three separate districts. The Senate also deleted the House provision concerning the Delaware district court and inserted in its place a change in the date of holding the spring session of the circuit court for Delaware from April 27 to the second Monday in June.[4] Moving Delaware to the end of the Middle Circuit allowed more time for holding the circuit court in Philadelphia.[5]

On June 6 the Senate passed an amended bill, which was in turn approved by the House, after the Senate receded from its amendment exempting all other marshals but the marshal in the district in which the Supreme Court was sitting from any service at the Court, even under special order.[6]

1. *Stat.*, 1:395. *DHSC* short title: District and Circuit Court Act of 1794.

2. See "An Act transferring, for a limited time, the Jurisdiction of the Suits and Offences from the District to the Circuit Court of New Hampshire, and assigning certain Duties in respect to Invalid Pensioners, to the Attorney of the said District," under date of April 3, 1794.

3. *HRJ,* 2:16, 49, 56, 66-67, 74, 87, 104, 133, 194, 198, 199, 211, 213, 215; *Annals,* 4:608-9; "Report on a motion of the 19th instant, respecting the attendance of the Marshal," made February 27, 1794, vol. 1, Reports of Select Committees, RG 233, DNA.

4. On March 28 Senator John Vining of Delaware had given notice to the Senate that he would introduce a bill altering the date of the Delaware circuit court. A bill was submitted to the clerk, but no action was taken on it before the House bill arrived in the Senate. *SLJ,* 2:58; Bill to alter the time of holding the Circuit Court in Delaware, March 28, 1794, Sen 3A-B1, Bills and Resolutions Originating in the Senate, RG 46, DNA.

5. It is not known who suggested this change or why, but the initiative may have come from state sources as both the federal circuit court and some Delaware state courts had meetings in late April. In light of later complaints by the justices about having to backtrack to Delaware after holding the circuit court in Richmond, it seems unlikely that the justices suggested the change. John D. Cushing, comp., *The First Laws of the State of Delaware,* 2 vols. (Wilmington, Del.: Michael Glazier, 1981), 2:1088, 1191; Samuel Chase to James Iredell, March 12, 1797 (q.v.); Justices of the Supreme Court to John Adams, August 15, 1797 (q.v.); Justices of the Supreme Court to Gunning Bedford, August 15, 1797, (q.v.).

6. *SLJ,* 2:102, 103, 104, 108, 113, 115; printed bill with manuscript Senate amendments and Vining's amendment, passed by the Senate June 6, 1794, Sen 3A-C1, Bills and Resolutions Originating in the House and Considered in the Senate, RG 46, DNA.

PRECIS

Section 1: district judges may appoint commissioners before whom appraisers may be sworn for giving testimony about ships or cargo seized by the United States.

Section 2: changes dates for holding district courts for Massachusetts, Pennsylvania, and Georgia; and changes the time of holding the spring circuit court for Delaware from April 27 to the second Monday in June.

Section 3: divides North Carolina into 3 districts: Wilmington, New Bern, and Edenton; causes begun in one district will be heard only in that district.

Section 4: effect of North Carolina division on arrest and bail.

Section 5: effect of North Carolina division on process already commenced.

Section 6: effect of North Carolina division on clerk's records.

Section 7: only the marshal of the district in which the Supreme Court is sitting must attend the Court; other marshals to be called by special order of the Supreme Court as needed.

Section 8: district court for Kentucky to be held at Frankfort, not Harrodsburg.

An Act making certain provisions in regard to the Circuit Court, for the district of North Carolina[1] —————————————

March 31, 1796

After presiding at the Circuit Court for the district of Virginia in the fall of 1795, James Iredell returned to Edenton, North Carolina to learn that for the second time in a year no circuit court had been held in the state. A statute was necessary to resolve the legal difficulties that resulted from the failure to hold the court.[2]

On March 24, 1796, Alexander Martin of North Carolina presented to the Senate a bill, written by Iredell, which provided for the legal procedures necessary to revive suits and process in and summon jurors to attend the North Carolina circuit court. The Senate passed it the same day; the House, two days later.[3]

1. *Stat.*, 1:450.

2. The failure of the fall 1792 circuit court for North Carolina had necessitated similar statutory provisions. See "An Act to alter the times and places of holding the Circuit Courts, in the Eastern District, and in North Carolina, and for other purposes," under date of March 2, 1793.

3. *SLJ,* 2:228-29, 229, 230, 231, 232; *HRJ,* 2:480, 481-82, 485, 487, 491; Original Senate Bill, March 24, 1796 (q.v.); engrossed bill, passed by the House, March 25, 1796, Sen 4A-B4, Bills and Resolutions Originating in the Senate, RG 46, DNA.

Original Senate Bill, reported March 24, 1796

A Bill making certain provisions in regard to the Circuit Court for the District of North Carolina.

Whereas a sufficient Quorum of Judges did not attend to hold the Circuit Court for the District of North Carolina for the purpose of doing business in June Term One thousand seven hundred and ninety five; and no Judge attended to hold the said Court in November Term in the same year; in consequence whereof certain provisions are now become necessary and expedient to prevent a failure of justice in the said Court.

Be it therefore Enacted, by the Senate and House of Representatives of the United States of America, in Congress assembled, That it shall and may be lawful for the District Judge of the State of North Carolina to direct the Clerk of the said Court to issue such Process for the purpose of causing Persons to be summoned to serve as Jurymen at the said Court at the Term to commence on the first day of June next, as had been before issued by the Clerk of the said Court for the like purpose returnable to June Term One thousand seven hundred and ninety five; that the Persons ordered by the said Process to be summoned for the said purpose shall be ordered to be summoned in the same proportion, and from the same Counties, as those Persons who were ordered to be summoned for the like purpose by process returnable at June Term One thousand seven hundred and ninety five: Provided, That if it shall appear expedient to the said District Judge that a different time of Notice shall be prescribed than that hitherto prescribed, ~~or practiced~~, he may cause ~~the same~~ such other time of Notice to be directed to be given as to him shall appear most conducive to Justice, and convenient to the Persons to be summoned: And the Marshall is hereby directed to execute the said Process so to be issued, and the Persons who shall be legally summoned to attend as Jurymen in consequence thereof, are hereby required to attend the said Court, under the like penalties for disobedience as if the said process had been ordered to be issued by the said Court in the ordinary method of proceeding; and the Marshall, and the Persons who shall attend as Jurymen in virtue of the said Process so to be issued, shall be entitled to the like allowances for their services respectively.

And be it further enacted, That all Suits and Proceedings of what nature or kind soever which have been commenced in the said Court, and not finished, shall be proceeded on at the ensuing Term in the same manner and to the same Effect, as if the said Circuit Court had been regularly held for the purpose of business in June and November Terms One thousand seven hundred and ninety five, and continuances had been regularly entered of all suits and proceedings in either or both of the said Terms, in which they were depending, in the usual manner of proceeding, as the case might be.

said
And be it further enacted, That all Writs and other Process sued out in the ∧Clerk's
of of the said Circuit Court[1]
office∧, according to the accustomed method, bearing Teste ~~June Term~~ in November
Term One thousand seven hundred and ninety four, June Term One thousand seven
hundred and ninety five, or November Term One thousand seven hundred and ninety
five, shall be held and deemed of the same validity and effect as if the respective
Terms of June and November One thousand seven hundred and ninety five had
been regularly held by a Judge or Judges competent to do business and continuances
in respect to Writs or other Process returnable to the two last mentioned Terms had
been regularly ~~and duly~~ entered.

AD (DNA, RG 46, Bills and Resolutions Originating in the Senate, Sen 4A-B1). In the hand of James
Iredell. Endorsed "Bill   Circuit Court   N° Carolina   March 23ᵈ   1796."
   1. The interlineation appears in the left margin of the bill.

PRECIS
Section 1: provides for summoning of jurors to attend the next session of the circuit
   court for North Carolina.
Section 2: revives all suits and process in the circuit court for North Carolina so as to
   be proceeded upon at the next session as if the spring and fall 1795 terms had
   been held.
Section 3: process bearing teste in November 1794, June 1795, or November 1795
   to be valid as if the June and November 1795 terms had been held.

An Act to repeal so much of an act intituled "An act to establish the
judicial courts of the United States," as directs that alternate sessions
of the Circuit Court for the district of Pennsylvania shall be holden at
Yorktown; and for other purposes[1] ————————————————————
   May 12, 1796

In December 1793 Chief Justice John Jay suggested to Senator Rufus King of
New York that alternating sessions of the circuit court for Pennsylvania between
York and Philadelphia should be abolished because "double places create double
Trouble."[2] Nothing more was heard until April 1796, when the Philadephia bar—in
an early instance of lobbying by the legal profession—petitioned the House to make
Philadelphia the only place for holding the circuit court. A committee report, citing
the circuit court clerk's certification that only one civil cause had ever been tried at
York, recommended "that a bill be brought in eliminating Yorktown" in the interest
of promoting "the speedy administration of Justice." The House and the Senate passed
the bill without amendment on May 6 and May 10, respectively.[3]

   1. *Stat.,* 1:463.
   2. *DHSC,* 2:434-35.
   3. *HRJ,* 2:526, 538, 541, 549, 550, 552; *SLJ,* 2:250, 250-51, 252, 253, 253-54, 254, 255; printed bill
passed by the House, May 6, 1796, Sen 4A-C1, Bills and Resolutions Originating in the House and Considered
by the Senate, RG 46, DNA. The petition of the Philadelphia lawyers has not been found. The House
committee report is found under date of May 4, 1796, in vol. 1, Reports of Select Committees, RG 233,
DNA.

PRECIS

Section 1: changes the meeting place of the circuit court for the district of Pennsylvania to Philadelphia only.

Section 2: process returnable at York to be returnable at Philadelphia.

An Act altering the Sessions of the Circuit Courts in the Districts of Vermont and Rhode Island; and for other purposes[1] ————————
May 27, 1796

In mid-April 1796, the House appointed a committee to report a bill that would alter the circuit court sessions in Vermont and Rhode Island. The bill, as passed by the House on May 10, added a fall term of the Vermont circuit court to be held at Rutland on November 7, and changed the dates of the district and circuit courts for Rhode Island. Only the provisions relating to the Rhode Island district court were amended by the Senate, which passed the bill on May 26.[2]

The addition of a fall circuit court in Vermont appears to have been at the behest of Senator Israel Smith of Vermont. To accommodate a new fall court on the Eastern Circuit, the date of the Rhode Island court was pushed back from November 7 to November 19, and the Vermont court was inserted between those in New Hampshire and Rhode Island. Although the order of holding the circuit courts was different from that of the spring circuit, it did preserve for justices residing south of New York the option of booking passage home by water.[3]

1. *Stat.,* 1:475.

2. *HRJ,* 2:511, 546, 547-48, 578, 580, 582, 583; *SLJ,* 2:253, 254, 268, 271, 273, 274, 276, 277.

3. Although the *Annals* for April 14 mentions only the district courts of Vermont and Rhode Island, it seems clear from the text of the resulting bill and the account in the House journal that the changes were made to accommodate the addition of a fall circuit court in Vermont. *Annals,* 5:951; *HRJ,* 2:511, 546; printed bill, passed by the House, May 10, 1796, and manuscript Senate amendment, Sen 4A-C1, Bills and Resolutions Originating in the House and Considered by the Senate, RG 46, DNA.

PRECIS

Section 1: changes the date and place of holding the spring circuit court for Vermont to Windsor on May 12 and creates a fall court at Rutland on November 7.

Section 2: alters the date of holding the fall circuit court for Rhode Island to November 19.

Section 3: changes the dates of holding the district court for Rhode Island to the third Tuesday of November, the second Tuesday of May, and the first Tuesdays of February and August.

An Act concerning the Circuit Courts of the United States[1] ————————
March 3, 1797

By 1797 the justices of the Supreme Court were embarking on their eighth year of circuit riding. Since 1790 they had made numerous efforts to streamline the system, usually in piecemeal fashion. Now they would try to revise all three circuits at once.

The bill seems to have been written by the justices and given into the care of James Iredell to shepherd through Congress.[2] It dealt with a variety of problems. On the Eastern Circuit, the justices had experienced continued difficulty getting to and from the hinterlands of Vermont. They attempted to solve this by beginning the entire spring circuit four days earlier, advancing by twelve days the date of the Connecticut court, and providing three more days between the Vermont and New Hampshire courts. They also moved the schedule ahead four days for the fall circuit. In addition, the fall session of the Vermont court was to meet after the Connecticut court—as it did in the spring, rather than after the New Hampshire court—as provided by statute in 1796.[3] This revision created a circuit that ran from New York City, north to Hartford and Rutland; east to Boston and Exeter; and south to Providence.[4]

Under the new plan, the Middle Circuit was also brought forward by a day and the spring session of the Delaware court was returned to its former date in April, preceding the Virginia court. The justices also wanted the Delaware court held at Wilmington only, rather than New Castle in the spring and Dover in the fall. This change, combined with one in Maryland that would have designated Baltimore as the only meeting place for the court (eliminating Easton), would have streamlined the circuit by eliminating travel on the Delmarva Peninsula and across the Chesapeake Bay to Annapolis.

Lawmakers, however, did not approve of all these alterations.[5] The Senate not only disagreed with the proposed change in the date of the Delaware spring court, it moved it even further back to June 27, and then struck out the proposed change in the places for holding the Delaware court. For its part, the House agreed to replace Easton with Baltimore in the fall circuit, but the spring court was still to be held at Annapolis.[6]

The justices' suggestions for altering the Southern Circuit fared better. They successfully argued that the South Carolina court be held at Charleston only rather than alternating with Columbia, thus eliminating some of the travel that made the Southern Circuit so distasteful. Congress also moved the spring circuit forward by five days.[7]

In addition to amending the sections dealing with the circuit courts, the House introduced three new sections. Two provided for changing the location of the district court in North Carolina back to New Bern only, as had been the case before 1792. The other altered the dates of the district court in Kentucky.[8]

1. *Stat.*, 1:517. *DHSC* short title: Circuit Court Act of 1797.

2. William Paterson to James Iredell, March 7, 1797, and Samuel Chase to James Iredell, March 12, 1797, (qq.v.) There is no surviving manuscript copy of the bill, but an important amendment, introduced between February 15 and February 28, is in the hand of James Iredell. *SLJ*, 2:324, 336; Amendment concerning Issuing Venires, February [15-28], 1797 (q.v.).

3. See "An Act altering the Sessions of the Circuit Courts in the Districts of Vermont and Rhode Island; and for other purposes," under date of May 27, 1796.

4. Printed Senate bill, Sen 4A-B1, Bills and Resolutions Originating in the Senate, RG 46, DNA. This new route in the fall was more consistent with the topography of New England, which made travel on a north-south axis along the river valleys easier than an east-west one across the mountains of Vermont and New Hampshire. As the first justice to complete the Eastern Circuit alone in the spring of 1795, James Iredell discovered that there was no easy route between Vermont and New Hampshire; that, in fact, it was necessary to travel by way of Boston and the relatively flat countryside of Massachusetts. In fall 1796 William Cushing was two days late arriving for court in Providence, after having crossed Massachusetts three times traveling east from Hartford to Boston and Exeter, west to Rutland, and then southeast to Providence. The

change in the fall circuit essentially validated the route Iredell had found necessary in the spring of 1795. After this act the only difference between the spring and fall circuits was that in the spring the Massachusetts court preceded that of New Hampshire, whereas in the fall the reverse was true. In either case the justices had to pass through Boston twice. See James Iredell to Hannah Iredell, May 20, 1795, and Circuit Court for the District of Rhode Island, November 19, 1796.

5. *SLJ*, 2:323, 324, 336, 348, 349, 350, 351; *HRJ*, 2:727, 728, 738-39, 743, 744.

6. Printed Senate bill and manuscript amendments, passed by the Senate February 28, 1797, Sen 4A-B1, Bills and Resolutions originating in the Senate, RG 46, DNA; Engrossed bill and House amendments, passed March 3, 1797, Sen 4A-B4, Bills and Resolutions Originating in the Senate, RG 46, DNA. Although the justices asked Congress to reconsider the date of the circuit court in Delaware, a House committee decided on June 9, 1798 that "it is not expedient at present to make any alteration." Vol. 2, Reports of Select Committees, RG 233, DNA; Justices of the Supreme Court to John Adams, August 15, 1797 (q.v.); Justices of the Supreme Court to Gunning Bedford, August 15, 1797 (q.v.).

7. Printed Senate bill, Sen 4A-B1, Bills and Resolutions originating in the Senate, RG 46, DNA; engrossed bill and House amendments, passed March 3, 1797, Sen 4A-B4, Bills and Resolutions Originating in the Senate, RG 46, DNA.

8. Engrossed bill and House amendments, passed March 3, 1797, Sen 4A-B4, Bills and Resolutions Originating in the Senate, RG 46, DNA; An Act for altering the times of holding the Circuit Courts, in certain districts of the United States, and for other purposes (q.v. under date of April 13, 1792). The change in the North Carolina district court back to New Bern only is also contained in James Iredell's "Alterations Proposed in the Judicial System" (q.v. under date of [ca. March 18, 1796]).

Amendment concerning Issuing Venires, reported February [15-28], 1797

and be it further enacted

Provided, That if in consequence of any alterations made by this Act it shall
of the
appear expedient to the District Judge of any Districts where such alterations are to
made as afores^d, 						Jurors
take place, that a new Venire should issue for the summoning of Jurymen to attend
the Circuit Court of such District which is to be first held after the present Session
of Congress, it shall be lawful for him to direct the Clerk of the said Circuit Court
								Jurors
to issue a Venire accordingly for the summoning of such number of Jurymen as the
said District Judge shall think fit, and from such parts of the District as shall appear
								People
to him most suitable to the convenience of the Citizens thereof, giving reasonable
notice of the time and place of attendance.

AD (DNA, RG 46, Bills and Resolutions Originating in the Senate, Sen 4A-B1). Text of the amendment in the hand of James Iredell; interlineations in a different hand. Attached to the original Senate bill and prefaced, "The Committee to whom was refered the 'Bill concerning the circuit Courts of the U.S.' Report that in their opinion the said Bill ought to be amended as followeth ... At the end of the Bill add the following sec^ts."

PRECIS

Section 1: sets the following dates and places of holding circuit courts: in New York on April 1 and September 1 at New York City; in Connecticut on April 13 at New Haven and September 17 at Hartford; in Vermont on May 1 at Windsor and October 3 at Rutland; in New Hampshire on May 19 at Portsmouth and November 2 at Exeter; in Massachusetts on June 1 and October 20 at Boston; in Rhode Island on June 15 at Newport and on November 15 at Providence; in New Jersey on April 1 and October 1 at Trenton; in Pennsylvania on April 11 and October 11 at Philadelphia; in Delaware on June 27 at New Castle and

October 27 at Dover; in Maryland on May 7 at Annapolis and on November 7 at Baltimore; in Virginia on May 22 and November 22 at Richmond; in Georgia on April 20 at Savannah and on November 8 at Augusta; in South Carolina on May 6 and October 25 at Charleston; and in North Carolina on June 1 and November 30 at Raleigh.

Section 2: repeals sections of earlier statutes and establishes the district court for North Carolina at New Bern only.

Section 3: allows process returnable to former district courts in North Carolina to be returnable to district court at New Bern.

Section 4: provides that all process issuing out of any of the former courts shall be returnable at new dates and places; and all suits and proceedings continued from former courts shall be continued to new dates and places.

Section 5: authorizes the district judge to issue venire to call a jury for the next circuit court held under this act.

Section 6: changes the dates of district court for Kentucky to second Monday in March, and third Mondays in June and November.

An Act for reviving and continuing suits and process in the Circuit Court for the district of North Carolina[1]

July 5, 1797

Thomas Blount of North Carolina informed the House on June 29 that the failure to hold the spring 1797 term of the circuit court for North Carolina necessitated the passage of a "law to compel process." The following day a committee composed of Blount, James Imlay of New Jersey, and William Gordon of New Hampshire, presented a bill. Both houses passed the bill without amendment on July 1, 1797.[2]

1. *Stat.,* 1:526.

2. *HRJ,* 3:58, 59, 59-60, 63-64, 65, 67, 69; *SLJ,* 2:381, 382, 383, 384, 385; *Annals,* 7:410, 421. A statute apparently was necessary to continue pending law suits even though the district judge, John Sitgreaves, had made provisions for calling a jury for the next session of the circuit court and had adjourned the court until the next term as provided for by the Adjournment Act of 1794. Circuit Court for the District of North Carolina, June 1, 1797 (q.v.), *North-Carolina Journal* (q.v. under date of June 1, 1797); Timothy Pickering to John Sitgreaves, September 6, 1797, Domestic Letters, RG 59, DNA.

PRECIS

Section 1: the district judge for North Carolina to issue process for calling a jury in the same manner and proportions as done for the previous term.

Section 2: all suits and proceedings in the circuit court for North Carolina continued to the November 1797 term.

Section 3: all other writs and process returnable at the November term of the circuit court for North Carolina.

An Act for reviving and continuing suits and proceedings in the Circuit Court for the District of Pennsylvania[1] ——————————
December 24, 1799

This act resulted from the failure of the October 1799 term of the circuit court for Pennsylvania. Because the Pennsylvania marshal had not properly renewed his commission, all his actions relating to the opening of the court and all the court's subsequent actions were void.[2]

The predicament required a legislative solution. That occurred when the Sixth Congress convened in December. Senator James Ross of Pennsylvania introduced a bill to revive all the suits and proceedings which had automatically been discontinued as a result of the court's failure. The Senate and House both passed the bill a week later on December 16.[3]

1. *Stat.*, 2:3.
2. Bushrod Washington to James Iredell, October 20, 1799 (q.v.).
3. *SLJ*, 3:8, 9, 10, 14; *HRJ*, 3:537, 538, 540, 543; Mr. Ross's motion, December 9, 1799, Sen 6A-B3, Bills and Resolutions Originating in the Senate, RG 46, DNA; original bill and committee report, passed December 16, 1799, Sen 4A-B1, Bills and Resolutions Originating in the Senate, RG 46, DNA; engrossed bill, passed December 16, 1799, Sen 4A-B4, Bills and Resolutions Originating in the Senate, RG 46, DNA.

PRECIS
Section 1: all suits and proceedings in the circuit court for Pennsylvania revived and continued.

Section 2: all writs and other process in the circuit court for Pennsylvania bearing teste date of April or October 1799 to be deemed valid.

Section 3: district judge to issue process for calling a jury to attend the April 1800 session of the circuit court for Pennsylvania.

APPENDIX C

Circuit Calendar: Dates of and Attendance at Court

SPRING 1795

Middle Circuit

New Jersey	Apr 2-4	Paterson	Morris
Pennsylvania	Apr 11-Jun 5	Paterson	Peters
Maryland	May 7-9	Wilson	Paca
Virginia	May 22-Jun 8	Wilson	Griffin
Delaware	Jun 8-9	Paterson	Bedford

Eastern Circuit

New York	Apr 6-7	Iredell	Laurance
Connecticut	Apr 25-May 5	Iredell	Law
Vermont	May 12-16	Iredell	Hitchcock
New Hampshire	May 27-29	Iredell	Pickering
Massachusetts	Jun 8-16	Iredell	Lowell
Rhode Island	Jun 19-27	Iredell	Marchant

Southern Circuit

Georgia	April 25-May 5	Blair	Pendleton
South Carolina	May 12-14	Blair	Bee
North Carolina	Jun 1	[no court held]	

FALL 1795

Eastern Circuit

New York	Sep 5	Cushing	Laurance
Connecticut	Sep 25-30	Cushing	Law
Massachusetts	Oct 12-19	Cushing	Lowell
New Hampshire	Oct 24	Cushing	Pickering
Rhode Island	Nov 7-12	Cushing	Marchant

Middle Circuit

New Jersey	Oct 2	Paterson	Morris
Pennsylvania	Oct 12-23	Paterson	Peters
Delaware	Oct 27-29	Wilson	Bedford
Maryland	Nov 7-9	Wilson	
Virginia	Nov 23-Dec 12	Iredell	Griffin

Southern Circuit

South Carolina	Oct 26-Nov 5	Rutledge	Bee
Georgia	Nov 8	[no court held]	
North Carolina	Nov 30	[no court held]	

SPRING 1796
Middle Circuit

New Jersey	Apr 2-5	Iredell	Morris
Pennsylvania	Apr 11-May 2	Iredell	Peters
Maryland	May 7	Iredell	Paca
Virginia	May 23-Jun 7	Iredell	Griffin
Delaware	Jun 8-15	Wilson	Bedford

Eastern Circuit

New York	Apr 5-20	Chase	Laurance
Connecticut	Apr 25-May 4	Chase	Law
Vermont	May 12-16	Chase	Hitchcock
New Hampshire	May 27-Jun 1	Chase	Pickering
Massachusetts	Jun 7-14	Chase	Lowell
Rhode Island	Jun 20-25	Chase	Marchant

Southern Circuit

Georgia	Apr 25-May 4	Ellsworth	Pendleton
South Carolina	May 12-13	Ellsworth	Bee
North Carolina	Jun 1-9	Ellsworth	Sitgreaves

FALL 1796
Eastern Circuit

New York	Sep 5-9	Cushing	Laurance
Connecticut	Sep 26-27	Cushing	Law
Massachusetts	Oct 12-15	Cushing	Lowell
New Hampshire	Oct 24-25	Cushing	Pickering
Vermont	Nov 7	Cushing	Hitchcock
Rhode Island	Nov 19-25	Cushing	Bourne

Middle Circuit

New Jersey	Oct 3	Wilson	Morris
Pennsylvania	Oct 11-15	Wilson	Peters
Delaware	Oct 27-29	[no court held?]	
Maryland	Nov 7-8	Wilson	Paca
Virginia	Nov 22-26	[no court held]	

Southern Circuit

South Carolina	Oct 25-29	Paterson	Bee
Georgia	Nov 8-16	Paterson	Clay
North Carolina	Nov 30-Dec 3	Paterson	Sitgreaves

SPRING 1797
Middle Circuit

New Jersey	Apr 1-4	Iredell	
Pennsylvania	Apr 11-29	Iredell	Peters
Maryland	May 8-9	Iredell	
Virginia	May 22-Jun 7	Iredell	Griffin
Delaware	Jun 27	Paterson	Bedford

Eastern Circuit

New York	Apr 1-8	Ellsworth	Troup
Connecticut	Apr 13-21	Ellsworth	Law
Vermont	May 1	Ellsworth	
New Hampshire	May 19-20	Ellsworth	Pickering
Massachusetts	Jun 1-13	Ellsworth	Lowell
Rhode Island	Jun 15-24	Ellsworth	Bourne

Southern Circuit

Georgia	Apr 20-May 2	Chase	Clay
South Carolina	May 6-16	Chase	Bee
North Carolina	Jun 1	[no court held]	

FALL 1797

Eastern Circuit

New York	Sep 1-5	Cushing	Troup
Connecticut	Sep 18-25	Cushing	Law
Vermont	Oct 3-7	Cushing	Hitchcock
Massachusetts	Oct 20-30	Cushing	Lowell
New Hampshire	Nov 2-4	Cushing	Pickering
Rhode Island	Nov 15-22	Cushing	Bourne

Middle Circuit

New Jersey	Oct 2	Paterson	
Pennsylvania	Oct 11	[no court held]	
Delaware	Oct 27-28	Paterson	Bedford
Maryland	Nov 7-11	Paterson	Paca
Virginia	Nov 22-Dec 4	Paterson	Griffin

Southern Circuit

South Carolina	Oct 25-28	Wilson	Bee
Georgia	Nov 8-17	Wilson	Clay
North Carolina	Nov 30-Dec 8	Wilson	Sitgreaves

SPRING 1798

Middle Circuit

New Jersey	Apr 2-9	Chase	Morris
Pennsylvania	Apr 11-20	Chase	Peters
Maryland	May 7	[no court held]	
Virginia	May 22	[no court held]	
Delaware	Jun 27	[no court held]	

Eastern Circuit

New York	Apr 2-6	Paterson	Troup
Connecticut	Apr 13-18	Paterson	Law
Vermont	May 1-7	Ellsworth	Hitchcock
New Hampshire	May 19-22	Ellsworth	Pickering
Massachusetts	Jun 1-8	Cushing	Lowell
Rhode Island	Jun 15-23	Cushing	Bourne

Southern Circuit

Georgia	Apr 20	[no court held]	
South Carolina	May 7-12	Iredell	Bee
North Carolina	Jun 1-9	Iredell	Sitgreaves

FALL 1798
Middle Circuit

Pennsylvania SS	Aug 6-7	Chase	Peters
New Jersey	Oct 1-3	Cushing	Morris
Pennsylvania	Oct 11	[no court held]	
Delaware	Oct 27-Nov 1	Cushing	Bedford
Maryland	Nov 7-8	Cushing	
Virginia	Nov 22-Dec 15	Cushing	

Eastern Circuit

New York	Sep 1-3	Paterson	Hobart
Connecticut	Sep 17-24	Ellsworth	Law
Vermont	Oct 3-9	Paterson	Hitchcock
Massachusetts	Oct 20-29	Paterson	Lowell
New Hampshire	Nov 2-3	Paterson	Pickering
Rhode Island	Nov 15-21	Ellsworth	Bourne

Southern Circuit

South Carolina	Oct 25	[no court held]	
Georgia	Nov 8-17	Washington	Clay
North Carolina	Nov 30-Dec 5	Washington	Sitgreaves

SPRING 1799
Middle Circuit

New Jersey	Apr 1-2	Iredell	Morris
Pennsylvania	Apr 11-May 18	Iredell	Peters
Maryland	May 7	[no court held]	
Virginia	May 22-Jun 7	Iredell	Griffin
Delaware	Jun 27-29	Paterson	Bedford

Eastern Circuit

New York	Apr 1	[no court held]	
Connecticut	Apr 13	[no court held]	
Vermont	May 1	[no court held]	
New Hampshire	May 20-22	Chase	Pickering
Massachusetts	Jun 1-11	Chase	Lowell
Rhode Island	Jun 15-19	Chase	Bourne

Southern Circuit

Georgia	Apr 20-May 2	Ellsworth	Clay
South Carolina	May 6-15	Ellsworth	Bee
North Carolina	Jun 1-11	Ellsworth	Sitgreaves

FALL 1799
Eastern Circuit

New York	Sep 2-6	Paterson	Hobart
Connecticut	Sep 17-26	Ellsworth	Law
Vermont	Oct 3-11	Cushing	Hitchcock
Massachusetts	Oct 21-26	Cushing	Lowell
New Hampshire	Nov 2	Cushing	
Rhode Island	Nov 15-20	Cushing	Bourne

Middle Circuit

New Jersey	Oct 1-7	Washington	Morris
Pennsylvania	Oct 11-22	Washington	Peters
Delaware	Oct 27	[no court held]	
Maryland	Nov 7-12	Washington	Winchester
Virginia	Nov 22-Dec 7	Washington	Griffin

Southern Circuit

South Carolina	Oct 25-29	Paterson	Bee
Georgia	Nov 8-15	Paterson	Clay
North Carolina	Nov 30-Dec 4	Paterson	

SPRING 1800
Middle Circuit

New Jersey	Apr 1-3	Chase	Morris
Pennsylvania	Apr 11-May 2	Chase	Peters
Maryland	May 7-16	Chase	Winchester
Virginia	May 22- Jun 4	Chase	Griffin
Delaware	Jun 27-28	Chase	Bedford

Eastern Circuit

New York	Apr 1-9	Washington	Hobart
Connecticut	Apr 14-18	Washington	Law
Vermont	May 1-9	Paterson	Hitchcock
New Hampshire	May 19-21	Paterson	
Massachusetts	Jun 2-10	Cushing	
Rhode Island	Jun 16-19	Cushing	Bourne

Southern Circuit

Georgia	Apr 21-28	Moore	Clay
South Carolina	May 6-9	Moore	Bee
North Carolina	Jun 2-9	Moore	Sitgreaves

FALL 1800
Eastern Circuit

New York	Sep 1-4	Paterson	Hobart
Connecticut	Sep 17-25	Cushing	Law
Vermont	Oct 3-11	Cushing	Hitchcock
Massachusetts	Oct 20-30	Cushing	Lowell

New Hampshire	Nov 3-4	Cushing	
Rhode Island	Nov 15-24	Cushing	Bourne
Middle Circuit			
New Jersey	Oct 1	Paterson	Morris
Pennsylvania	Oct 11-23	Paterson	Peters
Delaware	Oct 27-28	Paterson	Bedford
Maryland	Nov 7-8	Paterson	Winchester
Virginia	Nov 22-Dec 4	Paterson	
Southern Circuit			
South Carolina	Oct 25-30	Washington	Bee
Georgia	Nov 8-18	Washington	Clay
North Carolina	Dec 1-6	Washington	

APPENDIX D

Circuit Calendar: Places and Dates of Court Sessions
as Assigned by Statute

COURT	SPRING SESSION	FALL SESSION	STATU
Conn.	Apr 22-New Haven	Oct 22-Hartford	9/24/89
	Apr 25-New Haven	Oct 25-Hartford	3/3/91
	Apr 25-New Haven	Sep 25-Hartford	4/13/92
	Apr 25-New Haven	Sep 25-Hartford	3/2/93
	Apr 13-New Haven	Sep 17-Hartford	3/3/97
Delaware	Apr 27-New Castle	Oct 27-Dover	9/24/89
	2d Mon. of June-New Castle	Oct 27-Dover	6/9/94
	Jun 27-New Castle	Oct 27-Dover	3/3/97
Georgia	May 28-Savannah	Oct 17-Augusta	9/24/89
	Apr 25-Savannah	Oct 15-Augusta	8/11/90
	Apr 25-Savannah	Nov 8-Augusta	4/13/92
	Apr 20-Savannah	Nov 8-Augusta	3/3/97
Maryland	May 7-Annapolis	Nov 7-Easton	9/24/89
	May 7-Annapolis	Nov 7-Baltimore	3/3/97
Mass.	May 3-Boston	Nov 3-Boston	9/24/89
	May 12-Boston	Nov 12-Boston	3/3/91
	May 12-Boston	Oct 12-Boston	4/13/92
	Jun 7-Boston	Oct 12-Boston	3/2/93
	Jun 1-Boston	Oct 20-Boston	3/3/97
N.H.	May 20-Portsmouth	Nov 20-Exeter	9/24/89
	May 24-Portsmouth	Nov 24-Exeter	3/3/91
	May 24-Portsmouth	Oct 24-Exeter	4/13/92
	May 27-Portsmouth	Oct 24-Exeter	3/2/93
	May 19-Portsmouth	Nov 2-Exeter	3/3/97
N.J.	Apr 2-Trenton	Oct 2-Trenton	9/24/89
	Apr 1-Trenton	Oct 1-Trenton	3/3/97
N.Y.	Apr 4-New York	Oct 4-Albany	9/24/89
	Apr 5-New York	Oct 5-New York	3/3/91
	Apr 5-New York	Sep 5-New York	4/13/92
	Apr 5-New York	Sep 5-New York	3/2/93
	Apr 1-New York	Sep 1-New York	3/3/97

N.C.	Jun 18-New Bern	Nov 8-New Bern	6/4/90
	Jun 1-New Bern	Nov 30-New Bern	4/13/92
	Jun 1-New Bern	Nov 30-Wake Courthouse,	3/2/93
	but after fall 1793 term all courts to meet at Raleigh		
	Jun 1-Raleigh	Nov 30-Raleigh	3/3/97
Penn.	Apr 11-Philadelphia	Oct 11-York	9/24/89
	Apr 11-Philadelphia	Oct 11-Philadelphia	5/12/96
	Apr 11-Philadelphia	Oct 11-Philadelphia	3/3/97
R.I.	Jun 4-Newport	Dec 4-Providence	6/23/90
	Jun 7-Newport	Dec 7-Providence	3/3/91
	Jun 7-Newport	Nov 7-Providence	4/13/92
	Jun 19-Newport	Nov 7-Providence	3/2/93
	Jun 19-Newport	Nov 19-Providence	5/27/96
	Jun 15-Newport	Nov 15-Providence	3/3/97
S.C.	May 12-Columbia	Oct 1-Charleston	9/24/89
	May 12-Columbia	Oct 25-Charleston	8/11/90
	May 6-Charleston	Oct 25-Charleston	3/3/97
Vermont	Jun 17-Bennington	[No fall court]	3/2/91
	May 12-Court to alternate	[No fall court]	3/2/93
	between Windsor-Bennington		
	May 12-Windsor	Nov 7-Rutland	5/27/96
	May 1-Windsor	Oct 3-Rutland	3/3/97
Virginia	May 22-Charlottesville	Nov 22-Williamsburg	9/24/89
	May 22-Richmond	Nov 22-Richmond	3/3/91
	May 22-Richmond	Nov 22-Richmond	4/13/92
	May 22-Richmond	Nov 22-Richmond	3/3/97

If the day appointed by law falls on a Sunday, the court opens on Monday.

Bibliography

(see also short title list)

"Abstract of Bertie County Wills." *North Carolina Historical and Genealogical Register* 2 (July 1901): 3.

Adams, Charles Francis. *The Works of John Adams.* 10 vols. Boston: Little, Brown, 1850-1856.

Allen, William B., ed. *Works of Fisher Ames.* 2 vols. Indianapolis: Liberty Classics, 1983.

American Antiquarian Society. "Index of Deaths in *Massachusetts Centinel* and *Columbian Centinel, 1784-1840.*" Typescript. 12 vols. Worcester, Mass.: American Antiquarian Society, 1952.

Anderson, Frank M. "The Enforcement of the Alien and Sedition Laws." *Proceedings of the American Historical Society,* December 1912, pp. 115-26.

Bacon, William Plumb, ed. *Ancestry of Albert Gallatin ... and of Hannah Nicholson.* New York: Press of T. A. Wright, 1916.

[Bage, Robert]. *Hermsprong; or, Man as he is not.* 3 vols. London: Minerva Press, 1796.

Barnes, Robert William, comp. *Marriages and Deaths from Baltimore Newspapers, 1796-1816.* Baltimore: Genealogical Publishing, 1978.

Barry, Richard Hayes. *Mr. Rutledge of South Carolina.* New York: Duell, Sloan and Pearce, 1942.

Bee, Thomas. *Reports of Cases Adjudged in the District Court of South Carolina.* Philadelphia: William P. Farrand, 1810.

Bemis, Samuel Flagg. *A Diplomatic History of the United States.* 3d ed. New York: Henry Holt, 1950.

Bernstein, Richard. *Are We to Be a Nation? The Making of the Constitution.* Cambridge: Harvard University Press, 1987.

The Biographical Encyclopædia of Pennsylvania of the Nineteenth Century. Philadelphia: Galaxy Publishing, 1874.

Bourguignon, Henry J. *The First Federal Court: The Federal Appellate Prize Court of the American Revolution, 1775-1787.* Philadelphia: American Philosophical Society, 1977.

Briggs, L. Vernon. *History and Genealogy of the Cabot Family, 1475-1927.* 2 vols. Boston: Charles E. Goodspeed, 1927.

Brigham, Clarence S. *History and Bibliography of American Newspapers, 1690-1820.* 2 vols. Worcester, Mass.: American Antiquarian Society, 1947.

Broughton, Carrie L., comp. *Marriage and Death Notices from Raleigh Register and North Carolina Gazette, 1799-1825.* Baltimore: Genealogical Publishing, 1966.

Brown, William Garrott. *The Life of Oliver Ellsworth.* New York: Macmillan, 1905.

Brownell, Elijah Ellsworth. *Rutland County Vermont Genealogical Gleanings.* Typescript. Philadelphia, 1942.

Campbell, John H. *History of the Friendly Sons of St. Patrick and of the Hibernian Society for the Relief of Emigrants from Ireland: March 17, 1771-March 17, 1892.* Philadelphia: Hibernian Society, 1892.

Cappelli, Adriano. *Dizionario di abbreviature latine ed italiane.* 6th ed. Reprint. Milano: Hoepi, 1973.

Carroll, John A., and Mary W. Ashworth. *George Washington.* Vol. 7, *First in Peace.* Completing the biography by Douglas Southall Freeman. New York: Charles Scribner's Sons, 1957.

Carter, Clarence E. "Zephaniah Swift and the Folwell Edition of the Laws of the United States." *American Historical Review* 39 (1934): 689-95.

Carter, Edward C., et al., eds. *Latrobe's View of America, 1795-1820: Selections from the Watercolors and Sketches*. New Haven: Yale University Press, 1985.
——. *The Virginia Journals of Benjamin Henry Latrobe, 1795-1798.* 2 vols. New Haven: Yale University Press, 1977.
Cooper, Thomas. *An Account of the Trial of Thomas Cooper, of Northumberland.* Philadelphia: John Bioren, 1800.
Combs, Jerald A. *The Jay Treaty: Political Battleground of the Founding Fathers.* Berkeley: University of California Press, 1970.
Cote, Richard N., ed. *Dictionary of South Carolina.* Vol. 1. Easley, S.C.: Southern Historical Press, 1985.
Cunningham, Noble E., Jr., ed. *Circular Letters of Congressmen to Their Constituents, 1789-1829.* 3 vols. Chapel Hill: University of North Carolina Press, 1978.
——. "The Jeffersonian Republican Party." In *History of U.S. Political Parties.* Edited by Arthur M. Schlesinger, Jr. 4 vols. New York: Chelsea House, 1973.
Cushing, James S. *The Genealogy of the Cushing Family.* Montreal: Perrault Printing, 1905.
Cushing, John D., comp. *The First Laws of the State of Delaware.* 2 vols. Wilmington, Del.: Michael Glazier, 1981.
——. *The First Laws of the State of Georgia.* Part 2. Wilmington, Del.: Michael Glazier, 1981.
Daughters of the American Revolution. *DAR Patriot Index.* 3 vols. Washington, D.C.: n.p., 1966-1986.
——. *Lineage Book.* 144 vols. Harrisburg, Pa., 1895; and Washington, D.C., 1896-1935, n.p., 1895-1935.
Dexter, Franklin Bowditch. *Biographical Sketches of the Graduates of Yale College.* 6 vols. New York: Henry Holt, 1885-1912.
Dictionary of South African Biography. Johannesburg: National Council for Social Research, 1968.
Duffy, John. "An Account of the Epidemic Fevers that Prevailed in the City of New York from 1791 to 1822." *New-York Historical Society Quarterly* 50 (October 1966): 333-64.
Duncan, William. *The New-York Directory and Register, for the Year 1795.* New York: Thomas and James Swords, 1795.
Elliot, Jonathan, ed. *The Debates in the Several State Conventions, on the Adoption of the Federal Constitution, as Recommended by the General Convention at Philadelphia, in 1787.* 2d ed. 5 vols. Philadelphia: J. B. Lippincott, 1876.
Elsmere, Jane S. *Justice Samuel Chase.* Muncie, Indiana, Janevar Publishing, 1980.
The English Reports. 176 vols. Edinburgh: William Green & Sons, 1900-1930.
Ferguson, Russell J. *Early Western Pennsylvania Politics.* Pittsburgh: University of Pittsburgh Press, 1938.
Fitzpatrick, John C., ed. *The Writings of George Washington from the Original Manuscript Sources, 1745-1799.* 39 vols. Washington, D.C.: Government Printing Office, 1931-1944.
Foner, Eric. *Tom Paine and Revolutionary America.* New York: Oxford University Press, 1976.
Ford, Paul L., ed. *The Works of Thomas Jefferson.* Federal Edition. 12 vols. New York: G. P. Putnam's Sons, 1904.
Gay, Frederick L. "John Gay, of Dedham, Massachusetts, and some of his descendants." *New England Historic Genealogical Register* 33 (January 1879): 45-57.
Gershoy, Leo. *The French Revolution and Napoleon.* New York: Appleton-Century-Crofts, 1933.
Gibbs, George. *Memoirs of the Administrations of Washington and John Adams, Edited from the Papers of Oliver Wolcott, Secretary of the Treasury.* 2 vols. New York: W. Van Norden, 1846.
Goebel, Julius, Jr. *Antecedents and Beginnings to 1801.* Vol. 1 of *The Oliver Wendell Holmes Devise History of the Supreme Court of the United States.* New York: Macmillan, 1971.
Gordon, Armistead C. "The Stith Family." *William and Mary Quarterly,* 1st ser. 22 (July 1913): 44-51.
Gregorie, Anne King. *History of Sumter County.* Sumter, S.C.: Library Board of Sumter County, 1954.

Green, Harry C., and Mary W. Green. *The Pioneer Mothers of America*. 3 vols. New York: G. P. Putnam's Sons, 1912.

Griswold, Glenn E., comp. *The Griswold Family: England-America*. 3 vols. Rutland, Vt.: Tuttle Publishing, 1935.

Griswold, Rufus Wilmot. *The Republican Court; or, American Society in the Days of Washington*. New York: D. Appleton, 1864.

Gutstein, Morris A. *Aaron Lopez and Judah Touro: A Refugee and a Son of a Refugee*. New York: Behrman's Jewish Book House, 1939.

Gwathmey, John H. *Historical Register of Virginians in the Revolution: 1775-1783*. Reprint. Baltimore: Genealogical Publishing, 1973.

Harbottle, Thomas B. *Dictionary of Quotations*. London: Swan Sonnenschein, 1909.

Harrison, Richard A. *Princetonians: A Biographical Dictionary*. Vol. 3. *1776-1783*. Princeton: Princeton University Press, 1981.

Haskins, George, and Herbert Johnson. *Foundations of Power: John Marshall, 1801-15*. Vol. 2 of *The Oliver Wendell Holmes Devise History of the Supreme Court of the United States*. New York: Macmillan, 1981.

Haw, James, et al. *Stormy Patriot: The Life of Samuel Chase*. Baltimore: Maryland Historical Society, 1980.

[Hawles, John.] *The Grand-Jury-Man's Oath and Office Explained; and the Rights of English-Men Asserted. A Dialogue between a Barrister at Law, and A Grand-Jury-Man*. London: printed for Langley Curtis, 1680.

Hawkins, William. *A Treatise of the Pleas of the Crown*. 2 books. 4th ed. London: E. Richardson and C. Lintot, 1762.

Hayes, Lyman Simpson. *History of the Town of Rockingham, Vermont*. Bellows Falls, Vt.: published by the town, 1907.

Henderson, Dwight F. "Treason, Sedition, and Fries' Rebellion." *American Journal of Legal History* 14 (1970): 308-17.

Higgins, Anthony, ed. *New Castle on the Delaware*. Delaware Federal Writers' Project, American Guide Series. Reprint. New Castle Historical Society, 1973.

History of the Cauld Lad of Hilton. Reprint. Newcastle upon Tyne, England: Frank Graham, 1968.

Holcomb, Brent, comp. *Marriage and Death Notices from The (Charleston) Times, 1800-1821*. Baltimore: Genealogical Publishing, 1979.

———. *South Carolina Marriages, 1688-1799*. Baltimore: Genealogical Publishing, 1980.

Hollowak, Thomas L. *Maryland Genealogies: A Consolidation of Articles from the Maryland Historical Magazine*. 2 vols. Baltimore: Genealogical Publishing, 1980.

Holly, H. Hobart. *Descendants of Edmund Quincy, 1602-1637*. Quincy, Mass.: Quincy Historical Society, 1977.

Hunt, Gaillard, ed. *The Writings of James Madison*. 9 vols. New York: G. P. Putnam's Sons, 1900-1910.

Hurd, D. Hamilton, comp. *History of Rockingham and Strafford Counties, New Hampshire, with Biographical Sketches of many of its Pioneers and Prominent Men*. Philadelphia: J. W. Lewis, 1882.

Ifft, Richard. "Treason in the Early Republic: The Federal Courts, Popular Protest, and Federalism During the Whiskey Rebellion." In *The Whiskey Rebellion: Past and Present Perspectives*. Edited by Steven R. Boyd. Westport, Conn.: Greenwood Press, 1985.

Jackson, Ronald Vern, and Gary Ronald Teeples, eds. *South Carolina 1800 Census*. 2nd ed. Bountiful, Utah: Accelerated Indexing System, 1975.

Jacob, Giles, comp. *A New Law Dictionary*. 10th ed. Revised by J. Morgan. London: W. Strahan and W. Woodfall, 1782.

Jay, Stewart. "Origins of Federal Common Law: Part One." *University of Pennsylvania Law Review* 133 (June 1985): 1003-116.

———. "Origins of Federal Common Law: Part Two." *University of Pennsylvania Law Review* 133 (July 1985): 1231-333.

Jones, Hugh P. *Dictionary of Foreign Phrases and Classical Quotations.* Reprint. Boston: Long-wood Press, 1977.

Judicial Conference of the United States, Bicentennial Committee. *Judges of the United States.* Washington, D.C.: Government Printing Office, 1978.

Kaminski, John P. "'Outcast Rhode Island'—The Absent State." *this Constitution: From Ratification to the Bill of Rights.* Washington, D.C.: Congressional Quarterly, 1988.

Keith, Alice Barnwell; William H. Masterson; and David T. Morgan, eds. *The John Gray Blount Papers, 1764-1833.* 4 vols. Raleigh: State Department of Archives and History, 1952-1982.

Kelyng, John. *A Report of Divers Cases in Pleas of the Crown, Adjudged and Determined; In the Reign of the late King Charles II.* London: printed for Isaac Cleave, 1708.

Kirkland, Thomas J., and Robert M. Kennedy. *Historic Camden.* Columbia, S.C.: State Company, 1905.

Kline, Mary-Jo, ed. *Political Correspondence and Public Papers of Aaron Burr.* 2 vols. Princeton: Princeton University Press, 1983.

Koch, Adrienne, and Harry Ammon. "The Virginia and Kentucky Resolutions: An Episode in Jefferson's and Madison's Defense of Civil Liberties." *William and Mary Quarterly,* 3d ser. 5 (April 1948): 145-76.

Lee, Francis B. *Genealogical and Personal Memorial of Mercer County.* 2 vols. New York: Lewis Publishing, 1907.

Lee, Helen Bourne Joy. *The Bourne Genealogy.* Chester, Conn.: Pequot Press, 1972.

Lefferts, Elizabeth Morris, comp. *Descendants of Lewis Morris of Morrisania.* New York: Tobias A. Wright, 1907.

Leffingwell, Douglas. "Alsop Genealogy." Typescript. Library of Congress, 1928.

Lemmon, Sarah M., ed. *The Pettigrew Papers.* Vol. 2, *1819-1843.* Raleigh: North Carolina Department of Cultural Resources, Division of Archives and History, 1988.

Loomis, Dwight, and J. Gilbert Calhoun, eds. *The Judicial and Civil History of Connecticut.* Boston: Boston History Co., 1895.

Lowell, Delmar R., comp. *The Historic Genealogy of the Lowells of America.* Rutland, Vt.: Tuttle Company, 1899.

Lutz, Earl. *A Richmond Album.* Richmond: Garrett & Massie, 1937.

McCormick, Richard P. "Political Essays of William Paterson." *Rutgers University Library Journal* 18 (June 1955), pp. 38-49.

Magrath, C. Peter. *Yazoo: Law and Politics in the New Republic.* New York: W. W. Norton, 1967.

Malone, Dumas. *Jefferson and His Time.* Vol. 3, *Jefferson and the Ordeal of Liberty.* Boston: Little, Brown, 1962.

——. *The Public Life of Thomas Cooper, 1783-1839.* New Haven: Yale University Press, 1926.

"Maryland Politics in 1796—McHenry Letters." *Publications of the Southern History Association* 9 (1905): 374-88.

[Maryland.] *Votes and Proceedings of the House of Delegates of the State of Maryland, 1794.* Annapolis: Frederick Green, 1795.

Mease, James. *The Picture of Philadelphia.* Reprint. New York: Arno Press, 1970.

Meginness, John F. *History of Lycoming County, Pennsylvania.* Chicago: Brown, Runk, 1892.

Miller, John C. *Crisis in Freedom: The Alien and Sedition Acts.* Boston: Little, Brown, 1951.

——. *The Federalist Era, 1789-1801.* New York: Harper & Row, New American Nation Series, 1960.

Miller, Richard G. "The Federal City, 1783-1800." In *Philadelphia: A 300-Year History.* Edited by Russell F. Weigley. New York: W. W. Norton, 1982.

Minick, A. Rachel. *A History of Printing in Maryland, 1791-1800.* Baltimore: Enoch Pratt Free Library, 1949.

Mitchell, Stewart, ed. *New Letters of Abigail Adams, 1788-1801.* Reprint. Westport, Conn.: Greenwood Press, 1973.

Monaghan, Frank. *John Jay.* New York: Bobbs-Merrill, 1935.

Monaghan, Frank, and Marvin Lowenthal. *This Was New York*. Garden City, N.Y.: Doubleday, Doran, 1943.

Moore, John. *Edward. Various Views of Human Nature, taken from life and manners, chiefly in England*. Mount Pleasant, N.Y.: W. Durell, 1798.

Mordecai, Samuel. *Richmond in By-Gone Days*. New York: Arno Press, 1975.

Morris, Richard B., ed. *Encyclopedia of American History*. New York: Harper & Brothers, 1961.

Mouzon, Henry, et al. *An accurate map of North and South Carolina*. Paris: Le Rouge, 1777.

The New Columbia Encyclopedia. Edited by William H. Harris and Judith S. Levey. New York: Columbia University Press, 1975.

[New Hampshire.] *Laws of New Hampshire*. Vol. 6, *1792-1801*. Concord, N.H.: Evans Printing, 1917.

[New Jersey.] *Laws of the State of New Jersey*. Newark: N. Day, 1800.

North Carolina Reports. Edited by William H. Battle. Raleigh: Turner and Hughes, 1843.

O'Connor, John E. *William Paterson: Lawyer and Statesman, 1745-1806*. New Brunswick, N.J.: Rutgers University Press, 1979.

Ogden, Mary D. *Memorial Cyclopedia of New Jersey*. 3 vols. Newark: Memorial History Co., 1915-1917.

O'Neall, John B. *Biographical Sketches of the Bench and Bar of South Carolina*. 2 vols. Reprint. Spartanburg, S.C.: Reprint Co., 1975.

Papenfuse, Edward, et al. *A Biographical Dictionary of the Maryland Legislature, 1635-1789*. 1 vol. to date. Baltimore: Johns Hopkins University Press, 1979.

Parsons, Eliza (Phelp). *Woman As She Should Be; or, Memoirs of Mrs. Menville*. 4 vols. London: William Lane, 1793.

Platt, Virginia Bever. "Tar, Staves, and New England Rum: The Trade of Aaron Lopez of Newport, Rhode Island, with Colonial North Carolina." *North Carolina Historical Review* 48 (1971): 1-22.

Powell, William S., ed. *Dictionary of North Carolina Biography*. Vol. 1. Chapel Hill: University of North Carolina Press, 1979.

Presser, Stephen B. "A Tale of Two Judges: Richard Peters, Samuel Chase, and the Broken Promise of Federalist Jurisprudence." *Northwestern University Law Review* 73 (1978-1979): 26-111.

Preyer, Kathryn. "Jurisdiction to Punish: Federal Authority, Federalism and the Common Law of Crimes in the Early Republic." *Law and History Review* 4 (Fall 1986): 223-65.

Raymond, Thomas. *Reports of Divers Special Cases Adjudged in the Courts of King's Bench, Common Pleas, and Exchequer*. 2d ed. London: Henry Lintot, 1743.

Register, Jeannie Hayward, comp. "Marriage and Death Notices from the [Charleston] *City Gazette*." *South Carolina Historical and Genealogical Magazine* 26 (April 1925): 128-35.

Reynolds, Emily B., and Joan R. Faunt, comps. *Biographical Directory of the Senate of the State of South Carolina, 1776-1964*. Columbia: South Carolina Archives Department, 1964.

Rogers, George C., Jr. *The History of Georgetown County, South Carolina*. Columbia: University of South Carolina Press, 1970.

Rowland, Henry A. "A Sermon, Occasioned by the Death, and Delivered at the Funeral of The Honorable Oliver Ellsworth." Hartford: n.p., 1808.

Sanchez-Saavedra, E. M., comp. *A Guide to Virginia Military Organizations in the American Revolution, 1774-1787*. Richmond: Virginia State Library, 1978.

Seed, Geoffrey. *James Wilson*. Millwood, N.Y.: KTO Press, 1978.

Shurtleff, Nathaniel B. *A Topographical and Historical Description of Boston*. Boston: Alfred Mudge & Son, 1871.

Simpson, Henry. *The Lives of Eminent Philadelphians, Now Deceased*. Philadelphia: William Brotherhead, 1859.

Slaughter, Thomas P. *The Whiskey Rebellion*. New York: Oxford University Press, 1986.

Smith, Charles Page. *James Wilson: Founding Father, 1742-1798.* Chapel Hill: University of North Carolina Press, 1956.

Smith, James M. *Freedom's Fetters: The Alien and Sedition Laws and American Civil Liberties.* Ithaca, N.Y.: Cornell University Press, 1956.

South Carolina Genealogies. 5 vols. Spartanburg, S.C.: Reprint Co., 1983.

Spence, Wilma Cartwright, comp. *Tombstones and Epitaphs of Northeastern North Carolina.* Baltimore: Gateway Press, 1973.

Stephens, Thomas. *Stephens's Philadelphia Directory for 1796.* Philadelphia: W. Woodward, 1796.

[Stewart, Joseph A.] *Descendants of Valentine Hollingsworth, Sr.* Louisville: John P. Morton, 1925.

Stiles, Henry R. *A Supplement to the History and Genealogies of Ancient Windsor, Connecticut.* Albany: J. Munsell, 1863.

Surtees, Robert. *The History and Antiquities of the County Palatine of Durham, [England].* 3 vols. Sunderland, England: Hills and Co., 1908-1910.

Swift, Zephaniah, ed. *The Laws of the United States of America.* 3 vols. Philadelphia: Richard Folwell, 1796.

Trial of Samuel Chase. 2 vols. Washington, D.C.: printed for Samuel H. Smith, 1805.

Tyler, Donald H. *Old Lawrenceville: Early Houses and People.* N.p.: by the author, 1965.

[United States.] *Acts passed at the Third Congress of the United States of America.* Philadelphia: Francis Childs, 1795.

——. *Laws of the United States of America.* Philadelphia: Andrew Brown, 1791.

U.S., Department of Commerce and Labor, Bureau of the Census. *Heads of Families at the First Census of the United States Taken in the Year 1790: North Carolina.* Reprint. Salt Lake City: Accelerated Indexing Systems, 1978.

——. *Heads of Families at the First Census of the United States Taken in the Year 1790: South Carolina.* Reprint. Bountiful, Utah: Accelerated Indexing Systems, 1978.

University of Pennsylvania. *Biographical Catalogue of the Matriculates of the College, 1749-1893.* Philadelphia, 1894.

Van Rensselaer, Sarah R. *Ancestral Sketches and Records of Olden Times.* New York: Anson D. F. Randolph, 1882.

Walker, Lewis Burd, ed. *The Burd Papers: Selections from Letters Written by Edward Burd, 1763-1828.* Pottsville, Pa.: Standard Publishing, 1899.

Webber, Mabel L., comp. "Dr. John Rutledge and His Descendants." *South Carolina Historical and Genealogical Magazine* 31 (January 1930): 7-25.

Wharton, Francis. *State Trials of the United States During the Administrations of Washington and Adams.* Philadelphia: Carey and Hart, 1849.

White, Frank F., Jr. *The Governors of Maryland, 1777-1970.* Publication no. 15. Annapolis: Hall of Records Commission, 1970.

Whitney, Emma St. Clair. *Michael Hillegas and His Descendants.* Pottsville, Pa.: privately printed, 1891.

Williams, Thomas J. C. *A History of Washington County Maryland.* Reprint. Baltimore: Regional Publishing, 1968.

Williams, William Peere. *Reports of Cases Argued and Determined in the High Court of Chancery, and some special Cases Adjudged in the Court of King's Bench.* 2 vols. London: E. R. Nutt and R. Gosling, 1740.

Willis, Eola. *The Charleston Stage in the XVIII Century.* Reprint. New York: Benjamin Blom, 1968.

Wood, Gertrude Sceery. *William Paterson of New Jersey, 1745-1806.* Fair Lawn, N.J.: Fair Lawn Press, 1933.

Worth, Gorham A. *Random Recollections of Albany, From 1800 to 1808.* 3d ed. Albany: J. Munsell, 1866.

Zahniser, Marvin. *Charles Cotesworth Pinckney: Founding Father.* Chapel Hill: University of North Carolina Press, 1967.

Index

(Note: identifications of persons first mentioned in volume 2 of the *DHSC* are noted within parentheses.)